ARTHUR MEIGHEN
Volume Two

And when Athens shall appear great to you, consider then that her glories were purchased by valiant men, and by men that learned their duty; by men that were sensible of dishonour when they came to act; by such men as, though they failed in their attempt, yet would not be wanting to the city with their virtue, but made unto it a most honourable contribution.

PERICLES' FUNERAL ORATION

THE RIGHT HONOURABLE ARTHUR MEIGHEN, P.C.

ARTHUR MEIGHEN

A Biography by

ROGER GRAHAM

II

AND FORTUNE FLED

CLARKE, IRWIN & COMPANY LIMITED

TORONTO   1963   VANCOUVER

CONTENTS

PREFACE

THE FIRST VOLUME of this biography, *The Door of Opportunity*, closed with the appointment of Arthur Meighen as Prime Minister of Canada in the summer of 1920. In the present one I have attempted to tell the story of the following few years, the most crowded and crucial of his public career, ending with the convention of 1927 which chose R. B. Bennett as his successor in the leadership of the Conservative party. A third volume will deal with the remaining period of his life, which came to a close with his death in 1960 at the age of eighty-six.

It is a pleasant duty to record my indebtedness to the very many people who have helped me in one way or another, while absolving them of all responsibility for what the following pages contain. I desire again to express my gratitude to Mr. Meighen himself for his unfailing kindness and encouragement during the last decade of his life, to Mrs. Meighen, to their daughter, Mrs. Don Wright, and their two sons, Mr. T. R. Meighen and Mr. M. C. G. Meighen. Dr. Eugene Forsey read this volume in manuscript, as he did its predecessor, and contributed more, both in that and in other ways, than any words of mine could adequately acknowledge. I am grateful, too, to my colleague, Professor Michael G. Fry, who made available to me certain documentary material he had gathered for his own doctoral dissertion on the Anglo-Japanese Alliance and who read Chapters III and IV, offering a number of valuable criticisms.

Others whose assistance I wish specifically to mention include the late Chief Justice Albert Sévigny, the late Hugh Clark, Hon. E. L. Patenaude, Hon. T. A. Crerar, Hon. C. G. Power, Hon. M. Grattan O'Leary, Mr. Arthur G. Penny, Mr. John A. Stevenson, Mr. Arthur Ford, Mr. A. W. Merriam and Mr. W. T. Lucas. Mrs. Louise Morgan, secretary to Mr. M. C. G. Meighen, has been helpful in a number of ways and for this I am in her debt. My sincere thanks are owing to members of the staffs of the Public Archives of Canada (in particular Dr. W. Kaye Lamb, Dominion Archivist, and Mr. W. G. Ormsby, Head of the Manuscript Division), the Library of Parliament, the University of Toronto Library, the Reference Division of the Toronto Public Library, the Saskatchewan Provincial Archives, the Saskatchewan Legislative Library and the University of Saskatchewan Library. I also gladly acknowledge the advice given me and the interest taken in my work by Mr. R. W. W. Robertson, Editor of Clarke, Irwin & Company Limited, as well as the editorial assistance of Miss Isabelle Strong, who prepared the index and saw this volume through the press.

The University of Saskatchewan allowed me a year's leave of absence to complete the writing of the book and a very generous grant from the John Simon Guggenheim Memorial Foundation permitted me to work during that period in an atmosphere unmarred by financial stringency.

The most important and deserved acknowledgment I have left to the end. My wife not only listened to and constructively criticized the first draft of the work, but typed the manuscript, labour for which no sanction can be found in the marriage contract. More that that, while it may place a terrible burden of responsibility upon her to say so, without her constant encouragement the book would not have been completed.

ROGER GRAHAM

University of Saskatchewan
August 1963

AND FORTUNE FLED

1920-1927

It has fallen to me to lead this party through three general elections. . . . Fortune came and fortune fled; but, believe in my sincerity when I say that this is no reason for sympathy. It is only the lot of all of us, at least of all who strive—the joy of the upward struggle, the successes, disappointments and defeats. Perhaps it has been my fate to have had more than the average on both sides of the account, but I promise you there is going to be nothing of bitterness carried forward after the page is turned.

ARTHUR MEIGHEN

CHAPTER ONE

A TROUBLED LEGACY

E GUSS PORTER, Member of Parliament for West Hastings, looked up
at the drab, grey sky over the picnic grounds near Stirling and
wondered whether it would stop showering before the speeches started.
The elements had not been kind to the Porter Picnic that year;
yet as many people—about six thousand in fact—thronged the grounds as
he could remember seeing at any of his picnics in the past. Not for
nothing had Porter represented this riding continuously for almost
twenty years. He knew these people, knew that they had come from far
as well as near, from Madoc and Marmora, Belleville and Trenton, from
Ivanhoe and Moira and Plainfield and Tweed. In their buggies and
their wagons, in their Buicks and Overlands and Model T's, they had
converged on Stirling. Horny-handed farmers and their tidied-up wives
mingled with the people of the towns, labourers and railwaymen, merchants and tradesmen. Proud young bucks, arm-in-arm with their
giggling girls, strutted to and fro, heedless of the rain. Youngsters of
every age and shape ran slithering in the mud, conspired with their
friends, organized impromptu games or begged their parents for a
spending nickel. To all these people, old and young, the Porter Picnic
was an event looked forward to each year, a carnival, a respite from
drudgery. Of course it was also an occasion for rousing political oratory
and for rubbing shoulders or shaking hands with such men of power,
such bearers of fame, as had accepted Porter's invitation to attend.

This time, this Wednesday afternoon in August 1920, he had a real
drawing-card, which helped to explain why so many had braved the
inclement weather. Arthur Meighen was to deliver his first political
address since becoming Prime Minister of Canada a month before. The
great majority of those at the picnic were seeing and hearing him for
the first time, since he was a westerner who had done most of his stump-
speaking in that distant land beyond the Lakes. But probably most of
them knew something of his record and his reputation; perhaps they
recalled the days of confusion and uncertainty when the successor to
Sir Robert Borden was being decided upon and the reports—all too
true—that most of Meighen's colleagues in the Government did not want
him to succeed. Even had none of this been known to the crowd, how-

ever, Meighen's office and the fact that he was the youngest man ever to hold it were enough to assure him a large and expectantly curious audience.

A gusty shower of rain fell as the speeches began but almost nobody seemed to mind or want to go home. Instead they stood there dripping or huddled under big black bumbershoots while Guss Porter and various other speakers had their say. By the time it was Meighen's turn the rain had considerately stopped and as he took his stance at the front of the platform the throng eyed him appraisingly. They saw a very thin, fragile-looking figure of average height dressed in a somewhat rumpled dark suit; but it was the face above the high, stiff collar with its knotted polka dot tie that most commanded attention. There was a gauntness, almost alarming, about that face, with its rather pronounced cheek bones, its long, straight nose and, rising over the deep-set blue eyes with sharply creased crow's-feet at the corners, its high dome of thought from which the greying hair had begun to recede. The face bore an expression of brooding intensity, of care-worn fatigue, as though even more than the weight of governing a country rested on the slight shoulders of the man. The impression of high seriousness was heightened as he began to speak, quietly at first, then in more resounding, emphatic tones, a slight rasping huskiness affecting his sonorous voice as he warmed to his task. The conventional opening remarks were disposed of quickly, as though he wanted to waste no time in coming to the real meat of what he had to say, and then he spoke for an hour, earnestly, sparing of gesture, his words forming a faultless, felicitous prose.

The Stirling speech was the prototype of the many that were to follow in the next few weeks as Meighen discharged the obligation imposed upon him by his new office to confront the people face to face. He was by now a very familiar figure on the platforms of the western provinces; elsewhere, especially in Quebec and the Maritimes, he was much less well known at first hand. But everywhere, and most of all in his own prairie country, he was in demand as a speaker. People wanted to hear the new Prime Minister, to size him up as the picnickers at Stirling had done, and party workers across the land counted on him to rally the faithful. In fulfilling this duty he did not spare his energy, which was very much greater than his frail appearance would have led one to expect. After the Porter Picnic he was on the road much of the time, living out of a suitcase and suffering from his inability to sleep well on trains. On August the thirteenth he spoke in Toronto and on the seventeenth at a pleasant homecoming in St. Marys, the town of his childhood. A week later he was touring the Maritimes and on September the sixth he was in Quebec city, joining with Cardinal Bégin and Premier L. A. Taschereau in unveiling a monument to George Etienne Cartier.

He addressed a meeting in Kingston on September the ninth and one in Windsor on the thirteenth. Accompanied by his wife, he spent the weekend of the twentieth in Montreal, whence the two of them set out on a tour of the Eastern Townships. On October the twelfth he went to Elgin County in Ontario where a by-election was being fought and two days later boarded his railway car for a swing around the West, in the course of which he travelled eight thousand miles, visited twenty-two towns and cities and made forty speeches, seven of them in one day. Finally on the way back to Ottawa he stopped again in Toronto for a meeting at Massey Hall, where every seat was filled and a large crowd milled around on the street outside, trying to get in.

Indeed large crowds turned out to hear him everywhere and this was a satisfaction that compensated for the discomforts of travelling. They were not all as enthusiastic as the one in (and outside of) Massey Hall but Meighen was glad of this. "I do not know that I enjoyed the Toronto meeting very much," he wrote, "as I feel more at home . . . where the audience is adverse and particularly before a country or Western audience whose attitude of mind I better understand."[1] If a hostile or at least a sceptical crowd was more stimulating than one already convinced, he could not complain on those trips of a want of stimulation, especially in the West and Quebec.

In fact the political pot was boiling madly everywhere in Canada in 1920 and this helped to account for the great numbers who attended Meighen's meetings. The war had had a cataclysmic effect on politics, disturbing traditional loyalties and dissolving the old two-party system. The formation in 1917 of the Union Government, a coalition of Liberals and Conservatives who favoured compulsory military service, had led to the alienation of Quebec from the rest of the country. The result was that in the election of 1917 three-quarters of the seats won by the defeated anti-conscriptionist element of the Liberal party loyal to Sir Wilfrid Laurier were in that province, while the Union Government elected not a single member in the French-speaking ridings. The major task facing William Lyon Mackenzie King, who was chosen as Laurier's successor in 1919, was to make the Liberal party a truly national party once again. His aim was to maintain its position in Quebec while seeking to recover the ground it had lost in English-speaking Canada during the war, by luring back into the fold those Liberals who had deserted Laurier to support the coalition. By the same token Meighen's task was to foil King in this endeavour and also to rebuild his own party as a national structure by regaining a position of some strength in Quebec. There, conscription had made the Conservative party anathema among the French Canadians. Not only that, railway nationalization, reluctantly embarked upon by the Borden government, had estranged much of the English-speaking business class of Montreal. It was in part the belief that Meighen was unsuited by temperament and disqualified by his close connection with such unpopular wartime policies for the successful performance of this task that made many of the ministers oppose his selection as Borden's successor.

A complicating factor in the general post-war situation was the rise of a powerful movement of agrarian discontent. This found its political expression through the new National Progressive party led by Thomas A. Crerar, a onetime Liberal who had joined the Union Government as Minister of Agriculture. The failure of that government to reduce the tariff as much as he thought it should be caused Crerar to resign his portfolio in 1919 and around him in the House of Commons congregated a group of farmer members, mainly from the West. The grievances and demands of these Progressives were numerous and diverse but one central, concrete issue on which they could all unite was the tariff. The platform of their party called for the repeal of some duties, the reduction of others, free trade with the United Kingdom within five years and reciprocity with the United States. Clearly the strength of the Union Government among the farmers of the West, who had supported it overwhelmingly in 1917, was being quickly sapped after the war as they moved into the Progressive camp. And it was just as clear that if the Progressive party remained a distinct and potent force in Canadian politics there would be slight chance of Mackenzie King's being able to restore the Liberal party to its once powerful position in western Canada. King therefore set out to persuade the Progressives that there was no important issue of principle or policy separating their party from his own.

Meighen's reaction to the rise of Progressivism was very different from King's, as was his approach to the complex political situation as a whole. This was demonstrated in his 1920 stump speeches from one end of the country to the other, in which four themes stood out. Each was intended to assist in carrying out the decision of the Union Government caucus in 1919 to maintain the coalition, and the first of them was a defence of that government, of which Meighen regarded his own as a continuation and for the actions of which he assumed full responsibility. It was obvious, however, that the basis of the coalition now would have to be very different from the sense of urgency about the war which had produced the political realignment of 1917. Indeed it was necessary, in order to offset the loss of strength in some quarters, the West particularly, to gain the support of many who had opposed the Union Government in the past. A new issue must be found on which like-minded Liberals and Conservatives could unite and the re-unification of the Liberal party by King be prevented. Meighen was sure that the tariff was such an issue, that Liberal protectionists—and they were legion—could be convinced that only by their combining with the Conservatives might the National Policy of moderate protection be saved.

This, then, was his second theme: the clear and present danger to the protective system in the platforms of the other parties, both Liberal and Progressive. He had already indicated in Parliament the use he would make of this issue and his remarks on the subject during his speaking tours, repeated in practically every speech from Truro to Victoria, were much the same as those he had made in the Budget debate of the last session.[2] Emphasizing his own belief that not only Canada's prosperity but her very existence depended on the preservation of a moderately protective tariff, he reiterated the charge that Progressives and Mackenzie King Liberals were secretly leagued to destroy it. All Canadians concerned about the future of their country, he repeated over and over, ought to rally behind his government. In some places this was a popular message; at the Massey Hall meeting, Meighen remarked, he felt that he had been carrying coals to Newcastle. Outside of the prairies there were countless thousands, business and professional men, trade unionists, and farmers too, for whom defence of the National Policy was a paramount cause. Even out there in the happy hunting-ground of Crerar's Progressives there were not a few who shared Meighen's attachment to protection. But the large audiences which came to his western meetings and applauded his words belied the real opinions of the great majority of prairie people. Upholding the tariff in the West was assuredly not like carrying coals to Newcastle; it was more like offering spirituous liquor to an assembly of prohibitionists.

The danger of doing so was impressed upon the new Prime Minister by several of his friends. He should refrain from using the word "protection" in his western speeches, R. L. Richardson of the Winnipeg *Tribune* warned him. "It is the red rag to the western settlers' eyes. . . ."[3] "Distinguish between 'high protection' and 'protection,'" urged J. A. Calder, a member of his Cabinet. "I find our Liberal friends [in the West] continue to speak of you as an old time Tory protectionist of the worst type. You must get this idea out of their heads."[4] C. A. C. Jennings of the Toronto *Mail and Empire* had a somewhat different suggestion. Instead of emphasizing the tariff while speaking in the prairie country Meighen should "boldly claim the leadership of Western Canada. It will gratify a large number of people to have you thus identify yourself with the West as the public man who has most right to the confidence of the people there, as the one in the best position and of the most sincere mind to serve the West."[5] But Meighen was dubious about this. "As to my western trip," he replied, "and the pressing home of a claim to leadership there, I am afraid I am not very well qualified by nature to take the role assigned. I intend to argue the trade issue and to convince, wherever there are minds to be convinced."[6] He agreed with Calder that he should stress again, as he often had in the past, that he favoured only the moderately protective tariff then in force. Under that tariff, he informed a Winnipeg importer who questioned the wisdom of protecting industry, the "degree of protection we have in Canada now is not only the lowest we have ever had but is the lowest of any country in the world and that means all except Great Britain."[7] When W. A. Buchanan, M.P., a Liberal supporter of the Union Government, wrote a friendly letter conveying his inability to endorse Meighen's tariff policy, the latter answered: "I cannot for the life of me see how a policy more limited as to tariff than that upon which I frankly and clearly stand can expect to be actually maintained in Canada. I could not hold any conviction more strongly than I hold this conviction."[8] So, despite the unpopularity of the old National Policy on the prairies, of which he was well aware, Meighen was determined to make its maintenance the major element in his programme and strategy. He knew there were serious risks in this, that the West might feel he was writing off its support as expendable. But as he put it, in "all campaigns a man's duty is not to seek out what is most pleasing to his audience, but to sound the note that is true and to try to impress the lesson that is going to do the most good."[9]

In any case, however repugnant his defence of the tariff might be to prairie people, it seemed to offer the best hope politically in the rest of the country, especially in Quebec where his party was so woefully weak. He well knew the huge dimensions of the barriers he would have to surmount there, the immense store of resentment and prejudice against him and his government among the French Canadians. The political isolation of Quebec, and this was his third theme, must be brought to an end; there must be a reconciliation of the two peoples. The interest of party and country alike demanded it and Meighen lost no time in extending the olive branch. In speaking at a homecoming in Portage la Prairie early in August he had declared: "We have two great races. The fundamental institutions of Canada are just as dear to the one race as to the other. The peril of every nation has been to divide on lines of race, or lines of religion, or lines of social caste. If we do not come together to reach a better understanding and a better unity on things that are vital and essential to the state, there will be a heavy penalty paid."[10] These views he reaffirmed more than once in the following weeks. Speaking at Sherbrooke in the Eastern Townships, he referred to and denied categorically insinuations and accusations that he was an enemy of French Canada. He had, he said, no desire to see Quebec either isolated or anglicized and he would be happy indeed to include more French Canadians in his Cabinet if the voters of Quebec would but furnish the means. National unity must be restored but it must be the unity of diversity, not of assimilation.[11]

And finally he warned wherever he went against the gusty winds of insidious radical doctrine that had been blowing so strong since the end of the war. As the great Winnipeg general strike of 1919 had demonstrated, he thought, people were allowing themselves to be seduced from their attachment to old beliefs, tried and true, by the glittering promises of new ideologies. Much of this, he was convinced, was the result, direct or indirect, of the Russian Revolution, which so many otherwise sensible people evidently regarded as an emancipation from tyranny and a harbinger of a good new world. In one of his speeches he invited his listeners to look closely at Russia under the Bolsheviks. "There is nothing there," he assured them, "but a disordered, dishevelled, suffering, seething chaos of humanity, with assassination on top and starvation underneath."[12]

From this mood of unsettlement and dissatisfaction Meighen sought to call the country back to an acceptance of the sound Puritan values on which he had been nourished and which thus far had served him so well. He assured the boys of Bishop's College School at Lennoxville, Quebec, that "hard work was the only thing that could get a man anywhere,"[13] and he explained at Truro:

A truly great future is ahead of Canada if we only keep our heads and seriously believe in the doctrine of work. Work after all is the normal condition of men—I mean of every man—and it is the best answer and antidote to Socialistic, Bolshevik and Soviet nonsense. . . .
The great task before the people of Canada is to get back not to old conditions but to old time sanity of thought and action, to get back to our old high standards of living and character—standards handed down to us by our forebears. We have been living for the last six years in a highly abnormal and artificial age, and the sooner we get to normal conditions the better it will be for all of us. . . . We intuitively sense that we are living in a new age, and yet in our hearts we know that much of that which is new is superficial and transitory, some of it unreal and based upon insecure foundations. The public mind is confused with a veritable Babel of uninformed tongues. A great many people seem to have lost all sense of values, of proportion and of numbers; extravagance in thought is as great as the undoubted extravagance in living. It is an age of indulgence, in Isms and theories. Thousands of people are mentally chasing rainbows, striving for the unattainable, anxious to better their lot and seemingly unwilling to do it in the old fashioned way by hard honest intelligent effort. Dangerous doctrines taught by dangerous men, enemies of the State, poison and pollute the air. We are asked to believe not in so many words but in fact that we should have class domination instead of a true democracy with government of all classes and for all classes. Some there are—by no means few numerically—who would so order things in this country that all men be placed on the same plane, irrespective of brain power, energy and industry; who would have all

men on a dull, drab, grey level which would be destructive to all hope, ambition and human progress.[14]

While this was appropriately conservative doctrine for the leader of a Conservative party, its political usefulness was open to doubt when the winds of change were blowing as they were in 1920. There was danger in equating, or seeming to, the old and familiar with the "normal" and desirable, a danger pointed out to Meighen in a candid but friendly way by John Nelson, Managing Director of the Vancouver *World:* "I am rather disposed to think that too frequent insistence upon a firm attitude to 'the forces of unrest' and 'thoughtless change' may be misunderstood. I find that the number of references which you have made of this nature are being used to prove that you are reactionary and belong to the old Tory school which resents change. It would be very unfortunate if that view were to gain general circulation or to prevail. . . . I do not know how it is in the east but out here there is a remarkable loosening of all old affiliations. I have an impression that a political leader would do well to ignore the past and to focus his attention and his ideals on the future."[15] Of course Nelson might have agreed that the future must be in some measure an extension or reflection of the past and that one of the tasks of statesmanship was to transmit to the future what was worth preserving from history. Meighen believed as strongly as he believed anything that the ideals and attitudes he offered at Truro and elsewhere were an invaluable heritage whose preservation it was the duty of responsible men to ensure. If this be reaction, he might have said, let my enemies make the most of it. And, as Nelson had said they would, they did.

There was still another topic that kept cropping up in Meighen's speeches in this 1920 tour of the country: the utter hypocrisy, absurdity and contemptibility of William Lyon Mackenzie King. He pursued King so relentlessly, with such savage, ironic scorn, that the pursuit sometimes embarrassed even his own supporters. More than once he was advised that it would be better to ignore King, or at any rate to pay less attention to him, and concentrate instead on the constructive aspects of Conservative party policy. Dr. Howard P. Whidden, a Conservative member of Parliament and President of Brandon College, quoted a letter he had received from a prominent former Liberal business man. This gentleman remarked that "many voters have no politics at the present time and do not know where they should align themselves." He had attended a recent meeting in Winnipeg which Meighen and Calder had addressed and it seemed to him "that both ministers were more combatative [sic] in their utterances than good judgment would justify." Meighen had "delivered a very able address. I could not help feeling, however, that his speech would have wielded a much greater influence had he not devoted so much time in criticism of the leader of the opposition—Mackenzie King. This view is largely shared by many of his personal friends who heard him on this occasion." Presumably Whidden shared it too, since he took the trouble to forward these comments,[16] and Meighen's reply suggests that he also recognized the element of truth in it. "I have tried more than once," he wrote, "to give my speeches a forward looking view rather than a combative tendency but I fear I am not quite as great a success in that as I would wish to be."[17]

The advice to ignore King a little more, or to treat him somewhat more gently, may well have been wise since an onlooker at a contest is apt to acquire a lively sympathy for the contestant who seems badly overmatched, as King appeared to be in the early phase of his struggle with Meighen. Not only that, no one in public life, surely, at least no one who had risen to the position King now occupied, could be quite so preposterous and unworthy as Meighen made him out to be. This may well have been the reaction of a good many uncommitted voters who, observing King from a greater distance and more casually than Meighen did, were perhaps repelled by the ferocity of the latter's onslaughts. But Meighen held King in such great detestation that it would have required superhuman forbearance and self-control on his part to resist the temptation to pillory the leader of the Opposition whenever he had a chance. In any event, to undermine confidence in King was essential to the success of his strategy. He knew that King had won the Liberal leadership in 1919 by only a narrow margin after several ballots. It was evident that a great many Liberals had little liking for him and if that little could be destroyed these people would be more likely to hearken to Meighen's message about the tariff and follow him instead of King.

Between forays into the country Meighen grasped whatever time he could in his office to deal with the normal tasks of his position and also with the special problems that faced him. First and foremost of these latter was the situation in Quebec and he lost no time in trying to improve matters in that province. One thing and one thing only was clear about Quebec: he would have to start practically from scratch. His party had almost nothing in the way of organization there, even less in the way of popular approval and few prominent French-Canadian figures who were not thoroughly discredited in the eyes of a majority of their compatriots. His only French-speaking minister was Postmaster-General P. E. Blondin, who now reposed in the Senate, safe from the hazards of elections. At the provincial level the old Conservative party had sunk almost out of sight, having been ground down by the Liberal steamroller during Sir Lomer Gouin's fifteen years as Premier which had just ended. There was little or nothing to be hoped for there from Meighen's standpoint. Nor had the national party any organization in the province worthy of the name. Its effectiveness had been declining for many years; 1917 had given it the *coup de grâce*. All that appeared to be left was a small, hapless collection of party workers, most of them resentful and jealous of one another, none of them with the stature to rise above this sorry, squalid state and assume a commanding position as Meighen's coadjutor. From the outside it looked as though there were as many factions in Quebec Conservatism as there were Conservatives. "The difficulty of getting organization under way in the Province of Quebec," Meighen observed, understating the matter, "is far greater than anywhere else. There is the complexity due to there being both French and English to consider. . . . There is also the question of some irresponsibles. . . ."[18]

It was true that both French and English had to be considered; it was equally true that they could not seem to work together. Meighen was informed by a supporter in Montreal that he and a group of his friends had decided to organize "an exclusively English-speaking Club," it having been unanimously decided "after a great deal of careful thought . . . that the English-speaking people could much better co-operate with their French Canadian compatriots by the formation of a purely English-speaking club than by amalgamation with them." The club had already had "phenomenal success," as was attested by the fact that the President of the Montreal branch of the Canadian Manufacturers' Association had joined it.[19] But surely this was a novel form of "co-operation" and not a very hopeful one in a province where the Conservative party was by now too exclusively an English-speaking remnant whose leaders had no prestige among the French population. This was impressed upon the Prime Minister by many, one of whom wrote: "Gentlemen like Ballantyne, Sir Hugh Graham[20] (This one not very hot for you as told me lately his good friend Bob Rogers,) Senator [George G.] Foster, Doherty, could play the strings behind the stage but believe me dear Mr. Meighen they better not show thelselfs [*sic*] outside West Montreal. It is hard what I am telling you but it's the fact, it is the truth. You must not forget that Quebec is a latin province, a french [*sic*] province. For god sake act accordingly. This is not understood by the above named gentlemen."[21]

The difficulty of bringing the two ethnic groups together was by no means all. Within each group there were any number of back-biting jealousies and antagonisms. Factionalism was particularly rampant among the French Canadians but their English-speaking counterparts were far from being a unit. Each group had its pro-Meighen faction and its anti-Meighen faction and each faction in each group was divided into a great variety of cliques, the existence of which had no discernible basis other than personal antipathy and suspicion. All in all the Conservative scene in Quebec was an arid wilderness of demoralization, despair and irresponsibility. Almost every day letters reached Meighen's desk complaining about the lack of organization, the dearth of leadership, the absence of co-operation. One of these was from a Montrealer who described himself as "a life long Conservative and one who has taken part in many political campaigns throughout Canada. . . ." His object in writing was to give his opinion of the new National Liberal and Conservative organization which had been set up in Montreal.

You are no doubt aware that the Liberal-Conservative party have not had a serious Organization in the Province of Quebec since 1896. Since then the Conservatives have gradually lost ground from year to year. We cannot possibly go back any further.

The little stir of 1911 was due to Henri Bourassa's activity on the Navy question, which was far from being the principal issue at that election. A few Nationalists sprang up and were not long in starting trouble in the ranks.

Since 1896 the Liberal-Conservative Organization has been in the hands of a few Lawyers only—a little pack who would not listen to any suggestions, nor pay due attention to public opinion. They would only sit around the Central Committee table and send us to battle throughout the country without any real preparation. If we happened to make suggestions or to tell them what was needed we were told that we were rebels. We would do the work,—they would get the credit and reap the benefit. They never made any real live effort to stir up and rally the McDonald [sic], Cartier and Chapleau Old Guard and offer a straight front. These few Lawyers simply used the Organization to keep their names before the public and wait for a Judgeship or some other appointment.

What is wanted is an Organization composed of real democratic workers, representative of the different classes of the electorate—not of one class only. Great Orators are not what is needed to start. What is needed are Practical politicians who know the mentality of the Quebec Farmers and who will go throughout the rural Districts and rally our old leaders of groups and have a quiet talk with them; convince them that the Liberal Conservative party will come back in the province of Quebec. The leaders of groups have got to be convinced through the rural Districts before any big movement can be started.

A dozen or so of young Lawyers have started the "Idée-Libérale-Conservatrice Association" who in turn deliver lectures to other Lawyers, but all these Lectures would not cut any ice among the Farmers or the working men. It is the Farmer we must get after in the Province of Quebec and not the Lawyer.

In Montreal there are two classes of Liberal-Conservatives. The Aristocrats and the Democrats. The new Organization is already in the hands of the Aristocratic Lawyers who will talk at Banquets only and make the others work at Election time. They have complete control of the Organization. A rumor is already circulating that 7 or 8 of them are receiving fat salaries as Organizers and are running their private Bureaus at the same time.[22]

Not only was there no organization worth speaking of, there was not a dependable party press any more. *La Patrie* and *Le Matin* of Montreal, *L'Evénement* of Quebec, a few other lesser journals here and there, gave the Government a qualified and hesitant support, daring to defend Meighen against the more outrageous slanders, venturing to question the more extreme Liberal and Nationalist opinions. But compared with the thundering, confident tones of such papers as *Le Devoir* and *Le Soleil*, *Le Canada* and *La Presse*, their voices were still and small and their audience was of slight proportions.

None of this was new in 1920, of course. It had been more or less like this for years and Meighen knew when he succeeded Borden, if he knew anything at all, that in Quebec he would have a terribly hard row to hoe. But it had to be hoed, however hard the ground, and he was forced to concern himself more directly and continuously with the Quebec situation than he would have liked and to endure for years the welter of conflicting advice and the noise of intra-party strife that beat upon him from that province. Unfortunately there was little he could do except counsel unity and strive to use whatever personal influence he had to reconcile the factions in the face of their determination to remain irreconcilable. He could also cling, of course, to the belief that the Conservative party in Quebec, despite its baffling vicissitudes, need not be completely written off. Surely, one had at least to hope, there must still be a nucleus of true *Bleus,* surely life could be breathed into the sickly frame and the party rescued from its sad condition. Into the wilderness Meighen stepped warily, looking for signs of life amongst the shattered remnants of the army. "What I have tried to do," he explained to a correspondent in Montreal, "is to establish relations of confidence with four or five including both French and English in the province and to act when and as they advise."[23] But he knew that this kind of collective leadership and consultation could work only if all the leaders whom he consulted agreed with one another, or at any rate were prepared to compromise. This was certainly not the posture of all the would-be leaders in Quebec. What he was really looking for, what he really needed, was one man, a dominating individual, some new Cartier who could rally the party, create an *esprit de corps*, build an organization. The agent of resurrection must, needless to say, be a French Canadian; more than that, he must be someone who had disagreed with Meighen about conscription. Assuredly French Canada would follow no one else in the climate of opinion then prevailing. Had he been free to choose Meighen would have preferred to work, and would have worked, with Albert Sévigny, formerly Speaker of the House of Commons and briefly one of Borden's ministers, who had gone down to defeat in the election of 1917 bravely holding aloft the banner of conscription. Sévigny's courage in the crisis

had cost him the utter eclipse of his political career. He had no following
of consequence, no prospect, at least for years to come, of redeeming himself in the eyes of his people. The same was true of Blondin. The one
hope seemed to be E. L. Patenaude, who had resigned from the Borden
government in protest against conscription and had resumed the practice
of law in Montreal. Patenaude's stand on the great issue of 1917 gave
him prestige in Quebec. He possessed both ability and integrity. He
was respected by the English-speaking business community as well as by
his own people and, all in all, could be accounted the leading French-
Canadian Conservative. Could he be induced to enter national politics
again at Meighen's right hand?

In the late summer of 1920 he and the Prime Minister held a series
of conversations, the object of which was to discover common ground.
At their conclusion Meighen asked Patenaude to set forth in writing the
essential principles which he thought must be adopted to re-establish
amity between French- and English-speaking citizens. This Patenaude
did. He began by saying that he had

> noted with lively satisfaction your sincere desire to establish your new
> Government on peace and concord. You rightly believe that it will
> be impossible to build anything truly solid unless the two great races
> which principally compose the Canadian nation are at last re-united
> on the ground of understanding and conciliation, and it is to this
> necessary *rapprochement* that you will devote your foremost efforts.
> The enterprise is one of political wisdom and no one would be
> happier than I to see it achieved, and even to contribute to it to the
> full extent of my power.

He had not, he continued, any particular authority to speak for French
Canada but believed he could accurately express its point of view. The
French Canadian, in spite of certain wrong-headed members of the group,
was a loyal citizen. He had long since accepted British allegiance and
neither regretted it nor sought release from it. "In the absence of affection,
self-interest commends it to him." The French Canadian, though, was
first of all a Canadian.

> He feels an interest in the progress, not alone of the part he inhabits,
> but of the whole of Canada. Certainly he is misunderstood when it is
> claimed that he seeks to isolate himself. On the contrary he asks
> nothing but to work in concert with his fellow citizens of other races
> for the greatest advancement of the country. But at the same time
> he claims, in this country whose first occupant he is, to have the right
> to develop according to his traditions . . . not alone in such corner
> of the country as may be thought to have been assigned to him, but
> in the whole of Canada. That is all that the French Canadian people
> ask: liberty to develop according to its traditions and an equal par-
> ticipation as much in the costs as in the advantages of good govern-
> ment.

Having stated these generalities, Patenaude came to particulars, listing six "practical propositions":

1. The free life and development of the two races—across the country—in harmony—but without fusion and without assimilation.

2. Protection of the rights of the minority, be it Catholic, be it French.

3. Interpretation of the Act of Confederation and of the laws which concern minorities in a generous sense following the spirit which animated the Fathers of Confederation.

4. Recognition of both languages in all acts emanating either from Parliament or from the Federal Government.

5. To encourage the diffusion of both languages throughout the country, without prejudice, however, to the jurisdiction of the provinces in matters of education.

6. Proportional representation according to population

A. In the Cabinet, the French element of the province of Quebec must be represented by at least three ministers and that of the rest of the country by at least one minister, and this representation in every case must be increased according to population.

B. In the Senate, the French element of each province must have one or more representatives as its population may justify, and following numerical proportion.

C. In the judiciary.

D. In the various public positions.

The political party, Patenaude concluded, which, basing itself on these propositions, would undertake to give French Canada "a reasonable measure of justice and which will offer it real guarantees of sincerity can be assured of its support, and Canadian history has already shown the value of its support, as much from the standpoint of loyalty as from that of usefulness."[24]

Over a month elapsed before Meighen was able to answer this. He had been away on his trip through the Eastern Townships and on his return was engrossed in other matters for the time being. In replying he began, as Patenaude had, with some general observations.

The importance of your letter is such that I desire to express my sentiments on points raised therein not only with care but with frankness and clearness. As stated to you more than once in conversation, I regard as a first object of public policy in Canada the improvement of relations between the two great races that mainly comprise our population and the maintenance of good relations so established upon a secure and lasting basis.

In the achievement of the purpose defined in the preceding paragraph, there will be required first a full and vivid recognition on the part of both our French and English speaking people of the paramount need of concord. This condition, in my opinion, is already met to a degree that has not been reached before. The more general and impressive recognition of this, our peculiar and vital necessity, should be the aim of every man and woman who loves Canada. That such harmony can be realized and sustained only on the premises of common attachment to British connection is, I am glad to know, conceded alike by our English and French speaking people. As you say in your letter, this attachment has its roots not only in affection but in interest.

You observe as well that the object we have in view, namely, the establishment of better relations and their consistent maintenance can be attained by a recognition on the side of each of the unassailable right of the other to share in substantial proportion to numbers, the privileges and obligations of government and administration. With the truth and fairness of your contention I cordially agree. Experience has surely taught us that both races must be permitted, if they desire, to develop in line with their respective traditions and that there should be on the part of the Government no influence exerted to force any process of fusion or assimilation. As therefore each race progresses as you express it "according to its traditions" it is manifest that the best results will flow from a sharing on the general basis of numbers of the responsibilities of government and administration. I have stated this general principle not as one to be regarded as a mere ideal or vision but as an active principle to be carefully regarded in practice, to be interpreted in a liberal spirit and not to be departed from in any substantial degree except for unavoidable cause.

Meighen now proceeded to deal *seriatim* with Patenaude's enumerated conditions. Concerning the first, he wrote, his attitude had been defined in the preceding part of his letter. As for minority rights, those "guaranteed by the Constitution must be held sacredly inviolable." With respect to the British North America Act, the importance of a generous interpretation "on the part of both the great races cannot be over stated. A mutual desire not to contest the last inch of ground or the farthest meaning of each phrase and sentence but instead a liberal reading of the spirit of the Constitution would dissolve virtually all the causes of discord." Going on to the fourth demand Meighen wrote: "I am not clear as to what is meant by 'Acts emanating either from Parliament or from the Federal Government' as of course Statutes can only emanate from Parliament but I readily subscribe to the recognition asked for believing same to be now conceded not only by practice but by the terms of the Constitution."

Thus far the reply had been sympathetic and agreeable but when Meighen encountered Patenaude's reference to encouraging "the diffusion of both languages throughout the country" he balked. Personally, he said, he favoured "to the utmost possible extent the acquaintance of our people with both English and French." But what could the government of Canada do toward that end? "The jurisdiction of the Provinces in these matters is so clearly defined and indeed so exclusive that anything in the way of Federal interference would appear to be very likely to fail of effect if not indeed to do positive injury." Quebec could hardly desire the infringement of provincial rights. Finally Patenaude had laid down the principle that there should be French-Canadian representation in proportion to numbers in Cabinet, Senate, judiciary and civil service. As far as the Cabinet was concerned Meighen agreed. There should be, he wrote, not less than three French-Canadian ministers. It was through no wish of his that there was now only one and he would be glad, also, if a minister to represent French Canadians outside Quebec could be found. As for the Senate, he had not realized that there was dissatisfaction with its makeup on ethnic grounds but would be happy to correct any unfairness of this sort there might be. Respecting the judiciary and civil service the first criterion must be the ability to serve of those appointed but even here he thought the general principle of representation by population was sound. "At no time," he said in concluding his answer, "and under no circumstances have I given expression to sentiments that vary at all from those outlined in this letter. I have always sought and so long as I am in public life shall continue to seek to instill an appreciation of the very real and thorough going democracy that is ours, of the privileges we enjoy as Canadians and of the obligations that accompany those privileges and cannot be separated therefrom. I have no sympathy with any spirit of self-asserting ascendancy much less of [sic] any spirit of antagonism or distrust."[25]

As soon as he had drafted this letter Meighen had to leave on his western tour. It was agreed that in his absence an effort should be made through C. J. Doherty, the Minister of Justice, to have Patenaude modify the terms of his letter in certain particulars. Patenaude did so, deleting his fifth proposition to which Meighen had taken exception and amending the fourth so as to make it clear that he had in mind, not statutes only, but other official documents as well. On Meighen's behalf Doherty rephrased his reply to suit these changes and the revised answer was sent to Patenaude.[26] There, however, the matter apparently rested. If the object of the conversations and correspondence had been to persuade Patenaude to join the Government, failure was the result. Presumably Patenaude wanted explicit consent to his stated principles before he would come in; presumably, too, Meighen's reply was not deemed to go far enough to satisfy French Canada. In addition, perhaps, Patenaude decided that to work with Meighen was to play with fire in Quebec; his fingers might be burned and he was a cautious man. Just what kind of fire might be kindled was suggested by the comments of the Liberal French-language press on national politics and the incumbent Prime Minister. Of these some excerpts from an editorial in *Le Canada*, published while the negotiations between Patenaude and Meighen were in progress, were not untypical.

Obviously, the object of Mr. Meighen's trip to the Eastern Township was to convince the Quebec people that never has he been a fanatic and that he is most sympathetically disposed towards us.

We must base on his past record our appreciation of Mr. Meighen; who can gainsay that Mr. Meighen has been the prime mover of the infamous campaign of calumnies and disparagement aimed at Quebec during the war? . . .

It was then that a group of tories, of whom Mr. Meighen was chief, induced Premier Borden to introduce a conscription measure and to form a coalition arraying against Quebec all the English speaking provinces.

We have to-day the evident proof that the measure of conscription was not adopted to satisfy the exigencies of the war, but that it was aimed at Quebec. . . .

But that is not all.

The scandalous frenzy which characterized the conscription campaign has not been forgotten. What outrageous calumnies have not been poured out of overflowing pages, paid by funds provided by the conservative association which filled the press of Canada with full-page advertisements so as to secure the triumph of the coalition.

Neither has the outrageous "War Elections Act", concocted by Mr. Meighen and by him fostered in the House, been forgotten; an act enabling him to practically prepare a list of select voters who alone were entitled to cast their voting papers in the ballot-box.

Nor have the provisions relative to the soldiers' vote passed out of memory, which allowed to preferred constituencies the distribution of votes cast by our soldiers in home or overseas camps.

And, by the way, let it not be forgotten that Mr. Meighen stands indebted to that law for whatever majority remains to him in the House.

And what about the famous ciphered telegram in which Mr. Meighen, speaking of "scarlatine" and "prunes", was asking Mr. Borden to assign votes to a certain constituency in need of them.

This vast conspiracy of calumny, outrageous laws and stolen and manipulated ballots was directed against the province of Quebec; and Mr. Meighen was at the bottom of it all.

How can he have the presumption to proffer the glad hand to us?

His assumed attitude and his false smile can but draw to himself the contempt and derision of our citizens.[27]

The writer of this editorial could certainly speak with authority on the art of calumny but Patenaude undoubtedly knew that misrepresentation of this kind would have a powerful effect on public opinion. In any event he remained aloof, evidently convinced that the time was not ripe to challenge the Liberal hold on his province.

Nothing could have been more discouraging to Meighen than this because, leaderless, the party in Quebec was doomed to continued impotence. That in itself was bad enough but it would have the further effect of making it more difficult to enlist support for the Government among Quebec's Liberal protectionists. If Quebec Conservatism became once more a force to be reckoned with they might be won over but they would hardly flock to what was clearly a hopeless cause, to a party both prostrate and lifeless. Still, regardless of the handicaps to be overcome, converts from the Liberal camp must be won if at all possible and to this purpose Meighen addressed himself.

One method of accomplishing it was to keep hammering away in Parliament and before the public at the danger to the protective system inherent in the rise of the Progressive movement and in King's wooing of the western voters. If the people of Quebec could be convinced that the tariff was in fact imperilled, conscription might be, as it ought to be, forgotten, at least to some extent. Another way was to do what Borden had done in 1919, seek out and attempt to win over important individual Liberals.[28] It still looked like good tactics to try to exploit the division between the faction in Quebec of which Ernest Lapointe was increasingly the recognized leader and which ranged itself behind Mackenzie King, and the more conservative wing, with Sir Lomer Gouin its chief representative, which had no use for King's "radical" proclivities and looked askance at his flirtation with the Progressives. But to widen this breach some other method than a direct approach to the wary, inscrutable Gouin would have to be tried. Meighen was certainly no more *persona grata* with him than Borden had been and was hardly likely to succeed where Borden had failed. Thus, although he was advised by some to make his overtures to Gouin, he preferred a different approach. He would seek out, not Gouin, not Rodolphe Lemieux nor Jacques Bureau, assuredly not Lapointe, all of whom Borden had approached, but one or two others, lesser men perhaps in the councils of their party but men of standing nevertheless whose adherence would be valuable.

These tactics were not popular with many a Quebec Conservative and Meighen received several letters begging him to make no compact with the enemy, to pin his hopes, rather, on the tried and true Tories of the province.[29] However attractive this argument may have been sentimentally, it was hardly practical politics to act on such advice. Accessions from the Liberals had to be won unless the Government was prepared to write Quebec off as irredeemable, which no responsible party leader could contemplate doing. The one big question for Meighen was whom he should go after. What prominent French-speaking Liberal protectionists were most likely to be converted? In the plentiful advice Meighen received in this connection and in the multitudinous rumours that circulated three names figured most. One was that of P. J. Veniot, a New Brunswick Acadian and Minister of Public Works in that province. Veniot, indeed, declared in an interview with a newspaper reporter that he had been invited to join the Meighen government but the Prime Minister denied this categorically in the House of Commons. He had, he said, made no overtures to the gentleman nor had anyone been authorized by him to do so.[30] The case of the second individual was somewhat different. L. J. Gauthier, a Liberal who had represented St. Hyacinthe-Rouville in the Commons since 1911, was an outspoken critic of Mackenzie King and a stout defender of tariff protection. Amidst speculation that he was about to join the Cabinet, Gauthier declared his support of the Government during the session of 1921 and crossed the floor of the House. Here was an eager recruit indeed but opinion was sharply divided as to how useful and desirable he was. Meighen was cautioned by many against making Gauthier his colleague and when the Ministry was reconstructed his name did not appear on the list.

The real prize coveted by the Prime Minister was George H. Boivin, Member of Parliament for Shefford County in the Eastern Townships. Boivin's obvious ability, his personableness and his comparative youth— he had just turned thirty-nine at the end of 1920—stamped him as a coming man. Following the 1917 election he had been chosen Deputy Speaker of the Commons, there being no French Canadian among the Government's supporters, and he had earned the respect of both sides for his impartial courtesy and good sense. It was known that he had no love for Mackenzie King, that he feared the radicalism of the Progressives and that he was a staunch upholder of the National Policy. With Boivin beside him Meighen might have a lieutenant from Quebec to rival Lapointe.

In the spring of 1921 the two men discussed the situation. Boivin was asked to join the Government and in due course agreed. On the very day he was to be sworn in, however, he suddenly changed his mind, having been convinced at the last minute that to ally himself with Meighen would be to put an end to his political career. One of his leading supporters, Ludger P. Bernard of Granby, came to Ottawa at the request of Boivin, who told him what he intended to do. Boivin said that he admired Mr. Meighen, that he had been a Laurier man but was not a King man and he asked Bernard what his chances of being re-elected as a member of Meighen's Cabinet would be. Bernard told him that he would have no chance whatever. The two of them then went to Meighen's office and Bernard repeated what he had said to Boivin. Thereupon Boivin withdrew his acceptance of office and that very hopeful prospect of recovery in Quebec was rudely extinguished.[31] For some time Meighen clung to the thought that Boivin might sooner or later be won over. "I sincerely hope," he wrote to him several months afterwards, "we will yet be found side by side in the public service."[32] It was a hope never to be fulfilled.

In the meantime, Parliament had met on February the fourteenth. It was, of course, the first opening Meighen attended as Prime Minister and, though neither he nor anyone else could foresee such a thing, it was also to be his last. Never again would he take his place at the Governor-General's right hand in the Senate chamber while His Excellency read the speech from the throne. Never again would the words that fell from His Excellency's lips express Meighen's thoughts. Indeed, not again after that session would Meighen sit in Parliament as leader of the Government. After his unbroken succession of advances to the top his time of troubles was about to begin, though as yet there was no inkling of the dark and disappointing future that was in store.

This session did not prove to be a particularly happy one from the Government's point of view. Its legislative programme was pushed through but on some of the votes the margin was uncomfortably narrow. The confidence of the Opposition parties appeared to grow as the session progressed, whereas the morale of the Government supporters, their will to fight, seemed to be fast fading away. A noticeably dispro-portionate amount of the talking on behalf of the administration was done by the Prime Minister, while his colleagues and followers sat silent or absented themselves from the House. Complaints reached the ears of the Opposition about this, that Meighen was not giving others a chance to express themselves or to demonstrate their ability.[33] He had been warned on this score before the session started by a friend in Vic-toria who wrote:

> The rank and file members of the house should do more fighting. The general runs the show, but many of the rank and file could do some fine bayonet work on King and Crearer [sic], and it would do a lot to put ginger into the people.
> The Ottawa idea seems to me that the members and the senate [sic] and House consider themselves ring-side onlookers at a gladia-torial combat between yourself and King & Crearer, and it would stiffen the people up if you would order a general engagement horse foot artillery and bombs in which all can contribute something.
> Don't do all the hard work yourself as you are too prone to do, but incite others to take a hand on occasions.[34]

This was sound advice, and Meighen knew it, but the fact was that no one else on his side of the House carried a bayonet nearly as sharp and highly polished as his own. Another correspondent put his finger on part of the difficulty: "There are those who say that your Cabinet needs strengthening. It is a common, if exaggerated declaration that yours is a one man Government and that you do all the work."[35] It was all too true that the Cabinet did badly need strengthening, for it was a far less imposing group of men than the coalition ministry formed in 1917, of which it was supposedly a continuation. Sir Robert Borden, Sir Thomas

White and Newton Rowell, along with Meighen the strongest men in that coalition, had all left, though Borden and Rowell still appeared in the House from time to time. Several others, some of them able parliamentarians, had either moved into opposition or retired from politics altogether. Few of those who remained or had been brought in were men with much parliamentary experience, first-class ability and real taste for controversy. Aside from Meighen the best House of Commons man left in the Government, the doughtiest fighter, was Sir George Foster and he was almost seventy-five years old. Nor did there seem to be an abundance of vigour and enthusiasm for the fray among the private members. There were few if any eager, ambitious young men of the sort Meighen himself had been when he first entered Parliament in 1908. It was as though most of them were playing out the string, waiting for an eclipse of their party whose approach could already be sensed.

Nevertheless, while there certainly was a dearth of superior debating talent among his followers, it is probably true that Meighen failed to make the best use of what talent there was. His own pre-eminence as a parliamentarian, his own almost unlimited liking and capacity for hard work were in this sense a handicap to him as a party leader. The work had to be done well, he could do it better than others. For years past he had been accustomed to performing far more than his share of the parliamentary labour of the Government and it was natural for him to continue to do so. He lacked the patience to sit quietly by and listen to someone else do a mediocre job of expounding a piece of important legislation or the forbearance to remain silent while others lost an argument that might be won. Thus without any desire to exclude them from the limelight and monopolize it for himself, he did the lion's share of the talking simply because he was a great deal better at it, and knew he was, than anyone else. As one of his ablest and most respected opponents has put it,

> Meighen was so thorough and had such a grasp of the questions which came before the House that he felt he had to express himself and to express the views of the Party. It would be unfair, I think, to say that he didn't want to give a chance to . . . others on his side. . . . I don't think that Meighen would ever have made a good player on a team, not that he was selfish but rather than divide the work decided to do it himself, possibly without thinking that these others also might have had ambitions to receive publicity and to shine in the public eye. But let it not be forgotten that Meighen's work and his aptitude for work were possibly the greatest assets which the parliamentary Tory Party had. Perhaps one of the fatal defects of his character was his inability to distribute work rather than his desire to hog it and to get the credit for it.[36]

Whether or not these mutterings of the members about not being given a chance were justified, and probably for some this was just a convenient excuse for inactivity, they were symptomatic of a demoralization from which, by the spring of 1921, the National Liberal and Conservative party, in Parliament and in the country, was evidently suffering. From outside its ranks it was being severely buffeted by criticism and ridicule, blamed for all the ills and accused of all the sins that man is heir to. Worse than these attacks, which after all had to be expected, was a serious division within the party and a fairly widespread lack of confidence in its leadership and its programme. The root of this feeling was not a personal antipathy to Meighen, though of course there were some who were jealous and resentful of him or who believed he was not temperamentally suited to be a party leader. What was really at the bottom of it was that a good many Conservatives had never become reconciled to the policy of trying to preserve and solidify the coalition with as many Liberals as might be willing, once the war was over. Indeed, some of them had bitterly opposed coalition in 1917 and all of them were convinced that with the return of peace to the world the time had come for Canadian politics to return to partisan warfare of the old, familiar style. In the minds of these folk one was born a little Liberal or else a little Conservative and that was all there was to it. To them it was a law of nature that the two breeds must fight like cat and dog to the end of time as they had since the beginning of time. They therefore found themselves at odds with Meighen's strategy of trying to find new strength for the party among Liberals who disliked or were suspicious of Mackenzie King.

There were a good many things with which these people were dissatisfied, for one thing the new name of their party: National Liberal and Conservative. An awkward, wordy mouthful, that! Meighen shared their attitude on this. The name had been suggested by Calder in order to give the two elements in the party due recognition but to Meighen it seemed unnecessarily long and cumbersome. The old "Liberal-Conservative" would have suited him better, though he accepted the new label in the hope that it might make it easier for many Liberals to come over. To the unregenerate Tories, however, it was an absurdity and an affront, as was the purpose it symbolized, of making permanent bedfellows of natural enemies. On this, and on this perhaps alone, they would agree with one of those natural Liberal enemies, Ernest Lapointe, when he commented to an Ontario audience *à propos* of his opponents' new designation: "They are trying to put the two names together, Liberal and Conservative. What of these two names? They cannot be combined, for one is that [sic] absolute contrary of the other. The one is virtue, the other is vice, politically. The one is beautiful. The other is ugly. The one is progressive. The other is reactionary. The combination of the two is nonsense. It is impossible."[37] No Conservative, of course, would accept Lapointe's apportionment of vice and virtue and all the rest of it but some would say "Amen" to his main proposition.

To object to the name was simply one way of saying what a great many Conservatives felt at that time, "No more truck or trade with the Grits!" A good deal of evidence reached Meighen that this sentiment was fairly prevalent. A few days after he became Prime Minister he heard from General S. C. Mewburn, a Liberal who had been Minister of Militia in the Union Government. There were plans afoot to hold a large political picnic in the Hamilton district, the hope being that it would attract people from all over western Ontario. Mewburn thought Meighen might be willing to speak at it. "A meeting will be held before long regarding it," he wrote. "I have urged some of my friends not to make it a Conservative picnic if they decided to go ahead. If this could be pulled off, would it appeal to you?"[38] "Of course I have had a flood of invitations to speak everywhere," Meighen replied, "and I did not know so many Picnics were on the go in this agitated and dissatisified nation. Your idea seems to me a good one."[39] But it did not seem so good to the Conservatives of the Hamilton district. Some days later Meighen sent Mewburn another note: "I see they are getting up some Conservative picnics on old time lines for, I think it is, the 28th. I am sorry they are taking this line, but I do not think it will have any material results."[40]

Of course the effects of this brand of Conservative partisanship were not confined to excluding Liberals from picnics. F. B. McCurdy, who was fighting a by-election in Colchester, Nova Scotia, urged Meighen not to defend the record of the Union Government in the speech he was going to give at Truro on McCurdy's behalf. "I take it that we do not want to spend our energies in apologizing for, or defending, as the case may be, what is past and gone. I can assure you that Union Government is extremely unpopular in Nova Scotia and particularly among former Conservatives." Since a Farmer-Labour candidate was his only opponent in the by-election he hoped, McCurdy added, to get some Liberal votes but "it would be an offence if the record of Union Government were put forward as a reason why they should support me."[41] McCurdy won the election, in spite of the fact that Meighen ignored his advice, but was probably correct in believing that there was a deep-seated aversion among Nova Scotia Conservatives to Unionism in theory and practice.

One could expect such an attitude in that province, where intense partisan loyalty might almost be part of one's genetic makeup, but it was just as much in evidence elsewhere, for example in Toronto where Mr. Edmund Bristol, whom Meighen had asked to take charge of organization in central Ontario, was in hot water with the Central Liberal-

Conservative Association. The organizing secretary of this body informed Meighen that its president, Mr. Edworthy,

> is forwarding you a letter asking you to meet the members of the executive at the Albany Club. . . . A meeting of the Organization Committee was held last evening and Mr. Edworthy . . . told the members that Mr. Bristol had approached him . . . to arrange for a meeting of the leading Party workers in Toronto. . . . There was a good deal of hostility shown by some of the members toward Mr. Bristol and it was pointed out that as the Central Association had gone on record as being determined to get back to straight Party lines, that [sic] Mr. Edmund Bristol was therefore an outsider and not entitled to any consideration by the Association.

To consider a man with Bristol's impeccable Conservative credentials an outsider was carrying things rather far. Of United Empire Loyalist descent, he was a past president of the Conservative Association of Toronto and had sat in the House of Commons as a Conservative since 1905. He was an Anglican, an affluent lawyer with extensive business interests. He belonged to the right clubs, the York and the Albany, to say nothing of the Royal Canadian Yacht Club and the Toronto Hunt Club. If he could not qualify as a Conservative, who could? The answer was, apparently, that in the eyes of the ultra-orthodox no one could who had, like Bristol, aligned himself with this ill-conceived half-caste, the National Liberal and Conservative party.

But to the Torontonians there was more to the matter than restoring party purity and keeping renegades like Bristol out of the party picture. The organizing secretary added some candid observations in his letter to Meighen.

> I might say that there are two things that are worrying the Party workers here, or to put it more correctly, one trouble subdivided into two headings; 1st, the Civil Service Commission: the boys want the old patronage system back, and they declare that the Grits that we have been fighting for the last 25 years have secured positions in the Post Office and the Customshouse, and at the same time we have great Party men who have been trying to secure similar positions who have not been successful. Secondly, they want the Purchasing Board abolished and Government contracts given as before the war.[42]

The same resentment of Liberals' being given too many plums and enjoying too much influence was expressed frankly to Meighen by a Belleville lawyer, who wrote:

> There seems to be a distinct feeling that we are counting too much on the prospect of Liberal votes because of some Liberals being in the Cabinet and of some Liberals receiving favours from the Government, whereas the only Liberal support we can get is that support which will come to us anyway by reason of the Policy. This has a disheartening effect among Conservatives and some say the Government is a Conservative Government run for the benefit of a few

Liberals who cannot deliver any results. Possibly the rewards that have gone to Liberals have not been numerous but some of the appointments of the Civil Service Commission and of the Government have given rise to this view, and there are Conservatives who, consequently, feel like giving the Government a whack.[43]

This yearning to get back to "straight Party lines" and to reopen the channels of patronage closed by wartime reforms was typical of many a Conservative party professional in all parts of the country. In taking their stand against continued co-operation with elements of the Liberal party they were playing into the hands of Mackenzie King, whose object was to lure as many errant Liberals as possible back into the fold, and they were a constant source of embarrassment and annoyance to Meighen. This was especially true of their unofficial leader and chief spokesman, Robert Rogers of Winnipeg. "The hon. Bob" had been one of the casualties of Union Government in 1917, his resignation from the Borden Cabinet having been virtually a prerequisite to the entrance of the Unionist Liberals in whose eyes he personified the most reprehensible features of Toryism. He had opposed the coalition in the first place, he was one of the first to demand its dissolution once the war was over and since then he had worked steadily, if surreptitiously, to spread the gospel that the Government must become again a purely Conservative one and fight the next election as such. There was no love lost between Rogers and Meighen. The latter had been one of the first advocates of coalition during the war and with Rogers' resignation from the Government in 1917 had supplanted him as the leading western Conservative. Now he was attempting to consolidate a party which would be in actuality as well as in name Liberal and Conservative, a project for which Rogers had not the slightest sympathy. Working mainly from his office in Winnipeg but with frequent trips hither and yon in search of support, Rogers set out to discredit both the project and the Prime Minister, appealing to Conservatives wherever he went to raise the old pure blue flag.

Some of Meighen's friends in Manitoba took the trouble to keep him up to date on Rogers' doings. One of them wrote:

> I think it wise that you should be informed of the activity against you be the Old Guard of the Conservative party in Winnipeg.
> I have therefore decided to communicate the following information.
> Some two weeks ago at a small meeting they put a resolution repudiating you as leader of the Conservative party.
> About a week ago a notice appeared in the press calling a meeting of the Conservatives of the city. . . . Talking over this advertised meeting with Mr. R. G. O'Malley we concluded from information we possessed that the real object of this meeting was to prosecute further propaganda against you. We consequently decided that

some of your Conservative friends should attend the meeting and
take part in the discussion, if our assumptions were correct, with
the object of frustrating their purpose. Mr. O'Malley and I therefore saw a number of your friends and had them present at the meeting. . . .

  The Hon. Mr. Rogers gave a lenghty [sic], carefully prepared address against you and your Government. . . .

O'Malley had replied, "heroically and ably" defending Meighen[44] but
clearly Rogers was in no mood to be deterred. "Mr. Rogers' supporters,"
another Winnipegger told Meighen, "are holding meetings once a week.
These meetings, however, are not very largely attended but it is clear
that a real effort is being made by Mr. Rogers to create an organization
in Winnipeg, opposed to the Government."[45] And this was confirmed
in still another letter: "The Hon'l Robert is very busy these days working
along the lines of the duty of reforming the old Tory party and not being
tangled up with the Liberals or Union Liberals."[46] Meighen answered:
"I noticed in last night's Montreal Star that following a long series of
telegrams the Hon. Robert Rogers had hurried East and would hold
conferences in Montreal, Toronto and Ottawa. The report further
stated that his office has been for a long time a scene of vast activity, his
staff being busy day and night. Having had none too light or exhilarat-
ing a day I was glad of this piece of news at night."[47]

  So highly regarded was Rogers' organizing and electioneering prowess
(not for nothing had he earned the title of "Minister of Elections")
that some people thought it essential that there be a *rapprochement*
between him and Meighen before the Government went to the country.
Dr. F. L. Schaffner, a Manitoba senator who periodically sent the Prime
Minister advice couched in the peremptory tones of command, wrote:
"Elections cannot be long delayed. To be brief I want you and Bob
Rogers to get together. *Now you need him,* you have no one else to take
his place. . . . Now Arthur you must know that 'Bob' with all his faults
we love him still, and he possesses qualities that serves [sic] well in running
elections, and dealing with men. I think he knows more people from
coast to coast than any other man in Canada. . . . You are saddly [sic] in
need of an organizer of the Rogers stamp. . . . 'Nuf said.' "[48] Enough
said, but more easily said than done. How was this reconciliation to be
effected? Meighen responded: "I have had discussions with the party
you name and not only have no objection but would be glad indeed to
have his co-operation and help. He has not, so far as I can see, been
disposed to render this help in the past—rather the reverse. I know he
has very many friends and always will have."[49] Since to both Meighen
and Rogers "co-operation" would mean playing the game his way,
Schaffner's suggestion, however sensible, was less than realistic.

  He was, however, entirely realistic in mentioning the need of organization. It was this with which practical politicians like Rogers and his friends from coast to coast were primarily concerned. Organization, they thought, was more important in winning elections than all the principles and platform eloquence in Christendom. They knew that the organization of the Conservative party had collapsed with the establishment of the Union Government, which, quite rightly, they blamed for that collapse. The organization, after all, had been geared to the proposition that Liberals were mortal enemies who must be beaten and it was not adaptable to the strange situation which prevailed during the 1917 election when some Liberals for once were on the right side. For the wartime election a sort of *ad hoc* Unionist organization had been set up. Once that contest was over it promptly fell apart, while in the meantime the organizational apparatus of the Conservatives, which had not functioned in a campaign since 1911, had practically ceased to be. In this respect the Liberals now enjoyed an advantage, for their party machinery had been kept in working order during and after the crisis of 1917 by the Laurier loyalists. The problem was serious not only at the national but at the provincial level as well. W. H. Dennis of the Halifax *Herald* explained to Meighen why the Nova Scotia Conservatives had been disastrously defeated in the provincial election of July 1920, when their representation was cut from a dozen to two. ". . . When the election was announced, the Conservative party—which has been in a state of chaos since Union Government was formed—was without organization. They failed to rally their forces together—there was *NO* real leadership and *NO* enthusiasm."[50]

With another national election approaching enthusiasm was necessary and so was organization. So, the Rogers Tories would have said, was some real leadership for they had little faith in Meighen's ability in that respect. But the only enthusiasm they could feel was for the old Conservative party, which they wanted to revivify and reorganize. Like Ernest Lapointe they thought it quite absurd to believe that one could be a National Liberal *and* Conservative and as far as they were concerned there had been too much catering to the Grits in an effort to nourish this hybrid monster. Let it die, and when it did the Conservative phoenix, which had destroyed itself in 1917, would be born anew and rise splendid from the ashes. To Meighen this idea seemed utterly quixotic, not to say idiotic. Commenting on the antics of the Rogers group, he wrote: "The talk some of those fellows go through in Winnipeg is really remarkable. They do not seem to have done very much careful reasoning."[51] There certainly was one cardinal fact the Tory diehards seemed to overlook: the sole hope for the Government lay in gaining Liberal votes because the nadir of the Conservative party as such was at hand.

Just how embarrassing and dangerous to the Government the activities of these recalcitrant Conservatives might be was shown by one episode which reached its lamentable climax shortly before Parliament convened in February 1921. A favourite argument of these people, and in this they were at one with Mackenzie King, was that the 1917 union of Liberals and Conservatives had been effected solely for the more vigorous prosecution of the war and that the administration elected at that time ceased to have a mandate from the people as soon as the war was won. According to this view it was dishonourable for the coalition to perpetuate itself and to embark upon a programme of peacetime policies for which there was no public sanction. Almost the first letter Meighen received when it became known that he would succeed Borden was from J. H. Burnham, the Tory member of Parliament for Peterborough West, who announced that he had resigned his seat and at some length explained why.

> In congratulating you upon your elevation which you will remember I prophesied some years ago I must not forget that in 1917 I was elected by members of all parties in West Peterborough who responded loyally to the general invitation of Sir Robert Borden to Canadians to join together for the one and only purpose then before Canada viz., the united and successful prosecution of the war. When the war ended I expected Sir Robert Borden to return to pre-war political conditions and ventured to intimate the necessity of so doing by going to the cross-benches. A new appeal to the country was a necessary redemption of a promise both express and implied made to the country. Why was a Union Government formed if it was not for a temporary purpose? This return to pre-war political conditions has been delayed at Ottawa but cannot in honour be longer delayed by me. Relying upon my good faith and upon the improbability of my taking an improper advantage of the general support given to me as standing for a war government during wartime I am in honour bound to hand back the trust then handed to me by so many of my constituents who altogether differ from my views of the proper peace-policy for Canada. If I stand again it will be as a moderate protectionist and as one also out to fight the growth of atheism in this country and the sinister modern disregard of liberty. Let us go to the country and begin the new era by an honourable acknowledgment of our duty to those who trusted us and suspended their political principles for the sake of unity in war as we must do now for the sake of justice and good faith in time of peace. With much of this I have no doubt you will agree. My resignation has been sent to the Speaker.[52]

Burnham had this published in the press with the result, he reported a couple of days later, that "scores of old Liberals who were bitterly reproached for having put us in power wh[ich] we now refused to give up, are overjoyed at my letter since it removed this reproach from them here at least."[53] For some reason he neglected to see that Meighen's reply to his letter was also published.

> I readily accord you full credit for sincerity of purpose in the step you have taken. Your reasoning however I cannot follow. The immediate and paramount duty of the Government elected in December, 1917 was the prosecution of the war to the full extent of Canada's power. Its further duty, however, was the implementing of the complete legislative programme outlined in its platform, much of which was unconnected with the war, and as well, the proper conduct of all public business coming before it during its term of office. There was no promise express or implied that such term of office should be subject to other limitations than those constitutionally appertaining.
> You urge in your letter that we go back to pre-war political conditions. I do not think a progressive country ever goes back to old and past conditions in the political or any other sphere and it is my earnest hope that this young country, building upon the foundations so firmly laid in the trials of war, and upon the measure of unity then achieved, will go forward to a still greater unity and a larger national life. It is only by seeking steadfastly this goal that the Government can command, and commanding, deserve the support of forward looking Canadians.[53]

To this Burnham retorted: "The promises I refer to were made on the platform by Borden & I heard him. However if you *will* run your head against Public Opinion it is of course your own business. Your whole outfit will be wiped out."[54] He followed this up by offering to debate publicly with the Prime Minister the propriety of his resignation, which Meighen declined to do,[55] and then, evidently seeing that he might not have the backing of the Government in the by-election his resignation had necessitated, he wrote again:

> Your adoption of the old Conservative policy of Protection reconciles me to your course although the change of party name has greatly displeased the Conservative party & has ruined the old organization.
> I can carry W. Peterborough where my action has been generally approved & if you would care to consider the matter of my representing you here in the election I am willing to do so.[56]

Meighen could not let pass unchallenged the condescending insinuation that he had just become a convert to "the old Conservative policy of Protection." He answered:

> I have your letter. . . . Nothing in any pronouncement with regard to tariff matters which I have made since your resignation, differs in the faintest degree from the opinions expressed on this same subject in the speech I made on the Budget, and on many previous occasions. The speech on the Budget was made months before your resignation. I cannot, therefore, see how anything I have said since on the subject

of the tariff can have had anything to do in bringing about a change in your attitude towards me now.

As to candidature in Peterborough . . . that is a matter entirely for the electors for that County, and not for me, to decide.[57]

As it turned out Burnham was not recognized as the Government candidate; a local convention nominated Roland Denne instead. However, Burnham insisted on running, as Meighen described it, "in support of the Government's general policy, and, as he calls himself, a 'straight Conservative.' I feel the right thing to do is to support only a candidate who has confidence in the administration and to go in and support him with zeal and courage. That we are going to do."[58]

All told there were five men in the field. In addition to the two Conservatives, "straight" and otherwise, the Liberals, Labourites and United Farmers each nominated a candidate and all the zeal and courage available did not suffice to get Mr. Denne elected. The Liberals won the seat handily with Denne in second place and Burnham in third. The results indicated, as one angry politician put it to Meighen, that "if we had had but one candidate . . . we would have won, and we can put the disaster down to saphead Burnham."[59] It was small consolation, though, to know that it could have been won; the fact was that it was lost, an industrialized district where Meighen expected his tariff message to be whole-heartedly welcomed. True, the protectionist vote had been divided between the two Conservatives and probably a good many working men had found the Labour nominee's emphasis on unemployment, the high cost of living and the power of the bosses more to their liking. But even those who agreed with Meighen about the protective tariff apparently disagreed with him that it was in danger. H. H. Stevens, campaigning for Denne, reported from the scene: "I am working to get a number of leading business men & prominent citizens to come out openly as such on the tariff question. It is hard as they are saying it is not an issue."[60] Meighen, having striven in speeches at Peterborough and elsewhere to show that it was the only issue, found Stevens' report most discouraging. If this kind of indifference prevailed in Ontario the outlook was dismal indeed, since that was one of the two provinces in which defence of protection was expected to be most popular.

The other, of course, was Quebec where the tariff question was supposed to overcome the popular obsession with conscription. In May 1921 this means of making headway there was put to a test in a by-election in the County of Yamaska on the south shore of the St. Lawrence. The seat was opened by the death of the incumbent Liberal. He had won it in 1917 by a large majority but big Liberal majorities had been the rule in Quebec in the wartime election and Yamaska was looked upon by the Conservatives as fair fighting ground. A. A. Mondou, who had narrowly won the riding in 1911 as a Conservative-Nationalist but had not contested it in 1917, was again the Conservative candidate. He denied, however, that he was the Government candidate, claiming that he opposed the Government that had introduced conscription as "a punishment for Quebec's anti-imperialism."[61] He denounced conscription ringingly and promised that if elected he would press for the repeal of the Military Service Act. At the same time he described himself as an independent protectionist supporting the Government's tariff policy, which he suggested was now the real issue. Of this he failed to convince the electors. In spite of his repudiation of conscription and his disavowal of any connection with Meighen and the Government, Mondou was beaten by the largest majority, except for 1917, in the county's history.

In brooding over this setback some people contended that Mondou would have fared better had he faced up to the conscription issue, frankly identified himself with the Government and fought like a man. "If our party," one of them told Meighen, "could only find 2 or 3 fighters like Chapleau, or Caron and before that like Cartier and Taché, men who did not know what fear was, and grabbed the bull by the horns and put the fear of God into the Electors. The politician who faces the storm with determination to make his opponents dance, gets, in a short time the upper hand."[62] And Senator Blondin wrote:

> Ever since the 1917 election, a strong current of opinion has prevailed amongst our Montreal and Quebec friends, that it would be a mistake to defend the past actions of the Union Government, and that we should try to make the people forget the war and conscription, by speaking only of the present and of the future.
> I have always contended and pleaded with my friends that it was useless to dodge the question of conscription, which the Liberals would certainly not fail to make the paramount issue of the coming battles in Quebec.

He had, Blondin said, suggested this approach before the Yamaska by-election but Mondou preferred to take the opposite tack. The failure there, the Senator thought, showed that his advice should have been taken and he now proposed to stump the province to educate its people about conscription.[63] Meighen was in complete agreement that this was much the better way. He intended to follow it himself in his own appearances in Quebec. Until the misapprehensions and prejudices connected with the conscription question could be cleared away, as he hoped to do, Quebec would never grasp, as it must grasp, the urgent significance of the tariff issue. How slow the educative process was, how ingrained the misapprehensions, how irrelevant the tariff controversy seemed to the people of Quebec, he was soon to discover.

CHAPTER TWO

THE ANXIETY OF OFFICE

L ATE IN September 1920, in answer to one of Senator Schaffner's lengthy advisory epistles, Meighen wrote:

> If there is one thing more than another which has impressed me since I took this office it is the necessity so strongly urged by you in this letter of keeping a cheerful mind under all circumstances. If one is not able to do this to a fair extent anyway he would break under the load before very long. I want to assure you that this task and indeed the task of all Ministers for that matter, but of course the task of the Prime Minister in particular, demands an intensive concentration hour by hour and moment by moment [that] it is hard for one who has not some experience in it to realize. If you were close by for even a few days you would enthusiastically come to the conclusion that one requires the assistance and loyalty of his friends and furthermore that without a very generous and consistent loyalty from his friends no one could possibly succeed and indeed anything like a strong and useful government could not be carried on. I believe and am cheered by the belief that when it is over and I can feel that I have done my duty without flinching and to the utmost of my capacity, the memory of it all will be worth while and a real pleasure. Until it is over though I have no hope at all that the anxiety of office will cease to do what it is doing, namely, quite submerge my sense of enjoyment.
>
> I intend, and will succeed if resolution is worth anything, in refusing [sic] to be over-worried but I want to say to you, and I know I can say it freely, that what makes this the most difficult of all is the disposition on the part of those from whom I think I should expect co-operation and support to listen rather . . . to the enemy.[1]

In view of all the evidence of discord within the ranks and of the decline of his government it was not surprising that Meighen sometimes felt disheartened but one would never have guessed, watching and listening to him in the House of Commons, that he felt anything but pleasure in his work. On his feet in the House, where it was less a matter of managing men than of debating policies, he was in his element, was always supremely confident. There he was not dealing with anything so slippery as the machinations of Bob Rogers, so baffling and impenetrable as the bottomless morass of Quebec politics, or so uncontrollable as the righteous folly of "saphead Burnham." In the House one argued according to well-defined rules about more or less precise questions with men whom one directly confronted. One could really come to grips with public issues as well as with one's opponents. Matters could be pinned down and decided one way or the other, finally and conclusively. There was an order, a rationality about the business of the Commons which was absent from the business of leading a national political party.

Meighen had always derived a certain exhilaration from his parliamentary life and, depressing as the general situation in the country seemed to be, the 1921 session was no exception. There was in particular one new experience on that February afternoon when Parliament opened which, repeated day after day, was to become as familiar as it was—for Meighen—stimulating and enjoyable: for the first time he confronted Mackenzie King directly across the aisle. Of course the moment King re-entered the House in 1919 Meighen had singled him out as the special object of his wit and scorn. Now, with the one having risen to the place coveted by the other, the rivalry of the two men was brought into sharper focus. A contest of opposites without equal in Canada's past was about to begin. Sir John A. Macdonald, to be sure, had differed very markedly from the series of Reform leaders he outlasted: the tempestuous George Brown, the sternly moral Alexander Mackenzie, the sensitive, scholarly Edward Blake. The dissimilarities, too, between Sir Wilfrid Laurier and Sir Robert Borden had been too many and obvious to pass unnoticed. But none of those earlier contrasts was as starkly complete as the contrast between Meighen and King. These two were completely incompatible—Presbyterian Puritans both, perhaps, but of different breeds for all that.

The antithesis was nowhere so brightly illuminated as in the House of Commons and the 1921 session cast a good deal of light upon it. For one thing it brought out King's habit of ancestor worship. Always prone to treat the party battle as a monumental moral struggle between the forces of good and evil, he tended to romanticize his grandfather's role but much more to romanticize his own. William Lyon Mackenzie had valiantly contended against a government of Tory tyrants who had held the people and their representatives in high contempt and ridden roughshod over their rights and liberties: thus the folklore of the past. William Lyon Mackenzie King, his residuary legatee in the never-ending strife, must carry on the good, eternal fight against the powers of darkness, now led by Arthur Meighen, the spiritual descendant of those arrogant and autocratic Tories of another day. There was a new Tory despotism in power now. Putting on his favourite raiment as defender of the Constitution and democracy, King rode out to do it battle, his bludgeon of verbosity raining *clichés* and platitudes on every hand. He preferred to deal, not with particular questions of policy, but with general constitutional

principles, with the abstract, not with the concrete. His understanding of
those principles was usually in inverse proportion to his fondness for them
but by concentrating on them he was enabled better to practise the art
of sanctimonious demagoguery in which he had no peer.

His first joust with the windmill occurred in the throne-speech debate.
The ministers, he declared in an amendment to the motion for an address,
"do not possess the confidence of the House or of the country, and . . .
their retention of office constitutes a usurpation of the powers of popular
government."[2]   And what proved that they were usurpers?   In a long,
declamatory and often irrelevant oration King undertook to explain.
The present Parliament had been elected to deal with war, not peace,
issues.   There was a new Prime Minister.   Many members of the Union
Government had now disappeared, either through death or resignation.
The Government of 1921 was therefore not the Government returned
to power in 1917; neither it nor this Parliament had a mandate and
consequently there should be an immediate appeal to the people.   Why,
said King in his peroration, in what Meighen presently described as
"those last fifty awful sentences,"[3] the only difference between the
usurpation of power in Russia and its usurpation in Canada was that in
the one case physical violence and in the other legislative violence had
been employed.   During the war, he asserted, parliamentary government
had suffered so much that now the country was "witnessing open defiance
of the most fundamental of all principles of free government, namely:
the right of the people to control their own Parliament."   In 1917, he
went on, "the people thought they were returning patriots to power.
They find in office to-day only office seekers, and office holders, those who
love the loaves and the fishes, who make broad their phylacteries, who
enlarge the border of their garments, who love the uppermost rooms at
feasts, and the chief seats of the synagogues, and greetings in the markets,
who make clean the outside of the cup and of the platter, but within are
full of extortion and excess."[4]

In rising to answer Meighen began, as was to be expected, by paying
his personal respects to the leader of the Opposition.   King at the outset
of his own remarks had complimented the Prime Minister on his elevation to that office, remarking that to him

> on personal grounds it was . . . a source both of pride and of plea-
> sure to learn that His Excellency had chosen as his first adviser
> one who in university days was a fellow undergraduate, and whose
> friendship, through a quarter of a century, had survived the vicissi-
> tudes of time, not excepting the differences of party warfare and
> acrimonies of political debate. . . . I shall strive with him to pre-
> serve the highest traditions of our public life, and to be governed
> in all things by its amenities, and never by its animosities.[5]

Was this hypocrisy, this reference to their long "friendship," or did King really believe in its existence? They had never been friends at university, at least to Meighen's knowledge, in fact had hardly known each other there. They had gone their separate ways after graduation, moving in different worlds until the election of 1908 threw them both into the House of Commons. Meighen had never been a friend of King when the latter was Minister of Labour and had had nothing to do with him since his disappearance from the House in 1911. If this for King constituted friendship, he was a friendless man indeed. In any event Meighen's response gave the idea short shrift. "I have," he said, "known the leader of the Opposition for, I think, something over a quarter of a century. I think I understand his public opinions and I think I can clearly get the meaning of his speeches; and I assure him here and now that if the essential humour of his addresses is always to be so thinly covered by a veil of argument and satire, as it was this afternoon our relations will never be disturbed in Parliament."[6]

As for the address by King to which the House had just listened, Meighen promised to try to extract and deal with what there was of substance in it. "I will have to drag the substance from under a mass of hyperbole, but the effort must be made. I may have the aspiration—but if I have I certainly have not the talent—to rival my hon. friend in the power of declamation, a power that he has exercised throughout most of his life and which he has brought to some degree of perfection." Having thus returned the personal compliment, Meighen launched out on a point by point refutation of King's argument about usurpation and the necessity of an immediate election. It was true, he admitted, that winning the war had been the overriding issue in 1917 but who had ever heard of the idea that as soon as an issue had disappeared a government must seek a fresh mandate? In any case the Union Government had been pledged, not only to win the war, but also to deal with post-war reconstruction, which it was now endeavouring to do. For it was in effect the same government, despite some changes in personnel, carrying on the same policies as it had under Borden. Also, by King's reasoning, if a government elected in wartime should go to the country when the war was over, then one elected in peacetime should go to the country when war broke out. Yet in 1914 the Liberals had deprecated in the strongest terms any idea of holding an election then. Why the very same Opposition leader who now denied that the Government had any mandate to touch the tariff had demanded only a year ago that it undertake a tariff revision. The tariff, said Meighen, was a great issue, no question of that. The Government had taken its stand unmistakably in defence of protection. Let the Opposition take a stand too; let it make up its mind where it stood, instead of supporting here protection, there a revenue tariff and somewhere else free trade. If and when that happened and the issue was joined it would be time to talk about elections. Meanwhile charges of usurpation and despotic disregard for popular rights were so much dishonest clap-trap which should deceive no one. As long as the Government enjoyed the confidence of the House of Commons it was entitled to govern until Parliament's term expired. If the House wanted to withdraw its confidence, well and good. All it had to do was vote for King's amendment now before it. If, however, it voted confidence in the Government, then King would have more time to nurse his only real grievance which was that he was out of office, or as Meighen paraphrased it, "that you should not be there—that I should be there instead of you."[7]

Despite the fact that his amendment was defeated, despite the verbal trouncing Meighen had given him, King returned again and again during the session to his favourite theme, lecturing the ministers about the principles of responsible government. On one occasion, referring to a number of vacancies in the House, he belaboured Meighen for not saying when by-elections would be held, at the same time wringing his hands in lamentation over the fact that the people in those ridings were without representation.

> As Prime Minister of this country my right hon. friend has a great responsibility and a solemn trust imposed on him, and as part of that responsibility and of that trust it is his duty to take this House and the people of Canada into his confidence in very considerable measure, on matters of great public concern, and in this connection to state at the present time in a frank, open and straightforward manner what he intends to do in order to give these constituencies their rights to representation.[8]

Meighen's tart answer was a thrust that sank deep:

> Mr. Speaker, I am sure if any improvement of character or conduct on my part could be looked for as a result of the scolding from the leader of the Opposition . . . , I rise very much chastened and purified by it. I recognize the privilege of being given lessons in candour and honesty and frankness at the hands of my hon. friend.[9]

Not only was the Government in power by usurpation and in defiance of the Constitution, not only did it refuse to hold by-elections and generally treat the rights of the people with contempt, but, said King in the Budget debate, it was kept in office by that powerful group of oligarchs whose ambition to dominate the state threatened the very foundations of democracy. It was nothing new, of course, to accuse the Conservative party of being the creature of big business; that sort of thing had been the stock-in-trade of Reformers and Liberals for generations. But by the time King got around to voicing it, it had become nothing more than a demagogic shibboleth, sanctified by incessant ritualistic repetition. As events were soon to show, his accusations along this line were singularly, almost comically, inappropriate and untrue. They did, however, fit in nicely with his self-assumed role of the St. George of democracy, and also with the tradition of righteousness of which he thought his grandfather and himself to be the chief exemplars. Mounting his charger, King swept in to slay the dragon.

> The self-same interest [he declared] which caused members of the Government to cling to office despite honourable obligation and constitutional right, has operated in like manner to cause certain members of the financial, manufacturing, transportation, and distributing interests to continue to look to Government for special favours and special privilege, and in return to support the administration by direct methods as well as indirect in its retention of power against the will of the people as a whole. Thus we have come to have in Canada, on the one hand, a Prime Minister and a ministry to whom usurpation of office and the exercise of autocratic methods in Government belong as a sort of natural right, and, on the other, a small circle, a sort of little oligarchy of interwoven financial, manufacturing, transportation and distributing interests, prepared in return for a continuation of favour and special privilege, to use their wealth and influence to keep the Administration in power, and thereby constituting in a very true sense the real though invisible Government of this country.
>
> We have, in other words, political power united with plutocracy in a band of self-interest, the former the visible symbol of authority, the latter the governing and directing force in the State. We have a Government, democratic in form, but autocratic in behaviour, and back of that Government, and vastly superior to it in many respects, we have the privileged coterie of wealthy and influential men . . . who are not satisfied with sharing in the control of industry and the State, but wish to dominate both. They are for the time being able to exercise this domination at their own free will, for the Administration owes its existence to their dictation and its continuance in office to the powerful influence which in a multitude of directions, they are able to exert. There is the real situation with which this country is faced at the present time. That is the danger to Canada at the moment . . . that we have on the one side the selfish groups united together working for their joint ambitions, and, on the other, the great body of the people left to look after themselves.[10]

King was too shrewd to name the dominating oligarchs, to enumerate the special privileges they allegedly enjoyed or to point to any specific evidence that they controlled the Government. For his purposes it was enough to make the accusation in general terms and hope that the populace would be impressed. Unfortunately Meighen was not in the House to hear and answer these horrendous allegations; he was fulfilling an engagement out of town. The answer, however, came in the election campaign a few months later when he found himself engaged in battle against the topmost representatives of that oligarchy of which, according to King, he was the willing, servile accomplice.

These animadversions of King on the Constitution, on responsible government and democracy, his high-flown professions of faith and his dire warnings of autocracy, Meighen regarded not only as utterly ludicrous in themselves but as a smokescreen deliberately emitted to conceal what he was sure was the one real issue—the tariff. King, striving still to gain the favour of both western free traders and eastern protectionists, was anxious to avoid being forced to take a definite stand on trade policy. Temperamentally, of course, he was averse to taking a definite stand on anything except general principles generally accepted, but the tariff question held a particularly large number of pitfalls for the unwary. The Government was firmly, irrevocably committed to protection; the speech from the throne had stated that it must be "consistently maintained." It appeared, therefore, that the ministers had decided that western support on a large scale was expendable as far as the next election was concerned. No matter how moderate the protective tariff or how reasonable the defence of it offered, the very word "protection" was anathema to the farmers out there. On the other hand King could not afford to commit himself consistently and unreservedly to free trade or even to a tariff for revenue only. To do so would be to estrange hopelessly many Liberals in Ontario and Quebec. Therefore from his point of view the right thing to do was to play down the tariff question, saying what seemed to be the appropriate thing about it in each section of the country, and to concentrate on other matters, even if spurious issues had to be manufactured for the purpose.

While King pursued this strategy Meighen tried to keep the subject of the tariff always to the fore and in his own speech in the Budget debate of 1921 sought, as he had in the corresponding debate the year before, to expose the essential falsity of King's position. If the Liberals came to power and had to make a tariff, he said in effect, there must inevitably be a betrayal, either of western opinion which King so carefully cultivated when he was in the West, or of eastern opinion without whose support no government could be maintained. In particular he heaped scorn upon the insincerity of King's efforts to convince the West that he would substantially reduce the tariff and upon the witless willingness of some Progressives in the House to accept his promises at their face value. Meighen's speech nettled his opponents—Crerar described it as "an exhibition of cheap political vaudeville for over two hours and a half"[11]—but the future would demonstrate the essential truth of what he said.

The Opposition's financial critic, W. S. Fielding, had introduced the customary amendment during the Budget debate and to this Meighen devoted most of his attention. It was a long and artfully ambiguous amendment, regretting the declaration that the tariff should be protective and affirming that the aim of policy should be to encourage industries based on Canada's natural resources, "the development of which may reasonably be expected to create healthy industries, giving promise of enduring success. . . ." It pointed out that the tariff was a tax and should be lowered in order to reduce the cost of living but added a significant few words of caution: in any readjustment "regard must be had to existing conditions of trade, and changes made in such a manner as will cause the least possible disturbance to business."[12]

This anaemic declaration was made to order for Meighen's gift of satire. He would, he said, address himself "with such brevity as is possible, to a discussion of the amendment, the challenge to the Budget, if you may call it that—although the word has a virility and masculinity that makes it wholly inapplicable to this amendment." The House had been led to expect that the Liberals would incorporate in the amendment the tariff resolution adopted at their 1919 convention, with its clarion call for the abolition of duties on this and that and the reduction of duties on other things. Where was the 1919 platform now, asked Meighen; on the scrap heap? As for the Progressives, they had not moved their tariff platform in the House of Commons either and would no doubt vote for this namby-pamby Liberal amendment. Michael Clark, once a Liberal and then a Unionist but now in the Progressive camp and a doctrinaire free-trader, had said that his group was in the same boat with the Liberals as far as the tariff was concerned. But just the night before the chief whip of the Progressives, Levi Thomson, had told the House what they wanted: free food, free cement, free farm implements and so forth. Could anyone find any of these things in the amendment before the House, or anything else that was in the platform of the Farmers party adopted in November 1918? "Oh," exclaimed Meighen, "I would like to have been present when this amendment was being fixed up. I would like to have been around when the pruning, and the sandpapering, and the varnishing, were being applied to the verbiage in order to get the amendment in such shape that they could all get in on the vote." The Progressive leaders, he charged, in their willingness to support the Fielding amendment, had made themselves "a political annex" to the Liberal party, "servile tools and minions of the official Opposition, ready to do whatever they are bid to do . . . an adjunct, an annex, and a dilapidated annex at that." Small wonder Mr. Crerar was annoyed!

In this whole matter of the tariff, Meighen proceeded, the two Opposition parties were engaged together in a process of "hocus-pocusing," of "circuitous sinuosity."

> Why not throw the mask away? Why not join right up? Am I to be told that I am anxious to keep these people divided? I was paid

that compliment by the leader of the Opposition last session. "Oh,"
he said, "you would like to divide us." I do not want to divide
them. I think if I did that is just what would unite them. Why do
they not unite? I do not care whether they divide or unite if they
will really and finally say where they stand and remain there. If
they want to unite let them do so. Let them throw away both platforms and frame one on which they can both stand and then remain
on it; but do not let them say that one is still back on the 1918 platform and the other on the 1919 platform, when, as a matter of fact,
each of them has in this House discarded them both.

Now the Liberals were very fond of posing as believers in low tariffs for
the benefit of western Canada. Even Fielding, who everyone knew was
a protectionist, talked about decreasing the cost of living by reducing
customs duties. But what had he done while he was Minister of Finance
under Laurier? He "found a protective tariff in effect, and he kept it
in effect—he scarcely changed it at all. Any change he made one could
scarcely see with a microscope." In fact when the Liberals came to
power in 1896 they started out by lowering the tariff by precisely seven-
tenths of one per cent. Of course they had abolished the duty on barbed
wire, binder twine and cream separators and admittedly those three items
were necessities for many farmers. Nor was that all by any means; there
was a long list of other reductions as well. Meighen read the list, from
a Liberal campaign pamphlet:

> Degras oleostearine,
> Florists' stock, as follows:—corns, tubers, rhizomes, auracaria,
> spiraea,
> Indian corn,
> Seed beans from Britain,
> Rape seed-sowing,
> Mushroom spawn,
> Artificial limbs,
> Asphaltum (refined),
> Religious tracts,
> Clay crucibles,
> Cyanogen,
> And another one if any hon. member can pronounce it: Q-u-e-
> b-r-a-c-h
> An hon. MEMBER: Sandpaper.
> Mr. MEIGHEN: Then follows:
> Extract of nut galls; Fashion plates,—
> I went through the entire list, and outside of the three that I
> have named I admit I found one that I think in this age of decay
> mighty fairly be described as a necessary of life, and that was—false
> teeth.

The reduction of seven-tenths of one per cent, Meighen conceded, had
just been the beginning. By the time the Liberals went out of office in
1911 the average tariff on dutiable goods had plunged—by all of another

two and one-half per cent—to 26.7 per cent. What was it now, in 1921? Exactly 21.2 per cent, Meighen claimed, and this when the revenue needs of the state were over three and a half times as great as in 1911. In the face of these facts Liberal allegations about the present oppressiveness of the tariff as a tax hardly made sense. Why even Rodolphe Lemieux had accused the Government of standing for high protection, Lemieux of all people, one of the leading spokesmen of a province where practically everybody, including himself, was a protectionist. "I wish he were in the Chamber," said Meighen, "so that I might ask him upon what authority he made that statement. . . . He makes it upon no authority at all. This Government stands for the tariff that is in existence to-day, and in any adjustment that will be made we will admit the principle of protection and we will apply it, but only to the extent that we have applied it during our term of office here, namely, to the extent essential to ensure production in this country and to enable producers to compete with similar businesses in other countries." A policy of moderate protection, he asserted, was manifestly the only course for Canada to follow. "Anything else under existing world conditions would be madness itself," especially in view of an impending and probably drastic upward revision of the American tariff. "The United States, by reason of its tremendous size and industrial potency, exercises inevitably a very great influence over our commercial conditions and destiny, and we must have regard to what it does, regard ten times greater than any concern they need have for us."[13]

These words and Meighen's entire approach to the tariff issue mirrored authentically the sentiment and policy of Canadian protectionists since the days of Sir John A. Macdonald. For Meighen it was in part a conscious hewing to the line first drawn by Macdonald but much more a conviction based on dispassionate analysis that one of the prices of Canada's very existence was the maintenance of a national economy, the possession of an economic life seperate from and as far as possible independent of that of the United States. It was the task of statesmanship to distribute the cost and the benefit of the tariff as widely and as fairly as possible but the protective principle could not be abandoned without running the risk of grave economic and social dislocation and of perilous political consequences. It remained to be seen whether the public still shared this view of the matter and whether Meighen could convince enough voters that a Mackenzie King government would in fact discard the National Policy.

With King in the House long disquisitions about the menace of despotism and the blessings of parliamentary government were to be expected. So were renewed arguments about the tariff, now that the West was up in arms, with Liberals and Progressives vying with one another to see who could say the nastiest things about protection. But there was another subject—the railway problem—to which the legislators had by now become so thoroughly accustomed that without extended reference to it no session of Parliament in those days would seem really complete. For all the debates of the past several years, all the Acts passed and the monies paid out of the Dominion treasury, the nationalization of the railway derelicts was still not quite accomplished. And beyond its accomplishment lay yet the formidable task of completing the consolidation and organization of all the publicly owned lines into one national system. Not surprisingly Meighen, "the father of railway nationalization" as he was sometimes dubbed by enemies of the policy, was most eager to see this work completed at last. He knew that it would not be completed without great anxiety, delay, discouragement and powerful opposition. As he wrote, "We have quite our share of difficulties, but this one is the most stupendous."[14]

By the spring of 1921 a good deal of progress had been made towards consolidation and integration. The Canadian Government Railways, comprising the Intercolonial, the Prince Edward Island Railway, the Hudson Bay Railway (as yet uncompleted) and the National Transcontinental, were being operated, along with the Canadian Northern and the Grand Trunk Pacific, as the Canadian National Railway System under a single board of directors, with D. B. Hanna, formerly of the Canadian Northern, as President. During 1921 economies arising in considerable measure from unified management resulted in an operating deficit fifty-five per cent and nearly twenty-one million dollars less than the deficit of the previous year.[15] This was a creditable achievement in view of the fact that to a considerable extent the component parts of the system had originally been planned to compete with, rather than to complement, one another and in view, also, of the very complexity of coordinating so vast and far-flung a network of lines of over seventeen thousand miles. In his annual report for 1921 Hanna wrote: "The three year period during which the present board has administered the Canadian National Railways has been full of operating difficulties and most disturbed economic conditions. In this period three separate groups of railways have been organized into one smooth working system."[16] What chiefly remained to be done in the early months of 1921 was to incorporate the Grand Trunk Railway into the national system but this had to await the report of the arbitration board which was to determine the value of certain classes of Grand Trunk stock.

The agreement of October 1919, providing for the acquisition of the Grand Trunk by the Crown, had stipulated that the arbitrators must complete their work within nine months of their appointment, subject to the right of the Government to extend the deadline should it so desire. The agreement also laid it down that, pending receipt of the arbitrators' report, control and management of the company should be vested jointly in the existing board of directors in London, which would continue to discharge a portion of its usual powers, and in a committee of management, appointed by the Government and representing the Grand Trunk and the Canadian National Railways. This awkward and cumbersome arrangement was a compromise. The directors had argued that they could not relinquish control because they had a duty to look after the equity of the shareholders until the arbitration board had reported and that in any case they required access to the records and accounts of the company to prepare their case for presentation to the arbitrators. The Government, on the other hand, wanted to see the Grand Trunk united with the other railways, as far as operation was concerned, without further delay.

The arbitrators were duly appointed on July the ninth, 1920, the day before Meighen was sworn in as Prime Minister. Sir Walter Cassels of the Exchequer Court was chairman, Sir Thomas White represented the Government and no less a personage than William Howard Taft, former President of the United States, was the nominee of the company. For the first six months of its existence the arbitration tribunal did nothing, thanks to the unpreparedness of counsel for the Grand Trunk. With less than three months to go to the deadline when proceedings finally started on February the first, 1921, it was obvious that a report could not be produced within the allotted time. The question then arose, should the Government exercise its power to extend the time limit and, if so, on what terms? The decision reached in this regard at once involved Meighen in yet another controversy with the redoubtable Sir Alfred Smithers, chairman of the Grand Trunk's board of directors.

The decision was communicated to Smithers in a letter sent by J. D. Reid, the Minister of Railways, less than a week after the arbitrators had at last got down to work. The Government, Dr. Reid wrote, would be willing to extend the time on condition that the "embarrassing, inconvenient and expensive" system of joint administration by the board of the company and the committee of management be abolished and possession and control vested entirely in the Crown. Reid was probably not surprised by Smithers' rejection of this suggestion. Denying that the Grand Trunk was responsible for the delay in the arbitration proceedings and stating that the shareholders would never agree to relinquish their stock before the arbitration was finished, Smithers proposed a three months' extension with no strings attached. The Government refused to consider this. "It is imperative in the public interest," the Minister replied, "that the Government railway system should be unified

and put on an economic working basis immediately and this essential
requirement will not be met by unconditional extension of proceedings."

The outcome of this disagreement was to all intents and purposes a
foregone conclusion since the Grand Trunk was, as usual, a suppliant for
large funds from the Dominion treasury. Grand Trunk estimates total-
ling nearly ninety million dollars were before the House of Commons
but Reid informed Howard Kelley, president of the company, that "the
Government have come to the conclusion to make no further advances
on account of the Grand Trunk Railway . . . until we have some definite
and satisfactory assurance as to when the road is to come into our possession. In the absence of a satisfactory arrangement of these questions,
the Grand Trunk Railway must finance on its own responsibility from
this time on." To expect this, as Reid and Kelley knew equally well, was
to look for blood from a stone. In fact so hard-pressed was the company
that its treasurer blandly informed the Deputy Minister of Railways
that the Government would be expected to provide funds to meet certain interest payments due April the first, amounting to more than three
million dollars and including over one million dollars on debentures
which the company heretofore had always paid itself. When Reid remonstrated that the operating profits of the system must surely be sufficient to pay these charges, he was assured by Kelley that the company
had not sufficient cash. If true this was a damaging admission; if the
Grand Trunk was unable to meet the interest on its debenture stock the
value of its common and preferred shares, which was under arbitration,
could not amount to very much. However, Reid refused to believe that
the company was in quite such dire straits, pointing out that its budget
showed $32,000,000 to meet cash requirements and reminding Kelley
that he and Smithers had always emphasized the sufficiency of earnings
to take care of debenture interest payments.

As the first of April came nearer the Government appeared to be adamant in its refusal to provide funds for these charges. The desperate
Smithers now went over Reid's head to the Prime Minister. Was it
true, he asked Meighen, that the Government would not take care of
these obligations now coming due? "If so, position is most grave and I
shall be compelled to make public statement which will be most painful
and distressing." If default occurred it would be regarded in London
as a default by the government of Canada and justly, said Smithers, "as
the Government by Act of Parliament undertook to acquire Grand
Trunk, thus rendering Company powerless to finance itself." He was
addressing Meighen as head of the Government, his cable concluded,
"in the hope that you will avert what will be nothing short of a catastrophe."

This appeal fell on deaf ears and Meighen cabled a reply that should have removed all lingering hope on Smithers' part that the Government would relent, pay the interest and modify its stand on the matter of immediate possession. "Conduct of arbitration proceedings by Grand Trunk," he told Smithers, "has been dilatory and unsatisfactory." In December and again in January he had urged the company to speed up the preparation of its case in the arbitration and had warned it not to expect an extension of the time allowed for the hearings to be completed. The Grand Trunk must be united with the other Government railways as soon as possible. As long as the company expected to be financed with public funds it had no right further to postpone relinquishment of possession and control, "and we refuse to accede thereto." The agreement governing acquisition of the system by the Crown expressly provided that the company should do its own financing until it actually surrendered possession, "but if, as you assert, company cannot do this, then obviously you should not any longer insist on possession and control." Unless and until the company surrendered its properties to the Government there would be no more cash advances from Ottawa. When Smithers answered that he had not the legal power to transfer possession, Meighen informed him that if Kelley were authorized to execute its terms a Bill creating the legal power would at once be introduced in Parliament. "It is only upon these conditions," his message ended, "that Government can extend time or make further advances."

Instead of capitulating at once in the face of this ultimatum, Smithers had Kelley and F. H. Phippen, one of the Grand Trunk's legal counsel, frame an argumentative reply. In a lengthy letter they rehearsed the terms of the 1919 agreement, denied that the company was in any way to blame for the delays in the arbitration, affirmed the Government's duty to make further cash advances until the arbitrators had reported and asserted that the directors could not lawfully hand over the property without the prior consent of the shareholders.[17]

With the matter in this inconclusive state the nine months allotted to the arbitration ended and the proceedings lapsed. Ten days later Meighen introduced a Bill in the House providing for revival of the arbitration on condition that possession of the railway be surrendered at once by its directors. He accompanied his explanation of the measure with a review of the financial and other assistance given the Grand Trunk and the Grand Trunk Pacific since 1903, acknowledging that his government's policy had caused great indignation in England, especially among holders of Grand Trunk preferred and common stock, the market prices of which had plummeted. While understandable, he said, their attitude was entirely unwarranted. The Government had lived up to all its undertakings, unlike the parent company and its defunct offspring, and in addition had advanced to them a sum which, counting interest unpaid, now amounted to nearly $140,000,000, practically all of which was due, to say nothing of the large volume of their securities it had guaranteed. Was it unreasonable in the light of these facts to insist upon immediate possession? Meighen argued that in the public interest transfer of the property must be no longer delayed. "If the Grand Trunk as a government property is to be operated to advantage," he declared, "it must be operated in full unison and concert with the Canadian National railways. They should no longer be operated in any degree as distinct systems, but as one system. This advantage the Dominion is entitled to now, and, in the judgment of the Government, the Grand Trunk authorities are entirely without justification in seeking to withhold it."[18]

The Bill having been passed, it became the basis of a new agreement providing for the resumption of the arbitration, the transfer of possession, the removal of the head office of the Grand Trunk from England to Canada and the resignation of the board of directors. This was approved at a meeting of shareholders in London and signed on May the thirteenth. In quick succession the directors resigned, were succeeded by a new board appointed by the Government, and the arbitration hearings recommenced.

Meanwhile this game of cat and mouse between the Government and Smithers had brought the long-standing controversy over public ownership, which had simmered continuously ever since the nationalization of the Canadian Northern in 1917, once again to a rolling boil. Montreal, home of the Canadian Pacific Railway as well as Canadian headquarters of the Grand Trunk, was, as always, the focal point of the opposition and thence early in April came additional fuel for the fire. Its source was most eminent: Lord Shaughnessy, who had retired as President of the C.P.R. in 1918 but was still one of its directors. On April the sixth, 1921 he addressed to Meighen the following letter:

> National railway affairs are, I am sure, to you a source of constant anxiety. To my mind the railway question involving, as it does, such an enormous draft on the annual revenue of the country with no prospect of any improvement in the near future is the most momentous problem before our country at this time.
>
> I fear very much that the Grand Trunk transaction will prove disappointing and expensive, and if it were my case I would go a long way to secure the consent of the Grand Trunk shareholders to the abrogation of the statutory contract.
>
> I am enclosing a memorandum giving in rough outline my opinion as to the only process through which the atmosphere can be cleared. Some people, whether they believe it or not, will find in my suggestions a selfish desire on the part of the Canadian Pacific to control the railway situation. The Canadian Pacific bogey has served its turn on every occasion in the past thirty-five years, when schemes like the Canadian Northern, Grand Trunk Pacific and others of the

same type were being urged upon Parliament with a disregard of the cost to the country that must have been based upon lack of knowledge or misinformation.

The Canadian Pacific has no fish to fry, and I am not sure that my plan would be viewed with favour by the Executive, the directors or the shareholders. Everybody connected with the Company would prefer to see its status undisturbed, but it is impossible to accept with equanimity a situation which makes a demand on the public treasury of $200,000. per day, without any compensating advantage.

My memorandum, as you will observe, merely brings up to date on very much the same lines a similar paper that I prepared about the end of 1917, and sent to Sir Robert Borden. I was informed that he read it to his cabinet ministers, but he never discussed it contents with me beyond expressing the opinion . . . that apparently creating a Canadian Pacific monopoly the plan would not be acceptable to the country. Even if there were foundation for that theory at the time, the current of events since 1917 may have resulted in a decided change of sentiment.

I am submitting the memorandum to you with the best intentions in the world for such consideration as you may think it deserves, and would request that, with the exception of your colleagues, of course, its contents be considered confidential for a few days at any rate.[19]

The plan outlined in Shaughnessy's memorandum embodied a very radical departure from Government policy and it is hard to believe that he entertained any real hope that Meighen, so much the author of that policy, would accept it. He proposed that the nationalization of the Grand Trunk be halted and that system left with its private owners. It should be relieved of all its obligations with respect to the Grand Trunk Pacific, which it had failed to honour in any event, and be granted easy terms for the repayment of its debts to the Crown. The railway properties of the Canadian Pacific should be segregated from its other assets and added to the Canadian National Railways. The national system thus enlarged would be administered by the existing management of the C.P.R. for a term approaching perpetuity. The shareholders of the Canadian Pacific should be compensated for the surrender of their railway property with a fixed annual dividend to be guaranteed in perpetuity by the state, supplemented by an additional amount when the finances of the national system should warrant it. All deficits would be met out of the national treasury but the management of the railways must be completely free from political interference or control.

Shaughnessy, after discussing his plan in person with Meighen, amended his letter in some particulars at the Prime Minister's suggestion and, together with the memorandum, it was published in the press on April the twenty-fifth.[20] His ideas elicited a good deal of favourable comment, especially in Montreal where in some circles there was a compulsive determination to find some alternative to what the Government seemed bent on doing. On the other hand Meighen was warned by various people of the dangers inherent in the Shaughnessy plan and was himself quick to recognize its many interesting implications. To a friend in Ontario he wrote:

> You will see on reading Lord Shaughnessy's memorandum that it is not a suggestion for the Government to acquire the C.P.R., it is a suggestion embodying the transfer of the National Railways to the C.P.R., the management of the railways by the Company, the Government paying the deficit whatever it is, and guaranteeing the C.P.R. shareholders their dividends, but having nothing to say as to who should constitute the management or as to what obligations are incurred. I do not find the approval very general but there are a certain number who would approve of almost anything if it comes from a source they favour. I have every respect for Lord Shaughnessy but he has been a long time with the C.P.R.[21]

What Shaughnessy described as "the Canadian Pacific bogey" was more than that in Meighen's mind. Frequently in the past he had asserted that the only probable alternative to the policy of public ownership was control of all the important and potentially profitable lines by the C.P.R. A Canadian Pacific monopoly, he thought, was still a real and present danger which must be avoided and for that reason Shaughnessy's proposal was quite unacceptable. Equally unacceptable was the idea that the Government must shoulder large financial obligations, in paying dividends and making up deficits, while at the same time relinquishing all authority over the basic policies of the railways. The publicly owned system, Meighen agreed, must be wholly free from political interference in its day-to-day management and operation. But neither the Government nor Parliament could assume their inescapable financial responsibility for the affairs of a Crown corporation and at the same time divest themselves of ultimate power over it. For these reasons he dismissed the Shaughnessy plan as totally impracticable. In doing so, he was soon to discover, he further alienated and outraged powerful interests which once upon a time had regarded the Conservative party as their own and had supported it through thick and thin.

Among those who warned Meighen to beware of Shaughnessy's suggestions was Sir Joseph Flavelle, who expressed the opinion "that if this course were followed, both the Canadian Pacific Railway and the Government would be subject to deep suspicion that the transaction was not on the square."[22] For years Meighen had held Flavelle's business acumen, administrative ability and sound common sense in high regard. Just now he was particularly ready to listen to Sir Joseph's views on railway policy, for Flavelle was his first, one might say his only, choice as head of the consolidated Canadian National Railways which would come into being with the completion of the Grand Trunk arbitration. The offer of the position was extended orally by Meighen in March and after thinking it over and consulting some friends, Flavelle turned it down. The job, he wrote, should go to someone who believed in public ownership on principle, which he did not, and he feared "that through an impossible idealism in administration, I would render myself unhappy and bring embarrassment to the Government." In addition "urgent family reasons" and his advancing years made it undesirable for him to accept so heavy a task.[23] This decision was a blow Meighen had hoped against hope he would not have to suffer. "The responsibility I have to discharge is heavy," he replied, "and the one element which quite outweighs all others is the proper handling of our railway problem. The solution would have been well under way had you been able to accept the post."[24]

Meighen's disappointment was tempered somewhat when Flavelle agreed to become chairman of the interim board of directors of the Grand Trunk, which replaced the old board in London and was to act until the amalgamation of the Grand Trunk with the other national railways. This was encouraging, not only because of the important service Flavelle could render in that capacity, but also because it seemed to open up the possibility that his involvement in railway affairs might act as a spur and a challenge and induce him to reconsider the matter of the permanent headship. The interim board, which besides Flavelle included E. L. Newcombe, Deputy Minister of Justice, A. J. Mitchell, Vice-President of the Canadian National Railways, J. N. Dupuis of Montreal and Howard Kelley, who remained as President of the Grand Trunk, took office on May the twenty-sixth. Its task was clarified by an exchange of letters between Flavelle and Meighen shortly before that date. The former, asking for instructions, wrote:

> I presume it is unwise, as it is unnecessary, to speculate upon what is involved in the service you desire from the proposed Interim Board for the Grand Trunk System. I suppose that the Board in London, which the new Board replaces, interfered but little, if any, in the administration of the system in Canada. It may be that you simply desire the Board to be Trustees to hold the property until re-organization of the whole system of National Railways, and that it is your intention that the active officers of the Grand Trunk shall be directed to work with the active officers of the National Railway System, as at present organized, and that your new Board will fill a merely nominal position. If, on the other hand, it is your thought that the new Board will play any part in directing the early closer co-operation between the Grand Trunk and the present National System, I suppose the duties of the new Board, for the time they are in office, will require careful consideration in harmony with the plan which you have in mind.[25]

Meighen explained that Flavelle and his colleagues were expected to play no merely nominal role. "My intention," he said, "is that the new Board shall play a real part in directing the early closer co-operation between the Grand Trunk and the present National System, pending the appointment of a new Canadian National Railway Board to operate the entire Government Railways."[26]

As Flavelle began to address himself to his new task, comments on his appointment were by no means entirely favourable. That he had the confidence of the business world, at least in Toronto and its hinterland, there could be little doubt. But during the war he had been accused of shameless profiteering and these charges had left a residue of popular prejudice against him. Also, in Montreal there were mutterings, which in time became clearly audible, that his acceptance of the Grand Trunk chairmanship presaged his selection as chief of the Canadian National Railways and this, it was felt, might be detrimental to Montreal in view of his connections with Toronto financial interests. Indeed it was widely assumed, and not only in Montreal, that the interim chairmanship of the Grand Trunk was a stepping-stone to the top executive position in the complete national railway system. Meighen could not have been anxious to quell rumours to this effect or to forsake the hope that they might turn out to be true. Flavelle, however, was quick to clarify his stand on the matter, which had not changed since the end of March, and in another letter to the Prime Minister stated that under no circumstances would he become President of the C.N.R.[27]

At the same time he impressed upon Meighen the importance of finding someone for the position quickly and suggested various possibilities. One was Mr. Justice W. E. Middleton of the Ontario High Court of Justice, whom Sir John Aird of the Canadian Bank of Commerce had suggested to Flavelle for the job. Neither the latter nor Meighen, however, seems to have taken that nomination very seriously. More carefully considered were Home Smith, Chairman of the Toronto Harbour Commission, and W. N. Tilley. Flavelle was especially enthusiastic about Tilley, who, though a comparatively young man, was one of the leading members of the Toronto bar and had had extensive connections with railway matters, most recently as one of the Government counsel in the Grand Trunk arbitration. His qualifications were impressed upon Meighen by Flavelle in various communications, the last of which read:

> Covering Tilley.
> He dines with me alone to-night, the purpose being to tell me the plans he had made for his life, the hopes he had had for his future and, generally, reasons why he could, and reasons why he should, not consider the senior executive position of the New National Railway Board, if it were offered to him.[28]

This sounded suspiciously as though Flavelle had told Tilley he was recommending him but Meighen was not going to be rushed into making an offer, even though he had much respect for Tilley. Since Flavelle, in whose capacity he had the greatest confidence, had declined to serve, he preferred, knowing the importance of choosing the right man, to think about the various possibilities carefully before committing himself. Furthermore, while he recognized the force in Flavelle's argument that the chief executive of the railways, whoever he might be, should take part as soon as possible in making plans for the final unification of the lines, Meighen knew that in all probability a good deal of time would elapse before the Grand Trunk could be completely merged with the other roads. The arbitration hearings would occupy a good many weeks yet, the preparation of the arbitrators' report would take quite a few more, and there might be an appeal from their decision to the Judicial Committee of the Privy Council by one side or the other, as the agreement with the Grand Trunk allowed. There was therefore, he decided, no urgently pressing need for an appointment and he had faith that in the meantime Flavelle, Hanna and their associates would further the operational unification of the lines in every possible way. Thus he let the matter ride, with the result that by the will of the voters he forfeited the power of making the appointment to Mr. Mackenzie King.

CHAPTER THREE

PROBLEMS OF EMPIRE

T HESE DOMESTIC issues with which Meighen had to grapple during the first troubled year of his premiership had either been produced or aggravated by the war. But the war had had other consequences as well with which he was to be no less concerned, for it had brought about a significant, if still somewhat ambiguous, change in Canada's position and status in the world. The well-known constitutional developments—formation of the Imperial War Cabinet, representation of the Dominions at the Peace Conference, their signing of the treaties and their separate memberships in the League of Nations—had elevated the Dominions to a place never before occupied by dependent states. Constitutionally they occupied a kind of no-man's-land, in recognized status and popular opinion less colonies than before but not yet quite sovereign states.

Uncertainty regarding Canada's exact constitutional position, coupled with her great material growth since the end of the nineteenth century, her by no means negligible contribution to the Allied war effort and the growing pride in their country felt by Canadians, stimulated a great deal of discussion about the Imperial relationship and the direction its evolution would or should follow in the future. The growth of national feeling, which was markedly in evidence during and immediately following the war, was also, no doubt, in part a reflection of the temper of the times in the western world at large. Nationalism had come into full flower and the map of post-war Europe showed a number of new states whose existence rested on the principle of national self-determination. To Canadians it seemed incongruous that their great and growing country should have a less exalted status in the society of nations than, say, Latvia or Yugoslavia. Still, few people subscribed to the view that Canada ought to secede from the British Empire and set up shop as an independent republic; to the vast majority that was neither practicable nor desirable. The real issue was not between outright independence and continued membership in the Empire, but rather how the Empire should be organized or, perhaps, whether it should be organized at all. There were some who still dreamed the dream of Imperial federation but that vision had faded since the hey-day of Joseph Chamberlain; federation seemed hardly more feasible or attractive to most Canadians than separation. The problem was how to reconcile the integrity of the Empire with the autonomy of the Dominions. More specifically, could so scattered and heterogeneous a commonwealth of free nations devise a single foreign policy suitable to them all in such a way as to permit the Dominions an influence in its determination commensurate with their size, power and self-respect? Some concluded that this, in fact, could not be done. These folk, the professional autonomists of whom Mackenzie King became the leader, believed that the Dominions should be as free in setting their own foreign policy as in their domestic affairs, that an effort to maintain the diplomatic unity of the Empire might be inimical to the freedom and the best interests of its self-governing members. Others, of whom Sir Robert Borden was representative, assumed that there had to be one foreign policy for the whole Empire but argued that the time had gone by when the policy could be made in London and the Dominions expected to endorse it as a matter of course. Means must and could be found to enable Great Britain and the Dominions to formulate the policy in concert, as they had to some extent during the last two years of the war and at the Peace Conference, so that the views and interests of the Dominions might achieve expression in measures to which they were together committed.

On this issue, as on nearly all, Meighen was with Borden. By inclination and necessity he had heretofore devoted himself for the most part to domestic matters and there had been more than enough problems in that sphere to keep his exceptional talents at work. Imperial and foreign affairs had been looked after in recent years almost exclusively by Borden and Rowell, with some assistance from Doherty and Foster. Meighen had never fancied himself as an international statesman, despite his attendance at London in 1918, where after all his chief business had been the negotiations with Smithers of the Grand Trunk rather than the not altogether pressing agenda of the Imperial War Conference.[1] Like most English-speaking Canadians of his generation he had a strong emotional attachment to Great Britain and was apt to assume that her lead in world affairs ought generally to be followed. He looked with mingled respect, admiration and apprehension towards the United States. The League of Nations he regarded tolerantly, though with more sceptical detachment than many, believing that foreign policy should be in harmony with its Covenant but inclining almost instinctively to the view that greater hope for peace was to be found in the diplomatic unity of the Empire and the maintenance of concord between Britain and the United States. Canada, he believed, had a right to be heard, whether at London, Washington or Geneva, with respect to matters affecting her but this did not mean that her path and that of the mother country should be allowed to diverge widely one from the other. Rather, through discussion the two should be able to walk the same path together.

In short, his opinions about these great concerns were quite conventional. He was neither an advanced nationalist nor the imperialist extraordinary he was often depicted as being, especially in Quebec. He was a Canadian Conservative in the tradition of Macdonald, in whose wisdom he had been taught to believe as a child. Circumstances had altered subtly since Sir John's day but the fundamental conditions of Canada's existence had not. She must still strive to be what he had sought to make her, a British nation in North America, closely allied with the mother country but at the same time, by the dictates of geography, closely related to the United States. If these opinions were conventional, they were also in Meighen's case generalized merely; immersed as he had been in other affairs, he had never been faced with the necessity of applying his general convictions to particular cases or of assuming individual, special responsibility for decisions reached in the realm of Imperial and foreign relations. When he became Prime Minister and Secretary of State for External Affairs in 1920, however, that necessity confronted him.

One of the decisions bequeathed to him by Borden was that Canada should have her own diplomatic representative in the United States. In May 1920 the House of Commons had been informed by Foster, Acting Prime Minister, that the United Kingdom and Canada had reached an agreement, of which the United States had been informed and which it approved, that a Canadian Minister should be appointed. He was to be a kind of second-in-command at the British Embassy, acting on behalf of the British Ambassador during the latter's absence but at all times negotiating independently with American officials on instructions from Ottawa with regard to any matter affecting Canadian-American relations. The official announcement was careful to say: "This new arrangement will not denote any departure either on the part of the British Government or of the Canadian Government from the principle of the diplomatic unity of the British Empire."[2]

As no appointment was made before Borden's retirement, Meighen fell heir to the task of finding the right man for the job. He had, of course, concurred in the policy and was now anxious to implement it. He was less interested than some others in the theoretical implications of the step, as symbolizing a more elevated national status for Canada; what attracted him was its obvious utility. Two-thirds or more of the business of the British Embassy in Washington was Canadian business, with which the Embassy staff was not well equipped by training or experience to cope effectively. This meant that there had to be a great deal of running down to Washington by Canadian officials to get things done and much of that could be avoided if there were a Canadian Minister with his own staff on the scene. Anyway, it was rather preposterous that formal communications between the governments of two countries with a common boundary of nearly four thousand miles should have to travel circuitously through the Foreign and Colonial Offices in London. The inadequacy from Canada's standpoint of traditional channels of official communication with the United States was forcefully explained to Meighen by Sir Charles Gordon, Chairman of the Canadian War Mission in Washington, and also Director-General of War Supplies there for the British government.

> From what I have seen of the workings of the British Embassy, during my stay in Washington [Gordon wrote], I should say that the knowledge which they have of Canadian affairs is decidedly limited. Most of the staff have never been in Canada, and I do not think that either the Ambassador or any of his staff, are in a position to deal with Canadian affairs first-hand. I think perhaps they know a little less about Canada, as a rule, than they do of other parts of the world, because as a rule a number of members of the staff have at least served in Embassies or Consulates in other countries. This lack of knowledge with regard to Canada, becomes apparent at once to the heads of the various Government departments of the United States, when any representative of the British Embassy calls upon them with regard to Canadian affairs. My experience in Washington was that United States officials, in important positions, want to meet Canadians when they have to deal with matters pertaining to Canada, and that it is not satisfactory for them to communicate by way of London, to Ottawa.[3]

In the 1921 session of Parliament an item of $60,000 for Canadian representation in the United States appeared in the estimates. In defending it Meighen took his stand on the practical advantages such representation would bring. "We take this step," he said, "not because we are a nation and merely to express our nationhood. We take it for the service it is going to be to us. We take it because it will be a help to us, but it does illustrate the growing nationhood of the country . . . It does illustrate the development of this country as an integral portion of the Empire; it illustrates the evolution of the Empire as an Empire. But it is not merely for the purpose of so illustrating it that we take the step. If it has no purpose and utility it should not have been done."[4] Most of those who took part in discussion of the subject in the Commons endorsed the principle of a Canadian representative at Washington, though some on the Liberal side expressed reasonable misgivings about the dangers and uncertainties which stationing him at the British Embassy and making him the deputy of the British Ambassador might entail. This feature of the plan, which had been proposed by the British government, would, they argued, give him a dual responsibility and perhaps put him—and Canada—in an invidious position. But Meighen did not regard that part of the arrangement "as of first importance. I do not know that there would be any probability of difficulty arising due to that, but if it did, there would be no difficulty in making modifications in that regard."[5]

As to the policy itself, the idea of appointing a Canadian Minister to Washington, there were some objections to it from both sides of the House. Fielding again embarrassed Mackenzie King and other autonomists in the Liberal party, as he had two years earlier in criticizing separate Canadian representation at the Peace Conference, by affirming his conviction "that we have got as far as we need to go to-day. We are right at the very verge of Independence. . . . My view is that this proposal of an ambassador at Washington is not a useful one. . . . We have to-day, in the making of commercial treaties, all the power we ought to have or that is any good to us."[6] A similar objection was voiced by W. F. Cockshutt, a Conservative, who saw the proposal as "the thin edge of the wedge of separation"[7] and this fear may have been fairly widespread. Later on R. B. Bennett confessed to Meighen that he had "always been afraid of this Washington business except it was dealt with by say making R. L. B[orden] British Ambassador. I do not think at this moment we would be doing a good service for either Canada or the Empire by taking the action proposed."[8] Bennett's views did not always reflect widely held opinion and they might well have changed radically had he been offered the position. Still, there was undoubtedly a certain amount of uneasiness abroad concerning the possible effects of the policy on the Imperial relationship.

However, Meighen's hand was not stayed by these prudential objections. When asked by Ernest Lapointe why no appointment had been made, he answered: "There is one reason and one only, namely that the Government has not been able to decide as to the best man and when I speak of that, I mean available to occupy this very important post."[9] Most definitely he disagreed with the Fielding-Cockshutt point of view.

> I cannot [he told the House] follow the reasoning which leads to the conclusion that we must maintain colonial status or else march towards the disintegration of the Imperial structure. That does not appeal to me in any degree. Indeed, the Imperial structure has multiplied in strength as the different Dominions of the Empire have elevated themselves step by step beyond the colonial status. Nor do I think that this will be the end of the evolution of the Dominion into nationhood. I cannot conceive that even the relationship that this establishes would be adequately expressive of what the position of this Dominion should be in relation to the rest of the Empire when, say, we have a population here equal to the population of the United Kingdom. All this will take care of itself with the passage of time.[10]

Being balked in his efforts to get the "best man" for various positions was becoming a familiar experience for Meighen. Patenaude had refused to take charge of the Conservative party in Quebec; Flavelle had refused to take charge of the National Railways. There was similar disappointment in the quest for a Canadian Minister to Washington. In the public speculation about who would be selected quite a few names were mentioned: Borden, Rowell, Lord Shaughnessy, Sir Charles Gordon, Flavelle, C. A. Magrath—a fairly imposing roster. The actual choice was a good deal narrower, however. Borden, in poor health, was evidently determined to remain in private life, aside from an occasional visit to his seat in the House of Commons. Two years earlier he had been offered and had declined the position of British Ambassador to the United States; he would hardly be content as Canadian Minister with a status apparently somewhat less than equal to that of the office he had already refused. Rowell had some time since announced and acted upon his intention to return to the practice of law; he was not available. Shaughnessy was elderly and physically infirm, while Gordon does not seem to have been seriously considered. As for Flavelle, Meighen hoped when he began to consider the Washington appointment that Sir Joseph would accept the railway position. There, the Prime Minister probably believed, he would render more important service than he could at Washington.

One attractive possibility was Sir Robert Falconer, President of the University of Toronto. In a conversation between Meighen and Rowell his name was mentioned and Rowell agreed to sound him out without intimating what was in the wind. The result was a strong recommendation, in which Flavelle concurred, that Falconer be asked to take the post.[11] In thanking Rowell for his views Meighen assured him: "There has been no change whatever in the Government's intention as to appointing a representative at Washington." He was glad that Rowell had let him have Flavelle's opinion, as there "are few men whose judgment of other men's capacity is better than Sir Joseph Flavelle's."[12] However, the position does not appear to have been offered to Falconer, who in many ways would have made an excellent spokesman for Canada at Washington. The matter seems to have hung fire until the autumn of 1921, when Meighen seriously considered Magrath, chairman of the Canadian section of the International Joint Commission. Before going ahead he wanted to consult Borden, who was then representing Canada at an international conference in Washington. Meighen wired him: ". . . am considering appointment Magrath to Washington post. Suggest salary fifteen thousand dollars which believe he would accept. Kindly consider this suggestion and give me your views. Would be here Thursday or Friday if you could come and discuss matter personally."[13] Borden answered that the work of the conference would prevent his coming to Ottawa but he believed Magrath would be a good choice. However, Meighen should keep in mind three considerations.

> First.   After delay of eighteen months since announcement in Parliament is it wise to make appointment on eve of general election. [Second.] Salary proposed should be supplemented by such allowance as would enable Canadian representative to maintain position among other members of Diplomatic Corps. Salary of fifteen thousand dollars without allowance would leave him in unfortunate position, unless supplemented by large private means. Washington most expensive city in the world. British Ambassador has house and allowance of seventeen thousand five hundred pounds which is seven times amount of his salary. Third. Chairman of the Canadian section International Joint Commission should devote his whole time and energy to [work] of commission and you should be sure he possesses such quality of tact and good judgment as would maintain the high standard established by Magrath. I regard this Commission as a most important and even vital factor in maintaining good relations and understanding between the two countries.[14]

This was enough for Meighen. Magrath was not appointed and there was still no Canadian Minister in Washington when the Meighen government left office at the end of December.

The prevailing uncertainty about the general drift of Imperial relations when Meighen succeeded Borden has already been noted. The war had brought a measure of centralized co-ordination in the shape of the Imperial War Cabinet, though "Cabinet" was something of a misnomer since its members had no collective executive powers and were severally responsible to different legislatures. With the end of the military crisis that had called this body into being the sense of urgency was dissipated; in the more relaxed atmosphere of peace close co-operation based upon steady consultation between Britain and her Dominions began to seem less essential to the statesmen of Whitehall than it had before, and certainly less so than it continued to seem to Borden and Meighen. Agreeing as the latter did with Borden that the Empire must speak with one voice, but a voice whose tone and language were decided by discussion among its self-governing states, he regarded constructive participation in Imperial councils as one of the most profoundly important duties of his new office. Before his government went down to defeat he was to have a splendid opportunity to show how effectively he could perform that duty.

However, at the outset of his term as Prime Minister there were no set plans for future sessions of the Imperial Cabinet or of the Imperial Conference. Everyone seemed to take it for granted that one or both of these bodies would be convened before very long but when and for what precise purpose was not entirely clear. The one definite commitment was a resolution of the Imperial War Conference of 1917, which had been moved by Borden and seconded by Jan Christian Smuts, in the following terms:

Resolution IX
Constitution of the Empire

The Imperial War Conference are of opinion that the readjustment of the constitutional relations of the component parts of the Empire is too important and intricate a subject to be dealt with during the War, and that it should form the subject of a special Imperial Conference to be summoned as soon as possible after the cessation of hostilities.

They deem it their duty, however, to place on record their view that any such readjustment, while thoroughly preserving all existing powers of self-government and complete control of domestic affairs, would be based upon a full recognition of the Dominions as autonomous nations of an Imperial Commonwealth, and of India as an important portion of the same, should recognize the right of the Dominions and India to an adequate voice in foreign policy and in foreign relations, and should provide effective arrangements for continuous consultation in all important matters of common Imperial concern, and as the several governments may determine.[15]

Late in April 1920 the Dominion governments were reminded of this by the Secretary of State for the Colonies, Lord Milner. Replying to a Canadian proposal that the next meetings of the Imperial Cabinet and Imperial Conference should be held in Ottawa, he reported that the Prime Ministers of the other Dominions thought it would be impossible to hold any sessions in 1920 and that W. M. Hughes of Australia would prefer a meeting of the Imperial Cabinet to be convened in London the following year. However, Milner continued, there appeared to be agreement by all concerned that the constitutional conference referred to in Resolution IX ought to take place in 1921 and he suggested that it might be held in Ottawa. This suggestion was evidently met with silence in the Canadian capital, where the immediate political future looked most uncertain. Sir Robert Borden was convalescing in the southern United States; it seemed likely that he would shortly retire, as he had more than once expressed a wish to do.[16] It was not known who would succeed him and he may have hesitated to accept an engagement for a constitutional conference which he might be unable, and his successor unwilling, to keep. However, in response to further cables from Milner in August, after Borden had retired, the Governor-General replied: "My Government are doubtful whether the proposed Constitutional Conference can with advantage be held New Year. They are impressed with the importance of the issues to be discussed and if possible determined at such a Conference. They think that their consideration at the Conference should in Dominions at least be preceded by the fullest opportunity for discussion by the people concerned as represented in Parliament and also in Press."[17]

It is probable that this attitude reflected the change of leadership in Canada. Borden, having sponsored the idea of a constitutional conference, would hardly have counselled further delay two years after the end of the war had he remained in office. Naturally he was prone to think of himself as an architect of the Commonwealth, whereas his comparatively youthful and inexperienced successor had no pretensions or ambitions of that kind. Such a conference would have suited Borden's tastes and talents very well; he would have been happy to assist in formulating a definition of the new Imperial relationship that time and events had produced. Meighen, on the other hand, was temperamentally inclined to shy away from abstract definitions, as well as from the belief that the creation of new constitutional machinery, for "continuous consultation" or any other purpose, was the way to deal with particular individual problems that might arise from time to time. No doubt it was desirable and ought to be possible to improve communications between the various member states; no doubt there were certain general principles that ought to govern Imperial relationships and the manner in which the self-governing countries of the Empire determined their common policy. But these were hardly matters of such urgent significance as to require either broad statements about formal status or an elaborate renovation of the Imperial structure. Not only that, it seemed certain that if definitions of status were arrived at in a constitutional conference there would be widespread dissatisfaction with them no matter what they were. If this proved to be the case Meighen's heavy political burdens would be added to and he was already sufficiently weighed down. Public opinion on this question was by no means clearly formed and certainly far from united. All in all, therefore, he thought it better to refrain from general declarations about status and from the designing of new Imperial apparatus. Canada, he was sure, could make her voice clearly heard and her influence unmistakably felt under the existing order of things.

The project of a constitutional conference was shelved temporarily in the summer of 1920 but by early November it had been agreed that the Prime Ministers should meet in London in the following June, and that they might then prepare the ground for a later meeting on constitutional subjects, as well as explore in a preliminary way some of the matters that might come before it. At the ensuing parliamentary session in the spring of 1921 Meighen outlined for the House of Commons the agenda that had been proposed for the Prime Ministers' Conference. The British government, he reported, had originally suggested, in addition to preparations for a later examination of constitutional questions, "a general review of the main features of foreign relations, particularly as they affect the Dominions," consideration of whether the Anglo-Japanese Alliance ought to be renewed and "preliminary consideration, preparatory for the proposed Constitutional Conference, of some working method for arriving at a common understanding as to policy in such external affairs as concern all parts of the Empire." Subsequently the United Kingdom had suggested several additional topics, all of which except one—naval, military and air defence—were of a purely technical nature. Australia and India had also each proposed one topic. None had been suggested by Canada.[18] Meighen had already expressed to the Colonial Secretary his misgivings about the inclusion of some of these, explaining that he would not be accompanied by experts, and he told the House he thought it unlikely that any of them would be "closely discussed." In all probability, he said, the London meeting, which was not a regular Imperial conference but a "special meeting of prime ministers" which "should not be of a prolonged character," would be devoted to the four major subjects mentioned.

A day was set aside for a debate on these things by the House, the first time this had been done before an Imperial conclave, and it occupied the afternoon and evening of April the twenty-seventh. That there was widespread interest in Imperial relations was shown by the large attendance of members, more than two-thirds of whom were present. Borden led off, reviewing the growth of Dominion autonomy and emphasizing the importance of the principles enunciated in Resolution IX. It was the speech of an elder statesman who, from the height of his experience and wisdom, could view the problems of the Empire in a calm, dispassionate way, but it had not much directly to do with the particular items of the conference agenda which Meighen had announced. Borden was followed by Mackenzie King, who brought the attention of the members back to the agenda itself, and especially to the subject of defence policy. Several weeks earlier, he reminded the House, the Prime Minister in answer to a question had mentioned "naval policy based upon the principle of co-operation" as among the subjects likely to be canvassed at the conference. Now, in contrast, Meighen relegated "naval, military and air defence" to a subordinate position among a number of additional subjects that had been suggested but which probably would receive little attention. Yet Mr. Lloyd George was reported as having stated in the British House of Commons "that it was too much to ask of these small Islands that they undertake the whole burden of the defence of a gigantic Empire in every sea, and that at the forthcoming conference of Prime Ministers of the Dominions in London the whole problem of Imperial Defence must be considered." Lloyd George had added, according to the newspaper dispatch from which King quoted: "There must be . . . co-ordination not only between the various services, but between the several parts of the Empire."[19]   Could the House, asked King, not have some explanation of this apparent discrepancy between the statements of the two Prime Ministers?   Would "naval policy based upon the principle of co-operation" be before the conference or not?   Borden had remarked that he thought "the occasion [of this conference] altogether inopportune for considering the problems of imperial defence or the responsibility to be undertaken by the various parts of the Empire in that respect."[20]   King agreed and implied that he feared an effort would be made by some at London to secure commitments to Imperial defence from the leaders of the Dominions, and beyond that, acceptance of new constitutional arrangements intended to tie the Empire more tightly together.   True, he acknowledged, Meighen had said that "any proposals resulting from the Conference and affecting Canada must be subject to the approval of the Canadian Parliament."   "We understand," said King, "that in representing Canada at this conference my right hon. friend will in no way commit this Parliament or this country with respect to any of the subjects that are upon the agenda."   Nevertheless, although he had this understanding, he thought it desirable that the limits of the Prime Minister's authority should be clearly spelled out.   Hence he felt constrained to present a motion defining those limits, which read in part:

> . . . At the coming conference no steps should be taken in any way involving any change in the relations of Canada to other parts of the Empire; and . . . in view of the present financial position of Canada, no action should be taken implying any obligation on the part of Canada to undertake new expenditures for naval or military purposes.

This was not a motion of want of confidence in the Government, King stressed.   On the contrary, it was offered so "that my right hon. friend's hand may be strengthened when he goes overseas" by "clearing up any doubt in my right hon. friend's mind as to the scope of his authority or as to the scope of the conference itself. . . ."[21]

Meighen, in whose mind there was no doubt about the scope of his authority, was unable to see the motion in this light.   ". . . If the hon. member has confidence in the Government," he snapped, "and especially in the Prime Minister as regards this conference, I do not know why the motion is advanced."   How could it be other than an expression of want of confidence, when coming from the leader of the Opposition, "it seeks to place manacles on the hands of a representative of this country going to attend a Conference of Prime Ministers of the Empire"?   Such a motion was unprecedented in Canada or the other Dominions and was "out of harmony with the whole principle of conference."

Suppose the motion which we are asked to take this afternoon, and which we are requested, I fear with some satire, to assume is in no way intended to embarrass the Government, but rather to be of assistance to the Government in this great task—suppose the action we are asked to take . . . is to become a practice to be followed by the other Dominions, and that it is to be pursued not only as to the special subjects enumerated in the [motion], but as to other subjects (because if we are right in directing as to one we are right in directing as to another); suppose that it is to be followed to its logical conclusion . . . and that the delegates go to the conference directed by their governments along certain lines, or along all lines, then why do they go there at all? What is the conference for? Has not the conference been blasted at the hour of its conception? Indeed, the step we are asked to take this afternoon is the first step towards making the consultative and conference principle of no value at all in the promotion of the common interests of the Empire.[22]

Respecting defence policy Meighen made it clear, without mentioning Lloyd George by name, that he did not agree that "the whole problem of Imperial Defence must be considered." On the contrary, he said, the "whole question of armaments the world over is such at this time that it seems to me little progress could be made in the way of conferring between parts of an Empire as to just what the armament programme of that Empire should be. In my view each country would do well to leave the door open to take such steps as circumstances that may develop will render necessary, and such as may seem to grow logically out of the solution of the major question—whether we are going to have some understanding as to the reduction of armaments or whether we are not."[23] Nor did Mackenzie King or anyone else in the House need to fear that Parliament or the country would be committed to anything at the conference.

The leader of the Opposition asks me to be very clear and to leave Parliament in no doubt as to whether anything can be done, as he expresses it, "of a final, binding or other nature" unless ratified. Well, I can speak as regards the "final and the binding," but I am not sure that I can speak as regards the "other", until I know what the "other" is. Nothing can be done of a final or binding nature— nothing whatever. This stands to reason, because this is a conference—this is not an executive. Even the War Cabinet was not an executive; it was a consultative body and nothing more. . . . It was a consultative body, this is a consultative body—a body whereby the various units that compose the Empire can meet, get each other's opinions, learn each other's conditions, then come back to the parliaments from which they are sent and, in the light of the information there gained, in the light of the impressions there driven home upon them, in the light of knowledge as to conditions, not only in their own country but in the world at large, make such recommendations to their home parliaments as to them seem best suited to meet the need. . . . I can give the assurance, with all the emphasis that I can

command, that no step whatever will be taken binding this country
—indeed, no step can be taken, whatever might be the will of the
representative of Canada, which would have force or effect before
ratification by the Parliament of this Dominion.[24]

But even so categorical an assurance did not satisfy the Opposition.
Later, towards the end of a long speech by Rowell, one of the few men
in the House who had devoted close attention to external affairs, King
interrupted to put a question. Did Rowell not agree that the statement
by Lloyd George which King had read earlier was at variance with
Meighen's? "How will the Prime Minister," asked King, "reconcile the
position he will take at the conference with that of the Prime Minister of
Great Britain . . . ?" To which Rowell gave the obvious answer: "Other
prime ministers are not responsible to the parliament and people of
Canada; the Prime Minister of Canada is. They are responsible to their
own parliaments; he is responsible to this. He is not responsible for
what they say; he is responsible for what he says and does." He was prepared, added Rowell in what may have been intended as a rebuke, he
was sure the House was prepared, "I believe my hon. friend [King] is
prepared," to trust Meighen as other Prime Ministers had been trusted
in the past, "to preserve and protect all Canadian interests while seeking
to promote the spirit of unity and hearty co-operation among all the
states of the Empire."[25] Rowell urged King to withdraw his motion but
to no avail; the House divided and the motion was defeated by thirty-
two votes.

During the debate remarkably little attention was paid to what proved
to be the main business before the conference—the Anglo-Japanese Alliance. Judging by his rather short speech, Meighen regarded this as the
most important and pressing subject on the agenda. At least it was
precise and concrete, the kind of issue he enjoyed grappling with, rather
than amorphous and abstract as so much of the discussion about Canada's
place in the Empire and the world seemed to him to be. But if, in setting
aside a day for this debate he hoped to receive illumination or guidance
from Parliament regarding the Alliance, he must have been disappointed.
Neither Borden nor Mackenzie King made any reference to it whatsoever,
although Meighen undoubtedly knew that the former at least was opposed to its renewal. Nor did Rodolphe Lemieux or Ernest Lapointe,
aside from King the chief spokesmen on the Opposition side. Michael
Clark of Alberta, speaking for the Progressive group, recognized that it
was "about the only great subject that seems to be taking my right hon.
friend to London at this time," but argued that the trip was unnecessary,
that on this question "an exchange of two or three despatches on each
side should . . . make it perfectly plain to the Imperial Government what

the mind of this Government is. . . .."[26] Indeed, the debate as a whole consisted almost entirely of general observations regarding Imperial relations, with the Opposition speakers especially showing a preoccupation with Canada's autonomous status and a desire to see the country remove itself from the dangerous jungle of world politics. There was little evidence that the members of Parliament had any great interest in or understanding of concrete problems of foreign policy. Clark probably spoke for many when he said: "My own feeling is that this country and the world have had all the foreign policy they want for a number of years."[27] This was rather like saying that the world had had enough of weather but the remark reflected a mood of post-war disenchantment, a desire to retreat into isolation, that was undoubtedly widespread.

In any event only Meighen and Rowell made any real reference to the Japanese treaty, the former hinting briefly and obliquely at the stand he would take in London, the latter offering a slightly more extended analysis of the problem. The future of the Alliance, said the Prime Minister,

> is a subject of great and definite moment . . . and if there is one Dominion to which, more than another, the question of the renewal is of importance, it is to the Dominion of Canada. I say that with particular reference to the relationship this Dominion bears, and must always bear, as a portion of the British Empire standing—if I may say it—between Great Britain on the one hand and the United States on the other. I need not enlarge upon how serious, or even how momentous, is the deliberation that must take place as regards the question of the renewal of that treaty. The importance of it arises from the interest of the United States therein, and the interest of Great Britain and of Australia and other parts of the Empire; but the importance of it to us arises, in a very great degree, out of the very great interest of the United States in the renewal or the non-renewal thereof.[28]

Rowell, after quoting some of the major provisions of the treaty, offered an opinion which Meighen shared though he had refrained from expressing it: "The Government of this country cannot ignore the feeling that does exist in the United States in reference to this alliance. I submit for the consideration of the Government . . . that . . . in the interests of good relations all round . . . this treaty should not be renewed, at least in its present form."[29]

Even though the Alliance and its future received somewhat more attention from the press of Canada than it did during the one-day debate in the Commons, the apparent indifference of the parliamentarians was matched by general public ignorance and apathy about the matter. This state of mind was not very surprising, of course. In the past neither Canadian governments nor Canadians in general had shown a great deal of interest in Asia or in Far Eastern affairs, except for the popular feeling in British Columbia against oriental immigration. It was this issue, always a burning one on the Coast, that had led to the only real foray into Far Eastern diplomacy by Canada when in 1908 Lemieux, then Minister of Labour, had negotiated an agreement with Japan under which that country agreed to restrict the emigration of its people to Canada. Although Canadian trade with the Far East was increasing and although Canadian churches were active in missionary work in that region, all the ties of tradition and sentiment, and most of the ties of commerce, had led the gaze of Canadians, when they looked beyond North America, eastward across the Atlantic.[30] Now, in 1921, the government of Canada was compelled to take greater cognizance of developments in the western Pacific, and for the best of all possible Canadian reasons: those developments clearly would affect in a vital way, and perhaps detrimentally, the relations of Great Britain and the United States. Instinctively, yet with reasoned deliberation, Canada moved to prevent that calamity.

The Anglo-Japanese treaty grew out of an agreement reached by the two countries in 1902, the purpose of which was to stabilize the situation in the Far East and especially to check the spread of Russian power and influence in that region. Its precise object was to safeguard British interests in China and Japanese interests in China and Korea. It bound each signatory to neutrality if the other became involved in a war with a third power, and to military intervention on the side of its ally if the latter were at war with two or more states. The scope of the pact was widened by a revision negotiated in 1905 during the Russo-Japanese War. The purposes of the treaty were stated to be three: to maintain peace in eastern Asia and India; to ensure "the independence and integrity" of China so as to preserve equal opportunities for the commerce and industry of other states in that country; and to safeguard the territorial rights of Great Britain and Japan in eastern Asia and India "and the defence of their special interests in said regions."

With Russia defeated by Japan and gripped by an internal convulsion, the most potent menace to the *status quo* in the Far East, at least in British eyes, became the German Empire. The 1905 treaty required of the two parties, not merely neutrality, but armed intervention by the one if the other should be attacked by a third power. The treaty was to run for ten years but in 1911 another revision occurred. This new version, which was submitted to the representatives of the Dominions for their approval at a meeting of the Imperial Defence Committee, was also to be of ten years' duration with the proviso that if neither country gave notice of abrogation at least twelve months before the expiry of the ten years, the treaty would continue in force until one year after such notice had been given. The main alteration in substance in 1911 was the addition of a provision, Article IV, that neither signatory would be obligated to go to war against another power with whom it might have concluded a general treaty of arbitration. This change was made at the insistence of Great Britain, where there was a growing fear that the Alliance might lead to war with the United States. Negotiation of a general arbitration treaty between the two English-speaking powers was then in progress. This failed to secure ratification by the United States Senate in 1912 but two years later, shortly after the outbreak of war in Europe, Great Britain and the United States agreed by treaty, duly approved by the Senate, to establish a permanent international commission that might investigate disputes between them if ordinary diplomatic processes failed. This was regarded by the British as a general treaty or arbitration within the meaning of Article IV of the Anglo-Japanese treaty of 1911 and Japan was so notified.

This seemed to remove the possibility of war between Britain and America arising from the operation of the Alliance.[31] Nevertheless, it remained unpopular in the United States, probably because it seemed to establish something resembling an Anglo-Japanese condominium in the western Pacific, where for many years, and especially since the acquisition of the Philippine Islands, the Americans had had important commercial and strategic interests of their own. Dislike of Japan and suspicion of Japanese ambitions were widespread in the United States, where friendship for China with its new republican regime established in 1912 was growing. It appeared possible that Chinese and Americans, with a common antipathy towards the Japanese, might draw closer together in opposition to Great Britain and Japan. This prospect could not be regarded with equanimity in Whitehall, to say nothing of the East Block in Ottawa.

On the other hand, recognition of this American attitude was balanced in Britain and the Dominions, especially in Australia and New Zealand, by appreciation of Japan's contribution to the winning of the World War. She had entered the war promptly on the side of the Allies; the presence of her naval forces in the western Pacific had freed British ships for service elsewhere and her navy had also rendered valuable service in convoying Australian and New Zealand troops to the battle fronts. It seemed less than courteous—and also less than wise—to turn one's back on a loyal and powerful ally and to repudiate an alliance which by 1921 had operated to the satisfaction of both parties for nearly twenty years. Furthermore, the security of the Australasian Dominions, exposed and geographically isolated from other friends as they were, might be endangered if Japan, with her numerous people, her warlike spirit and her formidable navy, were antagonized.

Nevertheless, while these were compelling arguments, a very different situation had come into being with the end of the war. Germany, like Russia, had ceased to be a menace in the Pacific; the dangers against which the Alliance had been directed were gone. At the same time the United States had emerged as the newest and most redoubtable of the world powers, with a vital interest in the Far East. It was one thing for Great Britain to enlist Japanese co-operation against Russian or German expansionism; it was quite another to try to maintain a diplomatic system from which the United States was excluded or to which she was hostile. This hostility, bound to be disturbing from the British standpoint in any event, was made doubly so by the clamour in some circles in the United States for the expansion of its sea power to the extent necessary to give it a navy second to none. Such an enlarged navy, some of whose components were either under construction or authorized by Congress when the war ended, would presumably be deployed mainly in the Pacific, with which American strategists were preoccupied. The only possible adversaries against whom it might be used were the other two Pacific powers, joined by solemn treaty. One of these, Japan, responded to American policy by announcing a naval building programme of its own; in the other, Great Britain, pressure was brought to bear upon the Government to follow suit.

It may be that the naval arms race involving the three Pacific states, of which so much was heard at the time, was more an illusion than a fact. The time was not propitious at the end of an exhausting war to end war to undertake vast new expenditures for naval armaments. The Japanese programme seems to have moved little if any beyond the planning stage while in the United States, though a big navy lobby was active, there was a pronounced and politically effective revulsion of public opinion against arms expansion. Similarly in Great Britain domestic difficulties and financial stringency were not conducive to popular acceptance of the need for enlarged naval power.[32] Nevertheless, the fear did exist, however unfounded it may have been, that a naval arms race was in progress, or at least impended, and this fear had an important effect in determining the policies of various countries, including Canada, at that juncture.

It was not surprising in view of this situation that the future of the Anglo-Japanese Alliance became closely related to the question of naval power in the Pacific. Nor was it surprising that in certain quarters, and not least in Canada, the idea took root that the existing bilateral treaty should be superseded by some multilateral agreement concerning Pacific affairs as a whole, and that a conference of all the major powers with a stake in the Far East should be convened in an effort to work out a generally acceptable settlement. This seemed to offer the one hope of limiting naval armaments and stabilizing a potentially dangerous situation. Above all, from the Canadian point of view, it offered the means by which Great Britain and the United States could be brought into accord and the danger of a rupture between them over the Pacific question removed.

The first official suggestion that such a conference be held appears to have come from Ottawa. In the middle of February 1921 Meighen sent a cable to Lloyd George, arguing that "every possible effort should be made to find some alternative policy to that of renewal" and emphasizing "the need of promoting good relations with the United States." The attitude of that country, he asserted, must be given the closest attention.

> In view of her tendency towards abandonment of attitude of isolation generally, her traditional special interest in China which is as great as ours and of the increasing prominence of the Pacific as a scene of action, there is a danger that a special confidential relationship concerning that region between ourselves and Japan to which she was not a party would come to be regarded as an unfriendly exclusion and as a barrier to an English-speaking accord.

Therefore, he went on, the objectives of the Empire in the Far East must be pursued in a different way. The Alliance should be terminated and an effort be made to arrange a conference of the Pacific powers, Japan, China, the United States and the British Empire, with each of the Dominions represented in the Empire's delegation. It was essential to know in advance of the June meeting of Prime Ministers what chance there might be of organizing such a conference, and especially to learn the views of the new administration of President-elect Harding, who would shortly be installed in the White House.

> Accordingly we suggest that a representative of the Canadian Government should get in touch with the new President and his Secretary of State as soon as possible after their inauguration and discover through informal confidential conversations whether any such policy is feasible. For this purpose I would nominate Sir Robert Borden who is willing to act.
>
> This method of approach seems most appropriate, first, because the concern of the Pacific Dominions in the question is in reality more vital than that of the other parts of the Empire, and, second, because the proposal seems best calculated to succeed in Washington if put forward by Canada. We attach importance to the idea of putting it forward as looking to a Pacific Conference.[33]

In his reply Lloyd George agreed that it was desirable to "carry the United States with us in whatever course we decide on." However, he thought there were considerations "against immediate adoption of your proposal." The complete freedom of action of the Prime Ministers at their forthcoming meeting should not be prejudiced in any way. Their hands might be tied by even an informal approach to the United States, especially if the idea were received favourably in Washington, and in any case no such approach could be made without the consent of all the Dominions. A conference of the Pacific powers might be an ultimate solution but many questions concerning Great Britain's interests and the foreign policy of the Empire would have to be settled before any overtures could be made to the Americans. Thus, Lloyd George argued, the whole situation ought to be thoroughly canvassed by the Prime Ministers before any soundings, however informal, were made in Washington.[34]

Meighen submitted this message for analysis to Loring G. Christie, legal adviser in the Department of External Affairs and the member of its small staff upon whom he relied most closely and continuously for advice respecting Imperial and foreign affairs. Christie, a protégé of Borden, possessed not only extensive knowledge but an exceptionally clear mind and altogether was much more the leading figure in the department than its Under-Secretary, Sir Joseph Pope. In a lengthy and powerful critique of Lloyd George's cable Christie asserted that the nub of the question was "whether . . . it is more desirable to move towards a policy of British-American cooperation or away from it." Britain's rejection of the Canadian suggestion seemed to point to the latter course, which would be absolutely disastrous, and Christie convincingly built up the case for a prior informal approach to Washington by Canada, on her own behalf solely and without committing herself or her partners in any way. If, he contended, the Prime Ministers assembled without knowing whether the Americans might be willing to take part in a conference on Pacific and Far Eastern questions, they would have only two choices: to renew or to discontinue the Alliance with Japan. It would be helpful to know whether in fact a third choice existed.[35] The substance of Christie's memorandum was communicated to London but apparently elicited no reply.[36]

Although the suggestion that Borden be sent on an exploratory mission to Washington was given short shrift by Lloyd George, the proposal of a Pacific conference received attention in London. In May the British Cabinet discussed at some length the future of the Anglo-Japanese Alliance and the possibility of bringing together the interested powers at a gathering of the kind envisaged in Ottawa. Out of this discussion came a plan to be submitted to the Dominion prime ministers. The President of the United States should be asked to summon a conference on the Pacific and Far East but only after it had been made clear to Japan and the other countries concerned that the United Kingdom did not intend to drop the Alliance. The intention, in fact, should be to renew it for some period of less than ten years, in such modified form as would make it consistent with the Covenant of the League of Nations and acceptable to the United States. If the conference proved to be possible, well and good; but whether it did or not the Alliance must be renewed.[37] The British ministers evidently believed that all the Dominions, even Canada, could be persuaded to endorse this course of action but they were in for a rude awakening.

During the closing weeks of the parliamentary session which ended on June the fourth Meighen snatched what time he could to make his final preparations for the coming Conference of Prime Ministers. It was not easy to find many uninterrupted moments for that purpose. Political problems pressed upon him from all sides; delegations demanded to be heard; public functions required his attendance and private correspondence his attention; of course, also, there were the daily sittings of the House from which he was seldom absent. But with his habit, cultivated for many years, of working long hours, with his ability to turn from one subject to another and then to still another without losing his train of thought on any, he found no great difficulty in getting ready for what he already knew might be a contentious and even disagreeable encounter around the table at 10 Downing Street.

As something of a tyro in the field of international affairs he naturally placed much reliance on the counsel of certain associates whose experience and interest lay particularly in that field. First among these was Borden, whose greatly superior knowledge of and standing in world diplomacy Meighen was the first to acknowledge. Indeed, the contrast between the two men in this respect led to the suggestion "in the Press, and elsewhere, that Sir Robert should accompany Mr. Meighen to the Conference and give him the benefit of his experience, but the ex-premier . . . wisely decided that Mr. Meighen should find his own feet."[38] It would have been quite out of character for Meighen to act on this proposal, even had Borden been willing, for to do so would be a tacit admission of his own inadequacy. With his usual confidence he felt fully equal to the task of representing Canada. He was not intimidated by the prospect of having to lock horns with a group of men all of whom were older and wiser in the ways of world politics than he, and some of whom would no doubt disagree with his views. This, indeed, was the kind of challenge he always welcomed and he did not fancy himself in the role of a ventriloquist's dummy. Furthermore, he was now Prime Minister, possessed of the power and responsibility the office entailed. Borden's presence in London might make it seem that Meighen was in some way seeking to delegate his power and evade his responsibility; this in his mind would be the cardinal sin.[39] Nevertheless, he had great respect for Borden's knowledge and judgment and a number of consultations between the two men doubtless did much to shape the arguments which Meighen took with him to the conference.

Another man with considerable influence was Rowell, whose speech in the Commons debate foreshadowed in many respects the stand adopted by Meighen on various matters in London. There was not the close personal relationship between these two that there was between Meighen and Borden but Rowell's experience and ability made his views count. Early in February he had visited Washington and talked with a number of leading Republicans who were close to Warren G. Harding. In a letter to Meighen he conveyed their dislike of the Anglo-Japanese Alliance.[40] Both to this report and to Rowell's remarks in the House Meighen must have paid close attention. But the person upon whom he depended most in preparing for the trip to London was Loring Christie, who, in conversations with his chief and in a number of memoranda written in his characteristically lucid style, provided a great deal of ammunition—the specific arguments and data—that Meighen was to fire off with telling effect.[41] In addition he accompanied the Prime Minister to England and attended some of the conference sessions, thus giving Meighen a counsellor at his elbow to help him confront the impressive array of Cabinet ministers, high military officers and senior civil servants who from time to time appeared in the meeting room at the behest of Lloyd George.

Another man, an outsider, who later claimed to have exercised a powerful influence on Meighen (and on others) was Bertram Lenox Simpson, an Englishman who in 1916 became a political adviser to the President of China. In March 1921 he set off from Peking on a mission for the Chinese Foreign Office to lobby with important people in strategic places against the Anglo-Japanese Alliance. About the end of April he arrived in Ottawa and on May the third kept an appointment in Meighen's office. Though warned by a secretary that the interview could last no more than five minutes since many others were awaiting their turn, Simpson by his own account so gripped the Prime Minister that he stayed for an hour, talking all the while. "Mr. Meighen," he wrote afterwards, "was instantly aware that here was a matter which derived its importance from its many-sided and far-reaching implications which had been hitherto ignored" and, "his keen mind already on the alert, no doubt made a momentous mental decision." At the close of the interview Meighen asked Simpson to submit a memorandum on the subject of China's attitude to the Alliance and this Simpson did.[42]

While Simpson sought to give the impression in his highly coloured and frequently inaccurate narratives of events that he had been instrumental in shaping Canada's policy and in bringing about the abandonment of the Alliance in favour of a new order in Far Eastern diplomacy, his actual influence was undoubtedly of much more modest dimensions. The contents of Meighen's cable to Lloyd George in February showed that the Canadian government had determined its attitude long before he appeared on Parliament Hill. In any case Meighen was not apt to arrive at "a momentous decision" after one brief conversation with a complete stranger from Peking. The most that can be granted is that Simpson's memorandum may have supplied additional grounds on which renewal of the treaty could be opposed from the standpoint of China, and this assuredly was one of the foundations on which Meighen was to base his submission that the Alliance should be discarded.

But his main argument was, of course, the dangerous effect that renewal would have on American opinion and on Anglo-American relations. Was there, one wonders, pressure exerted on him directly from the United States to take this stand? Fragmentary evidence exists that there was. Shortly after the Prime Ministers' Conference William Howard Gardiner, a member of the executive committee of the American Navy League and a leading advocate of naval expansion by the United States, claimed in a letter to Senator Henry Cabot Lodge that he "had much to do with forming Canadian opinion against the Alliance. . . ."[43] He also told J. W. Dafoe of the *Manitoba Free Press*, as Dafoe reported years later to Professor J. Bartlett Brebner of Columbia University, "that the views of the American Government had been imparted unofficially to Mr. Meighen, and I judge from what he said that he had been active in this connection, probably in an unofficial capacity."[44] "I have a supplementary piece of information along similar but decidedly more dramatic lines," Brebner answered, "which I wish I could pass on to you but which I acquired accidentally from a source which I could not possibly betray." He thought it would be worth knowing what relation, if any, Gardiner's activities bore to Simpson's and remarked: "There certainly were a number of unofficial gentry playing about on the international stage at that time."[45]

It is impossible to know what Brebner's "decidedly more dramatic" piece of information was but there seems to be no good reason to attach quite as much significance to Gardiner's influence as he did himself. Of course he can hardly be dismissed as just another Lenox Simpson. Gardiner was a close friend of Lodge, one of the most powerful figures in American politics enjoying great influence with President Harding. That Meighen was anxious to have an authentic expression of American opinion concerning Far Eastern affairs was shown by his desire to send Borden to Washington for consultation. That suggestion may conceivably have been prompted by Gardiner, though it is not clear just how early he became active in "forming Canadian opinion." There may have been puzzlement in Ottawa that with his Navy League connections Gardiner should be working against an alliance whose termination would remove a strong argument for American naval expansion, but his association with Lodge made him a man not lightly to be ignored. Still, it seems probable that he exaggerated his own influence with the Canadians, to which he attributed Canada's adoption of a policy that he happened to favour. That policy, it is reasonable to conclude, was based on a Canadian assessment of the situation. Gardiner's representations in all likelihood influenced the assessment by providing a reliable indication of American opinion. But that he was able to exert a determining pressure on such men as Meighen, Borden and Christie is not easy to believe.

Preparations for the meeting in London included, not only some intensive study on Meighen's part, but also a number of adjustments in the Meighen household. It was early decided that Mrs. Meighen would accompany him. She was always eager to meet new people and see new places and she would be of inestimable help to him in a number of ways, not least in fulfilling the social engagements they would be obliged to accept. In her absence the children would have to be looked after. The eldest, Ted, a self-reliant youth going on sixteen, was already at work out West on Senator Billy Sharpe's farm. As for Max and Lillian, it was agreed that when school was out at the end of June they would accompany their mother's cousin, Lillian Seale, who was in Ottawa visiting the family, to her home in Manitoba. That would take care of the youngsters and the house would be looked after by the two maids.

It was not difficult to arrive at this settlement of things but further complications were caused by the presence in Ottawa of Meighen's parents and by the suggestion that his mother should seize this opportunity to travel to the Old Country she had never seen and visit relatives in Ireland and Scotland. Not long before, the elder Meighens had sold their farm at St. Marys and come to live in an apartment just down Cooper Street from their son's home. They had done so at his urging, acquiescing in his belief that his father, over seventy years of age and in none too robust health, should no longer attempt to look after the farm. There was a special, compelling reason, one of his own causing, why Meighen wanted to remove his parents from St. Marys. In a moment of misguided generosity he had given his father a car, thinking this would provide more convenient and comfortable transportation than the horse and buggy. But almost at once he regretted the gift as he began to hear frightening reports, which he substantiated with his own eyes, of his father's conduct behind the wheel. The main street of St. Marys crosses the valley of the Thames and at both ends of it there are steep hills. Joseph Meighen would come into town in his new conveyance and roar down the hill towards the business district, forgetting the brake pedal and crying "Whoa!" as was the habit of a lifetime, while the townspeople watched his hurtling progress with mingled awe, fear and indignation. His son was afraid he would kill or maim someone, perhaps even himself, and thus urged the move to Ottawa, knowing that the car would be left safely behind.

There was no thought of Joseph's going on the trip across the sea in 1921; he expressed no desire to, perhaps feeling unequal to the uncertainties of the voyage and a long stay in strange surroundings. Mary Meighen, on the other hand, with her physical vigour scarely diminished and her interest in the wider world still very much alive, obviously wanted to go but seemed less than sure that she ought to. "Arthur," she kept asking with her mind on the Irish troubles then raging, "is it safe for me to go to Ireland?" Or: "Isabel, do you think I will sleep on the trip?" Her daughter-in-law, losing patience with such dithering uncertainty, finally answered: "Well, if you don't sleep you will see just that much more!" "So I will," the old lady agreed and that settled that, though even on the dock at Quebec she was still expressing misgivings over her audacity. Meighen's father moved into the Cooper Street house to stay with Miss Seale and the two children; after they departed for the West the maids would look after him. As Meighen stood with his wife and mother, ready to leave for the railway station, he said: "Now Father, see that the house is all locked up at night." This instruction was scrupulously carried out each night before Joseph went to bed—at eight-thirty. And each night after his grandfather had retired Max crept down to unlock the front door so that Miss Seale, if she had gone out, would be able to get back in.

Meighen's intention had been that they should ride in the comfort of his private railway car from Ottawa to Quebec but when the train arrived at Montreal he was met by a group of local Conservatives who insisted that he should go the rest of the way in a motorcade. This would be a much more impressive means of proceeding through the countryside and, besides, it would enable him to make two or three politically useful stops along the road. And so they set off in several automobiles on a hot, dusty, tiring drive, pausing here and there to allow Meighen to do his duty to the party with a few well-chosen words and a few well-placed hand-shakes. When he returned to his office two months later he found on the desk a reminder of this comfortless safari from Montreal to Quebec: a bill for the entire expenses of the motorcade, which presumably he was expected to pay out of party funds but which, having no such funds at his disposal and preferring to save such as might exist for more productive purposes, he paid out of his own pocket.

The cavalcade brought them to Quebec city on the evening of June the sixth. The next afternoon, after attending a luncheon in his honour given by delegates to the annual convention of the Canadian Manufacturers' Association, then in session in Quebec, Meighen with his two ladies and one of his secretaries, C.H.A. Armstrong, boarded the *Empress of Britain.* Several good friends were already installed there, waiting for the ship to cast off and move out into the St. Lawrence. Loring Christie was present and in his custody the numerous documents being taken for study during the voyage and reference during the conference. Two journalists whom Meighen knew were on hand, Grattan O'Leary and John A. Stevenson. Both were going to cover the conference, the former as correspondent for the Canadian Press News Agency. Meighen's Minister of Agriculture, Simon Tolmie, was bound for England on a mission of special importance to the Canadian livestock industry. In 1892 an embargo had been placed on the importation of Canadian cattle into Great Britain because of an outbreak of foot-and-mouth disease in Canada. Though the disease had long since been wiped out the embargo remained, despite numerous efforts by Canada to have it removed. Early in May 1921 the British government appointed a Royal Commission to look into the cattle import question and Tolmie was to testify before this body in the hope of recovering a share of the British cattle market for Canada.

It was an uneventful voyage as far as the elements were concerned, aside from some trouble with fog and icebergs which caused a delay of one day in reaching Liverpool. Certainly it was a far more comfortable one for Meighen than his passage to the Imperial Conference of 1918, when the sea had been heavy and he had been almost continuously sick. This time, according to O'Leary, he proved to be an excellent sailor and "entered into the various activities of shipboard with avidity." An ocean voyage, it is said, can strangely affect one's behaviour. Thus it was that Meighen, not normally an early riser, was one of the first to reach the deck in the morning; that, usually indifferent to organized games, "he spent a great deal of time playing shuttlecock . . . at which he exhibited considerable skill"; that, ordinarily not fond of dancing, "he was among the most enthusiastic of dancers. . . ." But one of his activities was more in keeping with his usual fancy: ". . . Later in the night," O'Leary wrote, with a sly jibe that Meighen would greatly enjoy, "[he] would disclose his puritanical upbringing by playing the second worst game of bridge on the boat."

One not unwelcome change from his usual existence was that he had to deliver only one speech during the seven days afloat. This was his impromptu contribution to the programme at the customary concert for the benefit of the Seamen's Home in Liverpool. He extolled the work of the British mercantile marine and the maritime glories of the British race, his words calling forth "both enthusiastic and practical response." The majority of the passengers were Americans and English people, who "were agreeably surprised at his complete absence of side and affectation and toward the end of the voyage the premier was quite the most popular figure aboard." It was always thus when politics was remote, when there was no controversy in the air. Then the gentler side of this unpretentious democrat's nature expressed itself, revealing his irresistible charm, his droll humour, his considerateness and warmth of feeling for others. Then the brooding asceticism of his countenance would be softened by a smile, the sharp edge of his wit rounded by a more jovial merriment, his intensity of mind and action relaxed in conviviality. Those even briefly exposed to this aspect of the man looked upon him with affection; for those long exposed affection might border on idolatry. In the midst of the journey there was an unexpected demonstration of the regard even his casual acquaintances of shipboard had for him. One of the passengers, a Canadian, gave birth to a son and promptly announced that he would be called William Meighen Smith. So touching a gesture, so signal an honour called for prompt, appropriate acknowledgment and Meighen visited the mother to express his appreciation, presenting her with a suitable gift.

What with all this varied activity the Prime Minister's customary regimen of almost ceaseless work was pleasantly disrupted. However, there was work to be done and he found the time to do it. Sometimes by himself, sometimes with Christie, he studied his documents and turned over once more in his mind what he intended to say at the conference and how it could best be said. With Tolmie he discussed the British cattle embargo and reviewed the brief the Minister would present to the Royal Commission. There was time also to read books from the ship's library; time to walk around the deck and then around again, a necessary pleasure for an almost compulsive walker; or time simply to sit in a deck chair talking to his friends, while watching the Atlantic, fortunately in one of her less boisterous moods, slide steadily by. In this pleasant way they came to Liverpool on June the fourteenth. There Meighen and his party were greeted by the Lord Mayor and, after a brief stopover, entrained for London.[46]

He was the youngest and the newest of the Dominion prime ministers now assembling there, and the least well known. True enough, some would remember him from his visit in 1918 but on that occasion Borden had dominated the Canadian delegation. All the others—J. C. Smuts of South Africa, W. M. Hughes of Australia, W. F. Massey of New Zealand —were veterans of the international stage and Smuts in particular had an enviable and deserved reputation as a Solon of world politics. But relatively little was known of the thought and character of the new Canadian leader. His name, of course, was familiar, and not favourably so, to some British financiers and stockholders as the man who had nationalized the Grand Trunk Railway, but on the whole he was an unknown quantity. Readers of the *Manchester Guardian,* a small but influential minority, had recently been given, to be sure, some indication of his ideas on Imperial relations. He was asked by the newspaper to contribute to its centenary number in May a statement on "The Place of the Dominions in the Empire: the Outlook for the Future." His contribution revealed something other than the archaic Tory imperialism to which, his opponents in Canada often alleged, he was in thrall.

The Dominions, readers of the *Guardian* were told, were conscious of their growth and development, which had accelerated in recent years. This had given rise to much discussion of their status and "there is now fairly general agreement that . . . the relations between the constituent parts of the Empire must be based upon a conception of complete freedom and equality in national status." In possessing at that time no absolutely certain or fixed status the Dominions were unique. "Other western countries enjoy or endure no such speculative exercises; their constitutional position is fixed and universally taken for granted. The result in our political life is much discussion, often exceedingly interesting, but often on the other hand unduly distracting, and the strain put on the conduct of public affairs by this factor alone must be experienced to be fully appreciated." The solution of this problem would not be found in "the erection of new mechanisms of Government. . . . It suggests at once the idea of centralization, a conception which, if it can be said ever to have been seriously considered, is now generally recognized to be outside the realm of practical things, and which indeed is directly counter to the principle on which our Commonwealth has based its prosperity and even existence." The practical need would be met, "not so much by novel devices in state organization, as by clearly understood and definitely accepted declarations of principle, which shall obviate the uncertainties and distractions to which allusions have been made, with improvements in so much of the form and content of the existing mechanism as may be found to be obsolete." With regard to the actual substance of the Empire's foreign policy there "is . . . a primary and unalterable condition by which every proposal must be tested, and that is that we are a world wide group of communities, composed of various elements and living upon different continents separated by the greatest distances." Therefore policy "must be conceived on broad and simple lines, intelligible to all the nations of the Empire. Unless it is so understood and the relation to the interests and welfare of all is apparent, it can scarcely command the common assent that is essential to success. . . . A course of policy concerned intimately or predominantly with the complexities of one continent would not meet that condition."[47]

Such, for the information of an English audience, were some of Meighen's general views on the Empire. They were neither novel nor startling, certainly, though his elaboration of some of them at the conference was to cause considerable stir. But what about the man himself, what was he like? John Stevenson, a few days after he arrived in London with the others, tried to give at least part of the answer in a piece he wrote for *The New Statesman*.[48]

At the Conference he will be a debutante among a tribe of dowagers, but it would be a profound error to regard him as a political *jeune fille*. Mr. Arthur Meighen is one of the most interesting personalities on the North American continent, and his character constitutes a curious enigma. By origin, tradition and early practice a Tory, he displays at intervals streaks of Liberalism, and betimes amazingly Radical proclivities. . . . He is a masterful authoritarian, who has a passion for efficiency, and has not learnt to suffer fools gladly. He will use to the limit the powers of the State to repress ebullitions of democratic discontent, but at the same time he is not afraid to mete out stern justice to powerful capitalist interests. Within the last two months he has brought the directorate of the hapless Grand Trunk railway to heel, and has refused to be intimidated by the usual moans about the terrible damage certain to befall Canadian credit in London if the course he laid down was pressed. On most questions he is far in advance of his exceedingly stupid and very derelict party, and he has established his position as the recognized master of Parliament. In his social habits he is the most democratic Premier that Canada has known since that lover of good cheer, Sir John Macdonald, died. He plays golf with his tailor, and sends his children to the national schools. He has been heard to declare that he would rather spend six hours with even his present Cabinet than one hour at a dance, and social functions are a nightmare to him. He is a product and a very creditable product, of the Ontario small town, which is not much different from the Gopher Prairie of Mr. Sinclair Lewis's *Main Street*, and he is shot through with its Puritanism, its anti-militarism, its sense of the quality of human values and its detestation of pretentious arrogance.

That despite his inexperience in international politics this was certainly no *jeune fille*, his fellow conferees were shortly to discover when the debutante sat down with the dowagers to argue the great issues of Imperial affairs.

CHAPTER FOUR

DEBUTANTE AND DOWAGERS

INSTALLING HIMSELF in Claridge's Hotel in Mayfair, Meighen waited for the opening of the conference, which had had to be set back a few days because Lloyd George was suffering from an indisposition. The London papers, he noticed, were not giving much attention to the forthcoming deliberations of the Prime Ministers. He knew there were good reasons for this. What with serious economic difficulties besetting their country, widespread labour unrest unsettling her peace, a government that seemed likely to fall at any moment and violent disorder bordering on civil war in Ireland, it was not surprising that British editors, before the Conference of Prime Ministers had even begun, had scant space for what by comparison must have seemed the remote and academic concerns of the Empire. And there were still other matters of pressing importance that demanded immediate, earnest consideration. " . . . Problems of the Empire," Grattan O'Leary reported, "for the moment are wholly subordinated to the races at Ascot and the defeat of England by Australia in the test match at Lord's."[1] The admirable English sense of proportion was making itself felt.

While he waited Meighen dealt with a steady stream of cables from Ottawa, saw his mother off for Scotland and kept the first few of a series of engagements that were to occupy him for luncheon and dinner almost every day throughout the visit. He had hoped in vain that these social obligations could be kept to a minimum, that the conference would be brief and business-like so that he might get back to Canada and attend to things. Only three or four of the many invitations that had reached him before he left home had been accepted but once he got to England the demands on his free time multiplied and the conference stretched out as though it would never end.

There were some invitations that could not possibly be declined, of course: a state dinner at Buckingham Palace in honour of the King and Queen of the Belgians; a few nights later a state ball at the Palace; luncheon with the Prince of Wales at St. James's Palace; and, scarcely less commanding, lunch with the Duke of Connaught at Clarence House. Nor could Meighen very well turn down the invitation to dine with the Benchers of Gray's Inn or with the Empire Parliamentary Association

82

at the Royal Gallery of the House of Lords. Most assuredly he had to be present at Buckingham Palace to be formally sworn of the Imperial Privy Council and just as definitely he could not refuse, nor had he any wish to, the freedom of the City of London or the freedom of Edinburgh, both of which were proffered. These latter two ceremonies remained among the Meighens' most cherished memories of that visit to Britain, especially, perhaps, the one in London, enacted as it was with such ancient ritual and pageantry.

Entering a carriage drawn by four horses, with liveried coachman and footmen, they set off for the Guildhall, the horses' hoofs clattering splendidly on the pavement. The Lord Mayor, the Aldermen and Councilmen of the City were assembled, along with a number of distinguished guests. The Chamberlain commended Meighen for the freedom of the City, extended the right hand of fellowship and then the certificate of freedom in a golden casket bearing views of the Parliament Buildings, Ottawa, the Houses of Parliament at Westminster, the Horseshoe Falls of Niagara and Crow's Nest Mountain in the Canadian Rockies. After Meighen's short speech of acknowledgment, in which he described London as "the centre of gravity of the world," the company repaired to the Mansion House for the Lord Mayor's luncheon. There, a toast to his health having been proposed and drunk, Meighen responded: "I confess myself in profound ignorance of the duties of the office to which I have been raised, and I intend conscientiously to maintain that ignorance; but I will promise to make an early acquaintance with the privileges pertaining thereto, and to avail myself of them to the full. In ancient times, I understand, these privileges were very substantial indeed. They involved freedom from taxation and freedom from the fear of destitution, two attributes which in modern times seem to mean one and the same thing."[2]

A short while later a ceremony somewhat similar to the one in London was performed in Edinburgh and Meighen was now doubly free. After freedom again food—a bill of good Caledonian fare: *Ananas au gingembre; Saumon de la Tay froid; Sauce Mayonnaise; Côtelette d'Agneau princesse; Pouding glacé au Macédoine de Fruits; café.* Then, of course, toasts and speeches, the plain Canadian accents of the guest contrasting with the rich Scottish burrs of his hosts. And afterwards, a visit to Edinburgh University, where the honorary degree of Doctor of Laws was conferred on the visitor.

Along with these command appearances and ceremonial occasions there were a great many less formal and less public functions: one day dinner with Winston Churchill, who had taken Milner's place at the Colonial Office in January, and another, luncheon with Leopold Amery, his Under-Secretary; Baron Byng of Vimy, Canada's Governor General-designate, and Lady Byng entertained at their home in Belgrave Square and a few nights later the Meighens were guests of General Smuts. One evening there was a party at Cliveden, country home of the remarkable Nancy Astor, M.P., who had assembled a glittering array of people to meet the visitors from the Dominions. One of the guests was Lady Kennet, formerly Lady Scott, widow of the Antarctic explorer, who noted in her diary: "There was a dinner at Lady Astor's and great fun." J. L. Garvin, editor of *The Observer,* had escorted her into dinner, she noted, "but my greatest fun was with Meighen, the Canadian Premier, ridiculously young and so alive. I danced with him with a crowd looking on and I didn't care a blow. I loved it. He told me of his difficulties in Canada, all the different races and the Americans too. He is an adorable one."[3]

Although the golf links offered nothing quite so attractive or lively as the likes of Lady Kennet, Meighen much preferred them to the dance floor and managed to work in a few games in England during his busy round of activity. It is improbable that his English companions were any more impressed by his skill at the game than his friends in Canada, who had much fun at his expense over his very individual approach to the sport. However, he did distinguish himself unforgettably in one of his English golfing expeditions. Usually he remembered to provide himself with the proper clothes and necessary equipment before setting out but this time, according to John Stevenson, he appeared somewhat late on the first tee, fresh from a session of the conference, without a golf bag and attired in striped trousers, black coat, wing collar and dress shoes. In this garb, ignoring all remonstrances, he played a stylish round, borrowing the club needed for each shot from some other member of the foursome.[4]

The conference was opened at twelve noon on June the twentieth with a general survey of the world situation and the state of the Empire by Lloyd George.[5] Touching upon Far Eastern matters, he avoided taking a stand on whether the Alliance with Japan should be renewed, contenting himself with a few words of praise for that country's help during the war, a nod towards China with her desire for "sympathetic treatment and fair play," and the statement, hardly unexpected, that "friendly co-operation with the United States is for us a cardinal principle. . . ." Neither the friends of the Alliance nor its critics would find much to please or annoy them in his non-committal words. With regard to Imperial relations he said in effect that the Empire was one big happy family and deprecated suggestions that Great Britain wanted to revolutionize and centralize its structure. Existing machinery for consultation and co-operation, he thought, worked very well but he would be glad to have suggestions for improvement, as well as proposals for making clearer to everyone the equality of status as partners of the United Kingdom which the Dominions now enjoyed.

Following Lloyd George each of the visiting Prime Ministers and Srinivasa Sastri, representing India, made an opening statement of his own. Meighen came first, speaking for the senior Dominion immediately Lloyd George had finished, the others the next day. Meighen's remarks were the briefest—he spoke for only ten minutes—the least elaborate and the least eloquent of them all. He made no disclosure of his attitude on any important topic and implied that he thought lengthy opening speeches should be avoided in order to expedite consideration of concrete questions. This view did not seem to be shared by the others, especially Hughes and Massey, who, possibly because they had come halfway around the world to get there, demonstrated equality of status by delivering longer addresses than Lloyd George.

The whole of the Wednesday sittings was devoted to a lengthy exposition of British foreign policy since the war by the Foreign Secretary, Lord Curzon, and on Thursday this was discussed by the others. Hughes, Smuts and Massey devoted considerable attention to particular aspects of policy in Europe, the Middle East and Asia but Meighen, less knowledgeable on these matters than they, confined himself to a disquisition on how the foreign policy of the Empire ought to be made. That it must be *a* policy and not a number of separate ones determined individually by each of the member states was for him a basic assumption but, given that assumption, it was proper to examine the principles governing the formulation of the policy. Up until that time, he pointed out, the only body which had directly advised the Sovereign and therefore had directly implemented policy on behalf of the entire Empire in the field of foreign relations was the government of the United Kingdom, and that government was responsible solely to the Parliament of the United Kingdom. But the character of the advice tendered, the wisdom of the policy, was obviously of vital importance to the Dominions, since in the event of war, which might be the consequence of policy, they would all be liable to attack whether they chose to take part in the war or not. Ways had been found in which the Dominions might be consulted and their advice sought with regard to specific aspects of foreign policy and matters had reached the stage where in certain instances the views of a Dominion with a special or exclusive interest in the particular case had determined the policy adopted. One could scarcely exaggerate the importance for the future of the Commonwealth, said Meighen, of the British government paying close and respectful attention to the representations of the Dominions before charting its course in world affairs, and even relying entirely upon the views of any one of them that happened to have a paramount interest in the question at issue. Nor was it, he asserted, overstating the matter to say that a Dominion might refuse to be bound by a policy to which it had not given its consent.

From all this he drew three conclusions. First, there should be conferences as nearly continuous as possible attended by responsible delegates from Great Britain, the Dominions and India with the purpose of establishing the general principles governing the foreign policy of the Empire. Secondly, the government of the United Kingdom, though it bore final constitutional responsibility in advising the Sovereign, ought nevertheless to take into account at all times the opinions of the governments of the Dominions and of India in devising and applying that policy. Thirdly, with regard to any aspect of policy of special importance to one of the Dominions, the influence of that Dominion in deciding policy should be commensurate with the importance of the decision to it.

Enlarging upon these conclusions, he suggested that the principles underlying the foreign policy of a Commonwealth of such diversity required to be simple and comprehensible, with a universality of application that would make them acceptable to all. By way of illustrating what he meant, he declared that the policy of the Empire ought to be to work for the success of the League of Nations in every way and, to that end, it ought to shun treaties or alliances setting up groupings of states which might revive the balance of power diplomacy of the pre-war years. Later in the conference he went further than that and asserted that the Canadian people would not support any plans for the defence of the Empire if they felt that its foreign policy was not in keeping with the aims and authority of the League. As for his third point, about the right of a Dominion to set the policy in certain circumstances, he had in mind, of course, Canada's paramount interest in the relations of the Empire with the United States. At some length he explained why he thought Canadian opinion should be conclusive in this sphere. Canadians, living in constant contact with the Americans, dealing with them continuously in multifarious ways, not only would be most vitally affected by Empire policy in that direction but were in the best position to decide what that policy should be.

While Meighen presented his three conclusions as descriptive of an existing procedure which ought to be more scrupulously adhered to, some of the others did not see them in that light. Lloyd George described them as constitutional proposals, which Meighen curtly denied they were, and later in the conference Hughes angrily asserted that if one Dominion were to determine the policy of the Empire in a matter of special concern to it, the unity of the Empire would inevitably break down. Undeniably there were inherent difficulties in Meighen's postulates. For one thing, he did not explain how more continuous consultation, to which everyone paid lip service, was to be achieved in practice but assumed that that would be worked out in due course. For another, he did not make it clear how, if the sole constitutional responsibility for the foreign policy of the Empire were to continue to be that of the United Kingdom government to the United Kingdom Parliament, that government could accept the views of one or more of the Dominions with which it did not agree. Responsibility for decisions must carry with it power to decide. Nor was he, on the other hand, willing to contemplate the possibility, which had been discussed by some authorities, of each Dominion government separately advising the Sovereign on foreign policy and assuming responsibility to its own Parliament for its advice; that, in his view, would probably destroy the unity of the Empire in the world. Finally, he did not appear to recognize, in presenting his third and most far-reaching conclusion, that often it would be anything but easy to agree which Dominion should have a predominant influence in determining the course to be pursued by all in concert. Probably he looked upon the fate of the treaty with Japan, about to be considered, as a case in point. He approached that matter basically from the standpoint of its bearing on the relations of the Empire with the United States, and therefore as a subject on which Canada's views were entitled to prevail. But Australia and New Zealand looked at the treaty from a different standpoint—of their own security in the Pacific. Might not they, because of their location on the globe, claim that here was a problem in whose solution they had a peculiarly vital stake? The great question, of course, was whether the members of so scattered and diverse a Commonwealth could together arrive at a common foreign policy suitable to them all. Meighen would have answered emphatically that this was indeed possible, that all differences of outlook could be resolved by discussion around the conference table. Given proper consultation, given the chance to hear one another's arguments, there was no reason why intelligent statesmanship should not be equal to this task, no reason why it should not become clear to all which member of the Commonwealth in any given case ought to have its opinion prevail. He was shortly to discover when the Japanese treaty came up for consideration how far apart, how nearly irreconcilable, were his own views on that subject and those of the Prime Ministers of Australia and New Zealand. This chasm eventually was bridged, more or less to the satisfaction of all concerned, but as much perhaps by the intervention of fortuitous circumstances as by the discovery through discussion of a genuine consensus.

All this talk about foreign policy, of course, was closely related to the project of the constitutional conference envisaged in 1917, since the purpose of such a conference would be so to rearrange things that the Dominions might have a greater influence in deciding the concerted policy of the Empire. One of the chief tasks before the Prime Ministers in 1921 was supposedly to lay the groundwork for this later gathering. Meighen's scepticism about it has already been referred to and he expressed it vigorously when the subject came up for consideration on July the eleventh. He contended that it was both unnecessary and inadvisable, because of the unsettling effect it would have politically, to announce that constitutional changes were contemplated; this would cause dissension and debate as to whether there should be changes and, if so, what they ought to be. It would be better, he argued, not to lay down any agenda for a constitutional conference or even to hold a conference advertised as such. When the Prime Ministers met again in a regular Imperial Conference (a term Meighen preferred to "Imperial Peace Cabinet" which was in vogue in Britain) they might be able to consider changes in constitutional relationships which seemed desirable then. He did not, he emphasized, think those relationships were entirely satisfactory as matters stood. Some way would have to be found to enable the Dominions to participate more effectively in setting foreign policy because a failure to do so might lead to the disintegration of the Empire with each of the self-governing states going its own way. One method of improvement was to continue in peacetime the right granted during the war of representatives of the Dominions sitting with the British Cabinet when matters of common import were under consideration. If greater advantage were taken of this right the Dominions might participate more fully in the formulation and control of policy. But the existing structure was not in need of profound change, only of refinement, and no specially designated conference was needed to accomplish that.

In general the others present shared this attitude, although Smuts proposed to no avail that certain tentative constitutional propositions might be drawn up to be mulled over before another conference was called. The final decision of the Prime Ministers effectively administered the *coup de grâce* to Sir Robert Borden's cherished Resolution IX. In their own resolution on the subject they affirmed their belief in the importance of continuous consultation; they expressed the desire that Prime Ministers' meetings should occur annually "or at such longer intervals as may prove feasible"; they sanctioned the existing practice of direct communication between the Prime Ministers of the United Kingdom and the Dominions, with the equality of status it implied, in preference to the former reliance on the more roundabout route from Dominion Prime Minister to Governor-General to Colonial Secretary to United Kingdom Prime Minister: and they decided that the right of the Dominions "to nominate Cabinet Ministers to represent them in consultation with the Prime Minister of the United Kingdom" would be maintained. But the really substantive sentence in their resolution was the flat statement that "having regard to the constitutional developments since 1917, no advantage is to be gained by holding a constitutional Conference."[6]

This decision, understandably, was a disappointment to Borden. Delivering the Marfleet Lectures at the University of Toronto in the following October, he was severely critical of the conference for not reaching a more positive conclusion. ". . . it can hardly be said," he declared grumpily, "that its pronouncement is progressive or even illuminating."[7] And, he added, although the Dominions were represented at the Peace Conference and had signed the peace treaties, "I have yet to learn that since the conclusion of peace their right to 'an adequate voice in foreign policy and in foreign relations' has been recognized in any effective or practical way."[8] It all hinged, of course, on what one meant by "adequate," "effective" and "practical" but Meighen might well have blinked in astonishment upon reading Borden's strictures. After all, as Sir Robert well knew, there had just been a dramatic demonstration in connection with the Anglo-Japanese Alliance of how a Dominion could effectively influence policy in a very practical manner. What Canada had done on that question she or one of the other Dominions, Meighen thought, might do again in the future. Where Borden wanted a conference on the constitution of the Empire so that the rights of the Dominions in making foreign policy might be officially spelled out, their equal status officially defined for all the world to know, Meighen's view was that it was enough to enjoy the substance of influence, to be able to play in practice as he did in 1921 a real part in directing the Empire's course. In his mind there were no problems affecting the relations of the self-governing states of the Empire which intelligence, fair-mindedness and some improvement of existing consultative procedures could not solve. Adherence to his three "conclusions" would dispose of issues of foreign policy as they arose. Conferences were needed, and as frequently as possible, to deal with important concrete matters; a conference to formulate a constitution for the Empire, to try to define in fixed terms a relationship which, based as it was on convention and custom, would no doubt continue to change slowly in the future as it had in the past, was not to his mind necessary or consistent with the best traditions of the Britannic community.

The Japanese Alliance, the chief subject to come before the conference, was first formally introduced for debate by Curzon on June the twenty-eighth, though both Hughes and Massey had referred to it at some length in their opening addresses, expressing their desire for its renewal. After sketching its history and giving some of the arguments

both for and against its continuation, the Foreign Secretary recommended that it be renewed in such altered form as consultation with the United States, China and the League of Nations might render necessary.
Referring to Meighen's proposal of the previous February that a conference of Pacific powers be convoked, Curzon suggested that the Empire,
in renewing the treaty, should at the same time make clear its willingness
to participate in such a gathering.   Thus the plan decided on by the
British Cabinet in May was laid before the Prime Ministers.

The moment for which Meighen had carefully prepared had arrived
as he opened the debate on Curzon's recommendation on the morning of
the twenty-ninth.   All the talk at the conference thus far had been in a
sense general and preliminary but the real meat of the business, the most
urgent of the concrete issues, had now been reached.   Essentially his
speech was an enlargement of his February cable to Lloyd George.   At
the outset he declared bluntly that he was opposed to the renewal of the
Alliance in any form and then went on to expound his reasons.   The
first was that the menace of Russia, which the original agreement of 1902
and the treaty of 1905 had been framed to meet, had disappeared, as had
the menace of Germany, so real when the treaty was re-negotiated in 1911.
The purpose of any treaty must be to deal with an actually existing situation; inasmuch as the situation had radically changed and the earlier
dangers were no longer present, the perpetuation of the treaty would be
pointless.   Nor could its renewal reasonably be advocated in order to
meet some hypothetical future contingency, such as a Russo-German
combination, to the possibility of which Curzon had alluded.   Indeed,
Meighen suggested, to continue the treaty might be to invite the very
combination of those two countries it was desirable to prevent.

Secondly, he denied that Japan had faithfully observed the terms of
the Alliance, as was so often alleged in her favour.   True, she had fulfilled her obligations during the war but assuredly she had not honoured
her convenant to ensure "the independence and integrity" of China and
to maintain the "Open Door" there.   On the contrary, as the Foreign
Secretary himself had pointed out, Japan had gained effective control of
southern Manchuria, excluding the "commerce and industry" of other
nations in violation of the treaty; similarly she had seized control of
Shantung Province and thus far had not carried out her promise to relax
it; in 1915 she had addressed twenty-one demands to China which, if
accepted, would have made the latter her vassal.   Added to all this was
her annexation of Korea, Formosa and the Pescadores.   To continue the
treaty, under cover of which Japan might further add to her conquests,
would be to make the British Empire an accomplice in such acts and
thus reduce its moral standing with the rest of the world.

Furthermore, Meighen continued, it was indisputable that China, whose "independence and integrity" were supposed to be guaranteed by the treaty, was resolutely opposed to its renewal. The friendship of China was not to be despised nor should the commercial and other interests of the Empire in that country lightly be put in jeopardy. To renew the Alliance with Japan would be to alienate China and throw her more and more into the arms of the United States; thus a Sino-American combination might form in opposition to that of the British Empire and Japan. This, in fact, was one of the evils of the alliance system, that it led to the confrontation of gigantic aggregations of power. Better far than the entanglements resulting from such bilateral alignments would be a settlement of Pacific problems negotiated by and acceptable to all the states concerned. It was not a question of casting Japan into the outer darkness, of turning one's back on her. She had rights in the Pacific that could not be denied; the Empire needed and must seek to retain her friendship. But her rights could be protected, her good will preserved by other means than the continuation of an Alliance which, in Meighen's eyes, was full of peril for the future.

The greatest peril, of course, was the estrangement of the British Empire from the United States, and on this point he dwelt at considerable length. He admitted that the fate of the Japanese treaty was important to all members of the Commonwealth but asserted that Canada had a special right to be heard with respect to its bearing on British-American relations. Canada not only understood the United States better than others but if war should ever ensue between the Empire and the Republic, Canada would be the Belgium of such a conflict. Curzon had said that any renewal of the treaty must be in a form acceptable to the United States but, Meighen replied, even though the Americans might not object to the specific terms of the treaty, they would be antagonized by the fact of its existence. Suppose it contained a clause, as the present one did, which in effect would exclude the possibility of armed conflict between the English-speaking peoples. Would not the Japanese expect a benevolent neutrality on the part of the Empire in the event of war between them and the Americans? Might they not, therefore, with greater impunity under the guard of the Alliance continue their career of conquest with what would be regarded in the United States as the connivance of the British nations?

Meighen then referred to the passage by the United States Senate on May the twenty-fifth, with no dissenters, of a resolution introduced by Senator William E. Borah authorizing and requesting the President to invite Great Britain and Japan to a conference for the purpose of reducing naval armaments in the Pacific.[9] This indicated, he said, not only American willingness to negotiate, but also the hope in the United States that the Conference of Prime Ministers would take some constructive step to facilitate a multilateral agreement as to armaments. Renewal of the Alliance with Japan would in effect close the door on such negotiations, for the Americans, finding themselves excluded from a pact embracing the other two Pacific naval powers, would go their own way and continue the buildup of their maritime strength. Agreement with the United States to prevent a continuation of the naval arms race would be much easier to achieve if the Empire were not formally allied with Japan.

In February, Meighen went on, he had suggested to Lloyd George that Canada sound out the United States as to the possibility of a general conference of the Pacific nations. The suggestion had been turned down but he still thought such overtures should be made and at once, before the treaty with Japan expired. It was his understanding that expiry would occur, failing renewal, on July the thirteenth and this understanding seemed to be shared by all those present. Although the treaty of 1911 contained a clause providing for its continuation beyond the stipulated ten-year period until twelve months after either party gave notice of abrogation, in July 1920 Great Britain and Japan notified the League of Nations that they regarded the treaty in its present form as incompatible with the League Covenant. In London this notification was regarded as a denunciation of the treaty and therefore notice of abrogation. This interpretation does not appear to have been fully accepted in Tokyo, though the Japanese tacitly fell in with it by taking part in negotiations for a three months' extension of the Alliance beyond July the thirteenth, 1921. There seems to be no doubt that everyone around the conference table at 10 Downing Street when Meighen launched his attack on the treaty assumed that it would lapse in two weeks' time unless the temporary extension were approved. The Canadian government had been informed by the Colonial Office in January that as things then stood the Alliance would terminate on the thirteenth of July. Hughes of Australia was evidently under the same impression; in his opening address to the conference he declared: "It is not a thing to be settled in the future, but now. . . . It is an urgent matter. It must be settled without delay."[10] Curzon in recommending renewal warned that there were only a few days left in which to reach a decision before the expiry of the treaty and the very fact that the Foreign Office was engaged in arranging a short extension indicated an assumption that it would lapse at the middle of July.

Meighen, stating that the Canadian government had never approved this brief extension, argued that it should not now be approved. Instead, he urged, the possibility of a Pacific conference should be immediately explored with the United States and other interested countries in the hope that at least agreement to hold a conference of that kind could be obtained before the treaty lapsed. The most recent dispatch from the British Ambassador in Washington, he pointed out, testified that the American Secretary of State, Charles Evans Hughes, was opposed to any arrangement of Pacific affairs in which the United States was not included. Surely the voice of the Secretary must on this matter be listened to as the authentic voice of his country; surely what he had said to the Ambassador indicated, as did the Senate resolution, that the Americans would answer favourably a call to a conference on Far Eastern questions.

When Meighen had finished the floor was taken by the Australian Prime Minister, whose patience, one imagines, must have reached the breaking-point as he listened to Meighen's discourse. William Morris Hughes was a tiny, scrappy, bantam cock of a man with a big voice and an impressive gift of emotional eloquence which, when he was aroused, flowed from his lips torrentially. With a remarkably varied background as drover, farmer, cook, sailor, prospector, trapper, teacher, labour organizer and politician, he was accustomed to the rough-and-tumble of life. "His powers of expression were definitely unique," Meighen recalled long after this encounter. ". . . he . . . was a waif of a man . . . but bound up in that emaciated frame was a character, fearless, resolute and masculine to the last degree."[11] Hughes greatly enjoyed a fight, he was a good fighter and clearly he believed the survival of the Anglo-Japanese Alliance worth fighting for. He therefore set out, indulging in some violence of tone and language and considerable misrepresentation of Meighen's case against the treaty, to blow that case over with the gusts of his anger. No sooner had he a full head of steam up, however, than Meighen slipped out of the room to keep his luncheon engagement with the Prince of Wales. Thereupon, perhaps hoping it would cool his excited passions, Lloyd George tactfully suggested that they adjourn, as it was most important that Mr. Meighen hear what Mr. Hughes had to say. That afternoon Meighen heard it: that *he* was speaking more for the United States than for his own country; that he had offered no practicable alternative to the treaty he was so eager to abandon; that the Americans were by no means sure to adhere to any general agreement, while in Japan the Empire had a loyal, trusted ally. With savage scorn Hughes ridiculed the vague voice of the United States he alleged Meighen had said they should listen to. Although he admitted that the friendship of the United States was essential, his speech was strongly anti-American and he vigorously rejected the idea that the foreign policy of the Empire should, in effect, be decided in Washington.

After Hughes the others spoke in turn. Smuts was in favour of renewal, with suitable reservations and safeguards of the sort Curzon had mentioned. Massey, as large in frame and deliberate in manner as

Hughes was small and impetuous, supported the latter in his own gentle-manly, debonair fashion and Lloyd George, when his turn came, also pronounced for the treaty. This, of course, was not surprising since his Foreign Secretary had already done the same. The really noteworthy feature of Lloyd George's speech was, not what he said as to the merits of the Alliance with Japan, but rather his bland announcement that he was unconvinced it would expire on the thirteenth of July unless extend-ed. He had, he said, referred this question to the Law Officers of the Crown and he now called upon Viscount Birkenhead, the Lord Chan-cellor, to give their opinion. Meighen remembered Birkenhead from his previous visit to London and had renewed the acquaintanceship ten nights earlier at the Gray's Inn dinner where Birkenhead had proposed his health. He recalled being greatly impressed in 1918 by the man's acuteness of mind. He now had cause to be impressed all over again, for the Chancellor, in a dazzling feat of legal legerdemain performed with just the right air of insouciance, demonstrated that the notification to the League of Nations had not after all constituted denunciation of the treaty, which would thus continue in force until one year after notice of abrogation had been given. This startling dictum removed an im-portant assumption on which the discussion thus far had been based, rendered pointless the negotiations, almost completed, for a three months' prolongation of the Alliance, and cut part of the ground from under the feet of Hughes and Meighen, both of whom had emphasized the one thing on which they were really in agreement—the necessity of an im-mediate decision.

By engineering this extraordinary about-face with the help of the Lord Chancellor, Lloyd George was apparently playing for time to allow some sort of compromise to be achieved, though with two such men as Meighen and Hughes facing one another across the table he may well have wondered what the chances of compromise were. If the con-ference decided to endorse the treaty it was obvious that the diplomatic unity of the Empire would be destroyed, for Meighen had made it abun-dantly clear that Canada would not be bound by an agreement of which it did not approve. If on the other hand a formal decision to abrogate were reached at once, Hughes would go home angry and embittered, Massey would at least be put out, and Japan would be much offended without there being any assurance that the kind of conference Meighen advocated would take place. The beauty of Birkenhead's pronounce-ment was that it made it needless to choose either of these stark alterna-tives. Furthermore, it might help to reassure the Japanese, who were probably somewhat unsettled by reading the highly circumstantial ac-counts of the conference proceedings appearing in the press, because it meant British acceptance of their contention that the treaty remained operative despite the notification to the League.

Although Meighen found the shift of the British position in this regard rather disconcerting, since it demolished his argument that a Pacific conference must be sought before the treaty lapsed, it considerably strengthened his hand in other ways. It could no longer be objected that such a conference could only be promoted at the cost of repudiating the treaty, which, it was now realized, would continue in force while the Pacific powers conferred. Japan might the more willingly attend a conference on the Far East, and friends of the Alliance, in Australasia and elsewhere, could with less reason object to a conference of that sort while the Alliance remained unimpaired. On the morning of July the first Meighen returned to the attack. He curtly dismissed Hughes' animadversions of the previous day as a gross caricature of his position and bluntly accused Lloyd George of having acquiesced in it. Then point by point he briefly recapitulated his case, asserting again the ultimate importance of the friendship of the United States and emphasizing that there was nothing whatever to be lost, and perhaps a world of good to be gained, by pursuing the project of a really representative meeting on Pacific questions. As the others followed him one by one it became clear that the balance of the scales had changed, that Hughes, not he, was now the minority of one. Hughes remained obdurate, in another highly charged oration, but Smuts, Massey and Lloyd George veered sharply towards Meighen's position. The path in that direction had been nicely smoothed for them by the Lord Chancellor's pronouncement; they could sanction the kind of conference Meighen desired, knowing that the Alliance would continue in effect until formally denounced. And they were the more willing to take the path, perhaps, having had a night to reflect on the pith and substance of Meighen's arguments, of which they had now heard a cogent summation.

In any event it was agreed that Curzon should sound out the Japanese and American ambassadors and the Chinese Minister, in that order, as to whether their governments would care to participate in a Pacific conference, the intention being that the British Empire would issue the invitations if the responses to these inquiries were favourable. While this decision brought to an end the debate on the Anglo-Japanese Alliance it did not, of course, end the Alliance itself. It was further agreed, over Meighen's objection, that notice of abrogation of the treaty with Japan should not be given until after the proposed Pacific conference. If that gathering proved successful the need for the treaty would disappear; if it failed, however, the treaty would be continued in such altered form as to make it compatible with the League Covenant. Here was a victory for Hughes of Australia and a defeat for Meighen, who argued to no avail that it would be madness to make Japan in effect the arbiter of the projected conference. She would be enabled to sabotage it if she wished, he contended, secure in the knowledge that the Alliance would survive. To place Japan in so powerful a position would hardly make the conference idea appealing to the United States.

However, while Meighen had to bow on that issue, the decision to seek a meeting of all the major Pacific powers amounted to a signal triumph for him in his first important appearance in Empire councils. Had he been less uncompromising, had his exposition of the case against the treaty been more timid and equivocal, had he yielded ground in the face of the broadsides from Hughes and the sniping by others, renewal of the Alliance in some modified form, as originally proposed by Curzon, probably would have been endorsed and Birkenhead would never have been brought in to perform his dexterous re-interpretation of inter-national law. It is an overstatement to describe the episode, as one authority has done, as "the first notable occasion of a Dominion formula-ting the policy of the British Empire,"12 but it *was* one of the rare occasions on which Canada has in reality acted out her much-celebrated role as interpreter or linchpin between Great Britain and the United States. It also demonstrated that the charge often levelled against Meighen in Canada of being ready to follow blindly wherever Britain led, ready to sacrifice Canadian interests on the altar of Empire, was less than just. As he remarked acidly, after Hughes had accused him of looking at the treaty from the American standpoint rather than from that of the Empire, that accusation was certainly a novel one to be laid against him. In fact his action was dictated by the enlightened self-interest of Canada and also, he firmly believed, the real interest of the whole Empire, for which, no less than for its senior Dominion, the good will of the United States was the most fundamental of necessities. It may be that any Canadian Prime Minister would have had to take essentially the same stand but Meighen brought to the conference table his own special gifts which there stood him and his cause in good stead: a superb-ly analytical mind, a striking clarity of expression, an ironic wit and a genuine enjoyment of controversy. In short he showed why he was the master of the Canadian House of Commons and his performance was described to John Stevenson by Sir Robert Horne, Chancellor of the Exchequer, as "the most powerful piece of political advocacy he had ever listened to."13

Meighen's victory at the conference table was sealed on the anniver-sary of Confederation. It is highly unlikely, though, that he spent much time reflecting on the coincidence (if it occured to him) or in seeking some deep significance in it.14 It was enough that he had won the day and in any case he had other things to think about: the further business of the conference, which was by no means over; the unwelcome news, with all its troubling political implications, of the overwhelming defeat of the Government candidate in a by-election in Medicine Hat a few days earlier; a weekend trip to France the next afternoon; and, most immediately, a Dominion Day reception and dinner at which he would have to act as host. One of the distinguished guests at the dinner would be the Japanese Ambassador. In the light of what had just taken place at the conference one wondered how *he* would be disposed towards Canada and her Prime Minister. However, there was no need to worry; the Ambassador spoke and acted with impeccable oriental courtesy. There were several pleasant speeches, full of compliments to Canada and kindly references to her statesmen, including an especially charming one by Srinivasa Sastri, for whom Meighen and his wife during this visit to London conceived a particular affection.

The visit to France was occasioned by Meighen's having promised to unveil the newly erected Cross of Sacrifice at Thelus Military Cemetery, Vimy Ridge. On Saturday he and Mrs. Meighen took the train to Dover and crossed the Channel to Calais, whence they were driven to the town of Arras in the ancient province of Artois. The town bore many signs of the havoc it had suffered, with the jagged edges of ruined buildings standing out bleakly against the sky. Overnight they lodged in a hotel, one whole side of which had been knocked off by shell fire and was still missing, and on Sunday drove the short distance to Vimy Ridge, scene of a glorious but sanguinary Canadian attack on Easter Monday, 1917. Climbing to the crest of the Ridge they looked upon a sweeping panorama of quiet, fertile countryside stretching towards the horizon. It was a beautiful summer's day, calm and warm. Not a cloud marred the bright blueness of the sky. The ripening grain in the fields around swayed and rustled softly in a gentle breeze and through the clear air rang the sweet, joyous song of a lark. Peasants from a nearby village came in their Sunday best, talking in subdued tones among themselves and bearing bunches of red poppies and blue cornflowers to place upon the graves of the warriors. It was hard to associate the violence, the death and destruction of war with so sunny and peaceful a scene. But the white crosses in geometric array were proof too positive of the most recent human tragedy this storied land had seen, this land, which, as Meighen phrased it in his short address, had "resounded to the drums and tramplings of many conquests. . . ." As he spoke his few moving words of tribute to the dead and unveiled the Cross of Sacrifice, their monument, he saw his hope that "the long, ghastly story of the arbitrament of man's differences by force" had been closed forever reflected in the faces of those who listened: bereaved parents on a mournful pilgrimage; Canadian and French officials, civilian and military; and in the background the local people, the men with caps doffed, not understanding his words but comprehending his meaning.[15]

During the week following the climactic meeting on the first of July the summoning of the Pacific conference was arranged, though not quite in the way that had first been planned. The Prime Ministers had approved on Friday Curzon's scheme for making informal overtures to the three diplomats, beginning with the Japanese Ambassador. As naught save imminent catastrophe would induce a gentleman to transact business on a weekend, nothing apparently was done until Monday when, it seems, Curzon got little encouragement from the representative of Japan. Evidently he did not broach the matter to George Harvey, the American Ambassador, until Tuesday. At this point, amid circumstances that are not entirely clear, a change of tactics occurred.[16] Curzon proposed to Harvey that the United States should issue invitations to a conference on the Far East and promised British co-operation in making it a success. Harvey agreed to cable the gist of Curzon's proposal to Washington and to send a full account of their conversation by surface dispatch. Whether it was Harvey who suggested that the initiative should be made to appear to come from Washington or Curzon, reconsidering the situation after the meeting of July the first, who simply revived the procedure approved by the British Cabinet in May, the change was concurred in by all those who hoped the conference would materialize. If the invitation were to come from London the isolationists and Anglophobes of the United States, who had campaigned successfully against America's joining the League of Nations, would inevitably arouse with great effect the fear of being ensnared in the sinuous machinations of British diplomacy. There were now signs that the United States was preparing to emerge from her North American shell into which she had retreated in post-war disillusionment. To those who welcomed this tendency it was supremely important to allow her government to take the initiative, or to appear to do so, lest American public opinion be needlessly alarmed by the danger of further involvement in a war-prone world.

No official word of this activity in London reached Washington until July the eighth when Harvey, with some prodding from Curzon, at last sent off his cable to the State Department. But some inkling of it had reached Charles Evans Hughes through press dispatches and on July the seventh Lloyd George, under close questioning in the House of Commons about policy in the Far East, intimated that discussions with other countries were going on and that he hoped to be able to make a statement in a few days after replies to a British message were received from the

United States, China and Japan. As Harvey had not yet transmitted the message to his government, the Foreign Office was compelled, at the cost of adding to the confusion and contradicting the Prime Minister, to announce that no reply was expected from Washington since there was nothing for the American authorities to reply to. However, Lloyd George's statement, along with substantially accurate newspaper accounts of what had been going on in the Prime Ministers' meetings, convinced Hughes that the British planned to promote a large conference on the Far East and this galvanized him into action.

The new Republican administration of Warren G. Harding was caught between the devil of the big navy enthusiasts in its own party and the deep blue sea of widespread public opposition to large-scale expenditures on armaments. So strong was public opinion on this issue, so effectively was it organized and brought to bear upon Congress, that the Borah Resolution referred to by Meighen in his opening attack on the Japanese treaty was passed overwhelmingly by both Houses. Its passage placed squarely upon Harding the onus of calling an arms limitation conference. He had already subscribed to the idea of a conference of this sort in principle but thought it should be deferred until American naval power had increased sufficiently to permit negotiation from a position of unchallengeable strength. The verdict of Congress, however, indicated that the step could not be that long delayed without discrediting the administration in the eyes of the American people. But Secretary Hughes appears to have been spurred into action on July the eighth by the rumours emanating from London, which he used to convince the President that delay would be disastrous. "Rushing to the White House, he told the President that 'if the British get ahead of us in calling any kind of conference our show would amount to little.' Harding agreed."[17] Thereupon Hughes drafted cables to his ambassadors in the United Kingdom, Japan, France and Italy, asking them to ascertain whether those countries would attend an arms limitation conference in Washington.

The cable to Harvey passed in transit the one he had promised Curzon three days earlier to send to Hughes. Harvey conveyed Curzon's suggestion that the United States summon a conference on the Far East "and added that the British were about to make public the steps they had taken toward calling the conference. He therefore urged that the President issue a statement to the press which would indicate that the United States had already taken the initiative. Otherwise, Harvey concluded, Harding would be robbed of his 'rightful credit,' and would appear in the unfortunate position of following the lead of Great Britain."[18] Just why credit rightfully belonged to Harding is far from clear, to say the least, and Harvey's remarkable suggestion that an American initiative be publicly claimed, when as far as he knew when he sent his cable there had been no such initiative, was of dubious propriety. However, as Hughes had already acted, Harvey's fear of Great Britain seeming to be the leader at this juncture proved to be groundless.

Hughes' cable referred only to a meeting on the limitation of arms and one not confined to the Pacific powers. He had in mind, therefore, a very different type of conference from the one Meighen had been advocating and Curzon had suggested to Harvey should be sponsored by the United States. However, on receipt of Harvey's cable of July the eighth Hughes and Harding decided that their proposed conference should be broadened to include the whole field of Far Eastern and Pacific affairs. If this were not done and Curzon's proposal were made public, the American government would appear to be dragging its feet, to be shunning an opportunity for negotiating on a broad front a settlement of important outstanding issues. Accordingly on July the tenth Harding issued the following statement:

> The President, in view of the far-reaching importance of the question of limitation of armaments, has approached with informal but definite enquiries the group of Powers heretofore known as the Principal Allied and Associated Powers—that is, Great Britain, France, Italy and Japan—to ascertain whether it would be agreeable to them to take part in a Conference on this subject to be held in Washington at a time to be mutually agreed upon. If the proposal is found to be acceptable, formal invitations for such a Conference will be issued. It is manifest that the question of limitation of armaments has a close relation to Pacific and Far Eastern problems, and the President has suggested that the Powers especially interested in these problems should undertake, in connection with this Conference, the consideration of all matters bearing upon their solution, with a view to reaching a common understanding with respect to principles and policies in the Far East.[19]

This announcement was brought by Harvey on the day it was issued to Chequers, the Prime Minister's country home where the Dominion leaders and their wives were the weekend guests of Mr. and Mrs. Lloyd George, and the next day Lloyd George happily announced this fortunate turn of events to the House of Commons.

Thus the lines of British Empire and American policy converged—but they did not quite meet. The Prime Ministers had sanctioned a small conference of the major Pacific states. It now seemed that what would take place in Washington was a very large conference at which the political problems of the Far East, with which the men in London were largely concerned, might become confused with and subordinated to the question of armaments, which was the overriding concern of the United States. In order to prevent this happening Lloyd George, after consulting at length with his Dominion colleagues, proposed to the

Americans that there should be a preliminary meeting on the Far East of the four main countries concerned. If this were held in London almost immediately it would be possible for all the Prime Ministers to attend. This they thought very desirable since probably none of them, with the possible exception of Meighen, would be able to get to Washington in the fall. This was rejected by the United States, which presumably feared that such a gathering might detract from the importance of its own conference. Efforts to find some other way in which Far Eastern questions might be considered prior to the Washington meetings all proved abortive owing to American opposition, with the result that there took place in Washington two simultaneous conferences on separate but related questions and embracing different groups of countries, the one on political arrangements in the Pacific, the other on disarmament. This seemed to the Prime Ministers much less than the ideal way of handling things but at least the door was now open to a solution of Far Eastern problems which would, without giving offence to Japan, permit the replacement of the Anglo-Japanese Alliance by a multilateral agreement.

In his account to Parliament of the events culminating in Harding's invitation Lloyd George left the impression that the invitation had been prompted by the conversation between Curzon and Harvey and the latter's cable to the State Department; the inference to be drawn, therefore, was that credit for the American action properly belonged to the British nations. This was not wholly accurate in view of the fact that Hughes had sent his feeler about a disarmament conference before hearing from Harvey. Nevertheless, it is clear that the first initiative had been taken by the Prime Ministers, although they yielded it in deference to the President and the exigencies of American politics. Their endorsement of Meighen's plan, which prompted Curzon's overtures to the diplomats, acted as a catalyst in Washington. Because Harvey was dilatory in communicating Curzon's proposal, that endorsement was known only unofficially in Washington, but it was known. It induced a sense of urgency in Secretary Hughes and precipitated an invitation which, however, would probably have been forthcoming before very long in any case. Both in this respect and in the broadening of the agenda of the Washington Conference beyond the subject of armaments, the decision reached at the conference in London was important. Since he had been instrumental in bringing his colleagues to that decision, Meighen had a significant influence, not as author of the Washington Conference—that distinction he would not have claimed—but with respect to its timing and scope. Furthermore, that there had been no formal renewal of the Anglo-Japanese Alliance, a fact for which he was largely responsible, greatly facilitated the action of Harding and Hughes in calling the powers together. Had the Prime Ministers sanctioned renewal of the Alliance as Curzon had proposed at the outset of their deliberations, even in the modified form he suggested, there would have been less likelihood of American public opinion supporting multilateral negotiations in which the two chief rivals of their country in the Pacific region would participate as partners in a newly reforged union. The old Alliance remained in effect, of course, after the Conference of Prime Ministers was over but everyone knew its days were numbered should the conference at Washington result in the desired settlement of Far Eastern questions.

A few days after the American invitation was received Meighen commented on it in a letter to a number of Conservative publishers and editors in Canada:

> I know that no one in Canada will be more grateful than you at the one great result that has already followed the Conference. I mean Mr. Harding's message and the consequent Disarmament Conference which will be held in Washington. This is undoubtedly one of the great events of the last half century and it dare not wholly fail. The fact that the message came and that the Conference is now sure to follow is, in far greater degree than is generally understood, due to our deliberations here. There are certain portions of our discussions which, of course, must be kept secret for the present at least, but whatever part, be it small or important, that Canada has had in so directing her course as to lead to this goal will be to me a proud and cherished memory. We have had many other subjects under review as well, but none so important.[20]

One of these other subjects was Imperial defence, always a highly explosive matter in Canada where there was much fear in some quarters that Great Britain might seek commitments from the Dominions, as she had on occasion in the past, to some form of integrated, centrally controlled naval defence scheme. It was this apprehension in part that had inspired Mackenzie King's circumscribing motion during the House of Commons debate on April the twenty-seventh. In fact fears on that score proved to be unwarranted, though unquestionably there was a hope in Great Britain that some day some way would be found of distributing more evenly among the member states of the Empire the burdens of its defence. At the conference, though, the question seemed to pale into relative insignificance beside the great issues of foreign policy which were its main concern. The impending meetings in Washington on disarmament provided an ideal excuse for doing nothing about defence in the meantime, and nothing was what the Prime Ministers decided to do. Their resolution on the subject read:

> That, while recognizing the necessity of co-operation among the various portions of the Empire to provide such Naval Defence as may prove to be essential for security, and while holding that equality with the naval strength of any other Power is a minimum stand-

ard for that purpose, this Conference is of opinion that the method and expense of such co-operation are matters for the final determination of the several Parliaments concerned, and that any recommendation thereon should be deferred until after the coming Conference on Disarmament.[21]

The importance of Canada's part in helping to pave the way for a settlement of Far Eastern and disarmament questions was attested by a number of English newspapers, such as the *Times,* the *Daily Telegraph* and the *Evening News,* which gave Meighen much of the credit for bringing on the American decision to call the Washington Conference. The Liberal *Manchester Guardian,* which had campaigned strongly against renewal of the Japanese treaty, praised Meighen for the same reason and expressed the hope "that this will not be the last imperial conference in which he will take part."[22] That hope, of course, found no echo in the breasts of Canadian Liberals, who by and large approved of Meighen's actions at the conference as far as these were known but understandably derived little satisfaction from the accolades he received. Some Liberal newspapers denied that he deserved any special credit for the results of the meetings and rather harshly took Grattan O'Leary to task for having greatly exaggerated Meighen's influence in his "hero-worshipping" dispatches. Criticism of Meighen's conduct in London, as distinct from depreciation of his influence there, came from some ultra-Tory circles on the ground that he had been too much the spokesman of the United States and too adamantly nationalist in his pronouncements on the making of Imperial foreign policy. But most Conservatives in Canada naturally held a different opinion. "I suppose," wrote his old friend Fawcett Taylor from Manitoba, "you won't object to my telling you that your friends here are all highly delighted with the reception that you received in the Old Country, and with the deservedly prominent place which you occupied in the conference of Premiers. Your name is on everybody's tongue just now. I wish we could count them all as ballots for the next election."[23] "I appreciate very keenly what you say about my work Overseas," Meighen answered. "I do not think I did any harm, but I did not dominate the Conference at all as some of the reports would indicate."[24]

There was one respect in which Meighen was later accused, by some who approved generally of his actions and attitudes in London, of having failed in his duty there: that he had not safeguarded the right of Canada to be adequately represented at the Washington Conference. When he left London he had some hope that he would be able to attend the conference himself, but shortly after arriving home he concluded that the state of domestic politics made this impossible. He therefore asked Sir Robert Borden to act as Canadian delegate and Borden consented.

Nothing had been said during Meighen's presence at the Prime Ministers' meetings about Dominion representation at the gathering in Washington but he took it for granted that each of them would have a member
on the British Empire delegation. He was not disturbed by the fact that
when the formal invitations to the conference were issued on August the
eleventh none arrived in Ottawa; by tradition invitations, even to meetings at which one or more of the Dominions might wish and expect to
be represented, went only to Great Britain. The important thing to
Meighen was that Canada have a place in the British delegation and be
enabled to participate, not that her status be officially acknowledged by
a separate invitation to attend. As always where Imperial relations
were concerned, he was more interested in the substance than the form.

Assuming that Canada would be present at the conference but lacking precise information as to the arrangements proposed, Meighen cabled
Lloyd George late in August:

> Would be glad to receive information by cable concerning Wash-
> ington Conference indicating position with regard to Agenda
> scheme of representation proposed and other aspects of arrange-
> ments particularly with regard to procedure contemplated for hand-
> ling Far Eastern and Pacific questions. Shall be glad if you will
> arrange to furnish us by mail with copies of relevant correspondence,
> memoranda, and papers prepared by experts for use at Conference.
> I hope also you will arrange to telegraph us any important develop-
> ments.[25]

When at the end of five days there was no answer to this, Meighen sent
Lloyd George another cable marked "Private and Personal," saying that
he was "most anxious to know method by which it is proposed to provide
for representation of Canada in British Empire delegation."[26] The non-
committal reply which Meighen received perhaps reflected the expectation
of the British government, which George Harvey detected in a conversation with Lord Curzon, that the latter and Lloyd George would represent the entire Empire at the conference. That there was such an expectation is confirmed by a message from Lloyd George to Meighen early in
October in which it was stated, to Meighen's great surprise, that it had
been "arranged at recent Imperial Conference that His Majesty's Government should represent the whole Empire at Washington."[27] He knew that
he had not been privy to any such arrangement and was unable to
understand how, in the light of the whole debate at the Imperial Conference, the British authorities could have entertained the belief that
unitary representation had been agreed upon or would be acceptable.

Whatever initial objections Lloyd George may have had to according
the Dominions their places in Washington were soon dropped and he
asked the Dominion governments to nominate their representatives.
Meighen promptly submitted Borden's name, with Loring Christie to

serve for Canada on the secretariat of the conference. When it was announced in the press that Canada would have a member on the British Empire delegation Meighen received a cable from General Smuts, arguing that the Dominions should not send delegates unless they received their own invitations from the United States. The United States, Smuts pointed out, had not ratified the peace treaty "to which we are signatories as component independent States of British Empire. On the contrary agitation in Congress against our independent voting power in League of Nations was direct challenge to our Dominion status. This is first great international Conference after Paris and if Dominions concerned are not invited and yet attend, bad precedent will be set and Dominion status will suffer. If a stand is made now and America acquiesces, battle for international recognition our equal status is finally won."[28]

When this arrived in Ottawa Meighen was away campaigning and the message was directed to Sir James Lougheed, the Acting Prime Minister. Lougheed consulted Bordon, who agreed with Smuts in principle but saw no hope of separate invitations being secured. Negotiations on this point between London and Washington would be required and, as the conference was scheduled to open on November the twelfth, these could not possibly be concluded in time.[29] At Lougheed's suggestion Meighen cabled Smuts to this effect. A copy of the latter's protest had gone to Lloyd George, who sent a reassuring message to Meighen through the Colonial Secretary. In Lloyd George's view, to press for direct invitations to the Dominions at this late stage would cause annoyance in Washington and create an undesirable atmosphere on the eve of the conference. However, he proposed that any agreements arrived at by the conference should be signed separately by the representative of each Dominion on behalf of his own government, which would give each of them the power to reserve assent and thus demonstrate their autonomous status.

This was communicated to Meighen on the hustings and he wired Christie: ". . . please prepare and submit to Lougheed and Borden reply along lines of acquiescence in position taken by Foreign Office. Unless such lines seem objectionable to you or to them or require conditions send cable accordingly."[30] Christie thereupon prepared a cable, agreeing to the procedure suggested but emphasizing that it was "essential that Dominion representatives should hold same status as at Paris and that this status must not be allowed to be prejudiced by proceedings at Washington conference."[31] In fact, however, the Dominions were not represented at the Washington Conference in quite the same way as they had been in Paris. At the Peace Conference each of them had had a place on the British Empire delegation, which participated in all the sessions on behalf of one of the principal powers. But each had also had separate membership on the same basis as other smaller states with the right to attend sessions where matters directly concerning them were under consideration.   In this respect their individuality and status had been recognized in a way that was not repeated in 1921, when they were treated only as component parts of a single entity, the British Empire.   Meighen, unlike Smuts and Borden, devoted little attention to the formalities of status and was fully content that the Empire should appear and act as a unit, provided that Canada's influence could make itself felt.   Thus he did not share Smuts' concern over the lack of official recognition in the form of a separate invitation from President Harding.   As long as Canada was assured of a place in the delegation from the Empire he was satisfied.

It is clear that the Americans had no objection to the Dominions being represented at the conference in this way; indeed, Secretary Hughes seems to have desired their presence and to have taken it for granted that they would be on hand.   Any early doubts about the expediency of including them seem to have been confined to London rather than Washington.   However, once the right of the Dominions to take part was conceded, as it soon was, the British government began to consult with them as to Empire policy at Washington and to provide the data that Meighen had asked for and on the basis of which a concerted policy could be worked out.   All differences of opinion about policy among the states of the Empire were not resolved before the conference began, but as far as possible the ground was prepared by telegraphic consultation for the united stand they would eventually take.   Among the cables that arrived in Ottawa from London was one that displayed a real recognition of the need for consultation, about which there had been so much talk, as well as a scrupulous respect for the autonomy of Canada. It also indicated that in one important way the forthcoming conference might be a good deal bleaker than such gatherings in the past.   The ponderous machinery of official communication by one Prime Minister to another through the Colonial Office and Rideau Hall was put in motion to send a secret message in cipher:

> Following from the Prime Minister for your Prime Minister. Begins.
> I think you may like to know that so far as our section of the British Empire Delegation to Washington is concerned, I have decided that in view of liquor restrictions in force in the United States of America no alcoholic liquor should be taken for use in official entertainments.   Individual members however are at liberty to make their own arrangments for taking liquors.   Ends.[32]

This flurry over Dominion representation at the Washington Conference was still in the future, of course, as Meighen began to prepare for his departure from England.   He had booked passage home for July the twenty-first but was detained in London while the fruitless negotiations for a preliminary conference on the Far East were proceeding. It was July the thirtieth when he and Mrs. Meighen (his mother returned separately) at last sailed from Liverpool on the *Carmania*. The Prime Ministers' Conference was still in progress but there was no business remaining to be dealt with that required his presence, while in Canada a host of matters demanded his attention. For one thing he wanted to be on hand to greet the new Governor-General, Baron Byng of Vimy, who was due to arrive at Quebec on August the tenth, but that pleasant ceremonial duty was really only a pretext for his departure. The political skies over Canada were ominously lowering and the first distant lightning bolt had struck in the Medicine Hat by-election. He must get back to prepare as best he could for the approaching storm. On July the sixth he had received a cable from Borden which left him in no doubt about the seriousness of the situation: "Secret Private Personal. I venture to urge the vital importance of your return at earliest possible moment. The situation is extremely difficult and affairs are drifting somewhat dangerously. It is my firm conviction that these decisions should be taken in immediate future."[33] If Borden, of all people, thought domestic politics should be given precedence over an Imperial conference, the situation in Canada must be serious indeed. It appeared that Meighen would not have a wholly pleasant homecoming but when the *Carmania* docked at Halifax on August the sixth he was able to tell a group of waiting reporters as he disembarked, "I like to travel but the part of it I like best is the coming home."[34] And he added:

> I will give you one thought that the experience of the past few weeks has impressed on my mind. I have been impressed with the real value, the undoubted necessity of these Conferences. It is not a mere platitude, much less an empty patriotic boast, to say that Great Britain is the greatest factor in the world to-day for preserving peace. The influence of the British statesmen in the councils of the world is greater because the Dominions and India are within the Empire and because she reflects, or wants to reflect, their views as well as her own. So far as Foreign policy is concerned, I do not think there are many in Canada who would have this country decline the invitation to come and help. We must walk with the nations of this Empire or walk away from them. The gospel of isolation is the gospel of separation under a thin disguise. I believe in the British Empire.[35]

After spending a night at Halifax and a couple of days in the seclusion of Metis, Quebec, the Meighens moved on to Quebec city to be on hand for Lord Byng's arrival. As a large welcoming crowd cheered and a band played, His Excellency and Lady Byng came down the gangplank to be welcomed by Meighen and the Premier of Quebec. Afterwards at a Government luncheon Byng, with disarming candour, said something to which some of the things that were to befall him in the next five years lend a certain poignancy: "I've never done anything like this, you know, and I expect I'll make mistakes. I made some mistakes in France, but when I did the Canadians always pulled me out of the hole. That's what I'm counting on here."[36] His diffidence may have arisen in part from knowledge that he had not been the first choice of the Canadian government. They had not the slightest objection to him on personal grounds, of course, and the fact that he had for a time commanded the Canadian Corps in France gave him an honourable association with Canada which no one else in sight for the Governor-Generalship possessed. However, in Ottawa it was apparently believed that a civilian rather than a military personage would be a more appropriate choice. Consequently, though Byng had earlier been recommended to the King by certain "responsible Canadians" of identity now unknown and had expressed his willingness to serve, consultations between London and Ottawa were begun to find someone else.[37]

Late in February 1921 Meighen had agreed to a suggestion by Winston Churchill at the Colonial Office that the latter submit a list of possible successors to the Duke of Devonshire, whose terms was nearly over, with an assessment of their respective qualifications. When nothing further was heard from Churchill, Meighen cabled him on March the sixteenth and again on the twenty-second. Consultation seemed to be anything but continuous, for on March the twenty-eighth there had still been no further word on the subject from London. Thereupon Meighen sent off a wire to Sir George Perley, Canada's High Commissioner, which betrayed his exasperation. "No letter has been received, nor even an explanation of delay in spite of fact that urgent reminders were telegraphed to Colonial Office. . . . Please make representations and cable me as matter is most urgent."[38] As it happened Perley's representations were unnecessary. The delay was explained by the fact that Churchill was touring Mesopotamia and Palestine with even more urgent matters on his mind than the tenancy of Rideau Hall, but on March the twenty-fifth he finally found time in Jerusalem to write Meighen the promised letter. Of the various persons who had been suggested he recommended either the Earl of Desborough or the Earl of Lytton, since Canada apparently would not favour the appointment of Byng.[39]

It took six weeks for this letter to reach Ottawa. While it was *en route* Meighen, backed up by Borden, had proposed to the Duke of Devonshire that he remain as Governor-General for a further period. The reason for this may have been that Meighen desired to postpone an appointment until he had a chance to discuss the matter personally with Churchill during the Prime Ministers' Conference, possibly because he hoped to secure someone of even more exalted station than any of those who had been mentioned.[40]   However, Devonshire had made plans to return to England and declined to stay longer in Canada.[41] Disappointed in this move, Meighen then notified Churchill that Canada would approve Lord Desborough, who, however, refused the position when offered it.   Churchill, communicating this decision to Ottawa, proposed Lord Lytton but the Canadians evidently rejected that advice, perhaps because they did not want to run the risk of another refusal.   The upshot was that with Meighen's approval Byng, who was already committed to acceptance, was formally offered the post and on May the twenty-sixth the appointment was duly made.

And so here he was, a forthright, modest, honest soldier.   His first words in Canada were of his inexperience in this new kind of work but his main fear, one he had expressed when first approached informally about going to Canada, may well have been the inadequacy of the salary and allowances to enable a man of modest personal means like himself to make ends meet, rather than his inadequacy for the job.[42]   After all a Governor-General was just a constitutional monarch, though of less than regal stature, who acted on the advice of his responsible ministers, showed himself to the people and supported worthy causes.   Full of good will and with none of that desire to influence policy or that condescending air of superiority to the Canadians exhibited by some of his predecessors, Lord Byng could surely look forward to a stay in Canada unmarred by controversy or unpleasantness.   But it was not to be so.   Neither His Excellency nor his Prime Minister, as they shook hands on the dock at Quebec and watched while Lady Byng was presented with the inevitable roses by the inevitable little girl, could have even faintly imagined what a rough road they both would travel before Byng's term was over.

CHAPTER FIVE

BACK TO EARTH IN OTTAWA

BACK AT his desk in Ottawa Meighen turned his attention at once to assessing the political situation. He knew from gloomy reports he had received in London, especially following the disaster at Medicine Hat, that the situation had not improved during his absence. Before going to England he had been pondering whether there should be another session of Parliament before a general election. He had been inclined to think, like most of those who wrote him about this, that there should be, despite the clamour set up by the Liberals and Progressives for an immediate appeal to the people. While there was life, there was hope that matters might improve if that appeal were delayed until the latter part of 1922—as was constitutionally possible. There might be at least a partial economic recovery, a revival of trade, a decline in unemployment, and with all this a lessening of vociferous discontent which was so much in evidence and boded so ill for his government. A more popular Budget than the one Sir Henry Drayton had presented in the session just over might be managed. Also, it might help if Quebec were given as much time as possible to realize that conscription was now a thing of the past. Canadians everywhere might come to appreciate the significance of the tariff issue. Time might allow the Mackenzie King Liberals and the Progressives to make that compact Meighen had been predicting, thus facilitating the polarization of political forces on the tariff question he desired. Finally, a redistribution of seats in the Commons on the basis of the 1921 census would have to be made. Those provinces entitled by their population to increased representation would legitimately feel aggrieved if a new Parliament were elected under the existing distribution.

On the other hand, deferring the election entailed the risk that things might go from bad to worse before it was held. Perhaps, as some argued, it would be better to go to the country as soon as practicable after Meighen's return from England and salvage as much as possible. A redistribution would undoubtedly give larger representation to the Prairie Provinces, which would hardly be advantageous to the Government, while Ontario, where it was strongest, would probably lose a few seats or retain only the same number as before. As for the ethical objection, that a Parliament elected before redistribution would not be representative, no opponent of the Government really could complain of this since both King and Crerar had demanded dissolution without delay. When Meighen sailed for England in June he had not made up his mind. The ministers were sharply divided in opinion, as were the private members. The one thing they were agreed on was that a decision ought to be reached promptly but the decision was for Meighen to make and he was not yet ready to make it.

The result of the Medicine Hat by-election tipped the scales against delaying the general election until the following year. In a two-way fight between a Government candidate and a Progressive the latter won with a majority of nearly ten thousand. There had been bigger majorities than that in some constituencies in the 1917 election when party lines had broken down but with these few exceptions the winning margin in Medicine Hat was the largest in the history of Canadian politics up until that time. Even before the seat was made vacant by the death of Arthur Sifton in January 1921, Meighen began to receive letters from people in the riding advising him that if there was to be a by-election, as seemed certain in view of Sifton's failing health, it should be held without delay. One of them wrote that if this were done there was "no risk in opening up this Riding" for the simple reason that there would be a small vote, as many farmers would not be able to get to the polls in the wintertime and the urban people would support the Government.[1] However, this advice was not followed. Instead the by-election was put off until June the twenty-seventh, not only allowing the aroused and well-organized farmers to get to the polling places but, as it happened, coinciding with the crest of the agrarian wave that was to sweep a United Farmers government into office in Alberta three weeks later.

The Government candidate was a Conservative, Lieutenant-Colonel Nelson Spencer, a respected citizen of the city of Medicine Hat with a distinguished record in the war. No Liberal candidate was nominated but the Liberal press of western Canada and the Liberal organization in the riding supported Robert Gardiner, nominee of the United Farmers of Alberta. While this meant that the whole anti-Government vote would be concentrated behind Gardiner, the absence of a Liberal candidate was not wholly unwelcome to Meighen because it seemed to bear out his contention that Mackenzie King was in league with the Progressives. He was sure there must be many Liberals in the West, as elsewhere, who feared Progressivism and would support the Government against it when these were the only alternatives. This thought was in his mind when he wrote Spencer just before leaving Ottawa for the Old Country.

... Medicine Hat occupies naturally quite a place in my thoughts.

> The importance of success there can scarcely be over-estimated. I do not think there is anything that I can say that you have not thought of yourself but this I will emphasize, the support of Liberals is essential. The utmost care should be taken that nothing is done to alienate that support. The attack should be on the whole Farmer party, Farmer political methods, Farmer Leaders and Farmer policy. I do not mean personal attacks but I mean that their public career and public inconsistency should be unremittingly exposed. Nothing should be done that would make it appear necessary for leading Liberals to disavow their desire to see you elected.[2]

When the Prime Minister got to London he found waiting for him a cable from his secretary in Ottawa reporting optimistically on the outlook in Medicine Hat,[3] so he was by no means prepared for the staggering news that reached him when the returns were in. "The Medicine Hat majority," he wrote to C.A.C. Jennings, "was certainly a stunning blow and my first impulse was to say 'well if the people of Canada want Ivens, Wood and the Farmers platform, they have a right to have the whole combination and should be given a chance without delay.' "[4] Whether Medicine Hat proved that Canadians in general wanted that "whole combination" was doubtful but it was the most telling symptom thus far revealed of popular dissatisfaction with the Government. Not only had Spencer been crushed in the rural districts, he had failed to carry even his own city; the Liberal support on which he and Meighen had counted so heavily had failed to materialize. This "frightful defeat," this "serious catastrophe," wrote H. H. Stevens who had worked on Spencer's behalf, resulted from "a combination of organized Farmers, Red Labour and Liberals who had one common interest and that was to defeat the Government." But, he implied, it was not enough to denounce this unholy alliance. He saw "the imperative need of a new policy as far as the North West is concerned. I do not think that protection or free trade amounts to a row of shooks. . . . I am convinced of this, that some new line of action must be taken if we hope to hold any portion of it."[5] This did not seem to appeal to Meighen, who thought that what was needed was not a new policy but a more defiant, resolute fight against western radicalism.

> I have received many reports [he replied to Stevens] as to the condition of the public mind through the prairies. It is simply appalling the success that propagators of discontent have had in disturbing political views throughout the country, chiefly by unblushing and persistent falsehood. It is just possible that they have over-shot the mark and that the evidence of their swash-buckling spirit, manifested in recent contests, will alarm men of all classes in other parts of the Dominion. One thing is certain, if this does not result then the chastening effect of a few years' experience will bring the country to its senses. I am prepared personally for

either consequence, but my unsparing endeavour will be to fight this movement and beat it now.[6]

Whether it should be fought in a general election or first of all in another session of the existing Parliament was what he had to decide. After Medicine Hat, as before, the ministers and members were divided on this question with, his friend Senator Billy Sharpe reported in a lengthy memorandum on the general political situation, a majority of the Cabinet, nearly all the Conservative members and most Conservatives in western Canada in favour of deferring an election until 1922.[7] The remaining vacancies in the House of Commons they thought should be filled through by-elections. But the arguments for going to the country without calling Parliament again were compelling ones, made more compelling by the fiasco in Medicine Hat. Coming on top of Peterborough and Yamaska, it indicated that the Government might well lose any further by-elections, which would not only damage it severely in the country but reduce its majority in Parliament to the danger point. Perhaps it would be wisest, bad as the whole situation was, to appeal to the people before it got worse as it seemed likely to do. One of those who strongly urged this course was Sir Henry Drayton, who wrote to Meighen in London:

I do not like bothering you with domestic issues when you are so busy overseas but think that I ought to. I have spoken to you before about re-organization and election. I am becoming more convinced than ever that my views are correct. . . .

I expected Medicine Hat to go against us but I did think that Spencer would have had a majority in the city and a very substantial one. The fact is, he is beaten and beaten in his own town I think that the general outside opinion is that we are simply drifting and nothing kills a party more surely than drift. . . .

I think that what Canada wants more than anything else, is to find out what she intends doing and where she is at and she won't get this without a general election. . . .

Both King and the farmers have demanded an immediate election. They cannot very well object to it but even if they did I am convinced that the general public interest requires a premier, whoever he may be, who in the trying times ahead of us ought to be furnished with a clear fresh mandate and be free of troubles in the House.

I have already told you that in your own personal interest it is very much better for you to go down, if go down you must, in a general election on some principle, than run the risk of being counted out in the House. . . .

I am absolutely certain that putting through redistribution, having particular regard to Ontario which must lose seats, will give you a great deal of trouble in the House. You would have difficulty in getting even your supporters to vote for the elimination of their own counties.

In my view there ought not to be any bye-elections. I think they will merely further weaken the Government. I do not for one moment think that the prospects for success at a general election are at the moment promising. I am certain that they are better than they will be next spring as everything points to a bad winter. I am also of the view that the returns for the present fiscal year and the next Budget, if there be no election, will but further add to the unpopularity of the Government.

Theoretically we ought to have a redistribution before there is an election. That is what ought to be done but to my mind the general business interest of the country requires settled conditions. People want to know what the tariff will be. . . . The business community in Canada to-day are very largely living from hand to mouth. I am afraid they are drifting just to the same extent as general public opinion thinks the Government is.

Then, apart from the question of public good, which I hope is the real motive actuating me in writing you, and I believe it to be so, and to get down to the political question about which I admit I know very little or nothing, my view is that every day the Government continues makes Mackenzie King just so much the stronger. . . . The temper of the public is such that I do not think the Government gets credit for anything it may do. It is practically certain that there is nothing that the Government can do which will at once bring back good times and a contented populace. At one time I thought it was in the public interest to hold on so that matters could get settled. They have settled to a point. I think there is to-day much less danger of Bolshevism than there was but I do not think there will be any improvement in future brought about by merely deferring an election.

I just repeat my former advice. You ought to go to the country as a brand new Premier (and remember your newness is wearing off) with a brand new cabinet.[8]

It did not take Meighen long, once he got home, to recognize the force of these arguments and before the end of August he had made up his mind to go to the country some time ere the year was out. Nor did he disagree with Drayton about the need to reconstruct his Cabinet, though whether he could make it a "brand new" one was doubtful. He was a novice at the difficult art of Cabinet-making, having inherited all but three of his ministers from Borden. With varying degrees of reluctance they had consented to serve under him but some, at least, on the understanding that they would stay on only until the dissolution of Parliament. He knew it would not be an easy task to find suitable replacements for those who would retire or to make the new Cabinet sufficiently representative of the various ethnic, religious and sectional interests in the country. The chief difficulty lay in Quebec, of course. The only French Canadian in the present Cabinet was Senator Blondin and he was bent on retiring. It was essential to find several French Canadians of real standing in their province but, considering the state of the party there, it would be far from easy to find them, to say nothing of getting them elected in their constituencies. Most of all in Quebec, but everywhere in the country, really strong men who were willing to serve were at a premium, reluctant to identify themselves with what appeared to be a doomed cause. No Prime Minister ever had to rebuild his Cabinet under less auspicious circumstances.

But rebuilt it had to be and for several anxious weeks Meighen devoted himself largely to this work. All the ministers put their resignations into his hands and he accepted those of six: Sir George Foster, C. J. Doherty, J. D. Reid, P. E. Blondin, J. A. Calder and R. W. Wigmore. It was rumoured that C. C. Ballantyne desired his to be accepted, too, and that Hugh Guthrie hoped for a judgeship but Meighen, striving to preserve the Liberal flavour in his government, could ill afford to dispense with the services of these two Liberal Unionists. Ballantyne was quoted in the press, which for days on end was full of speculation about the makeup of the new Cabinet, that "strong pressure" was being exerted on him to remain[9] and Meighen was certainly no less anxious to have Guthrie do so. In the end both consented to stay and, in addition to them and the Prime Minister, the reconstructed ministry sworn in on September the twenty-first contained seven members of the old one: Sir Henry Drayton, Sir Edward Kemp, F. B. McCurdy, S. F. Tolmie, Gideon Robertson, Sir James Lougheed and E. K. Spinney. There were twelve new men all told when the solicitor-generalship was filled a little later: J. A. Stewart, H. H. Stevens, R. B. Bennett, L. G. Belley, Rodolphe Monty, J. W. Edwards, R. J. Manion, J. B. M. Baxter, L. P. Normand, Edmund Bristol, J. R. Wilson and André Fauteux.

Although by no means the strongest Cabinet ever assembled, it was a reasonably representative body. However, only four of its twenty-two members—Ballantyne, Guthrie, Spinney and Manion—had ever been identified with the Liberal party; the Conservative element of the National Liberal and Conservative party clearly predominated. Also, it was rather heavily weighted with Ontario men, eight in number, but as before every province except Prince Edward Island had at least one representative. There were now four French Canadians, instead of the solitary Blondin as formerly, but it was doubtful that either the number or the identity of these choices would inspire much enthusiasm in Quebec; the absence of anyone of Patenaude's stature or Boivin's popularity was most apparent. Among the four only Belley, a Quebec city lawyer, had ever sat in Parliament, where he represented the riding of Chicoutimi-Saguenay from 1892 to 1896. Monty and Fauteux were both well known in Montreal, where each practised law, and to some extent in the province at large but neither had previous administrative or legislative experience. The same was true of Dr. Normand, a physician from Three

Rivers. One could hardly be optimistic about the likelihood of their being able successfully to challenge the massive Liberal power in their province, personified by such men as Gouin, Lemieux and Lapointe. Among the other newcomers a few, notably Bennett and Stevens, were men of real vigour, ability and experience but even if all their colleagues had possessed these qualities in equal measure, the Government could hardly have survived the election now in the offing.

Meanwhile the campaign had been officially opened by Meighen on September the first at London, Ontario, where he announced that he would advise a dissolution of Parliament. This was the first of about two hundred and fifty speeches he was to deliver between then and polling day on December the sixth. Very little of this effort was devoted to his own constituency, where he was able to spend only two or three days. In Portage la Prairie he had to rely for re-election almost wholly on the efforts of his friends, his personal reputation and the prestige of his office. There were two men in the field against him, A. M. Bannerman of the Liberals, whom no one seemed to take very seriously, and Harry Leader of the Progressives. Leader, who farmed near the village of Burnside, was a threat but Meighen's supporters did not see in him a really formidable rival for a Prime Minister. Neither, apparently, did some of the Progressives in Portage, who, so Meighen was told, had hoped in the beginning to persuade Crerar to run against him. He had received a note from a crony, Jack Garland, about this.

> They are going to make a great effort to get Crearer [sic] to run here they put one over me by haveing [sic] him open our Fair so I took my medicine sizeing [sic] up the odds and at once conceived the idea that we should put on a small track event the first day told them that an immense crowd would come to hear Crearer and that we would charge 50 cents that after noon [sic] to the Grand Stand as we needed the money they fell for it and past [sic] a resolution to that effect as we had not in previous years charged first day.
> Crearer waited and waited Billie Miller rang the Horse bell but he had to start and opened the Fair with a grand stand filled to the extent of about *thirty people* it was absolutely emptied they would not pay 50 cents the first day, say it was good. . . .[10]

This incident may have given Crerar pause but no doubt there were more powerful reasons for his decision to stay in his own riding of Marquette.

For two months Meighen was almost constantly on the road, crossing and re-crossing the country by rail, speaking in theatres, armouries, opera houses and concert halls, and sometimes in the open air, shaking hands and drinking coffee and talking to the local politicians about candidates, strategy, organization and policy. He could not possibly speak everywhere he was asked to but he pushed himself to the limit of his endurance, wherever he went attracting large crowds, many of which displayed a heartening enthusiasm. He was not misled by this; though ever professing confidence in the outcome, as he had to do, he recognized that the odds were against him but this only made him the more determined to throw himself into the contest with the last ounce of energy he possessed. Then, come what might, victory or defeat, he would have the satisfaction, the truest satisfaction this life offered, of knowing he had done his best and had spared no effort. Assuredly a herculean effort was needed, not only to appeal to the populace but to instil some verve and vigour into the faithful. Bedevilled as the party was by internal friction, lack of organization and the demoralizing foretaste of defeat, his presence was counted on by the campaign managers, and not least by himself, to rally the forces and work up some zeal for the battle.

How badly they needed rallying was all too evident. It was exasperating to sit in his office and read, more than a fortnight after his London speech, that the party in Nova Scotia was "without organization and in many of the constituencies suitable men were not in sight as candidates."[11] He could only reply wearily: "Convention should be called at the earliest possible date, and organization should begin in the Constituencies forthwith. There is no reason why it should not—organization cannot be directed from here. It must spring from the energies and convictions of the people."[12] No less discouraging news came at the same time from Toronto in the form of a gloomy letter written by C. A. B. Jennings of Saturday Night Press. He had attended a meeting in the King Edward Hotel presided over by Edmund Bristol. The people at the meeting had come "for information and inspiration, and from my observations they got neither. . . . Here in Toronto we appear to have run to seed and the officers of the different wards are mostly employees of the city and can see nothing but patronage. They are sore on Union Government. . . ." As for Bristol, he "is one of the most unpopular men in public life today." Jennings was writing "because something must be done at once to remedy things" and presumably he expected Meighen to do whatever that undefined something was. Probably he meant that Bristol should be sacked but that remedy, if such it was, was not taken.[13]

The ward politicians of Toronto were not, of course, the only ones preoccupied with patronage. Interest in contracts and appointments was always high among the faithful and, though the reform of the civil service in 1918 had very greatly reduced the number of rewards that could be dispensed, the Government still had at its disposal a good many positions, prestigious and otherwise, for which there was an incessant and often indiscreet competition. Meighen's papers, like those of other public men, testify to the immodest eagerness with which some individuals pressed their claims. A passage in one of the first letters he received after becoming Prime Minister was not untypical: "Now I trust that you will not think that I am an office-seeker but in plain words I say I am entitled to the vacant senatorship of British Columbia."[14] But the clamour always became louder and more insistent before a general election, when a government tended to dispose of most of the favours in its possession. There were good and obvious political reasons for this practice but it had the effect, at least in 1921, not only of putting an extra burden of decision on Meighen's shoulders at a time when he was exceptionally busy, but of intensifying the rivalries of the aspirants and thus creating division and friction within the party at the very moment when unity and co-operation were most necessary. Every important appointment, to the Senate for example, involved consideration of a variety of factors: the merits of certain individuals, the claims of different districts or ethnic groups or religious denominations or occupational classes to representation in the upper House. And, obviously, no matter what choice was made someone was bound to be hurt and resentful.

Meighen's difficulties in this regard were well illustrated by the contest for a New Brunswick senatorship, which came to a head shortly after the election campaign opened. The main issue here was the rival claims of the North Shore and the southern sections of the province. Ten or a dozen claimants submitted their credentials to Meighen but the choice seemed to narrow down to three men—W. S. Montgomery from the north, J. D. Palmer and F. B. Black from the south. Montgomery and his friends argued that he was personally entitled to the position and also that the North Shore, which had no member in the Senate, had always been overlooked when appointments were being made. Early in September the Prime Minister received a peremptory and threatening telegram from Montgomery:

> If report true Black or Palmer for Senate you will see the whole North Shore lined up to defeat you. We are entitled to Senatorship. I know the feeling and no one can stop it if you turn the tide against you. Do not forget that we are on the map. . . . All right thinking Conservatives in the South say the appointment should come to the North Shore and if you do not give us justice you will have to assume responsibility for making a total wreck of the party in New Brunswick.[15]

Similar messages had been coming into Meighen's office from other districts of New Brunswick and he almost regretted that there were such things as Senate appointments to bother one. "If the reasoning of your telegram is correct," he told Montgomery, "then we would be a great deal better without Senatorships at all. Not one, but several, have written me from other parts of the Province threatening just as dire results if districts that send us no support are, as they put it, rewarded instead of districts that do. My only desire is to try to do the right thing and I must frankly say threats are not very convincing."[16] The appointment finally went to Black and in the election all the northern counties returned Liberals. This seemed to vindicate Montgomery but it is barely possible that the results would have been much the same had he not been passed over.

One of the aggravating factors in New Brunswick, as in every province, was the anger of many Conservatives, by now all too familiar to Meighen, at the favours bestowed by the Government on Liberal Unionists. The last New Brunswick senatorship had gone to one of these and the Tories, whether from north or south, were determined that this time that kind of mistaken generosity should not be repeated. It was most depressing for Meighen to hear from so many directions in the midst of the campaign and afterwards that a lot of old Conservatives still harboured their resentment and suspicion of the Government's Liberal supporters. Although unity and a co-operative spirit were essential now that the electoral gage was down, their dander was still up. One of them wrote from British Columbia: "The real Conservatives throughout this Province . . . will not rally under any other banner except a Conservative one. It is a by-word with all true Conservatives that under the regime of the Union Government and the hybrid name of National Liberal and Conservative party, that [sic] the true Conservatives received no consideration whatever and that the heads of the party catered to Grits and nothing else."[17] Another protested the appointment of H. M. Mowat, a Liberal Unionist, to the Ontario High Court of Justice: "Many old friends of the Government feel quite disappointed to see . . . that apparently the policy of rewarding new friends in priority to old is still to be recognized as the proper thing to do. After eleven years in office (for the Conservative Party has been the back-bone of the Government for eleven years) all the members of the Board of Railway Commissioners, five members of the Supreme Court of Canada and nearly half of the Supreme Court of Ontario are old time opponents."[18] The same kind of disgruntlement was reported to Meighen through his secretary by the new Minister of Railways, J. A. Stewart, who found in central and western Ontario a lively complaint that those sections of the province were not fairly represented in the Cabinet. Meighen may well have groaned when he read the reason for this: none of the three Ontario men from west of Kingston who held portfolios—Guthrie, Manion and Robertson—was a Conservative. Furthermore, adding insult to this injury, the Quebec representation in the Cabinet, these people thought, was much too large![19]

The Liberal Unionists still loyal to the Government did not, of course, see the matter in this light. One of them, W. A. Charlton of

Toronto, wrote Meighen to say that he had "seen some items in the Toronto papers stating that they think the Conservatives here are catering too much to the Liberals, that this is a great mistake." In fact Meighen "would be wise to have a few leading Liberals who are thoroughly loyal to your Government taken into the counsels of those working in your interests."[20] The Prime Minister agreed with this but no more knew than Charlton did how the ultra-Tories were to be persuaded to admit these friendly Liberals to their counsels. "You are quite right," he answered, "as to the wisdom and indeed justice of the fairest and most cordial treatment of Liberals who really would like to support us. . . . I know that there is a certain narrowness in some quarters but I earnestly hope that our Liberal friends . . . will not feel that I am responsible for it. The exact contrary is the case."[21]

There was, to be sure, more narrowness than one would like, and not only in Ontario. From Regina came word that Conservatives there wanted to keep James Calder as much as possible out of the campaign in Saskatchewan. The impression was "fairly strong," one of them explained, "that if he were allowed to institute campaign proceedings here, he might insist upon the tail wagging the dog or in other words, upon the small Liberal element in the campaign predominating. Indeed there is a very strong lack of confidence in Mr. Calder locally which MAY possibly be of such an influence as to offset any advantage which might be gained through conducting the campaign as a Union campaign rather than a straight Conservative one."[22] With what patience he could muster Meighen replied that Calder, whose only desire was to win the election, would undoubtedly recognize that most of the Government's support in Saskatchewan would come from Conservatives, who therefore ought to predominate in the organization and the campaign. But, he went on,

> we will need Liberal support and certainly we ought to get it. We are getting it in very encouraging sections [?] from other points of the compass. I hope our friends will not forget that this support we must have.
>
> No doubt at all our platform is the platform of '78 and of '91 and James A. Calder like many another man of brains who has applied himself to the task of understanding the needs of this country, has become just as firm a believer in the platform as you or I or anyone else.[23]

". . . the platform of '78 and of '91. . . ." In every one of his speeches, from London on September the first to Windsor on December the fifth, he insisted that, as in those earlier elections, the issue that transcended all others was whether or not Canada would continue to have a protective tariff to safeguard her, mainly against the vastly superior economic power of the United States. "If," he said in a speech at Portage la Prai-

rie, "I can but get the people in this country to see that the issue is
Protection or no Protection, the battle will be won."[24] But try as he
might, he was never able to make this the dominating question as it had
been on those occasions in the past. In 1878 the issue had been clearly
drawn between Alexander Mackenzie's tariff for revenue and Sir John
A. Macdonald's National Policy. In 1891 it had been clearly drawn
between the Liberals' promise of absolute free trade with the United
States and the Conservatives' devotion to "the Old Man, the Old Flag,
the Old Policy." But it was by no means as simple as that in 1921.
Between the Progressives and the Government, to be sure, there was a
world of difference on the tariff question because both had well-defined
policies to which they adhered. There could be no mistake about it,
anyone who supported the Government would vote for a continuation
of the protective system; anyone who supported the Progressives would
know, much as they differed among themselves about some other subjects, that he was voting for the abolition of tariff protection with all
possible speed. Crerar, while denying Meighen's contention that the
tariff was the only issue, seemed to think that it was by far the one of
greatest significance, that the lowest possible tariff and reciprocity with
the United States were what Canada needed most of all.

Mackenzie King, on the other hand, was anything but willing to have
the campaign revolve around the trade question. "In the mind of the
Prime Minister," he said, "it may be the issue; in the mind of the people,
however, the issue is the Prime Minister himself and what he and his
colleagues represent of autocracy and extravagance in the management of
public affairs."[25] It was characteristic of King that he preferred to emphasize the moral guilt of his opponents, rather than real matters of
public policy, and what a guilty man was Meighen! Not only did he
rule autocratically and spend extravagantly, he had usurped power in the
first place and had used it to serve, not the people, but only the great
corporate interests of big business and high finance whose servile minion
he was. He had ignored Parliament, ruling by Order-in-Council, so
that "the only difference between Mr. Meighen and Lenine [sic] and
Trotsky is that the latter use physical violence to retain power, while
Mr. Meighen uses legislative violence."[26] And then, having blared
forth these accusations everywhere he went, having called Meighen
usurper, autocrat, subverter of the Constitution and puppet, he wrote
complacently to his brother a few days before the election, "I have gone
through the campaign without saying one unkind or harsh expression
I am aware of. . . ."[27]

The beauty of sweeping charges of this kind was that they made an
impression without having to be substantiated and enabled King to
pose as the righteous avenger of the people's wrongs. It is always popular

to sound the note of outraged virtue; it is often effective to drag red
herrings across the trail, to invent issues where existing ones do not
suit. The campaign afforded one particularly neat example of King's
penchant for this sort of thing. Quite by accident he discovered on his
way back to Ottawa from a swing around the Maritimes that vast
quantities of munitions were being imported into Canada by her mili-
taristic Prime Minister and his cohorts. This alarming intelligence he
revealed to the public as soon as he got home in the form of a long letter
addressed to Meighen but clearly intended mainly for the newspapers,
where the Prime Minister saw it for the first time. A careful reading of
the letter makes clear its purpose.

> On my return journey from the Maritime Provinces, on the
> afternoon of the day before yesterday, as the train stopped at Levis,
> Que., I took advantage of the few moments' wait at the station to
> walk as far as the Levis Wharf. Observing that one of the vessels
> of the Canadian Government Merchant Marine, the "Canadian
> Runner," was docked at the wharf, I walked to where the vessel was
> in order to see the nature of the cargo being unloaded. To my
> surprise, I found that the ship's cargo was composed, apparently
> exclusively, of munitions of war in the nature of "high explosive"
> shells. From thirty to forty soldiers in uniform were engaged in
> unloading the vessel. On the landing and embankment, over an
> area comprising several hundred square yards, boxes upon boxes,
> filled apparently with these high explosive shells, were piled one
> upon the other to an average height of about four feet. In addition,
> on a railway siding paralleling the wharf, I counted nine box
> cars into which the explosives were being loaded, all of which were
> more or less filled. There appeared to be many more car loads of
> shells aboard the ship. The boxes I saw were marked, "Fire or
> destroy before 6, 25", the meaning evidently being that beyond
> June 1925 the effectiveness of the munitions would not be guaranteed.
> On inquiry, I was told that the munitions had come to Canada
> from England; that they were being distributed to Ordnance stores
> throughout Canada—not to ocean ports such as Esquimault and
> Halifax only—but to supply depots and stores in all the provinces,
> including the city of Quebec itself. I was further informed that the
> SS. "Canadian Runner," of the Canadian Government Merchant
> Marine, was the fifth vessel of the Government fleet to have come
> from England laden with high explosives of the character described,
> and whose cargoes have been unloaded at and distributed from, the
> port of Levis since the return from England of yourself, Mr. Guthrie,
> the Minister of Militia and Defence, and Mr. Ballantyne, the Minis-
> ter of Marine and Naval Affairs.
> Were Parliament in session, I should of course deem it my duty
> immediately to question yourself and your Ministers with regard to
> this whole matter. Parliament, however, is dissolved. Under the
> circumstances, it has seemed to me that my obvious duty to the
> people of Canada is to bring this matter at once to your attention,

and to address to you in public the questions which, had Parliament been in session, I would have addressed to you across the floor of the House of Commons.

1.   Am I right in believing that it is at the instance of the Government of Canada that the Canadian Government Merchant Marine steamer "Canadian Runner" has been employed to bring to Canada the munitions of war being unloaded at Levis this week, and that they are being bought and paid for in England out of monies contributed through taxation by the people of Canada? If the munitions being unloaded from the "Canadian Runner" are not for the Government of Canada, or are not being paid for by the Government, for whom are they intended, and how have they been obtained?

2.   Is the British Government in any way a party to the shipment of these munitions, and does the shipment owe its origin directly or indirectly to action taken by the conference of Premiers recently attended by you in London?   In justice to the British Government, I think a very clear statement should be made by you as to this.

3.   To what points in Canada or elsewhere are the said munitions being distributed, and to what uses is it intended they shall be put?

4.   Is it true that other shiploads of munitions have been brought to Canada from England or abroad during the present year; and if so, what quantities have come to our shores since Parliament adjourned in June last?

5.   Finally, if these munitions are for the Government of Canada, on what authority of the Parliament of Canada, and under what appropriation of Parliament have these or any other munitions been purchased outside of Canada during the present year?

Amplifying the last question, King went on to point out that the public accounts for the fiscal year 1919-20 showed that out of a grant approved by Parliament for demobilization expenditures nearly four million dollars had been spent outside Canada for ammunition.

... If, without any authority of the Parliament of Canada in the way of specific appropriations for the purchase of ammunition, the colossal sum of $3,784,279.82 was expended overseas during 1919-1920, out of a vote designated *demobilization appropriation,* what, may I further ask, may not be expected in the way of like purchases and payments out of the demobilization appropriations which the Government obtained from Parliament for the two fiscal years since 1919-20, the details of which owing to the Government's policy of withholding information and delaying the publication of reports, are not as yet accessible to the public, and will not be available before another session of Parliament?

Was any of the demobilization vote for the current year, he asked, being spent for the munitions being unloaded at Levis?   And then he concluded:

You will realize that, in view of the approaching International Conference on Disarmament at Washington, the extent of unemployment in Canada during the past year and at the present time, and the representations made to the returned soldiers with respect to public monies available for purposes of relief, these questions are all-important, and are deserving of an immediate and explicit reply.[28]

Meighen was in western Ontario and as soon as he read this in the London paper he wired Ottawa: "I must have by mail concrete answers to each question embodied in King's letter. See that letter is sent me signed by Minister [of Militia and Defence], Acting Minister or Deputy, containing these answers put in best possible form as I wish to incorporate this letter in my reply to King."[29] He then dictated the following note to King:

> I see by the morning press that you have written me a letter, dated Ottawa, October 21st, making a long series of inquiries as to munition supplies which you discovered at Levis. This letter has not yet reached me, its publication being evidently deemed more important to you than its communication to myself.
> You ask for an "immediate and explicit reply" to the various questions set out. This you shall have. The matter concerns the Department of Militia and Defence and I am disposed to think you could have obtained the information by inquiry of that Department. However, I have no objection to making the inquiries myself and as soon as the facts are in my possession I will give them to you without delay, and will hope that in future you will be equally explicit in making replies to questions I have put to you. Please accept my assurance that no time shall be lost in removing from the public mind the wholly erroneous impression which your letter is designed to convey.[30]

King did not bother waiting to receive the promised explanation before announcing his own conclusions to all and sundry, and his conclusions did not seem to change after he *had* received it. On October the twenty-sixth he stated: "Talk about disarmament! The Government has adopted the very reverse. They are bringing in war materials to an extent we have never known before, and to an extent greater than it is possible to use. Wherever available accommodation can be found they are putting these high explosives."[31] Newspapers supporting King were quick to take up the cue. "What answer can Sir Robert Borden make [at the Washington Conference]," asked the Toronto *Globe*, "when the representatives of the United States ask why high explosives by the ship-load are coming to Canada three years after the close of the Great War, and at a time when a representative of the Canadian people is asking the nations to disarm?"[32] While he waited for Guthrie's reply Meighen made light of King's insinuations that a massive military buildup was under way, that Canada was re-arming at a time when disarmament was everywhere else in the air. "Let me hasten to assure Mr. King," he said, "that he is not in the least danger from these explosives. They are for use in the active militia, and as far as I know he is not in it."[33]

On October the twenty-fifth Meighen received the letter from Guthrie[34] and immediately sent off his answer to King, both to King himself and to the newspapers.

> Your letter of 21st October reached me last night. It had, of course, been published in the press Saturday morning. As promised in my acknowledgement of Saturday, I obtained the information at once from the Department of Militia and Defence and now append below answers to your questions as furnished by that Department.
>
> I need only add that no reports whatever have been withheld from publication or delayed in production in Parliament. On the contrary as very fully disclosed in discussion last session, reports have been brought down with the utmost possible despatch and more promptly than was done when you were a member of the Government. As the information given below will be of interest to those who read your rather remarkable letter in the press, I am giving like publicity to this reply.

He then listed the questions with the answer to each in turn. To the first the answer was:

> No war material of any kind has been purchased by the Government since the Armistice. On the outbreak of war all available war material was shipped to England and handed over to the War Office, Canada receiving a credit of war material equivalent to the amount turned in, upon which she could draw for the use of her forces as required. During the war, war material was purchased under the authority of Parliament, for the use of the Canadian forces and became the property of Canada, and used by our Overseas forces. After the Armistice, by agreement with the War Office, practically all Canadian owned war material Overseas was turned into British Army Ordnance Depots; Canada being given a credit of war material free of cost upon such depots and the right to draw her own proportion to meet the requirements of her active Militia. In the spring of 1920 Canada's requirements were forwarded to the War Office and since that time, as cargo space became available on ships of the Canadian Government Merchant Marine, shipments which were Canada's own property were made to Canada. The shipment lately arrived at Levis, Quebec, by the steamship "Canadian Runner" is one of these.

The second question was answered as follows:

> The only relation that exists between the British Government and Canadian Government on these shipments is that the British Government, owing to the fact that they had stored in Ordnance stores all shipments of such munitions belonging to all Colonies, they [sic] were the custodians of these munitions and ship them as cargo space becomes available. The meeting of the Prime Ministers in June last had nothing whatever to do with the arrangements or the shipment.

As for question three:

> The war material is consigned where accommodation can be made available in the various Military Districts in Canada and is to be entirely used for the training of that portion . . . of the Canadian Army called Artillery; and already a large portion has been used during last year's annual training. . . .

And number four:

> No other shipload has been brought to Canada during the present year. Several partial cargoes were received early in the present year, and the bulk of them has been used for annual training during the year 1921-22. Since Parliament prorogued in June last, 2355 tons of war material have arrived in Canada.

And finally the reply to the fifth question:

> As all the ammunition received from the War Office which had been placed in depot for the Canadian Government in England [was] to replace stock issued at the beginning of the war and to replace the number of rounds as per standard scale owing to Canada, there was no need of any purchases and Canada simply received the proportion to which she was entitled.

With regard to King's queries regarding the use made of demobilization appropriations for the purchase of ammunition, it was explained that the amount referred to by King as having been spent for that purpose in 1919-20 was to pay for ammunition whose purchase had been authorized by Parliament but the accounts for which were not received until after the Armistice. Parliament had voted that amount of money for the express purpose of disposing of those accounts. In actual fact no money intended for demobilization expenditures had ever been spent on ammunition.[35]

Accompanying Guthrie's letter to Meighen was a memorandum which suggested that the danger, if there was any, was rather different from the one which King had invented out of whole cloth after he took his constitutional at Levis. "When all ammunition and shipments are received from England," the memorandum read, "the reserve in Canada will be 500 rounds per gun which constitutes one day's supply. It is desired to point out that this is a dangerously low reserve and it would be unwise to give this statement to the public as it would show how weak our position really is."[36]

Militarism, autocracy, unsurpation, extravagance, favouritism, corruption: issues such as these, though spurious and supported by little or nothing in the way of real evidence, enabled King to put the Government on the defensive and in some measure divert public attention from the tariff question. Meighen, trying to drive his wedge into the Liberal party, kept repeating that Progressivism and Mackenzie King's Liberalism were one and the same thing. Some credence was given this view by King's reiterated assurances to rural voters that the Progressive party and the Liberal party were not separated by any real difference of principle. Their aims were so similar that they should join in securing the coming triumph over the common enemy. "We have now to consider whether it is to be a triumph for a name or for a principle. I would like the Progressives to point out wherein the principles for which they stand differ from those of the Liberal party as advocated in their platform."[37] The farmers ought to recognize "that a great deal more can be done to attain the ideal they cherish by co-operation with the other forces of progress which form the Liberal party, than by becoming identified with an organization of class aims and ambitions."[38] An important part of the ideas cherished by the organized farmers, judging by their plat-form, was "an immediate and substantial all-round reduction of the customs tariff," successive increases in the British Preference which would lead to free trade with Great Britain in five years, acceptance by Canada of the reciprocity agreement of 1911 with the United States, and the outright abolition of the tariff on various goods. Did King's words mean that he was prepared to go that far, or even as far as the platform of his own party and carry out its explicit pledge to repeal the tariff on many things, reduce it by half on clothing and footwear and increase the British Preference to fifty per cent? Well no, he did not mean exactly that, even though Meighen tried to give the impression that he did. The Liberal platform, it turned out, was not to be taken too seriously or at any rate too literally. "I consider the platform," said King, "as a chart to guide me, and with the advice of the best minds in the Liberal party as a compass, will seek to steer the right course. The platform was laid down as a chart."[39]

King's references to the tariff issue, which he could not avoid men-tioning altogether, were masterpieces of ambiguity. He believed in a revenue tariff, he kept saying, not in a protective one. But apparently he adhered to the Laurier-Fielding tariff, which, he neglected to mention, was both protective and to all intents and purposes still in effect. He thought "the Tariff should be revised in the interests of the consuming class and not the monopolists and the big, selfish interests."[40] And again: "The Protective tariff has led to profiteering on the part of its friends. Mr. Meighen stands for the interests who support him. He would revise the tariff in their interests. We stand for the rights of the home and the people and would revise the tariff from the viewpoint of their rights."[41] However, he wanted "to build up, not to destroy, the industries of the country, and no industry doing a legitimate business need have fear."[42] The tariff could "be made low enough to permit

goods to come in and yet give sufficient Protection. Tariff for revenue
only should be the object."[43] About the only thing all this proved was
that Meighen was mistaken in asserting, as he frequently did, that the
issue was between protection and free trade. But, except for the doctrinaire free-trader, there was something for everyone in what King had to
say on this subject.

On the hustings, as earlier in Parliament, Meighen often warned the
Progressives not to believe King when he implied that he would reduce
the tariff; they would be betrayed if they trusted in him. This assertion
was at cross purposes with his major argument that King would join
with the Progressives in an assault on the National Policy but its accu-
racy was indicated by an interesting letter the Prime Minister received
from a prominent Toronto business man, E. H. Gurney of the Gurney
Foundry Co. Ltd.

> Sir Joseph Flavelle has telegraphed me, asking that I give you the
> substance of an interview which took place between W. L. McKenzie
> [sic] King and myself on Saturday last, November 5th.
> The meeting was not planned by Mr. King, because I was walk-
> ing along King Street and he was coming in the other direction and
> apparently in a great hurry. He stopped when he saw me, and asked
> if he could call and see me at some early time. I told him that
> while I would be glad to see him, he must understand that he and I
> were joined in battle at the present time, and that I was doing what-
> ever lay in my power to help you and defeat him. I then asked him
> if he still wished to see me.
> He said that that was just why he did wish to see me. He stated
> that the larger business interests of this town and elsewhere were
> making a fundamental mistake in supporting the Conservative
> cause at the present time, for the reason that there wasn't even a
> remote chance of the Conservatives being returned to power. He
> said that in view of this alleged fact, support given to the Conserva-
> tives increased the probability of the election of a Progressive
> government, from whom we would have everything to fear as far as
> tariff was concerned; and he stated that we had nothing to fear in
> respect to tariff measures, as proved by the record of the Laurier
> administration, as far as the Reform Party in Canada was concerned.
> He desired to see me at a time when he could quietly set these
> facts in front of me, and presumably to secure support for the Re-
> form Party. I said to him that I did not admit his premises for a
> minute, and that I hoped and expected that the election would
> demonstrate that his hypothesis was entirely incorrect. He then re-
> marked that he might have expected that any member of a family
> which had been so consistently in the Conservative ranks as our
> own might not respond to this appeal, but that he hoped other
> business men who were presently engaged in your behalf would see
> the correctness of the position he was taking, and would cease to
> take action which would, in his opinion, strengthen the hands of

the Progressive Party at a critical time as far as tariff issues are concerned in this country.

This was the substance of our conversation. I have not attempted to give it to you word for word, because, while I am perfectly certain as to its substance, I could not be sure of the precise wording which Mr. King employed.[44]

Of course King had an excellent reason for confusing and obscuring the tariff question, for not wanting it to become the dominant issue in the campaign. His biographer writes: "Party unity and with it national unity could never be achieved by harping on such a divisive issue as the tariff." Leaving national unity aside for the moment, certainly the issue was divisive of the Liberal party, which was split down the middle over it. A great many Liberals in the West and the rural parts of Ontario had moved into the Progressive camp; King wanted to lure them back. Others in very large number were protectionists; King could not afford to alarm and alienate them. "To move too far towards protection would make any entente with the Progressives out of the question, to move too far towards free trade would drive the Liberal protectionists into alliance with the Conservatives."[45] Thus his position, if such it could be called, was somewhere in the middle, exactly where no one could be sure. By avoiding explicit statements on this divisive question and concentrating on the alleged sins of the Government, about which all Liberals and Progressives could agree, King avoided falling into the tariff trap which Meighen set for him and helped to frustrate the latter's purpose of winning over the protectionist element of the Liberal party.

It is asserted that in doing so he served not only the cause of party unity but the larger cause of national unity and furthermore that "Mr. Meighen could afford to be explicit simply because he had abandoned one of the primary functions of a party leader, namely, the discovery and maintenance of areas of common agreement which would enable him to build an effective party on a national scale."[46] But this was exactly what Meighen was trying to do with the tariff issue, to build a national party. He knew his policy would not appeal to everyone or to all sections of the country but he believed the function of political parties and party leaders was to crystallize issues, not obscure them. There would always be differences of opinion about national policies, and quite properly so; it was the glory of the democratic system that such differences could be debated reasonably in the open and decisions reached peacefully, without violence or disorder. But politics could only be intelligible if politicians, especially leaders of national parties, gave some guidance to public opinion and stated with some precision and consistency what their policies were. The Liberals, he said sarcastically, were talking "protection on apples in British Columbia, Free Trade in the Prairie Provinces and the rural parts of Ontario, Protection in industrial centres in

Ontario, Conscription in Quebec, and humbug in the Maritime Provinces."[47] In other words, they were trying to re-establish themselves as a national party without any national policies and with nothing to offer but confusion. To Meighen it seemed that the electors, as intelligent human beings, should be presented with clear alternatives to choose from, alternatives arising from actual matters of policy which the public had to make up their minds about. King preferred to deal in mistier issues, in grander if irrelevant alternatives with moral overtones: good or evil; autocracy or democracy; autonomy or colonialism; militarism or disarmament; national disintegration or national unity; executive despotism or parliamentary supremacy; private avarice or the public interest. These were choices on which everyone could agree, for no one would consciously vote for evil in any of its known forms, but they were false alternatives in the actual context of Canadian politics, whose coinage was debased by their incessant reiteration. If national unity rested upon the avoidance of issues that were "divisive," as all real issues are, and "the discovery and maintenance of areas of common agreement" such as these, the country would be united by nothing more than the common befuddlement of its citizens.

At the height of the campaign a minor episode occurred which brought some consternation to the Meighen household and caused the head of the family rather acute embarrassment. It seemed to suggest that while Meighen, unlike Mackenzie King, had only one message to preach about the tariff—the message that it should be high enough to encourage the sale of Canadian products in Canada—he did not exactly practise what he preached. In October Mrs. Meighen bought a baby grand piano—made by an American firm. This news was divulged to its readers by *The Canadian Music Trades Journal* and before long Meighen's private secretary, George Buskard, received a polite remonstrance from the general manager of the Canadian Manufacturers' Association, J. E. Walsh, who explained that Canadian piano makers were feeling somewhat aggrieved that none of their instruments was deemed worthy of gracing the Prime Minister's living-room. Meighen was away from Ottawa at the time so Buskard mentioned the matter to Mrs. Meighen "but, of course," as he wrote Walsh, "did not care to enquire as to the reason for her purchasing other than a Canadian made instrument."[48] The reason was perfectly simple: she had bought it because she liked it and had never thought of asking about its place of origin.

When Meighen got home a few days later he found on his desk a rather stiff protest from the president of the Sherlock-Manning Piano and Organ Company against the purchase of the American piano. Although he had some other rather pressing matters on his mind, and cared as little about pianos as he did about motion pictures, stylish dress or dogs, he recognized both the enormity and the implications of his wife's crime and so took the trouble to dictate an apologetic reply. A friend in Toronto, whence he had just returned, had brought the subject to his attention:

> ... his intimation was the first I ever had that the piano Mrs. Meighen bought was not made in Canada. No doubt I should have looked after this but with the pressure under which I live I really gave no attention to it at all and took it for granted that, as she was buying it here, it was a Canadian instrument. Certainly it would never have been bought if I had given the matter sufficient attention to ascertain the facts.
>
> Am sorry indeed for this circumstance. I may add that until I examined it after the inquiry I had never been near enough to see even the name of the piano.[49]

Fortunately the case of Mrs. Meighen's piano did not become a major issue in the campaign, though it was at least as good a one as the case of the Levis munitions, and the piano itself continued to occupy its place of honour in the Meighen home.

In bearing down so heavily on his tariff theme Meighen knew very well that, for the time being at least, he would please relatively few people in western Canada. That was a risk he believed he had to take, both for the sake of gaining strength elsewhere and because the national interest, as he conceived it, required the maintenance of the protective system. It would be both dishonest and insulting to the intelligence of the western voters, in his view, to try to hide his opinions behind a veil of ambiguity as King did. The West, or at least a great many westerners, he believed, could eventually be educated to appreciate the necessity of protection. When that was accomplished Progressivism, with the elimination of the protective tariff as one of its major objectives, would wither away as quickly as it had blossomed. But Meighen also had another song in his western repertoire, one that he thought might sound more pleasant in the ears of the prairie farmer. It was a policy respecting the marketing of wheat, a subject that seemed to be almost as important to the farmers as the tariff itself.

It was a subject to which Meighen was by no means a stranger in 1921, since this was one of the many matters outside the scope of his own department with which he had been directly involved under Borden. During the last two years of the war the wheat crop had been bought and disposed of at fixed prices by a Government agency, the Board of Grain Supervisors. With the end of the war it was anticipated that the traditional open market would function once again and the Government prepared early in 1919 to relinquish its power to control the trade. However, in July of that year it decided to continue the state marketing of wheat under a somewhat different form for the crop about to be harvest-

ed. This decision resulted from the realization that the open market in
the world wheat trade was not going to be restored as quickly as had
been expected. The sale and purchase of wheat still remained under
Government control in most countries with the result that there was no
world price determined from day to day by the functioning of the free
market economy. The operation of the free market in Canada depended, in the normal course of events, upon credit supplied by the banks
to those who bought and handled the grain, so that the farmers might
be reimbursed and other expenses met before the crop was actually sold,
most of it overseas. But in 1919 the banks, through the Canadian Bank-
ers' Association, informed the Government that they could not finance
the handling of the crop in the usual way because of the abnormal and
uncertain conditions prevailing. As Meighen explained it to a farmer
in Manitoba: "Owing to the absence of any regular market Overseas,
against which financing could be done, the banks had taken the position
that, unless the Government in some way got behind the situation, they
could not finance the crop so as to secure movement of same. The railways also urged that unless the Government got behind the situation in
some way, the crop would not move."[50]

It was these representations, rather than its assessment of public opinion on the prairies, which precipitated the Government's decision to remain in the business of buying and selling wheat for another year, or as
Meighen put it, which were "behind our taking action at all"[51] and
abandoning the intention of allowing the free market to reopen. As a
matter of fact western opinion was sharply divided on the issue in 1919.
It was not surprising that people in the grain trade were by and large
opposed to continued Government control; ". . . it is scarcely to be expected," Meighen remarked, "that those who hope to make profits in
the wheat crop, would be very enthusiastic about the Government's handling of the crop this year."[52] Nor were the organized farmers all lined
up against the Winnipeg Grain Exchange on this question as they had
been on so many in the past. Those in Manitoba and Alberta generally
advocated or were ready to accept a return to the open market, allowing
the price of wheat to find its natural level. That level, they confidently
believed, would be very greatly higher in the existing circumstances of
large demand and relative scarcity than it had been in the past. Since
the relationship between supply and demand now favoured the producers, that relationship, in their opinion, should determine the price.
On the other hand the Saskatchewan Grain Growers' Association, speaking for the province which produced most of the wheat, had demanded
that the Government market the 1919 crop at a guaranteed minimum
price, and so had the Canadian Council of Agriculture which claimed to
speak for the farmers as a class across Canada.

While pressure from the banks and railways prompted the Government's wheat marketing policy in 1919 they made no effort to dictate the way in which it should get "behind the situation." There were various possible methods, about which Borden's ministers disagreed among themselves, but the scheme adopted was the one advocated in the Cabinet by Meighen, who apparently had a good deal to do with working it out, "in two or three hours" as he later remarked.[53] By Orders-in-Council under the War Measures Act, trading in wheat futures on the grain exchanges was prohibited and a Wheat Board created with monopolistic powers of purchase and sale. It was to buy the 1919 crop at a guaranteed minimum price, subsequently set at $2.15, and dispose of it to the best possible advantage in the world markets. The farmer upon delivering his grain would receive an initial payment plus participation certificates entitling him to share further in the proceeds from the marketing of the crop in proportion to the quantity and grade of wheat he supplied. The men appointed as members of the board, some of whom had served on the Board of Grain Supervisors, were representative of the farmers, the grain trade, the millers and the railways. A few months after its creation the Wheat Board was given a statutory basis by an Act passed in the autumn session of Parliament.

Announcement of the policy evoked a decidedly mixed response, to nobody's surprise. Those farm organizations that had demanded such action welcomed it, but it was reported to Meighen from Manitoba that "for the *moment* the policy which you have adopted is the most unpopular among the western farmers of any act of any Government. They are simply frantic and are damning the Government by the yard."[54] This attitude presumably reflected the widespread belief that the price the farmer would receive would be substantially less than if it were determined by the free play of economic forces. At the same time a very strong agitation against the policy was conducted by the Winnipeg Grain Exchange and its President, John E. Botterell. Just how chagrined the grain merchants were was revealed to Meighen by Drayton, who had recently succeeded Sir Thomas White as Minister of Finance.

> I am having some trouble in connection with the Victory Loan [Drayton wrote] with regard to the Grain Exchange people. While there has been a good deal of dissatisfaction in what we have done this year among the Grain Exchange members, I find the real trouble is that they fear what was done is to be turned into permanent policy. . . . You have had so much to do with this matter that I would appreciate a memo from you upon the subject, bearing in mind the fact that the Grain Exchange people in the past were large subscribers to our Loans and that this year they are holding off.[55]

But Drayton got little in the way of reassurance with which to disarm the grain people and revive their practical patriotism. Meighen answered:

> . . . I do not think it would be wise to make any intimation what-
> ever to the Grain Exchange people as to what our policy regarding
> wheat might be next year. They are very quick to cling to an inti-
> mation and read into it all manner of binding obligations. They
> should not be allowed to extract from us any embarrassing restraint
> whatsoever, as the price of their doing what everybody ought to
> do with regard to the Victory Loan.[56]

By the time the question of how the 1920 crop was to be disposed of
came to a head just after Meighen became Prime Minister, there had
been no change in the attitude of the Winnipeg Grain Exchange, but
the farming community in the West was now much more solidly in
favour of the Wheat Board continuing to function. There had been
general satisfaction with its performance, which seemed to demonstrate
the advantages of a single public selling agency. However, the abnormal
conditions leading to its formation had disappeared and in addition the
Government received legal advice that with the lapse of the War Measures Act it no longer possessed the constitutional power to operate a
compulsory state marketing system. Therefore, despite strong pressure
from farm organizations, the Government decided to abolish the board
and announced that the crop would be disposed of through the normal
channels. The unpopularity of this move among the western farmers
increased as the price of wheat dipped in the autumn of 1920 and their
demand for the resurrection of the board became more shrill and insistent as prices declined still more in the summer of 1921. They complained bitterly that the Government had intervened in 1919 at a time
when wheat prices were on the rise and likely to rise still higher, and now
returned to a policy of *laissez-faire* when prices were falling off. They
equated state marketing with price stability, believing that it would
bring them an assured return of a greater amount than they would receive
through the pricing mechanisms of the open market. Since the Government, they argued, insisted on giving artificial protection to certain
classes of producers, it should in all justice protect the wheat producers
from the hazards of their position.

This problem engaged Meighen's attention during the latter part
of 1920 and the early months of 1921, and a number of anxious letters
went out over his signature as he solicited advice about what, if anything, the Government might do. He did not think the price of wheat
was within its control. "No Government," he wrote, "could possibly
undertake to fix a price for a commodity such as grain or, indeed, any
other commodity, and any public man who would hint that such could
be done, for the sake of obtaining support, would be a political quack."[57]
However, he agreed that the farmers had reason to be less than completely
satisfied with the customary marketing process. ". . . the methods of
handling our Western grain," he observed, "have not for a long time

appealed to me as the best that could be devised. Indeed, the time I gave to working out the Wheat Board plan was the result of my conviction on this subject. The farmer at distant points and far from the railway is put under severe handicap and, as well, there is, in my judgment, an element of uncertainty as to marketing greater than is absolutely unavoidable. Of course, the element of chance cannot be eliminated, but there is more of it than there ought to be." However, as the western farm organizations were talking about forming their own cooperative wheat pools for the marketing of the crop, Meighen claimed that action by the Government just then would be misconstrued.

> Ever since this idea was evolved it has appeared to me that consideration of any action on our part might well be deferred until the success or failure of the Farmers' programme for handling their own wheat could be judged. If the Government were to take any action or announce its intention of taking action now, immediately the cry would go out that we were doing so to circumvent the Farmers' plan. Indeed, the usual thing has happened already and newspapers have sought to strike the Government by telling the Farmers that we were out to anticipate their scheme and put another in its place.[58]

But it was one thing for farmer organizations to endorse the principle of co-operative wheat pools and another thing to get the pools established. To do so would take both considerable time and a good deal of money and the immediate concern of the farmers was with the disposal of the 1921 crop. The Wheat Board, they insisted, must be re-established to handle it and Meighen was bombarded with telegrams and letters from individuals and farm locals, urging that course upon him. There was great disappointment in the West as the months passed and no action was taken to revive the board. During Meighen's absence in England the agitation on the prairies for its revival became more and more frenzied and dissatisfaction with the Government's wheat marketing policy, or lack of it, was no doubt one of the factors which produced Robert Gardiner's tremendous victory in the Medicine Hat by-election.

Meighen's response was to propound early in the general election campaign, in a speech at Portage la Prairie, the establishment of a new Wheat Board without the monopolistic power exercised by the old one. It would function in the same way as that board had in 1919, buying grain from the farmer, giving him an initial cash payment along with participation certificates entitling him to share in the pooled receipts from the sale of the crop. But there would be no compulsion; it would be for the individual farmer to decide whether he would sell to the board, to one of the privately owned companies or to a farmer-owned concern. Thus the grain exchanges would continue to function, prices would be set by the normal mechanisms of the market, but any farmer who wished to could share in such economies and other advantages as might lie in the operation of a Government selling agency, whose sole purpose would be to bring the largest possible income to the farmers who patronized it.

Politically the purpose of this voluntary wheat board proposal was to widen a cleavage already existing within the ranks of the Progressive party, in much the same way that Meighen tried to divide the Liberals on the tariff issue. It was known that some leading Progressives, including Crerar himself, were strongly opposed to state marketing as a permanent policy. They believed, consistently with their dislike of tariff protection and like the good nineteenth-century Liberals they were, in the free market economy. Crerar had accepted the Wheat Board of 1919 to meet a temporary situation while expressing the hope "that within the period of another year at any rate these restrictions may be removed . . . and we shall get back to normal conditions once more."[59] He opposed Meighen's plan in 1921 on the grounds that the official Progressive platform did not advocate a Wheat Board, that more would be achieved by a reduction of freight rates, especially on grain, and that the best course was co-operative marketing by the farmers with financial help from the Government, rather than the Government involving itself in the wheat business. It was alleged by his opponents that Crerar's attitude on this stemmed from his position as President of the United Grain Growers' Limited with a seat on the Winnipeg Grain Exchange, that though his company was owned by farmers he naturally looked at the marketing problem from the same standpoint as other grain merchants did, resisting intervention by the state which might reduce profits from the trade. In any event his position, as already noted, was consistent with his belief in the free market economy, just as Meighen's was with his willingness to use the power of the state on occasion to reduce its hazards. As for Mackenzie King, he too was consistent in having no clear policy respecting the marketing of wheat. He resolutely refused to commit himself as to whether he would establish a Wheat Board and dismissed Meighen's plan out of hand as an election dodge, implying that the only reason the Prime Minister had come up with it was that he knew his government was going to be defeated and would therefore not have to redeem his pledge.

The wheat question came into focus in the midst of the election campaign when a series of letters was published in the press between Meighen and E. A. Partridge of Sintaluta, Saskatchewan, a venerable and influential figure in the history of farmer organization and collective action. Writing in his capacity as secretary of the wheat board committee of the Sintaluta Grain Growers' Association, Partridge demanded the re-establishment of the Wheat Board "under the old management, and with all the powers conferred upon it by the original Orders-in-Council, left unimpaired by restrictions or qualifications." It must have a "strong-

willed, capable, honest, public-spirited man at the head of it, armed
with dictatorial powers" for "the crisis facing this country is ample
warrant for the creation of such a virtual dictatorship. . . ." Meighen's
voluntary scheme, Partridge added, would "find few friends among farmers and will be hopelessly inadequate to cope with the situation." He
had "no reason to doubt your desire to secure the common good, or to
think that you are not seriously concerned to find an adequate remedy
for the unfortunate conditions surrounding the business of grain growing." He therefore hoped that Meighen would "get together to solve the
problem with Mackenzie King and Crerar," to whom he was also writing.[60] Meighen replied:

> You . . . observe in your letter that the plan I proposed . . . at
> Portage la Prairie . . . will be hopelessly inadequate to cope with
> the situation. I do not observe, however, anything in your communi-
> cation to show why it would be inadequate. I may say that I should
> scarcely be surprised that Associations which have assumed political
> functions and very hostile political activities should take the attitude
> you describe towards any proposal that I make. They took just the
> same attitude towards the Wheat Board when, after much effort on
> my part, it was established. It is their apparent consistent policy
> to attack everything this Government does or proposes to do irres-
> pective wholly of its merits. I am confident, however, that the
> farmers of Western Canada are more interested in the merits and
> advantages to themselves of the Grain Board as I proposed to
> establish it than they are in serving the political ends of what has
> become a partisan organization.
>
> You state in your letter that you have written also to Mr. Mc-
> kenzie [sic] King and to Mr. Crerar. You have definitely requested
> me to commit myself to the re-establishment of a Board with exclusive
> monopolistic powers such as the Wheat Board possessed. Would
> you kindly inform me whether you have made a similar request to
> Mr. Crerar and if so please be good enough to let me know his reply.
> I would ask also that you inform me whether you have made a similar
> request to Mr. King and would be obliged as well to know his reply.
>
> I draw to your attention and through you to the attention of all
> interested, that I have made a definite concrete proposal for the
> handling of the Grain business. I am not aware that either of the
> gentlemen you refer to has yet made any proposal, and will be most
> interested to learn what such proposals are when they come and
> what the attitude of the organization above referred to will be
> toward them. My policy is before the people and it is for them to
> accept it or reject it.[61]

Partridge answered this with a six-page letter, dilating on the general
theme that the real reason Meighen refused to reconstitute the old Wheat
Board, as Partridge thought he would like to do, was that he was afraid
of big business, which was opposed to the compulsory state marketing of
wheat and which held both the old parties, and through them the coun-

try, in thrall. The farmers were the victims of an alliance between business men and politicians which had to be broken before the interests of agriculture could be effectively advanced. In addition Partridge offered a number of specific criticisms of Meighen's plan, which the latter dealt with in his own reply.

> . . . I have considered the objections which you urge to the Grain Board plan which I propose—a plan under which the farmer can dispose of his grain either through the Government Grain Board operating on the same lines as the Wheat Board of 1919-1920, or, if he chooses, through a private selling agency such as those now existing. You say that this means the continuation of expensive grain machinery composed of buying companies and exchanges which must be paid for. Though this is true, they will be paid for only by those who choose the second method, not by those who choose the first. The first method, therefore, is a means of relieving those who desire from such burdens. You say, as well, the Grain Exchange members would leave no stone unturned to discredit the State system. I am not clear as to what harm that will do. It should do none. If they would so act, they would probably act still more determinedly against the old Wheat Board if re-established. . . .
>
> Your statement that my motives in undermining the establishment of the Grain Board are open to suspicion is one I need not deal with, as I do not think it is worthy of yourself and the reputation you enjoy. Your assertion that the purpose of the creation of the Wheat Board was to prevent a rise in the price of wheat is wholly and, may I say, unpardonably wrong. The order creating the Board made it expressly the duty of the Board to get the highest price that could be obtained, and as a matter of fact, you know that the farmers did get the highest prices that could be obtained. The intervention of the Government was the result of a temporary and exceedingly difficult world situation in the wheat market, as was fully and faithfully explained at the time.
>
> Much of your letter is based on false assumptions which I think an impartial inquiry on your part would soon dispel. If the production of goods by manufacture is a profiteering enterprise, this could easily be cured by the farmers themselves, through their companies, entering the manufacturing field, say, for the making of implements and thus, by reducing profits which you say are abnormal, to a fair margin, compel all others to do likewise. There is no barrier to prevent any man or any set of men launching on this line of endeavour. There is, and has been, no barrier. . . .
>
> You suggest the establishment of a wheat board now by Order-in-Council, without statutory authority but with the consent of Mr. Mackenzie King and Mr. Crerar. Any wheat board so established would be illegal and could be dissolved by injunction on the application of grain companies or others immediately it was created.[62]

It was one thing to win an argument with E. A. Partridge, as Meighen did in this exchange of letters; it was another to persuade a great number of prairie farmers that they ought to vote for the only party that had a wheat policy. As Crerar was evidently out of step with the rank and file of the farmers on this matter and as King had no policy except the usual promise to give the matter earnest consideration, Meighen hoped that his proposal would attract the votes of those who wanted action. But he was to be sorely disappointed. Few westerners seemed to take the voluntary wheat board idea very seriously. The farmers could not dissociate the policy from the man who advanced it and to them, conditioned by years of indoctrination, Meighen and his party were so completely the creatures of the "big interests" whose vast power was inimical to the welfare of the West that nothing Meighen proposed could be looked at without suspicion. As one Winnipegger had long since explained to him, "Most of our Western friends look upon you somewhat as a 'Tory' of the old school, and more or less retroactive."[63] Nor did he help to give himself a more popular image in the West by his constant emphasis on maintaining the tariff and his strong attacks on the Progressive party as a class movement infiltrated with men of "Bolshevist" tendencies. In the temper of western Canada at that time, to attack the Progressive party and its leaders was tantamount to attacking the West, which for the moment was in no mood to traffic with either of the old parties, and Meighen's bitter-tasting tariff medicine was made no more palatable by his promise to do something about the marketing of wheat.

However, it is doubtful whether the Government would have fared much better on the prairies had Meighen been, like King, more conciliatory towards Progressivism and more equivocal about the tariff, or had he seemed less "retroactive" to so many westerners. For the time being the artful, "unifying" ambiguities and the pious moralizings of King were no more attractive to the West than the more explicit and down-to-earth declarations of Meighen. Furthermore, had the latter come out for the restoration of the old Wheat Board that Partridge and many others desired, his party would still have been badly trounced in the West. As it was Government candidates polled about sixteen thousand more votes in the three prairie provinces than the Liberals, though this was accounted for mainly by the absence of Liberal candidates from a dozen prairie ridings. But the significant fact was that the old parties were swamped under a deluge of Progressive ballots which buried King as deeply as it did Meighen. Therefore the issue between the two men would be decided elsewhere, and chiefly, of course, in the two central provinces where the preponderance of political power lay.

CHAPTER SIX

"ECRASONS MEIGHEN, C'EST LE TEMPS"

T HE ONE province above all others in which Meighen counted on the
tariff issue to attract support was Quebec, but his strategy there failed
completely. He discovered that as far as that province was concerned
King had been right when he said that the issue was not the tariff but
the Prime Minister himself and his many crimes against the people. Of
course his chief crime in the eyes of French Canada was conscription.
As Blondin after the Yamaska by-election had warned him they would
do, the Liberals in Quebec fought the campaign mainly on that question,
contributing to the cause of national unity by harping on the most divisive issue of them all. When it was all over one of the defeated Government candidates wrote to Meighen: "The only question discussed by our
opponents in the District . . . was 'CONSCRIPTION'—some of them
going so far as predicting a War within two months and telling the
mothers and sisters that their sons and brothers would be called again."[1]

The high significance of the election for Quebec was explained by
Premier Taschereau in a speech at Arthabaska. "The present election,"
he said, "is the most important we have had since Confederation: questions are being argued that are vital for our race. Quebec has been
isolated; we have been treated as pariahs. But the day of revenge has
arrived and Quebec must recover its place at the hearth of the nation."[2]
But revenge for what exactly? For innumerable discriminations, indig-
nities and barbarities allegedly inflicted on French Canadians during the
war. Take for example the case of the lumberjacks who enlisted in forestry battalions. Their harowing fate and the callousness of the Government's treatment of them were described by George Parent, a leading
Liberal newspaperman and politician. "These men," he told a meeting
in the city of Quebec, "had been promised that they would remain in
those battalions and they left with that guarantee. Some time later,
however, came the 1917 elections. Those men were still engaged in
forestry work, but some one heard that they were to vote for Laurier
and thousands of them were sent to dangerous zones where death was
sure. One day a colonel, on being told that an investigation was possible
for such cases, answered, 'dead men don't talk.' This was done under

the Borden Government but the responsible man was Meighen."[3] *Mon Dieu!*

The issue in Quebec was indeed Meighen, half-man, half-monster, and *Le Canada* of Montreal sounded a note reminiscent of Voltaire in a streamer of large black letters across the bottom of one of its pages on election day: "ECRASONS MEIGHEN, C'EST LE TEMPS."[4] The same journal remarked with bitter scorn that Meighen

> asks our population to FORGET EVERYTHING except the tariff.
>
> But the people will not forget the record of Mr. Meighen, this record of ruin and hatred, present in all memories. . . .
>
> Mr. Meighen was formerly the soul and moving spirit of the Borden regime. All the scandals and the turpitude of that regime during the war are recalled. There was speculation in military supplies, in munitions, in the equipment of the armies, in EVERYTHING.
>
> In 1917 the Borden-Meighen party was so discredited that it was marching to certain defeat.
>
> It was then that Mr. Meighen had recourse to that famous coalition and conceived the Union Government—against the province of Quebec.
>
> One remembers the campaign of 1917, which Mr. Meighen took pains to organize.
>
> Quebec was denounced as the disloyal province, traitor to the Empire and our people were treated like dastards and cowards.
>
> During that time the farmers of the English provinces were promised that their sons would be exempt from CONSCRIPTION, which was only for Quebec.[5]

Commenting on a campaign poster bearing a picture of Meighen, *Le Canada* declared:

> Mr. Meighen is depicted in his provocative attitude of 1917, his brow creased, his fingers crooked, declaring solemnly: I desire unity in the hearts of the Canadian people.
>
> This sudden love for the people, this dream of the pacifier, is in marked contrast with the campaign of disunion which he directed four years ago and in the course of which, thanks to his appeals to prejudice and hatred, he succeeded in stirring up eight provinces against a single one.
>
> Today he begs for unity because he provoked a near war between the races a few years ago.[6]

Le Soleil of Quebec city, another leading Liberal organ, also appealed to French Canada to crush its infamous enemy. Nothing less than survival, it announced, was at stake.

> Since this great struggle in which we are engaged is one of revenge, liberation and of life or death, would it be desiring too much to ask of the *élite* in each county that they aid the masses in accomplishing this primordial and urgent duty?

We want to believe that there will not be found in our national *élite,* which includes the spiritual and civil leaders of our cities and our villages, a single man who wishes to perpetuate in our country this despotic regime under which the people have groaned, above all since 1917; thus it is only fair to demand that the *élite* give an example and co-operate with the candidate of the Liberal party in order to free our country from the bondage of an odious dictatorship . . . which is perhaps nourishing still more malicious designs. . . .

LIFE OR DEATH[7]

There was also another *élite,* the members of the second sex, most of whom would be voting for the first time. "The Women Can Save the Country," cried *Le Soleil* at the top of one of its editorials.

We do not dare think that the women voters of our province would cast their votes in favour of this regime which has re-established in Canada the Family Compact of autocracy and financial plutocracy.

Let the women electors . . . review then in their memories all the evil this Government has done for four years; let them recall to their thoughts the days of anguish of the time of conscription and the high cost of living. . . .

How many families have seen want and others misery seated on their hearths in the course of this period, while the arch-millionaires accumulated millions and ran riot?

Let the women, spouses, mothers, fiancées, imagine then what might come if the Meighen Government were re-elected. Mr. Meighen does not hide from it: he is the father of conscription; then is it to be thought that again tomorrow conscription will not be demanded to help England by him who has tied us to England?[8]

There was, indeed, a kind of Meighen phobia in Quebec which gripped people and made them anathematize him more bitterly than any other public man since Confederation. Anti-Meighenism was dinned so much into the political air of the province that even intelligent, worthy and relatively good-natured politicians became the prisoners of their own propaganda. One day during the 1921 campaign C. G. Power and Ernest Lapointe were driving to a meeting in one of the country parishes down river from Quebec city. "It was a beautiful Sunday morning," Power has recalled, "and I was watching the scenery as we proceeded. Turning to Lapointe, who I suppose had been preparing his speech for the day's performance, I said to him, 'This is indeed a beautiful country and the scenery magnificent.' Ernest, waking up from consideration of his speech turned to me and said, 'Yes, too damn good a country to let Arthur Meighen run it.' "[9]

Meighen was well aware, of course, of the horrendous things that were being said about him in the Province of Quebec. It was a mystery to him how muckraking tactics such as these served the great object of national unity to which the Liberal party and its leader were professedly devoted heart and soul. It seemed to him that they were deliberately perpetuating and exploiting disunity for political purposes and fabricating charges against him which were utterly without foundation in fact. He watched Mr. King going around the country perorating about how the Liberal party desired "unity of class and class, creed and creed, race and race, Province and Province, East and West,"[10] and at the same time saw Mr. King's lieutenants in Quebec busy themselves in feeding the fires of racial passion and bitterness with inflammatory eloquence of tongue and pen.

While Meighen found it hard to reconcile these means with the end that King said his party was serving, he had no trouble in deciding how he would behave during his own appearances in Quebec. The best way to defend himself, his government and his party against outrageous slander was not to engage in recrimination, which would be undignified and unworthy of his audiences, or to try to refute individual calumnies like the alleged slaughter of the innocent foresters, which would only give them wider circulation. At the same time he did not intend to ignore the general and oft-repeated allegation that he bore an animosity against French Canada, that policies with which he was identified, such as conscription, had sprung from his hatred of the French-Canadian people. Silence about this on his part might be interpreted as admission of guilt and he wanted to plead not guilty as emphatically as possible. Or he might, remaining silent, appear to be shirking his responsibility for unpopular measures, which he had no wish to do. And so in his Quebec speeches he reviewed and defended the policies of the Government during and since the war, including conscription. The Military Service Act might be regarded by French Canadians as the blackest of his many sins but he was unrepentant. "I favoured conscription," he told the people of Shawinigan Falls. "I introduced the Military Service Act,[11] I spoke for it time and time again in the House of Commons, in every province of the Dominion. I did it because I thought it right. It was applied in my own province in just the same way as in every other province of the Dominion."[12] To defend conscription so openly was thought by some to be foolhardiness but he knew the issue could not be avoided and believed that French-speaking Canadians were not immune to the attractions of honesty and courage.

He had need of some courage at his meetings in Quebec for they were marked by disorder and at times violence threatened. Before his first campaign speech in Montreal posters were distributed around the city saying, "Meighen is coming. Bring eggs."[13] When he arrived at the Monument National he found it jammed with nearly four thousand people, with many more outside on the street unable to get in. The police, anticipating trouble, were out in force, practically surrounding the hall, but the only disturbance was caused by one man in the gallery who confined himself to making rude noises and obscene gestures and left when he discovered these activities displeased the crowd. However, in a later tour of the province Meighen encountered a little more excitement. At Three Rivers on November the seventh a group in the back of the hall tried to drown out his speech by yelling and whistling but he persevered and won the sympathy, if not the votes, of the audience. Two nights later he was speaking at Sherbrooke when he was suddenly interrupted by the noise of shattering glass, as a rock came hurtling through a window, sailed over his head and struck the canopy above the platform. "Don't bother about the window," said the Prime Minister, "we don't care what they knock down. They certainly will not knock us down."[14]

The Sherbrooke rock, though dramatically expressive of an ugly mood, was anti-climactic. The real climax of Meighen's electioneering in Quebec had come, fittingly enough, in her capital city the night before. There, in his first political address in the ancient capital, he had spoken to a huge throng of eight thousand which packed the armouries on the Grande Allée. It was a representative cross-section of the French Canadians with, of course, a smattering of English-speaking folk, people of sundry ages, both sexes and every occupation: men of affairs in the city, well-to-do, sleek and dignified; farmers from the nearby townships in ill-fitting Sunday suits; river pilots and boatmen; dockers and cabbies; shopkeepers and tradesmen; journalists and politicians; students and teachers and articled clerks; and assorted females—modishly furred matrons, spinsters and housewives, office girls, waitresses and chamber maids. Practically all of the throng were opposed politically to the man they had come to see and hear and as they waited for him to appear the air in the cavernous drill hall vibrated with suppressed excitement, with a tense expectancy that this night would produce a confrontation of Prime Minister and people long to be remembered.

At last, to the applause of part of the crowd, the platform party made its appearance, the band of the Quebec garrison struck up "God Save the King" and the meeting got under way. The chairman, C. A. Chauveau, first called upon Wilfrid Laliberté, Government candidate in Drummond-Arthabaska, who was given a rough ride, the audience interrupting him with catcalls, cheering and applauding ironically when he mentioned Laurier and Mackenzie King. Meighen's friends began to perspire nervously, wondering how *he* would fare against the boisterous spirit of the crowd. After a few minutes poor Laliberté, realizing he was getting nowhere, remarked: "You are anxious to hear the Hon. Mr. Meighen." This was the most popular thing he had said and someone called out, "Send him on right away. We're in a hurry!" After a few more sentences and several more interruptions Laliberté took his seat and was followed by J. A. Scott, an esteemed resident of the city, who introduced Meighen in French as "the greatest man in the country," "the man who always says the same thing, in Ontario and in Quebec."

During these preliminaries the Prime Minister had been assessing the audience. He felt a bit lonely up there on that platform, knowing that most of them reviled him as a villain and that he was unable to speak to them in their own tongue. However, he was used to facing unruly, hostile crowds and he enjoyed it. After thirteen contentious years in the House of Commons and on the hustings he was an old, accomplished hand at dealing with hecklers, and the kind of interruptions that had just disposed of the hapless Laliberté held no terror for him. On the contrary he rather liked being heckled, matching wits and words, and had often turned it to his own advantage in the past. So he started out bravely with a few carefully rehearsed words in French which were well received, expressing his appreciation of the warmth of his welcome to the city and his regret that he could not give his speech in the language they all understood. He then began to speak in English, affirming his desire for reconciliation and amity between the peoples of Canada and denying that he had ever said anything in the least defamatory or derogatory about his French-speaking fellow citizens. He had repeatedly challenged his opponents, who were spreading vile slanders about him through the country, to find in the record of his career any evidence of his alleged bias against Quebec. They had completely failed to do so for the good and simple reason that no such evidence existed. The record was there for all to see; he did not regret what he had said and done in the past but was prepared to be judged by it and judged severely. Here he paused for a moment and gazed defiantly out at the audience, his arms folded. There was a burst of applause and as it died away a voice from the gallery called out,

"Ton chien est mort quand même."[15]

"I beg your pardon," answered Meighen, turning to the gallery, "but I don't understand French very well. If anyone has an objection to make, a question to put, I would ask that it be put in English and I shall undertake to answer it."

From that moment on the speech became, not the one Meighen had intended to deliver, but rather like a dialogue between him and individuals in different parts of the hall. Questions and comments, upwards of fifty of them, came thick and fast: about the tariff and railways and the merchant marine; about agriculture, taxes and unemployment; about the adoption of the closure rule in the Commons; and about the Levis munitions, mention of which provoked gales of laughter. For the most part the interruptions were good-natured—legitimate question reasonably posed—and to each Meighen gave his reply in simple, concise words, looking directly towards the questioner. The answers did not win unanimous approval, of course, and were not couched in language intended to please or mollify. Some of them provoked sarcastic jeers, cries of "Non, non!" (which brought counter-cries of "Chut! Chut!") and someone bleated loudly like a lamb. On the other hand his remarks elicited frequent applause; one friendly soul called out in broken English, "You're alright," and Meighen could sense that all these interruptions and his handling of them were earning him a measure of sympathetic respect which in the beginning he would not have thought attainable. At least he had shown them that he for one was not going to be intimidated and take to his heels in ignominious retreat.

The dialogue went on for about an hour. Finally when the applause greeting one of his answers had subsided Meighen took a step forward, stood with arms akimbo, looked somberly out over the audience and said provocatively, "Well, gentlemen, any more questions?" For several seconds there was a profound silence in the vast room while the crowd digested this challenge. And then a thunderous roar of applause, a resounding ovation that went on and on in spontaneous tribute to the courage of the slight, gaunt, harrowed-looking, solitary figure standing there in defiance of them all. His friends relaxed and smiled, breathing sighs of relief that what had looked at the start of the meeting like becoming a disastrous rout had turned instead into a personal triumph for their leader. After a few more remarks Meighen sat down near his wife, who also, as one reporter phrased it, had conquered the audience with her smiling grace, and again there was almost delirious acclaim. In all the din and tumult it proved impossible for L. G. Belley, who was supposed to speak next, to make himself heard at any length and he soon gave up after saying that even Laurier had never had a meeting like this in the city of Quebec. The meeting was declared closed, the band played "O Canada" and "God Save the King" and several hundred members of the audience converged upon the platform, pressing around Meighen to shake his hand.[16]

It was a moment of dazzling success, of almost dizzying satisfaction which the incident at Sherbrooke the next night did nothing to efface. "In the opinion of all his listeners, Liberal and Conservative," said *L'Evénement,* which at this stage was editorially neither one nor the other, "in the opinion even of his interruptors . . . the Prime Minister of Canada accomplished the greatest *tour de force* that has ever been accomplished by a politician at an election meeting."[17] "In such an adverse situation," added the *Chronicle,* which at the time was editorially Conservative with reservations, "only a great man could hold his own and only a very great man gain mastery."[18] The judgment of *L'Action*

Catholique, a paper unfriendly to the Government, was less glowing but not unfair: "Mr. Meighen . . . leaves an excellent memory in Quebec. . . . He has given a very marked impression of being a man of intellect and a leader."[19]   Among those who watched the performance that evening with a certain awe and wonderment was C. G. Power, who since 1917 had observed Meighen's impressive forensic power from the opposite side of the House of Commons. "It would be difficult," he wrote many years later, "to imagine any one placed in a similar difficult position being able to overcome the obstacles which Mr. Meighen overcame that evening. I can only account for it by the thought that he appeared to be alive, resourceful, sure of himself, unafraid. . . . I have witnessed many of our most turbulent contradictory meetings, but never has it been my privilege to witness such a demonstration of sheer strength of a fighting personality."[20]   But, as *L'Action Catholique* emphasized, it was a personal and not a political triumph for the Prime Minister. "If he was before an audience four-fifths of whom had political ideas contrary to his own, and of whom he could convince only a part, he spoke before French Canadians in whose veins flows the blood of the rugged fighters of Fontenoy, and who never fail to do homage to courage and boldness."[21]

How many he had convinced remained to be seen but Meighen, though immensely pleased by the success of the Quebec meeting, was not so naïve as to think that all those who applauded him would translate their plaudits into votes on December the sixth. He might have echoed the words of Sir Wilfrid Laurier at a meeting in Toronto: "Ah, my friends, you applaud me but you do not vote for me." Still, he was sure that his tour through the province had done him and his cause no harm and this was borne out by the opinions of others, some of whom, though, were misled by the demonstration of respect from the crowd in the drill hall. "You have the confidence of the members of your own Party," one of them wrote in an optimistic appraisal of the Government's chances in Quebec, "and the affectionate admiration, on the part of men and women, which will prove a great asset for you in the future. After this there is no part of this Province to which you cannot go and expect a kindly reception, and a sincere welcome, and if, by the grace of the Gods, you are able to get a reasonable support from Quebec, and hold on to the Government, you will be able to develop, in this Province, the old enthusiasm which was for so long the back-bone of the Conservative Party."[22]   This was an encouraging word but Meighen was doubtful that the gods would dispense so much grace, that one spontaneous ovation, however tumultuous, could be taken to show a widespread readiness to vote for the instigator of conscription. "The reports from Quebec," he observed cautiously, "are good—indeed so good I find it hard to understand them."[23]   These reports were, in fact, the product of wishful thinking and faulty intelligence; Quebec was not yet ready to forget and forgive. Conscription and the other grievances of French Canada, magnified and distorted by Liberal propaganda, constituted for the moment at least an insuperable obstacle to Meighen's progress in that province.

His hope had been that by stressing the danger to the protective system he could make many people in Quebec forget conscription and come over to his side, particularly some of the leading figures of the Liberal party along with the following they commanded. The Quebec Liberals were divided into two rather distinct sections between which there was a decided tension. The one, in which Gouin was the dominant figure, was composed of men who were essentially conservative in outlook, who abhorred the kind of radicalism represented by the Progressive movement, were as devoted as Meighen to the maintenance of the National Policy, and looked upon Mackenzie King with a mixture of suspicion and contempt. The other group, which followed Lapointe, were more liberal in attitude, less closely identified with the large business interests of their province, less frightened of western radicalism and much more closely associated with King, who owed his election as Liberal leader largely to their efforts. Meighen's objective was to deepen this split and to detach as many as possible of the Gouin Liberals from King. An attempt to do this had been in progress for a long time before the autumn of 1921; it had been conducted mainly by Calder, who in various interviews with Gouin had tried to persuade him to throw in his lot with the Meighen government.

The effort had been entirely fruitless and one reason undoubtedly was, as Calder had foreseen in opposing Meighen's selection as successor to Borden, that Meighen was *persona non grata* to most of the people of Quebec.[24] Gouin was too shrewd a politician to tie himself to a man as closely connected as Meighen was with wartime measures that were utterly odious in the sight of his compatriots. He saw, as clearly as Patenaude did and as Boivin had been made to see at the eleventh hour, that to align himself with Meighen might be to commit political suicide, that aroused popular passions directed against Meighen as the blood-stained man of conscription might well sweep to oblivion all those in Quebec who espoused Meighen's cause. If a Conservative of Patenaude's stature refused to be drawn in, it was hardly likely that Liberals of standing and ambition would consent. When Gouin accepted the Liberal nomination in a Montreal constituency on October the twentieth, all hope of an alliance between him and Meighen before the election vanished. Sir Lomer evidently preferred to count on his influence and that of his friends to control the tariff and other policies of their own party if it were returned to power, rather than to cast in his lot with a man as venomously execrated and reviled as Meighen was in Quebec. Thus the concentration by many Liberal orators and much of the Liberal press in Quebec on disruptive national issues from the past helped to prevent the disruption of the Liberal party in Quebec which Meighen was trying to accomplish.

But the Prime Minister was under a further handicap in attempting to appeal to the Gouin Liberals and, indeed, to all convinced protectionists in Quebec, whether Liberal or Conservative. Not only was his name anathema to the mass of French Canadians because of conscription, he was also deeply suspect because of his close connection with the public ownership of railways, a policy which caused almost as much excitement and anger in certain Quebec circles as conscription did in others. Consequently he had to contend, as well as with the massive, organized hostility of the French-Canadian people, with a concerted attack on his government and on himself personally by a powerful group of English-speaking Conservatives, who desired not only his defeat in the election but his removal as leader of the National Liberal and Conservative party. It was a favourite theme of Mackenzie King and of the Progressives that Meighen was the slave of big business, the captive of that powerful group of oligarchs who aspired to control the country. In the midst of the 1921 campaign, however, he found himself embroiled in a struggle with the biggest of the big interests in the city of Montreal, with those great aggregations of corporate power which allegedly controlled him and his administration. Far from regarding him as their pliant, useful accomplice, they looked upon his removal from office as necessary in their own and in the public interest.

In the forefront of the anti-Meighen movement conducted by some of the tycoons of Montreal was Hugh Graham, Baron Atholstan, a man whose career cries out for investigation—by someone with a knowledge of abnormal psychology. Immensely rich and successful, he was the owner of several newspapers, chiefly *The Family Herald and Weekly Star* and the Montreal *Daily Star*, which he and his father had established shortly after Confederation. In the early 1920's the former had the largest circulation of any Canadian publication and among the daily newspapers the latter was second only to *La Presse*. The Montreal *Daily Star* under Graham's guidance was given to tub-thumping campaigns and bizarre crusades which made the other main English-language paper in the city, the *Gazette,* seem by contrast even more sedate and respectable than it was. Graham had obtained (some would have said extorted) a knighthood in 1908 through the good offices of Sir Wilfrid Laurier and a peerage in 1917 on the recommendation of Sir Robert Borden. The latter, writing in his diary, sized up the *Star*'s owner as "a singular mixture of cunning and stupidity. His great weakness lies in his belief that he can hoodwink others. . . . Evidently he is consumed with immense desire for peerage. Speaks of it as a bauble hardly worthy of his acceptance."[25]

Baron Atholstan was noted for his large philanthropies (his detractors claimed these were not as large as they were made to appear in the columns of the *Star*) and his petty conspiracies. During the South African war he had insured the lives of Canadian soldiers to the extent of $1,000,000. To celebrate the marriage of his daughter and only child he donated $250,000 to charity and gave his employees double pay for the week. He took a special interest in the problems of disease, providing $100,000 for cancer research and the same amount for the establishment of the Montreal Anti-Tuberculosis and Public Health League. Many other worthy institutions and well-intentioned groups profited from his generosity, from McGill University to the Society for the Prevention of Cruelty to Children.

But Atholstan was not content to be merely a benefactor of mankind. Obviously he aspired to play a dominating role in politics from behind the scenes, as a puppet-master manipulating the politicians. Meighen, after suffering much at Atholstan's hands for a number of years, wrote to a good friend in Nova Scotia: "I cannot think of any institution in Canada whose history is more putrid and whose conduct more uniformly despicable than . . . the Montreal Star. Aside from the moral aspect of his course, the degree of sagacity and judgment used by its owner in public affairs has been a converging minimum which long ago passed the zero point. I know of nothing upon which his judgment is worth anything except how to run the character of newspaper which has been for so many years under his charge."[26] Atholstan, said Meighen, was "a political intriguer in a class by himself,"[27] a "circuitous, gumshoe sort of person"[28] who "could turn a corner so fast you could hear his shirt tails snap."[29] He "had a passion for being inscrutable. He wanted to be sought after and he wanted to be feared."[30] And, it may be added, he wanted someone other than Arthur Meighen to lead the Conservative party. To that end his conspiratorial talents and the news and editorial columns of the *Star* were faithfully devoted between 1921 and 1926.

In this desire Atholstan was by no means alone among the Montreal magnates, though he seems to have played a more or less lone hand and certainly employed methods uniquely devious and unscrupulous in seeking to attain it. The *Gazette,* perhaps in lesser measure and undoubtedly in a less sensational manner, was also hostile to Meighen, presumably reflecting the views of much of the city's business community and in particular those of the Canadian Pacific Railway-Bank of Montreal group whose mouthpiece the *Gazette* was. As for the leading members of that group, it is difficult to document their part in these matters since their deliberations were no doubt carried on orally and in private. It would be interesting, for example, to know just what part, if any, E. W. Beatty, who in 1918 had succeeded Lord Shaughnessy as President of the C.P.R., played in the Montreal politicking of the 1920's which was largely inspired by dislike of railway nationalization. We are told by Beatty's biographer that "as President of the C.P.R. we see him opposed to nationalization while as a patriotic Canadian he wished every success to this new railway venture."[31] But from the same source one gets the impression that Beatty believed that what was good for the C.P.R. was good for Canada and there is no doubt that he thought, as did Shaughnessy, that the existence and competition of a publicly owned system was bad for the C.P.R. His fear of what it might mean for his company Beatty had expressed to Meighen in the autumn of 1920. ". . . the results of the Company's operations during the current year," he wrote, ". . . are, to say the least, very discouraging: in fact they are so discouraging that I would not care to make them public." Then later in his letter he continued:

> While I would not desire to suggest to you any considerations which you might conceivably give effect to in determining your railway policies, I feel strongly that a straight statement from the Government that it will not discriminate either for or against the C.P.R., would have a salutary effect. Toronto and a portion of the West is [sic] full of the idea that because of its possession of the National Railways the Government should use every weapon in its power against the Canadian Pacific while, in the East, there is apprehension that it will do so. A declaration of judicial neutrality would, I think, put the former partisans right and relieve the latter of their unfounded apprehensions.[32]

Before receiving this letter Meighen, in fact, had affirmed that very principle, that the Government must hold the balance even between the two systems, and he was to do so again. This may not have satisfied Beatty but in any case, whether or not the latter was personally implicated in any scheme to oust Meighen from power in the country and the party, the Prime Minister received numerous warnings before the election that the influence of the C.P.R. organization was being brought to bear against him. It was perhaps this which led him to remark that he was "more and more convinced that it is not the failure but the success of the National Railways that is feared."[33]

Meighen's unpopularity among the bigger bigwigs of Montreal, most of whom by the traditions of their class were inclined to support his party in national affairs, seems to have been caused chiefly by their belief that he was most unsound on the railway question. This subject loomed so large in the minds of some of them as to amount almost to an obsession and they apparently came to the conclusion that Meighen had to be put out of the way before the problem of the railways could be solved to their satisfaction. To these men anyone more radical than Warren G. Harding, their favourite American President, was a dangerous revolutionary and no one had been so prominently active as Meighen in framing, explaining and defending the various measures giving effect to a policy which the *Star* described as "that discredited and ruinous fantasy of the most demented form of Socialism, viz.:—Government ownership of railways."[34]

Related to the Montrealers' dislike of public ownership was their suspicion that the Conservative party under Meighen, as under Borden, was too much influenced by financial interests in Toronto, represented mainly by the Canadian Bank of Commerce and the National Trust Company. This alleged influence was personified best by two men prominent in public life, Sir Joseph Flavelle and Sir Thomas White. Flavelle was president of the trust company and a director of the bank. White, before he joined the Borden government in 1911, had been general manager of the National Trust and after his retirement from politics in 1919 became a director of that company and vice-president of the Bank of Commerce. It was felt in Montreal that this Toronto group, which included besides Flavelle and White such others as Sir Edmund Walker, Z. A. Lash and E. R. Wood, had been instrumental in forcing Borden and his colleagues to embark upon the treacherous sea of public ownership by acquiring the Canadian Northern Railway in 1917, and that that step had been taken to save the Canadian Bank of Commerce from disaster.[35] The continuing influence of these men was to be seen in the appointment in 1920 of White as the member representing the government of Canada on the Grand Trunk Arbitration Board and in the choice of Flavelle as chairman of the Grand Trunk Railway in 1921, pending its amalgamation with the other Government lines. As some incidents of the 1921 campaign in Montreal were to show, Meighen was viewed by St. James Street as being too much under the baneful domination of Toronto, a charge that could be used to good political advantage in Quebec.

There were other counts against him as well, of course. For one thing, as the *Gazette* explained later, "Quebec will not have Mr. Meighen." It was fruitless to argue that the charges made against him about conscription and so on were untrue; the important fact was that they were believed to be true by the mass of French-Canadian voters. It was idle to hope that the Conservatives could effectively combat the kind of propaganda used against them as long as Meighen remained leader of the party. Until someone else took command the party might as well write the province of Quebec off as virtually a dead loss.[36] In this connection it is fair to remark that neither the *Gazette* nor the *Star* made any effort to refute the absurd calumnies about Meighen which were spread broadcast through Quebec. Sometimes they reported them in their news columns but never did they devote editorial space to exposing the cynical mendacity of Liberal campaign methods in that province. In fact there were relatively few Conservatives in Quebec who cared or dared to defend Meighen; it was not the popular thing to do.

Meighen, then, was looked upon in Montreal as a hopeless political liability as far as Quebec was concerned. At the same time, paradoxically, to some people in the city he was suspect as being too lukewarm where the mother country and the Imperial connection were concerned. For example, the *Star* was severely critical of his stand on the Anglo-Japanese Alliance at the conference in London. Lord Atholstan was an imperialist of extraordinary emotional fervour and before the conference convened his newspaper waged an intensive editorial campaign in favour of renewing the Alliance. When Meighen took the opposite line the *Star* made no attempt to hide its displeasure. The Prime Minister, it remarked disgustedly, "had a chance to show . . . that a Conservative leader regards it as a duty and a privilege to co-operate with the British Empire in policies which its responsible officials think essential to Imperial safety." Instead he had sided with the United States against the United Kingdom, Australia and New Zealand; he had failed in his duty and refused the privilege.[37]

These were some of the reasons why Meighen was looked at askance by the moguls of Montreal. Anxious for their support and yet not willing to give ground where his policies and convictions were at stake, he tried to appeal to them, as to Quebec generally, with his favourite argument about the present danger to the protective tariff. Had he succeeded in convincing Quebec of this danger it is conceivable that railways, conscription and imperialism might have become less dominating political factors there than they were. But his argument made little impression in Quebec where the 1919 Liberal platform was not taken very seriously and where it was widely held that a province with sixty-five seats in the House of Commons had the best possible guarantee that its economic interests would not be endangered. Also, Meighen was handicapped in trying to arouse the business men of Montreal by Gouin's decision to enter the lists as a Liberal candidate. As the *Gazette* pointed out, Sir Lomer had "the respect, the confidence of all classes in Quebec" and was "solid and steady and sane in matters political."[38] Assuredly he enjoyed the trust of the business class, a great many of whose Conservative members had supported him during his fifteen years as Quebec's Premier. They looked upon him as one of their own, as his election in 1920 to the boards of directors of the Bank of Montreal and the Royal Trust Company indicated. They were confident that any government of which he was a member (and if the Liberals won the election he would undoubtedly be in the Cabinet) would pursue a safe and sound course with respect to the tariff. Hence Meighen found it difficult to attract to his protectionist banner that element in Montreal, some of whom were Liberals and others Conservatives, for whom the retention of the National Policy was at once an economic and an emotional necessity.

The tariff, then, in the opinion of the business men was not really an issue. The overriding fact in their minds was that the Conservative party, with Meighen in the forefront, had needlessly and to its eternal shame led the country down the garden path towards the public ownership of certain railways; the overriding necessity was to rescue the country from the consequences of that ill-conceived and disastrous policy. If this could be done through the Conservative party by inducing a change of heart in its leader or by wringing some concessions from him, well and good; if not, other means would have to be found. In September, shortly after the commencement of the election campaign, Lord Atholstan tried a gambit of characteristic effrontery, evidently in the hope of bringing Meighen around. His Lordship's journalistic and financial support was important to the Conservatives of Quebec. This he knew and they were willing to admit. He was, of course, in a position to dictate the terms upon which such support might be offered and in 1921 the terms included a willingness on Meighen's part to give ground on railways. Atholstan scribbled in pencil on scraps of paper drafts of a series of letters which he intended the Prime Minister to send out over his signature. These indicate something of the oddities of Atholstan's mind. Various persons were to be urged to solicit his co-operation because "with reference to literature and some other important matters Lord A's help is invaluable." In other letters Meighen was to promise to make amends concerning what were evidently minor matters of Government policy which annoyed Atholstan and some of his friends. To humour this inscrutable schemer, because it *was* important to have his good will if possible, Meighen duly dispatched these notes, some of them in the words Atholstan had supplied, others in amended form. But the key letter in the series was another matter, intended to take control over railway policy out of Meighen's hands. It was to be sent to Senator George G. Foster and A. J. Brown, both prominent Montreal lawyers with extensive business connections, and to Atholstan himself, whose draft of it read as follows:

> In any matter subject to my control or my influence directly or indirectly in respect of the Railway problem, I will take you into consultation and will associate with you one other probably Sir Robert Borden and myself and thoroughly thrash out all possible plans for the relief of the country of as much of the annual deficits

as possible and what any three of us agree upon as the best solution will have my earnest support under all circumstances. In the meantime I ask you to give earnest study to the question from the standpoint of the country's interest. In addressing the public I will say it is too soon to condemn pub[lic] ownership but if the deficits continue something must be done and it may be very drastic.[39]

For Meighen to have sent out this communcation would have made him Atholstan's captive and subject to blackmail. It was not sent and the public reference to railway matters suggested by Atholstan was not made. Early in October, replying to a letter from Brown bearing the same suggestion that the Government should consult with Atholstan, Foster and him, the Prime Minister expressed his willingness to do so but added: "It is understood, of course, the Government must take into consideration the views of, and consult with its supporters in Parliament. . . ."[40] Since their views, like Meighen's own, were averse to the changes so much desired in Montreal, it must have become evident to Atholstan, Brown and Company that nothing was to be gained by trying to work through the Conservative party as then constituted and led.

When Atholstan spoke in his draft letter of "possible plans for the relief of the country," he no doubt had in mind the proposal, already mentioned, which had been submitted to Meighen the previous April by Lord Shaughnessy. Meighen was not prepared to give serious consideration to the plan but some other politicians were. In fact, so it seemed to the press barons and financiers of Montreal, the Quebec Liberals were more alive to the gravity of the railway problem than the Prime Minister and, in their vigorous and consistent opposition to nationalization, had adopted a more correct and more truly conservative stand than the Conservative party itself. Gouin, for instance, was an outspoken critic of public ownership and on his influence, chiefly, the Montrealers pinned their hopes for a new policy. A week before Gouin announced his candidature in Montreal, Meighen received from J. A. Stewart a report that had come to Stewart from that city.

> The story runs as follows:—Lord Shaughnessy through Sir Lomer Gouin is now supporting Hon. Lyon McK. King in Quebec and the East, as well as in Ontario, with an idea that King's party will carry at least 62 seats if not the whole 65 in Quebec and from 17 to 22 in the Lower Provinces—while they count on carrying 60 in Ontario and a few scattered ones in the N.W. Provinces—which would give them a clear working majority over all the other groups if combined (nice?). Then Hon. King, in return for Shaughnessy's important help, has given positive assurances, if returned to power, [that he] would turn over the National Railway to the C.P.Ry. bunch to run them [sic] in a manner as already outlined in the press by Lord Shaughnessy some time ago and which plan does not seem to have been favourably considered by the Government. Following this up there

was a three hour conference yesterday (October 5th) between Lord Shaughnessy, Sir Lomer Gouin and Mr. Beatty . . . and much of the conversation was overheard by a special party above suspicion, who vouches for the absolute truth of the above story and conference and to-day Sir Lomer is wearing "the smile that won't come off."[41]

Although it was often possible to receive whatever impression one desired from what King said, it seems most improbable that he gave the "positive assurances" referred to in this communication since, publicly at least, he was as unwilling to make commitments concerning railway policy as he was to be definite about the tariff or the marketing of wheat. The most he would say was that public ownership should be given a fairer trial than it had been thus far under the Borden and Meighen administrations and he was far too canny to make promises to Shaughnessy or Gouin which he knew would be generally unpopular everywhere except in Quebec. But Shaughnessy may well have shared the delusion prevalent in Montreal business circles that Gouin rather than King would dominate a Liberal government and certainly there could be no doubt in the minds of the Montreal people that Gouin's approach to the railway problem was the essence of wisdom. In a campaign speech at the end of October he declared: "The Railway question is of paramount importance now. Unless it is settled there will be a national tragedy. . . . Our roads show immense deficits while privately owned roads over the same territory can declare dividends. . . . And so long as we run nationally-owned roads so long will our debt increase. The problem must be settled, no matter who wins. If the Meighen policy continues we will certainly have a national disaster."[42] Of the same view was Rodolphe Lemieux, who stated explicitly: ". . . only one solution has been proposed, and that is the one given by the most competent man on this continent, Lord Shaughnessy. I prefer a monopoly to bankruptcy."[43] Walter G. Mitchell, Quebec's Provincial Treasurer until he became a candidate for the House of Commons in 1921, was equally critical of the course that had been followed and many other Liberal candidates in Quebec came out against public ownership.

This was unquestionably a source of embarrassment to Mackenzie King in the rest of the country and he was moved to state that Lemieux, in endorsing the Shaughnessy plan, had been speaking for himself.[44] This inspired a scathing editorial in the *Star,* which referred contemptuously to the "Boy Leader" who owed his position to the Quebec Liberals and who would lose it if he got too far out of step with them.[45] Indeed, in Montreal Gouin rather than King seems to have been looked upon as the real leader of the Liberal party and the man whom the forthcoming election would place in a dominating position at Ottawa. The expectation appeared to be, not, as Stewart had been informed, that the Liberals would win a clear majority, but that none of the three groups would do so. The *Star* explained that the formation of a government would have to be preceded by "negotiations" in which Gouin would presumably be the key figure,[46] and the *Gazette* predicted that his control of the large Quebec representation would "enable him to command the situation."[47] In fact a major realignment of political forces would have to take place so that Liberals and Conservatives of sound business judgment and common sense could combine to save the nation from financial ruin. A leading Montreal Conservative, C. H. Cahan, probably spoke the mind of the city's business class when he said: ". . . the financial and economic problems, which so sorely beset us, will undoubtedly necessitate entirely new political alignments; thoughtful and experienced minds of both the old political parties must break from former party affiliations and co-operate to preserve the solvency of the country."[48]

An inkling of what the Montreal oligarchs had in mind in the way of new political orientations may be gained from a memorandum presented to Meighen by Senator W. H. Sharpe in August. Reporting on opinion as to when the election should be held, Sharpe wrote:

> The Bank of Montreal and the C.P.R., and many of our friends in Montreal are in favour of an election this fall, and they claim if you have an election this fall and come back with 75 or 80 members you can make a deal with Quebec members who during the election will be solid against us. I have met friends of the Hon. Mr. J. L. Parent, who stands very close to Sir Lomer, and at my request, they have had several meetings and decided to meet you and have an understanding before an election is called.
>
> Also you should certainly have a meeting with Mr. Beatty and the President of the Bank of Montreal, for they control Sir Lomer and a large number of the members from Quebec, and I am told Sir Lomer will come into the Government with you after the election.[49]

Sharpe did not go on to specify the terms of the proposed "deal" but it is probably safe to assume that one of them would be a revision of railway policy, perhaps along the lines of the Shaughnessy plan. This Meighen would be asked to concede in return for an alliance with the Gouin Liberals and the voting strength in the House which their accession would bring. In some respects he must have found this an enticing prospect, for after all his whole strategy was directed towards winning over as many Liberal protectionists as possible. Furthermore, as such a reconstruction of political groupings would probably bring the low tariff Liberals and the Progressives together against the combined protectionist elements, the tariff could more easily be made the chief national issue as Meighen thought it should be.

On the other hand there were serious disadvantages to be considered. For one thing, of course, a coalition with Gouin would antagonize

French-Canadian Conservatives who had been fighting him on the provincial level for years. However, this was a risk Meighen would have deemed it necessary to take had the coalition been possible on acceptable terms. There was also the danger, though, that such an alliance might alarm and alienate Conservatives in other provinces. Some of them had had enough of coalitions since 1917 and desired to see traditional party alignments restored as fully as possible. Many of them, too, were inclined to fear the influence of Quebec, not only of French Canada but as well that of the great business interests alleged to be behind Gouin. Furthermore, Conservative opinion outside Quebec was on the whole favourably disposed to the railway policy then in force. Finally, a bargain with Gouin, if it involved a new departure with respect to railways, would necessitate a repudiation by Meighen of a major policy of the Borden government. As a member of that government he assumed responsibility for all its actions and was prepared neither to revise nor to repent them.

On balance these disadvantages of a union with the Gouin Liberals outweighed any advantages it might bring and the understanding which Sharpe and many others had envisaged failed to materialize. In any case there is no evidence that Gouin was really willing to join with Meighen on any terms and once he had thrown down the gauntlet by declaring that "if the Meighen policy continues we will certainly have a national disaster," Meighen could not unite with him except at the cost of disowning everything he had done in the field of railway affairs. The only thing he could do was defend his policy and strike back at Gouin. Thus transportation was added to conscription as one of the main issues in the campaign in Quebec and Meighen was forced to give up his last hope of keeping the tariff question to the fore.

Among his supporters were some who argued that it would pay dividends to make railway policy the chief issue in the rest of the country as well, in order to exploit the general popular approval of public ownership. Since the attempt to detach the Quebec Liberal protectionists from their party was clearly a failure, why not try to take advantage of the widespread fear that Gouin's influence might bring about the destruction of the National Railways in the event of the Liberals forming a government? T. A. Russell, a high-school classmate and lifelong friend of Meighen, wrote from Toronto to suggest "that an aggressive campaign on the Railway situation would . . . be well received, as I understand your policy contemplates the strongest possible support in building up the National system of Railways, which are now the property of the country. I believe you would gain a great deal by clearly stating this and contrasting it with the policy of the French wing of the Liberal party, which is so noticeably pro-C.P.R."[50] Similar advice came from Tom Blacklock, Ottawa correspondent for the *Gazette*, a close friend of Meigh-

en and a shrewd political observer. Just before the Prime Minister set
out on his tour of Quebec early in November Blacklock wrote:

> . . . I would strongly advise that you accept Gouin's challenge and
> in the Quebec speeches hit him without mercy. It will strengthen
> you both in Quebec and the rest of Canada. There is no doubt that
> the future of the National Railways as a political issue will over-
> shadow the tariff during the last two weeks of the campaign. There
> is also no doubt that the C.P.R. is actively engaged in organizing
> opposition to you. I firmly believe that you must state clearly in
> Quebec your position on National Railways and also not hesitate
> a moment in criticizing Sir Lomer Gouin. The bold course in Que-
> bec will win you both there and in Ontario.[51]

In his Quebec speeches Meighen did deal with railway matters, attacking some of Gouin's declarations on the subject and defending his own
measures. But he did not go far enough to suit Blacklock, who wrote
again, urging him to bring the railway question more vigorously to the
fore in the remaining days of the campaign and warning him against
any kind of deal with Gouin, which Blacklock thought some Conservatives
were still trying to arrange.

> I have always been convinced that the great issue was the con-
> solidation and preservation of the National Railway System. . . . It is
> indisputable that the future of the National Railway System is men-
> aced by Sir Lomer Gouin's support—the Canadian Pacific Railway
> and allied Montreal corporate interests. Eight provinces favor the
> retention of the National Railway System but those eight provinces
> are not voting on this issue while the great province of Quebec is
> being mobilized to attack and destroy that system. . . .
> The Canadian Pacific is using its whole power and prestige
> against you. Right here in Ottawa every non-union C.P.R. employee
> is against you, and in Montreal the C.P.R. organization is in compact
> with your enemies. Why should you hesitate to force them into the
> open and make the co-ordination and preservation of the National
> Railways the supreme issue? The C.P.R. cannot do more against
> you than they have done and will do.
> A Meighen-Gouin coalition would mean your political ruin.
> Opposition is much preferable to office with the suspicion that
> would be attached to such coalition. Gouin is a tool of the C.P.R.;
> would return the Grand Trunk to former owners; would destroy
> the National Railway system; is opposed to your imperialism, and the
> enemy of organized labour. Can you afford such association? Such
> a coalition could only be accomplished at a price—the fulfillment
> of the desire of the C.P.R., and everybody knows of that desire. A
> coalition would be a betrayal of the Quebec Conservatives to their
> bitterest enemy Gouin, and the terms of the pact, a betrayal of the
> Nationalization advocates throughout the Dominion. Yet I can tell
> you that its accomplishment is the desire and aim of some of your
> closest political associates.

I firmly believe you must make the issue—Canada vs C.P.R. You may not win but you would make impossible a Liberal-Farmer coalition; make possible a bonne Entente between Conservatives and Farmers; and would preserve the National Railway System by exposing the C.P.R. conspiracy. . . . Do not become a party to any scheme that means either co-operation or coalition with Gouin. He represents corporation Quebec; you must remain representative of progressive Canada.[52]

To this rather gamy missive Meighen replied: "In pointing out the direction to me, I think you are right as to just what words should be used now. There is room for no other opinion."[53] But he must have had in mind another bit of advice he had received a day or two earlier from Calder, who was somewhat more cautious but no less astute than Blacklock. ". . . hit Gouin &c hard on the railway question without dragging in the C.P.R. if this is possible," wrote Calder. "I know it is difficult and that if C.P.R. passes the word along the result may be disastrous. Personally I would take the chance if it is well handled."[54] Calder failed to explain how Gouin could be attacked without dragging in the C.P.R.; that would take some conjuring in view of Sir Lomer's close association with the men who ruled the company. Thus to "hit Gouin &c hard" might amount to making the issue "Canada vs C.P.R.," as Blacklock advised and Calder thought might be disastrous.

A pronouncement by Meighen came a few days later as a result of action by C. Grant MacNeil, Dominion secretary of the Great War Veterans' Association, who was greatly exercised over the plottings of the Montrealers. After talking the matter over with the Prime Minister, MacNeil wired him: "I have decided to act on the matter discussed with you last Wednesday. My motive is prompted by [sic] the sincere conviction that you should make a clear cut unequivocal declaration against the conspiracy."[55] The action he took was to send identical telegrams to Meighen, King, Crerar, Gouin, Beatty and Sir Vincent Meredith, President of the Bank of Montreal. They were asked to comment on the following charges:

... it is alleged that an alliance has been formed under the leadership of Sir Lomer Gouin between the Quebec Liberal party interests, the Canadian Pacific Railway interests, the Bank of Montreal interests and Wall Street interests to accomplish through traitors in all parties:
1. Confusion in the public mind on election issues to minimize the possibility of a party majority on December sixth, thus enabling manipulation for Government through coalition.
2. The betrayal and downfall of Hon. Mackenzie King as leader of the Liberal party to enable accession to the post of Sir Lomer Gouin supported by Hon. W. G. Mitchell and a Quebec bloc.
3. The betrayal of the Right Hon. Arthur Meighen from within

his party for the purpose of enforcing agreement to coalition with Sir Lomer Gouin on the terms dictated by the latter, failing which the elimination of Mr. Meighen.

4. The corruption of the "key men" in the Progressive Party to undermine confidence in the integrity of its leaders.

5. The formation of a coalition Government which would acquiesce in the return of the Grand Trunk Railway to its former owners and the ultimate disposal to American Railway interests as well as the looting of the Canadian National Railways to the point where transfer to private corporation control would be welcomed by the tax-payers.[56]

The other recipients of the telegram denied all knowledge of any such conspiracy but Meighen answered:

> There is ample evidence that first two parties referred to Sir Lomer Gouin and leading Quebec Liberals, are determined on transfer or disintegration of present National Railway system. Proposals of Lord Shaughnessy on same subject have been expressed in a memorandum now public. Beyond that I do not know views others referred to.
>
> Whether downfall of Hon. Mackenzie King as leader is sought on behalf of Sir Lomer Gouin, backed by a Quebec bloc, is for them to say.
>
> Personally I have been loyally and splendidly supported by all Parliamentary followers and candidates for Parliament in our behalf and judging from every indication am being now supported by the great mass of the people. The policies stated in your message to be subject of attack after election are policies established and put into effect by the present Government. I have defended them through many sessions against every assault. By those policies I stand and no combination or manoeuvre will turn me from my course.[57]

Apparently this attack on Gouin and Meighen's unequivocal declaration of adherence to established railway policy were too much for Lord Atholstan. On November the thirtieth the *Star* became openly hostile to the Government in a manner that provided a sensational climax to the campaign. Until then its stand on the approaching election had been somewhat ambiguous. It had expressed its contempt for King and for much of that remarkably variable platform on which he was appealing to the people. On the other hand it had refused to endorse the Government, its leader or its candidates. Rather it had urged the voters to support candidates who believed in protection and "economy," the latter probably being in the *Star*'s vocabulary a euphemism for the Shaughnessy plan. What Atholstan obviously desired was the election of a large bloc of Quebec members of the Gouin-Lemieux-Mitchell variety but until the end of November his newspaper refrained from openly attacking the Meighen government. Meighen's reply to the MacNeil telegram presumably provoked the extraordinary roorback which the *Star* used in the closing days of the campaign to ensure the defeat of Conservative candidates in Quebec, and in Montreal more especially.

In its issue of November the thirtieth it gave front-page prominence to what purported to be a dispatch from its Ottawa correspondent. This was headed:

S T A R T L I N G   R U M O R !

REVOLUTIONARY RAILWAY CHANGES SAID TO BE CONTEMPLATED

Measures Calculated to Tie the Hands of the New Government

The "dispatch" stated, "on authority that would be recognized as unimpeachable that the Railway board contemplate making immediate and important changes in the staffs of the Government railways. The report is that Montreal . . . is to be deprived of many of its best railway men; and it is suspected that Sir Joseph Flavelle may be behind the new policy."[58] In succeeding issues these assertions were repeated and amplified, leaving the impression that the plot was to remove the head office of the Grand Trunk from Montreal to Toronto preparatory to making the latter city the headquarters of the consolidated National Railway System. A similar rumour had been spread in Montreal the preceding summer and the *Gazette* at that time had angrily declared it to be the settled policy of the Government and Flavelle to make Toronto the capital of the Canadian National Railways.[59] But the rumour had been laid when Flavelle wrote a categorical denial to the *Gazette*.[60]

With the revival of the charge by the *Star* the Liberals in Quebec were quick to catch their cue. The party's publicity committee took full-page newspaper advertisements to proclaim: "Montreal Threatened. Destruction of One of Its Greatest Assets."[61] Gouin asserted that a vote for the Government would be a vote for the removal of the National Railways headquarters from the city and the loss of 50,000 of its population.[62] Herbert Marler, a candidate in Montreal, declared at a public meeting, and no doubt the rafters rang, that he would not tolerate the withdrawal of railway headquarters from his city.[63] It seemed evident, as J. A. Stewart remarked to Meighen, that the purpose of the *Star*'s allegations "was to provide new material for Gouin and other Quebec speakers."[64]

In view of the known attitude of the C.P.R.'s proprietors to the railway problem and the reports that they were organizing their employees to vote against the Government, it was not surprising that they were suspected of having had something to do with the fabrication of the *Star*'s sensational charges. Bearding the young lion in his den, one of Meighen's close friends in Montreal, Lorne Webster, on his own initiative went to see Beatty about this. Whether he believed in the complicity of the C.P.R. or wanted to give Beatty a chance to deny it is not clear. As Meighen was in western Ontario at the moment, Webster reported to Lougheed, who passed it on to the Prime Minister's office which in turn transmitted it to Meighen, that Beatty had denied seeking to influence any of his company's employees. If the Prime Minister would like to send any message to Beatty, Webster would be glad to convey it.[65] This brought a wrathful response from Meighen:

> . . . Do not feel like conveying any message to any of these people stop. Conduct of Star and others in concocting base cruel false-hoods injure us Montreal will await its own punishment stop. Before I give any assurance anywhere I will know who are parties this diabolical outrage besides the Star stop. Advise Webster accordingly who may pass it on if he sees fit.[66]

Both Meighen and Flavelle, of course, denied absolutely that there was any truth whatever in the "startling rumor" and the former demand-ed that he be shown the proofs which the *Star* claimed were available. A week after the election Meighen went down to Montreal with Stewart. On the train they happened to meet Flavelle, who joined the party. The three were met at the Ritz-Carlton Hotel by Lord Atholstan and A. R. Carman, editor of the *Star,* and were driven to the office of Howard G. Kelley. What ensued can best be told in Meighen's own version which he wrote to Calder.

> Today I went down to Montreal to see the "proofs". Jack Stewart went with me, also Sir Joseph Flavelle happened to be on the train, and I took him up as well. We were met at the Ritz by Lord Atholstan, Carman, the Editor, and a witness, I suppose he was, by the name of Rowat. They took us to Kelley's office and the scene there was really absurd beyond words. Kelley and Carman cut a sorry figure and looked the part. They asked me what questions I had to ask and I said "None; I was there to be presented with those proofs." After a lot of stupid stammering Kelley pulled out a key and got a sealed envelope from a vault con-taining letters that I had already seen and that referred only to the retirement of a few officials. Not a word even contemplating or suggesting the removal of one man out of Montreal. I took a record of them, told them there was no evidence there that would impress a child out of the cradle. Kelley admitted there never had been a suggestion to move anybody from Montreal. Lord Atholstan was quite debonair but the others looked the part of convicted humbugs. I had the satisfaction of telling them that the entire episode was the most despicable conduct I had ever known in my life. This they took without rebuke as well as other sentences of an equally flatter-ing character.[67]

So very debonair was Atholstan, so completely unruffled, that as the little meeting in Kelley's office was coming to an end he invited Meighen out to lunch! The invitation was as distasteful as it was surprising and Meighen curtly declined.

The letters referred to had passed between Flavelle and Kelley and concerned the pending retirement of four Grand Trunk vice-presidents, who Flavelle proposed should not be replaced in the interests of economy and in view of the approaching amalgamation of the Government railways.[68] Nothing in them, as Meighen told Carman, "bore the remotest relation to the allegations, which by way of super-structure your newspaper built up through successive issues just prior to the election, upon the slender and purposely fashioned foundation of an Ottawa 'despatch'. . . . Indeed nothing referred to in the corespondence affected Montreal as a City, any more than it affected Honolulu."[69] In this opinion the *Gazette* concurred.[70] Its proprietors had little love for Meighen and still less for his railway policy but they did operate a newspaper and not a sheet whose news columns could be brazenly prostituted for an immediate political advantage. But the *Gazette* and those it spoke for did share Atholstan's view that it was desirable to supplant Meighen with some other leader of the party, and as Meighen settled down to play the new role of leader of the Opposition he was soon to learn that his troubles in Montreal had only begun.

CHAPTER SEVEN

IN PURSUIT OF A PHANTOM GOVERNMENT

O NE OF those who watched these events and the campaign as a whole with great interest and much sympathy for Meighen was Sir Robert Borden, who was still engaged in the work of the Washington Conference. On December the second he wrote his successor, praising his efforts and at the same time trying to prepare him as gently as he could for the defeat Borden seemed to sense was in the offing.

> May I be permitted to say that your effort from the commencement of the campaign has been admirable and that your position before the people of Canada has undoubtedly been greatly strengthened by the unfailing courage, the sincerity and frankness, as well as by the conspicuous ability with which you have discussed public questions. Whatever may be the result of the polling you will have nothing to regret. . . . I do not put much faith in any prophecies or conjectures as to the probable result. The conditions are too uncertain and complex to justify confident anticipation; if any person's prophecy may turn out to be approximately correct it will be because he made a lucky guess and not because he realised or understood all the factors entering into the result.
> Even if that result should be much less favourable than you now anticipate do not let it discourage you in the least. Behind you there is a splendid record and before you a great career in public life whatever the people may decide on Tuesday next. I was about your age when I was reluctantly forced into the leadership of the Liberal-Conservative Party, then at the nadir of its fortunes. For more than eleven years I wandered in the wilderness of opposition amid discouragements and difficulties much greater, I believe, than any that you have hitherto encountered. Looking back upon the years spent in opposition I remember they were sometimes very weary but on the whole I do not regret them.[1]

To this letter Meighen replied on election day: "I think exactly as you do about the contest. Prediction is of no value whatever. I do feel, however, that if we are in for surprises it will be from the Farmers. The crusade carried on for so many years has produced temporarily at least more results than I had anticipated. A strong class feeling prevails, fostered by vicious and unscrupulous literature. Whatever happens we have conducted a good fight and in a manner to which no Canadian can take exception. I feel we are on very solid ground."[2]

A few short hours after writing this he discovered how little solidity the ground had as it opened up to bury his government in overwhelming defeat. Sitting in his office, with Mrs. Meighen, Lillian and Max to keep him company, he learned the bad news as it came in, first from the Maritimes, then as the polls closed and the counting was completed across the country, from Quebec and Ontario, from the prairies and finally from British Columbia. Various friends and colleagues appeared, to say whatever few encouraging words could be found at such a moment. But nothing they said could give much cheer and Meighen had need of all his stoic fortitude and pride, all his disciplined reserve, to accept with a good heart the crushing verdict of the people. In its newspaper advertising the publicity committee of his party had played up heavily the slogan, "Canada Needs Meighen." A decisive majority of the voters, however, had not grasped this need and the party elected only fifty members, as against sixty-five Progressives and 117 Liberals. Six of the nine provinces returned no supporters of Meighen and seventy Government candidates lost their deposits. The Prime Minister himself, along with ten of his colleagues, suffered personal defeat. Each of the sixty-five Quebec ridings elected a Liberal. The Conservatives were completely shut out also in the three prairie provinces where the Progressives won all but six of the forty-three seats, with the Liberals capturing three and Labourites three. No fewer than thirty-seven of the fifty Conservative victories were in Ontario but even there Liberals and Progressives carried off twenty-one and twenty-four seats respectively. In the Maritimes the Government won five of the eleven New Brunswick ridings but none in either Nova Scotia or Prince Edward Island. Only British Columbia remained in the Conservative fold, giving seven of its thirteen seats to Government candidates. The one Yukon seat also went to a Conservative.

The distribution of the popular vote told a somewhat different story, one slightly less discouraging from Meighen's standpoint. There were the usual striking disparities between the proportion of ballots and the proportion of seats given to the various parties. Thus, for example, in the country at large Conservatives polled thirty-one per cent of the vote and won only twenty-one per cent of the seats while the Progressives, whose popular vote was less by over 200,000, took twenty-eight per cent of the seats. In Quebec the Conservatives attracted a fifth and in both Nova Scotia and Prince Edward Island over one-third of the votes, even though they failed to return a single member in any of those three provinces. The most glaring discrepancies were in Meighen's own Manitoba. There the Progressives picked up four-fifths of the seats with less than half of the popular vote while the Conservatives, with more than a quarter of the ballots polled, obtained no seats at all. However, all this was cold comfort and no amount of mulling over the figures could obscure the fact that the public had rejected Meighen's bid for a mandate with no uncertain voice. Even though the Liberals were just shy of a clear majority it was obvious that Mackenzie King must be given a chance to form a government and Meighen, though constitutionally entitled to meet the new House of Commons as Prime Minister and await its verdict, at once submitted his resignation to the Governor-General. There were some who urged him, in the words of one of them, "to *sit pat* for a considerable time, even till the time of the calling of the House, rather than surrender,"[3] their view being that he might now be able to effect an alliance with the protectionist Liberals, especially those from Quebec, or else, perhaps with Crerar. But Meighen would have none of this. "Your suggestion," he answered one such letter, "seems based on the thought that by coalition with another group the present Government could, at this juncture, be justified in retaining office. In this I cannot agree. The verdict of the people on the 6th of December was undoubtedly adverse to the Government and under these circumstances I immediately deemed it my duty to offer my resignation. I have since been holding office merely at the request of the Governor General, in order that the leader of the largest group, Mr. King, might be able to form an administration."[4]

On the very day this was written, more than three weeks after the election, the new government was sworn in, "the consummation of many delays," Meighen told Billy Sharpe, "after much shifting of position and general comedy executed by Mr. King."[5] King had been engaged in delicate negotiations concerning the makeup of his Cabinet. His purpose had been to effect a union of the Liberals and Progressives by including Crerar and other Farmer members in the Ministry, while at the same time giving due representation to the anti-Progressive element in his own party, especially the Gouin wing of the Qubec Liberals. It was a feat of balancing that did not quite come off. Crerar, who, Meighen remarked, "is, of course, historically a Liberal and in general sympathy—or might I say in prejudice—is about as much of a Liberal yet as there is in the country,"[6] was apparently willing, even eager, to join King in the Government. But Meighen found it hard to believe that he would be able to do so. "From our standpoint I would think such a step on his part would be most advantageous. It would simply be the throwing off of the mask and the betrayal all at once of the whole Farmer movement."[7] It might also, and no doubt King was fully alive to this danger, alienate the conservative, protectionist wing of the Liberal party and open the way to an understanding between it and the Conservatives. Thus King had to tread most warily, which by every instinct, inclination and experience he was superbly equipped to do. As it happened, however, many of Crerar's followers, especially in Alberta and Ontario, were opposed to any kind of coalition or fusion with Mackenzie King and a series of conferences among the Progressives and between them and the Liberals failed to bring about the union that King so greatly desired. As a result his government was less representative of the prairies and of rural Ontario than he had hoped to make it. The most he was able to secure was a promise that the Progressives would support all "progressive" legislation introduced by his government and that they would not become the official Opposition, thus avoiding the appearance of direct conflict between the two parties.[8]

Christmas came and went and still these grave deliberations continued, giving Meighen, still in office as head of a caretaker government, time to assess his own position and consider his future course. He was, though not very greatly surprised by the downfall of his regime, sorely disappointed by the humiliating decisiveness of its rejection at the polls. He knew that the debacle would be widely blamed on him, despite his gallant and prodigiously vigorous campaign, and that many would see in it proof that he would have to resign as leader of the party in order to permit its recovery. He contemplated this course, which may have been made more tempting just then by the fact that to political disaster was added bodily misery. "Have been having teeth extracted," he wrote Sharpe "and generally having a rather uncomfortable and painful time, but there doubtless will be better days ahead."[9] However, while the attractions of retirement were undeniable, he quickly turned his back on that course. He would sorely miss the Commons, where he felt so much at home, and he had a score or two to settle with King, whose victory in this round surely did not signify his ultimate triumph. There were other reasons, too, for staying on the job, reasons Meighen explained to a friend in Winnipeg.

> . . . A man is not much good who, after a period of unbroken success, cannot stand one reverse, however sharp and decisive. If I felt that I had the right to retire, you may be sure I would gladly do so. It is perhaps probable that at no future time could I retire with better advantage to myself. I am still young enough to establish a law practice which would be remunerative. However, speaking with the utmost frankness, I do not feel that I have such a right and if I were to do so I would be justly open to the charge of being a quitter in adversity and of having abandoned those who loyally stood by me. What is going on is pretty hard even for us to know. The Prime Minister Elect is of a different temperament from me. He is always sincerely convinced of the excellence of his own position and genuinely sanguine of everything. It is a happy state of mind but one that unfortunately is not a legacy of mine. Doubtless he has difficulties but, putting myself in his position, they do not seem

anything like as formidable as those I have had for a long time to surmount.[10]

Later on he wrote to Howard Ferguson, Conservative leader in Ontario: "The very truth is that I have little if any ambition to keep in the public eye or take further part in public life, but I have a determined ambition to be true to men who have been true to me. . . . In fact, it was that consideration that decided me to continue after the reverse of December. Having decided, there will be no wavering on my part— though there may be mistakes."[11]

Early in 1922 the possibility of practising law on a part-time basis arose and Meighen gave this serious consideration. T. A. Russell told him that there was an opening in the firm of the late Robert MacKay in Toronto which he could fill if he wanted to. The prospect appealed to him but, as he explained, "the difficulty is this. I do not see how I can retain the duties of Leader of the Opposition and undertake to give any substantial time to the practice of law. I would certainly like to do so."[12] Nevertheless, he went to see MacKay's nephew, who was in the firm. "The proposition he made to me involved the giving of a minimum of four months each year to the firm's business. The share of remuneration was entirely satisfactory—indeed, in my judgment, unwarrantably high and I so expressed myself to Mr. MacKay."[13] After pondering the offer for another week Meighen finally turned it down and so informed Russell:

> Well, I wrote Mr. MacKay on Thursday last finally declining to make an engagement now. I have made up my mind if I did it would not be long before it was made the basis of complaint, and as you know one cannot hold the post I now occupy without having to meet with criticism. I therefore want to give the least possible excuse for it.
>
> I cannot say how reluctantly I came to this conclusion, or how grateful I feel to you for putting the opportunity within my reach.[14]

If Meighen were to be an effective leader of the Opposition the first requirement was to find him a seat in the House of Commons. He felt very badly to have lost out in Portage, with all its cherished personal associations, and his supporters there were appalled and embarrassed that he had been worsted by a nonentity like Harry Leader. But Meighen wrote one of them:

> I certainly do not feel the least resentment to the people of Portage la Prairie. Our cause was not represented by any newspaper, and bitter and poisonous misrepresentation was poured into the minds of the people by antagonistic papers. They catered to all manner of prejudice. Times were hard in the west on account of cruel weather conditions, bad crops, lowering of prices, accompanied by rather high production costs and freights. In addition to the

above I was only able to give two days to the county, and encountered as well a special difficulty with the French Canadian part of that constituency. That my supporters there should have been able to bring me so very near to victory, under these circumstances, was very much to their credit.

The time is coming rapidly when the people of the West will see how they have been deceived, and will have little difficulty in concluding that through all these years I have faithfully served this Dominion.[15]

As Portage was no longer his another seat would have to be found for him, since Meighen had no wish to be what he had once described King as being before the latter entered the House in 1919, "outside leader of the outside party in this country."[16] The customary procedure to get him back into the Commons was outlined by Borden. "In the ordinary course there should be a meeting of the Conservative members, at which you should not be present, and an unanimous resolution should be passed urging you to remain in the leadership and undertaking to provide you with a seat. That course was taken in 1904 when I was defeated in Halifax."[17] But the ordinary course, Meighen explained, would not serve very well in the present circumstances. "To do as you suggest involves my staying out until perhaps the middle of the session. We could not get our Members together and our defeated candidates as well, who, I think, would expect and demand to come just before the session. A resignation then for the purpose of my contesting the seat would involve my being out for, say, forty-five days of the session. This is an objection but it does not appear to me so great as it does to the other Members of the Government."[18] It was the view of these people, and Meighen did not really dissent from it, that his presence at the outset of the session was most desirable in order to give direction and confidence to the fifty Conservative survivors of the election. With his knowledge of affairs and debating ability they stood some chance of scoring points against the new administration and catching it off balance. It was important that the Opposition start off well with all its guns firing; Meighen's absence would mean the muzzling of its most powerful weapon.

This agreed upon, it remained to decide how a seat should be opened for him. Normally the sitting member for the riding selected would submit his resignation to the Speaker of the House, who would declare the seat vacant. It would then be for the Government to cause a writ to be issued for a by-election. But at the moment there was no Speaker and would not be until the new Parliament met and elected one. By that time King would be in office and could hold up the issue of the writ for as long as six months if he wished. A member might resign before there was a Speaker by delivering to any two other members of the House a declaration of his intention to resign. These two would address their warrant to the Chief Electoral Officer for the issue of a new writ, which must accordingly issue within six months. However, no member could resign while his election was being lawfully contested, or until after the expiry of the time during which it could be lawfully contested on grounds other than corruption or bribery. A petition contesting the election of a member might be presented any time within twenty-eight days after his election was made official by his return being published in the *Canada Gazette*. But even after that his election could be contested; the law stipulated that a petition might be launched up to fourteen days after receipt by the returning officer in his constituency of the return and declarations of his election expenses, which were often long delayed.[19]

The first batch of returns from the 1921 election were gazetted on December the twenty-third. Therefore no member could legally resign before January the twentieth, at the very earliest. Again, King would then be in office and able to delay the issuing of a writ until July the twentieth. If he did so Meighen, by the time he got a seat in the ensuing by-election, would have missed the entire session of Parliament. Consequently, the only way in which a constituency could be opened in time for him to be elected before Parliament assembled was to appoint one of the elected members to an office of emolument under the Crown, which would automatically make the seat vacant. In England the accepted procedure for opening a seat in the Commons was to appoint its occupant to the Stewardship of the Chiltern Hundreds, a purely nominal post of ancient origin which was retained in modern times expressly for the purpose of arranging parliamentary vacancies. The lack of any comparable office in Canada meant that the opening of a riding for Meighen immediately could only be accomplished by appointing one of his supporters in the House to some post in the regular civil service.

On December the twenty-seventh, two days before the change of government, A. C. Casselman, the newly elected member for Grenville in Ontario, was appointed to a minor position in the Department of Soldiers' Civil Re-establishment at a salary of fifty dollars per month, from which he resigned the next day without having drawn any salary whatever. In this way the Grenville seat was opened, and at the same time a writ was issued for a by-election to take place on January the twenty-sixth. Announcement of these actions sent King into one of his constitutional tantrums, and the moral indignation he could so easily muster was poured into a statement he issued to the press: ". . . such a violation of constitutional procedure can scarcely fail to bring the severest censure upon Mr. Meighen. . . . Just whether this high-handed and unwarranted course on Mr. Meighen's part can be defended on technical or legal grounds remains to be seen. That it is morally indefensible I do not hesitate to say. One thing is certain, the Canadian public will not fail to recognize, nor Canadian political history to record, that Mr. Meighen's last act as Prime Minister, like his first, was one of usurpation."[20] Reading this outburst in the newspaper, Meighen was rather surprised that even Mackenzie King could be quite so preposterous and he wrote in a letter:

> I see that Mr. King has issued one of his many "parentia menti" fulminating against the autocracy of opening a seat. A technical appointment is the historical British-Canadian way of enabling a member to resign prior to the election of a Speaker. The member retires practically immediately after appointment. Why any supporter of myself should not be allowed to do so is a mystery to me. Indeed the senseless utterances of this man pass comprehension and it is indeed difficult to understand how he has advanced in spite of them.[21]

A little later on King explained that had Meighen "consulted me I would have assisted him to secure a seat. . . . But . . . the will of the people must be respected. In the last election the people expressed their will in no uncertain terms."[22] The last part of this curious utterance seems to imply that it was the popular will that Meighen not have a seat in Parliament, in which case Mr. King had no right to have other ridings opened for him after his personal defeats in 1925 and 1945. But the first part gives the impression that Meighen erred, not in seeking a seat, but in doing so without first consulting King, who after all was now the leader of the largest party and was about to assume office. It was apparently the lack of such consultation that flouted the will of the people. Assuming that Meighen had consulted King, what could the latter have done to help him find a seat? He could have agreed to Casselman's appointment on the twenty-seventh of December had Meighen sought his approval, or on or after the twenty-ninth he could have appointed Casselman himself. It may be doubted that he would have done either but in any event it probably never occurred to Meighen, since the appointment was a purely nominal one, that there was any reason to consult King at all. Had Casselman resigned after the election of a Speaker, King could have helped by issuing the by-election writs promptly and seeing to it that Meighen was not opposed by the Liberals in Grenville. There was no other way in which he could render assistance. The only difference resulting from the method Meighen employed, in preference to the customary but at that moment impossible one, was that he would be present when Parliament opened instead of being out of the House for at least the first several weeks of the session. Perhaps it was this rather than the alleged violation of the Constitution that really chagrined King. As for the popular will, the voters of Grenville, having elected a Conservative, presumably would not object to the leader of the party being substituted as their representative.

But the Prime Minister-elect, according to his own account and that of his biographer, was not the only one angered by Meighen's method of finding a place in Parliament. "Lord Byng, for his part, was most unhappy at the role he had been compelled to play in this political legerdemain. Meighen had made him a participant in what he thought was a discreditable act: and Byng's sense of fair play was outraged by this last minute attempt to circumvent the wishes of those whom the people of Canada had chosen. He had protested—which was, of course, his right—but in the end he had acquiesced. . . ."[23] This passage is based, and in one particular inaccurately so, on an entry in King's diary which relates what purported to be a conversation between him and the Governor-General just before the new government was sworn in. According to this version Byng had refused to approve a number of other appointments Meighen had recommended after the election but reluctantly signed the Order-in-Council appointing Casselman to the civil service. King quoted him as follows:

> . . . Mr. King, I want to give you my entire confidence, to tell you everything. I shall keep nothing from you, if there are matters I want to speak about I shall do so quite frankly, then when you have decided I shall have nothing more to say. . . .
> . . . When Mr. Meighen placed before me the order regarding the seat in Grenville I did not like it, I felt tho' that he was my constitutional adviser, that I was acting in a constitutional way in taking his advice, because it was a matter personal to himself I did not like to raise a further question. I tell you this Mr. King that you may know my whole mind.[24]

It would appear from this that Byng did not actually protest the Casselman appointment and according to Meighen he signed the Order-in-Council without demur. When King's account of the incident was published Meighen wrote: "I say without the slightest hesitation that Lord Byng never expressed any hesitation to me or gave me the slightest reason to think that he had any hestitation." He also denied that he had recommended other appointments subsequent to the election.[25] Certainly had Byng objected Meighen would have explained, if he did not in any case, his reasons for proceeding in this manner and one must have enough regard for His Excellency's intelligence to assume that the explanation would have satisfied him. There seems to be some reason to doubt the credibility of King's story. Since Lord Byng while he was in Ottawa had the reputation of being discreet and tight-lipped in his dealings with Canadian politicians he would be out of character in pouring out his heart to King as he allegedly did in this conversation. However, he may have been swayed by King's pronouncement in the press and if the conversation as described did take place it is evident that the Governor-General misinterpreted Meighen's action as completely as King did, attributing to it a constitutional and moral significance it wholly lacked.

Mr. King's official biographer has attempted to draw a parallel between this constitutional "issue" of 1921 and the constitutional convulsion of 1926 in which the same three men were involved. The general problem faced by Byng in each case, he wrote, "was in many ways the same. He perceived in each dispute the same desire to gain a political advantage; he was shocked by the same appearance of what to him was unfairness and lack of generosity; he felt the same need to offer his protests and remonstrances; and he was tempted by the same impulse to substitute his own judgment for that of his constitutional advisers and in so doing raise his voice on behalf of the absent opponent who was unable to defend himself. The two cases, of course, presented a number of different and distinguishing features, and Lord Byng added yet another: in the first dispute he followed the advice of his Prime Minister, and in the second he rejected it."[26]

Leaving aside the fact that, if King's account can be believed, Byng *did* refuse Meighen's advice respecting other appointments, one may well wonder what conceivable "unfairness and lack of generosity" towards an "absent opponent who was unable to defend himself" there was in Casselman's appointment. The only thing King had to defend himself against in the matter was Meighen's presence in the House of Commons but surely there was no reason why Byng should feel called upon to assist in that defence. That the appointment was made by a defeated government is quite beside the point, since its only purpose was to vacate a seat as promptly as possible, and neither parliamentary supremacy nor responsible government was flouted in the least degree. Indeed there *were* a great many differences between the two cases of 1921 and 1926; there were so many, in fact, that no valid comparison can be made between Meighen's perfectly proper and constitutional advice respecting the Grenville riding, for which there was ample precedent, and King's entirely improper, unprecedented and unconstitutional advice four and a half years later that Parliament be dissolved so that it might not pronounce its censure of his government.

Winning the Grenville by-election was the least of Meighen's worries as he moved into the office of the Opposition leader (which became his through Crerar's refusal to take it) and prepared to reorganize what remained of the National Liberal and Conservative party to travel the long road back. The Liberals did not nominate an opponent but the Progressives did, no doubt, Calder assured him, because "King and Crerar put their heads together to see you were opposed. Neither of them wishes to see you in the House."[27]   Whether or not there was such collusion, the action of the Farmers meant that Meighen, on a much less strenuous scale, had to begin campaigning all over again. However, the seat was won handily with the help of others, especially Casselman and Howard Ferguson, who represented the riding in the Ontario legislature. Sitting for an Ontario constituency and keeping his fences mended there presented a few minor problems for Meighen after his many years' association with Portage la Prairie.   In some respects customs were different from those out West and he felt a little uncertain in dealing with the local people.   Some months after his election he wrote to Ferguson, enclosing three letters asking for donations.   A Women's Institute wanted to provide a ladies' rest room at Prescott; the Kemptville Annual Exhibition and the Merrickville Agricultural Society wanted contributions towards defraying their general expenses.   "Be good enough to tell me what you think I ought to do," he besought Ferguson.   "I do not know what scale you adopt here.   These fairs are a new one on me!   I feel somewhat like helping out the rest-room."[28]   Ferguson's reply indicated that it was not a question of which one should be assisted but how much each one would be.   He reported that he gave fifteen dollars to the Merrickville fair and twenty-five to the Kemptville fair.   The Institute he had sent ten dollars and fifteen had gone to the Grenville County Plowman's Association, of and from which Meighen had apparently not yet heard.[29]   Whether this merely provincial scale could be adopted by the federal member Ferguson did not say but it was evident that not all of Meighen's largesse could be lavished on the enterprising ladies of the Institute.

In comparison with the one that had just passed, with all its hurly-burly of electioneering and before that the concentrated drama of the Imperial Conference, the year 1922 was a relatively uneventful one for Meighen, though not without its moments of excitement and its quota of controversy.   Relieved of the responsibility of office, he was able to devote himself more continuously to the affairs of the party and to preparing for the next electoral contest with Mackenzie King when he might attain his measure of revenge.   How large the job of reconstruction was the election had made all too clear, as, indeed, had many of the reports reaching Meighen during the campaign.   It would take all the extra time now at his disposal, all the effort of which he was capable, to regenerate the party and it was his realization of this that made him decide not to be a part-time lawyer in Toronto.

One of the many problems that confronted him was the necessity of establishing his own authority as leader.   No doubt the great majority of Conservatives, even most of those who were critical of his judgment

in certain respects, believed that he should continue to lead and took it
for granted that he would.   But in the post-mortems after the sixth of
December there was a marked disposition in some quarters to lay blame
for the disaster at his door.   He was not surprised that this sentiment
was much in evidence in Montreal and among the Robert Rogers coterie
in Winnipeg, or that it was shared by the ultra-Tory malcontents of
Toronto and their mouthpiece, the *Telegram*.   Nor did it astonish him
that J. H. Burnham, who had never forgiven Meighen for running an
official Government candidate against him in the Peterborough by-
election and who, like Rogers, had been defeated in the general election,
should join in the grumbling chorus of complaint.   Just after the New
Year Rogers set out on one of his frequent trips to Toronto and Montreal
to proclaim once again the need to resuscitate and reorganize the Conservative party.   The period of "suspended animation" since the formation of the Union Government was at last over, he announced, and the
time to get back to "straight party lines" had come.   There should be a
national convention at which questions of policy and leadership could be
settled and a little bone and muscle built onto the wasted frame of the
party.   "Maybe you have heard of the antics of the Hon. R.R.," Meighen
wrote to Billy Sharpe.   "He and Ham Burnham have burst out again.
They want a Convention so that a really good leader can be chosen.   Bob
has been down to Toronto, giving interviews, also to Montreal, but Ham
reserved his explosion for Peterboro [*sic*]."[30]   An angry account of the
activities of the Rogers group reached Meighen from a loyal supporter in
Winnipeg.

> Many people have always smiled at me in my anxiety about the
> machinations of the Hon. Mr. Rogers and his friends, but I am sure
> that they had a lot to do with our failure in Winnipeg. . . . You know
> the sneers of a man labelled a friend is [*sic*] often more productive
> of harm in an election than the active hostility of a score of avowed
> opponents.   Now every where I went during the campaign I found
> these nominal friends of the party sneering at the "half-grit" organi-
> zation we had and with which they said they had to consort.   Again
> and again my appeal to attend committees and meetings was met
> with: "Confound it. . . . Why can't we have the old friends so we can
> all pull together?"   They simply wanted an excuse and they thought
> they might make me ashamed of my new associates.   How in h-ll
> they expected us to replace desertions except by gaining recruits
> from the Grits I don't know.   Did they expect us to line up with
> the mugwumps and the bolsheviks?
> Even now that the elections are over these Rogerites here are
> not letting up on their scheming.   I enclose you a clipping from
> the Tribune showing that a meeting has been held in which the
> avowed purposes enunciated are to revive the old party, but the
> true purposes of which are to restore the prestige of Mr. Rogers.
> This meeting was called by invitation sent only to a hand-picked

lot from which was scrupulously eliminated every known Meighen man. . . .

Now as far as South Winnipeg is concerned this will get us no where unless something can be done to assure us that the ultimate purpose is not to injure Arthur Meighen. Personally I have nothing against Mr. Rogers, but unless he will call his hounds off you and let it be fully understood that he is to cease his plans to railroad you I will do everything I can to disrupt any organization got together in Winnipeg by him or his henchmen. Strategically it is subversive of success that we should have these dissensions and if the party could accept Mr. Rogers into its councils again in such positions as he is suited [to] it would do us an immense service. I discount all his claims as an administrator, as an orator, as an organizer and deny him absolutely any place as a statesman, but he is capable as a manipulator of men. His cunning and his ability to worm himself into peoples [sic] confidence make him enormously useful to the party.[31]

There was a lot of talk by people like Rogers about returning to "Conservative principles" from which, they implied, Meighen had departed. The Montreal *Star,* commenting on the election results, declared that "the cure is to get back to Conservative principles,"[32] and when Rogers appeared in Montreal early in January, and was no doubt closeted with his good friend Lord Atholstan, the *Star* revealed that the Conservative party had not been defeated because "THERE WAS NO CONSERVATIVE PARTY IN THE LAST CAMPAIGN. . . . Only by giving proof of its sincerity of purpose can . . . a party win respect and only under leaders of discernment, faith and ability can it command success."[33] The *Gazette* also endorsed Rogers' opinions and attempted to define the much touted principles which allegedly had been abandoned: ". . . the maintenance of British connection and absolute self-government; Protection to domestic industry; private ownership and operation of public utilities under Government regulation; an energetic Immigration policy; maintenance of Provincial rights, protection of minorities and respect for rights of property."[34] Save for the reference to utilities, in which the *Gazette* may have meant railways to be included, there was really nothing here to which Meighen, or for that matter most Canadians regardless of party, would take exception in principle. However, the inference to be drawn from these Montreal pronouncements was that he had been untrue to the essence of the Conservative creed which it was his duty to expound and to defend. Referring to these manifestations of discontent with his leadership, Meighen wrote: "My purpose is to take such steps as will put beyond any question my own status; this one thing I am determined upon."[35]

The step he took was to request all National Liberal and Conservative senators, members of Parliament and defeated candidates to a meeting in Ottawa on March the sixth, three days before the opening of Parliament, at which he would submit his resignation. While he was prepared to continue as leader and though his having found a seat in the Commons might make it more difficult to supplant him (a fact which may help to explain Mackenzie King's indignation at the Casselman appointment), those present would have an opportunity to replace him with someone else if they so desired. If they chose to do that he would have no complaints; if they confirmed him in the position his critics would be silenced, at least for the time being.

It was, however, not only his own position that was at stake. For every Conservative like Rogers or Atholstan or Burnham who wanted to get rid of him there were probably a dozen opposed to that but nevertheless in sympathy with the view that the old Conservative party should be officially re-established. These people tended to blame, not so much Meighen's conduct as leader, but Union Government for the catastrophe of June the sixth. Although Meighen had favoured that coalition and helped in its formation, and though he had since repeatedly affirmed the desirability—in fact the utter necessity—of appealing for Liberal support, he was generally regarded as a Conservative at heart than whom there was no better leader in sight for the grand old party of Macdonald that was waiting to be reborn. Union Government had wrecked the party, demolished its organization, sapped its spirit. Now the remnants of the Union Government had finally gone down to ignominious defeat, the coalition had died its own death, and few Conservatives could bring themselves to weep over the corpse. As the Ottawa *Journal,* one of the staunchest of Conservative papers, put it, the party should "get back to what it really is—Conservative."[36]

The existence of this sentiment was not least evident to those relatively few former Liberals who, like Calder, had stayed with the Borden and Meighen governments after the war, instead of gravitating back to their old party or into the Progressive ranks as most of their fellows had done. Calder, explaining why he thought he should stay away from the meeting in Ottawa, wrote to Meighen: "Among the 'Old Guard' there are those who have an idea that I was to some extent largely [sic] responsible for Union Government and that the events following were disastrous to the Conservative Party. There are still those who look on me with suspicion—as a sort of special agent of the old Grit party and that I have never been averse to seeing Borden and yourself get into trouble. . . . Consequently I am inclined to the view that it would be just as well for me to keep in the background till you have things settled with the members elect."[37]

Meighen thought about this and reached a contrary conclusion. "I think the weight of the argument is the other way," he replied. "There are some 'die-hards' of course, and suspicious people, but really there are not many, and the best way to get rid of them is to pay no attention, but stand right up with us from the very beginning."[38]   This did not convince Calder, who wrote again, now shifting the ground of his argument:

> . . . Somehow or other I cannot help but feel that King is liable to land in all sorts of difficulty within a year or so and there is a possibility that I may be able to help more if I do not too closely identify myself with that first meeting.   At the same time I want you to know more or less confidentially that I have not the slightest use for King or his bunch and that further I am anxious to assist you in any way I can.   Briefly—it is all a question of tactics. . . . Sooner or later the Gouin & Lapointe factions in Quebec must clash—and when the time comes there will be something doing. Every effort should be made to widen the cleavage between them.

Thus if Calder preserved a semblance of his old Liberal affiliations by avoiding a meeting where the Conservative party would probably be resurrected in all its purity and where sentiments of Conservative "straight partyism" would probably prevail, he might have more influence among the Liberals of Quebec when the long-awaited rupture between the two factions at last occurred.   He might be able to lead the losers in that struggle to Meighen's door.   It was an ingenious argument but a specious one.   Calder had been trying for three years to work that magic in Quebec without success and it seemed unlikely that those he was after in that province would much care whether he had been at a particular meeting or not, however provocative its decisions might be.   Calder's tactics were never given a chance; Meighen repeated that he wanted him on hand and Calder came.[39]

Another matter Calder raised in his letter was the name of the party. Dislike of "National Liberal and Conservative" was widespread and he agreed that it should be discarded.

> . . . It is too big a mouthful.   The name was originally suggested by myself but only after consultation with a good many friends— both Tory & Grit.   The majority at the meeting will undoubtedly be in favor of the old names—Liberal-Conservative or Conservative so as to maintain the tradition of John A.   Of course it makes no difference to me but I am strongly of the view that it would be wise to drop the old name "Conservative" altogether.   It does not appeal to the masses or the foreign born.   I would prefer the name "Unionist" with all its war traditions.[40]

This suggestion was surprisingly naïve, coming from one of Calder's usual percipience.   Most critics of the existing name were determinedly Conservative, wanting to get away from the Unionist tradition as completely as possible, while in Quebec, to which he attributed particular importance and where for several years he had been trying to strengthen the party, the label "Unionist" had evil connotations which would be a serious handicap to any party to which it was attached. In any event, as he had foreseen, the meeting voted to restore the old name, "Liberal-Conservative." It had originally been devised to signify the coalition of hitherto opposing elements; now it was being adopted again, this time to signify the repudiation of a coalition. Meighen approved of the change—he had never liked the awkward title Calder had contrived—but not the motive that prompted it. He still believed, now more than ever, that much of the added strength his party required would have to be sought among disenchanted Liberals. His troubles with the ultra-Tories on this score were not yet over.

In addition to performing this symbolic interment of the coalition principle, the meeting approved a motion that there be a national convention of the party and appointed a committee to make the arrangements. There seems to have been uncertainty as to whether this should be a leadership convention of the type Rogers and others apparently desired. Meighen was unanimously re-elected leader at the meeting without any intimation that this was to be subject to confirmation by the convention but his opponents perhaps believed that the overriding authority of the latter body might be used to reopen the leadership question. They could bide their time and meanwhile try to educate Conservative opinion across the country to see the need for a change. Commenting on his re-election, Meighen wrote: "I think I have more doubt myself about the wisdom of the action taken than anyone else seems to have. Indeed I would be happier to-day if the decision had been otherwise in that regard."[41] But all his actions since the general election had indicated his intention of staying on and certainly there were some other people who were far less confident than he of his ability to lead the party back to power.

Leading a stricken party requiring to be rebuilt brought a great many trials and tribulations Meighen's way, some of them of baffling complexity, but there was at least one worthwhile compensation in having been ousted from power, aside from the fact that Mackenzie King was on the defensive for a change. Meighen was now able to find a little more time to devote to the study of the French language, which he was determined to be able to speak, if not fluently, at least with some measure of assurance. He had learned a little bit of schoolbook French as a youth but hardly more than enough to give him a nodding acquaintance with it and it was only when he took Borden's place in 1920 that he resolved to seek greater proficiency in the tongue. During the hectic months that followed, however, he was able to do little in that regard. In the election campaign he began his Quebec addresses with a few carefully prepared words in French but this was not enough, only a kind of ritual gesture. Those meetings made him acutely aware of his handicap, so after the fall of his government he set about to overcome it as fully as he could. In the House of Commons he had always greatly envied and admired the facility with which so many French Canadians spoke English, the real felicity with which some of them could express themselves in it. He once complimented Lapointe in the Commons on "the extraordinary command he has attained of a language not his own," though he felt constrained to add in the next breath: "I wish I could compliment him on the logic of his address in general."[42] He knew he would never be able to speak French anything like as well as Lapointe spoke English; such proficiency was simply unattainable at his age and with his limited time to devote to that work. Certainly he never intended to address Parliament in French, as did once in a long while one or other of the English-speaking members from Quebec. He did, though, become sufficiently confident to ask occasional questions in French of some member who was holding forth in that tongue and another time, but not by intention, he displayed at slightly greater length his knowledge of the language. In the course of a speech he said that he wanted to quote a paragraph that was in French but would translate it. Immediately there were good-natured objections from across the aisle and demands that he read the original. He did so, "and to their credit more than to mine they applauded heartily."[43]

He set about to learn to speak French, not by taking formal instruction, but by reading as much of it as he could, listening to it being spoken by others and carrying on conversations in it, rather haltingly, with his friends from Quebec. He realized that the best way to make progress would be to spend some time in a place where nothing but French was heard. Accordingly in the spring of 1922 he wrote to Sir William Price of Quebec city, saying that he and his family wanted to spend three weeks in July at Tadoussac, at the mouth of the Saguenay River. Where could he write to rent a cottage there? "I may say I want to spend most of my own time with a French family to help me with the language."[44] Price was in England but his secretary very helpfully suggested a number of places. One was the Tadoussac Hotel, operated by Canada Steamship Lines, and to it Meighen sent an inquiry. The hotel, it turned out, had just the right thing for so eminent a person. He could, its manager informed him, have a suite of two rooms for $260.00 weekly or another suite at $240.00. Meighen's answer ran to two paragraphs.

> I have your letter of the 6th instant.
> Kindly do not consider me in connection with the rooms.[45]

Fortunately other, if less princely, accommodation turned up and he

was able to get some of the practice he desired. In addition his two
sons, and especially Ted, became interested during this stay at Tadoussac
in learning French so in 1924 Meighen wrote a characteristic letter to a
local lumberman they had come to know there.

> You will no doubt remember myself and family being at Tadoussac in the summer of 1922. My oldest son Ted at that time discussed
> with you the chance of his being taken on in your party for a month
> or so in the summer principally to enable him to improve his
> French. He did not write you in time enough last year but has
> written me expressing the hope that he would get on this year. I
> do not want to impose on you in any way at all and, indeed, his
> desire, as well as my own, is that he help in your work in every way
> and his hope is there will be work he can do, no matter what kind
> it is, that will make him useful. If, however, there is not work he
> can do to earn his way, then I certainly would want to pay you for
> his keep. . . .
> I might add that my second boy, who is now bigger than I am,
> Max, fifteen years of age, wants to go for the same purpose. I do not
> suppose that you can be bothered with two, but if you can he certainly would like to go too.
> Please write me as to what you think can be done and in case
> you do take them I hope you will never speak a word of English
> to them but see that they either talk French or nothing.[46]

Thanks to such encouragement, to his parents' decision that after graduation from Royal Military College he should attend Laval University, and
to a subsequent sojourn in Paris, Ted Meighen in time became perfectly
fluent in French. His father was not so fortunate. He never learned to
use the language with genuine ease but his pronunciation was adjudged
acceptable and by 1923 he was delivering short addresses in French.
Most of these were solemn utterances where he was attempting to lay
the ghost of conscription but on one occasion at least he spoke in a lighter
vein, the vein of gentle humour, more of which he was sometimes
admonished to display in his political speeches. As one of his journalist
friends, Brenton Macnab, put it to him, "Why don't you crack a joke
once in a while in your speeches? You've got it in you; let it come out."[47]
When dealing with public issues corrosive rather than jocular humour
seemed to be the only type of which Meighen was capable, but in congratulating the newly elected president of the Press Gallery at the Gallery
dinner in 1924 he let a bit of the other kind some out, poking fun in
French at his own efforts in that tongue and also at the assembled
reporters.

> The task which I have chosen in life is of so serious a nature that
> it is only on the rarest occasion that the lighter shades can be allowed to enter either into conversation or into speech. Happy is the
> man who can command humour on all occasions. For my part it
> is sometimes hard to have my humour understood when expressed

in English and I am sure it would be impossible to have it understood when expressed in French. Some days ago I invited the member for Labelle, Mr. Bourassa, to reverse the process which he invariably adopts of supporting the Government in English and attacking the Government only in French. This occasion seems appropriate for me to make a proposal to Mr. Bourassa. If he will adopt the plan which I advise him to I will undertake to do the same myself and whenever it becomes my duty to oppose the administration I will speak in English and when it is my duty to support the Government I will speak in French.

The function of the Press Gallery is to add to the importance of Members of Parliament. This is done both by laudation and by execration. With the Canadian Press [news agency] it matters not whether the speech is good or bad, the report is the same in either case. The saddest hour in the life of a member of Parliament is to rise to speak and to see only the C.P. representative in the gallery. A man might as well speak in the Senate.[48]

Meighen's ordinary custom when speaking in English was to have no notes, except perhaps certain statistics or quotations he intended to use. But in preparing for these French-speaking occasions he took understandable precautions, drafting the speech in English and having it translated into French, then assimilating the French text in his mind so as to be as little dependent on his manuscript as possible. He recalled later having spoken in 1926 at the Montreal Forum for twenty-nine minutes in French without once looking at his manuscript but admitted that "this was more a feat of memory than . . . a true measure of my command of the language."[49] Another time he had to perform the same kind of feat unexpectedly. He and Grattan O'Leary went together to a banquet meeting in Quebec which Meighen was to address. When he went to change his clothes for the dinner he discovered that his dress shirt had not been packed. O'Leary, more diminutive in stature, offered to lend him his and with some difficulty Meighen got into it. In the excitement of this crisis he forgot to put the text of his speech in the pocket of his dinner jacket and was seated at the head table before he discovered it was missing. He wrote a rather frantic note to O'Leary, who without a proper shirt was hovering discreetly on the outskirts of the crowd, and O'Leary obligingly went up to Meighen's room to get the speech. There were papers scattered all over the room but nowhere could O'Leary find what he was looking for so he went back down to the banquet hall and reported his failure. A less confident man would have extemporized some remarks in English, but not Meighen. When called upon he stood up and spoke in French for twenty minutes, delivering word for word the address he had prepared.[50]

There were excellent political reasons, of course, behind the desire to improve his French and he was sneered at by some for being governed by such motives. A few hostile Quebec newspapers jeered at his clumsy attempts, intimating that *les Canadiens* would not be taken in by them, and the *Free Press* of Winnipeg, which at the time regarded Meighen as the author of all crime, described with what was supposed to pass for wit how he would probably conduct himself henceforth at meetings in typical western communities:

> Ten minute address in the English language, ten minutes in French, five minutes in Polish, five minutes in Ukrainian, two minutes in Cree, two minutes in United States, one minute of shillelagh waving, three minutes Highland Fling.[51]

Meighen would not deny that he was learning to use French in order to improve his position in Quebec, though he was unable to see why he should be derided for this. But he was prepared to defend bilingualism on principle, as an attribute desirable for Canadians generally. He told an audience in London, Ontario, where the message could not be expected to be especially popular:

> . . . I cannot withhold a tribute to our fellow citizens of the French race for the wonderful manner in which they acquire a mastery of the two great languages of our country, English and French. I believe myself in the teaching of both these languages in this Dominion. I believe in having our young boys and girls thoroughly taught in English and thoroughly taught in French as well. It would be a good thing for Canada if this could be done and I say before this audience in London, although the subject is within provincial and not federal jurisdiction, that I for one would favour as strongly compulsory the teaching of the two languages as I would favour compulsory military service or compulsory anything else.[52]

This conviction, as well as political considerations, may have had something to do with Meighen's policy of donating a number of medals to French schools in Quebec and Ontario, apparently for proficiency in English. (There is no evidence of his having given medals elsewhere for proficiency in French.) In the summer of 1924 he received from one of the winners a letter of thanks which, though its genuineness was beyond dispute, indicated that incentives were indeed needed and also raised some misgivings about educational standards:

Hon. Arthur Meighen,
Conservative Leather,
House of Commons,
Ottawa

Honourable,

I thank you, very much for the beautiful medal that I had honour of to receive at the price's distribution.

By this alone medal, I fell amply recompensed for my good application at work during the year school.

Honourable, accept my sincery thanks at the name of my father and meantime know that the first one, that you give, was to a liberal girl and the next came to me, to a conservative girl, being arrived the first of all the convent with ninety-eight on one hundred for the year. I wish you the same thing for next election.

Yours very truly,

(sgd.) Germaine Bellemare

Please excuse the mistakes I made done in my letter.[53]

To this Meighen responded warmly—in French.

It was over ten years since Meighen had last sat on the Speaker's left but the shift to the Opposite side of the House required no great change in his parliamentary manner or debating technique. During the decade his party had been in power he had always acted on the principle that the best means of defence was to attack. Mackenzie King still sat across from him, though their positions had been reversed; Meighen would simply go on attacking the man and his ludicrous ideas, as he had derived considerable satisfaction from doing ever since King had come back to the Commons in 1919. Now, of course, he could enjoy the luxury as Opposition leader of waiting for the Government to present its measures, to take responsibility for policy—if it had any policy. King, as it were, would have to come to him and he anticipated many opportunities of making the little man squirm. King would rediscover, if he had forgotten during his absence from office since 1911, that there were restrictions and embarrassments in the exercise of power; he would learn that it was one thing to issue fine, high-flown pronouncements while in opposition, to preach grandly about the moral basis of politics and so on, and another to be true to his well-advertised canon of morality while having to formulate acceptable and workable laws in this most imperfect world. There was bound to be confusion, uncertainty and inconsistency in the actions of any new government until it found its feet. Meighen was sure that there would be more than the usual amount of these weaknesses in any government headed by Mackenzie King. And so he waited to pounce, the rapier of his mind at the ready; whatever he had of ironic wit and savage scorn, of logic and memory, of knowledge and force of conviction would be devoted to exposing, not only the pretensions and hypocrisies of his rival, but all the flaws which he was confident the next few months would reveal in the new regime.

As leader of the Opposition in the Commons Meighen acquired the reputation of being a master of purely destructive criticism and this was held against him, not only by those who were subjected to it, but also by some Conservatives in the country. They thought that little was gained by his pitiless pursuit of Mackenzie King, that it left the impression that he was a vindictive partisan bent on destroying King, rather than a moderate, constructively minded statesman who was primarily interested in the welfare of the nation. They had faith in the power of positive thinking; in their minds the way to political success lay not so much in the relentless exposure of the follies and misdeeds of the Government and its leader as in the forward-looking advocacy of new policies and new methods. There should be a little less invective and more sweet reasonableness, more constructive criticism of what the Government was doing so that the Conservative party might appear as an alternative government and not merely as a carping, captious, professional Opposition.

It was true, of course, that Meighen possessed an extraordinarily acute critical faculty. "Usually my critical mind finds at least a shade in which I can differ from almost any argument," he once remarked.[54] It was equally true that not since the days of Edward Blake and Sir Richard Cartwright at their best had any Canadian government had to endure so much probing, scathing analysis or as much clever sarcasm as Meighen brought to bear on the King administration in 1922 and afterwards. Certainly no party leader had ever been so mercilessly treated as King was by Meighen, though the treatment seemd even crueller than it was because of King's inability to cope with it in the House. King had his moments there but in general the unevenness of the verbal contest was so marked, Meighen's lordly superiority in debate so obvious, that there was a certain sympathy for his victim and a disposition to think that Meighen overstated his case, that King could not be quite that bad after all. Of course it was the "destructive" criticism, the onslaughts against the Prime Minister and his colleagues, that caught the headlines and lingered in the memory. Meighen's "constructive" criticism, his suggestions, of which there were many, as to how Government Bills might be improved or his calm, closely reasoned pleas for other courses than the ones being followed—these went largely unnoticed. But at all events, in his view of the matter, it was not the duty of an Opposition to help the Government improve its measures. Politics, when everything was said and done, was a contest in which power was the prize; the duty of the Opposition, both in its own and in the public interest, was to place the Government's exercise of power under close scrutiny, attacking at the weak points with all the ammunition it could muster. Its criticism might be thought destructive, especially by those whom it damaged, but unless it was resigned to remaining out of office indefinitely, it must try to destroy confidence in the Government. Anyway it was often necessary to destroy a ramshackle edifice of thought or action in order to build something better in its place.

Thus, in Meighen's mind, the essence of politics was controversy between contestants for public confidence and power, a verbal combat in which no quarter should be asked or given. Those who entered the lists must be able to defend themselves or expect to be unhorsed by the long, sharp lance of argument. This outlook was natural and appropriate to the most brilliant political controversialist in Canada's history, who had not yet really encountered in 1922—despite the recent election—the overwhelming, baffling, deeply troubling fact that it was possible to win the arguments and still not gain the prize.

Although the 1922 session was a good deal less turbulent and acrimonious than most of those during the past ten years, Meighen's critical faculty found much to keep it occupied. Even more than when he had been Prime Minister the performance of his party in the House was a one-man show. With its ranks reduced to fifty and with many of its old stalwarts absent through defeat or retirement, it could not well be otherwise if the Government were to be faced with the most effective Opposition possible.[55] And real, sustained criticism would have to come from the Conservatives rather than the more numerous Progressives. Some of Crerar's followers shared his desire to co-operate with the new administration; others had no interest in the conflict of Government and Opposition, disliking as they did the whole apparatus of the party system, and were concerned in the main with getting from the Government what they thought farmers generally, and especially their own constituents, wanted. They did not think of their party, or "movement" as many preferred to call it, as an alternative government. So a concerted attack on the general policies and attitudes of King and his colleagues could not be expected from them, whose support King needed and hoped to obtain, but from the Conservatives; this meant in effect that it would come very largely from Meighen himself. Some of the latter's forty-nine followers were of little use in the House. They not only accepted his dominating role there with good grace but expected even more of him than he was willing or able to do and he found it hard to get them to pull their weight. His astonishment knew no bounds when one of the back-benchers, explaining that he would be too busy to do so himself, asked him to write a few speeches for him to deliver in his riding between sessions of Parliament. Meighen had to explain that he, too, would be rather busy.

In addition to standing out like a solitary, towering peak among his own followers he seemed to be more conspicuous, to focus more attention upon himself without even trying, than anyone else in the House. A reporter for the *Manitoba Free Press*, "T.B.R.," after drawing for his readers a word-picture of the Commons chamber, wrote:

And in this confection of blended tones and hues and half-tones and velvet shadows, you observe Mr. Meighen—the Right Honorable Arthur Meighen, Leader of the Opposition. There are a hundred men and more in the chamber, but your eye finds Mr. Meighen. He has the face, the visage, the countenance. You see it first. And you attend. If you were drowsy before, you are awake now; if you have been heedless, you become heedful; if reckless, cautious. You discover your hand is moving. Instinctively it is groping for a weapon. You observe his pale, thin alarming face. . . .[56]

He took part in the customary two large "show-piece" debates of the 1922 session, of course, on the speech from the throne and the Budget, but in neither broke new ground. In the former he reviewed the election campaign, ridiculing King and his followers for the irreconcilable variety of their many arguments and promises; in the latter he scornfully contrasted what now turned out to be the trade policy of the Government with the 1919 platform and the things that during the campaign various Liberals had pledged would be done, while at the same time reaffirming his own fidelity to the protective system. But there were other occasions during the session that illustrated better his accomplishments as a parliamentary debater and some of the many contrasts between him and Mackenzie King, occasions which brought out in particular the differences between the views of the two men respecting the operation of parliamentary responsible government and the nature of leadership in a democratic state. Before long he became convinced that what he had suspected would be the case was indeed true: that leadership to the new Prime Minister really meant following where the prevailing winds of opinion might take him, instead of having a policy of his own by which he was prepared to stand or fall. King had often spoken of his respect for public opinion and the rights of Parliament but he seemed to carry this philosophy to the point where he was prepared to wait for public opinion working through Parliament to determine the policy of his government. That, argued Meighen, was wrong, entirely inconsistent with the British and Canadian parliamentary tradition. In the nature of things the House of Commons could not formulate policy and should not be expected to; that was the responsibility of the Government, which must devise and recommend the measures it thought best so that Parliament might pass judgment on them. This was the proper role of Parliament, to consider and pronounce upon specific policies brought before it. In that sense Parliament must, to be sure, decide. But neither it nor the public, save perhaps in most exceptional circumstances, could be asked to spell out for the Government in advance what the Government ought to do. Only a Cabinet with no mind of its own would shirk its responsibility by insisting that Parliament make up its mind for it, and that was the kind of Government, said Meighen, that Canada now possessed. At one point in the session he delivered a pithy description of how policy was being made:

> We have heard of government by conviction; we ought really to have government by conviction; but what have we now? We have government by listening. The Prime Minister bereft of opinions himself listens sometimes at an angle of 45 degrees, sometimes at an angle of 90 degrees, [that is, to the Progressives, who sat down the chamber next to the Conservatives, or to his own followers] listens for the whisper of the corridor, listens for the threats and the growls around, and then all these noises are gathered together, fused into one and the conglomerate emission becomes the tune that he calls the Government policy.[57]

If exaggerated, this nonetheless did indicate one of the significant dissimilarities between King's method of making up his mind and the practice which Meighen tried to follow and believed to be correct.

The contrast was illuminated during two debates in particular, one on certain estimates of the Department of Militia and Defence, the other on whether the manufacture, importation and sale of oleomargarine should be permitted in Canada. In presenting his estimates on April the twenty-fifth the Minister of Militia, George P. Graham, declared that they had "been pared down to a point as low as is compatible with national safety. . . ."[58] The second item in the list requested $1,400,000 for summer training of the militia. C. G. Power, the Liberal member for Quebec South, moved that it be reduced by $1,100,000 on the grounds that the country could not afford the money, that the nine days' training proposed would be useless, and that in any case, as there was no likelihood of war, training of this sort was needless. After some discussion, during which a certain amount of Liberal and Progressive support for Power's amendment and of Conservative opposition to it was expressed, the House adjourned for the night without a decision having been reached. That was the last that was heard of the item for two weeks. When it again came up for consideration Graham made a short statement. "It is the desire of the Government, of course," he said, "to meet the wishes of Parliament, for Parliament is supreme." Consequently after the previous discussion of militia training he had once more conferred with his officers and was now prepared to recommend a reduction of $700,000 in his original militia estimates, including a cut of $400,000 in the item for summer training. The Government therefore moved, in amendment to the Power amendment, that the sum of $1,400,000 at first asked for be diminished by $400,000 only.[59]

Thus a rather unusual situation had developed. The official Opposition was supporting the Government's first estimate, from which the Government had departed. It appeared that after the earlier debate on the item Graham had been instructed, either in a Cabinet meeting or by the Prime Minister personally, to effect a further lowering of his estimates. Although presumably these, as originally presented, had been approved by the Government and though Graham had said at the outset that they had been brought down to the bare minimum, the evidence of opposition by some of its own supporters, all of them from Quebec, and by the Progressives had forced the Government into retreat. The change of policy in this particular was defended with the argument that it reflected the will of Parliament but as only eleven private members had spoken by the time the change occurred and no vote had been taken, who was to say what the will of Parliament was? The situation was made to order for Meighen. After giving at some length his own reasons for thinking any reduction undesirable, he asked:

> But where are we to-night? We are asked to take $400,000 off a vote which the minister declared was indispensable to the safety of this country, which the Minister of Marine and Fisheries (Mr. Lapointe), seated at the council table, agreed was the very lowest that the Government could reach compatible with the safety of our people, which the Prime Minister . . . agreed was the lowest that they could justify the presentation of to Parliament. . . . That is the position which the Government has taken to-night. Why has it taken that position? Because there was disagreement behind; partly that, partly because there was agreement here. I wonder which it really was. The hon. member for St. James (Mr. Rinfret) says that he is all the more determined to cut these estimates down because we support them. Fine public spirit! He attacks us as Tories trying to hold to the old Tory policy. A bitter, long deliberated virulent attack he made on us this afternoon, and all for what? Pray, what was our offence? Our offence was supporting the minister whom he was elected to support. And as usual he feels that he has clinched his argument when he denominates us Tories. That appellation ends the discussion in the mind of the hon. member. I never put very much store by names; I put far more store by deeds and records, and I would rather belong to a party under any name on earth, a party that stands to its principles through storm and through sunshine, through adversity and through prosperity, in power and out of power, and that applies those principles in progressive legislation to meet the needs of the hour as the hours advance, than belong to a party which, though called in honour of the angels of heaven, cannot describe its principles for the life of it, can only sermonize in language of evasion and of mystery and cannot adhere to any policy for a single session or even from week to week.
> . . . What has transpired? There was a threat from the hon. member for St. James; there was rebellion in the heart and on the lips of the hon. member for South Quebec (Mr. Power), supported by the determined and dogmatic pacifism of the hon. member for Laprairie and Napierville (Mr. Lanctot) — and now he nods assent. Apparently there is mutiny still in his heart to-night. Consequently, these estimates were postponed in order to give the Government

sufficient time to change its policy and its principles. They did not need to be postponed very long. All were gathered into the composing room and the operation proceeded. . . . Some hon. member . . . gave the Government credit for living true to one of its preachings in the late campaign,—namely that the Government was going to be a committee of Parliament; the Government was going to find out the will of Parliament and then put it into effect. Well, if the Government is merely going to come to Parliament and ask Parliament what shall be the policy of Canada, if Parliament is to take the initiative and dictate a programme item by item to the Government, then in all respect, I do suggest, to hon. ministers, that they might reduce their salaries. . . . Is that responsible government? Is that the character of government that commands the respect of this country? Is that the sort of government that they have or have ever had in Great Britain? Is that traditional British government? If it is, then I do not know what British government is. It is not "democracy", surely not, to come here with a policy and, upon hearing someone rebuke from behind, get up and say, "very well, this is the course we decided on, but if you don't like it we will go back and fix up something else." This is a guess-work government. They canvass how many votes they can get by one line of action, and if they find by a counting process that they are wrong, they go back and guess again; and if they discover that they are still wrong they withdraw for cogitation and for caucus and then make another attempt.

An hon. MEMBER: Order.

Mr. MEIGHEN: Some hon. member says that is out of order. Well, it is certainly out of order in other British countries. No! wobbling of that kind is not "democracy." Do not let us besmirch the name of "democracy" by describing that sort of thing as democracy. It is impotency; it is helplessness; it is drift, sterility and inefficiency.

. . . I think the minister really believes at this moment that he would be doing better by the country as Minister of Militia to stand by the estimates he first proposed. I believe he wants to do right by the country—if he had the strength essential to his office. But he should have courage as strong as his desire is pure. Instead, he now returns coerced by his followers, driven and bludgeoned by them; for nothing else can explain his course.[60]

The same issue of the respective powers and duties of Government and Parliament arose a little later in the debate on oleomargarine. For many years before the war the product had been banned but the ban had been lifted during the war and, as a result of action by Parliament since, had still not gone back into effect. That it should go back into effect permanently was the substance of a resolution introduced in May by A. W. Neill, an Independent from British Columbia. The resolution was discussed for a day and defeated on a non-party vote, 83 to 57, the Prime Minister having stated that the Government wanted to get the opinion of the House on which, presumably, to base a policy. Clearly at that stage the Government lacked a policy for W. R. Motherwell, the Minister of Agriculture, emphatically supported the resolution while Fielding, the Minister of Finance, just as strongly opposed it.

Late in June Motherwell moved another resolution, this one as the basis of a Bill to be brought in, providing for extension for a further year of permission to manufacture, import and sell margarine. S. W. Jacobs, a Liberal who represented a predominantly working-class riding in Montreal, objected to the limitation of one year and asked why the matter could not be settled permanently. Motherwell explained that it was a "new question" to half the members of the House and besides, ninety-five members "were either absent or did not express themselves" on the Neill resolution. "Consequently we did not feel justified in settling the matter once for all." Meighen then asked Jacobs whether he was satisfied with this explanation and Jacobs said he was not. The discussion that followed had nothing to do with the merits of margarine but a whole lot to do with the theory and practice of responsible government. Meighen touched it off by saying:

> I can give the explanation, I think, that the Minister of Agriculture . . . failed to give, and I will oblige the hon. member for George Etienne Cartier (Mr. Jacobs) by doing so. It is because the Government does not know its own mind on the question. This House has debated the question, and this House has decided. The Minister of Agriculture is against the measure, but he comes here introducing it. . . . He was against the admission of oleomargarine a month ago. Unless he has changed his mind since, he is against the bill he is introducing. Other ministers are in favour of the admission of oleomargarine and its manufacture. The Government has no information on the subject, but they cannot conform to constitutional practice in this matter. If they did it would mean that one of them would lose his salary, and everything in constitutional practice must bow to that consideration. The Minister of Agriculture introduces a bill with which he has no sympathy at all, against the whole principle he has declared himself in the most emphatic language. He comes here as the sponsor of the measure in the House, rather than taking the ordinary course of resigning from the Administration, which is the usual course in every government, according to constitutional practice. . . .
>
> Mr. MACKENZIE KING: I do not understand why the hon. leader of the Opposition . . . should work himself up to this state of mind, in view of what took place when this question was discussed previously. I think I said that the members of the Government were not all of one mind on this question. We were quite prepared to have the House discuss it, to have it debated, and to be guided by such action as the House might take. . . . It is perfectly true there was not a very full attendance of the House at the time. Under the circumstances, the Government does not think it wise to extend the act beyond the period of one year, but we feel, in going that far,

we are implementing the promise we made to be guided by the views of hon. members. . . .

Mr. MEIGHEN: The explanation of the shilly-shallying policy is about as good as the explanation of the Minister of Agriculture. The attendance during the oleomargarine debate was just as good as the average attendance during any debate this session. The Government pledged itself to be bound by the opinion of the House. The Government now says we must be bound, not by the opinion of the House, but by some who did not express an opinion, or who were not here. . . . This method of action is always going to follow, if the Government shirks its responsibility, saying "We have no opinion, or we have two opinions, or ten opinions, and cannot get together, and, therefore, we will wash our hands of the whole thing, and whatever parliament says we will do. If that is the attitude, then we are going to have shilly-shallying. The hon. minister of Marine and Fisheries (Mr. Lapointe) pounds his desk in applause at the assertion that the Government has no opinion on the question. What are we coming to in this country?

Mr. LAPOINTE: No more autocracy.

Mr. MEIGHEN: There is just as much reason in everything they do as there is in their action in regard to oleomargarine. Why did we not have the Government coming to Parliament and saying "We do not know what to do about the tariff, we have no opinion on that." Really they had not any, but they thought they had, and they came here with two or three tariffs. They should have said "We have no opinion on that, so we will just throw the whole thing into the air and everybody can say what he likes and vote as he likes, and after it is done we will act as clerks and put it into the act." That is the administration we have—afraid to face its responsibilities or to discharge them, and the country suffers in consequence, and is going to suffer in future.

Mr. MACKENZIE KING: My hon. friend's argument would be for the abolition of Parliament, and for the establishment of autocracy.

Mr. MEIGHEN: No. The function of Parliament is to pass on the Government's proposals, after the Government makes them, and the duty of the Government is to come to Parliament with its proposals upon which it can unite. If it cannot unite, then it is for those who cannot come to a conclusion to leave the Government. The function of the Government is to come to Parliament with definite proposals on public questions, submit them to Parliament, and ask for its judgment upon them. That has been the practice in the world, and in this country, until we had the present phantom of a government in office.

Mr. MOTHERWELL: Mr. Chairman, the committee must not take my right hon. friend too seriously. He is just having one or more [sic] of his political catfits. The policy of the Government is embodied in this bill and in this resolution. A mandate was given by the House, and I am coming here with the bill, obeying the mandate. What other course could I take? Absolutely, no other course. It does not matter whether I believe it or not. I am obeying in a democratic way the mandate of the House. A vote was taken in the House where 95 members did not express themselves; it was on a Monday, when a large number of members were away. There are limitations to that mandate, and we have put limitations in this resolution by putting it in force for only one year. Even my hon. friend should be able to see that and, what is more, I am satisfied that if we had a reasonably full House, or if the vote were taken on any other day than Friday or Monday, there would be a different result.

An hon. MEMBER: Can you prove that?

Mr. MOTHERWELL: No, I cannot prove that. That is another reason why there is a limitation in this bill, and what is more, this is a new kind of House. There are 133 new members here, more than half the House. We had some general knowledge of oleomargarine, but we had not discussed it as we discussed it here. We had not taken the responsibility of action that we did here. We did it in a hurry. We had not more than five months to consider the question. . . .

Mr. MEIGHEN: Pretty quick.

Mr. MOTHERWELL: We refuse to be rushed. It is too important a question. Furthermore, the dairying interests are becoming more extensive and more important every day in this country, and as long as the charge of those interests reposes in my hands, I am going to protect those interests. I am going to defend them. I believe those interests are jeopardized by the suspension of that law that was in existence in this country for a quarter of a century. On the other hand in order to give hon. members of this House an opportunity to express their views, we are bringing this bill down to-day in good faith, restricting importation to one year. . . .

Mr. MEIGHEN: I hardly know at what end of the tangled scheme [sic] to begin, to bring some gleam of light from the conglomeration of adjectives and nonsense to which the hon. minister has just given vent. The minister, among his other defects as a public man, cannot apparently distinguish between impertinence and argument. To describe his course on this subject or any other, is really some task. To picture the grotesque position he is in, particularly in his own constituency and throughout western Canada, would really demand some powers of invective as well as a command of adjectives. I do not think I should attempt the task. Sometimes the claims of mercy are really stronger than the demands of justice.

Mr. BUREAU: You ignore those claims very often.

Mr. MEIGHEN: Does the minister think that this is a case for mercy?

Mr. BUREAU: No.

Mr. MEIGHEN: What is the Minister of Agriculture trying to say to Parliament to-night? He says: We are carrying out here the mandate of Parliament, but the reason that Parliament mandated us to do this was that Parliament was not here, and if Parliament had all been here, they would have mandated us to do the opposite. One only needs to state that to expose it. Nobody except the Minister of Agriculture can utter such a fallacy with a sraight face in Parliament.

Then he says: We have another reason. We are doing this because there is nothing else for us to do after that vote. Why, of course, but why did he not come down to Parliament with his policy before the vote? Why did he not follow the course that governments worthy of the name always follow? That is what I ask. Then he says: I won't make this legislation permanent. Why? Because these suspensions are damaging to the dairying industry of Canada, and as long as I am here, I am going to protect that industry. Really, I was sorry for the minister that he could not think of a better word than "protect." He usually manages to avoid that, but it slipped from his lips to-night. I am going to protect that industry, he says, and this suspension is damaging to the industry. Here we have the sponsor of the legislation saying: The bill I am bringing down here is damaging to the interests I am going to protect. That is the position he is in, but it is not anything more ignominious than the position he is in with respect to every other question of consequence that has come before this Parliament. . . .

Mr. CRERAR: . . . the Government is to be commended a great deal for seeking the opinion of Parliament on measures that come before it.

Mr. MEIGHEN: Certainly, but the measure must come before Parliament. They asked the opinion of Parliament before the measure was brought down.

Mr. CRERAR: That is all very well, but if the view of my hon. friend is held to the letter, it simply means that a dozen gentlemen composing the Government of this country will decide in Cabinet Council what is good for the country, and then come to Parliament and say; you must take this or turn us out.

Mr. CASGRAIN: Toryism.

Mr. MEIGHEN: That is right.

Mr. CRERAR: My right hon. friend says that is right. That certainly is the essence of Toryism.

Mr. MEIGHEN: It is the essence of Gladstonian Liberalism, too.

Mr. LAPOINTE: Never, Gladstone consulted Parliament.

Mr. MEIGHEN: After he brought in his measure. . . .

The Government is virtually standing up and asserting "We are so helpless, we are so powerless, that we ask that the ordinary constitutional principles be abandoned. We ask that we be mere clerks of the House of Commons; we ask that we do not have the responsibilities of government at all; we ask that we be allowed to sit here and ask Parliament, by a vote, to decide what we ought to do as a government. We will be good enough to take that down, and we will be good enough to carry it out and draw $10,000 a year each to do it." You cannot carry on government that way. . . . Parliament has its functions of course. Has the British Parliament for the last five centuries had no functions? Has it none to-day? It is [sic] merely an automaton? The minister knows better. Parliament's function comes after the government has declared its course on matters of government policy. Parliament has its function to review this. . . . it will be a distastrous thing if governments are to be relieved of responsibility for coming forward with definite principles as to government policy, submitting those principles to parliament for parliament's approval, and taking the constitutional consequences of their own action. If the hon. member (Mr. Crerar) looks with sympathy, or looks with leniency, upon the present course then he just absolves the government from all constitutional consequences and he will get just the kind of government that that action merits. Does he not want to keep responsible government? Surely responsible government is something that is worth preserving.

Mr. MACKENZIE KING: I do not propose to take up the time of the House. The discussion is really out of order, but it deals with a fundamental question. . . . The whole evolution of constitutional government has been that it is gradually subjecting the executive to the will of Parliament and there is an effort to make Parliament more and more an expression of the will of the people. I contend that is exactly what we are attempting to do to-day and if it means further evolution in giving expression to the constitutional rights of the people we will do all that we can to develop that evolution.

Mr. MEIGHEN: I will not let the Prime Minister put me in the position of saying that a government is not answerable or subject to the will of parliament. Undoubtedly it is subject to the will of parliament expressed at the proper time.

Mr. MACKENZIE KING: How do you know the will of Parliament if you do not listen to it?

Mr. MEIGHEN: After the government has brought down its proposals to Parliament it can listen to the will of Parliament. Governments run in a constitutional manner have always done that.[61]

Just how far King was prepared to go in abiding by the will of Parliament was nicely illustrated by the discussion of another matter bearing on constitutional practice, a discussion which gave Meighen one of his numerous chances to impale the Prime Minister cruelly on the sharp point of his scorn, holding him up, wriggling, for all the world to despise. A. R. McMaster, the Liberal member for Brome in Quebec, presented a resolution to the effect that ministers of the Crown should not be directors of banks or of trust, insurance, transportation or large public utility companies, and that no other companies in which they held directorships should do business with the Government. At the previous session he had brought in a private member's Bill giving effect to this principle but going even further by requiring ministers to resign all directorships in any companies within fifteen days of accepting office. The Bill had been warmly supported by King, with appropriate declamations about democracy being threatened by the power of the big interests; Meighen had just as warmly opposed it and it was defeated.

King's behaviour on the more limited resolution that McMaster now proposed suggested that one's perspective underwent a marked change when one moved from opposition into power. He now disapproved of actually applying the principle McMaster was trying to establish. Why? Well, for one thing there were various British opinions and precedents against it; for another, the House of Commons had already decided the year before that it should not be applied and that verdict, said King, was good enough for him. There might, of course, be instances where the public interest would be damaged by "certain gentlemen holding directorships" while they were ministers.

> But I can also see where a passing of a resolution such as is proposed by my hon. friend to-night, might deprive the country of the services of some of the ablest business men in Canada and this at a time when special knowledge of financial and commercial conditions is most needed in the management of public affairs. . . . As between myself and my colleagues, and between the Government and the country, the relationship I wish to have maintained is that of "Trust me all in all, or not at all." That is the attitude I hold towards every member of the Government, and it is the attitude I believe which every member of the Government holds towards myself. While we began with confidence in each other's integrity and ability, I may say that at this moment that confidence has ripened into implicit trust. Inasmuch as the support of my hon. friend's motion would seem to make it necessary for me to reflect upon the honour and integrity of any hon. gentleman associated with me in the cabinet, I must decline absolutely to vote for it.[62]

Though nauseated by King's sanctimoniousness, Meighen was not surprised by his change of heart; he knew perfectly well the reason for it. But he was astonished that anyone would argue, in effect, that a decision of a former Parliament could not or should not be reversed. "If the experience of the last two months," he said when King sat down, "had not rendered me utterly impervious to all sentiments of amazement, it would require at least the space of a few half hours to recover sufficiently from the speech of the Prime Minister . . . in order to address this House." Pointing out that he himself had opposed McMaster on this subject the year before and was still opposed, he went on:

> But against the course the government took [last year], the leader of the present Government stood and voted, and every indication of opinion that he made was to the effect that he not only favoured the bill but would go further than the bill went and would include within its sweep the leader of the Progressive party and the leader of the Opposition as well. That was the declaration of principle and of faith that the present leader of the Government made to this Dominion, and upon which among other things he appealed to the electorate for support. . . . I am afraid my resources of ridicule would be entirely insufficient if I came to examine the reasons that the leader of the Government advances. He says: "Yes, it is true I sup-

ported this bill a year ago." He did all right—he did more; he supported a bill that was sweeping, drastic and complete, going a great deal further than this resolution goes. He declared that he wanted it to go even further. "Oh, yes," he says. "I voted for it, but I have kept in mind ever since the fact that the House voted it down. . . . I declared my principles; I declared my belief; I submitted to this nation where I stood upon the question, but—save the mark—I cannot stand there any longer, because the House voted it down." Well, this will come surely with a thud of despair to those hon. members of this House, if any are left, who expect the present administration under the present Prime Minister to adhere to anything they have declared for in the last five years. Did not the House vote them all down? . . . But more: "Now," he says, "I stand on British precedent." May I ask what precedent he stood on a year ago? He has spent a lot of time on the subject; he has analysed the argument presented by the hon. member for Brome. Back centuries he has gone, and he divides into four categories all of those who have ever discussed this question in the British House. Some who have discussed it, he says, are indifferent to it altogether—do not care anything about it. Others who have discussed it believe it should be left to conscience and to honour. Others, on the contrary, believe that there can be nothing done about it, even though they are not indifferent. And the fourth class, the Gladstone-in-his-prime class and the Campbell-Bannerman class—they believe that the decision should be left to the Prime Minister of the country; and of course my hon. friend, now that he is prime minister of the country, is right step in step with the Bannermans and the Gladstones, believing it should all be left to himself. I really admired the skill; rather I admired the plenitude of verbosity with which the hon. Prime Minister contrived to have this question lost in the fogs of the past, to have it buried in the recesses of history. How much better his memory was of what Gladstone said, of what Campbell-Bannerman said or of what Balfour said, than of what he said himself. How much better his memory was of the decision of the British House and of debates in the House of Lords in the time of Pitt and Walpole than of the debate last March in the Commons of Canada and of his own vote on that occasion.

"Oh," he said, "when I came to form my Government I found out that my individual opinion should not pervail." Why, he had told us before that he had abandoned his opinion in deference to the decision of this House. Which of his two statements is right? I am inclined to think that the conclusion is that he has no opinion, and never had any real opinion; indeed, I think those words apply to him as respects almost every subject of public policy in this country. "I found," he says, "that if I stood by that resolution I would have only a mediocre government; I could not form an administration of the conspicuous abilities of the hon. members who sit around me now."

I might have had a government of Sinclairs and of Motherwells, if I may abandon the rule for a moment, but I could not have had for example the hon. Minister of Customs (Mr. Bureau), I could not have had the hon. Minister of Justice (Sir Lomer Gouin), and I could not have had the Solicitor General (Mr. McKenzie). I could not have had such men as the hon. minister without portfolio from Quebec (Mr. Dandurand), I could not have had the minister without portfolio from Renfrew (Mr. Low), nor could I have had my distinguished friend the Minister of Railways and Canals (Mr. Kennedy). All these great men, six or seven or eight, perhaps more, directors of companies and members of his government to-day he would have had to leave out of his cabinet, and because he had to decide between their superhuman capacities and his principles, without a moment's hesitation he abandoned his principles.[63]

Moments such as this were as frequent as they were painful to King, who would sit hunched over his desk jotting on a piece of paper with the stub of a pencil, while the red flush of anger mounted the back of his neck. He came to hate Meighen, no less bitterly than the latter held him in contempt; it was a very personal hatred of one man for another and not merely of the things Meighen allegedly stood for, of "autocracy" and his manifold other crimes. His real crime was that he made King feel fearful and inferior in the House of Commons, that he subjected him there to repeated embarrassments and humiliations. No one, of course, would appreciate being ridiculed as Meighen ridiculed him but King appeared to be unusually sensitive to serious criticism of himself. Perhaps this was because he did not yet feel absolutely sure of his authority in the Liberal party; perhaps, also, he was so convinced he was the instrument of the Lord that he looked on such criticism as the next thing to blasphemy. And, blasphemous or not, Meighen's attacks went straight to the mark. It was hard to repulse them or turn them aside with an argument equally logical or penetrating, hard to dispute his facts or refute his reasoning. There was what Grant Dexter, who watched the struggle between the two men from the press gallery as correspondent of the *Manitoba Free Press*, later described as an "un-get-aroundable"[64] quality in what Meighen said in the House, which made his self-assurance and sometimes derisive manner all the more unforgivable to his opponents. The effect he had on them was described by Dexter:

> Meighen would carry his controversial speech to the point where he really infuriated the Liberals. Mackenzie King . . . would bow over his desk and you could see the blood coming up his neck. . . . His neck would swell and you could see that he was just furious. The members would be the same and they would begin to mutter and growl. Nobody would *say* anything. Meighen—I have seen him many times—. . . would stop in the course of a speech and say "You're growling over there. Now anybody there speak up. If you have anything you want to say, *say* it; don't behave as your ancestors did ten thousand years ago."[65]

Usually no one accepted such invitations but sometimes somebody did, running the risk and often incurring the penalty of being cut down with a few mercilessly thrusting words.

Although Meighen's most trenchant probings, his most exquisite sarcasm and biting scorn were directed towards the words and deeds of Mackenzie King, the ministers, of course, came in for their share, and especially Motherwell, whom Meighen seemed to take particular delight in tormenting. Nor were the Liberal back-benchers immune, whether or not they chose to come to grips with him. If the occasion arose, no matter how seemingly trivial the issue, he would needle them for their inconsistencies, humorously but with a certain edge in his tone, drawing upon the recesses of his memory to point out sardonically how different their attitudes had been when their party was in opposition and his in power. Thus, for example, when Charles Stewart was conducting the estimates of his department, Interior, through the Committee of Supply, as Meighen had done in days of yore, a minor item was arrived at.

Grant to Alpine Club of Canada, $1,000

Mr. MEIGHEN: I really think the minister should not have the heart to ask for this $1,000 for the Alpine Club in the absence of the hon. member for Brome (Mr. McMaster).

Mr. LAPOINTE: Oh, have a heart!

Mr. MEIGHEN: I recall the battle that he waged in this House year after year . . . to save the suffering people of this country from this awful imposition of a thousand dollars—a thousand dollars that he saw passing from the treasury into the pockets of the rich and the powerful to enable them to enjoy the scenery of the Alps of Canada assisted by the hard earned savings of the people of this country. The hon. member is absent to-night but I know it could not have been by intention, because even this session I find that the memory of the filching from the treasury that had been done by this Alpine Club has not passed from him. I can recall well that he reminded me of it only about two weeks ago; but here when there is an opportunity to save the nation from this imposition he is absent from his duty. I will not, I am sure, appeal to the minister in vain when I ask him just to let this item stand in order that the House may be treated once more to the lugubrious eloquence of the hon. member for Brome.

Mr. STEWART (Argenteuil): I also have a recollection of being attacked on a similar vote in the legislature of the province from which I come, and knowing the sympathetic mind and heart of the right hon. gentleman I am sure he will agree to allow this item to pass realizing what we have both suffered in the past in this connection.

Mr. MEIGHEN: Are none of the other critics going to speak at all?—because the hon. member for Brome was not alone.

Mr. LAPOINTE: Yes, he was alone.

Mr. MEIGHEN: Oh no, my recollection is much more intimate than that of the Minister of Marine and Fisheries. I am sure that the hon. member for Laprairie and Napierville (Mr. Lanctot) was one of his coadjutors and I see him now in his seat.

Mr. LANCTOT: I am here.

Mr. MEIGHEN: And silent.

Item agreed to.[66]

CHAPTER EIGHT

"READY, AYE, READY!"

THE DEBATE over whether Canadian militiamen should receive summer training, which prompted Meighen's attack on "guess-work government," ranged in a general way over the larger issues of peace and war. Much of what was said was a compound of optimism and isolationism, reflecting faithfully a very wide segment of public opinion. The world, some of the speakers seemed to think, had moved into a new era in which there was no need for military force of sizeable dimensions, for, as one of them put it, "history has proven that war is a gigantic and dismal failure. . . ."[1] The way to avoid conflict, they believed, was to disarm but if, unhappily, a new war should erupt in the distant, troubled parts of the globe, Canada need not be involved. Removed from danger as she was by oceans on three sides and the huge protective strength of the United States on the other, without enemies or ambitions that would incur enmity, she had nothing to fear and therefore no need of more armed force than was necessary to maintain internal order. Rather than spend money on a wholly non-productive militia for which there was no use, the hard-pressed taxpayer should be relieved or these funds be diverted to socially useful purposes. This would at once benefit the people of Canada and raise the country's stature by setting an example for all mankind to follow. This last argument, as plausible as it was fatuous, was well expressed by J. T. Shaw, a Labourite from Calgary. "I think it would be a very becoming and splendid thing," he said, "if this young country, inspired by new ideals and a desire to set a standard to the rest of the world, could say that we, at least, are prepared to disarm to the uttermost. If we did that, I am satisfied that our action would constitute not only a challenge but an inspiration to peoples in other parts of the world, less fortunately situated than ourselves."[2]

Meighen's views on the matter were rather different and, as was often the case with what he said, a great deal less popular. After much talk of new social orders emerging, of the evils of "militarism" and the wrongfulness of force, his remarks no doubt struck many members of the House as old-fashioned and dangerous, as decidedly "Tory." Being neither an optimist nor an isolationist, he was swimming against the tide of opinion, a tide he was sure would bring disaster if it continued to run in that direction. He started out by disclaiming any right to speak from the standpoint of military knowledge or experience and any intention of indulging in prophecies of the shape of things to come. Rather he wanted to

> say something . . . as to what appear from the story of the past, from the ordinary layman's reading of history, as being sound principles that a country like this should follow in determining what should be the measure of its military organization.
>
> . . . If we are going to march toward what my hon. friend calls a "great, new social order" merely by cutting out our defence; if we are going, as he says, to put Canada in the lead at this great climacteric in our history—put Canada in the lead in ushering in a new and better order in this world by the easy process of dropping the military estimates—why, then, I would want to drop them all; I would not tolerate a dollar. But I have not observed that, in the past or to-day, nations that do not gird on their armour and play the part of men in the world, but rather lolled back in self-indulgence, have been leaders either toward a new social order or toward any other order.
>
> . . . Now if by having a military organization we are only getting ready for war; if we are only taking a step to precipitate another conflict such as the war from which we have emerged, then let us stand for none at all; let us have nothing whatsoever. But while every one hopes—at least every one would like, though he may not dare to hope—that there would be no more great wars, I do not think the sensible people of the world are of the opinion that the British Empire and other nations of like character are going to hasten that time merely by themselves disarming, throwing away all means of self-defence. . . .
>
> If we are to get past the time of war, to my mind there is only one path we can tread that is likely to get us there. It is for those nations that undoubtedly have no militaristic purposes, that undoubtedly are not animated by sentiments of revenge or by ambitions of conquest, to stand together . . . in a world policy, endeavour to bring other nations into line with themselves, and all as one group be in a position to make their policy and their pacific purposes reign. . . . to the extent they are able to stand together, to the extent they are able to support their opinion by that reserve of force which alone in world politics creates influence and supports opinions, they are real contributors to the peace of nations.
>
> There is nobody in the British Empire, there is nobody in the United States, there is no considerable, respectable body of opinion in either of these great countries which believes for one minute that even though they stand together, they can get anywhere unless they have very considerable forces behind their opinion. . . . Such being the case surely it follows that we, as an integral part of the British Empire, must maintain a fair share and proportion of that means of defence which all the Empire must sustain. Surely that follows. Surely that is incumbent upon us out of regard for our self respect, out of regard for the very manhood of our people.

Then the question is, how far can you go? Where should you stop and be sure that you have not gone too far, but that you have reached the right line? Well, it is a difficult matter; it is a very difficult matter to decide. Opinions differ as to the state of the world; opinions differ as to the share incumbent on the different peace-seeking countries of the world; opinions differ as to the share of the various nations of the Empire. Some say that the late war so exhausted humanity that even if it would, through the perversity of human nature, it cannot wage a conflict for many years to come. I fear, though, that the state of the nations to-day affords not quite so good ground for the optimism of that class of people as it did even a few months ago. I do not think we can look to the horizon in the direction of Europe and be quite so sanguine, so certain, that the world is very far from war. . . . there is just about the antithesis of harmony in the whole European atmosphere at this hour. Very well, that is the condition, deplore it as we will, struggle against it as we will . . . nevertheless, that is the condition that confronts us.

They had been told by some, he went on, that Canada was made safe by geography, that the Monroe Doctrine would protect her from harm. Was it not proper, then, that Canada, now spending less per capita on defence than any other country, and a great deal less than the United States, should carry a proportionate share of the burdens of North American security. But this was a delusion, that location and the engirdling arms of the United States would preserve Canada from harm.

Surely the Great War, if it taught us anything, taught us this, that any considerable war of the future will be such that no nation knows whether it will be possible for it to withhold its hand and its part in that war. Surely it taught us . . . that the British Empire can be maintained only to the extent that it stands united, and that we are secure here as a part of that Empire only to the extent that the whole Empire is secure. If any one doubts that, let him get up and say so. For myself, my reason cannot bring me to the conviction that there is any security at all for us save in the security of the Empire of Britain.

We are asked, where is the foe? Where is the enemy that is going to attack us? Let me put the answer this way. . . . We are told we have no foes. Had Canada any foe in 1913? But foes came. The world is smaller to-day than it was two or three hundred years ago, and as time goes on the relations of continents and nations become closer, the dependence becomes closer, and the security of the one depends more and more on the security of the other; the peace of each depends more and more on the peace of all. . . .

. . . We are told the militia is a non-productive body and that we have a large debt to-day; that we have a tremendous interest burden to carry year after year, and that consequently we should cut down the militia. That argument proceeds upon the hypothesis that the militia, the defence force, is a mere luxury—that the reason it is maintained by a nation is because that nation has some money to throw away. The militia organization is maintained not for luxury, not in any sense merely to appease the parading ambitions of any class of people. It is maintained by a nation first to maintain law and order within the country; and second, to be a nucleus around which the national force can gather if danger comes from without. Those who preach that we ought to cut down because our debt has grown have a wrong conception of what the militia is for. We ought to maintain—and I admit it is very difficult to tell just where the line should be drawn—we ought to maintain a militia not proportionate to our debt, but proportionate directly to the need for the militia itself, proportionate to the size of the purposes the militia is to meet.[3]

On the basis of these general observations Meighen went ahead to argue, vainly of course, that there should be no reduction in the militia estimates.

In the spring of 1922, with the Washington Conference successfully concluded, the League of Nations in being and expectations of a peaceful future still running high, Meighen's arguments no doubt seemed to many both perverse and academic. His attachment to Empire solidarity was not shared by the administration then in office, though it was paid lip service from time to time by the Prime Minister. His conviction that peace and security depended upon the willingness and ability to act collectively with other countries, even to the extent of using force, was widely questioned. Many did not agree with him that it was a profound and perilous delusion to put one's faith in the protective guarantees afforded by geographical isolation. The post-war tendency to recoil from Europe with all its rivalries and tensions, the abhorrence of further involvement in world power politics, the genuine and deep-seated desire for peace at almost any price left a large, though indeterminate, number of Canadians quite out of sympathy with the kind of sober realism to which Meighen in this speech attempted to give expression. To them it was simply unthinkable that Canada should again allow herself to be sucked into the maelstrom.

In the autumn of that year a situation arose with a shocking suddenness that made this eventuality seem uncomfortably close. It arose in the Near East, a part of the world about which the majority of Canadians knew little and cared less. The Chanak crisis resulted from a series of events in Turkey which were related to the question—all-important in Great Britain—of control over the narrow water passage which separates Europe from southwestern Asia and links the Black Sea with the Mediterranean. The Treaty of Sèvres, signed in August 1920, provided for a neutral and demilitarized zone on both sides of the Dardanelles and the Bosporus in order to prevent Turkish control of the Straits. The treaty was signed by a representative of the Sultan's government, which was virtually a prisoner of the Allies in Constantinople, but was repudiated by the revolutionary nationalist government at Ankara, headed by Mustapha Kemal Pasha, which by the late summer of 1922 enjoyed *de facto* power over practically all of Asiatic Turkey. British, French and Italian forces were stationed in the neutral area forbidden to the Turks but their respective governments were by this time in evident disagreement over policy. It seemed probable that Mustapha Kemal, emboldened by knowledge of this dissension among the Allies and by decisive victories in Anatolia over the Greek army, which had been encouraged by Great Britain to attack his forces, might order his soldiers to move towards the neutral zone at Chanak, at the narrows of the Dardanelles, and seek to occupy it in violation of the treaty which he had from the outset refused to acknowledge. The rout of the Greeks was completed during the first two weeks of September and Kemal, with 80,000 men under his command, stood ready to move against the small European garrisons occupying the last strip of Asia Minor still under foreign control.

The collapse of the Greek army was a severe blow to Lloyd George, whose pro-Greek, anti-Turk policy had not been wholly acceptable to his colleagues, let alone much of the British press and public and Britain's major allies. The failure of the policy meant that Kemal Ataturk, instead of having been disposed of by Greek arms, was now poised to seize the Straits and move into Europe. That, Lloyd George and most of his ministers were agreed, must be prevented. As Winston Churchill later explained, "We intended to force the Turk to a negotiated peace before he set foot in Europe."[4] British warships were ordered into the Dardanelles to prevent a crossing to the European side by the Kemalist army, and British troop reinforcements began to move towards the scene. Churchill was instructed to cable the Dominion governments to explain the situation, inform them of Britain's intention of defending the neutral zone and inquire, in the language of his cable, whether they "wish to associate themselves with the action we are taking and whether they would desire to be represented by a contingent."[5] The message added that a declaration of support by any or all of the Dominions might help to prevent actual hostilities.

This was dispatched to the various Governors-General on the night of Friday, September the fifteenth. The next day the Lloyd George Cabinet decided to issue a statement for the information of the British public. This was also drafted by Churchill and went out verbatim to the news agencies of the world. It revealed that a message had gone to the Dominions "inviting" them to send contingents, and that similar invitations had gone to France, Italy, Roumania, Bulgaria and Yugoslavia. The importance of control of the Straits was emphasized and the old spectre was raised of the Turk in Christian Europe, laying waste property and human life. It is hard to resist drawing the inference that this provocatively worded statement was designed, not only to inform the British public and unite it behind the policy, but also to influence public opinion in these other countries in such a way that their governments would find it difficult to turn the "invitation" down. If this was the object it was only partly achieved. France and Italy, instead of deciding to strengthen their forces, in a few days withdrew them entirely, leaving a handful of British troops alone at Chanak to face the Turks apprehensively from behind their barbed wire. The Balkan countries were not sufficiently interested to become actively engaged. As for the Dominions, New Zealand at once promised to send a contingent and Australia, more deliberately and with some qualifications, followed suit. Participation does not seem to have been seriously considered in South Africa, except in the event of a major conflict breaking out, and Prime Minister Smuts contended that the cabled inquiry from London had really been directed primarily to the Australasian Dominions, to which the Near Eastern situation was of prime importance, and had gone to Pretoria and Ottawa only as a matter of form.[6] Although this opinion was confirmed in a second message from Churchill to the Canadian government, both it and one from Lloyd George stressed that, as the latter cable put it, "A definite statement . . . that Canada will stand by the Empire . . . will do much to ensure maintenance of peace."[7]

The first British cable inquiring as to the attitude of the Dominions arrived at Rideau Hall in Ottawa at ten o'clock on the evening of September the fifteenth. Probably it was assumed in London that it would be decoded immediately and forwarded to Mackenzie King without delay. Instead it was put aside until the next morning when the deciphering was done and the message arrived belatedly at the Prime Minister's office at three o'clock in the afternoon. By that time the British press statement had already been published in the newspapers and the first intimation King had that Canada had been "invited" to send a detachment to the Near East came when a reporter asked him what reply would be sent to the British message. King was justifiably annoyed that the whole matter had become public property and that everyone knew the substance of a secret cable sent to him before the cable ever reached his desk. Clearly this was a case where there should have been direct communication between Prime Ministers, in the manner approved by the Imperial Conference of 1921, instead of through the traditional channel of the Governor-General's office.

Unfortunate as this mischance of delayed transmission was, the failure of the British government to keep the Dominions up to date on developments in the Near East was much more serious. "Continuous consultation" seems to have gone by the board. There is nothing to indicate that

King sought information about a situation which from newspaper reports was known to be rapidly deteriorating; undoubtedly he preferred not to be kept informed. Rejecting the concept of a single foreign policy committing the whole Empire, he was content not to be consulted and in this way to avoid responsibility. However, the fact that he had received no warning prior to the middle of September that a crisis impended and the further fact that there had been no effective consultation between London and the Dominions with regard to British policy *vis-à-vis* Turkey was a grave violation of the principle, frequently reiterated, that the foreign policy of the Empire must be made in concert, that those affected by the consequences of policy must share in its determination.

Churchill's message of September the fifteenth placed King in an awkward position and instinctively he equivocated. Dependent politically as he was so largely on Quebec, whose opposition to further involvement in the machinations of British diplomacy he fully appreciated, and upon the Progressives, whose pacific sentiments were no secret, he was not in a position, even had he so desired, to reply to the "invitation" from London with a forthright affirmative. Nor, on the other hand, could he fail to take into account the considerable body of Liberal opinion in the country that would be alienated by an abruptly negative response. His reply, therefore, was non-committal: Parliament would have to sanction the sending of troops and he would be glad to have further information to enable the Cabinet to decide whether Parliament should be summoned for this purpose. As he wrote in his diary, "I shall not commit myself one way or the other, but keep the responsibility for prlt.—the executive regarding itself as the committee of prlt."[8] The next day he added, describing a Cabinet meeting: "We debated long over question of giving moral 'support' & approving attitude. I felt that involved whole question of participation in European wars & held back on it."[9] The view expressed by Lloyd George and Churchill that a declaration of readiness to fight was the best way to prevent a fight did not appeal to King. What if the Turks were not suitably impressed by such a demonstration of Empire solidarity and moved on to the attack? It was the kind of risk King was not prepared to run. Not only that, he thought the Progressives and his Quebec followers might be brought together under the stress of the crisis against their "common foe, the jingo-tory-militarist. I believe we have found the basis on which the Progressives of Western Canada may be brought into real accord with the Liberals of the Province of Quebec and other parts of the Dominion."[10] Divergent social philosophies and economic interests had thus far prevented such an assimilation, which King dearly wanted to achieve. It might now be facilitated by agreement on foreign and Imperial affairs but only if there were no commitments to support Great Britain at Chanak.

Publication of the British press statement on the sixteenth of September caused a great stir in Canada and a deep division of opinion was at once revealed. Those who favoured a declaration of solidarity with Britain have been dismissed as "a number of church groups" and "an element with strong British sympathies,"[11] but this, with its implication that their response was purely emotional, scarcely gives an accurate impression of the extent or the basis of the sentiment. That the issue transcended party lines was shown by the variety of editorial comment, with some Liberal papers joining the majority of Conservative ones in advocating an affirmative reply to the British inquiry. While some warlike sentiments found expression, while some people doubtless instinctively demanded that Canada make common cause with Britain, there was a lot of sober consideration by the editors of the responsibilities that Canada of her own volition had recently assumed in the world and of the possibility that one might have to be ready to fight in order to preserve the peace.

During the first few days of the crisis Meighen remained silent. He probably soon reached the conclusion that the Government's action, or inaction, constituted, as he was shortly to describe it in a letter, "a selfish, halting exhibition of procrastination and impotency. . . ."[12] However, he stated in a speech on September the twentieth: "This being a grave question of Foreign policy, it is the duty of every good citizen to give the Government every opportunity to live up to the sterling aspirations of the British Empire. I am giving them that opportunity."[13] His forbearance was likely also caused by the fact that he was to address a luncheon meeting of the Toronto Liberal-Conservative Business Men's Club on the twenty-second. Better to wait until he was before that large and enthusiastic audience when circumstances would be auspicious for a public declaration of where he stood.

The banquet room of the King Edward Hotel was crowded with five hundred men who, when Meighen was introduced, greeted him with a resounding ovation and a lusty rendition of "For He's a Jolly Good Fellow." The first part of his address was devoted to a discussion of railway affairs and a criticism of the Government's policy in that regard. No business man could fail to be interested in this subject, of course, but the audience was really waiting to hear what, if anything, he would say about the crisis in the Near East. He did not disappoint them. Having mentioned briefly the events that precipitated the crisis, he said:

> There is much of destiny hangs upon the decision of the present
> hour in this country. From this week in September may date a
> struggle on the outcome of which may depend, not only our place

in the world, but also the influence of the Empire in her power for good and peace. There are those who write and talk as though Great Britain were not our good partner and friend but our chief antagonist, an imperious, designing mistress, seeking to lead us to our ruin. I do not attribute that attitude to a large section of those who are opposed to me. That would be unfair. But there are many such.

After referring to the importance of the Straits, to their neutralization by the Treaty of Sèvres, and to the danger inherent in allowing Turkey again to control them, as she had to the detriment of the Allies during the war, Meighen launched into what proved to be the most famous utterance of his entire career, an utterance quoted (in part) by Mr. King's biographer as evidence of that "jingo-Tory-militarism" from which King, fortunately, was engaged in saving the nation. With the audience hanging on his every word and frequently interrupting him with salvoes of applause and gusts of cheering, Meighen declared:

> Britain is not prepared to surrender that prize of victory, because she wishes to secure that the future may belong to peace and not to war. She sends a message to the Dominions, not a mere indifferent inquiry as to what was the mind of Canada, but a message to see if the Dominions were solid behind the Motherland. The exact wording of the message we do not know, but judging from the evidence that was its purport. From Australia and New Zealand the British Government got messages of co-operation in defence of the Treaty of Sèvres. Those messages have been met with an expression of gratitude from the Government, which, it is reported, intends to abide by her position. We were a party to the Treaty of Sèvres and the trials and sacrifices that made it possible. There is no suggestion at all that we should send armed forces across the sea. Britain merely sought a declaration of solidarity on the part of the Dominions (Applause) —the existence of which the war has demonstrated once and for all. Let there be no dispute as to where I stand. When Britain's message came then Canada should have said: "Ready, aye ready; we stand by you."

This was an echo, and deliberately so, of Sir Wilfrid Laurier's words in the special war session of Parliament in August 1914: "When the call comes our answer goes at once, and it goes in the classical language of the British answer to the call of duty: 'Ready, aye, ready!' "[14] The echo was greeted with a great outburst of cheering that came in successive waves and compelled Meighen to pause for some moments. When the noise had subsided he went on:

> I hope the time has not gone by when that declaration can yet be made. If that declaration is made, then I will be at the back of the Government.

Again he had to halt while the audience vented its enthusiasm with renewed cheers and applause, after which he resumed:

> By that course we do not bring the country nearer war. We take
> the best step in our power to ensure that war shall not come.
> (Applause.) Can anyone divine what is to be the result of a policy
> by which we determine for ourselves whether or not we leave to
> Britain, or share with her, the defence of treaties to which the honor
> as well as the signature of this country is pledged? Can anyone
> divine where it is going to lead us, or what will be the effect of the
> procrastinations of this week we are passing through? By any con-
> sequences of my decision I am prepared to stand.[15]

While the immediate occasion on which these remarks were made was
a triumphant success, the political consequences of his declaration were
to prove more far-reaching and less favourable, especially in Quebec,
than Meighen could have imagined as he listened to the noisy acclaim
that greeted his words. Did not "ready, aye ready" mean that he was
ready to follow blindly wherever Britain led, to plunge his country
into wars that were not of her making over issues that did not affect
her, to sacrifice Canadian blood and treasure on the altar of British
imperialism? Was his speech, in short, not the classic expression of
"jingo-Tory-militarism"? Meighen had said, Mackenzie King later
contended with utter disregard for the facts, that "this country ought
to go to war with Turkey—and go to war why? To drive the Turk out
of Europe. . . . The right hon. gentleman bravely and heroically shouted
that the answer should have been, 'Ready, aye Ready,' and that it was
our job to get into the fight."[16] Such was the nature of the charges made
against him, charges that were to become embedded in the conventional
interpretation of that period of history. But the propositions expressed
or implied by Meighen were quite different: that those who have successfully waged war and concluded peace have the right and duty to enforce
the peace by collective action; that covenants entered into are not to be
lightly and expediently discarded; that Canada was in and of the world
whether she liked it or not. These propositions were not in harmony
with the prevailing temper of the time but subsequent experience was
to indicate that they were by no means wholly invalid.

It has been suggested that Meighen might have spoken with more
restraint had he been in office instead of in opposition[17] and, to be sure,
the responsibility of power in a democratic state has had a wondrous way
of imposing restraints on men. While he was perhaps less prone to that
kind of caution that others, had he still been Prime Minister he could not
have failed, and yet remained true to the principles he had enunciated at
London the year before, to protest vigorously against the entire lack of
prior consultation concerning policy in the Near East. In fact by the

time he made his Toronto speech he could have inferred from a statement King had given to the press that there had been no such consultation and this ought logically to have softened Meighen's strictures on the Government. For, as he himself had emphasized at the Imperial Conference, the solidarity of the Empire in the world must rest upon discussion and agreement in determining the course it would pursue. Conceivably, though this is by no means certain, had he still been in office he would have shown more desire than King did to be kept abreast of developments in the Near East, prompting communications from London on the subject and offering his own views in return. However, the fact remained that the British government had grossly neglected to communicate with the Dominions and to solicit their opinions. Did not this negligence indicate a bland assumption on the part of Lloyd George that he would continue to call the tune of foreign policy and that the Dominions, if the need arose, would help to pay the piper?

Perhaps it did and if it did Meighen should have been the first to deplore that attitude. But was this the really vital issue in the whole Chanak affair? He was convinced at the time and remained ever afterwards convinced that it was not. The real point, in his mind, was that Canada, as part of the Empire and in common with her allies, had determined on a policy, embodied in the Treaty of Sèvres, respecting the future of the Straits, a policy she was in honour bound to do her part in sustaining. Whatever one might think of British policy in Turkey since the war and of Britain's failure to consult and inform the Dominions, the fact remained that the Turks were now threatening to assert their sovereignty over the Straits, which Canada for one had expressly denied to them in the treaty. To Colonel J. B. Maclean, the Toronto publisher, Meighen wrote:

> I am afraid you and I are not of the same view of the wisdom, in the common interest, of denying to Turkey the key of the Dardanelles. Canada like all the Allies, thought wise at the Peace Conference to divest the Turk of control. I for my part have not changed my mind on this subject, and if Canada has, her Parliament has certainly shown no evidence of its altered position. Nor does it appear to me that British public opinion favours any other policy in this regard than that embodied in the Peace Treaty. There are sections and probably very important sections of British opinion which are of the view that in maintaining the British stand for the neutralization of the Straits errors were committed. This may be right or it may be wrong, but on the question of the object to be reached, I do not think there is any substantial difference of opinion.[18]

But after all, it was argued, the Treaty of Sèvres was a dead letter; the new regime in Turkey had repudiated and refused to ratify it and as a result formal ratification by His Majesty on behalf of the Empire had been held up.[19] Consequently it had never really come to life and Meighen should "have known that there could be no obligation on Canada to uphold the terms of a stillborn treaty."[20] But Meighen, with his "jingo-Tory-militarist" obsessions, emphatically rejected this interpretation of the matter.

> . . . The shameless excuse that we had no obligations under the Treaty of Sèvres [he wrote] and consequently did not require to stand by Britain in a just cause embodied in that Treaty, is too manifest even to deceive those who want to be deceived. As between the Turk on the one hand, and the Allies including Canada on the other, there is no enforceable treaty as such because of the failure of Turkey to deposit ratifications, but as between Britain and her Allies, and especially as between Britain and Canada, the achievements represented in the Treaty of Sèvres and the obligations there entered into are as sacred as any part of the whole war settlement.[21]

Implicit in the assertion of King and others that the treaty was moribund was a principle with far-reaching implications: that if a defeated nation refused to accept a treaty of peace, or if the treaty were repudiated by a new regime coming to power, its terms were rendered wholly inoperative and unenforceable. If this principle were recognized there would be little likelihood that those vanquished in war would ever again ratify a settlement imposed upon them and the victors would be both deprived of the right and absolved of the responsibility to secure the peace they had established. War would therefore become even more pointless and wasteful than many people already thought it to be. King no doubt would have disowned so sweeping an interpretation of his argument, an argument which presumably can be considered only a rationalization of his stand on Chanak. However, even if one admitted, as everyone did, that there would have to be a new treaty with Turkey, it was going rather far to argue, in effect, that it was proper to surrender to the Turks before the new treaty was negotiated that control of the Straits and that access to Europe which had been denied them. To do this would be to weaken immeasurably the bargaining strength of the Allies at the conference table and to place in jeopardy the future of a waterway which was of the utmost importance to many countries, and not to Great Britain alone.

Hostilities did not break out between Turkey and Great Britain in 1922 and Mackenzie King thought it very probable that Canada, by having put a damper on the enthusiasm of a British government hell-bent for war, deserved a good deal of the credit for this. "I believe," he told Parliament later, "that the attitude which Canada took . . . had a very wholesome and restraining effect at a very critical moment, and no one can say that the attitude of Canada . . . did not avert a war in the world then. I do not go so far as to say that it did. . . ."[22] Others have attributed the decision of the Turks not to attack the neutral zone to the evident determination of Great Britain to defend it and also to the firmness and tact of the British commander on the spot. "The British Government," said Smuts of South Africa, "has acted with great firmness and has saved, without bloodshed, the Empire and the world from a very grave trouble."[23] This view of the matter, however, was widely disputed in Great Britain itself, where the crisis precipitated, though it did not wholly cause, the defection of most of Lloyd George's Conservative supporters, thus bringing about the downfall of his coalition ministry on October the nineteenth. In any event before this change of government occurred discussions had been opened with Turkey looking towards the negotiation of a new treaty to replace that of Sèvres. These led to the summoning of a conference at Lausanne, Switzerland, out of which came the Treaty of Lausanne as well as a separate Straits Convention, which provided for their continued demilitarization and control by an international commission.

The Dominions were not represented at Lausanne, either on their own account or in the British delegation, and none of them seems to have made any effort to secure representation. The Canadian government had no desire to take part in the conference. King was worried lest it be invited to do so and when no invitation came one of his ministers exclaimed, "Thank God!"[24] With the precedents of the Paris and Washington conferences in mind the British government no doubt expected a strong protest against the exclusion of the Dominions and the Colonial Secretary explained that France had objected to their being invited. But there was no protest, nor even a demand by any of the Dominions that, as at Washington, they be given places on the British Empire delegation, to which neither the French nor anyone else could have taken exception. They were promised that they would be kept informed of the progress of negotiations, as the British government assumed that they would want to sign any treaty that might result as well as any separate agreement regarding the Straits. How ill-founded was this assumption in the case of Canada was revealed by King's response and his subsequent cables: not being a party to the conference she would not want any arrangements it might make submitted to her for signature, approval or consent to ratification and would accept only such obligations under any treaty or other agreement as her Parliament might decide. "King knew that the questions confronting the Lausanne Conference were of no real interest to Canada. . . ."[25] It was therefore only proper that Canada should entirely abstain from any association with its work. This was a logical position to take but it raised one difficulty: until the treaty was formally ratified by the King the Empire would remain technically at war with Turkey. The practice was for the Dominion governments to signify their concurrence in ratification. In Canada such signification was preceded by parliamentary approval of the treaty in question. In this case, however, Mackenzie King did not want to bring the treaty before Parliament, as he thought it of no concern to Canada, and would thus have no sanction for consenting to ratification. Consequently it appeared that owing to the Canadian stand, the Treaty of Lausanne would not become operative as far as the Empire was concerned. This awkward fact was at first ignored by the government of Canada when it was brought to its attention in December 1922.[26] As, according to King, neither the Treaty of Lausanne nor the Straits Convention imposed obligations of any kind on Canada, there was no reason why her government should concur in their ratification.[27] However, since the purpose of the treaty was to restore peace with Turkey, if it were not ratified on Canada's behalf, a state of war would legally continue between her and the Turkish Republic unless a separate peace were made between them, which King was not prepared to do. Recognizing this, he and his ministers, when again asked if they would not concur in ratification, replied that they could not without consent of Parliament but added: "With respect to ratification they will not take exception to such course as His Majesty's Government may deem it advisable to recommend."[28] In other words, Canada would legally be party to a treaty which her Parliament, and for that matter her government, had not approved. But, argued King, though bound in law Canada would have no moral obligation to uphold a covenant which she had not helped to formulate and had not signed. To put it differently, she would enjoy whatever benefits might accrue from the restoration of peace with Turkey without incurring any responsibility for defending the terms of the peace.

Anticipating a debate in the 1924 session of Parliament on these constitutional matters arising out of the Lausanne Conference, Meighen turned to Loring Christie for advice. As Prime Minister he had relied heavily on him and had never been disappointed. "On matters of external affairs," he told Christie afterwards, "I value your views more highly than any other I know. . . ."[29] Therefore now that Christie had resigned from the Department of External Affairs (he had stayed on for over a year after the change of government but had been ignored by King)[30] Meighen was glad to be able to call on him once again. Accordingly he wrote as follows to Christie, who was in England at this time:

> . . . The question then is what is Canada's status as regards the treaty. Without having given very close study to the subject, as yet, I am disposed to the view that Canada is in the same position that she would have been in years ago before the practice of Dominion

ratifications took effect. That is to say Canada is no longer at war with Turkey and the treaty applies to us in really the same way as if we had expressly ratified it. If this view is correct all the Government's conduct is in effect a reversion to the more primitive or Colonial relationship to the Motherland. . . .

The only other alternative I can think of, as applying to our resultant position, is that we are still at war with Turkey. This, it seems to me, will hardly stand up. I would certainly be grateful if you would send me your views. . . . how could we escape the obligations binding on the Empire if we claim the benefit of the other features of the treaty including the restoration of peace.[31]

In answer to this Christie obliged with a lengthy, closely reasoned but sprightly missive which agreed substantially with the views Meighen had expressed. In acknowledging it the latter wrote that he found it "difficult to convey to you my estimation of the value to me of this document. . . . It has clarified my whole thinking on the subject and now I feel as if I had a practical grasp of the matter reviewed."[32] How valuable it was is shown by Meighen's speech in the Commons in the debate on Lausanne, for practically all his major arguments were ones that Christie had presented in his letter. The debate commenced with a statement by King in which he reviewed the communications that had passed between London and Ottawa and offered his argument that Canada was only legally bound and not morally obligated by the Lausanne Treaty and the Straits Convention. Towards the end of his statement he made some general observations about Canada's future within the Empire, stressing the importance of autonomy and equality of status, and concluded by saying: "But what above all else is needed is a united Canada, a Canada that as a nation will stand as one, recognizing its responsibilities and its duties, as well as its rights, a Canada that will have one aim and one purpose, a Canada which is united within itself and finds its unity within the unity of the British Empire as well."[33]

With this point of view Meighen, who spoke next, could not disagree. There were, he remarked, "two pillars upon which the future can be erected." The one was self-government. "We must first of all insist, as we have always done, the insistence year by year becoming less necessary, on the full exercise of our full governing powers, on the most complete autonomy for this Dominion as respects matters which concern ourselves." But no less important was the second pillar. "We cannot build a future on the basis of autonomy alone. It is impracticable . . . and, further, it does not savour of honour. We must necessarily adopt the principle of co-operation. We must seek, by pooling our judgement . . . to gain common ground with the other Dominions and Great Britain as to what should be our general course in respect of foreign policy. . . . We must approach this . . . in a spirit of friendship and of confidence, we cannot approach it in a spirit of suspicion, distrust; if we do, we can never succeed." Now, he asked, had the policy of Canada respecting the Lausanne Conference rested on these twin pillars? His answer was an emphatic No. "We not only willingly, but apparently gladly stepped aside and let the British . . . take what line they liked. . . . We offered no presentation of view at all; we offered no assistance; we contributed not the least in directing the policy of the Empire upon lines that we considered honourable and safe. . . . Is that a spirit of co-operation?"

The Prime Minister, he went on, had made much of the fact that Canada had not been invited to the Conference at Lausanne. She had not been invited to Paris in 1918, either, or to Washington in 1921. But on both those occasions she had insisted successfully on being represented. Had the government of Canada this time similarly asserted Canada's rights? No indeed. Instead Mackenzie King had cabled the British authorities that the lack of an invitation "has been regarded by us as evidence that in the opinion of the countries by whom the invitations . . . were extended, Canada could not have been believed to have the direct and immediate interest which she was supposed to have in the Conferences at Versailles and Washington." Was it, then, for other countries to decide where Canada's interest lay? The Government's attitude, said Meighen, should have been: "It is for us to say whether we are interested in this treaty or not; we were interested in the war which makes the treaty a necessity, and we are interested in the conditions now which are to tell for peace or war in the days to come. . . ."

The fact that there had been no such response from Canada, coupled with the omission from the Prime Minister's speech to which they had just listened of any mention of the actual contents of the treaty or of the Straits Convention, indicated that in the view of the Government, Canada was in no way concerned with those matters in the Near East. But she was bound by these agreements made in the name of the Empire and if they should ever lead to war, as Meighen thought possible, she would inevitably be dragged in. Thus her government should have sought to influence policy, as had been done at the 1921 Imperial Conference, in such a way as to lessen the danger of war. It should first of all have demanded representation at Lausanne, which Meighen believed could have been won; but had it proved to be unattainable the Government ought during the negotiations to have made strong submissions to the British delegates concerning policy. ". . . I say," declared Meighen, "that the policy involved in the treaty itself and especially in the Straits convention is . . . a mistake and a policy from which it was the duty of this government to endeavour to avert the British plenipotentiaries. It was the duty of this government to see to it that they adopted such means of communication and internegotiation as are clearly open to them to present the viewpoint of Canada."

His explanation of why he was uneasy about the agreements arrived at in Lausanne showed that fear of European entanglements was not confined to Mackenzie King and the Liberal party.

> . . . I do not think the British Empire pursues a wise course in launching upon European commitments. . . . Great Britain . . . is not distinctly a European country. It is true she is within the orbit of Europe: but Great Britain is a world Empire. She bestrides the seven seas of the globe. At all points of her vast domain she has interests sensitive and peculiar, interests that may be involved sooner or later in commitments which she is making quite unconsciously and in good faith and which appear to affect the Empire only in Europe.
>
> . . . I believe that in order that Great Britain's position as a world power may be appreciated, and that she may most wisely determine her general lines of policy, the dominions of the Empire owe it to her to present their viewpoints on all subjects that concern the issues of peace and war.
>
> . . . I say therefore that it was our business to have taken the very best means which it was within our power to adopt to make known the viewpoint of this Dominion in this respect. We should have taken every means of seeking to divert British policy from any course which we felt, having regard to our peculiar circumstances, might lead to danger.

Meighen's argument about these "European" commitments missed the point that Britain's overriding concern with the Straits arose from her Imperial interests, but the main fact for Canada was that the Convention bound the whole Empire "to preserve that demilitarized zone. I would much prefer that it did not, and I do not believe it ever would have bound us if the will of Canada had been properly represented and pressed; but it does bind us to do that, and it binds us to take the consequences that may follow such action."

Or did it? What about King's distinction between Canada's legal position and her moral obligation? This was only the principle, retorted Meighen, which had been accepted for generations: that in the event Great Britain was at war Canada, though committed in law, would decide whether to take part and what the nature and extent of her participation should be. That freedom she still retained but had now casually surrendered the right, exercised since the war, of influencing policy. It was both wrong and dangerous, he argued, to make such a surrender on the supposition that Canada had no direct or immediate interest in the treaty with Turkey.

> . . . our future happiness and peace depend upon the rightness and the soundness of the terms of that treaty, as upon the rightness

and the soundness of the terms of other treaties. Are we not interested in the peace securities stipulated in that treaty? Were we not interested in the treaty of Paris? Were we not interested in the securities obtained at Washington? Of course we were. And we are interested in this treaty, perhaps not in any equal but in a like degree; and never will this country submit to having to sit outside when terms are negotiated concluding a war in which we have participated and fixing the securities on which the peace of the future is to rest.

It was too late now to object to the terms of the treaty; the time to have done that was when the Lausanne Conference was sitting and the Canadian government was being kept informed about what was being done. The Prime Minister had not even availed himself of the opportunity at the recent Imperial Conference to object to the decisions reached at Lausanne. Canada's influence had at no time been brought to bear as it should have been, since in any considerable war of the future she would in all likelihood be embroiled. The Government had permitted a reversion to the old colonial status under which Canada had been bound by treaties she had not helped to make. All the gains achieved since the war, the right to help determine policies which would affect Canada vitally, had been given up in the mistaken belief that to stand apart from affairs was the best way to remain secure and avoid the troubles of the world. Security was not going to be found that way, Meighen concluded.

> . . . you do not get out of difficulty by keeping your eyes blind to what is going on, you do not get out of difficulty by permitting Empire policy to pursue a line which is ultimately bound to involve us, you do not get out of difficulty by remaining heedless of whether such policy involves us or not. In matters that we are concerned with let us present our view, and let our view every time be dictated by the interests of peace, and of peace alone. This government has abandoned the whole undertaking, this government has abandoned all responsibility, this government has abandoned its duty to the people of Canada.[34]

The fundamental question at issue between King and Meighen in this debate and in the earlier controversy over Chanak was not whether there should be war or peace, not whether "jingo-Tory-militarism" should prevail; to deal with the matter in those terms is to perpetuate a bit of folklore that does not accord with the facts. The two men differed, rather, over how best to safeguard the achievements of war and preserve the benefits of peace. King believed that peace could be secured for Canada by isolating her, refusing to become involved where trouble might erupt. She should mind her own North American business, speaking no evil, seeing and hearing none except the twin evils of "jingo-Tory-militarism" and Imperial centralization, which one must have the wit to recognize, eloquence to denounce and courage to resist. If Canada kept out of other people's affairs and set a good example for the world, she would make the best possible contribution to the maintenance of peace.

This was in marked contrast to Meighen's conviction that peace could only be maintained through a system of collective security. Righteous words and ardent wishes were not enough. To retreat behind the barriers of distance was merely a futile effort to flee from reality. Canada had demanded, because she had earned, the right to take part in making the peace settlement and, having won the right, had also assumed responsibilities which neither honour nor self-interest allowed her to cast aside. She must be prepared to co-operate and to act with other nations, for the courage to act in the face of danger might be the only way to avert danger. In answering "Ready, aye ready; we stand by you," as he put it in his Toronto speech, "we do not bring the country nearer war. We take the best step in our power to ensure that war shall not come." In this shrinking world a threat to the peace anywhere might become a threat to the peace everywhere and those who threatened must be deterred by the presence of an adequate aggregate of force.

That force, both moral and physical, Meighen believed deeply, could be provided by the nations of the British Empire walking together and, wherever possible, in step with the United States. It was the Empire, rather than the League of Nations, in whose ability and will to act he had little faith, which afforded the basis for collective security. The Empire was one of the few subjects that brought to the surface the emotional side of his nature, those passionate feelings which normally he kept hidden from the public gaze. As he remarked at Vancouver shortly before the Chanak crisis flared up, "If there is any man who by birth, intuition, and aspiration is more fervently British than I am, I haven't yet made his acquaintance."[35] He believed with all his heart that the Empire had been, not blameless by any means, but all in all a force for good in the world. He was confident that if its member states continued to consult and act with one another, if together they honoured the obligations they had together assumed, the Empire could exert a stabilizing influence of great proportions and contribute in a profoundly valuable way to the peace and security of all the world. He would not admit that Canada should walk separately from Great Britain and the other Dominions, or that she could casually decide from time to time on her own account whether she would walk with them or apart. Her true destiny lay within this partnership, this living league of nation; only there could she play a really constructive part by helping to direct the policy of the Empire along proper paths.

Quite clearly there were points at which Meighen's concept of the Empire, which was essentially also that of Sir Robert Borden, was vulnerable to attack: his view of Britain's Imperial record was somewhat idealized and romantic; he underestimated the difficulties of maintaining the unity of the Empire by conference and consultation; with his own success at London in 1921 in mind he overestimated the degree to which Canada might be able to affect the Empire's course in the world. And logically, was there not a flaw in the argument he advanced in the 1924 debate on Lausanne that Canada, asserting her right to attend conferences and make treaties, could yet retain that freedom to contract out if war should ensue? Did not the right to help determine policy entail a full moral obligation to uphold it? This was the position he had taken respecting Chanak. He might reply that the freedom was in fact illusory, that Canada could not contract out in any way except theoretically and therefore should try to shape the policy of the Empire in such a way as to lessen the danger of war. But this was less comforting in the new age of anxiety than the doctrine that the responsibility to act could not be laid on those who declined the power to decide.

Although one might quarrel with Meighen's concept of the Empire, might question his assumptions, deny his convictions or dissent from his arguments, it was a concept not without nobility, no less realistic an approach to the problems of war and peace than King's isolationist escapism and perhaps wiser. But it was doomed to be discarded and replaced by the nationalist nostrum of no commitments, coupled with the amorphous internationalism of the League. Mackenzie King had begun his crusade to save Canada from the British Empire and to protect her people from the big, bad world. British statesmen seemed no longer to believe, if indeed they had ever truly believed, in the kind of Imperial concert in foreign affairs which Borden and Meighen both wanted to establish. The modern Commonwealth was just over the horizon and all that Meighen was able to salvage from the wreckage of his dream of what the Empire might have been was the reflection, affording but cold comfort, that a little more of the spirit of "Ready, aye ready" on the part of Canada, as of all the western democracies, might have done much in later years to save the world from a gigantic tragedy.

CHAPTER NINE

"THE WHISPER OF DEATH"

V ITAL AS were these matters of high policy in the field of external relations, they probably seemed of less immediate importance to most
members of Parliament and to Canadians generally than other subjects
closer to home. Excitement over the Chanak incident soon died down and
the later debate on the Lausanne Conference revolved around issues that
may well have struck many people as of no more than academic interest
to constitutional lawyers. The real stuff of politics was to be found
nearer at hand and, despite occasional excursions into Imperial relations
and foreign policy, the attention of Parliament was concentrated for the
most part on domestic questions, many of them hardy perennials. How
could the wheat crop best be marketed? Should race track betting be
prohibited? Ought a wharf to be built at Sacroiliac, New Brunswick, a
customs house at Tous les Saints, Quebec, a post office at Yellowtooth,
Saskatchewan? Had the tariff been reduced too little or too much? Was
public ownership of railways being given the fair trial the Liberals had
promised it? Was public ownership committing the country to perdi-
tion? Ought not a system of proportional representation to be established? Had Mr. King really said what Mr. Meighen said he had said,
and vice versa? And finally, a question bound to recur again and again as
long as those two gentlemen faced each other: was it the duty of the
Government to lead or to be led by Parliament?

The one big question, of course, that always concerned the politicians
was the weather—the political weather. Were there signs of a Conservative comeback or a Liberal decline? Would the Progressives be as big
a factor in the next election as in the last one? During 1923 Meighen
felt entitled to some confidence that the weather was improving. To be
sure it was still too early to make forecasts with any certainty and no one
knew better than he that enough troubles remained. That great dark
cloud continued to hover in the sky over Quebec and considerable over-
cast was to be seen elsewhere. But at least the sun was beginning to
penetrate and to shine more brightly on the Conservative party. For one
thing there were some encouraging by-election results, with Liberal
majorities from the general election being very drastically reduced in
two ridings (Essex North, Ontario, and Cape Breton North, Nova

Scotia) and two other seats (Halifax and Kent, New Brunswick) being captured from the Government. Not too much significance could be attached to these gains but they might be hopeful omens. In addition the Ontario Conservatives under Howard Ferguson won a sweeping victory in June, displacing the Farmers' government of E. C. Drury. Provincial results were not invariably a reliable barometer for national politics but Ferguson's triumph seemed to augur well for the federal Conservatives in the Banner Province. Even in Quebec the local Conservatives made some gains, coming out of a general election there with twenty seats instead of the five they had held previously. There were good reasons to discount the importance of this from the national standpoint but it was heartening to know that people calling themselves Conservatives could still be elected in that province.

Aside from this electoral evidence Meighen had some reason as the year wore on to take fresh heart. He was confident that he had more than held his own in the House of Commons in the two sessions since his government's defeat and he got the impression on his trips around the country that his criticisms of the King administration were beginning to have an effect on public opinion. At least there were signs of growing dissatisfaction with the Government and also persistent rumours of discontent with King's leadership within the Liberal ranks. The Progressives, too, those sixty-five warriors who had descended upon Parliament Hill with such confidence after their 1921 success, seemed to be having troubles of their own. Robert Forke, who had become their leader upon Crerar's resignation from the post, was a much less impressive figure than his predecessor and the movement was seriously divided over basic issues of political philosophy. But more heartening than the difficulties of its opponents was the reviving spirit of the Conservative party and especially the fact that progress was at last being made toward giving it an effective organization.

Meighen had always recognized the seriousness of this problem but it was not one that he was temperamentally well equipped to solve, with his essentially intellectual attitude to politics. He had no peer when it came to analyzing issues, amassing evidence, building up an argument and presenting a case. He was prepared to take the truth to the people in the belief that the truth would make them free—of the Mackenzie King regime. Of course he was realist enough to know that a party had to have more than a message or a policy and the men to expound it in Parliament or on the hustings. There had to be apparatus, machinery to arrange meetings, prepare publicity, provide canvassers, get out the vote and do all the thousand and one other things that must be done. And there had to be money to do them with. He knew this but was not in his element in that aspect of politics; there was as little likelihood of his being able to devise an organizational structure as there was that Mackenzie King would publicly denounce his grandfather.

Meighen's initial approach to the problem was to assert that organization had to proceed from the grass roots, that it was a local responsibility. There should be an organization in each province with which the national party could co-operate and which it could use for its own purposes as the need arose. "I never had very much sympathy," he wrote, "with the cries and tub-thumping very often made from different parts of the country, demanding organization, and this always proceeds on the assumption that organization must proceed from here and especially must be financed by some one else. Organization is fundamentally local, and we must proceed in harmony with our provincial parties, and have an organization locally effected and by provincial units."[1]   And again:

> . . . I think myself provincial and dominion politics should be kept distinct, but at the same time I do not think we could keep separate organizations—one in each province for provincial purposes, and another in each province for federal purposes. . . .My idea is that we should organize by provinces for provincial purposes and organize under the name "Liberal-Conservative"; that our federal plans should be merely to utilize at the proper time these provincial organizations. . . . I know that the working out of this is not free from difficulty.[2]

Difficulties there were, indeed, for this notion did not sit entirely well with some of the provincials. In Quebec, for example, it was clear that the Conservative leader, Arthur Sauvé, wanted to dissociate himself entirely from Meighen and the national party in order to rebuild the party provincially. Of course there were special circumstances in Quebec but even in Ontario Meighen's approach to the matter caused a good deal of grumbling. In the summer of 1922 several picnics and public meetings were staged jointly by the Ontario and national Conservatives, some of which Meighen attended to discourse on national politics. "Statements have come to me frequently," Howard Ferguson reported, "which indicate that there has been a feeling that the provincial party and the provincial campaign is being relegated to second place at these joint gatherings. My people of course, point out that the rehabilitation of the party at Ottawa must be brought about by success in the provincial election which will come on next year. Our members and those who are active in our organization think for that reason that provincial issues and provincial interests should be kept in the foreground."[3]   Meighen was surprised that this feeling existed. "I don't know how they got the idea that at our general meetings provincial matters are being subordinated, but if so I am ready to yield to any suggestion that will produce the opposite results. I am prepared to speak or to stay away, and if I speak to speak first, or second, or last, or anywhere else."[4]   But the difficulty could not be solved simply by his self-effacement. The real grievance, as Ferguson explained to Arthur Ford, editor of the London *Free Press*, was that the organization created by and maintained at the expense of the provincial party was being used gratis by the national Conservatives, sometimes without Ferguson or his people being consulted.[5] Apparently the doctrine of provincial autonomy and suspicion of federal encroachment extended even to the matter of party organization.

At any rate few people seemed to share Meighen's belief that responsibility in this regard could be devolved upon the provincial parties. He kept receiving complaints about the lack of national organization and demands that something be done. He was going to take steps, he wrote Billy Sharpe in some exasperation, "with a view to making organization possible on a sufferable basis. The thing is not sufferable now when every one looks to myself to get work done in every end of the Dominion."[6] However, he still seemed somewhat at a loss as to just what steps should be taken. In the spring of 1923 he had a conversation with H. H. Stevens, whose vigour and ability Meighen respected, and suggested that when Parliament was prorogued Stevens might undertake some organizational work. The conversation prompted Stevens, who had given the subject more hard-headed study than Meighen had, to put his ideas on paper.

> If I understand your idea correctly it was that I should visit the different districts, particularly of Alberta and Saskatchewan, meet our friends, deliver addresses and endeavour to have them perfect their organization, etc.
>
> I have given the whole question of Party organization very careful and long study, and especially your recent suggestion and beg to submit to you an outline of my ideas on the subject. Permit me to say very frankly that I believe it would be a mistake to follow the proposal made by you, that it would not result in any real good being accomplished and would leave us practically where we are today. I believe we must organize some central authority both for finance and organization purposes. You as leader, should be relieved of this burden without delay. Furthermore, no person can do effective work, such as you proposed, unless he had the full authority and approval of the Party. He should be publicly recognized as holding some definite position so that when he visits any section it is with the imprimatur of his party rank and position.

Stevens then enumerated half a dozen specific suggestions. As a stimulus to organization preparations should be started at once for the national convention it had been decided over a year previously should be held. With the approval of caucus Meighen should appoint a national council which would have the task of raising money for the party and of perfecting an organization. The council ought to have an executive committee to work closely with Meighen and to have control over party finances.

One person should be chairman of both council and executive and "be known publicly as such." A secretary and staff would be required to do routine work for the party under the direction of the chairman. Finally, these proposals or others should be carefully worked out and submitted to caucus for its sanction.[7]

Here was a plan that at least made some show of coming to grips with the problem and a beginning was made on its implementation as the 1923 session of Parliament drew to a close. With the consent of the caucus Meighen appointed a committee of M.P.'s whose task, as he described it, was "to devise, provide for, construct and maintain a federal organization. . . . It has had several long and useful sessions. It has chosen Doctor Tolmie as Chief Organizer, or rather as Chairman of the Executive for the Dominion of Canada, and he has accepted the work and will give his time wholly thereto from now on."[8] This, of course, bore but a faint resemblance to Stevens' proposals but it was at any rate a start which gave Meighen hope, along with the other favourable portents already mentioned, that the turning-point in the party's fortunes had been reached.

If it had been there was still a long distance to travel back to power, as Meighen knew full well. He was not one to underestimate the formidable obstacles that stood in the way, especially in the Province of Quebec, and one of these, the animus of the Montreal tycoons, must have come to his mind more than once during the parliamentary session of 1923 when the affairs of the publicly owned railways were among the most prominent topics of conversation. The consolidation of those railways into one system was just being completed when the session began. The decision of the Grand Trunk Arbitration Board, announced in September 1921 with Taft dissenting, that the preference and common shares of the company had no value, and the dismissal by the Judicial Committee of the Privy Council of an appeal from that decision, opened the way to the final incorporation of the Grand Trunk into the Canadian National Railway System. The existing board of directors, appointed by Borden and headed by D. B. Hanna, was dismissed in October 1922 and the resignations of the interim directors of the Grand Trunk, led by Sir Joseph Flavelle, were accepted. These two bodies were replacd by one board for the entire system and a new president was imported in the person of Sir Henry Thornton, a naturalized Britisher of American birth with a long record of railway operation in the United States, England and, during the latter part of the war, France.

The makeup of the new board was clearly determined in the main by political considerations and, with two exceptions in addition to Thornton himself, none of them had had any experience in railway affairs. Among others there was a fur merchant from Toronto, a former Liberal M.P. from Nova Scotia, a wholesale grocer from Prince Rupert and the president of the Trades and Labour Congress. "Let it never be forgotten," the deposed Hanna wryly commented to Meighen, "that every member of the Old Board was invited to serve; a clear case of the position seeking the man. Would that the same could be said of their successors."[9] There was much criticism of these appointments but the choice of Thornton was generally well received; obviously if experience counted for anything he must know his job. Meighen, however, was indignant about the removal of Hanna and his associates. In a speech at Toronto he wished Thornton every success but denounced the dismissal of a president who had already succeeded and the replacement of directors who had done credit to their positions. This, he said, was a flagrant example of political patronage since most of the new appointees had no qualifications except that they had contributed "services to the Liberal party."[10] This statement in turn brought criticism down on Meighen's head, even from some who normally supported him, causing, Sir Joseph Flavelle wrote, "a painful impression among many men whose judgment I know you respect." After all, remarked Flavelle, who had good reason to remember this, Meighen himself had planned to supplant Hanna with someone else and therefore was attacking the Government for doing what he would have done had he remained in power.[11] It was true, Meighen replied, that he had looked for a new president but, as none of those he had considered for the office possessed practical railroading experience, he had intended to retain Hanna as general manager. Furthermore, he had taken it for granted that the members of the old board of directors would be eligible for re-appointment to the newly constituted board once the unification of the railway system was effected.[12] Still, even in Toronto where the business interests chiefly identified with those who had been dismissed were centred, the appointment of Thornton was well received[13] and thus Meighen appeared in the guise of a petty, partisan objector instead of one who, having done so much in nationalizing the railways, was prepared to give the new C.N.R. regime every encouragement and every chance to make good.

As a result of these changes in management, Meighen was in an especially critical frame of mind concerning railway matters when Parliament opened at the end of January, and was determined to scrutinize with particular care whatever aspects of the C.N.R.'s affairs properly came within the purview of Parliament. However, though he found several opportunities to refer in passing to what he regarded as the improper replacement of the old board with the new, he did not make a major issue of it. His main speech regarding the general progress of the publicly owned system was marked by moderation of tone and language and an absence of that sharply controversial quality which so often characterized his utterances.[14] It followed a statement by the Minister of Railways, George P. Graham, who had recently been transferred from the Department of Militia and Defence. Meighen's object was not to attack the Minister or the Government but to show that the data Graham had presented vindicated public ownership and thus to defend himself and the railway policy with the development and application of which he had been so closely associated. His speech was an expression of optimism—over-optimism perhaps—about the prospects of the C.N.R. and it must have caused a lot of teeth-gnashing among the anti-public ownership fanatics of Montreal. The evidence presented by the Minister showed that during 1922 the condition of affairs had very considerably improved. Meighen welcomed this, noting of course that the improvement had taken place under the Hanna regime which had remained in office until near the end of the year. The improvement, he predicted, would continue. In the past the Grand Trunk had always been handicapped by being controlled from London, with a "board of directors sitting in an attic in the middle of that city," and by incompetent management under President Howard Kelley in Canada. Now that these evils had been removed and the Grand Trunk at last united with the other lines, there was a good prospect that the annual deficits would continue to diminish until they disappeared altogether.

That clearly was the tendency at the present time, he argued, citing some statistics for the years 1920 to 1922 inclusive. The operating deficit of the Canadian National Railways, excluding the Grand Trunk, had declined from thirty million dollars in 1920 to sixteen million in 1921 and nine million in 1922. The operating profit of the Grand Trunk in 1921 was four million dollars, lower than the previous year, but in 1922 it had risen to nearly thirteen millions. Taking all the lines together there was in 1922 a net operating profit of about four million dollars, "the first operating surplus that parliament has had reported to it since we came out of the valley of doubt and difficulty through which we had been struggling for many years in the solution of our railway problem."

Of course the C.N.R. was not out of the financial woods yet, because the huge fixed interest charges on its bonded indebtedness had to be carried. Taking the system as a whole these charges amounted to about fifty million dollars per annum. Therefore, considering both operating results and interest charges, there was still a large net deficit. But the encouraging fact was that, owing to the steady improvement from the standpoint of operations, these deficits had been very materially reduced and, Meighen confidently prophesied, would continue to fall as all the benefits of unified management made themselves felt.

> I wish [he said] . . . to impress upon the House really what is meant by these recurring deficits in order that all will understand—though I do not wish to intimate that all do not now—just what these deficits imply, and will not think that they imply more than they do. I am not unaware—indeed, if there is anyone in this country wholly and vitally and keenly aware, it is myself—that there are influences at work . . . to make the people or some sections of the people believe that these deficits mean something that they do not mean at all; that they have been brought upon us because of the folly of weak-kneed, blind and stupid politicians in bringing this country into the ownership of the national lines we have to-day.

The point overlooked by those who wrung their hands over these deficits, he went on, and who wept in agony over the impending financial ruin of the country was this: that a very large proportion of the indebtedness of the railways, which caused the deficits, was money owed to the Dominion of Canada; it was "not money that must be found in order to let the railways stand up and proceed and give service" but an investment that in time would bring returns. Elaborating on this point, the ultimate heresy in the opinion of his enemies among the tycoons of Montreal, he said:

> What I impress at the moment is this: That assuming we go ahead, as certainly we should—and we should go ahead with accelerated speed from this on, now that we are loosened from the London management and have only one system instead of two—assuming that we go ahead as we have been going for these three years, and reach the point where deficits cease, then we must remember that all these deficits of years gone by have been no loss to the people. Quite the contrary; when we get to the point where deficits cease and we commence an era of returns over fixed charges, at that point all the deficits of these previous years become interest bearing assets. Because they are in the form of loans they now add to the fixed charges year by year; when we overtake the fixed charges so increased from year to year and get to earning money over and above them, at that point we have gathered up all the deficits of the years that have gone and they have become assets, loans, securities, in the treasury of the Dominion, bearing interest to the people of this country. It is a common feeling—I have met many who hold this view, and I can hardly find fault with anyone reading some of the newspapers of Canada for doing so—that after we get past the era of these terrible deficits and reach the point where operation produces a revenue over fixed charges, then we shall have to look back and think of the money we have thrown away because of the folly of politicians . . . all of which is gone forever. The very contrary, let me repeat, will be the fact. When that time comes . . . all those deficits will take the form of mortgages in the treasury, bearing interest to the Canadian people.

But even if one denied that deficits could ever become assets, one could not say that the country would have escaped them if some other

railway policy had been followed. "As a matter of fact," declared
Meighen, "it is my belief we would have had to face one of two alternatives . . . either an utterly demoralized service given to the people of
Canada by the roads, or vastly greater sums to be provided by the parliament of Canada to hold the roads in private hands." The Grand Trunk
Pacific would have had to be "held on its feet by the bounty of this
parliament in loans of millions year after year, operated as an isolated
and almost trafficless road." Its parent, too, "the Grand Trunk, which
was at the end of its tether by the admission of its directorate in 1918,
would have been out of smelling distance of its tether long years before
this, and the shoulders of the Canadian people would have been under
the staggering Grand Trunk, holding it there by a bounty of millions
voted by this parliament year after year." As for the Canadian Northern,
it could eventually have become a paying proposition but would first
have continued for a number of years to require large public assistance.
It was pointless to argue about whether public ownership was in principle
a good or bad thing; what had to be grasped was that there were great
concrete advantages in the course that had been pursued.

> The tremendous advantage of what has been done is not the improve-
> ment due to and flowing out of the fact that we have government
> operation; it is the improvement that arises from the fact that all
> these staggering unit systems are now one system, a system that is
> balanced in the east and west of Canada, a system that would be
> attractive to any band of capitalists in the world, a system that has
> every hope and prospect of growing into a great success.

There was one other fact to which he wanted to call the attention of
the House: many of the lines composing the Canadian National Railway System had not been built primarily for commercial reasons. Some
had been intended to promote colonization, others to serve some strategic
or high political purpose. Still others had resulted from blunders and
miscalculations.

> Consequently, it is no more than blindness and folly to compare the
> results of a system so collected, of factors of so various a character—
> colonization, political blundering, non-commercial, all the others—
> it is folly to compare the results of a system so constructed, so brought
> together with the results of a system that was projected by business
> men in order that they might get business returns. So when we
> say that the Canadian Pacific, on the one hand, has a surplus and
> pays ten percent on its capital stock, and that the Canadian National
> Road, on the other hand, has a deficit . . . and pays nothing on its
> capital stock, when we say that and believe that by saying so we
> are making a comparison of private ownership as against public
> ownership we are only talking the language of children.

So much for the "childish" moguls of Montreal, who were fond of making just this comparison to prove how inefficient and disastrous public own-ership really was.

There was nothing childish, however, Meighen thought, in looking forward with optimism to the future of the railways. If they were given a chance "there is abundant hope; there is, indeed, serene and well founded confidence, that good results, all that has been hoped for, will come." But would they be given the chance to perform to the best advantage? He concluded by expressing one misgiving which arose from the impression forming in his mind that political pressures might be preventing a full realization of all the economies that the amalgamation of the railroads ought to make possible.

> There should, it seems to me, be very many more economies resulting from the amalgamation. I am not a railway man, nor have I had the advantage of consultation with men who are, but I venture to say this, with a lot of deference . . . I venture to say that if error is being made at this time in the reorganization because of the bringing together of the system, it is the error of over organi-zation rather than of simplicity. The results tabulated in the press so far would seem to indicate that an effort is being made to retain everybody possible, instead of an effort to get rid of all the overhead we can, and seek to make the system no longer top heavy. I hope I am incorrect in my diagnosis. The tremendous, almost endless, table of departments, and departmental heads, and sub-heads, and assistants to presidents, and assistants to vice-presidents, and all sorts of door-keepers and paraphernalia that has been presented to the public so far, fills me with some fear. It seems to me that we have not yet had assurance that the hand of the railway master is at work rather than the hand of the politician.

Meighen's concern with economy in railway management was not, it appeared, fully shared by the new President of the C.N.R. Sir Henry Thornton took hold of his job with that great gusto one had a right to expect of a man being paid fifty thousand dollars a year. He was dynamic, ebullient, imaginative. In the very numerous speeches he delivered in all parts of the country he exuded confidence and enthu-siasm from every pore. The largeness of his ideas about the future of the system was equalled only by the magnitude of the problem he faced in trying to make it a profitable enterprise. Its salvation, he firmly believed, would be gained, not by a policy of niggardly retrenchment, by trimming services, laying off men or delaying improvements, but by enhancing and expanding service. Boldness was required if the C.N.R. was to compete successfully with the C.P.R. and boldness Thornton certainly possessed in most uncommon measure.

An interesting illustration of this, one that caused the Government some embarrassment, came to light in the spring of 1923 when it was reported in the press that Thornton had bought the Scribe Hotel in

Paris as European headquarters for the C.N.R. Details of the transaction were entirely lacking and there was much puzzled speculation about just what use would be made of the building and about how the system, with its huge deficits, could afford to extend itself in this way. The matter came before the Commons on June the seventh.[15] Meighen was absent from the House that day but close questioning by Sir Henry Drayton extracted a few bits of information from the Minister of Railways. Sir Henry Thornton, Graham explained, had decided that the C.N.R. should establish itself in Paris. The C.P.R. already had a large establishment there; as a result it was getting the lion's share of the European passenger traffic through Canada and carrying the bulk of the European freight as well. Nobody in Europe had ever heard of the Canadian National Railway System because it had no proper office on the continent. Consequently, according to the story Thornton gave the Government, Europeans planning to visit in Canada or emigrate to Canada bought their railway tickets from the Canadian Pacific and European shippers apparently directed their goods over C.P.R. lines. All this in spite of the fact that the C.N.R. had traffic arrangements with both the Cunard and White Star steamship lines.

Early in 1923 Thornton learned that the Scribe Hotel was for sale and he decided that possession of this property was just what was needed, as Graham expressed it in the House, to put the C.N.R. "on the front street in the city of Paris." Since there were other prospective purchasers he had to act quickly. Unfortunately the statute under which he administered the system forbade him to make capital expenditures without prior authorization by Parliament and the Government. But speed and secrecy were of the essence in transactions of this kind, so Thornton devised an ingenious plan. He deposited $2,000,000 of C.N.R. funds, the price of the building, in the Bank of Toronto. With that as security the bank loaned the same amount to one A. Aronovici, the agent of the C.N.R. in Europe, who proceeded to purchase the Scribe Hotel in his own name. However, he was not supposed to remain in possession very long. A New York syndicate, Graham announced vaguely and with a certain lack of conviction, was going to buy the hotel from Aronovici, after which he would repay the Bank of Toronto. Once that was done the C.N.R. would be able to recover its two million dollars. According to terms being negotiated between the syndicate and the C.N.R., the latter would have the option of renting as much space in the hotel as it required for its headquarters on mutually agreeable terms.

The Opposition in Parliament could hardly be blamed for thinking that there was something rather odd about these goings-on, something of "circuitous sinuosity," as Meighen remarked when he entered the debate on its second day. It had not been the original intent, he suggested, to have the New York syndicate enter the picture at all. In all probability, and neither Graham nor anyone else denied this, Thornton had originally planned to leave Aronovici in legal possession of the property, with the Bank of Toronto holding its cash security on deposit from the C.N.R., until the capital expenditure was duly authorized. Then Aronovici would surrender title and the bank be repaid. However, when a loud public outcry was heard against the C.N.R. investing two million dollars of what were in effect public funds in Paris property, it had been decided to get up a syndicate to provide the money. This was surmise, Meighen admitted, because the House had been denied access to all the essential facts in the matter.

It was true that very little real information was forthcoming from Graham, largely because he himself knew almost nothing about the purchase. Thornton had made his plan and acted without consulting the Minister in any way and the first the Government heard of the whole deal was evidently the newspaper story that Thornton had bought a Paris hotel. Who were the members of the syndicate? Graham was asked. He did not know. Was the syndicate under written contractual obligation to buy the property from Aronovici? He did not know. Had any effort been made by the C.N.R. to rent suitable premises in Paris before getting involved in this complicated arrangement? He did not know. What rental would be paid to the syndicate for the quarters used by the C.N.R.? He did not know. And he firmly stated that even if he did know, he would divulge no more information to Parliament until the whole transaction had been finally consummated.

It was, perhaps, a consummation devoutly to be wished but it was never accomplished. The next year the Government grudgingly vouchsafed a few more facts. There was, it transpired, no New York syndicate and evidently there never had been one, certainly none with any standing or resources. Efforts to finance the purchase in London had failed. The total cost of the property, paid out of C.N.R. cash, was a good deal nearer three than two million dollars. Title to it was now held by a new company which was a subsidiary of a subsidiary of the Canadian National Railways. It had taken over sixty thousand dollars just to effect the legal transfer of title from Aronovici (who incidentally had now been dismissed) to this sub-subsidiary concern. The Scribe Hotel had been rechristened *Le Palais Canadien*. "I congratulate the government on the new name," said Meighen sarcastically. "Le Palais Canadien has a sonorous sound. It falls on one's ravished ears with a soft and dulcet effect. I am sure the very name will bring many clients to the system, and will attract tenants to the building. Sincerely do I trust that somebody will be induced to occupy it pending the triumphant day when we are able to rid ourselves of the Scribe Hotel and all its memories."[16]

None of these additional facts, however, had yet come to light when Meighen rose on June the eighth, 1923 to say his say about the Scribe affair. The House was in Committee of Supply considering a requested appropriation of $73,000,000 for the Canadian National Railways. He had not been present the previous evening when discussion of the Paris deal had started, he remarked, but he had read the Hansard "and I must commence by saying that there was revealed last night the most extraordinary transaction, I think, ever disclosed to this parliament." It was clearly set forth in the statute under which Thornton and his board of directors administered the National Railways that, while they were to be free from political interference in the management and operation of the system, they had no power "to expend or pledge the money of this country, for capital investment, save with the antecedent authorization of the Governor in Council. And the Governor in Council had its powers only when the money for the express purpose had been voted by this House." Therefore they had hit on the device of Aronovici and the syndicate—"to call it a subterfuge is to honour it. . . . This thing is a scandal, this is an outrage, and when this became known to the minister Sir Henry Thornton should have been called to book at once. . . . What right, I want to know, has he to put his hand into the treasury of Canada and apply $2,000,000 to get the National Railways 'on to the main street' of Paris?"

> Where are we to-day? We have the property. We have it in our own name in this shape: Mr. Aronovici has the title and has mortgaged the property to us. As everybody knows this course is merely a substitute for having it in the name of the Canadian National Railways. We hold the property to-day, a property that is a capital investment in Paris; and all we have is a hope, annexed to which there is not a line, so far as this House has been informed, that some time some people over in New York will take it off our hands. Who the people in New York are we do not know. . . . That is the position Canada is in. And the minister thinks it is all right.

There was no assurance, Meighen continued, that if Thornton's action in this instance were approved he would not do the same thing again; he could "pledge this country in Paris, Berlin, South America, or anywhere he pleases . . . and the minister will think it is all right." While the country had little, if any, confidence in the C.N.R. board of directors—"The proportion of them who should have been appointed is small"—it had welcomed Thornton himself and wanted to give him a fair chance. But confidence in him would be severely shaken when the facts about this matter were grasped by the public.

At this point the discussion turned to the question of whether the

law had been broken. Graham, no lawyer himself, cited the verbal opinion of the C.N.R.'s solicitor that it had not been, inasmuch as the purchase
had not actually been made by the railway itself. At best, retorted
Meighen, there had been a legal evasion of the law; quite clearly the
spirit of the law had been violated. Two million dollars of C.N.R.
money were pledged to a capital expenditure and would not be recovered
if the much-talked-about but thus far invisible syndicate failed to buy
the Scribe. Graham was rescued from this argument about the law by
Motherwell, who came charging in to assert, in effect, that the question
of legality was irrelevant. What really bothered Meighen, he charged,
what occasioned Meighen's attack on Thornton, was not that the law
had been broken but his fear

> that Sir Henry Thornton is going to make a better job of the manage-
> ment of our National Railways than did his predecessor. That is
> what is the matter with my right hon. friend.
> An hon. MEMBER: That is true.
> Mr. MOTHERWELL: Of course it is true, everybody knows
> it. I have been watching my right hon. friend's antics in respect to
> our National Railway system, his solicitous regard for its success;
> but every time there is any evidence of the system doing better than
> formerly, well, he is pretty nearly prepared to take some kind of
> cat-fit over it.

Instead of trying to make political capital at Thornton's expense, Motherwell went on, one should take a large and generous view of the matter.
After all a man of Thornton's calibre had to be given wide discretionary
powers to use according to his best judgment. He could not make the
National Railways a success otherwise, nor would he be content to stay
on as president. Instead of worrying about whether the law had been
broken one should wait to find out whether Thornton used his discretionary powers capably. "The transaction is not yet completed; it will
be time enough to denounce the government or to denounce Sir Henry
Thornton when we know how this thing ultimately turns out. We
believe it will turn out exactly as the Minister of Railways has predicted.
If it does then what difference does it make whether the transaction is
done this or that or the other way?"

This doctrine, subsequently reiterated with some embellishments by
Mackenzie King, had a larger implication than Motherwell may have
realized, namely, that the real question was not whether an action was
lawful but whether it had the desired result. Meighen replied:

> The illuminating address of the Minister of Agriculture . . . had at
> least this merit: It was not so long as the last one; also it was equally
> pregnant. His argument is that unless we allow the manager of the
> National Railways to dig into the treasury without the knowledge
> of the government or the authority of parliament, you cannot get

a manager worth while. I venture to suggest to the Prime Minister, if he is here, that he keep a close watch on the Minister of Agriculture; a minister who pronounces these sentiments and apparently believes them is a very dangerous man to have in charge of funds. There is a measure of discretion, of course, given to all the directors, but it is given in the law, not by ministers on the floor of the House. . . . The manager of the National Railways has no more right to flout the law than a clerk in a bank or anybody else—or the Minister of Agriculture. . . . The discretion, let me impress upon the minister, is fixed in the law, fixed so clearly that no one in the world could honestly evade it or transgress it.

Motherwell having been disposed of, the next major voice to be heard was that of Robert Forke. The Progressive group was split on the Scribe Hotel issue, as on so many that came before the House. Some of them, along with two Labour members, J. S. Woodsworth and William Irvine, were outspokenly critical of the transaction while others were disposed to let it pass. Forke in his few remarks seemed to be trying to straddle the fence which divided his followers but to be taking particular care not to fall into the camp which was opposed to the Government on the question. He had, he said, some misgivings about Thornton's action but was even more disturbed by the eagerness of some members of Parliament to make political capital out of the affair. He thought that some men present, including Meighen, knew more about it than they had said, that they were withholding information and not taking the House into their confidence. In short, he suggested censoriously, the Opposition was more interested in embarrassing the Government than in helping all members to understand the facts. As for the Paris deal itself, he said: "I take this point of view—I may be right or I may be wrong—there is some mystery here that I would rather not see in connection with this matter." How Forke, having said that, could arrive at the conclusion expressed in his next sentence was no less mysterious. "But the consequences are so great, the issues are so tremendous, in regard to the management of these railways, that I am willing to let the matter go at the present time. . . . I do not believe it is in the public interest that this matter should be debated at any further length. I believe that incalculable harm has already been done by this debate."

In view of these observations Forke had no right to be as surprised as he appeared to be when Meighen turned his guns on him a few minutes later.

> . . . I am going to enter a protest against the too oft repeated assumption of the leader of the Progressive party . . . that he is sitting in final arbitrament over the moral quality of the other people in this House; nor do I thank him for the suggestion that I have certain information of my own about this transaction which I am concealing from parliament. I should like to know his authority

for this suggestion. I tell him I know nothing about this, not one word, not a tittle of information, that he does not know if he has sat through the discussion in this House. I ask him, before he attributes to me concealment of facts known to myself for partisan purposes, that he have some authority for his words. He goes on and he states with an air of sanctimonious complacency, that we of the opposition have no right to proceed with our criticism because we are seeking party advantage. I do not pretend not to be seeking party advantage provided that it is legitimate and right, and I do not expect the leader of the Progressive party to pretend to parliament not to be seeking party advantage provided it is legitimate and right. Am I to be deterred from criticism of a transaction which I believe to be wrong and which I believe I can demonstrate to be wrong, because if we succeed in bringing wrongdoing home to the government, it would be detrimental to an opposing party? Are we continually to be taunted, when we make criticism or censure that we are acting merely in a partisan spirit and not doing our duty as members of parliament? What does he consider to be our duty?

Mr. FORKE: If my right hon. friend would ask only one question at a time, I would have some chance to remember it.

Mr. MEIGHEN: I proceeded on the assumption that the hon. member's mind can carry more than he thinks it can. I will put my questions one by one in future.[17]

The morning after this debate Meighen read a very hostile editorial in the Ottawa *Journal,* strongly criticizing the Opposition for the stand it had taken and ridiculing the idea that Thornton should first have had the consent of the Government before going after the Scribe Hotel. He then dictated a letter to P. D. Ross, proprietor of the *Journal,* lodging a protest against the editorial which, he said, had treated the attitude adopted by the Conservative party "in a tone not only of antagonism but of contempt." There were, he reminded Ross, two basic principles governing the management of the C.N.R. "Constant fidelity to the first, namely, noninterference in operation, is of no more vital concern to the success of the National Railways than an equally firm fidelity to the second,—the control of Parliament over capital expenditure.... I am sorry indeed that the Journal should countenance and still more that it should become the protagonist of the abandonment of the only safeguard which Parliament possesses over the vast proportion of Canada's finances."[18]

Ross' defence was not unlike that advanced by the Government. The editorial, he replied, had been written before he had read Meighen's speech in the House. "Had I known you would take the position you did so vigorously, some of the expressions in the article would have been modified." But he was not going to retract anything. He thought the Paris transaction would probably turn out well enough and in any event the "property is an asset which at worst could be sold again for a loss not likely to be large...." But aside from the merits of this particular action by Thornton, "a deep feeling lay behind the Journal's article. . . ."

> I mean this: Canada, in the National Railways matter, is trying the biggest experiment in public ownership the world has seen. The experiment is viewed with suspicion by half our people, including practically all of "big business" whose viewpoint, consciously or unconsciously, is chiefly that big business should be left as free as possible to exploit the Community. Our National Railways experiment, therefore, is beginning not only under tremendous financial strain, but under great public doubt. The most dangerous part of this doubt consists in the idea that the management may be inefficient. Anything that lends to accentuate such doubt is liable to have a disastrous effect on the whole experiment, and it seems to me that the doubt is being accentuated by the criticisms which have been meeting Sir Henry Thornton. . . .
>
> To sum up, I cannot imagine that any mistake Sir Henry Thornton can make at present can cost Canada so much or so need exposure as to call upon us to risk the loss liable to result from a course which may help to destroy public confidence at this early date in his ability and management.[19]

Meighen's rejoinder to this was a bit tart. "The hope of sale of the property without loss is, I may say, to my mind a strange defence for an illegal purchase. . . . I consider a strict and faithful holding of the Directorate and Management within the compass of their statutory authority just as vital to the success of and to public confidence in the National Railways as refraining from interference on the part of Parliament and Government with management or operation within the orbit of the Directorate's powers."[20]

The correspondence with Ross on this subject ended there but in the meantime Meighen had received the same kind of reproach for his legalistic attitude to the Scribe matter from Sir Joseph Flavelle, of whose good faith he had not the slightest doubt and whose judgment he usually respected above that of almost anyone else.

> I am concerned [wrote Flavelle] in the persistence of the critical attitude of the Conservative Party towards the Thornton administration of the Canadian National Railways. I am even more concerned at the willingness to bring the administration of these Railways into the field of party politics. This criticism and opposition commenced immediately following Thornton's appointment; hence the Paris incident does not stand by itself. If it did, I could understand the Leader of the Opposition directing attention to the statement that two millions of dollars had been advanced to a syndicate to acquire property in Paris, but even then being careful to support the policy of giving the Railway Board a fair opportunity to carry on and demonstrate its success or failure over a reasonable period of time. I am not sufficiently acquainted with public opinion to make what I say of value, other than in expression of my own view, but I will be surprised if there has not developed in the country a query as

to the wisdom of the Conservative Party putting itself on record as hyper-critical of the Thornton administration before it has had a chance to work out its plans. No party in Canada is wholly responsible for public ownership being wished upon us on this huge scale. A set of circumstances which became too strong for control forced the issue, and a Conservative Unionist Government gave expression to it by passing the necessary legislation which has given us the National Railway System.

I have been anxious, as I am sure others have been anxious, at the heavy expenditures by Thornton. It may be that he is a man of vision and capacity, who plans these heavy expenditures in the belief that the return will come in increased business which will warrant them. If he is right, and gives a demonstration of his wisdom and courage in the results secured, there will be general satisfaction and there will be no political credit to his premature critics. If he is wrong and makes a mess of it, or by reasonably common consent does not succeed, the opportunity for the Opposition to score against the Government will be present. An alert Opposition can sufficiently indicate the danger signals without being committed to antagonistic relationship with an administration which the country prays may succeed.

I am not in any way in Sir Henry Thornton's confidence. I have been consulted in no particular in relation to his plans. I have had no personal means of forming an opinion of his capacity. I have some little knowledge of his problems. I am indebted to you for this. I am jealous, however, that whoever administers the property, is given a fair chance to demonstrate his capacity before being subjected to sharp criticism. I am equally jealous that the Conservative Party shall not prejudice its position and permit the existing Government to score as the broad large friend of this necessitously publicly owned enterprise.

I write remembering that a layman on the outside does not understand the parliamentary game, nor has he knowledge which qualifies him to speak with authority as to the procedure whereby public or parliamentary opinion is affected. With a recognition of these limitations, I venture to put my views before you.[21]

Meighen answered this in a friendly but uncompromising tone.

. . . I feel by no means resentful but rather indebted to you for communicating with me on this subject. It gives me not only the advantage of your own opinion and the grounds therefor, but, as well, an opportunity of placing myself right as respects the course I have pursued in Opposition toward the Sir Henry Thornton regime.

In the first place, you are not right when you intimate that my criticism and opposition commenced immediately following Thornton's appointment. In the discharge of the task to which Sir Henry Thornton was appointed, I have never yet offered him any criticism whatever. This is true in the absolute unless a danger signal which I set up on the day of the delivery of the National Railways statement in the Commons . . . would be considered a criticism. In that speech

. . . I merely expressed a fear that there was developing an over-manning at the top. My criticism in the latter part of last November was grossly misstated in certain of the press. I made no attack upon Sir Henry Thornton whatever. I attacked the Government for throwing out of office a President who had succeeded, and a Directorate who had done credit to their positions, and I called on Sir Henry Thornton to come to Canada and take on the work to which he was appointed . . . I expressly stated that I knew nothing of his abilities, and that if he were fitted for the position, the salary named was in no way too much.

I think your letter now received is founded on a misconception of the functions of Parliament as distinguished from the functions of the National Railway Directorate. When under the late Government the policy of placing our National Railways under the Directorate control was adopted, certain carefully thought out principles were implanted in our law and form to-day the very basis and meaning of our National Railway Act. . . .

In this way we sought to combine freedom from parliamentary interference in operation, and the sane control by Parliament of capital commitments and of the money of the people. These principles were expounded by Sir Robert Borden as well as by many others in Parliament, and were consistently and rigidly adhered to throughout our tenure of office. The records of Hansard are replete with the most unambiguous exposition of these principles and of the law that embodies them on the part of leaders of all parties of the time, and as well they are replete with pledges of the firmest loyalty and adherence to them on the part of members of the [present] Government. . . .

I might add that the chief cry of the Opposition two years ago was that Parliament had been deprived of its rightful control of public affairs, particularly in the National Railways. We all know that Parliament had not been deprived of any control which it could exercise in the public interest. It would be folly, I know, for me now merely because of that cry to repeat the offence myself. This I have most scrupulously avoided doing. At the same time, he would be a poor Leader of the Opposition who would allow the enemy not only to permit the occupation by the Railway Directorate of the sphere rightly allotted to it by Parliament, but the invasion as well, of the sphere which Parliament has rightfully reserved to itself. I always have been and am still quite prepared that in the management of the property entrusted to their care, the President and Directorate shall be left unmolested, but if they are to have power to make investments of this nature, or indeed capital investments at all, that is equivalent to putting them in control of the whole finances of Canada. If as Leader of the Opposition I let such a thing as the purchase of a hotel in Paris go without a protest, I would be in a very weak position to attempt to take a stand when confronted with the accumulated results of such a policy.[22]

The positions of Ross and Flavelle on the one hand, as revealed in this correspondence, and of Meighen on the other were really irreconcilable.

The former were saying that there were larger issues than legality at stake, while Meighen would deny that there could be a larger issue than that. It was probably the Scribe episode in part which prompted the assessment of Meighen written by Flavelle a couple of years later: "Meighen is clever, destructive in debate, crushing in criticism, but there it ends. No one possessed of such qualities can command heart loyalty. He is by qualification intended for first lieutenant, in place of commander-in-chief. He should be the fighting mate of a big, simple human man, who would win the affection and command the respect of his party. He is the terrier who worries the other fellow, the auditor who discovers mistakes in the man of constructive imagination."[23]

It was a new experience for Meighen to be accused of an unfair and overly critical attitude towards the publicly owned system, and a disconcerting one when it came from men like Flavelle and Ross who were normally friendly to him. He was much more accustomed to being attacked as the man chiefly to blame for public ownership, as the friend and champion of the nationalized railways. The suspicion of him in certain places on this score had by no means disappeared in 1923. In fact at the very time he was defending his stand on the Scribe Hotel purchase he was about to encounter the beginning of a concerted and sustained effort to remove him from the leadership of the party, an effort motivated in part by a belief that a sensible reconsideration of the railway problem and the implementation of a different policy must await his departure. This was not all that was behind the attempted ouster but the belief was undoubtedly held by some opponents of public ownership that if the Conservative party returned to power, which seemed possible since signs of its recovery were visible, and if Meighen remained at its head, the country could never be rescued from the financial disaster which a continuation of present railway policy would bring. Meighen was still adamantly unrepentant on this subject and they could hardly see how any man who professed such opinions about the future of the C.N.R. as he did and argued in all seriousness that its deficits were really potential assets in disguise could be trusted to deal with the problem from a business-like point of view.

Rumours of dissatisfaction with Meighen's leadership on the part of the Montreal tycoons and of their desire to see him make way for someone else had been frequently aired ever since the general election but in 1923 this became more than a matter of mere speculation and surmise. Early in May the Montreal *Herald,* a paper of Liberal proclivities owned by a company ostensibly headed by Senator J. P. B. Casgrain but reputedly controlled by Lord Atholstan, proclaimed in large black type: "BIG INTERESTS IN CONS. PARTY AFTER MEIGHEN'S SCALP." The story under this headline, a dispatch from Ottawa, recounted that the opposition of the big interests to Meighen had come out into the open, that most of the Conservative senators, including Smeaton White, President of the Montreal *Gazette*, wanted a new leader for the party. "They do not forgive Mr. Meighen for having saddled the Dominion with public ownership, woman suffrage and low tariff. Their man is Sir Thomas White with Bob Rogers as general manager." Ah, there was "good old Bob" again! "It is freely stated to-day that should Mr. Meighen go, the big newspapers which support the Manufacturers' Association in Montreal, Toronto, Hamilton and Winnipeg will immediately start a virulent campaign against the Government."[24] For some time the *Herald* had been following a "soft" line on public ownership, perhaps because attacks on it would embarrass the Liberal government now in office. This admittedly was strange behaviour for a newspaper directed by Lord Atholstan but Meighen thought he knew the explanation. "The scheme," he told C. C. Ballantyne, "happens to be for Lord Atholstan to appeal to Liberals through the 'Herald', to become gradually content with the National Railways and as time goes on to become enthusiastic. All the while he is to appeal to Conservatives through the 'Star' to rise in rebellion against the Conservative leaders for, as he claims, being responsible for the National Railways. It is a game worthy of his Lordship."[25]

Whether or not this was Atholstan's game, there could be no doubt about the attitude of his major organ, the *Star*, which in the summer of 1923 launched a characteristically bizarre crusade to save the country from politicians and public ownership. A series of editorials was published, some of them prominently displayed on the front page, under the general title "The Whisper of Death." The burden of these manifestoes was that Canada, staggering under an immense debt produced mainly by railway nationalization, stood teetering on the brink of disaster. The first of them appeared on July the twelfth. "There are times when silence is treason," was its arresting first sentence and then it continued:

> Today in the boardrooms of powerful corporations, in the head-offices of great financial institutions, in exclusive clubs and wherever the men foregather whose business it is to know about the financial conditions of the country, a **THING is being said that threatens the life of this nation**—and yet the busy people of Canada, intent on making a living, are left in fatal ignorance of the impending peril.
>
> . . .
>
> It is time for emergent measures.
>
> . . .
>
> **What is needed is new blood.**
> Public life today does not seem to contain a man with the courage, the foresight, the public confidence which would equip him to rescue the Dominion from the rapids.
> . . . It is our misfortune in these latter decades that our great

men no longer seem to go into public life. They go into business, into finance, into transportation, into the learned professions.

But in a time of grave national crisis we must "dig them out." We must conscript ability, pluck, vision and statesmanship.[26]

On July the twenty-fifth the *Star* announced that there were "three possible ways out." The first was a "Coalition of National Safety. The getting together of the best elements in both the Conservative and Liberal parties. . . ." A second way lay in "strengthening . . . the Conservative party by the admission of strong men and improvement of the leadership." Still another possibility was the "strengthening of the Liberal party by the admission of strong men." The *Star* admitted that it had "an especial faith in the Conservative party because of its great traditions and past achievements." It was true that "nominal Conservative leaders" in recent years had been "found toying with Socialism and plunging into the adventure of Government ownership of railways" but "the great Conservative party of Canada is not dead, even if it does seem to be suffering from stagnation and astigmatism and amnesia at the head."[27] Similar jeremiads couched in lurid apocalyptic language, along with fierce attacks on the politicians who were really to blame for everything, continued to flow from the typewriter of the *Star*'s editorialist for several weeks. ". . . His Majesty's Loyal Opposition, which . . . is the constitutional party to propose drastic changes of policy, has nothing to offer but 'piffling' criticisms." ". . . if the very name of 'Canada' is not to disappear from the map, our men of courage and vision must bestir themselves and **seize the loose reins of government from the slack hands of professional Parliamentarians of both parties. . . .**"[28] **"Professional politicians are the most timorous, earth-bound and pariah-ridden cowards in creation."**[29] "We are 'bullish' on Canada, but terribly 'bearish' on her present breed of politicians."[30]

Although by no means the *Star*'s only target among the politicians, Meighen certainly was the chief one, the one most frequently singled out for abuse in the editorials, and he was justified in describing Lapointe's allegation that he had deliberately inspired the "Whisper of Death" pieces as an "adventure in mendacity."[31] He was a "piffling" critic of the Government who had "toyed" with socialism, a leader under whom the Conservative party had fallen prey to "stagnation, astigmatism and amnesia." Because it was that party which the *Star* counted upon to snatch the country back from the brink of bankruptcy, the first "emergent measure" presumably ought to be his replacement by one of those "strong men" the *Star* talked so much about. But the articles neglected to mention one of the worst of Meighen's many crimes, the stinging rebuke he had administered to Lord Atholstan in the presence of witnesses for the *Star*'s roorback on the eve of the general election. His Lord-

ship must have remembered that occasion as clearly as Meighen did,
though no doubt less fondly, and it was believed by some who knew the
plotting peer that his desire to have revenge for that humiliation had
more to do with the *Star*'s present hysterics than all the railway deficits
put together. It was suggested by one of these men, who had been talking
to Atholstan, that Meighen might make amends and produce a kindlier
tone of the *Star*'s editorials by writing Atholstan a letter, repenting in
some way the harsh things he had said during that stormy interview.
But Meighen declined to do this.

> . . . as to the "Montreal Star" situation. First of all, it is quite
> right that I expressed to you the opinion that from the standpoint
> purely of political success it would have been better had I suffered
> in silence and refrained from any characterization of [Atholstan's]
> conduct in the late campaign. At the same time, I would rather
> step out of public life than state to him or to any one what I know
> to be false, and I would do so were I to state or intimate that any
> statement of mine to him was in the least degree unfounded in fact
> or unmerited by himself. Knowing the whole circumstances as I
> do, a more bitter castigation, if such were possible, would have been
> well deserved on his part. . . .
> I do not think any letter I could bring myself to write would
> produce good results just now. I think he must first realize the
> failure of his campaign against me. My own judgment is, rightly
> or wrongly, that his campaign helps me in Montreal and west of
> that city. It may do some harm eastward, but I doubt very much if
> this will offset the advantage gained. I quite agree with you that
> the time should come when . . . an understanding would be the
> part of wisdom, and I am ready to play any honourable part to bring
> such understanding about.[32]

Judging by the comments in most newspapers, both Conservative and
Liberal (and including the Montreal *Herald*), the *Star*'s death whisper-
ings were not going to be taken too seriously. Its pronouncements were
received with a mixture of amusement and scorn by what it angrily
described as "the pap-fed, time-serving public prints."[33] But in one
quarter at least, and not unexpectedly, they were regarded as the pure
essence of distilled wisdom. Almost as though at a nod from Atholstan
there issued forth from the bailiwick of Robert Rogers in Winnipeg in
the middle of August a proclamation that a committee had been formed
there to arrange a national convention of the Conservative party. Rogers
was a somewhat unlikely saviour of the nation from the professional
politicians, among whom he had always been proud to number himself,
but there could be no question of the sincerity or the long consistency
of his desire to embarrass and discredit Arthur Meighen, who assumed
that this was the purpose of the declaration from Winnipeg. "I see a
Committee has been formed in Winnipeg to call a Dominion convention,"

he remarked. "Between this and the 'Whisper of Death' campaign, I am having an awful time holding my job!"[34]

It seemed no mere coincidence to Meighen that Rogers had again come out in the open just when the *Star* was in the midst of its emotional frenzy. He was sure, and so were others, that "the Hon. Bob" and the noble lord had together hatched a plan of attack against him. Some of Meighen's friends noticed that Rogers was now avoiding them altogether or meeting them with less than his usual affability. Brenton Macnab, who had published in *Le Matin* a savage attack on Atholstan after the first two "Whisper" articles appeared,[35] wrote: "I *suspect* Rogers & Atholstan have had an understanding of sorts. R.R. was different the last time I saw him."[36] Senator Lorne Webster, one of Meighen's most trusted political associates in Montreal, reported that he was seeing "our friend '*Bob R*' walking stately through our streets. He does not call on me—why?"[37] Arthur Ford, too, was "inclined to think that our friend Bob Rogers is working with Lord Atholstan in endeavouring to make trouble for you" by engineering a demand for a convention.[38] "The inspiration of the matter," Meighen answered, "was just as you divined."[39] It was widely believed that, while the Rogers clique and Atholstan's Tory mouthpiece were making all the noise, their desire to bring about Meighen's downfall was shared by the "big business" interests generally in Montreal. However, it was by no means certain whom they had in mind to take his place. Sir Thomas White, Sir Henry Drayton and Sir Arthur Currie were all mentioned, along with Howard Ferguson, whose vote-getting ability had been so impressively demonstrated in the Ontario election. And so, not surprisingly, was Gouin. According to the Toronto *Mail and Empire* Atholstan had him ticketed as the saviour of the country. Regrettably he had been unable to secure a radical change in railway policy on the part of the King government but he might be able to draw around him those "strong men," those "men of courage and vision," that "new blood" required to rescue Canada from her impending doom.

In singing out for a national convention the Rogers Conservatives of Winnipeg were not alone. Some others who joined in the chorus were under the influence of Rogers perhaps, sharing his suspicion of Meighen, his bitter memories of Union Government and of the post-war attempt to attract Liberal support. Arthur Ford reported to Meighen that there had been a meeting of the executive of the Ontario Liberal-Conservative Association which, he said, was attended mainly by ward-heelers from Toronto, and the talk had been all about a convention. He thought this reflected the influence of Rogers and Atholstan.[40] Conceivably Ferguson also had something to do with this; he may not have been immune to the allurements of national leadership, for which he was being touted in some places, and rumours of friction between Meighen and him were rife.

However, there were many others who had no thought of changing leaders but believed a convention was desirable. After all, the meeting of senators, members of Parliament and defeated candidates in March 1922 had formally resolved that there should be one and had appointed a committee to arrange it. That decision had not been rescinded and there was therefore an obligation to go ahead. As yet the committee had done nothing and had decided during the 1923 session of Parliament that it would continue to do nothing for the time being. This inertia was regarded by some men in the party as most unfortunate. Certain ones, such as Stevens, who had put the summoning of a convention at the top of his list of recommendations, thought that a gathering of the faithful would boost party morale and greatly assist the development of an organization. Some of Meighen's friends were convinced that a convention would resoundingly endorse and confirm his leadership, thus silencing his enemies. And Rodolphe Monty, one of his leading French-speaking allies, argued forcefully that from the standpoint of Quebec a convention would be particularly helpful in promoting party unity, though he does not seem to have shared the opinion of some Conservatives in that province that as long as Meighen remained leader the party would be in a hopeless position there. After a conversation with Monty on the subject Meighen went to Toronto to consult certain persons and the day after this visit reported to Monty that he had had long discussions of the question with White, Sir Edward Kemp and others. ". . . after leaving you," he wrote, "I decided to exhaust every possible effort to bring those who count in these matters to my point of view and went very far indeed in pressing the case yesterday." But the men in Toronto who counted were opposed to staging a convention.

> . . . I frequently wished through the discussion that you were there yourself. I put the matter from the standpoint of Quebec solely. I made it very clear that insofar as other adverse activities in further away parts of the country were concerned, I was not worrying at all, but that I had been thoroughly convinced by you that a convention would clear the air from the standpoint of Quebec no matter what its verdict should be and would give new life and unity to our party. . . .
> I think I may say that I succeeded in some degree in convincing them that some advantage would accrue from the standpoint of Quebec—at least I thought I had made that much progress. They were very determined though that there would be more harm than advantage. First of all they stressed very strongly the strained financial conditions of to-day. . . . They said it would be absolutely impossible to get the money to make the convention a success. At the same time they seemed equally convinced that if we just drive

persistently and vigorously along, hammering away, we will win the next contest.

On the question of financing a convention they were adamant. Also, they thought that a certain man [Rogers], one whom you and I have often discussed, would probably make matters very difficult for us at a convention by the proposing of resolutions on policy and other things which would be most embarrassing. I cannot say that I was greatly impressed with this latter fear because I say we can face these things and handle them. The first matter, that of finance, is, of course, the big practical thing.

Anyway these men gave me as well the view of others, and I am thoroughly convinced of this, that I cannot possibly bring on a convention except by an absolute public announcement of my resignation otherwise. They think this would result in demoralization and in a great weakening of my own personal strength because they think the public, and especially the Conservative Party, would conclude that I was over-sensitive and unsteady.[41]

Although the desire for a convention was shared by some Conservatives who, like Monty, were unconnected with the alleged Atholstan-Rogers plot, the only organized agitation continued to come from Winnipeg where it had originated. Because of Rogers' influence and his predilection for causing trouble, the motives behind the agitation were automatically suspect to Meighen and his associates. Even when Meighen was assured by some of those engaged in it that they had no designs against him personally, and that their object was rather to have a convention approve a new platform as was done every so often by provincial conventions, he was cautiously sceptical. The suggestion that a new platform was needed might in itself be construed as an expression of want of confidence in his leadership. If such lack of confidence were widespread a convention there ought to be, and he would step down if it decided that he should do so. But as dissatisfaction seemed to be concentrated so markedly in Winnipeg and on Montreal's St. James Street, he was not inclined to regard it as representative of Conservative sentiment as a whole. After talking to some of the Winnipeggers he wrote to Kemp:

You know the situation very thoroughly. The Winnipeg men, or rather quite a number of the officers of the Winnipeg Association, are very tenacious on the subject of a National Convention, and the subject must be disposed of in some straight forward and satisfactory way. Doctor Tolmie has been bombarded by them very forcibly on the question since he went west. Personally I am very strongly of the opinion as a result of my observations this summer that in general there is no feeling for a Convention at all. The Winnipeg men referred to above all tell me personally that they have no thought whatever of a change of leadership, and indeed Mr. Rogers has stated to a close friend of mine that he will nominate me himself. Nevertheless I confess I cannot understand their persistence on this

question. If they merely want to confirm my title all they have to
do is to get together and pass a resolution to that effect and the
trouble is over.[42]

Kemp's answer emphatically reiterated that a convention would be of no
use, either in formulating a policy platform or in clearing the air in
Quebec.

> For the life of me I cannot understand what reasons those who are
> advocating a Convention have to put forward. . . . Provincial Con-
> ventions surely cannot be a precedent for a Federal Convention of
> the Conservative Party. Provincial policies are simple matters as
> compared with policies for a Federal Political Party where there are
> so many divergent interests. There is no precedent for holding a
> Federal Conservative Convention. It is only the Liberal Party that
> have called such Conventions for the purpose chiefly of passing fake
> platforms. For the Conservative Party to allow itself to be drawn
> into a position of this kind is, in my opinion, nothing short of stupid.
> We all know what a difficult country Canada is to govern owing to
> its great area and conflicting interests. For a *Party* in opposition
> to try and lay down a political platform is only to furnish the enemy
> with ammunition to destroy it. . . .
>   The situation in the Province of Quebec is unique. . . . This
> Province is largely controlled by race and religion. The tide is
> running with the political successors of Sir Wilfrid Laurier because
> of their pride in him as a French-Canadian Prime Minister. The
> Grand Trunk Head Office question, Conscription, and "Big Inter-
> ests" (including Sir Lomer Gouin), all worked against our success
> in the last elections. A Federal Convention in my opinion, would
> not change this situation. If it is to be changed, some other method
> will have to be employed.[43]

The views of Kemp and others of like mind prevailed, whether for good
or ill, and there the matter rested.

Meanwhile, Meighen had been travelling a good deal around the
country during the summer and autumn of 1923. To begin with, three
weeks were spent in the Maritimes starting in the latter part of July,
during which he took part in the Cape Breton by-election and spoke in a
number of other places. He never felt quite as sure of his ground when
he entered the Atlantic provinces as he did when on the more familiar
soil of Ontario and the West, never quite so closely in touch with currents
of local opinion. The fact that there were no Conservatives in the Commons from Nova Scotia or Prince Edward Island made it more difficult
to keep abreast of affairs in those provinces and right now, when one of
the periodic agitations about Maritime rights and grievances was devel-
opping, he was uncertain just what climate of opinion he would find
there. Already he had been asked to telegraph five hundred words to the
Halifax *Herald*, giving his views about "what people of Maritime

Provinces can reasonably hope accomplish in a campaign for Maritime rights. What in your opinion are vital things we should concentrate on."[44] He had declined, saying that he "could not . . . do so in any other than rather platitudinous language which I do not like adopting."[45] The fact was, of course, that in common with everybody else he did not know how the manifold economic problems of the region could be solved within the framework of Confederation. This being the case, and wanting to avoid platitudes, he might be in an awkward position on his tour if he were expected to say something sensible about the matter. However, the visit went off without mischance. Addressing service club meetings which were non-political, he pleaded with his audiences to give a loyal trial to the National Railway System with which there was a lot of dissatisfaction in the Maritimes; at political meetings he castigated the King government as only he could do and he came home convinced that the outlook for the Conservative party in the Atlantic region was much brighter than it had been two years earlier.

Also most encouraging was a giant political picnic on Saturday, September the first at Cartierville, a suburb of Montreal, arranged jointly by the French and English-speaking Conservatives of the city. Preparations for this event had been going on for weeks and throughout the day the spacious grounds of Belmont Park were thronged with thousands of men, women and children enjoying the food, fun and games provided for all. The majority of them sported Meighen buttons, which struck the reporter from the *Gazette* as quite a phenomenon, considering that so many of these people "two years ago, or even one year ago, would have spurned the suggestion with indignation that they would be cheering for the Rt. Hon. Arthur Meighen." Arthur Sauvé and the other leading lights of the provincial Conservative party were conspicuous by their absence but Meighen was accompanied by Monty, Fauteux and Ballantyne. The speeches commenced at three o'clock in the afternoon. There were eight of them before Meighen's turn finally came but the crowd stayed on and when he finished speaking at seven-thirty there were still thousands of people gathered in front of the platform "ready to listen for any length of time the ex-premier might wish to speak." He began by talking for twenty minutes in French about his own problems in the province of Quebec.

> It will not be within my power, in the French language, or even in my own tongue, to thank you as I ought to thank you for this truly magnificent demonstration of your friendship and hospitality. A public man has much to endure, and of its buffetings and contumely I think you will agree I have not been spared—but there come times when all seems to be abounding good will, and such an occasion is this joyous afternoon. To this day I have looked forward for weeks and I assure you that its happy memory will linger with

me long indeed. It has been to me the greatest pleasure to meet many hundreds of you personally before the programme opened, and now I feel not as one from afar with a fog of misunderstanding between us, but as a man in the midst of his fellow citizens rejoicing in the opportunity of talking with them face to face.

No Canadian, wherever he lives, need come into this province of Quebec with any of the feelings of a stranger. I never do. . . . There is much I could wish for here in the way of better treatment politically, but nothing I could wish for in the way of better treatment personally.

Some of his opponents, he continued, had been saying derisively that he was going to

come to this platform today, to ask forgiveness for errors of the past. Well, I don't make any claim to have lived without error; but if I commit error, I am ready to take the punishment. All I want to say is that my public conduct has been dictated every day of every year by a desire to serve this country. In peace and in war I have advocated the same policy for the whole Dominion. If I have erred against you I have erred against Manitoba and against Ontario— the province of my adoption and the province of my birth. In times of peace, and in times of peril, I have done what I thought was best for Canada. One thing I ask you to remember. It is this: those who attacked me never had the task of governing Canada through the black nights of a terrible war—and they are not making any great success of governing Canada even now in the daylight of peace.

He then went on to characterize the treatment of him by his opponents in Quebec.

An unjust, an infamous campaign has been waged for years in this province trying to mass French-Canadian sentiment against me, on the ground, that I am hostile to their race. A more unjust fabrication was never invented by political malignity. Among my closest friends are French-Canadian public men, who have known me intimately throughout the fifteen years of my public life, and they know how false, how maliciously false is this whole wretched campaign. Not a word has ever passed my lips, not a thought, or an act has been mine to give even the shadow of an excuse for these attacks. I am told the good people of Quebec are getting very tired of this senseless fiction. You and I, you people of the French tongue and we who speak the English tongue—are joint heirs of this great Canadian heritage, your fathers and our fathers—the Cartiers of Quebec and the Macdonalds of Ontario—settled the terms upon which we live together as one nation. By these terms we abide. In the great compass of Confederation we are proud to stand united. We rejoice in your prosperity; we rejoice in your expansion. Let the expansion go on—let English and French multiply, and replenish the land—of the two great races let this nation be built and happy will be its lot on earth. The Conservative party which stood at the cradle of Confederation, will stand guard over the compact and protect with equal solicitude the rights of Catholics and of Protestants, of English and of French.

What, he asked rhetorically, was the purpose of this campaign of slander against him?

> To get men elected to Parliament. They must blind the people some way—and this way they have tried now for years! It is not only false, but it is vicious. Racial animosity is the worst kind of treason you can propagate in a country like ours—and I want these words to apply everywhere, in every province. These words I have already spoken in every province of this Dominion. Speaking today to thousands of my countrymen, I ask of you one thing and one thing only. Demand to know the truth, and see that you get the truth—and strike down every man who scatters mendacity and prejudice for the sake of votes.
>
> This appeal I make not only on my own behalf, I make it on behalf of our country. I am not necessary to the unity of Canada, but justice and fair play are necessary to the unity of Canada; they are necessary here and necessary everywhere. If the people insist on the truth and get the truth, they will give every man justice and fair play, and that is all that is due to a public or any other man.[46]

It was an eloquent plea but a useless, hopeless one. Those who heard it at first hand might cheer Meighen to the echo but his opponents found mendacity too effective a weapon to be discarded in favour of mere truth. The welkin in Quebec would soon be ringing once again with horrendous tales of his bitter, vicious, undying hatred of the French and all his hopes would wither, unfulfilled.

Shortly after the Cartierville picnic Meighen started out on a tour of the western provinces, across the territory that was more like home to him than any other part of Canada. His first meeting was at Portage la Prairie, whence he retraced his steps to Winnipeg to address the Kiwanis Club, whose members greeted him by singing:

> We are with you to a man,
> We will help you if we can,
> Howd'ye do, Arthur Meighen,
> Howd'ye do.

It was, he remarked, "the first pledge of unanimous support he had ever had from any audience in his long political experience."[47] For it to come from an audience on Bob Rogers' home ground just at that time must have made it especially heart-warming! Leaving Winnipeg, he spent the next few weeks criss-crossing back and forth between the towns and cities on the prairies: Regina, Moose Jaw, Yorkton, Weyburn, Prince Albert, Lethbridge, Calgary. He also made a quick visit to the Coast. In Vancouver J. A. Clark, Member of Parliament for Burrard, had invited a number of prominent men to dine at his home with Meighen. The

importance Clark attached to the occasion and to his guest of honour was
not lost on his cook, who, without Clark's knowledge, left the drapes
open and invited some of his fellow Chinese to assemble in the garden so
that they might have a glimpse of Canada's "king." Meighen was to
catch the midnight ferry for Victoria. He left the dinner party about
eleven o'clock, went to his hotel, had his luggage sent to the boat and
then sat down to write one or two letters. Engrossed in that work he
forgot all about the passage of time until, too late, he suddenly recalled
that he had booked passage to Victoria. He rushed frantically to the
dock, found the ship had already sailed, so returned to the hotel, re-
engaged his room and went to bed. In the morning he put on of necessity the tuxedo he had worn the night before, walked across the street to
a lunch counter and sat down unconcernedly to have his breakfast.
Hearing that he had been seen eating breakfast in his dinner clothes,
Clark got in touch with him and urged him to buy a ready-made suit
before boarding the next ferry. There was no need of that, Meighen
insisted. He had plenty of clothes in his luggage at Victoria and would
be there in a few hours; he would just wear what he had on. And that
is what he did.[48]

On his rounds through the prairies during this tour Meighen was
kept constantly busy meeting people, consulting with party workers and,
of course, delivering speeches, some at political meetings, others of a
less controversially partisan type. In Yorkton he appeared at the colle-
giate institute and left a characteristic message with the pupils: "Whatever you do, do it with all your might. . . . This is the single law of life
that is worth remembering." No one was ever hurt by hard work, which
was the inescapable lot of those who wanted to be happy and to succeed.
If success eluded them they ought not to blame others. ". . . the only
person who can stop you from success is yourself. . . ."[49]

Probably the high spot of his trip through the West, simply because it
was a new experience for Meighen, was his visit to a stampede at Raymond
in the ranching country near Lethbridge. The free-wheeling abandon
of the stampede atmosphere was not entirely congenial to a man of his
reserve and intellectuality but he entered into the spirit of the thing and
acquitted himself well. The local correspondent of the Lethbridge
Herald described the scene:

> It was a crowd in which was blended the old and the new west.
> The lean, ambling cowman with his broad hat, gaudy neckerchief,
> fur-covered chaps, and clanking spurs, rubbed shoulders with the
> man from the nearby threshing rig, hurriedly "dolled up" in his
> Sunday best, out with the wife and the kiddies and the "lizzie" for
> an afternoon of fun at the big annual celebration.
> Here and there were squaws with sober papooses eyeing you
> from the safe depths of their roving cradles. Bucks, a-straddle

good-looking saddle horses, rode over the grounds in groups, while schools of lean Indian dogs, emitting that camp-fire smell that is always a quick cure for "that tired feeling," roamed hither and thither, frequently giving [the cowboys] a little practice with the rope.

That was the kind of a crowd that Arthur Meighen celebrated with last Saturday. He disproved the report that he is a cold-blooded recluse. The ex-premier made himself very much at home, chatted with the farmers, nodded to the "punchers", smiled at the babies, and climbed on the fence and reached over to shake hands with Ray Knight, the big noise of this and a hundred other first-rate stampedes.

"I don't envy you your job, Mr. Knight," smiled Mr. Meighen as Ray gave him a welcoming grip.

"Nor I yours, Mr. Meighen. I'm quite satisfied," grinned back the big westerner, and everybody clapped.

And that meant that both these men—filling widely different positions in the life of the nation, and both vitally important—were quite satisfied with their jobs. Arthur would be as much out of place swinging a rope at a cunning range calf as Ray would be addressing an audience in Massey Hall.

Mr. Meighen proved himself a good sport. Much to the delight of the crowd . . . he mounted a saddle horse provided by the rodeo committee and for an hour mingled right with the boys around the chutes.

It was a master stroke.

And so it seemed to the local Conservative leaders of Raymond and Lethbridge, who were watching from the sidelines and among whom was Meighen's old friend and one time law partner, A. B. Hogg. "They were all smiles, and with good reason."

When it came time for him to give the inevitable speech, this one brief and non-political, Meighen stood up in an open touring car parked in front of the grandstand. He had uttered only a few words when a calf bawled loudly from one of the corrals.

" 'I note I have a rival in the yard,' smiled Mr. Meighen.

" 'Mackenzie King,' yelled someone in the crowd, and everybody laughed heartily. It was a jolly crowd."[50]

Meighen came back to Ottawa satisfied that almost everywhere things were looking up. The one major exception to the generally favourable position of things was, of course, the Province of Quebec and the two distinct but related aspects of that situation—the hostile sentiment of most French-speaking Canadians and the enmity of powerful elements in the Montreal business community—were to occupy more of his time and attention until the next general election, and afterwards, than any other political problem. He was not deceived, by the heartening mani-festation of good will at the Cartierville picnic or by the generally cordial reception given him everywhere he went in Quebec, as to the difficulty of winning the confidence of French Canada. ". . . none," he commented, "can receive public men better than the people in the Province of Quebec."[51] But it was one thing for them to extend hospitality, as they did so charmingly, and another to extend their active support. ". . . I anticipate," he wrote, "[a] wild and reckless anti-war; anti-imperial; anti-Meighen campaign when the time comes and have no delusions as to the difficulty of surmounting these obstacles which racialists are thus able to interpose."[52] As for the tycoons and their journalistic voices, the *Star* and the *Gazette*, evidence was to multiply rather than diminish of their desire to put some new man at the head of the Conservative party.

Not long after his return from the West Meighen received a letter about this side of the Quebec problem from J. B. M. Baxter, the New Brunswick Tory whom he had taken into his Cabinet shortly before the 1921 election. Whether Baxter was acting at Meighen's request as an intermediary between him and the Montrealers or they were attempting to use Baxter to put pressure on Meighen is not clear. In general the latter relied most on Lorne Webster and Ballantyne for advice about this problem. It is certain, though, that Baxter in the letters he wrote Meighen from time to time about the machinations of the magnates favoured making conciliatory overtures to them. He was emphatically and publicly on record as agreeing with them about public ownership, their governing obsession,[53] and this may account in part for his consistent advocacy of concessions and for the conclusion he seems eventually to have reached, without ever explicitly stating it, that if a suitable new leader could be found it might be best for all concerned if Meighen stepped down. At any rate he wrote from Montreal early in November to say that he had been talking to Lord Atholstan, the "Cardinal" as Baxter called him, to sound him out about the prospect of his giving financial and journalistic help to the party. He found that Atholstan disliked the King government (this would come as no suprise) but was rather vague as to just what he was prepared to do to help get rid of it.

> It is clear that the "Cardinal" is opposed to the present crowd; that he has *some* inclination to mix in the fight; that he would prefer to assist the party under another leader; that his last thought was that Ferguson might be a possibility but I think that the latter rather talked platitudes at his meetings here & that that line may not be followed up. . . .
>
> The . . . job is to convince the Cardinal that the best thing to do is to make a fight with you as leader, & that there is no other possibility. . . . I suppose . . . that in the end it will be a question of terms.
>
> Now the thing may come up directly with you at any time when neither I nor anyone else may be with you for consultation. If so, do not be stiff. Concede everything but your skin and vital prin-

ciple in order to get the assistance that not only you, personally, but the party, must have in order to win. Remember that there are several hundred thousand good Tories who are looking to you principally & to some others of us, in a subordinate capacity to bring them into power & do not let anything but the very gravest matters prevent the party getting all the assistance it can. We *must,* simply *must* get rid of Mackenzie King. After that we can take a long breath and begin all over again.[54]

The day after Baxter had talked to Atholstan and again a few days later the *Star* attacked the politicians in its familiar "Whisper of Death" style. The second of these effusions, which Meighen regarded as directed primarily against himself, was a two-column front-page editorial which read in part:

WANTED!

A Canadian Baldwin

By common consent, "the great emergency" has come to Canada.

There never has been a time in our history when we were in such dire need of courageous leadership, of far-seeing statesmanship, of constructive and recuperative achievement.

But we lack the men.

We have a ministry of mediocrities holding onto office by their finger-tips. It is a notoriously divided Government. . . . It may fall apart any day. . . .

Across the House, we have a divided Opposition, in neither wing of which has the country the smallest confidence. They are led by men either too little known [Forke] or too well-known [Meighen].

What is wanted is a Canadian Baldwin, who will lay down drastic policies of retrenchment, of balanced budgets, of cutting loose from ruinous railway policies, of adequate tariff protection, of pumping in selected immigration. . . .

Canada has not lacked for great emergencies or great men.

But are they all dead?

Have we lost the seed?[55]

This tribute to Stanley Baldwin, the tax-cutting, surplus-building, economy-minded British Prime Minister and Chancellor of the Exchequer, may have comforted that gentleman if it ever came to his notice (ironically his government suffered a severe reverse at the polls about a month after the editorial appeared), but it was not calculated to mollify Meighen or induce him to treat with Atholstan in the spirit proposed by Baxter. "If anything more were necessary," Meighen told the latter, "to fix my determination to hold this post up to the time of the Cardinal's death, these laughable efforts of his would be sufficient. From every source I hear that the paper has become really ridiculous. . . ."[56]

Ridiculous or not, the *Star* was not yet ready to call its dogs off

Meighen. A fortnight later he was touring the Eastern Townships and took occasion at Victoriaville to deny the charge frequently made that he was a hard loser and poor sport. "I am a cheerful loser," he said, "and have never spent two such happy years as since I left power." This inspired a particularly malicious editorial in the *Star* entitled "The Happy Warrior." Meighen, it observed, "probably runs less risk than any other possible leader of the Opposition of having his happiness ruined by being conscripted into office." Such risk as there was he "could wholly avoid . . . by resigning his position as Leader of the Opposition." The editorial then asked:

> Why doesn't he take this obvious precaution? There are material minds in the community who will say that there are ten thousand good reasons why he does not thus insure himself against disaster. Sir Wilfrid Laurier—who was one of the shrewdest politicians Canada has ever produced—invented the scheme of paying the nominal leader of the Opposition ten thousand dollars a year, in addition to his indemnity, just for being leader of the Opposition.
> That is, Mr. Meighen gets fourteen thousand dollars a year for remaining in his present position.
> Can this have anything to do with his happiness.[57]

Even for the *Star* this was a very low blow and at once other Conservative papers across the country cried "Foul!" rising to Meighen's defence with such vigour that there resulted more favourable comment than he had enjoyed for a long time. The Quebec *Chronicle* pilloried the "baronial broadsheet" of Montreal and declared that "the stench of the cess-pool from which this missile had been dredged up reeks in every line. . . ."[58] The *Star,* observed the Sydney *Post,* "was able to assassinate some Conservative candidates in Montreal in 1921, but Mr. Meighen is proof against its stiletto."[59] The *Standard* of Kingston, recalling the "Whisper of Death" calamity howlings, said that everyone had shrugged them off with the remark that " 'Athy' is raving again." But now "we have his Lordship breaking out in another direction. Not having made any headway in his endeavour to have Mr. Arthur Meighen supplanted as the Conservative Leader in the Dominion and a clothes horse of the noble Lord's choosing substituted in his place, our dear friend, the Lord, now proceeds to find fault with Mr. Meighen because the Conservative chieftain declares himself to be a 'good loser.' Of course that does not please 'Athy,' who cannot understand what a good loser means, and who thereupon proceeds to go into the editorial manure pile, which he seems to keep handy in his office. . . ."[60] The Calgary *Herald's* rebuke was no less pointed for being couched in somewhat more dignified language. Referring to the *Star's* innuendo about the ten-thousand-dollar stipend, the *Herald* said:

It is amazing that so unworthy a suggestion should come from any responsible Canadian newspaper. That it has been made shows the depth of the feeling against Mr. Meighen that animates the Montreal crowd.

If anything were needed to rally the Conservatives of Canada to firmer support of Mr. Meighen as leader of their party it would be supplied by these underground and mean attacks of the Montreal Star and the interests that paper represents. That he has inspired their enmity is sure proof that he has withstood their attempt to put over something decidedly more to their profit than to the profit of the people of Canada.[61]

Further evidence of a closing of the ranks behind Meighen elsewhere than in Quebec was afforded by the action of the Ontario Liberal-Conservative Association at its annual meeting in declaring its "unbounded confidence" in his leadership and pledging him its "undivided support." Similar expressions came from provincial conventions in Saskatchewan and Alberta in December. Meighen was accompanied to these meetings by Howard Ferguson, who explicitly disclaimed all desire to be anything more than Prime Minister of Ontario; so the threat to Meighen's position from that direction, if threat there had been, was ended. But more piquant by far than Ferguson's presence was the appearance of Robert Rogers on the convention platform at Saskatoon. Somehow he or someone on his behalf had wangled an invitation, unbeknownst to Meighen until it had been extended and accepted, and there was some rather worried speculation in both Ottawa and Saskatchewan about whether the "Hon. Bob's" intentions were honourable. Was his purpose merely to help breathe some life into the party in a province where it was certainly not very lively? Or was it more sinister, perhaps to lobby among the delegates for a national convention while sowing a few seeds of anti-Meighenism on what he hoped might prove fertile ground?[62]

These apprehensions proved to be unfounded. He had come to bury the hatchet and a polite, ritual reconciliation between him and Meighen took place. "I stand here to-day to compromise all my differences," said Rogers. "I thought and still think that my position in regard to the Union Government was correct, but we cannot live in the past. I have no further political ambitions, but I do now place at the disposal of the Conservative party for the remainder of my life whatever I possess of energy and ability."[63] Meighen responded by saying that he "was glad to be on the same platform with the Hon. Robert Rogers. For decades he has stood in the front rank and carried the standard in many a hard battle for the Party."[64] Rogers' statement was quite sincere, Simon Tolmie, who passed the word on to Meighen, was assured from Winnipeg. He did have one ambition but it was only to get into Parliament again. He "is reconciled to his position and . . . is quite ready to try a whirl in

South Winnipeg in the hope of rehabilitating himself in an advisory capacity in the Conservative rank."[65]   If true, that was good news for Meighen and probably it was true.   Rogers, realizing that there would be no national convention, that Meighen was going to stay in the saddle and that there were signs of a real Conservative revival, would not want to be on the outside looking in when the great day of victory came.

With the announcement of returns from the Halifax and Kent by-elections near the end of 1923, the sweet scent of victory did seem to fill the air.   In 1921 the Halifax seat had gone to a Liberal by a majority of nearly five thousand; it was now taken by a Conservative by a margin of nearly two thousand votes.   Kent had favoured the Liberal in 1921 by about fifteen hundred; in the by-election it returned A. J. Doucet, nominally an Independent but actually a Conservative, with a majority of two hundred.   For the first time since the general election the Opposition had a French-speaking member in the House of Commons and this brought cautious hope that its difficulties in French Canada were now on the wane.

CHAPTER TEN

"O GOD! O MONTREAL!"

BECAUSE OF these various developments the prospect as 1924 dawned looked fairly pleasing to Meighen everywhere except in the one province and it soon looked better still, even there, as signs of a possibly serious rift in the Liberal party were to be seen. The rift was caused, at least superficially, by disagreement over tariff policy and for a time put that issue at the centre of the political stage where Meighen had been trying unsuccessfully for several years to place it. During the 1921 campaign and afterwards Mackenzie King had tried to consign the tariff question to limbo by playing up other alleged issues such as autocracy, militarism and national unity. In speaking about the tariff he had faced in many different directions but his actual policy during the first two years of his administration was to leave the moderately protective system unimpaired. Although his personal inclinations may have been to lower the tariff, the influence of some of his leading colleagues such as Fielding and Gouin was exerted in the other direction, while the interests of Quebec, where most of his own party's strength lay, precluded any pronounced downward revision of the duties. This stand-pat policy allowed Meighen to have a good deal of sarcastic fun at the expense of the Government by contrasting its deeds with the glowing promises of the 1919 platform, but at the same time it left unfulfilled his predictions of a compact between King and the Progressives on the basis of substantial tariff reduction.

Early in 1924, though, there were signs that it was about to be fulfilled and that Meighen's long-desired union of Conservatives and protectionist Liberals might at last materialize. The practical difficulty facing King in his attempt to reconcile the views of the Progressives with those of his protectionist followers had been shown during the debate on the 1923 Budget, which was criticized by the Progressives for its failure to reduce the tariff and escaped rejection in the House by a margin of only nine votes. Meighen had often warned the Farmer members that they would be betrayed by King and they apparently now felt that the betrayal had occurred. They held the balance of power and therefore the fate of the Government in their hands. There was good reason to doubt that they actually wished to bring about its downfall, thus precipitating an early election, by combining with the Conservatives against it. However, because they were so largely a group of individuals rather than a disciplined, united party, their actions were somewhat unpredictable, and the fact that they had voted against the Budget indicated that unless concessions were made to them on the tariff the Government's position might become uncomfortably precarious. Thus King was in the position of having to make a definite commitment regarding the tariff, of having to choose between two alternatives: he had either to continue the existing policy, thus running the risk of alienating the Progressives completely and courting defeat in the House; or to make such reductions as might satisfy the Progressives and hope that most of his own supporters would acquiesce in this decision and stay with the ship. He chose the latter course and the speech from the throne at the opening of Parliament in February announced that reductions would be recommended, especially of the duties on agricultural implements.

This choice had been presaged, at least in the eyes of Conservative spokesmen and the Conservative press, by the resignation of Gouin from the Government early in January. His stated reason for retiring was ill health but it was widely believed that he acted in protest against a change in the tariff either already decided upon or about to be. Whether protest or not, his self-removal facilitated the change and rid the Cabinet of the man upon whom his friends in Montreal had confidently counted to prevent any serious departure from established tariff policy. The change was also made easier by the absence of Fielding, about whose illness there could be no doubt. Like Gouin he had been a conservative influence in the Government. Though he remained nominally Minister of Finance he was absent from the House throughout the 1924 session and, in fact, his distinguished parliamentary and administrative career was at an end. It is doubtful that King regretted very much the disappearance of either of these men, which left him, and with him Lapointe, in stronger command of the party than before. Fielding, his chief rival for the leadership in 1919 and the man designated by Laurier as his own successor, outshone King in Parliament, enjoyed exceedingly high repute from coast to coast, and held strong views on some matters which were quite at variance with King's. Gouin's outlook was more high Tory than Liberal; his retirement left the more liberally minded Lapointe as indisputably the leading spokesman for French Canada in the Government.

The announcement in the throne speech that the customs duties on agricultural duties would be lowered caused a lot of commotion, not least among the manufacturers concerned, and Meighen was given every encouragement from that quarter to take a strong stand against the reduction on the ground that it would be a severe blow to the industry.

Orally and by letter in the month of March they impressed upon him, as did trade-union locals and city councils in the communities affected, the dangers of unemployment and bankruptcy which the industry would face if the tariff were tampered with; and they plied him with memoranda giving the statistical data on which their alarm was founded. Officials of Massey-Harris Company, the leading Canadian implement maker, were most importunate of all in trying to enlist his support in opposing a step which, they claimed, would put the industry in Canada at the mercy of its American counterpart. They and other spokesmen for the manufacturers were especially apprehensive about the competitive power of the International Harvester Company, which J. G. Hossack, solicitor for Massey-Harris, told Meighen "is feared by every Company in America and Canada; to incur the displeasure of that Corporation means to go out of business." Hossack emphasized that he was "forwarding this information to you through my own personal interest in the industry and it does not represent an official communication from my Company. Indeed, I know that some of the Directors of my Company would prefer to treat with the King Government but I do not share that view and have not the least confidence."[1]

Before long Meighen began to realize that, despite their earnest representations to him, some officials of Massey-Harris did indeed "prefer to treat with the King Government" and to avoid creating a political issue which would embarrass the administration. He heard that one of them had assured J. A. Robb, Acting Minister of Finance, that the company had no real complaint about the tariff changes and when Robb at the end of April presented some further adjustments in the schedules the company's grievance evaporated completely. These adjustments, presumably resulting from pressure exerted by the implement makers and especially, perhaps, by Massey-Harris, provided for additional reductions in the duties on the raw materials they used. As these would lessen their cost of production, their competitive position was thereby improved. Although Meighen had been assured emphatically that no such palliatives would suffice as a remedy, Massey-Harris now issued a press statement which, far from expressing any objection to the Government's whole action regarding the tariff, said in effect that things would not be so bad after all if Canadian farmers would loyally buy implements made in Canada. With considerable justification Meighen felt that he had been led down the garden path by these people, who had urged him to attack the Government on their behalf and then had themselves suddenly capitulated.[2]

The agricultural implement industry, however, was not the one on whose behalf Meighen would have chosen to fight the battle of protection. As far back as 1911 he had argued eloquently and convincingly that this was one industry that was being given more tariff protection than it needed in order to compete with American manufacturers in the Canadian market, that the duties on implements should therefore be reduced and that their reduction would be consistent with the spirit and intent of Sir John A. Macdonald's National Policy.[3] Some lowering of these tariffs had been carried out between 1911 and 1921 and there was reason to think that now, in 1924, the implement industry was strong and efficient enough to require still less protection than it had been receiving. This, indeed, was the sum and substance of the Massey-Harris statement, which made it impossible to argue that the Government's policy would send the implement makers to the wall.

Whatever the genesis of this statement may have been, whatever discussions between Massey-Harris officials and the Government may have led to its issuance, its political value to the Government was not inconsiderable, for it lessened the danger of substantial defections by Liberal protectionists on the Budget vote. It made it easier for these people to reconcile their desire to uphold the protective system with their desire to maintain the Government and the great majority effected that reconciliation without difficulty. There were, though, a few defections, far fewer than the Conservatives had hoped for. Several Liberal members criticized the new policy and four of them—two English-speaking Quebeckers and two Ontarians—joined with the Opposition to vote against the Budget. More startling than the votes of these four bolters, however, was the resignation of a fifth, Walter Mitchell of Montreal. Mitchell had entered the Commons in 1921 after being Provincial Treasurer of Quebec under Gouin for several years. The business men of Montreal had looked to him almost as much as to Gouin to exercise a desirable influence on the general economic and financial policies, and especially on the tariff and railway policies, of the King government. If there was no proof that Gouin's resignation from the Cabinet was a protest against the tariff reductions, there was equally no doubt that Mitchell's resignation from the Commons was. He said so very explicitly in a letter to King which he made public the day before the vote was taken on the Budget.

The opening of Mitchell's riding of St. Antoine, where a by-election was set for September the second, created a nasty, complicated situation, in which Meighen unwillingly became involved, with consequences that were to provoke renewed attacks on him by the Montreal newspapers. It was an intricately tangled web that illustrated nicely some of the hazards faced by a party leader. The *Gazette* was insistent that Mitchell be returned to the House of Commons and urged the Conservatives to support him. Meighen, who had long fully realized that the co-operation of dissatisfied Liberals was essential to the success of his party in Quebec, was inclined to agree that this should be done provided certain terms were met. But his counsellors in Montreal were of a different view. Ballantyne, Webster, and Monty all thought a genuine Conservative should run in a riding that had returned Conservatives in every general election before 1921. Ballantyne sent Meighen a memorandum which, he said, was "based on information from a well known influential Conservative and bears out what I have been endeavouring to convey to you for some time." The memorandum explained, though far from clearly, that Mitchell's resignation was part of an elaborate plot hatched by persons unnamed in Montreal, the object of which was not to save the protective tariff but to do away with public ownership of railways. Meighen, argued Ballantyne, should go "very slowly towards bolting Liberals" who were playing that game.[4] Although it was by no means impossible that such a scheme had been worked out and though Meighen would ordinarily have refused to lend himself to it in any way, he was anxious just at that juncture to have the *Gazette* and those it spoke for on his side if this could be managed. ". . . I have not the least doubt myself," he told Ballantyne, "that this is in the back of the heads of a great many of the elect. However their assistance is welcome. When the time of dictation comes we will be prepared for that eventuality."[5] So, running the risk of offending his own friends and being accused of gratuitous interference in constituency affairs, he made up his mind that the party should support Mitchell if the latter would agree to his conditions. "If ever there was a case," he told Arthur Ford, "where a leader risked a great deal with his own party in order to hold the support of a newspaper I did so in St. Antoine, in my efforts to get Mr. Mitchell to stand where I could ask the Conservatives to support him."[6]

The stand Meighen insisted Mitchell must take was one of outright opposition to the Government. A mere statement of dissatisfaction with its tariff policy would not be enough; he must renounce his party. Support of Mitchell on these terms was acquiesced in by Ballantyne and Webster, and approved as well by Fauteux. The terms were also acceptable, Ballantyne reported, to Smeaton White of the *Gazette*. "Your decision in the matter about Mitchell coming out as a straight opponent of the Government is quite satisfactory to Senator White."[7] It was anything but satisfactory, however, to Monty and to many Conservatives of St. Antoine, who wanted to be able to vote for one of their own instead of for a Liberal like Mitchell. These people were determined to hold a nominating convention. When Ballantyne took this news to Smeaton White and told him how bound "some of our enthusiastic friends are to put a candidate in the field, he showed considerable heat, and stated that Mitchell would not likely run if this occurred but in his opinion the Conservatives would be making a mistake."[8]

To no avail Meighen attempted to have the convention postponed.

Aided and abetted by Monty, a faction known as the "Below-the-Hill" group, resentful of the dictation of rich and patrician business men like Webster and Ballantyne who on Meighen's behalf had tried to have the meeting delayed, went ahead and called it for the middle of June. F. W. Stewart, President of the English-speaking section of the Montreal Liberal-Conservative Association, sent Meighen a bitter account of what happened in the convention hall. He had moved a resolution that the choice of a candidate be deferred, explaining that this was the wish of the national leader. But Monty had stood up and spoken strongly in favour of nominating someone then and there. Stewart's resolution had been defeated and the convention had chosen Leslie Bell, a young Montreal lawyer, as Conservative standard-bearer in the by-election. ". . . we were overwhelmed," wrote Stewart ruefully.[9]

As it happened the convention in St. Antoine met on Meighen's birthday and the following day Monty wrote sweetly in a congratulatory note: "I believe that the electors of St. Antoine Ward have made you a nice birthday present in choosing, as conservative [sic] candidate, Mr. Leslie Bell, distinguished lawyer of Montreal."[10] As a matter of fact it was probably the least welcome present Meighen had ever received because, as Monty well knew, his wish was that no candidate at all be chosen as long as there was a chance that Mitchell would take the desired position against the Government. With a Conservative in the field Meighen's hope of being able to persuade him to do so was greatly diminished for he could no longer hold out to Mitchell the prospect of Conservative support on a large scale. The one thing that might clear the air was Bell's withdrawal from the race and this Meighen, with the help of his Montreal friends, set about to secure. Their method was to ostracize Bell; by refusing to have anything to do with him they sought to convey the sobering truth that he would not be able to count on the support of the official organization. ". . . things are working out nicely. . . ," Ballantyne reported not long after the nominating convention. "The policy of silence that we are all pursuing is having its effect and I believe in a week or two more Mr. Bell will drop out."[11] But this was much too optimistic. Bell wanted to be the candidate and regarded himself as the duly chosen one, Monty was all set to launch a big campaign on his behalf, and as the weeks went by there was no sign that either of them was prepared to give way.

Meanwhile, in conversations with Meighen, Mitchell had shown no real willingness to make a declaration of opposition to the Government's general record and policy and Meighen came to the conclusion that there would therefore have to be a Conservative candidate after all. But if the Liberals refrained from nominating someone against Mitchell, as Meighen feared they would, and if there were a two-way fight between Mitchell and Bell, the Conservatives in all probability would suffer humiliating defeat. Consequently Bell, whom Meighen regarded as a weak candidate, would have to be replaced by someone else. In the opinion of Webster and Ballantyne that someone else should be W. M. Birks, a business man of their own class, but Meighen, when Birks had earlier been suggested to him as a possibility, had expressed doubts as to whether he would have a strong appeal to the voters.[12] Now, with Mitchell evidently unavailable to the Conservatives on terms that they could accept and with Bell obstinately refusing to step down, Meighen turned to General Sir Arthur Currie, Principal of McGill University. If Currie could be induced to accept a nomination in St. Antoine a master stroke would be accomplished. For one thing, Bell would find it hard to oppose a man who stood so high in the public estimation and probably would consent to efface himself at last. For another, Currie was well and favourably known to the Montreal magnates, with some of whom he sat on the university's Board of Governors and on the board of the Bank of Montreal. The *Gazette* could hardly prefer even Walter Mitchell, one of its favourite public men, to so eminent a figure as Currie. More than that, if the latter agreed to run he would be enthusiastically endorsed by the Montreal *Star* and its owner, who, Meighen was aware, believed that the General would make an excellent leader of the Conservative party.[13] Atholstan, indeed, seems not to have shared Smeaton White's belief that the Conservatives should support Mitchell. Meighen received word that A. R. Carman, editor of the *Star,* whose thoughts faithfully mirrored those of his employer, believed that Bell should be asked to get out "in the interests of a better known and bigger candidate. He seemed to think that supporting Mitchell would show sign of weakness in the party, for with a proper candidate nominated, if the Conservatives cannot carry St. Antoine, it is no use to try to elect a Conservative Government."[14] Knowing what "better known and bigger candidate" Carman and Atholstan were thinking of, Meighen tried to persuade Currie to accept a nomination.

> . . . to this end [I] enlisted the help of Lord Atholstan. I reminded him that he had very definitely pressed forward the idea that Currie should be leader, and urged upon him the absolute necessity of a man aspiring to such leadership first becoming a Member of the Commons, getting the atmosphere and knowing the ways and rules of Parliament and thus qualifying for his high post. I told him that if Sir Arthur would accept nomination for this vacancy I would exert every influence to have him receive such nomination and to make his election assured, and then he would have opportunity in Parliament to show that he was the man to lead the Conservative Party. I visited Sir Arthur Currie and urged the same arguments on him; assured him that he would be welcomed by all our followers in the

House, and that the road to advancement would be open to him just as soon as he would demonstrate that he was best qualified to take the lead.[15]

"I did not know," Meighen added, "that he could not qualify, but may say . . . with the utmost sincerity that I had not the least fear of his competition."[16]

When Currie declined to be a candidate Meighen acted on the suggestion he had earlier deprecated and asked W. M. Birks to stand. Birks consented and was duly nominated at a meeting organized by Ballantyne and Webster. With two candidates in the field and the by-election only a month away the Conservative party had a great schism on its hands. Monty was infuriated by Birks' appearance on the scene. An angry passage at arms took place between him and Webster, who described the encounter in a letter to Meighen. Monty had been "as unreasonable as ever. He thinks I see too much of you and is not inclined to speak for Birks and still favors Mr. Bell. He even went to the length of suggesting that we had better hold a convention this fall and find out who the leader in the Province of Quebec really is. I had rather a hot time with Mr. Monty, but I informed him I was taking my instructions from the leader and I expected him to do the same."[17] Upon receipt of this Meighen, who was by now too deeply involved in the muddle to extricate himself, wrote to Monty, requesting him to get Bell to retire, which doubtless did nothing to improve Monty's temper.[18] Not long afterwards Bell did drop out with voting day only two weeks distant and, outwardly at least, the schism was ended.

Unfortunately the breach was repaired too late or too superficially to save the Conservative party from ignominious defeat on the second of September. Mitchell decided not to run and the Liberals nominated W. J. Hushion, a Montreal alderman. The margin of Hushion's victory was much narrower than Mitchell's had been in 1921 but even so the result was a grievous blow to the Conservatives. It was interpreted in Liberal circles as a mandate for that "freer trade and freer living for the great mass of the people" which Mackenzie King assured the voters of the riding his government stood for.[19] The downcast losers, on the other hand, attributed it mainly to the months of demoralizing internecine warfare between the Monty-Bell and Webster-Ballantyne-Birks factions. Meighen's original misgivings about Birks' suitability proved to be justified and Bell, who won the seat in the general election a year later, would probably have fared better against Hushion. Another cause of the Conservatives' defeat, according to the Ottawa *Journal,* was the "preference of hundreds of well-to-do among them for the invigorating breezes of Murray Bay and Metis, as against the plebeian and proletarian atmosphere of a democratic polling booth. While Mr. Birks' supporters were damning Free Trade . . . from the porches of the *Manoir Richelieu,* Mr. Hushion, like a good disciple of Tammany was fighting among the voters down around Bonaventure Station, and in politics the long distance fighter loses every time."[20]

The *Gazette* and the *Star,* however, had their own explanation: Arthur Meighen was to blame. It is always dangerous for a party leader to intrude on the affairs of a constituency and to try to dictate to the local people with regard to nominations for the House of Commons. Meighen might have been better advised to keep his hands out of the St. Antoine mess, although this was a case where he would be damned if he did and damned if he didn't. As it was his efforts to control the situation pleased no one. The fiasco in St. Antoine, said the *Star,* pronouncing judgment in its usual *ex cathedra* style, showed the absence "of any evidence of foresight on the part of those who had arrogated to themselves the role of leadership."[21] The *Gazette* waxed especially indignant over Meighen's failure to secure Mitchell's candidacy as a Liberal protectionist with Conservative backing. By demanding too much of Mitchell, in the form of avowed and total opposition to the Government, and by failing to prevent the nomination of a Conservative party candidate, Meighen was responsible, it seemed to believe, for this disastrous and wholly unnecessary reverse. In a long, gloomy lead editorial on "The Conservative Party" the *Gazette* concluded that the only salvation for the party lay in holding a national convention. "It is the simple truth that for long the practice has been to attain the office of leader by descent and not by election by representative delegates, and it may well be worth trying the latter method. For of a surety, whoever may lead the party when the fight is on will possess greater prestige, greater authority and greater popularity if he is the choice of a convention, and can rally to his support all who believe the policy he represents best calculated to promote the welfare of Canada. It would be folly to pretend that such a situation now subsists."[22] The Quebec *Chronicle,* whose support Meighen had generally enjoyed until now, echoed this pessimistic sentiment. After referring to his "austerity and isolation" and his inability to judge men accurately, it predicted that he would "remain a spectacular but impotent figure in our public life." The Conservatives, it said, "may stand by the leadership of Mr. Meighen, if they wish, but in doing so they will inevitably condemn the country to endure a further period of Progressive domination. . . ."[23]

When the *Chronicle* continued its campaign in succeeding weeks Meighen finally dictated a letter to its editor, Arthur G. Penny, whom he had always counted on as a dependable friend.

I am venturing after some hesitation to write you a few thoughts growing out of recent criticism of myself in the Chronicle. No one who knows me will say that I am over-sensitive to criticism: were such the case the extraordinary share which has been mine would have long ago made life insufferable. I do confess though that I felt very keenly the adverse attitude of the Chronicle commenced some months ago. More than all else together—for the other attacks I have no trouble in understanding—more than all these I was surprised and hurt that a paper under charge of Sir William Price and yourself should engage in a campaign for my retirement. Neither of you could have tried to put yourself in my position and get a grasp of what my resignation at the present time would mean. To desert my post now in the midst of struggles that follow a great reverse, while the members whom I lead in the Commons are all true and virtually all in the Senate, would be an act of cowardice and treachery which would make me a subject of execration and at which my children in later years would blush when the party records would portray it to posterity.

That the restoration of our party fortunes in Quebec after they were submerged and almost extinguished under the tragedies of the war is difficult no one knows better than I do. If the human being lives who can re-establish them in even a moderate length of time or more rapidly than I can, and who has any remote chance of being accepted as leader would to God you could locate him and start him on the path out of which leaders are taken. . . . Meantime a task inherently difficult, almost deperately so, is being enormously multiplied when newspapers of Conservative tradition and principles are undermining the measure of confidence I enjoy among the rank and file of the party. . . .

You personally; the late Sir William Price personally have for so long, until recent months, done so much to assist me that the change now is hard, very hard, to accept. You are under no obligation to me—quite indeed the contrary—all that I know. . . . perhaps you will tell me what error I have committed so fatal that confidence must be withdrawn. My other difficulties I understand and I can face them and depend on it I will.[24]

Penny replied with obvious mortification that he was no longer determining the *Chronicle*'s editorial policy; that that was being done by the paper's new proprietors.[25]

Fortunately for Meighen's peace of mind, as on former occasions when Atholstan had been after him, this anti-Meighen editorial barrage from Conservative papers in the Province of Quebec, and the public discussion it stimulated, produced a certain reaction in his favour. Brenton Macnab sprang to his defence with a series of articles in *Le Matin* and in the rest of the country friendly newspapers did the same. Resolutions came in from Liberal-Conservative Associations affirming confidence in his leadership, while friends and strangers alike sent him letters to the same effect. One arrived from his old St. Marys schoolmate, Fred McCutcheon.

I must confess I'm rather glad you have merited the outpourings of the wrath of the Montreal Tories. Any man that is entitled to their approval ought to have serious misgivings about his position. I presume the election in St. Antoine is only an excuse for the C.P.R. die-hards to make another protest against public ownership of Railways and nothing in your public life is more deserving of praise from the public of Canada generally than your outspoken unequivocal attitude on this question. You're a pretty good Tory and I'm afraid I'm not. . . . Wealth will always have undue influence in the councils of any political party but the Lord help the Tory party when Baron Atholstan and his friends dictate the policy and the leadership. "Purblind leadership" it will be with a vengeance.

Stick to the fight. Don't let it be one-sided. Say the things that you can so well that will give your friends a chance to cheer out loud.[26]

In acknowledging this Meighen replied:

. . . the task of leading the Opposition in Canada is an exceedingly trying one. Not so onerous as that of leading the Government, but more irritating. Your analysis of the Montreal situation is substantially correct. I think I see my duty and shall not be swerved from it, especially by those who have the least right to complain. At the same time I may confess to you frankly that to do so makes the work the labour of tenacity rather than of love.[27]

Another letter Meighen was both somewhat surprised and especially pleased to receive. It was from William Irvine, the Labour M.P. from Calgary, between whom and Meighen there was ordinarily no bond of common outlook.

Just a note [Irvine wrote] to say that I am glad you are out of favour with Sir Arthur Currie and the Montreal near-politicians. This is the best thing that could possibly have happened. It will serve to draw the West to your support; in fact, your few powerful enemies in the East are unwittingly re-establishing you in the West.

The man who dares to offend the Montreal interests is the sort of man that the people are going to vote for today. McDonald of Great Britain and Herriot of France are outstanding examples of that sort of man.

I congratulate you.[28]

The moaning over St. Antoine in the English-language press of Quebec had scarcely died down when an even more humiliating debacle occurred in November in West Hastings, Ontario. With one exception this riding had sent a Conservative to Ottawa in every general election since Confederation. In 1924 E. Guss Porter, who had held the seat continuously since 1901, on his responsibility as a Member of Parliament charged King's Minister of Labour, James Murdock, with having improperly used confidential information received by the Cabinet for his personal financial advantage. The charge was investigated by a parliamentary committee whose report exonerated Murdock. When the report was approved by the House, Porter resigned his seat and sought vindication from his constituents in the resulting by-election. Instead of being vindicated he was defeated, to the unbounded joy of the Liberals and the intense embarrassment of Meighen, who had encouraged Porter to proceed against Murdock and had vigorously supported him in the House and on the hustings. Both Porter and Meighen blamed the astonishing reverse in West Hastings on purely local factors, various extraneous issues and the liberal use of money by the Liberals. Porter, who seems to have had a keen eye for dishonesty, even alleged on what he claimed was good authority, that his opponent had paid some of his election expenses with counterfeit one-hundred-dollar bills![29]

To Meighen's critics, however, the disaster was further evidence of his failings as a party leader. It was noticeable that they had given him none of the credit for the striking victories in Halifax and Kent a year earlier but held him almost entirely responsible for the failure to win St. Antoine and the loss of West Hastings. The latter case, they claimed, showed that the people wanted, not picayune scandal-mongering, but constructive leadership and they interpreted this latest verdict of the electors as a clear expression of want of confidence in Meighen. The problem faced by the Conservative party, said the Montreal *Journal of Commerce*, was that "those who are leading the Party 'by the nose', as it were, lack the common-sense to drop a pilot whose eye for the rocks and shoals and quicksands of politics is not (to put it mildly) wholly unerring."[30]

One of the extraneous issues which in Meighen's opinion contributed to Guss Porter's downfall was outside the realm of party politics altogether, namely, Church Union. For many years a movement promoting union of the Methodist, Presbyterian and Congregational churches had been gathering momentum and had resulted in 1923 in an agreement between them known as the Basis of Union. To give effect to this agreement, legislation having to do with the property rights of the three churches had to be passed by Parliament, as well as by all the provincial legislatures, and in 1924 Robert Forke sponsored the necessary Bill in the House of Commons. There was no significant objection to the proposed union among Methodists or Congregationalists but the Presbyterians were sorely divided, with a sizeable element determinedly opposed to the disappearance of the church of their fathers and the spoliation of its property. Before coming to the House itself the Bill was lengthily considered in the Private Bills Committee, which heard arguments from the two groups of Presbyterians and the imposing array of lawyers retained by each side. The committee recommended certain amendments to the measure, notably one moved by the leading opponent of the Bill, William

Duff of Nova Scotia, which provided that the effective date of union should be postponed from June the tenth, 1925 to July the first, 1926 and might be still further postponed if a case already before the courts in Ontario arising out of the conflict within the Presbyterian church were not by then decided. When the Bill came before the House it was at once moved that the Duff amendment be deleted and June the tenth, 1925 restored as the effective date. It was on this motion that the main debate on Church Union took place.

Feelings ran high during the debate which was entirely on non-party lines, with each of the three groups in the House being divided, the Progressives less so than the others. Motherwell did take the precaution of circularizing his fellow Liberals before it began, admonishing them not to provoke a "possible maelstrom of litigation and religious strife, equally bad for both church and state, and certainly boding no good for the Liberal cause."[31] For this he was severely chastised by Duff, as ardent a Liberal as ever breathed, who complained that the Minister of Agriculture had "butted into the discussion like a billy goat at a billboard, and . . . warned Liberal members of parliament to be careful of what they are doing. I should like to know what politics have to do with this bill . . .?"[32]

Among the Presbyterians who took part in the debate were the Prime Minister and the leader of the Opposition. Their performances were characteristic of the two men and showed that King had both a lesser understanding of the subject and a better eye for the rocks, shoals and quicksand referred to by the *Journal of Commerce* than his rival. King expressed his disagreement with the Duff amendment, which he avoided mentioning explicitly, and then an hour later voted against the motion which was intended to remove that amendment from the Bill. Presumably the reason for this inconsistency was that he thought the crucial and hotly disputed question of whether the General Assembly of the Presbyterian church had acted within its powers in approving union should be submitted to the Supreme Court of Canada. An amendment to the effect that such a reference should be made had been ruled out of order on a technicality. He regretted that it had been because the matter, he thought, could be decided quickly by the Supreme Court without the necessity of lengthy litigation, the outcome of which would have to be awaited if the Duff amendment were accepted. If the Court found that the General Assembly's action was lawful, the opponents of union could not reasonably object to its consummation; if it found the action unlawful by reason of some disability which could be removed by legislation, those Presbyterians who desired union could request Parliament to enact any law necessary to permit the General Assembly to proceed. As doubt about the legality of the procedure existed, said King, it ought to be removed before the union was effected as a means of dissipating suspicion, resentment and ill will.[33] Thus, while appearing to believe that the churches should be allowed to unite, he managed to side with those who were opposed in their desire for a judicial determination of the legal power belonging to the Assembly. It was a typical "on the one hand, but on the other" speech in which he addressed himself to the country rather than to the question, a speech which would arouse no particular enthusiasm but give no one any real offence.

Meighen, in contrast, came out unequivocally for deletion of the Duff amendment and against any reference to the courts. He did not declare himself on the general subject of Church Union, which he favoured but believed to be not the business of Parliament, but in a closely reasoned presentation analyzed the questions actually before the House. It was after midnight when he rose to speak following King and as he had been engaged in a very acrimonious debate on another matter until three-thirty the previous morning, he did not, as he wrote afterwards, "feel in shape for any very great performance. . . . At the time I rather thought I did as well as I could, but after reading the speech myself I find that I do not think as much of it, and indeed prefer many others."[34]

If not his best speech it was at any rate by far the most powerful of all those advocating passage of the Bill in its original form. It was a good example of his exceptional ability to construct a reasoned argument, orderly, symmetrical, devoid of emotion and logically impeccable. And it illustrated nicely his belief that members of Parliament had a duty to pronounce themselves on one side or the other of a question, no matter how politically hazardous that might be, instead of trying to straddle the fence; in other words to lead and influence public opinion with whatever they had of knowledge and logic instead of being themselves directed by what they felt public opinion to be. He began by asking whether the power to unite with others resided in the Presbyterian church and answered that it did inherently because it was really nothing more than the power to alter doctrine. He then argued that the church, in the manner prescribed by its constitution, had delegated this power to the General Assembly which had lawfully exercised it. But even if the Assembly's power were questioned, he asserted, Parliament should accept the present motion before it, deleting the Duff amendment, and pass the Bill, inasmuch as the legally constituted authorities of the three churches had so requested. Nothing would be gained by waiting for a decision in the Ontario litigation, which might not even decide as to the Assembly's authority to act as it had, nor would anything be gained by a reference to the Supreme Court. If such a reference should establish at length that the Assembly had exceeded its powers, Parliament would inevitably be asked, and would not be able to refuse, to give that governing body of the church the necessary power and to pass the very legislation now before it. In other words, whatever the finding of the courts might be, the end result would be the same and Parliament might as well do now what it would have to do in any event. Meighen's address ended this phase of the debate and the motion expunging the Duff amendment from the Bill and restoring the date of union to June the tenth, 1925 was approved.[35]

While the Church Union question was in a real sense non-political, it could not be divorced entirely from politics and Meighen realized that he had deeply wounded, if not irrevocably alienated, a good many Presbyterians by his clear and forthright stand in favour of the Union Bill. The subject, he wrote shortly after the debate, "was one of the most embarrassing which has ever confronted Parliament. I quite agree that the great majority of those interested are on the side of union, but I am of the opinion that those opposed are the most determined and implacable. . . . While it is undoubtedly true that among those . . . having actual knowledge of the whole conduct of the matter the Prime Minister succeeded in losing the confidence of both sides, still it may be that throughout the country generally his course, if you call it a course, would result in his making less enemies than I have been compelled to make."[36] There was no doubt that Meighen had made enemies. "In taking this stand," one angry New Brunswick Presbyterian Conservative told him, "you could not dissociate yourself from your position as leader of the Conservative party. My resentment and sense of wrong are so keen that I therefore had no option but to decline to take any part in support of that Party, while you or Mr. Baxter, who apparently did not have stuff enough to take any part, are in [any] way recognized as leaders."[37] Another of the many letters of this tenor he received was couched in somewhat more excited language:

> By your voice and vote on the so-called Church union you—as Leader of my Party—cast to the winds of supposed popular propaganda on this question, every principal [sic] of British fair play to hundreds of thousands of Presbyterians, throwing your influence on the side of political Ranters lead [sic] by that camouflaged Grit Mr. Forke standing side by side with him when the vote was taken to obliterate the Church to which my wife and I gave our only son. . . .
>
> By your betrayal of the fundimentals [sic] of my political party, you gave support to the conduct of the Judases within my Church, and as they have destroyed the Sacred edifice, so you have alienated the fealty of thousands of partisans from the Conservative standard.[38]

Meighen knew, of course, that there were probably more of his fellow Presbyterians who approved of the position he had taken than objected but they would be less likely to support him politically on that account than the objectors would be to vote against him or, at best, to abstain from voting altogether. He noticed that most of those who took the trouble to write him appreciative letters about his speech were Methodists or Congregationalists. Still, he was pleased that the leaders of the movement for Union thought highly enough of the speech to order thousands of copies for distribution throughout the country and hoped that all thoughtful people who read it would see the reasonableness of his views.

He was soon to discover that anti-Unionists as well as Unionists could expect to suffer politically over this issue. Among those Conservatives who had sided in Parliament with Duff in opposition to the Bill was Guss Porter and Meighen was convinced that Porter's defeat in West Hastings was caused in part by that fact. Three days after the by-election he wrote to the Reverend E. Leslie Pidgeon of Winnipeg, one of the leading advocates and architects of Union.

> I am venturing to write you on a subject in the hope that you may be able legitimately to do something to prevent injustice in the future. In the recent contest in West Hastings quite a number of voters who had favoured Church Union voted against our candidate, Mr. E. Guss Porter, because of his opposition to that measure. This cannot now, of course, be helped, but I am given to understand by a prominent Unionist Presbyterian Minister of Ottawa that the intention is to do the same in the general election as respects Dr. Ross, Colonel McLaren, Gordon Wilson and others who were opposed to the Church Union Bill. In my opinion there is no justification for such a course. Mr. Porter, Colonel McLaren and the others who opposed the Bill were just as sincere in their opposition as I was in my support. It is true citizens have the right to estimate the conduct of public men. . . . I have never sought, and do not now seek, political capital out of the Church Union question, but in view of the wobbling indeterminate attitude of the Prime Minister as contrasted with the stand I took myself it is obviously and grossly unjust that because of this question my supporters should be defeated by Unionist votes.
>
> I am sure you will accept this view yourself and place it before any others where you think it necessary.[39]

Pidgeon replied that he would do what he "legitimately" could to discourage such discrimination and added:

> If there is one man in the House of Commons who should not suffer from the unionist, you are that man. We owe you a debt of gratitude and support that cannot be exaggerated and you may depend upon us to do all that we can to repay that debt.
>
> When I reported my experience at Ottawa to the Ministerial Association here, I gave them a vivid description of your wonderful speech and told them that the unionist [sic] owed their legislation to you more than to any other individual. . . .

One thing I want to make clear is that we are exceedingly appreciative of your attitude and assistance and earnestly desirous of preventing any inconvenience or loss coming to you from this movement.[40]

Meighen was naturally anxious to avoid doing anything more himself that might cause further "inconvenience or loss" and thus, when he was invited in June 1925 to send congratulations or greetings to the first General Council of the United Church meeting in Toronto, he declined. "It would be a pleasure to me to send the message," he wrote, ". . . but I think perhaps it is owing to some of my colleagues not to do so. As you know I strained the relations somewhat seriously in the action I took last session. This action it was my duty to take irrespective of consequences, but I don't think it is necessary for me to go further, that is in my capacity as a political leader. My personal sympathies are entirely with the cause of Union."[41]

For several years Meighen kept getting requests for copies of his Church Union speech and when his supply was exhausted he wrote to Dr. Pidgeon to ask whether the United Church had any copies available. Pidgeon replied that there was only one copy left and it was kept on file. "I had a number of them myself but was unable to keep a single copy. We never had anything in the form of literature for which there was such an urgent demand." He also took occasion to renew his earlier expression of gratitude to Meighen.

As I think back over the past I cannot remember another 40 minutes of such pleasure as I experienced while that speech was being delivered. I often say this to my friends in conversation and also with sincerity. May I say that I suffered more than will ever be known listening to speeches made from the floor of the House on the Bill that so persistently missed the principles at issue. Sometime [sic] I felt that if I could only spring up there and correct them it would have given me relief. But from ever you began [sic], every ideal I had cherished of a speech that would embody the vital principles of the issue were brought out in a way that was matchless and unanswerable.[42]

However significant the Church Union issue may have been as a factor in the West Hastings contest, the loss of that seat, coming so closely on the heels of the St. Antoine loss, intensified the desire in St. James Street to have the Conservative party drop its pilot, as the *Journal of Commerce* had put it. Early in December 1924 Meighen received two letters from Baxter, who was in Montreal sounding out opinion. He had been to see Atholstan one day and Senator White and his cousin, R. S. White of the *Gazette*, the next. Atholstan and the Whites, one would gather, were scheming separately and in their own different ways but were pursuing

essentially the same objective.   Baxter's first letter described the visit
with His Lordship.

> I have just spent 1½ hours with him at his house.   The usual
> preliminaries though not so long drawn out this time. . . . I told him
> I had talked with you and you said you would be glad to throw
> up the whole thing if it were not that it would be a desertion of
> the party also that you would gladly get behind any other man who
> could give a reasonable hope of success.   "Does he really mean it?
> Would he do that? is about the sort of comment that was made. . . .
> He suggests that if you came to him and were really enthusiastic in
> making the proposition that you would get behind some one else
> & give that some one else all your support and ask him [Atholstan]
> to call in a group to consult on the situation that then he would get
> people together; that there is no use looking for some one else until
> they can do so with the certainty that you were willing for some
> one else; that if we go as we are he believes we will be badly beaten;
> that if an attempt is made to get some one else and it fails then we
> must do the best we can with you—the latter seeming, to my mind, a
> bit illogical.
>
> I would suggest that you go to him in the way he wants.   There
> *is* no one else to be had.   You cannot take any man who is not
> sufficiently before the public today to be at once in all our thoughts
> and build him up in time for the next general [election].   The
> thing is impossible.
>
> I see some possible benefit in following his lead.   You make *him*
> in a sense and not yourself, responsible for the situation and for
> accomplishing something.   If he gets *real* men together and on
> consultation they find they cannot get any one else the very fact
> of their having tried will start some enthusiasm on their part and
> may bring about a real propaganda and a real push in the Province
> which up to the present is practically lacking.
>
> I do not think this thing is any trap at all.   I believe that he is
> sincere in his views and does not think that you can put the party
> through to a successful result.   When he finds that no one can be
> got I think that even he will want to make what he would probably
> term "the best of the situation" and that may mean, at least, some
> real aid from the standpoint of propaganda.[48]

The Whites, Baxter reported the following day, were in much the same
state of mind as Atholstan.

> I spent nearly two hours at the Gazette office this morning with
> the Senator and R. S. White.   There is a disposition in this quarter
> to throw the blame for St. Antoine on you—something that was not
> manifested even indirectly in my conversation of last night.   Other-
> wise the attitude seems to be precisely the same as to the necessity
> of your suggesting the consideration of a successor.   They seem to
> have in mind the General [Currie] & so far as I can ascertain do not
> know anything of what you told me about your efforts in that direc-
> tion.   Of course I was most careful not to let fall the slightest hint
> of anything that I knew.   I told them that if [it] were not for showing

absolute cowardice and abandonment of the party that you would, if you gave way to your personal feelings, get out at once & abandon the whole business of politics. Now, they simply do not believe that, or if they do, will not admit that they do. R. S. says it is just an excuse for not doing what you ought to do that you put your personal views above the party or expressions to that effect. Still, there seems to be under it all, a desire to get the party into winning shape. If no other can be got they wonder if an independent movement can be tried to break up Quebec with a coalition afterwards. I told them that such a movement would weaken the party elsewhere as we would not have a united front all over the Dominion. They see the force of that, I am sure and consider their suggestion a doubtful expedient.

I still thing the best thing to do is to get the whole lot of them together and go the limit by demanding that they shall get a leader—insisting that you will help in every way to get that leader and will serve under him to the full extent of your powers. Such a course will disarm them and bring some results, I believe. At all events the situation can be no worse than before. Last night it was suggested that you should be the power behind the throne with a new man. Today, while that exact expression was not used its equivalent was employed. Boiled down it seems to come to this—that they consider Monty & his group insufficient for the task and that *you* cannot get in others who would be superior—that that can only be done by bringing in a more or less nominal head who will be a sort of solvent of the situation. They say too that such a head must be a man of outstanding character & that no mere nonentity will do. Perhaps there *is* such a man in Heaven or—the other place! If so, it would be worth while to bring him back temporarily to the purgatory of this earth![44]

More than two weeks elapsed before Meighen answered these letters and when he did so he gave Baxter's suggestion short shrift.

I read and re-read several times the two letters you wrote me from Montreal. In one . . . you gave the language in which you described my view of my position, and you gave it in correct, faithful terms.

The corollary therefrom I was not fully able to grasp. Had you considered the position I would be in, and the party in Parliament would be in if to a number of men in Montreal I commissioned the task of making a selection? Naturally you had in mind that the selection would be submitted to the party in Parliament, but had you thought of the position one would be in who had to go to his followers and say that he had entrusted a group of men with the responsibility of making a selection to be submitted to them? I feel already I have said enough to you to indicate the indefensible position one would be in who took this course.[45]

Meighen-baiting had become a very popular sport in Montreal at the end of 1924 and one not confined to the proprietors of newspapers.

Their editorials attacking Meighen seemed to have a contagious effect and to stimulate a compulsive urge on the part of some people to join in the public elucidation of his inadequacies. One of those so affected was C. H. Cahan, who unburdened himself of a lengthy letter to the editor of the *Gazette*. It was a forceful, thoughtful and thought provoking screed which probably had been germinating in its author's mind for some time. It opened with the assertion that no effort should be made to bring in a new leader of the party "without the cordial approval and co-operation of Mr. Meighen. . . . It is only if Mr. Meighen should decide to retire from the Conservative leadership, and produce a suitable candidate, whom he and his associates are prepared to support, that any change could safely be effected before the next federal election contest." Cahan apparently wished that Meighen would do so but realized that he would not, for the letter went on to argue that instead of trying to exchange leaders it might be better to try to bring about a change in the one the party already had. If Meighen would just purge himself of his faults and become a new man there would be no need to worry about finding someone else. But before he could do this, of course, he had to know what his faults were and to enlighten him on this score was the task Cahan had set himself to perform. Fortunately Meighen did possess a few merits—they could be dismissed in one sentence—as a foundation on which to build: ". . . probity of personal character, a wide knowledge of political history, considerable parliamentary experience, and that ardent energy in advocacy and enthusiastic devotion to his work which are among the essential qualities of leadership." But the defects in the man were more interesting and important: ". . . his apparent indifference to changes of public opinion, his dislike of new ideas, his reluctance to analyze current economic problems to which he is not accustomed and which tend to disturb the fixity of his own preconceived opinions, and his seeming lack of discernment and tact in dealing with his fellow men."

Cahan proceeded to give illustrations of these short-comings. Meighen's use of the tariff issue was one. Public opinion had changed on that subject but Meighen persisted in presenting "the general policy of protection . . . as a dogma of political faith, which admitted of no reconsideration or revision." To go on talking about protection as a principle was not enough; people were now asking, "Protection to which industry, and to whom?" Another of Meighen's faults was "his over-weening desire to preserve a semblance of personal consistency in his political opinions."

> . . . when Mr. Meighen comes to Quebec, his addresses seem to sound a note of challenge to each of his hearers to find any flaw or fault in the conduct, during the war, of the administration of which he was a member; and he thus provokes a vote and division

upon issues which had best be deemed dead and buried, and upon which he can never hope to procure in this province a popular verdict favorable to himself and to his colleagues of the old regime.

In reality, the province of Quebec, which is the keystone of the confederacy, and the natural support of Conservative policy, is seething with a spirit of discontent with certain phases of the conduct of the present federal administration; and yet the Conservative electors of this province frequently express regret that Mr. Meighen seems to regard the consistency of his own personal history as of so much more vital importance than the future progress and prosperity of the country, that, instead of utilizing existing conditions as a means of restoring the Conservative party to place and power, he ignores the problems of the present and creates widespread distrust by diverting public attention to the dead issues of the past in respect to which he may never expect the approval of a large majority of the Quebec constituencies.

Meighen, continued Cahan, should be devoting more attention to the general problems of Canada, for example "to reconciling divergencies of political opinion" between the different provinces and sections of the country. "In no way could Mr. Meighen more successfully demonstrate his qualifications for premiership than by contributing by thought and deed to reconciling these internal domestic differences." Furthermore, the nation was beset by serious economic and financial difficulties—over-taxation, prodigality in public expenditure, inefficient utilization of resources, an excessively costly administrative machinery—solutions of which it was the duty of a party leader to seek or devise. "These matters are of more serious import to us than the peccadillos of individual ministers, or the personal fate of any political leader. We look to Mr. Meighen, not merely for partisan success, but for practical indications of a way out of the morass into which the country is placed."

> If Mr. Meighen will realize that he cannot succeed by himself alone; if he will place himself in closer contact with his fellowmen, profit by their experience and their counsel, and, withal, cultivate those qualities of mind and heart which inspire their confidence and co-operation, he may yet leave a name second to none in the political history of Canada.
>
> Mr. Meighen has now his opportunity. . . . His political future depends upon his ability to procure the hearty co-operation of all thoughtful members of his party; in a word, upon his adaptability for the office which has been committed to his charge.[46]

As soon as he had read this in the newspaper Meighen sent an appreciative note to Cahan, commenting on only one of the criticisms the latter had made.

> I am writing to thank you for the fair and thoughtful letter which you have today published in the Montreal Gazette. A contribution of this character cannot be otherwise than helpful to one who

desires to do his duty and who does not consider himself above criticism or impervious to advice.

On the subject of my too prolonged and sensitive attention to my past public conduct may I be permitted a word. It must be that the Press has overemphasized any remarks I may have made in this category. Rarely have I trespassed on the topic at all—not to the extent of one percent of the time occupied in speeches in Quebec. When one's foes devote almost all their energies to an explanation of one's alleged vulnerable and flagitious past sometimes a word in defence is necessary or one is assumed to be playing the role of a penitent.

Many times critics in Montreal have attacked me as not whole-heartedly and unqualifiedly protectionist. I am glad you have pressed to the front another view point.

Believe me, Mr. Cahan, sincerely appreciative—and with highest personal regards.[47]

His purpose in writing the letter, said Cahan in acknowledgment, was "to be helpful and nothing more. I have no personal political ambitions to serve."[48] But how he thought it would be helpful to advertize Meighen's defects in the columns of the *Gazette,* instead of writing him directly, Cahan did not say.

Cahan's epistle naturally attracted a lot of attention. One of those who wrote to him about it—probably one of a great many—was a Toronto business man, John J. Carrick, who had known Meighen for many years. They had gone to university together, together had sat in the Commons for a few years after 1911, and when Carrick had gone overseas in 1915 he had sold his house on Cooper Street to Meighen. The latter had learned from this long acquaintance that Carrick was somewhat subject to delusions of grandeur and that his words generally spoke louder than his actions. For some reason Carrick decided to send Meighen a copy of his note to Cahan. He agreed with what he took to be Cahan's opinion "that what we require now is not so much a change of leadership for the Conservative Party, as a change of attitude in our Leader to meet present conditions. Undoubtedly Arthur Meighen is very clever and the one criticism I would make of him . . . is that he is a rotten picker of men and has, unfortunately, some men about him who are very bad advisers, except in their own interests."[49] If he knew Meighen as well as he thought he did Carrick must have expected that there would be a strike at this bait, and so there was. Meighen wrote to him: "It would interest me very much and likely help me if you would tell me who the bad advisers are and what has been the bad advice. We could then get down to a concrete discussion. Please do not decline this invitation."[50]

The invitation was promptly accepted. "You know," Carrick answered, "that I have always associated with the biggest men of the country, and I think I am in a position, with my past political experience and business associations with both Liberals and Conservatives, to at least intelligently size up the situation." Worst of the bad advisers, he thought, were Ballantyne and Webster; neither had "the respect or the confidence of the great body of English electors," neither knew "anything of the traditions of the Conservative party. Both formerly favoured Laurier and both adhered to the Conservative party to further selfish personal and financial ends. In financial circles, their selfish and arrogant methods are held in contempt; and, except in so far as they may purchase political support, neither of them has any considerable political following. Decent Conservatives of the old party will not enter an organization under their leadership." On the other hand, Senator George G. Foster "is of the old school of Conservatives, very highly respected, and with very considerable political experience; but it is generally reported that you no longer seek his advice and counsel." In addition, Carrick thought, Rodolphe Monty and André Fauteux were not and never would be recognized as the real leaders of French-Canadian Conservatives. "There were hundreds of Conservative voters who declined to go to the polls in St. Antoine, because they utterly refused to countenance Ballantyne, Webster and Monty as leaders of Conservative opinion." In brief, a lot of people in the Province of Quebec were "discouraged with the present outlook; and they see no prospect of success, except in forming an independent organization, which will thrust aside existing local leaders, and you also if you continue to adhere to them. . . ."[51]

Meighen's response to this was to tell Carrick, in effect, to put up or shut up. He was, he wrote,

grateful to you for writing me so frankly. I asked for the names of the advisers of whom you complained and also for the advice given which was, as you say, bad. You have answered the first, not the second. Perhaps I should not call on you to answer the second as respects the two men you refer to because the fact is they have not given any advice. They make no pretence of being able to help direct the Conservative party, one of them being only a recent member of the Senate and the other not being in Parliament at all. I get advice from a very great many, but these are two men who never undertake that role. The fact is they have done as best they could what I have asked them to do, and that has been a work of a most difficult kind. I may say to you confidentially that both of them are anxious, and have been for some time, to retire from this work, and if you will undertake to carry it on instead I will gladly make a change. Further, if you will name me any one or two men reputable in your opinion who would do the work it is more than probable I would accept them. I am writing you in a confidential manner, of course, on this subject but I am in earnest. I know well the criticism that goes on but I would have thought that you having considerable experience in politics would remember that those who actually do things are continually pursued by criticism at the hands of those who do nothing. . . .

You refer to Senator Foster as one of the old school highly respected whose advice and counsel you say I no longer seek. With the first part I agree. I have a good opinion of Senator Foster. Parenthetically I may say that what you have stated in your letter of the other two men is very mild and complimentary compared with what some strong Conservatives have stated to me and written to me as respects Senator Foster. Furthermore I see the Senator just as often as I can. He is only too frequently absent from Montreal, and happened to be absent at the time I needed him most, namely, during the St. Antoine contest.

A word as to the French Canadian Conservatives of whom you speak. I don't think they deserve—at least I don't think one of them deserves—what you say of them, but before criticism of this kind is useful it is necessary that others be named who would be willing to devote the time and undertake the responsibilities which these men have given and carried, and who would be stronger and more acceptable. I have put this question many times and always with the result of hearing only names of men who after the utmost possible efforts could not be secured. You realize of course that the effect of the war and of Union Government was to paralyze and well nigh destroy the Conservative party in the province of Quebec. Resuscitation is not a matter of weeks or months; it is a matter of a long, arduous, patient toil. There are many who are sparing with their toil who have no modicum of patience, but have abundant stores of hasty and careless criticism.[52]

Carrick ignored the suggestion that he take over the work of Ballantyne and Webster. However, he told Meighen, "There is a very strong Montreal influence that I think I can help to get behind you. . . ." He explained the importance of this: "Quebec is the only province that is run from the top down and not from the bottom up. Both in matters of church and state a few at the top are in control. The Hierarchy controls the church and a few of the leaders the Province. If you can get a few of the big fellows behind you, at a cost not too great, you are sure to break into Quebec."[53]

Biggest of the "big fellows," by far the most formidable of the tycoons, was Sir Herbert Holt, President of the Royal Bank of Canada, a director of the C.P.R. and the controlling power in more other enterprises than perhaps even he could name off-hand. Carrick, who had "always associated with the biggest men of the country," sent Meighen copies of two letters he had written Holt and of Sir Herbert's reply. In one of his letters Carrick, without Meighen's consent, tried on his behalf to enlist Holt's assistance.

I have recently had an exchange of letters with Arthur Meighen with reference to the Quebec situation that is very interesting. At present there is, apparently, a Press combination between Senator

Smeaton White of The Gazette and Lord Atholstan of The Star to oust our Federal Conservative Leader. We have nobody to take his place, and as the country is seething with discontent, it looks as if the Conservatives have a wonderful opportunity to get back into power at the next Federal election.

You are the greatest individual financial power in Canada, and there is no reason why you cannot wield a similar influence politically. My association with Arthur Meighen is not only political, but dates back to school days, and while I appreciate that you have disapproved of some of his policies in the past, I know that he would welcome counsel and co-operation with you. I hope you will kindly give me an opportunity to discuss this with you when I am in Montreal.[54]

Holt, with his almost obsessive dislike of publicity and contempt for mere party politicians, may well have been astonished by the naïve suggestion that he should descend from his lofty eminence of real power to become embroiled in the noisy hurly-burly of these silly political games, especially to help a man for whose policies he had little use. His reply made it clear that he was one "strong Montreal influence" Meighen would have to get along without.

I note that you have exchanged letters with the Hon. Arthur Meighen regarding the Quebec situation. I think you are wrong in thinking there is a press combination between Senator White and Lord Atholstan to oust Meighen as Federal Conservative Leader, certainly as far as Senator White is concerned for I am sure he is only interested in the concern of the Conservative Party and, no doubt, considers that if Mr. Meighen is their Leader the Province of Quebec will probably return no Conservatives—and this all on account of the unfair blame they attach to him in connection with conscription, for which the whole Government of that time was responsible.

As you know, I am so fully occupied in the enterprises in which I am interested that, unfortunately, I have no time for politics. However, the time has arrived when somebody must take the political situation in hand, otherwise we are facing financial disaster in Canada.[55]

Through a most regrettable oversight Sir Herbert forgot to say who should do that, or how, but evidently he did not think Meighen was the man.

As a result of the loss of the two by-elections and the consequent criticism of his leadership, the year which had opened so promisingly for Meighen, in the rosy afterglow of the Kent and Halifax victories and with signs of a deep schism within the Liberal party, ended on a distinctly sour note. The setback in West Hastings he could lightly and rightly dismiss as a curious political phenomenon of no national importance;

the riding was recaptured by a Conservative less than a year later with the largest majority in its history. St. Antoine, however, was a different matter, for it brought out into the open one of the besetting problems of the Conservative party in Quebec—its demoralizing, anarchic, back-biting factionalism—that might well prove to have national significance. It looked to Meighen increasingly probable that the party would come out of the next general election on top in the country as a whole. If the Conservatives failed to win a reasonable number of seats in Quebec one of two things might happen: either they would be kept out of office altogether by the lack of a clear majority; or, if sufficiently successful outside of Quebec, they would have to form a government in which French Canada was not adequately represented. Meighen had no desire to be in that unenviable and dangerous position again. If this happened it would once more appear that Quebec was pitted against the rest of Canada, which would do neither the Conservative party nor the country —nor the Province of Quebec—any good.

Alas, it was easy to say that for the sake of all concerned (save perhaps the Liberal party) the gross imbalance of political forces in that province should be corrected but who was to say *how* this was to be accomplished? The time seemed to be ripe for its accomplishment because even in Quebec the King government, owing to its paring away at the tariff and the generally slow pace of economic activity for which it now had to bear the blame, appeared to be losing some ground. But the Conservatives could not expect to turn the declining popularity of the Liberals to their advantage until they had put their own house in order, something that all too obviously would take a good deal of doing. There were those, of course, who believed, as they always had, that it could never be done as long as Meighen remained as leader, an opinion which, naturally, he did not share. "You understand even better than I do," he told one of his French-Canadian followers, "my difficulties in the province of Quebec. They are great. In my judgment they are not greater than would be those of any other possible Conservative leader at this time. If I thought another would approach the task with greater advantages than myself then I really would have cause to reconsider my whole position." The real barrier to success, in his view, lay elsewhere. "There seems at the present time," he continued, identifying the barrier but understating its dimensions, "to be an incapacity on the part of our friends in that province to pull together."[56] Indeed the party was sundered by so many turbulent rivalries and jealousies, with such a variety of historical and personal causes, that it was next to impossible for an outsider to unravel them all, comprehend their intricate relationships and bring some order out of chaos rampant. No subject piled Meighen's desk so high with correspondence, none was so baffling and discouraging or preyed more on his mind.

To begin with there was no real unity of the French and English-speaking elements of the party, except superficially on special gala occasions like the Cartierville picnic. In the nature of things it was inevitable that they should work separately to a considerable extent but much of the time they seemed almost to inhabit different worlds. In addition each of these elements was subdivided into a number of factions which at best tolerated one another and at worst—seemingly the more normal condition—were at each other's throats. Meighen's unofficial representatives among the English-speaking Conservatives were the two men, Lorne Webster and C. C. Ballantyne, of whose influence Carrick had complained. Neither held any designated position or recognized authority in the party and neither, as Meighen assured Carrick, offered advice respecting its programme of public policy. At his request they had undertaken the important but thankless work of raising funds, assisting the development of an organization in any way they could, especially in the Montreal district, and generally promoting the party's cause among the English-speaking population. Although the nature and extent of their responsibilities were never exactly defined, as the confidants of the national leader both of them had a lot to say about the party's internal affairs in Quebec and Carrick had doubtless voiced a widely held opinion in saying that they lacked the trust and respect of many people there; theirs were the names most frequently mentioned to substantiate the oft-repeated charge that one of Meighen's major weaknesses was his inability to judge men. His retort to Carrick that those who did things were always criticized by those who did nothing was apt but did not dispose of the matter; while the unpopularity of Webster and Ballantyne was not wholly deserved—they did the best they knew how for the party in an extremely difficult situation—it was real enough and sprang from a number of causes. Both were erstwhile Liberals who, as Carrick remarked bitterly, had supported Laurier until 1917; they were therefore automatically suspect to some orthodox Tories who, in Quebec as elsewhere, were unable to forgive or forget Union Government. Also, the simple fact that they were Meighen's men and were not ashamed to say so was enough to discredit them in the minds of those who believed that the party's chief problem was its national leader.

But there was more to it than all this, of course. The approach of Ballantyne and Webster to party organization and management was not particularly conducive to popular enthusiasm or confidence in their judgment and methods. Neither was in touch, or appeared to make any real effort to be in touch, with the rank and file; neither recognized the importance of democratizing the handling of the party's affairs. They tended to view politics from the standpoint of wealthy business men, as both of them were, surveying the city and its populace, and beyond it the province, from the lofty eminence of Mount Royal or Westmount. They had the outlook of the oligarchy, the dominant minority, to which they belonged. To them important decisions were made, as it were, in smoke-filled board rooms because that was where important people were met. They were concerned with the manipulation of individual politicians, the promotion of this or that candidate, the courting of particular business men, newspaper proprietors or other persons of power and influence, the working out of a certain tactical manœuvre. In all fairness it must be added that it was no part of any duty or power assigned them by Meighen to take off their coats, roll up their sleeves and go to bat for the party among the middle and lower classes of the metropolis; in fact they were handicapped and suspicion of them was increased by their lack of officially designated authority to do anything. Nevertheless, they acted instinctively as members of a patrician *élite* who failed to appreciate the disconcerting fact that the plebeians were losing their willingness to follow obediently wherever the rich and powerful might lead. They both, and especially Webster, had and continued to have the confidence of Meighen; unfortunately the same confidence was not extended to them by many of those whose party fidelity and zeal were in need of encouragement.

The nomination of Leslie Bell in St. Antoine in the face of their opposition was an act of defiance indicative of the gulf that separated such men as Ballantyne and Webster from many members and supporters of the party. Also indicative was their decision to locate the Conservative headquarters in Montreal in the Mount Royal Hotel. When Meighen heard that this had been done with Ballantyne's approval he wrote to Webster to question the wisdom of the choice, saying: "I fear myself that the Mount Royal Hotel is somewhat grand and lofty as a place to attract the rank and file."[57] But Webster was not bothered by that drawback. "Everything considered," he replied, "I agreed to the Mt Royal Hotel for one year. I think it best meantime and saves considering the buying of property."[58] Meighen acquiesced in this, not wishing to impose his views on men on the spot whom he had entrusted with affairs in Montreal. He was far from convinced, however, and so were others who realized the obvious necessity of making the party organization more democratic. One of them wrote, referring to the use of the hotel: "Now, this is all well in its way but can you ever expect to get the 'shirt sleeve' brigade or the 'overall' men to go there? I doubt it. From what I can hear I think the method of procedure in Montreal is wrong. There they are working from the top down instead of from the bottom up. You need your Ballantynes and your Birks but you need much more the man on the street and you will never get him with an organization that functions from the exclusive Mount Royal Hotel." What was needed in Montreal, the writer of the letter continued, was "some reorganization . . . and the workers given more control of your party and not only be invited to co-operate but be given to understand that they are really necessary to party success. Branch quarters should also be established to the end that the workers may realize that Conservatism is not an exclusive Mount Royal Hotel organization but is a party of and for the people."[59] Meighen concurred in this wise advice with a hearty "Amen"[60] but was reluctant to interfere and the Mount Royal continued to house the Montreal headquarters.

Another factor that may have had a divisive effect on the English-speaking section of the party in Quebec, notably in Montreal, was the intense business rivalry, the competition for wealth and power between men who were ordinarily disposed to support the Conservative party in national politics. There has been little investigation as yet of this shadowy subject where evidence is hard to come by and thus one can only surmise that conflicts of this kind had political ramifications which added to the distractions from which the party suffered. Conjecture cannot be pushed to the point of assuming that one's personal business affiliations and interests would invariably or conclusively determine his political views and conduct. Still, it may well be that Meighen's reliance on Webster and Ballantyne, especially the former, a more considerable personage in the business life of Montreal, involved him indirectly to the detriment of party solidarity in the ruthless financial warfare of the city. Conservative business and professional men aligned with interests opposed to those with which Webster was connected might be the less enthusiastic about assisting a political cause which he was attempting to further. At any rate the many complaints that reached Meighen about Webster's influence in the party appear to have arisen from suspicion of his activities in the dog-eat-dog world of high finance. Whether or not such suspicion was justified—and Meighen had the utmost confidence in Webster's integrity and good faith—its existence was one of the many circumstances which had a deleterious effect on the vigour and morale of the party.

Great as was the disorder among Conservatives of the English-speaking minority in Quebec, it was far exceeded by the quarrelsome factionalism prevailing in the French-speaking section. Both from the standpoint of party fortunes and from the larger standpoint of national unity a Conservative recovery in French Canada was absolutely vital but it assuredly would never be effected as long as French Conservatives preferred to fight one another instead of what was supposed to be the common foe. Part of the problem was the apparently unbridgeable chasm that separated the provincial from the national Conservatives. Nowhere else in Canada was the distinction between "federals" and "provincials" so clearly drawn. The local party led by Sauvé had long since been abandoned by many Conservatives, especially the English-speaking ones, who had fallen into the habit of supporting the sound business administrations of Gouin and Taschereau. In Meighen's opinion this had had a most unfortunate effect on the party nationally. ". . . We cannot achieve federal success," he told Sir William Price, "in the absence of a strong provincial party. . . . The conduct of the 'Gazette' and 'Star' in abandoning us provincially many years ago has been the great factor in making our task impossible federally in the province of Quebec."[61] This obviously was an oversimplification, since neither of those two papers had great influence among the French Canadians, but in any event Price held out no hope of a change of attitude. "The English Conservatives," he explained, ". . . are not Conservatives locally—the French Provincial Conservatives have forfeited their confidence in the past and our people vote for the best man in Provincial Politics. I think if everything were known you would find that the 'Gazette' has acted the way it has in the past in Provincial Politics because it found it impossible to support our Provincial Conservative trash."[62]

For their part the "trash" dissociated themselves entirely from the national party, refusing to assist it in any way. Indeed, so anxious was Sauvé to prove that he had no connection with it or its leader that he went out of his way to attack the "federals," hoping thus to demonstrate his independence of them and his lack of responsibility for their alleged past crimes against French Canada. Meighen had objected to this practice in the spring of 1922, admonishing Charles Smart, one of the five Conservatives in the Legislative Assembly, that "it is a great mistake to denounce the Federal party in provincial contests, and, to my mind, never gets a provincial party any where."[63] There was to be a provincial convention soon, Smart replied, and a new platform would be drawn up. "Federal issues will be 'taboo' and I have it clearly understood . . . that there will be no more denunciations of the Federal party."[64] That was some comfort but Sauvé, much to Meighen's regret, still maintained his aloof, uncooperative, suspicious attitude. ". . . Mr. Sauvé," Meighen observed, "does not recognize the Federal Conservative Party."[65] Thus in Quebec there was an incongruous total divorce between the two levels of the party; neither really wanted to have anything to do with the other and all Meighen's entreaties, his pleas for concord, were in vain.

Among the French Conservatives who thought of themselves as "federals," not "provincials," as among their English-speaking counterparts, there were numerous rifts and divisions. Their apparent leaders were Monty and Fauteux, whom Carrick had singled out, along with Ballantyne and Webster, to support his claim that Meighen was "a rotten picker of men." Again Carrick had expressed a very prevalent opinion in saying that neither of the two possessed the requisite stature to lead. Many were asserting that some other French Canadian—the name almost always mentioned was that of E. L. Patenaude—must be induced to assume the leadership of the federal Conservatives in Quebec, someone with a greater reputation and larger following. Meighen was not prepared to admit that either Fauteux, for whom he had very considerable regard, or Monty, for whom he had somewhat less, especially after St. Antoine, fully deserved the scorn so freely heaped upon them. "When a party is down in a province," he remarked, "as we have been for ten years back, but especially for seven, it is inevitable, first, that those appearing as leaders would not be acknowledged as strong men, and, secondly, that other men would appear strong simply because during that period of submersion they did not play the part of leaders."[66] However, he recognized that neither of the two gentlemen had brought much strength to his reconstructed ministry in the autumn of 1921 and that neither now had sufficient standing among their people to organize and lead the necessary recovery in Quebec. Fauteux, in fact, did not aspire to be recognized as *the* leader in Quebec but Monty did and, more than that, assumed that he was so recognized by the people of the province. Early in 1925 Simon Tolmie reported to Meighen that he had been discussing organization with various people in Montreal, including Fauteux.

> . . . All of those whom I met . . . are firmly of the opinion that a committee should be created equally made up of English and French speaking people with eight representatives from Montreal, two from Three Rivers, two from Quebec and two from the Eastern Townships, making a total of fourteen. If we had been able to secure Mr. Monty's assent to this, things would now be on the way. Monty does not agree with this at all. He does not object to the formation of an English speaking committee nor to the selection of an English speaking Leader, but he states that such an organization would be useless as far as the French Canadians are concerned. He says they are not accustomed to anything of that kind, what they need is a Leader and he said the general feeling of the French Canadian in Quebec is to recognize him as "le chef". Some of those whom I met do not seem to take this view. Monty opened up his conversation with a statement that he had concluded to retire from public [life]; that he was disgusted with people running around carrying on organization behind his back and the delay that he had experienced in receiving monies that were due him for political purposes. I pointed out to him of course that he would be a great loss to the party after the consistent role he had played. Then he softened up a bit and he said that down at the Cartier-Macdonald Club and at public gatherings generally at Quebec he had been recognized as "le chef" and he knew of no one who would take his place in the event of

his retiring. He said if he were to remain certain things would be necessary. *First,* a letter from you endorsing him as Leader although he would have no objection to an English speaking leader also. *Second,* that there should be no interference with his section by the English speaking Conservatives. *Third,* that party monies promised to him in the past and still unpaid, should be given to him at once. Any further money promised should be promptly paid over so that he would lose no time running after it. He said in return for this he would take an active leadership in organization, would appoint his own men and carry on the party to success as far as possible in Quebec. In addition he would start a daily newspaper to be published in French and for which he would undertake to gather the necessary subscriptions himself from among his French Canadian people. He would also request a definite reply from you before February 4th, otherwise he retires but will still remain loyal to you.

I have imparted a brief outline of Mr. Monty's stand to one or two of the leaders. They appear to think that while he would be a great loss to the party, it would be the only thing that would clear the atmosphere and that his retirement would be a short way out of the difficulty.[67]

Meighen was unable to accept Monty's proposition. Certainly a sturdily Conservative newspaper would be welcome, if Monty were able to start one in a province where there was no dependable party press, especially in the French language. He agreed, too, that what was required in Quebec was one leader who might impose a peace on the warring factions, that collective leadership with no single man officially recognized as pre-eminent had been a failure. Meighen needed a coadjutor in that province, as Macdonald had needed his Cartier and King needed his Lapointe. But there was such evident and vocal lack of confidence in Monty that more harm than good might be done by placing him in command. In any case by the time Meighen received Tolmie's report discussions were already in progress with Patenaude in an effort to bring him back into the picture. If he came he would have to be *le chef;* if Monty were designated *le chef* Patenaude would not come. It was as simple as that.

Meighen, of course, shared the very general respect for Patenaude's ability and integrity. Nothing had caused him greater regret than the failure of his abortive effort to bring Patenaude into the Cabinet in 1920 and he was still fully prepared to welcome him back to the fight. In 1922 Patenaude had entered provincial politics and presumably deserved much of the credit for the quadrupling of Conservative seats in the Legislative Assembly, of which he now held one, in the election of 1923. The question was, would he even consider leaving his provincial colleagues to reenter the national arena? And if he would, what terms and conditions might he impose?

Overtures to Patenaude commenced shortly after the St. Antoine by-election and came from various directions. At Meighen's request Borden interviewed him and sent in a cautiously optimistic report. Patenaude "was very cordial throughout our conversation. There is no doubt of his good will, but his habit of mind is not aggressive, and he is probably unduly cautious." He recognized "the unfortunate character of the practical alliance between the French Liberals and the English Progressives," that "their ideals were wholly dissimilar and that the policies for which they really stand are quite antagonistic." Further-more, he was "disturbed at the influx of American capital and the con-trol of Canadian resources and industries by American capitalists: and he says this is greatly on the increase in his Province." While admitting that Meighen had been cordially received in Quebec, he did "not think that any material change has taken place such as would lead to different results in an early election. He considers that Mr. Meighen has not acted wisely in referring so frequently to compulsory military service, and he believes that Mr. Meighen's speeches in that Province should omit any reference thereto and should relate to future progress and development." Finally Patenaude had admitted to Borden "that it is the duty of leading men to change present conditions if possible, but he believes that this can only be done through some striking policy, some 'coup d'éclat', as he expressed it, which will divert the attention of the electors from the past and fix it upon the issues of the present. In any such case he will be prepared to spring into the fight. But without some such effort he is not hopeful."[68]

In the following weeks Meighen heard from various others who had been talking to Patenaude and they all thought there was a reasonable chance that he could be secured. R. J. Manion found him "quite friend-ly, but [he] has an impression that the Conservative party is not friendly to the French Canadians. . . . His main complaint is Regulation 17, and . . . I believe he would come out for us if that regulation could be wiped out."[69] There was, of course, no chance that this controversial regulation, which had bedevilled Canadian politics for many years with its curtail-ment of the use and teaching of French in Ontario schools, would be removed as long as it continued to be supported by the great majority in that province. If this was to be a condition of Patenaude's assump-tion of leadership in Quebec, all hope would have to be abandoned. A somewhat different estimate came from Armand Lavergne, who had been for many years one of the noisiest and most provocative of the French-Canadian Nationalist group but who was ready to assist a Con-servative resurgence under Patenaude's direction. In talking to the latter Lavergne formed the impression "that he certainly is tempted and more than open to conviction. Apart of [sic] the main points, which you know, about our imperial relations and the bilingual issue, I am inclined to believe that the greatest obstacle left in the way is that Patenaude is a C.P.R. man, and if that group could be won over, Patenaude would then be easily reached. He seems to think these people very hostile on account of the competition of the C.N.R. and that they lay the blame on you."[70] Another reference to the views of the C.P.R. group came in a letter reporting the opinion of Charles Duquette, Mayor of Montreal, that Patenaude's re-entry into federal politics was essential and that there should be a meeting between him and E. W. Beatty, "as Mr. Patenaude considers that Mr. Beatty's influence will have a specific result in Quebec at the next election."[71] There was no need for such a meeting to be arranged, Meighen answered, for "I am quite sure it has already been anticipated."[72]

If Beatty's influence was going to have "a specific result" in the election it was most desirable that it be favourable to the Conservative party, which had hardly received the support of the C.P.R. in 1921. Not only the C.P.R. people but others high in the business world of Montreal were apparently ready to support Patenaude as leader in Quebec under certain conditions. Webster informed Meighen that he had had some people to dinner; one of the guests had been "Financial Editor of the 'Star' for a number of years, and is a close personal friend of Lord Athelstan [sic]." He had told Webster "that the only man the French people will consider today is Patenaud [sic]" but did "not know whether Patenaud is enthusiastic about joining up with your followers."[73] From the St. James Street point of view Patenaude, if he could win enough French-Canadian votes, might serve a very useful purpose in facilitating a solution of the country's financial difficulties and especially of its railway problem. He might, indeed, prove to be the man whose political power would silence that haunting "Whisper of Death" which had so frightened Lord Atholstan in 1923. He possessed two essential assets: the esteem of his compatriots, who could be expected to support him in large numbers at the polls, and very sensible ideas about public policy. Whether or not Lavergne's description of him as "a C.P.R. man" was accurate, he was known to understand that present railway policy was driving the country rapidly towards disaster. In 1921 the Montreal tycoons had counted on conservative Liberals like Gouin and Mitchell to dominate the situation at Ottawa, to exercise a salutary influence on Mackenzie King with regard to railways, tariffs and public finance. That confidence had proved to be misplaced; Gouin was gone from the Government, Mitchell was gone from the Commons, the railway deficits continued to mount and the King government had sold its soul to the Progressive devil. The tycoons had then concentrated on getting rid of Meighen, hoping to control the Conservative party by replacing him with someone more amenable to their will. But he had had too much obstinate determination and too much support in the rest of the country; obviously he was not going to be shaken loose. Perhaps if things were managed in the right way, it now appeared, Patenaude might become the instrument through which financial common sense and realism could at last be made to prevail.

Some veiled hints of what was in the minds of the Montrealers concerning the coming campaign in Quebec began to reach Meighen shortly after the first overtures to Patenaude by Borden. In recounting his conversation with the Whites in December 1924, J. B. M. Baxter mentioned that they seemed to be thinking of "an independent movement . . . to break up Quebec with a coalition afterwards." Baxter made no mention of Patenaude as the man who might head such a movement but probably the latter's name had figured in the discussion. At any rate a few days later Baxter told Tolmie, who promptly passed the word on to Meighen: "I think that the Chief should devote his attention to Ontario and to the other Provinces right out to the Coast. We ought to get Patenaude in as the Chief from Quebec and leave him in charge of his Province making the campaign on his own lines and acting as the Cartier to Meighen's MacDonald."[74] Meighen was more than willing to have Patenaude emerge as the new Cartier and to leave Quebec in his charge; he was not, however, happy about the idea of an "independent" campaign in that province or about the degree of independence of himself which Patenaude, with the hearty encouragement of Meighen's critics in Montreal, was eventually to assert.

That turn of events, though, was still in the future as Meighen and Patenaude got together in the spring of 1925. Their discussions, first at Ottawa and at a later meeting in Montreal, brought out Patenaude's fear, which Manion had noted, that the Conservative party was hostile to the French Canadians. To set this fear at rest Meighen undertook to draft a letter which he hoped would fully satisfy Patenaude on that score.

> For some years back I have had the advantage at rare intervals of discussing with you the relations existing between the French speaking and English speaking people of this Dominion, and the basis on which you and I could co-operate with a view to the improvement of these relations and the consequent fortification of our national structure.
>
> You have impressed upon me the fact which I readily and gladly concede that our fellow citizens of French Canadian birth not only accept British allegiance but without any mental reservation are loyal to that allegiance. It is impossible for one to be associated long with the public life of Canada and not to acknowledge freely the further fact which you have so frequently impressed upon me that there is no desire on the part of those on whose behalf you speak to isolate themselves but on the contrary that they seek only

to work in concert with our fellow citizens of other races for the advancement of this country. They desire to develop according to their own traditions, and this not only in the province of Quebec but in every portion of this Dominion. I desire to say out of a sense of full conviction that I entirely accord the justice of their claim.

Pleasant as were generalizations like these, something more was needed so Meighen came to particulars, remarking that in his judgment "the people of this Dominion accede to and should accede to" certain propositions. These turned out to be the very principles which Patenaude himself had enumerated during their earlier correspondence in September 1920; Meighen now embraced them with none of the qualifications or reservations he had expressed in his reply on that occasion[75] and ended by saying:

> In all matters of parliamentary and public policy you and I are agreed. This has been abundantly evidenced by the result, especially of recent conferences. As a consequence recognizing the high place you occupy in public esteem in this Dominion I appeal to you to come to the assistance of your country at this time, join with the great Conservative party which now stands ready for battle on the lines laid down by its historical leaders. Take your place as a candidate in this contest, and a leader in our ranks and thus ensure the triumph of that party and the rescue of this country from its present disastrous condition and more disastrous tendency.[76]

Patenaude was anything but an impetuous, daring man and he was not going to be hurried into any premature commitments by Meighen's assurances or by the pressure that was brought to bear upon him by people in Montreal. On the contrary, "a master of silence" as Meighen described him,[77] he kept his own counsel, slowly and deliberately weighing all the factors. Week after week, month after month went by and still he did not declare himself, keeping the party in Quebec in a state of suspended animation while he made up his mind. His would be, by common consent, the most important political decision of the day. Meighen could only wait, and pray that he would decide aright.

CHAPTER ELEVEN

NATIONAL UNITY—A SPIRITUAL PROBLEM

IN HIS letter to Patenaude, Meighen mentioned that the Conservative party stood "ready for battle on the lines laid down by its historical leaders." This was a reference to the fact that the vital portion of the party's election platform was now before the public in the form of a resolution on fiscal policy which Meighen proposed to move in Parliament during its session in 1925. The core of the platform was still the maintenance of the protective tariff and he was still counting on that issue to lead large numbers of protectionist Liberals away from Mackenzie King. There had been a dismal failure to do that in 1921; perhaps now, if Patenaude came in, the people of Quebec would lose their suspicion of the Conservative party and support it in what it promised to do in the immediate future, instead of opposing it because of what it had allegedly done to them in the past. In Meighen's opinion there existed ample evidence, of which the lowering of agricultural implement duties was the most obvious but not the only example, that the Liberal party was doing what he had long predicted it would do—undermining Canada's historic National Policy as the price of Progressive support in the House of Commons. Now, much more clearly than in 1921, the tariff *was* the issue and he was determined this time to succeed in keeping it to the fore.

This determination, this constant emphasis on the subject, brought him considerable criticism from within his own party, particularly from western and to a lesser extent from Maritime Conservatives. They were inclined to agree with Cahan when he wrote in his letter to the *Gazette* that Meighen was too much disposed to treat the protective principle "as a dogma of political faith, which admitted of no reconsideration or revision." There was a good deal of truth in Cahan's remark. No Canadian politician, not even Sir John A. Macdonald when he first began preaching the gospel in the 1870's, had insisted so much, so strenuously or so consistently on the necessity of a firmly protectionist policy. On this subject Meighen was a doctrinaire, as much so as uncompromising anti-protectionists like Sir Richard Cartwright or Michael Clark had been on the opposite side of the question. If only Cartwright had been in the House of Commons in Meighen's day, *there* would have been the makings of a great debate!

Meighen's devotion to the protective tariff, which aroused Cahan's scorn and made some of his followers extremely restive, involved him in the spring of 1925 in a rather bizarre dispute which revealed the lack of political astuteness on his part which at times was the despair of his friends. He was invited to address one of the Hart House debates at the University of Toronto on the tariff issue, in accordance with the custom of asking distinguished figures from outside the university to take part. He refused to do so in a letter to J. B. Bickersteth, Warden of Hart House, on the grounds that it was not part of the function of a university to encourage this kind of discussion of public affairs and that professors were not "permitted" to give anything but a free trade slant in their lectures. Apparently to his surprise and obviously to his annoyance this refusal brought forth a strong remonstrance from C. H. A. Armstrong, who had served when Meighen was Prime Minister as one of his secretaries and was now practising law in Toronto. In a long and well-reasoned letter Armstrong denied that professors were not free to teach as they pleased and asserted that, like those of the Oxford and Cambridge Debating Unions, the Hart House debates were educationally useful, not a merely frivolous social diversion. "I have always been amazed," he wrote, "by the neglect of Conservatives to cultivate the enormous possibilities of the University field. Believing as I do that Conservative doctrines are to be deduced from moral and intellectual principles deeply imbedded in our history, why should not a Conservative leader discuss public questions in a constituency which is now itself historical, and where the best knowledge of history exists and is taught? Conservative leaders when they come to Toronto confine their addresses to the ward Associations which include electors whose allegiance is unshakeable [sic], and neglect a constituency whose influence ramifies into every county in this province, and into every province of the dominion. The Liberal leaders are fully seized of the importance of University opinion and will sedulously cultivate it." To this letter he had dictated Armstrong added the following in his own hand:

> This refusal to participate in the Hart House debates is poor political business, and the University Tories are outraged at it. For it should be remembered that, unlike its political leanings in the sixties, seventies, eighties, and nineties, when it was full of Scotch Grits, the University is now preponderatingly Tory. . . . Your letter will go before the debates committee and will leak out. I saw it because I know Bickersteth intimately. You are believed to represent the intellectual forces of this country against King's flabby ill-informed sentimentalism. But he will accept the invitation, and the contrast or result will have effects only too obvious. There is a

Gladstone Liberal Club in the University—but no Tory club of any kind. What's the use of forming one, they'll say, if the party leader doesn't think University Tories of any account? You could waste time better in the University, than in the ward associations of the converted. So let me implore you to write Bickersteth you misunderstood the nature and purpose of the debates, accept for an early autumn meeting, and come before King does. He can do little harm after you.[1]

Meighen's answer combined a partial recantation with a refusal to repent.

I received your letter of the 15th May. It may be that I wrote Mr. Bickersteth in the first place somewhat under the influence of a very unsatisfactory account given me by Mr. Sparks of the debate at the University in which he took part. I also have a very firm conviction that although the University have probably never interfered as to the teaching given in any subject at the University they have always managed to secure professors who gave the proper teaching.

Besides, I must say frankly again that I think under the conditions of Canadian public life our universities would be better to ban subjects of acute political controversy. This opinion may have been come to without thorough enough consideration, but I have expressed it to Mr. Bickersteth in one letter and have followed this up with another which was despatched before your communication arrived. . . .

I need only add that I had not thought of my letter being used in any public way, and much less did I think it would result in bringing down upon my head the thunderbolt which Captain Armstrong has launched against me. May I escape without further punishment.[2]

A few days later Meighen received another lengthy communication on the subject, this one from Professor Gilbert E. Jackson of the university's Department of Political Economy, who was also chairman of the Hart House Debates Committee. In very convincing fashion Jackson denied that there was any interference by the university in the teaching of economics or that any effort was made to inculcate free trade views.[3] "My letter to Mr. Bickersteth," Meighen replied, "was never intended as a general attack on Toronto University and little did I think it would give rise to the controversy which since has arisen. . . . It may be that the word 'permitted' as used in my first letter to Mr. Bickersteth was not well chosen and I quite accept your correction on this point. If it is not a fact, though, that the lecturers in economics actually engaged by the University have not [sic] been consistently believers in the free trade doctrine I would be surprised." Though there might not be any effort on the part of teachers to inculcate certain opinions students were inevitably influenced by the views of their teachers. "My old fashioned idea," said Meighen, ". . . is that an issue which has become the issue of Parliament in Canadian politics would be better not made the subject of public debate at the University."[4]

The idea was not only old-fashioned, it was misguided from a strictly party point of view and singularly inappropriate to someone of Meighen's intellectual bent. As one who prided himself, and justifiably, on appealing to the intelligence of people in discussing public questions, who continually urged them to be governed by their reason and not by blind prejudice, he might have been expected to rejoice that students were taking an intelligent interest in public affairs and to have welcomed the chance to give them one of his own logical, eloquent presentations. As a man who relied on reasoned analysis to convince the sceptical or the hostile, why did he not jump at the chance to speak to the kind of audience that was open to reason if any audience was? In truth Meighen was not entirely devoid of the contempt which men of affairs have been known to hold for universities as ivory towers whose inmates are out of touch with reality. But here was a chance to lay reality before them, to win converts to his cause, to grasp their loyalty and respect in a way that was uniquely his by the compelling power of his oratory, the quality of his mind, the sincerity of his purpose. His refusal to do so betrayed a disregard, by no means his alone, for the importance of the academic community and the community of youth which was to handicap the Conservative party long after its rival had begun to cultivate their good will and solicit their support.

Although he chose to shun the forum of the university, Meighen could not be blind to the fact that in the larger forum of the nation a good many voices were being raised among his own followers against what was claimed to be his too exclusive concentration on the tariff question. This protest came especially from the West and was more pronounced following St. Antoine and West Hastings. As two traditionally protectionist ridings had rejected the party of protection there was a marked disposition among western Conservatives, for whom the stand of their leader on this issue was a serious handicap, to demand some modification. Their view was that, because the Liberal party had already strengthened itself among the prairie farmers by its tariff reductions, notably on agricultural implements, it and it alone would benefit from the disintegration of the Progressive movement, now going on, if the Conservative party remained uncompromisingly the champion of protection. One of the letters Meighen received following West Hastings was from one of the least inhibited of his critics, Senator Schaffner. It was a long, bitter arraignment of Meighen and his leadership, the main complaint being that he harped too much on the tariff which, said Schaffner, was no longer regarded by the people as the main issue. A party leader, the letter implied, should find out what the voters wanted and then promise to give it to them, a proposition wholly abhorrent to Meighen. ". . . why go about all the time," the Senator wrote, "with a chip on your shoulder, and a deep desire to antagonize all except a few 'dyed in the wool' tories, why not extend your vision beyond a red hot Tory caucus, or a Tory meeting in Toronto, and endeavour to see and understand the needs of the great masses of this country? . . . Meighen you may as well admit the conservative cause was never at so low an ebb since Confederation."[5] Meighen's answer was remarkably even tempered.

> . . . I thank you for the generous references you make to certain good qualities which you feel I possess, and assure you that after reading your letter I never felt more in need of these qualities in my life. The number of faults seems to keep multiplying and sometimes one despairs of the leaven ever succeeding in leavening the lump.
> I have to bring myself to realize in answering not only that you have done me, on more than one occasion, very great kindnesses but also that you cannot go through my experiences even for a single day. If the latter were at all possible I assure you very confidently you would never write me the kind of letters which you have more than once indited.
> As to West Hastings, it was indeed a disappointment and a severe one. There were local conditions which apparently were unsuspected or at least were generally unknown, which accentuated our difficulties. . . . of all things on earth the one thing that was not the cause was the tariff policy of the Conservative party. The people knew quite well the time to vote on this issue would be later.
> I have inevitably some knowledge of the number of wise men who have arisen since the West Hastings defeat, and do not doubt you would meet some even in Winnipeg. . . .
> I am not, however, able to understand the tremendous emphasis placed upon West Hastings as relating to myself when I know that those who place this emphasis did not communicate corresponding views after Halifax and Kent. We have, I believe it is true, made gains in every election save the one.[6]

Schaffner was by no means a lone voice in the West on the subject of tariff policy, of course. During a tour of the prairies in the autumn of 1924 Meighen was advised by more than one local Conservative that he was devoting too much attention to that topic in his speeches. But he disagreed and apparently was not open to persuasion. "I know," he told one of them, "that another stand would be more popular in the West but a great party cannot shuffle and a leader worthy of the name never shuffles. We must build strength around the Conservative tariff policy on these prairies if Canada is to be made worth living in. In this task I am engaged and in this task I shall continue."[7] But how could he engage in it with any hope of success when, it seemed, a great many western Conservatives and some Conservative newspapers were dragging their feet?

The party in Manitoba, one of his good friends in Winnipeg informed him shortly after his return to Ottawa from this western trip, was not at all anxious to fight the next campaign in support of a protective policy. "It seems to me that you would be well advised to push some other plank to the front along with the tariff issue if you hope to make the slightest impression in Manitoba." Then came a gloomy recital of facts which indicated that the party there was demoralized and disunited, partly at least because of dissatisfaction with Meighen's too exclusive emphasis on protection.[8] Reaching him just when he was facing the challenge to his leadership from Quebec, this letter stretched his patience to the breaking-point and his answer betrayed his exasperation with those who thought he should do more trimming and tacking instead of sailing headlong into the wind.

> . . . I may as well acknowledge frankly that your letter, along with other evidence which I saw in Manitoba, has tested my tenacity to an unprecedented degree. Were it not that I am bound under present circumstances never to recognize discouragement the attitude of what was the Conservative Party in Manitoba would be next to fatal. It has had the effect of disturbing the belief I have hitherto honestly felt, that the fault was not my own. . . .
>
> You have encountered just what I encountered—the repeated assertion that a protective tariff policy is unpopular in the Prairie West and that consequently the fiscal principle, which has been the outstanding feature of Conservative policy for some forty years, and the chief issue in every election but one, must be subordinated and something else presented in its place. If those who make this assertion are correct then I am not the right man to lead the Conservative Party. With sixteen years of public life and federal affairs behind me, with a constantly increasing contact with the Canadian people and Canadian business from one end of the Dominion to the other, I have immovable convictions on this question both in its relation to Canadian well-being and the well-being of the Conservative Party. I do not think there ever was a time when the Conservative policy on this subject was so essential to Canada as it is today, and I do not think there ever was a time when an apparent weakening on the question on our part would be so fatal as it would today.
>
> It is not the only issue; that I well know. In one speech in Winnipeg I emphasized it chiefly for the reason that one has to do so both because of the effect in other parts of the Dominion, and, as well, because of the necessity of showing in the West reason for our faith, even to our closest friends. . . . For ten years my voice has been almost alone, whether on the part of public men or of the press, seeking to defend a fundamental Canadian policy in the Prairie West.
>
> The attitude of our friends on this issue on the Prairies is just the same as was the attitude of many of our friends on the conscription issue in Quebec. The effect of the unpopularity of our cause drove them to abandon our lines with the result that although all

are now ardently anxious to re-establish the Party's strength in that province, the task is Herculean, if not almost impossible. Had they stood by us in those days though in a hopeless minority the task now would be comparatively easy.[9]

Although, as this letter indicates, Meighen refused to countenance any suggestion that some issue other than the tariff be given first place in the Conservative programme, he did begin during 1924 to work his way towards a restatement of fiscal policy, a "reconsideration and revision" in Cahan's phrase, which he hoped would meet objections to the protective system. It was more than simply a matter of satisfying his own disquieted followers with some vote-catching promise, nor was it merely the West which objected. As on the prairies so in the Maritimes there was widespread and deeply rooted dissatisfaction with the effects, not of the protective tariff alone, but of national economic policies in general, in short with Confederation itself. It was such discontent that had given rise to the Progressive movement; although that movement was now losing its impetus as an organized political force the sentiment behind it was still very much alive. It was also this discontent that had inspired the recurring agitations for Maritime rights, most markedly in Nova Scotia, which had led on occasion to demands for secession from the Dominion. The difficulties of the Maritimes were more profound and complex than those of the West: the economy of the Atlantic provinces was stagnating, their industries languished, their port facilities lay mostly idle, their people left for greener fields. But like the prairie West they felt themselves to be in bondage to the central provinces, economically as well as politically, believed that they were being forced to pay high taxes, high consumer prices, high freight rates, in brief to bear the costs of national policies of which Ontario and Quebec were the chief, if not the sole, beneficiaries.

The problem, then, a fundamental, chronic Canadian problem, was to find some way of distributing more equitably among the various sections of the country the burden of maintaining and developing a largely unnatural, artificial national economy. There was no way, in Meighen's opinion, of getting rid of these burdens altogether if Canada were to remain one country and not be absorbed by the United States; certainly there was no possibility of discarding the protective system. But political leaders were in duty bound to present what human intelligence must be capable of devising—appropriate measures to lessen the disparities of costs and benefits falling upon the different regions of Canada as a result of the operation of basic economic policies. The search for such means had begun in Meighen's mind long before Cahan had referred in his letter to the importance of "reconciling divergencies of political opinion" between the two central provinces and the aggrieved, unhappy regions to east and to west.

In his search he had the benefit, of course, of much advice from both the prairies and the Maritime Provinces. He found the western viewpoint particularly well set forth by Charles Peterson of Calgary, editor of the *Farm and Ranch Review*, with whom he had a long correspondence on the general subject of fiscal policy, commencing in the spring of 1924 and continuing intermittently through the summer of 1925. While Meighen by no means agreed with all Peterson's contentions, he found his letters stimulating and derived almost as much enjoyment from this argumentative correspondence as he did from direct verbal encounters in the House of Commons. As he remarked to Peterson, "Whatever may be my duties . . . I am not going to deny myself the pleasure and personal advantage of a long distance debate with yourself on present Canadian questions. There is no correspondent on my list who keeps so close to the heart of the subject under discussion as you do."[10] Peterson was prompted to begin the discussion by a speech Meighen delivered at Windsor, Ontario, in April 1924 in which, while emphasizing the necessity of an adequately protective tariff, he advanced the proposition that the Atlantic region and the West were entitled to a compensating *quid pro quo* for their economic disadvantages. Just what form the compensation might take he was not then prepared to say but his admission that one was called for was what interested Peterson. He would like to support the Conservative party, the latter wrote, but "no intelligent man west of the Lakes and East of the mountains could do so." As a westerner he thought the party had "thrown that section of Canada overboard, frankly and callously, as the majority of the vote is still in the East." The Liberals' "policy of pretense" was no better. "Neither party has the slightest claim to any attempt to solve the subject in a just and statesmanlike manner. Pardon my plain speaking and do not get offended. The trouble with the Canadian statesmen is that they seldom hear the truth." No one could object to the principle of promoting industrial development but the traditional means of doing it were unjust and discriminatory. To prevent the country being split "wide open in the centre" there was need of "a higher quality of statesmanship than we have witnessed in Canada for a generation."[11]

Replying, Meighen admitted that the burden of sustaining the protective system fell disproportionately on certain sections but insisted that, "keeping in mind the general interests of Canada, as a single nation in competition industrially with other nations, such protection must still be maintained." He believed compensation might be provided by "the creating of transportation advantages accruing especially to the prairies and the Altantic Provinces."[12] Peterson encouraged him to develop this idea. ". . . you might possibly be able to appeal to the Western farmer on a clear cut policy of that sort. If it is a bargain between the industrial East and the agricultural West, with all the elements of fairness on both sides, no serious fault can be found with the policy. But it must be *candid* and *concrete*."[13]

The correspondence with Peterson lapsed for some months at this point but Meighen continued to work on the idea of sectional adjustments as a means of reconciling the national interest with divergent regional interests. He attached great importance to this restatement of fiscal policy because he intended it to be the party's major plank in the coming general election. By the end of 1924, though not yet ready to divulge his plan publicly, he had decided upon a constructive proposal designed to remove some western and Maritime grievances and to attract political support. "It is vital," he wrote to J. M. Imrie, managing director of the Edmonton *Journal*, "to get the Western people to feel that they are part and parcel of Confederation, that their fortunes are bound up with the fortunes of Canada and that they must think in terms of Canada. . . . In my judgment the basic element of . . . policy is a strongly Canadian tariff, but I do not for a moment rest satisfied in the belief that tariff must be its only element. It must be Canadian in every phase and I have in mind certain concrete moves, which are well worthy of review, as important factors in public policy. If only we could get the West to see that tariff is fundamental the great mass of our obstacles would be surmounted."[14] The need for some concrete policy was re-emphasized a few months later by Peterson, who returned to the fray with some more plain talk about the political outlook.

> You mentioned once a *quid pro quo* in the shape of certain transportation concessions west of Lake Superior. I have seen or heard nothing further on this subject.
> As matters stand today in the eyes of the public, your party has not the ghost of a chance on the prairies in an election. You have so far evolved no attractive western policy. You may, of course, carry the country without the West and for a time, at least, occupy the treasury benches in spite of the West, but no one knows better than yourself that the foundations for a great party are not laid that way.
> As I see it, a certain minimum of prairie support is *morally* essential to your party in the next election and any one who can indicate a fiscal policy which will be acceptable to the Western farmer, while at the same time preserving the principle of protection of industry, will apparently render your party no mean service.[15]

Such a reconciliation of agricultural and industrial interests, Meighen replied, would be at least partly effected by implementing the terms of a resolution he had placed on the Order Paper of the House of Commons.

This resolution, of which he sent Peterson a copy, expressed the Conservative party's revamped concept of fiscal policy and Meighen set immense store by it as one of the most important motions he had ever presented to Parliament.

The resolution was also intended to appeal to the Maritimes, about whose violated rights Meighen and the country heard a great deal of rather excited talk during 1924 and 1925. The loss of Kent and Halifax by the King government at the end of 1923 was indicative of a very prevalent discontent, which grew more and more pronounced in the following months. Meighen was urged by some of his followers in the Maritimes to exploit this sentiment to the full by identifying himself clearly as a champion of Maritime rights. Baxter, for example, sent him some advice which Meighen was as temperamentally incapable of following as any man could possibly be. ". . . you should," Baxter wrote, "make some quite definite pronouncement with reference to the case of the Maritimes. . . . I think it would be better to take a leaf out of King's book, if he has not got it so thumbed over by this time as to be undecipherable [sic] and make your promises in glowing generalities. Something must be done for them, but the mere specification of what can be done is . . . apt to produce disappointment. It is really the manner of this sort of thing rather than the matter that seems to catch the popular imagination."[16] Baxter should have known his man well enough by this time to realize that nothing would more certainly cause a rejection of his advice than the suggestion that Meighen imitate Mackenzie King! Nor was manner over matter an order of precedence of which Meighen would approve.

One of the most vocal, indefatigable upholders of Maritime rights was H. J. Congdon, President of the Maritime Club of Halifax, who for months on end beginning early in 1924 kept plying Meighen with entreaties to find a solution to the plight of the Atlantic provinces. "There are reasons," he wrote in a long exposition of the grievances of the region, "for thinking that the future of Canada is in danger and there seems to be no sense of honest dealing at all. Little provinces have no show at all for what are undoubtedly their just rights. Numbers alone count, and justice is blind. . . . We in these provinces by the sea, are determined to test Canada and find out whether might is right in Canada or not."[17] The first part of the test apparently was to ascertain where the leader of the Conservative party stood on this matter and Congdon raher peremptorily demanded an explicit statement by Meighen. The latter, though, was not going to be rushed into premature undertakings. He neither desired nor proposed to avoid the subject, he answered. "You ask, however, for so specific a reply that I simply will have to wait until

I get time to read the references you give, and think the subject out very thoroughly. This I purpose doing."[18]

One of Congdon's main arguments was that before Confederation Canadian politicians had promised that the proposed federal union of British North America would confer vast benefits on the Maritime colonies. At a number of banquets in various places at which the union was discussed John A. Macdonald, George Brown, George Etienne Cartier and others had prophesied in glowing terms that the trade of the interior would flow through Halifax and St. John, that free access to an expanding British North American market would revive Maritime industry and stimulate further great industrial development for which the natural resources of the region provided a basis. But this vision of economic expansion and material well-being had never become reality in the more than half a century since Confederation. The Maritimes, Congdon asserted, had a right to demand that it be made real because the promises uttered in all that expansive after-dinner oratory before 1867 were in the nature of binding commitments and must be viewed as part of the contract of Confederation. Because on those convivial occasions the politicians had said that certain things would happen, the Dominion, according to Congdon, was under an obligation, legal as well as moral, to see that they did happen.

This idea struck Meighen as altogether whimsical. ". . . I cannot concur in the contention," he told Congdon, "that speeches made anterior to Confederation can be read into the Confederation pact itself and thus made a contractual part thereof." All that the orators of that distant day had done was to express, "each in his own way, what the spirit of Confederation really was; what in broad terms was the guarantee to be set and what principles should animate public policy. . . ." Of course, he added, not everything had been done for the Maritimes, or indeed for some other sections, that might have been done and he was prepared to advance certain proposals to reduce transportation costs between the Atlantic provinces and the rest of Canada, as well as to place the ports of the Maritimes in a more advantageous position. These proposals, he thought, would go far towards solving the problem.[19] Congdon was not satisfied with this, however. "I regret that I am not impressed with your view of the Confederation pact," he wrote and went on: "I very, very much regret to say that I do not think that your letter would carry much conviction to the minds of the people of this Province, who are now fully imbued with the belief that we are not receiving our rights, and never have. We believe that there has been gross discrimination from the beginning. We shall need some very clear cut definite statements that these elements of unfairness will be redressed, and we shall need guarantees, as the French say."[20]

Meighen attempted to provide some "clear cut definite statements" in his resolution on fiscal policy, although obviously no mere resolution would placate emotionally aroused Maritimers like Congdon. But what would placate them? They were strong on complaints and accusations but short of specific proposals. What exactly did they think ought to be done? Meighen tried repeatedly to obtain from Congdon explicit suggestions but never succeeded. "The great difficulty I always have with Mr. Congdon and others," he told one of his colleagues in the House, "is to know just what definite legislative or administrative action they want from the Federal Parliament. I have proposed something definite and would be prepared to do a great deal more if shown that it was a practicable step. There is nothing I am seeking for more keenly than a solution of the difficulty of the Maritimes. I think the main line of remedy is proper aiding and cheapening of transport as definitely set out in my resolution."[21]

Although Meighen's resolution contained clauses designed especially to appeal to the western and Maritime points of view, in other respects it was ill calculated to arouse much enthusiasm in those quarters. Its central tenet, unequivocally stated, was protectionism and certain of its specific recommendations were bound to cause disquiet on that account, in the West especially. There were two things respecting trade which were most desired on the prairies: reciprocity with the United States of the type which had been defeated in 1911; and an increase in the amount of tariff preference given British goods entering Canada. The first of these the King government had offered to negotiate but had been rebuffed by the Americans; Meighen thought it both undesirable and unattainable and made no reference to it in his resolution. The case of the British Preference was somewhat more complicated. It had been inaugurated by the Laurier government in 1897 and continued ever since. Under it British goods were admitted into Canada at lower rates of duty than those imposed on imports from other countries. This concession was unilateral, with no corresponding preference being accorded Canadian goods entering Great Britain, where in fact the general policy of free trade was still largely in force. During 1924 considerable dissatisfaction with the British Preference developed among certain Canadian manufacturers, notably in the textile and boot and shoe industries, who claimed that they were being seriously injured by competition from British goods. This grievance was not solely a Canadian one. Both Australia and New Zealand, which had followed Canada's lead in granting tariff preferences to the mother country, found it necessary in response to pressure from some of their own hard-pressed manufacturers to adopt new regulations which in effect reduced the Preference. There were demands in Canada that the Government do the same, even that it abolish the British Preference altogether. This sentiment was endorsed by, among others, the Vancouver *Sun* which, displaying a singular ignorance of history, referred to "foolish British Preference tariffs, made by the Canadian Conservative Party" and then asked:

> Cannot we get in this country a Liberal statesman who will stop wasting his wind talking free or freer trade, or a Conservative statesman who will stop trying to tell us about the benefits of English preference tariffs?
> What Canada wants is a statesman who will think and talk in terms of Canada.
> This is not England. This is not United States. This is CANADA.[22]

Meighen, as he informed the publisher of the *Sun*, was rather mystified by the reference to himself in this article because the fact was that, while not prepared to do away with it entirely, he had no great love for the British Preference at all.[23]

Another possibility, less drastic than the outright abandonment of the existing Preference, was that trade within the Empire might be stimulated to the greater benefit of all by a system of reciprocally preferential tariffs between Britain and the Dominions. This would necessitate the return by the mother country to a policy of protection under which trade concessions might be granted to the Dominions. The Stanley Baldwin government committed itself in 1923 to such a reversal of historic policy but was defeated at the polls on the issue and the project therefore lapsed. There remained, however, a very substantial body of opinion in Great Britain that favoured such mutual preferences and there were many in the Dominions who supported this approach to intra-imperial trade.

Of these Meighen was one. He regarded the unilateral Preference as a breach in the tariff wall which endangered certain Canadian producers and he accepted the view that for every trade concession given by Canada to any country something must be conceded to Canada in return. In the same speech at Windsor which aroused Charles Peterson's interest he said: "I would make reciprocal treaties if I could and open every market I could without yielding the whole position. I would make a treaty with Britain on just the same basis as others. I do not believe in showing loyalty by giving industrial concessions unless we get something in return. I believe this country should, first of all and all the time, look after its own interests."[24] In other words, he explained to Sir Charles Hibbert Tupper who wrote deprecating any repudiation of the British Preference: "My opinion is that a protective tariff policy is basic and fundamental, and that no other policies should be permitted seriously to impair the tariff structure. Subject to this I think our tariff arrangements

should be inter-Imperial [*sic*] before all else, and that our present offer
of reciprocity to the United States should be abandoned, and an offer of
'preference for preference' within the Empire substituted in its place.''[25]
Whether the British government would be willing to treat on this basis
was, of course, somewhat doubtful, though the return of Stanley Baldwin
to office in the autumn of 1924 gave some hope that it might be. If it
refused would Meighen, once in power, discontinue the traditional preferred treatment of British goods entirely? Probably not, but even so his
adoption of the "preference for preference" cry would alarm many people
for whom the existing lower duties on British products were at once
economically advantageous and emotionally satisfying.

There were in his resolution, then, propositions intended to serve
and to attract support from a variety of divergent, even conflicting, interests, intended, that is, to express a conception of the national interest.
"It is no easy matter," he observed, "to get a resolution acceptable to all
sections of a party in a country like Canada. One's difficulty is that if
he seeks to make it too acceptable he tones it down until it is too qualified
and colourless. This I sought to avoid but must admit that I would
have liked myself to have been even more direct and striking."[26] The
difficulty was all the greater when one took a statement of policy of this
kind seriously, as Meighen did, and intended it to be taken seriously by
others as something to be implemented in every particular. To him it
was no vague expression of the substance of things hoped for, no vote-
catching collection of platitudes, no mere "chart" and "compass," as
Mackenzie King had described the Liberal platform of 1919. What the
resolution called for must be steps that could and should be actually
taken and Meighen, had he had the opportunity, would have taken them
as surely as summer follows spring.

The resolution was published in the press the day before the opening
of Parliament on February the fifth. It read as follows:

> That, in the opinion of this House, to meet the situation which
> has resulted from a strengthening in late years of the protective sys-
> tem the world over particularly in the United States; to give new life
> to industry and productive enterprise; to preserve and enlarge the
> Canadian market for Canadian farm products; to stimulate the devel-
> opment of Canadian resources by the Canadian people and thus
> create employment for the workers; to increase the traffic of our
> railways by which alone an all-round reduction of freight rates can
> be secured; and, as well, to provide added revenue and thus bring
> about a reduction of internal taxation, this Dominion requires an
> immediate revision of the Canadian tariff on a definitely and con-
> sistently protective basis.
> That such revision should apply to national products such as farm
> produce, fish, and coal with no less thoroughness than to manufac-
> tured goods.

That to the same ends steps should be taken to conserve for Canadian development our essential and irreplaceable resources in material and power.

That while every effort should be directed toward the establishment of a system of preference for preference within the Empire no preference should be given at the expense of the Canadian worker and all preferences should be conditional on the use of Canadian ports.

That a tariff commission should be appointed representative of the three great classes of Canadian industry, agriculture, manufacturing and labour and be entrusted with the duty of studying Canadian tariff problems in their every bearing and of making from time to time such recommendations to the government as it deems in the general public interest with the reasons therefor, and with power also, where it finds unfair advantage is being taken of protective duties, of making recommendations to be given effect by the government for removing or reducing tariff schedules or imposing special excise taxes upon products in respect of which such advantage is taken, and that its reports, findings, recommendations and reasons therefor be given to the public.

That to enable the products of the western and Maritime provinces to reach more readily the markets so developed the special transportation burdens borne by those provinces should be shared by the whole Dominion either by contributions to long haul freight costs or by assistance in some other form.[27]

Meighen was elated by the generally favourable response to this pronouncement when it appeared in the newspapers. "The most encouraging thing that has happened for a long time," he wrote excitedly to A. B. Hogg in Lethbridge, "is the reaction to this Resolution throughout Canada. Particularly from the West the response has been excellent, and from Alberta it has been best of all I have heard from a large city in the East criticism of the tariff commission proposal, but beyond that have not received a single criticism from any part of Canada. This is such a rare experience for a political leader that it deserves immortality. I hope it won't sound vain but the solid fact is that the people of Canada are slowly coming to the conclusion that the insistence on tariff of which I have been guilty in the last two or three years was not only right but crucially necessary."[28] But criticisms soon began to come in. Neither Peterson nor Congdon, each of whom claimed, and rightly, to represent widely held opinion in his own section of Canada, was satisfied. "It seems *tragic* to me," Peterson exclaimed, "that the conservative party has so completely cast agriculture overboard! You have taken your stand on high protection. Very well. But you have made no attempt whatever to square yourself with the *present generation* of farmer voters. . . ."[29] If you will read the resolution which was sent with my last letter," Meighen retorted stiffly, giving Peterson the benefit of assuming he had not done so, "you will not think that the

Conservative Party has cast agriculture overboard. Beyond what is therein contained I would very gladly have from you any suggestions as to what the Conservative Party, or any other party, can do which would be of special advantage to Canadian agriculture. There doubtless is something that can be done, and I want to know what it is."[30] With that the two men were off on another of their rounds of correspondence, exchanging long letters in which each reiterated and expanded his views but never coming closer together than one could expect of an adamant protectionist and an equally adamant anti.[31] As for Congdon, his anger at all the injustices perpetrated on the Maritimes and his contempt for the sops and morsels offered in the resolution exploded in another long summation of sectional grievances. "Have we," he asked rhetorically, "to fight for JUSTICE in a British country? Must we show our teeth in order to get fair play? What has become of the British sense of Justice and fair play? It is an infamous situation if we must beg or fight. How else can we secure our RIGHTS?"[32]

Getting the resolution before the public through the press was an easy matter but getting it moved and debated in the Commons was not so simple. It was on the Order Paper from the beginning of the session but each time it reached the top of the list of private members' motions on the days designated for their discussion it was so late in the day that there was virtually no time left. When Meighen declined to move it under these circumstances it was relegated to the bottom of the list in accordance with the Rules of the House. He requested the Prime Minister to set aside a day especially for its consideration but King refused, remarking that there were other private members with resolutions to move which were just as important to them as Meighen's was to him. Apparently no privilege might be granted the leader of the Opposition that could not be granted to all, especially in what was probably a pre-election session. Therefore he was unable to present his resolution in the form of a substantive motion, as he desired to do, so that it might be considered alone and on its merits. Instead he had to offer it as an amendment to a Government motion, thus in effect moving want of confidence. Since it was concerned with fiscal policy the natural time to bring it in as an amendment would have been in the Budget debate. However, because the custom in that debate was to allow the members to talk at will about so many irrelevant matters, he was afraid that the issues raised in his resolution would be obscured and perhaps entirely lost sight of in a dense fog of verbiage. So instead, after the Budget debate was over he made it an amendment to a motion on June the first that the House go into Committee of Supply.

His speech in support of the resolution was a classic statement of economic nationalism. It began with the argument, amply buttressed with statistics, that Canada had developed under and thanks to a protective system which to her great peril was now being whittled gradually away at a time when other countries were raising their own tariffs. Step by step it proceeded in orderly, precise fashion to elaborate on each of the propositions set forth in the resolution, each of the policies propounded. As so often when Meighen spoke, because he never refused to allow them, a great many loaded questions were thrown at him as he went along but these he handled with his customary effortless assurance, recognizing that they showed at any rate that he was being listened to, even by those he could not hope to convince. Towards the close of his address he summed up the substance of his faith in Canada and in the "Canada-First" policy he was advancing:

> After all, the main problem of Canada is a spiritual problem. It is a problem of getting all our people to see that we have only one country, that we have not a collection of unrelated sections. It is a problem of getting our people to see that the object of all is to help each, and that the success of one does not mean the failure of another. There are far too many in this Dominion who are of opinion that it is a great mistake if anybody is allowed to make money, that if a city is prosperous it is at the expense of the country, that if the industrial sections of the country are making money it is a burden on the back of the farmer. A more false conception it is impossible for anyone to realize. This country is competing with other countries. It is the whole country that is competing. It is not any section with any section of the same country; it is the whole Dominion that is fighting a great commercial battle and must fight it, whether we like it or not, with all the great industrial countries of the world. Therefore, we ought to adopt a course which gains the maximum advantage for the whole; and then, having gained such advantage we will be in a position to afford special assistance, carried by the entire country, for the benefit of those who have special burdens to bear. This seems to me to be the right line to pursue. . . .
>
> We have heard throughout our history sectional appeals. This was bound to be our experience in the very nature of things. We took vast territories, empires in themselves, stretching across a great continent and we undertook the task of welding them into one under a central government with the same general laws, the same rules of trade, the same fiscal system. These divisions which exist among us have been accentuated by the fact that for political purposes frankness has not always prevailed over the great distances which divide. But we were bound anyway to encounter years of strain and trial, testing to the utmost our powers of patience and resolve. Our one essential creed should have been to pursue that course which offered most to the aggregate whole, to gain the maximum national advance at all costs—and after that proceed to adjust advantages among ourselves in a spirit of equity and union.
>
> This sectionalism or whatever you like to call it we can never

ameliorate by following a policy which weakens the strength of the entire unit. Such a course we have experimented on now for three years—and the malady is worse than when we began. We have sapped the virility of our industry, we have drained out much of the best of our population, we have diminished our national estate. But the experience of these years will not have been in vain if it teaches us in every part of this Dominion the folly of such a plan.

We still have a great people, a great country, and a latent power for progress unequalled in this world. I believe unreservedly and unwaveringly in the destiny of Canada—the destiny our fathers decreed, the destiny which already many generations of Canadians have striven nobly to attain—that of a great free nation endowed with an abundant heritage, never dissipating it, never casting it away, never weakly surrendering it to make great any country but our own, making the most of our possessions, turning them ourselves to the uses of mankind and in the end finding our natural riches reflected in a grander and more varied civilization, in a larger national stature, in increasing millions of Canadian homes. I believe in the destiny of Canada as a British nation, as the strong son, the elder brother, in this commonwealth—to my mind, to my heart no other future is thinkable. And without questioning in the least degree the fidelity to that future of any member of this House, believing as I do that beside such a destiny there is for us only one alternative, I submit the great article of policy which my words to-day seek to expound as the firmest safeguard against drifting that other way. But apart altogether from every question of our relationship to the empire or to the world and thinking only of the people of Canada I present the principles embodied in this resolution as the best for ourselves, best for every interest, best for every province, the principles surest to lead to the union and progress of all.[33]

Mackenzie King followed with a few remarks. It was not a reply for he did not deign to deal with the arguments Meighen had brought out. Of course the Government was opposed to the resolution, he said, but the whole matter of fiscal policy had been so thoroughly canvassed in the Budget debate that it would be pointless to waste time in re-hashing it all again. But there was one particular thing he wanted to say before he sat down: "I am afraid the speech of my right hon. friend this afternoon, despite the patriotic words with which he concluded, being as it is an appeal for higher protection and still higher protection, can serve only to set the east against the west in this country again, to help make wider the differences that may exist between the Maritime provinces and central Canada, and if his policy were to be carried out [the country] would find itself just about where we were in the matter of national unity at the time when the present administration took office, a country again divided and disunited. . . ."[34]

After three Progressives, including Forke and Crerar, had spoken against the resolution and two Conservatives had supported it the debate came to an end. It was a less thoroughgoing discussion than Meighen had hoped for, mainly because the Liberals refused to take part, understandably choosing to give as little publicity as possible to what was in fact the Conservative platform. However, he was really addressing himself to the country more than to the House, where the overwhelming defeat of his motion was a foregone conclusion. The Liberals were joined by the Progressives and by J. S. Woodsworth, one of the Labourites, in rejecting the resolution 147 to 37. Woodsworth's Labour colleague, William Irvine, was not present for the vote but evidently the two were in disagreement. When Meighen had finished speaking Irvine scribbled him a note: "Your speech was as *great* as I expected it would be. No man with any regard for reason can escape the logic of your analysis. Please accept my humble congratulations for having added a dignity to *this* parliament which makes one feel proud to be a member of it."[35] Judging by the number of requests for copies of it which Meighen received, there were many people in the country who shared Irvine's opinion of the speech. These came from all sections but it was noticeable that there were relatively few from the prairies or the Maritimes. Whether his policy would encourage that unity of outlook which, no less genuinely than King, he so much desired remained to be seen.

Although the discussion of his resolution did not become the great parliamentary event he had hoped it would, the speech which so impressed Irvine showed Meighen's "constructive" side at its best, showed that he was more than a nagging, "destructive" critic of the Government. But the 1925 session also provided a golden opportunity to display his talent for so-called "destructive" criticism in all its devastating power and to demonstrate the service that talent could perform in the public interest. Late in 1924 the King government entered into an agreement with Sir William Petersen, an English shipowner, under which the Government would control freight rates on a fleet of ten vessels to be built by Petersen and operated by him on the North Atlantic between Canadian and European ports, the Government paying him an annual subsidy of $1,300,000 for ten years. In March 1925 this agreement was brought to Parliament for ratification. As was required in the case of any policy involving the spending of public funds, the first stage was the introduction of a resolution, to which the agreement itself was appended, and which, upon being approved, would be followed by a Bill implementing the terms of the agreement.

The Petersen contract, which had been signed by both parties to it before it reached the House of Commons, was heralded as a means of freeing Canadian producers and exporters from the exactions of the North Atlantic shipping combine, which by stifling competition in ocean freight rates kept them artificially high. As debate on the resolution proceeded it became clear that some of the Progressives had serious misgivings about the agreement and in the face of this the Prime Minister retreated. He had begun by saying that his government would stand or fall on the terms of the contract. Now he proposed, once the resolution was passed and before a Bill was brought in, to have a special committee of the House examine the agreement and suggest alterations if it so desired; it might, indeed, want to investigate the whole problem of ocean freight rates and recommend some other way of controlling them. All that the House would do in passing the resolution would be to endorse the principle of controlling rates and to open the way to an examination of the entire subject by the committee. In other words, the Government, having struck its bargain with Petersen, was ready to modify or abandon it in accordance with such recommendations of the committee as the House might accept. Instead of being determined to stand or fall on its policy embodied in the contract, as was proper in a system of responsible parliamentary government, it was clear from King's speech, as Meighen put it, "that the government is prepared to change its policy, to the left or to the right, provided it can save its precious existence."[36]

Meighen's speech in the debate on the resolution was a brilliant effort, one of the greatest debating speeches in the history of the Canadian House of Commons. He had been preparing for it for weeks, amassing as much information as he could from those who had expert knowledge of ocean shipping. After lampooning the Government for not having the courage to assume responsibility for its policy in Parliament, he set out to analyze the agreement with Petersen, which, he pointed out, was the matter actually before the House rather than, as might be gathered from King's remarks, the principle of controlling rates or the question of whether a special committee should be appointed. When he got through the Petersen contract was so riddled and tattered that no man in his right mind could have voted to approve it.

Meighen admitted that a shipping combine existed and that it fixed rates but denied that that practice would be effectively combated by the agreement. Petersen was to be paid a very large sum of money to build and operate the ten ships between Canada and Europe but nothing in the contract required him to provide a guaranteed number of sailings or to carry a single pound of Canadian freight at the rates the Government might set. Nothing in the contract would prevent American shippers from using his ships in order to have the advantage of those lower rates and such Americans would in effect be subsidized by the Canadian taxpayer. Not all Canadian exports could be carried in ten ships in any event, and some producers and exporters would be discriminated against by having to ship on vessels controlled by the combine. Control of rates on a small fleet of ten ships would have no effect on rates generally, which, furthermore, could not be regulated unilaterally by one country. International agreement was the only remedy and the Government would have spent its time better in working for some multilateral system of control. Anyway, why had the Government gone to Petersen in the first place? Why had it not put lower rates into effect on the ships of the Canadian government merchant marine, which were already under its control and some of which were in service on the North Atlantic? Those ships on the average were fully the equal in size and speed of the ones Petersen proposed to build and in some respects were architecturally superior. If more ships were needed they should be built in Canada in order to create employment. In the course of ten years Petersen would receive $13,000,000 from the Canadian treasury and there was not the slightest assurance in the contract of his giving anything in return.

Part way through the speech King interrupted to say that his silence thus far should not be construed as agreement with what Meighen was saying. "I want him to have the fullest latitude to make his case as strong as he can, and that is my only reason for not replying to these absurd views." "Silence does not necessarily imply consent," added one of King's followers. "But," replied Meighen, "silence in the case of the Prime Minister, who is never slow in interrupting, does imply that he has great difficulty in answering." That was not so, said King; he disagreed entirely with Meighen's arguments, "which are inaccurate and absurd." "That is always the answer of the controversialist who cannot give any reason for his position," Meighen retorted.[37]

There was, in fact, nothing that could be called a reasoned reply to Meighen's views. However, the resolution was carried and the special committee King had promised was duly appointed. On June the eleventh it reported, making a number of recommendations and advising that the Petersen contract not be implemented until further information had been obtained. The next day Petersen, who had come to Canada to testify before the committee, suddenly died. Five days after that Meighen asked King in the House whether the Government planned to bring in legislation based on the committee's report. "In view of the death of Sir William Petersen," said the Prime Minister piously, "we have not thought that it would be fitting to bring into the House at this time the discussion of his name in matters relating to his projects." Meighen scoffed at this. ". . . the death of Sir William Petersen . . . has nothing to do with government policy, and indeed does not affect the validity of the contract in the least. . . . This appears to be only an excuse to defer action." But, King replied, there was no completed contract and after all the committee had found that more information was required before the agreement should be proceeded with. "In other words," said Meighen, "it is dead."[38]

Dead it was, and deservedly. Nothing more was ever heard of the Petersen contract and Meighen may have been entitled to some of the credit for that. In the light of his analysis it would have been an act of effrontery for the committee to recommend approval of the contract or for the Government to press for its ratification. Ordinarily his criticisms went unheeded by the ministers but he had exposed the weaknesses of their policy in this instance so convincingly that even partisan animosity could not have overcome the sober second thoughts they were having about the bargain they had rashly made. Also, for those Progressives who had doubts and objections to which they were unable to give clear articulation Meighen provided a comprehensible, unanswerable array of fact and argument with which to buttress their position. They would be ready if the agreement again came before Parliament and they were a group the Government did not desire to offend. Meighen's speech was a work of demolition, destructive certainly; but never had any member of Parliament performed a more constructive service.

In his address on fiscal policy Meighen had spoken about Canada's "spiritual problem" of unity. There was, of course, the other side of the problem that had nothing to do with trade, tariffs or transportation, another aspect of national disunity where the barriers to be overcome were ethnic and cultural rather than geographical. Although he counted heavily on his fiscal policy to appeal to the people of Quebec, he realized that without a powerful French-Canadian leader to espouse the policy little headway would be made. All depended on what Patenaude would do, but when Parliament was prorogued on the twenty-seventh of June amid expectations of an early election the "master of silence" had still not declared his intentions. Meighen thought he might be waiting until Mackenzie King announced that Parliament was dissolved, and could see the merit in doing so. However, while Patenaude deliberated Conservative activity in Quebec was more or less at a standstill. Monty and Fauteux, knowing of the plans to supersede them, continued to hold meetings in various parts of the province but they lacked the authority to organize a concerted campaign. Meighen himself felt constrained to stay out of the Quebec picture until he knew what Patenaude was going to do, in order to avoid the appearance of interfering where he had asked Patenaude to take charge. It was a most awkward situation. ". . . I am being compelled to hold my hand in the province of Quebec," Meighen told Baxter, "and am having not a little difficulty in holding the confidence of our friends there while I continue to take no active part."[39] The danger was that if Patenaude should at length decide not

to come in it might be too late by then to organize any effective campaign in Quebec. One could only hope that he would appreciate this
and that the long delay simply meant that he was coming but waiting
for the most propitious moment to say so.

Some basis for such hope was afforded by reports reaching Meighen
from those who had talked to Patenaude or to his friends. From Regina
came word of a meeting between a group of Conservatives and a party
of French Canadians who had passed through, including Arthur Sauvé
and J. E. Laforce, a former Conservative organizer in Quebec. The
latter had said that the trouble in his province was "that the 'Chiefs'
were self-appointed 'Chiefs' and he referred to Monty et al. . . . Patenaude
as Sauvé's right hand man is apparently ready to get into the Federal
game again if there is a rearrangement and reorganization" but, "while
very strong in Quebec will not work under Monty." Laforce had also
expressed the opinion "that 'Bob' Rogers if sent to Quebec could do a
great deal towards getting everybody lined up. He says Rogers is very
popular in Quebec and has a good deal of influence there."[40] Patenaude,
answered Meighen, "is at the present time the strongest man in that
province. He knows my mind towards him just as well as I know it
myself. There are differences of opinion as to what can be done by the
party from Winnipeg to whom you refer. All I can say is that . . . he
has had every encouragement to use this influence and he cannot use it
too much to suit me."[41] As a matter of fact "good old Bob" had already
seen Patenaude, who, he reported, "is certainly in a much better frame
of mind than ever before" and "has promised me to come West a little
later on and make a few speeches."[42] This news pleased Meighen
exceedingly. "If he has promised to make the speeches indicated in
your letter . . . it is mighty encouraging and I think settles the situation
as far as he is concerned. . . . For some time back I have been quietly
confident that he could not resist the pressure to take the part which is
rightly his in the next federal campaign."[43]

Quiet confidence was all very well but outright certainty would be a
lot better. The summer wore on and still there was no clear signal from
Patenaude. J. S. Royer of Quebec city, who had been talking to him,
explained to Meighen that

> he is not yet ready, because he is not satisfied in himself that the
> people of our Province are fully ripe for a change. And for that
> reason, he seems to be thinking, over the most effective way to make a
> change. And as he also feels that the people of our Province are
> prejudiced against you, he thinks that a certain understanding could
> be arrived at, by which he and his friends and followers could be
> recognized by you and your party, as an element of a certain prestige
> in your government, and that over and above the protective tariff,
> which he endorses absolutely, you would favour the cancellation of

the british [*sic*] preference; that you would endeavour to improve the railway situation by some ways and means to be found; that more definite informations [*sic*] be given by you on your imperialist policy.[44]

". . . an element of a certain prestige" seemed to be a fancy way of saying "autonomous" or "independent" and Meighen greatly feared that Patenaude might seek to establish some special status for himself as a separate ally instead of throwing in his lot unreservedly with the Conservative party. If he did so he might antagonize the real Conservatives of the province and injure the party in the rest of the country, with the result that there would be less unity, not more. There was some alarm over the possibility that if he went so far as to form a new party there would be a repetition of what had taken place in the 1911 election when the Quebec Nationalists had aligned themselves as a separate group with the Conservatives in the rest of Canada against Laurier. That marriage of convenience had demoralized the Conservative party in Quebec and had soon dissolved. Meighen was warned by one supporter in Montreal that plans for an independent campaign in Quebec had "been discussed in committee and submitted for approval to the Nationalist group. If this information is correct we shall have a repetition of 1911 with all its shortcomings and . . . misunderstandings." If on the other hand, Patenaude "accepts you as the leader of the Opposition, I believe he will be a great help to you in this Province. But he must have the courage of stating his position regarding you, otherwise our people will not know what to do."[45] He would "strongly resist and decline to have anything to do with such a proposal," replied Meighen. "What I want myself is definite alignment with the Canadian Conservative party. . . . To bring this about I am exhausting every effort and if it is impossible for me to secure it absolutely, then I want the nearest possible approach."[46]

His efforts were confined in the main to trying to influence men who were close to Patenaude, as the latter was practically incommunicado as far as Meighen was concerned. One of these was Armand Lavergne, whose Nationalist history made his sudden prominence in the affairs of the party in Quebec look suspicious to many a genuine Conservative. "What is worrying me most now," Meighen wrote, "is just the line that will be taken by our much desired friend in Montreal when, as many expect, he will declare himself within a week or so. I think it is most important from every angle, and especially from the angle of the rest of the country, that we keep as closely together as possible, and indeed best of all that we should keep united."[47] The same message was imparted to Senator C. P. Beaubien, one of the relatively few French Canadians in the upper echelons of the Montreal oligarchy, who was closely associated with the tycoons in a business way and apparently was assisting them

in their efforts to draft Patenaude and direct his course.   Beaubien
visited Meighen's office for an interview which the latter described to a
friend in Montreal.

> . . . yesterday Senator Beaubien came in.   I wrestled with him
> for over an hour and had some effect but I do not think a very great
> deal.   He is quite confident that our friend will come out and head
> a Conservative movement in the province but was, especially when
> we opened up, very emphatic on the necessity of its independent
> nature.   What they have in mind is not by any means a repetition
> of the performance of 1911 or anything like that, but rather a
> repetition of the independent efforts of Cartier and Macdonald
> which finally converged together into a sort of dual government.
> Today I had a long distance message from Lucien Moraud,
> Quebec.   Our friends there are, he says, quite determined to take
> no part in any independent movement whatever.   He says that the
> Conservative party of Rimouski have got together and passed a
> resolution against any such step and are sending a delegation with
> the resolution to Montreal, and he is coming with the delegation.
> I fear there are going to be some difficulties to overcome.
> What is not being put before Mr. "P." is the very urgent necessity
> of his being advised as to the rest of the country and the possible,
> if not certain, serious effect of an independent movement, especially
> if it went the length of not acknowledging the Conservative leader-
> ship. . . . If Mr. "P." is fully advised, that is, if he has a chance to
> study carefully and get the facts about the rest of the country as
> well as P.Q. I am entirely confident that he will decide aright and
> conduct his work aright.   Between him and me there is no essential
> difference.   What I fear is that owing to our not being able to get
> together he may be accepting only partial information, some of it
> prejudiced, and possibly on that account make an error.   I know he
> will appreciate this viewpoint being urged on his attention.   It is of
> very great importance.   Senator Beaubien was entirely friendly and
> I am fully of the belief both he and Mr. "P." are acting in good
> faith and with an object we hold in common.   You can understand
> my anxiety particularly in the presence of such a wonderful oppor-
> tunity, for really the sentiment against the Government seems prac-
> tically universal.   Most earnestly do I hope they will keep as close
> to us as they possibly can; otherwise there may be difficulties far
> greater than we think.[48]

Among the eminent and powerful gentlemen in Montreal who were
bent on getting Patenaude to take charge of the Conservative forces in
Quebec none was more eager than Lord Atholstan and, knowing this,
Meighen with a pessimism born of bitter experience was inclined to
expect the worst.   Atholstan, reported one of his acquaintances, was
"fairly well committed to the financing of a campaign if Mr. Patenaude
is in it."[49]   And so, apparently, he was—on certain conditions.   The
campaign would have to be conducted along lines of which he approved,
with Patenaude's independence of Meighen the keynote.   Sir George

Perley, who was to contest one of the Quebec seats, passed on to Meighen an assurance Atholstan had given him that such a campaign would predominantly "be Conservative run on Canadian issues. Nothing derogatory to you would be said."[50] Meighen might extract whatever comfort he could from this extraordinary concession but he would have to accept the "independence" of Patenaude. Otherwise, His Lordship made it obvious in a letter to him (which also revealed one of the reasons why Meighen and Patenaude could not get together face to face), the party could expect support neither from his newspaper nor from his cheque book. This letter characteristically bore no date, no salutation and no signature but it was accompanied by Atholstan's card and its style and substance were unmistakably Atholstanian. Evidently it was composed some time during the late summer, the day after the Baron and Meighen had one of their infrequent conversations, either in person or over the telephone, and it scolded Meighen for having dared to dispute the wisdom of an independent Conservative movement in Quebec.

> You gave me a fright yesterday. The question of success depends entirely on your playing the game according to Hoyle and I see plainly you think you can contrive an improvement. The one reason why some of us are willing to strive is the fact that we can see victory if everything is worked to win irrespective of the personal feelings and sensibilities of anyone concerned. Of course the first necessity is P's willingness to take up the fight; the next is that there should not be the slightest appearance of anything like a frame up. Now P. will be here Monday. I advise you strongly not to have any intercourse personally or by letter. . . . It is better to talk plainly to the leader. Some will fawn on him and complaisantly concur in all he does. These are not helpers. They are sycophants. For my part I have no use for a mere moral victory that leaves the enemy in possession. Your mind has been warped I fear by men professing loyalty who all their lives have been in the enemy's camp. It is astonishing that you do not see the danger of misplaced confidence. If P. comes in right and you play the game we will win. In any event you are going to have accessions throughout the country but you are in imminent danger of having to content yourself with a moral victory. In sporting parlance a miss is as good as a mile. In other words if we don't win we are beaten. Finally, if P. comes in of his own volition and you are prepared to play the game as previously outlined, I will do the utmost of which I am capable. On any other basis I may as well tell you that I infinitely prefer leaving the whole thing to those who think they have a better plan and that is what I will do.[51]

It was entirely typical of Atholstan to say in effect, "Either we play by my rules or I won't play." This time the game *was* played by his rules and the game was lost, with the Conservative party having to content itself with that "mere moral victory" he had claimed he knew how to avoid.

While these complex, largely hidden negotiations were going on in Montreal and everybody waited to see whether Patenaude would jump and, if he did, where he would land, Meighen got involved in another little matter concerning Quebec which affords an illustration of how affairs in that province took up his time and tried his patience. It had to do with campaign material, with the possibility of exploiting Mackenzie King's alleged "pro-Americanism" to the advantage of the Conservative party. This tactic was first suggested to Meighen by his second cousin, Brigadier Frank S. Meighen of Montreal, who wrote that he had "spoken to a good many friends on this matter, and they all agree that a persistent propaganda along these lines will seriously damage the solidity of the '65' in the next election."[52] Meighen agreed that "the appeal in the next election must be for a determined stand on the part of Canadians of every Province to resist the silent processes of American absorption now going on."[53] This was enough encouragement for the Brigadier, who two months later came up with a full-blown plan which he unfolded with some excitement.

> . . . fear of Americanization is the great dread of the French clergy. Protection and conscription are in comparison minor issues to them, and I believe that it would be easy to stimulate that fear among them to such a degree that we could carry about 30 seats in this Province. It could be done this way. Have a series of pamphlets written exposing the American leanings of the Govt, and pointing out what danger there is to their language and church should American control come. Have copies of these pamphlets sent at regular intervals to every one of the French parish priests in Quebec, and as election time approaches have the pamphlets increase in frequency and strength, and I believe there would be an astounding change in Quebec, for as the priests think, the people vote, certainly in the rural districts. The cost of such propaganda would not be great, the writing and printing of say 5000 pamphlets each issue, and the services of two or three girls to address and stamp them. I have in mind also the man to write them—Olivar Asselin—than whom there is no better writer of polemics in Canada. He would go into it with delight I believe, as he is a very strong upholder of the French language, and in many ways has completely abandoned his extreme national ideas. In fact he is "plus Royaliste que le Roi", is a strong believer in monarchy, and is also anti-democracy, in other words almost a Tory.[54]

"The idea you have given expression to is an excellent one," Meighen answered. "I have taken the liberty of discussing it with two men whose opinions you would appreciate. One is Senator Beaubien. He is enthusiastic as to the possibilities of an effort along this line and thinks there should be no delay." However, Beaubien thought the pamphlets should be written by someone other than Asselin, who had had "a violent difference" with his former mentor, Henri Bourassa. The latter's *Le Devoir*

was the most influential newspaper among the parish priests and therefore "the identification of Asselin with the work would render its pene-
tration into the very places we want it most sorely to reach rather difficult." The Senator also suggested that the first pamphlet should be
published originally as a full-page newspaper advertisement signed by
certain eminent French Canadians, for example himself, Patenaude and
Senator Thomas Chapais, a venerable Conservative scholar-politician.
He would be glad, said Meighen, if his cousin would take the matter
up and see what could be done.[55]

In responding to this Frank Meighen recounted the experience of
an English-speaking friend of his who lived in a French-Canadian rural
district.

> He has had a talk with the priest of his parish (he is a Protestant
> himself but has the priest's confidence.) This priest was formerly
> Liberal but has become Conservative, and his opinion is to be
> trusted.
>
> He was asked which paper was most widely read by the clergy.
> "Le Devoir" was his answer. Asked regarding pamphlets and the
> effect they might have, he said they would have to be signed by
> some well-known French-Canadian. This would seem to indicate
> a man like Senator Chapais. He then went on to say that of course
> the parish priests could not take any official action without the
> approval of their Bishops. This is true, but in my opinion it is not
> exactly official action that is wanted, and I doubt if the Bishops
> would openly commit themselves to any party. What is wanted is
> the instillation in the minds of the clergy that their language and
> possibility their Church, is in danger. Then, without doubt, if they
> are seized of that idea, they will talk to their people, and the dam-
> age (to the Liberal cause) is done.
>
> I do not know whether you remember a scene in the opera "La
> Tosca" where Scarpia, by clever innuendo makes Tosca jealous.
> When he has finished he says aside—"The poison has worked; the
> effect is gained." I am not of course comparing you to Scarpia,
> who was a real bad lot, but the principle is the same.[56]

With this letter he enclosed a memorandum setting forth evidence of
King's American learnings that might be used. It was thin stuff, poison
worthy of a Scarpia: King often spent his holidays in the United States;
he had been partly educated there; he had been employed by John D.
Rockefeller, Jr. during the war. It was certainly taking a dim view of
the intelligence of the priests and their parishioners to think that they
would be converted to Conservatism by these revelations, true though
they undoubtedly were.

This material was so thin, in fact, that Beaubien, who had undertaken
to draft the first pronouncement in the series, did not deign to use it.
Indeed, his draft was as different from what either of the two Meighens
had had in mind as it could be. The soldier-business man Meighen had

been thinking of King's personal attachments to the United States, a kind of gossip campaign. The politician-statesman Meighen had been thinking of the underlying continentalism of King's policies, which in various ways, he was convinced, were breaking down the barriers that separated Canada from her giant neighbour. But Beaubien's mind was moving along other channels still. His draft made no reference whatever to the dangers of Americanization and was, intentionally or not, a complete perversion of the original concept. After reading a copy sent to him in Ottawa Meighen was inclined to wonder just whose side the Senator was on. In the document the other provinces, especially Ontario because of Regulation 17, were severely indicted for their unjust treatment of French Canadians; the nationalization of the railways was roundly condemned; statistics were cited to show the large exodus of people from Canada that had occurred between 1911 and 1921, when the Conservatives had been in office! In short, as Meighen pointed out to Beaubien in a friendly but trenchant criticism, the whole tenor of the production was such as to cast discredit on Conservative governments for what they had done or what had happened to Canada under their auspices.[57] Accordingly the Senator revised his screed and submitted it again to Meighen, who thought it an improvement over the first effort but still too much a rehearsal of Quebec's grievances.[58] If this was an indication, as it might be, of the kind of campaign Patenaude planned to conduct, he certainly would not be associating himself very closely with the national Conservative party.

By the time the discussion of propaganda reached this stage at the beginning of September, Patenaude was on the verge of parting the curtain of silence behind which he had been secluded for so long. On September the fifth Parliament was dissolved, shortly thereafter he announced that he would contest the riding of Jacques Cartier and on the twentieth he opened his campaign in the riding with a speech at Saint Laurent. The long-awaited definition of his position came early in the address. Disclaiming any intention of forming a new party, he said:

> I love, and I want to make known fully, the tradition and the principles which have made the life and the strength of the Liberal-Conservative party, founded by Lafontaine and Baldwin, which allowed Cartier and Macdonald to bring into being Confederation, and to launch it into the future.
> And because I love that tradition and those principles, and because I know that you also love them, I have wished to remain there, the better to inspire myself from them and to bring them forward, to the limit of my power. BUT I AM IN EVERY WAY FREE, I AM FREE FROM MR. MEIGHEN, EVEN AS I AM FREE FROM MR. KING.

The deep root that I have taken in the Liberal-Conservative party attached me so strongly to the old principle of liberty and breadth of view, that I feel well protected against prejudices and men. My past record will tell you that better than my words. And tomorrow, as yesterday, the errors even of our chiefs will not be able to uproot from me these old principles that earned for our party the reputation of being the protector of minorities.[59]

Was this the new Cartier speaking? Perhaps so; but the prototype had never gone quite so far as to declare that he was as free from John A. Macdonald as from George Brown. Pleased though he was that Patenaude was riding out to do battle, Meighen was understandably disquieted and disappointed by the repudiation of his own leadership. Still, there it was, one of the facts of life that had to be accepted. All one could do now was wait and see when the ballots were cast and counted on October the twenty-ninth whether the strategy of independence would pay the rich political dividends in Quebec on which its advocates counted with such assurance.

CHAPTER TWELVE

THE 1925 ELECTION

PATENAUDE'S DECLARATION of independence meant, among other things, that Meighen was unable to appear in Quebec during the campaign and some meetings that had been arranged for him had to be cancelled. The candidates in that province were not his or the party's, they were Patenaude's, as all the campaign literature made plain. The strategy was to persuade the voters to forget all about Meighen; he could hardly intrude where obviously he was not wanted. And Patenaude, having made his choice, must bear responsibility for the result, whatever it might be. "As to my not speaking in Quebec," Meighen pointed out after the election, "it became most unwise for me to do so after the Patenaude campaign took the direction it did. Had I done so then all sorts of imprecations would have been hurled at my head and I would have been held responsible for failure to get all sorts of imagined results."[1]

Meighen deeply regretted that this barrier had been set up against him just at a time when he thought he had begun to enjoy some rapport with the French Canadians. However, at least there was one redeeming feature: he was left with more time and energy to devote to the rest of the country. Almost everywhere the situation was encouraging. The brightest spot of all was Ontario, which he was sure would give a resounding majority to his party this time. British Columbia, too, the only province where Conservatives had won more than half the seats in 1921, seemed likely to do still better now. But that was not all. In the Maritimes the party's fortunes were most decidedly on the upswing, no doubt less because of its own appeal than because of the depression and the failure of the King government to satisfy the demand for Maritime rights. The whole Atlantic region had undergone a really remarkable shift of political forces at the provincial level, with the Conservatives displacing Liberal regimes in sweeping victories. This had happened in Prince Edward Island in 1923, in Nova Scotia and New Brunswick two years later. The result of the Nova Scotia election was the most sensational of all. The province had been ruled by the Liberal party for forty-three years continuously. When the legislature was dissolved in 1925 the Conservatives held only two seats; in the new legislature they held thirty-nine to the Liberals' three. So pronounced were the

changes in the three provinces that Conservative strategists and prog-
nosticators were convinced that they portended a corresponding shift of
the Maritimes to the Tory side in national politics as well.

Even on the prairies, and particularly in Manitoba, the picture looked
a good deal brighter from the Conservative standpoint than it had
four years earlier. The situation there was complicated by uncertainty
as to the extent to which each of the two old parties would benefit from
the breakup of the Progressive movement but the Conservatives could
at least feel sure that they would do no worse than the last time, when
they had won not a single prairie riding. Reports reaching Meighen
indicated that the chances for success were very good and he himself was
most desirous of contesting Portage la Prairie once again. He was told
that the Conservatives of Grenville would be glad to have him remain
there[2] and it was impressed upon him by some who wrote to him that he
ought to select a safe riding. As one of them pointed out, "our next
Prime Minister should not be bothered electioneering for himself in a
doubtful constituency, as he should be free from such worries, and devote
his time to helping the other members." Furthermore, there were "some
wealthy and influencial [sic] members of the Conservative party, who for
purely selfish reasons would like to replace you, as you are too honorable,
independent, and clever, to be used by them, so if you were defeated in
some fool western constituency you would be playing into their hands,
as a personal defeat always lowers the prestige at the time of a Public
man, and there is absolutely no sense of your taking this chance and
giving your enemies such an opening."[3] There was force in this argument but Meighen thought is was outweighed by other considerations,
which he mentioned in his reply.

> . . . You are entirely right as to the attitude of certain men in
> Montreal, but really of these men I have not the slightest kind of
> fear, and I am bothering less and less about them as the months
> and years have gone by. My reasoning is this: To fail to run in
> Portage la Prairie will not be conducive to a good effect throughout
> the country. It would be accepted virtually as a sign that I would
> count myself defeated in that riding. I know very well the moral
> effect on our candidates generally throughout Canada of my choice
> in this matter and I feel pretty confident that if we can carry the
> country we can carry Portage la Prairie . . . I am strongly disposed
> to go right back to my old home again and take my chances with
> the rest.[4]

Not only that, contenting himself with a safe Ontario seat would lend
credence to the view that the Conservative party was too much the party
of Ontario. And no doubt there was a personal reason as well for his
wish to run in Portage: he wanted to show that he could beat Harry
Leader and avenge 1921.

Many prominent Conservatives in Manitoba, however, were strongly opposed to Meighen's running in Portage and some of them went so far as to say that they would "not go into or take part in a fight" there. They regarded it as a very doubtful riding, largely rural as it was and with a considerable French-speaking population. A lot of money and a great deal of effort would have to be expended and it might all be wasted. Therefore they urged him to choose South Centre Winnipeg, a new urban, Anglo-Saxon, middle-class constituency created by the redistribution effected in 1924. "If necessary," he was told, "one meeting will do this constituency and one-quarter the contributions if what we hear about Portage avariciousness should be conceded."[5] Meighen seriously thought of going into South Centre Winnipeg but, as he explained to one of the anti-Portage group,

> I could not get out of my mind the thought that this would not be the right thing to do in deference to the good of the entire party. Have had communications from all over the country and it has kept growing on me as a result that if I fail to go to the real mat myself the impression will spread everywhere, first, that in my opinion the rural West is hopeless and even rural Manitoba, and, secondly, that I am somewhat wanting in that unwavering energy which a leader should possess. But most important of all I have it in my bones that if I choose any other resting place I will never think myself I played the game aright.[6]

Meighen's desire prevailed and he won Portage back, defeating Leader by a majority about five times as great as Leader's margin of victory in 1921.

In opening his campaign at Richmond Hill, Ontario, on the fifth of September, Mackenzie King felt called upon to offer an explanation of why he had advised a dissolution of Parliament, though no one was likely to quarrel with the advice in view of the fact that the customary four sessions of Parliament had been held since the last election.

> Is it sufficient [he asked] that as a Government we should continue in office, drawing our indemnities and salaries as members and ministers and enjoying the fruits of office when great national questions press for solution with which for want of an adequate majority we are unable satisfactorily to cope? . . . I have come to the conclusion that it is not in the national interest further to postpone the day when questions that are pressing urgently for a solution can be dealt with in a reasonable and satisfactory manner. . . . I refer now to all-important national problems that are pressing for solution, and which cannot be solved in a parliament constituted after the manner of the parliament elected in 1921, or by any government which does not command a substantial majority of the House of Commons. . . . The fourteenth Parliament of Canada . . . from

its record on divisions will be known as the Parliament of large majorities.[7]

On the face of it his description of the fourteenth as "the Parliament of large majorities" seemed inconsistent with his claim that "great national questions" could not be coped with "satisfactorily" by that Parliament "for want of an adequate majority" at the command of the Government. What he had in mind was the lack of a clear party majority, his dependence on the Progressives, whom thus far the Liberal party had been unable to absorb. At times, owing to Progressive recalcitrance, the Government's margin of voting superiority in the House had fallen perilously low and throughout the four years King had had to try to avoid doing anything that would seriously antagonize either the agrarian radicals or his own much more conservative followers from the central and Maritime provinces, especially those from Quebec. In practice this had meant trying to avoid doing anything at all and that, as he tacitly and rightly admitted, had not been conducive to the settlement of those "all-important national problems that are pressing for solution," none of which was new in 1925. He did not explain why the Government had allowed such an intolerable situation to last until now, why they had been content for four long years to draw their indemnities and salaries and enjoy "the fruits of office" (a strange phrase, surely, to fall publicly from the lips of a Prime Minister) while all those urgent problems awaited attention. Nor was he very precise in this or later speeches as to how, if given the clear majority he had lacked in "the Parliament of large majorities," he would tackle the four major problems he enumerated: transportation, the tariff, immigration and Senate reform.

Meighen fired off the first gun of the Conservative campaign before several thousand people at Wingham, Ontario, five days later and the performance was an excellent example of his style on the hustings: it was at once a lucid exposition of facts and figures (perhaps too many of the latter for some of his listeners) and a relentless attack on the enemy, laced with wit and sarcasm, sprinkled with ear-catching phrases. As was to be expected he devoted considerable attention to King's Richmond Hill speech and to King himself. His judgment of the Prime Minister was not surprising. "There never was a political leader," he said, "who was so utterly oblivious to hard, practical, immutable facts and so enamoured of time worn truisms, dusty platitudes and meaningless though prolific phraseology as the leader of the present Government."[8] As for the speech, he remarked, King ought to have reviewed "the actual accomplishments of his Government" and given "a clear declaration of principles which his party proposes to submit for public approval." But he had done neither. "From the first word to the last that speech can be read without finding reference to one single achievement, and for the very good reason that the page of achievements of the Mackenzie King Government is a blank. Within the four corners of the speech there is not a single sentence which declares a principle that any practical man can understand. The whole is an opaque mass of ill-founded and contradictory excuses."

Now Meighen took note of the paradox of governmental impotence in "the Parliament of large majorities."

> This Parliament, he says, has been a Parliament of large majorities. If that is the case may I quietly ask what more in the world did he need? It is true his majorities were mostly Progressive but did he not tell you, and did he not declare in every speech in Western Canada, that the Progressive platform and principles were identical with his own? He conducted his whole election in 1921 by courting a Progressive alliance, and he is going to conduct this one in exactly the same way if the Progressives allow him to do so. How is it, may I ask again, that though he obtained the votes of large numbers of the Progressives throughout the divisions of the last Parliament he couldn't enforce his principles if his principles were the same as theirs? The answer everybody knows. In the first place the principles he proclaimed in 1921 were only adopted in order to catch Progressive votes. The ridiculous impasse in which Mr. King found himself throughout the whole term of his Parliament was merely the product of his own dishonest campaign. The great national issues which he says must be settled could not be settled along the lines to which he committed his party. If they could have been he had a tremendous majority in Parliament by which his programme could have been translated into law. . . . The futility, the hopeless deadening impotence of the last Parliament was nothing else than the penalty for many long years of unprincipled political quackery.

At Richmond Hill King had made some finger-wagging references to Meighen, to which the latter proceeded to turn his attention.

> He told the people of North York that your humble servant . . . is the principal cause of the country's calamities. According to Mr. King I am a man of tremendous influence. The speeches I make affect the destiny of hundreds of thousands of people. The citizens of Canada are getting on, according to Mr. King, wonderfully well; they are prosperous and happy under his beneficent rule, but my speeches are so powerful they are convinced they are not getting on at all so they resign their positions, sell their homes, pack up their belongings and make off for the United States. My influence extends not only over all the provinces of Canada but, according to Mr. King it spreads across the Atlantic and moves great masses of humanity in every country of Europe. Because of the speeches of this awful Mr. Meighen the herculean immigration efforts of his Government amount to little or nothing. They try to convince intending immigrants from Europe that Canada is all right but the people of Europe believe me and won't believe Mr. King. This is

really a terrible state of affairs. I didn't think there was anyone living who could pay me such a compliment; but I would be happy if I were vain enough to accept it. But the fact is, as every child knows, that the whole thing is ineffable nonsense.

Coming to the four great national problems King had mentioned, Meighen paused first over the one that to him was transcendent, the tariff. In 1921, he charged, King and the Liberals had "flinched" that issue, saying different things about it in different parts of the country.

> For the four years since that contest they have feebly fumbled and floundered; they have stepped this way and they have stepped that way, and they have always threatened that with each succeeding year they would reduce protection and still more reduce it. . . . Throughout these four years of Mr. King's Government I have continued to the utmost of my energy in every part of Canada to drive home the biggest fact in the whole political being of our country, that a sound and strong and definite protective policy is the only means by which we can live and prosper. Mr. King now says, as if by way of complaint, that I have the same programme today which was defeated in 1921. He and his party flinched the issue and confused the electors of Canada under a tornado of misrepresentation. But whether it was defeated in 1921 or not the principle I preached then is a sound principle and true. I preach it now just as I preached it then and this time the people of Canada are not going to be befuddled by the twisting and shifting practices of Mr. King.

As for the other three issues, said Meighen, "I put this question to each one of you; I put it to the people of Canada. Is there any person in this Dominion, either man or woman, who knows today what the Government wants done on this transportation question, what the Government wants done on immigration, or what the Government wants done on Senate reform? Can any human being define now what the Government's policy is on any one of the three? Mr. King says he want a mandate on these three. What does he want a mandate to do? He has not told us and he is not going to tell us." On the subject of railways King at one place in his speech

> intimates that a system of government ownership in competition with a system under private ownership which pays the largest share of taxes in this country could not be defended and cannot long exist. This is for consumption in Montreal and anywhere else it may turn out to be popular. In another portion he says the two systems are going to continue, that he would never stand for amalgamation because he has such a horror of monopolies. This is for consumption in Ontario and in Western Canada or wherever it may prove to be popular. What I would like to know is this:—where is the common sense in making declarations like this one contradictory to the other, and then asking the people of Canada for a verdict? The fact is the Government has no proposal on the railway prob-

lem and is only introducing the question to sidetrack public attention from the great issues which the people have to decide.

And then there was immigration. "The only policy the Government has on immigration is to spend money without stint. . . . It is utterly ludicrous for the Prime Minister to intimate that the efforts of his Government would be greater if he had more of a majority in Parliament. Parliament has never hindered him in the slightest degree. What has hindered him is his policy. . . . What explanation has Mr. King for the fact that after all these efforts and this vast expenditure of money all we get is a trickling stream which rapidly finds its way through Canada to another land?" Finally Mr. King said he wanted to reform the Senate.

This old bird is provided with wooden wings and told to fly again. The people of Canada, says Mr. King, must decide the question of Senate reform. I make this assertion, and I challenge Mr. King to contradict it, that he has not one single proposal for reform of the Senate to which he dare commit his Government. If the public of Canada are to be asked to decide Senate reform they must be told how the Senate is going to be reformed. Mr. King once proposed a plan. That was in the early summer of 1924. He solemnly told the House of Commons that he intended to take measures which would make it impossible for the Senate to reject more than twice any bill sent up from the House of Commons. Let me ask Mr. King will he bind himself today to champion such a measure if returned to power? Last session I asked him on repeated occasions and he ran away from the question. Instead of introducing a measure or an address on the subject to Parliament he said all he would ask was authority to call a conference of the provinces. He got that authority but he never called the conference. I asked him if he were prepared to submit the proposal which he made the session before to this conference when it was called but he refused to tell me. He says now he wants a mandate from the people of Canada before he even calls the conference. Of all the humbug ever proposed this is the most transparent and absurd. Mr. King has called conferences many a time without even a mandate from Parliament. The fact is the Government has not one single proposal which it dare make on this subject of Senate reform. Let Mr. King tell the country what he wants done with the Senate for until he tells the country what he proposes to do it is all moonshine to be talking about the supposed issue of Senate reform.

Issues like these, Meighen declared, concluding this part of his address, issues on which the Government had no policy to offer, would be drummed up by King in the coming weeks to lure the attention of the public away from the underlying truth—the sterility, the futility of his administration.

A lot of aimless orating on these things is just so much shadow and vapor. Mr. King hopes by flying these kites to give the people something to divert their eyes. What he wants to do is to give Liberal candidates and speakers something to talk about instead of the record of his Government. But from one end of the Dominion to the other I believe the public of Canada have been watching. I know the people of Canada have been suffering and no contortions of Mr. King can turn their minds from the dismal pages of these last four years. Promises and pictures were all right for the last election but they won't do now. The time for performance came and the time for performance passed and nothing but a long series of blundering evasions is presented upon which the judgment of the electors must be heard.

The balance of the Wingham speech, the prototype of all that were to follow, was devoted to a discussion of railway policy and to an elucidation of his resolution on fiscal policy. To those who had heard him on these subjects before, or had read his remarks in Parliament about them, there was nothing new in what he had to say now. He was hewing to the familiar line of his arguments, secure in the belief that this was what ought to be expected of a public man.

Following their opening presentations the two leaders pursued one another around the nation, first through Ontario, then into the Maritimes, finally out across the West. On the prairies Robert Forke was also active, of course, making a last-ditch stand on behalf of the Progressives and ignoring the rest of the country. The central substance of Meighen's speeches was always the same: an excoriation of the King government to begin with and then an explanation of the corrective efficacy of the measures set forth in his fiscal policy resolution. In the Maritimes and the West, while stressing the need of a protective tariff, he laid particular emphasis on the benefits which would accrue to those sections if his proposed freight rate adjustments financed by the Dominion treasury were instituted. But in the West, and especially in Saskatchewan, the province that suffered most from high transportation charges, he found that such levelling adjustments were not thought to be enough. What was wanted there, as it had been for years, was completion of the railroad to Hudson Bay which, it was thought, would very materially reduce the burden of freight rates by providing an outlet to a tide-water port relatively close at hand.

The Hudson Bay Railway had been started shortly before the defeat of the Laurier government and construction had continued under the Borden administration until the war forced the diversion of resources to other purposes. Construction had not been resumed since the war, partly because of financial stringency and partly because the West was not politically powerful enough to offset the indifference or hostility to the project felt elsewhere in Canada. It was believed by many westerners, in whose minds the necessity of completing the road was an *idée fixe,* that powerful eastern financial and transportation interests had used their control over governments to block its completion. In 1925 less than one hundred miles of steel remained to be laid but on the portion already built large expenditures for repairs and improvements were required before the line would be fit for service. Furthermore, a big outlay would be needed on terminal and port facilities, whether at Fort Nelson, which had been designated the terminus, or at Churchill, where many people thought it should be. Meighen had always taken the position that there was an obligation to finish building the line and to put it in a serviceable state but that this work would have to be deferred until the financial conditions of the country improved.

This middle-of-the-road point of view, one slightly east of centre, earned him few plaudits. In the West his proviso about improved financial conditions was dismissed as a thinly veiled excuse for doing nothing. At the same time his declaration that the railway should be finished as soon as possible aroused a certain amount of ire in Montreal, something Meighen did with great ease and regularity. After one of his references to the subject, in a speech at Winnipeg in 1923, Ballantyne wrote to say that the statement "that you favored the completion of the Hudson Bay Railway, has caused a great deal of adverse criticism here."[9] What he had said, Meighen replied,

> was exactly what I said in Parliament last session. . . . I have at no time expressed my personal opinion as to whether the route will succeed from a business standpoint or not. I stated, though, that the country, through both parties, had solemnly pledged itself to complete this railway, and now that the bulk of the railway was done, the country would have to keep its word. Thousands of farmers have gone into those districts on the strength of these terms. . . . However, I stated that in our financial conditions to-day we could not justify going ahead with the large expenditures involved and we would have to wait until these financial conditions improve.
> The "Montreal Star" is continually misrepresenting me on this subject.[10]

From the West great pressure was put on the party leaders in an effort to get them to commit themselves to immediate completion of the road. The "On to the Bay" Association kept up an insistent propaganda, delegations descended on Ottawa, petitions were circulated, signed and presented to the Government. As G. H. Haney of Saskatchewan told one of the Conservative M.P.'s in 1924 in a letter which was passed on to Meighen, the "whole west is aflame with indignation over the delay. . . . It is possible for the Conservative party to win the next election if they promise the west the road NOW—and this despite the use of Forke or any implement, agrarian or otherwise."[11] With this Haney enclosed an open letter to Mackenzie King in the form of a poem which he had fashioned

in the white heat of indignation and which he signed "Fairfax."   It was
entitled "The Way to the Bay."[12]

> With the uttermost farthing ground out of the West,
>   Ere she lands her vast crops at the sea,
> You haven't a dime to spend on the line
>   That will make this great prairieland free.
> To our plea for "The way to the Bay," Mr. King,
>   You reply with a curt—"N.S.F."
> But you've money to spend on a tapering tower[13]
>   That may mark your political death.
> We will not desert the old flag, Mr. King,
>   Or the Empire that mothers the world,
> But you'll build us the line to the Bay, Mr. King,
>   Or—there'll be a new banner unfurled.
>
> You tell us the Senate sits hard on this scheme,
>   And we know that in this you speak true,
> But we've tired of the tricks of that barnacle crowd—
>   We look, not to them, but to YOU.
> YOU were given command of the fair ship of State,
>   To direct without favor of fear
> But you're letting the forecastle pilot the craft
>   With the sequel that wreckage is near.
> Then give us "The way to the Bay," Mr. King,
>   Ere the tide of secession up-rolls,
> Or we'll show you the way to the hay, Mr. King,
>   When our chance comes again—at the polls.
>
> You willingly father the Vanceboro line—
>   A matter of ninety odd miles—
> And the buying of hotels in La Belle Paris
>   Evokes nothing harsher than smiles.
> You've doubled the payroll on government jobs—
>   That is, your predecessors and you—
> But YOU are the man on the job, Mr. King,
>   And YOU get the blame—only you.
> You subsidize private-owned ships, Mr. King,
>   While our own lie awash at the quays;
> Could you not send these idlers up into the Bay
>   To carry our wheat o'er the seas?
>
> You could if you would—and you will, Mr. King,
>   Or we'll cut this Dominion in twain;
> And on whom, do you think, when the history's writ,
>   Will fall ignominious blame?
> On you, Mr. King. You are seized of our case;
>   You know that we pay through the nose
> For every dam'd thing, both forward and back,
>   From the grain we produce to our clothes;
> You know that it costs us a third of our crop

To land it at old Liverpool—
So give us "The way to the Bay," Mr. King—
Be the BOSS, use the old Golden Rule.

With the opening of the election campaign western demands for firm promises respecting the railway were intensified and King, speaking at Neepawa, Manitoba, was reported as promising that if in the election "he received sufficient Western support to enable him to carry out Liberal policies generally, completion of the Hudson Bay Railway would be one of those policies."[14] That at least was putting it in terms that everyone could understand, although it was King who would decide how much support was "sufficient." A few nights later Meighen referred to this promise at Saskatoon, where he addressed an audience of two thousand people who jammed Third Avenue United Church, overflowing into the choir loft, onto the platform and into Castle Gardens nearby, where his words were transmitted through the facilities of a local radio station. The completion of the railway, he said, should not have been held out by the Prime Minister as an election bribe. For his part, if returned to power he would ascertain as quickly as possible how much it would actually cost to finish building to the Bay. If reliable estimates indicated that the remaining steel could be laid and the whole line made serviceable for about three million dollars, as some thought was possible, he would undertake to have it completed before the time for another election arrived.[15] As King had attached no such figure to his promise, it was probably more convincing and attractive to western voters than Meighen's conditional guarantee. At any rate one of the complaints against the latter cherished by many a western Conservative for years to come was that he had refused to go far enough on this subject to compete successfully with King's bland assurances.

No matter where he happened to be during the campaign Meighen's thoughts were never very far from what was going on in the great province which for the time being he was unable to enter. So much hinged on the outcome in Quebec, so much of his own and his party's future, that he read avidly every bit of political news from that province he could lay his hands on. On the whole the news was encouraging. Patenaude by all accounts was waging a very effective battle. His meetings were well attended and aroused enthusiasm. His speeches were marked by force and eloquence and he seemed to be hammering away at the tariff question as Meighen had hoped and felt sure he would. Estimates of the success he would have varied but most observers thought he would win about fifteen seats and a few guessed that the number might be nearer twenty-five or thirty. But at the same time there were some most disquieting features in his campaign, features connected with his constantly reiterated insistence that he was "free from Mr. Meighen." Patenaude's own reason for taking this position was, of course, his belief, sincerely held, that it was the only way in which the confidence of the French Canadians could be gained; rightly or wrongly they would never support one of their own who was linked with the hated man of conscription. If they knew that in voting for Patenaude and his candidates they would be electing men free to follow an independent course at Ottawa, free to defend the rights of French Canada, free to give their support to a government or party or to withhold it, the solid Quebec Liberal bloc might be broken up.

According to this reasoning many electors who were Conservative by tradition and inclination but not willing to vote for Meighen would come out in their true colours to support an independent Patenaude. Also a lot of disgruntled Liberal protectionists would register dissatisfaction with King's tariff-tampering policies by casting ballots for Patenaude's men, as they would not do for Meighen's. Finally, it was thought, those of the Nationalist persuasion, who in the last two elections had voted Liberal for want of candidates of their own, might rally behind what Patenaude was clearly trying to identify as a movement peculiarly devoted to the interests of Quebec. The prominence as one of his lieutenants of Armand Lavergne, who became President of the Quebec Liberal-Conservative Association, suggested, or perhaps was merely intended to suggest that the Nationalist point of view was best represented by the Patenaude forces. Lavergne even thought that Henri Bourassa, possibly the most influential public figure in Quebec, might be won over or at least be persuaded to be benevolently neutral. He suggested in August, before Patenaude made his declaration at Saint Laurent, that Meighen when next in Montreal should call on C. H. Cahan, who had helped to engineer the Conservative-Nationalist alliance of 1911. Cahan, explained Lavergne, had "considerable prestige amongst the French with whom he is exceedingly popular. He is also a great friend of Bourassa's, on whom he has an influence which he could use at our benefit, to pacify Bourassa, who is very bitter and unfair to you and whose paper le Devoir is just now the only black spot on the Quebec horizon. If le Devoir were favourable or even only neutral we could carry the majority of seats in this Province. I think also Mr. Cahan would be a wonderful candidate in Montreal."[16] Meighen promised to see Cahan and added: "I note what you say as to Mr. Bourassa. Strange to contemplate I have never met Mr. Bourassa personally. He evidently thinks I am a bad lot."[17] So Bourassa did, and he was not to be "pacified." Le Devoir charged that Patenaude, backed by the Montreal Daily Star, was engaged in creating a parti Québecois which would be entirely inimical to national unity,[18] and throughout the campaign directed its editorial fire both against this movement and against Meighen. Although Bourassa was officially endorsed by the Patenaude organization when he announced that he would run for Parliament as an Independent, he disclaimed any connection with it and, once elected, supported the King regime.

In the minds of the mighty moguls of Montreal who gave Patenaude their wholehearted support there were, as far as one can judge, various good reasons for favouring the independence of him and his followers from Meighen. To some of them, Lord Atholstan especially, Patenaude's repudiation of Meighen might have the incidental advantage of weakening the latter in the country at large. Atholstan, in fact, wanted more than a declaration of mere independence and during the campaign entreated some of Patenaude's friends to obtain from him expressions of hostility to Meighen, which he refused to utter.[19] Meighen was aware of this. Atholstan, he remarked later, "was determined on the cleavage. . . . He used his every endeavour to drive in the wedge and separate us irreconcilably. This might have been expected and certainly was expected by me. Am doubtful, though, whether he had very much influence on Mr. Patenaude. Other influences were stronger than his. Mr. Patenaude did not go anything like the length that gentleman would have had him go."[20] But Atholstan after all was a unique phenomenon and his vindictive personal vendetta against Meighen probably did not interest most of the other big men of Montreal, small though their regard for Meighen may have been. To them, and Atholstan no doubt saw this also, the importance of Patenaude's independence lay in the effect it might have on public policy. If he succeeded in leading to Ottawa a sizeable contingent of men who were free from Mr. Meighen even as they were free from Mr. King, he might hold the balance of power and be able to barter the support of his group in return for certain measures much desired in Montreal. As the *Star* put it:

> No one imagines that Meighen—or any other possible Premier—will be able to take office without Patenaude's consent.
> AND PATENAUDE CANNOT GIVE THAT CONSENT TO ANY PREMIER—and stay in public life—WHOSE PREMIERSHIP WILL NOT BE ACCEPTABLE TO THE PEOPLE OF QUEBEC WHO WILL HAVE PUT IN PATENAUDE'S HANDS THIS FINAL POWER OF "VETO".[21]

Chief of the measures which Patenaude might thus be able to compel would in all probability be a new approach to the railway problem, possibly an amalgamation of C.P.R. and C.N.R. along the lines recommended by a Senate committee during the 1925 session of Parliament. This suggestion, opposed by Meighen and by many others on both sides of politics, was receiving a good deal of favourable attention in Montreal. Patenaude, while not openly advocating unification in his Saint Laurent speech, showed that his views were generally similar to those prevailing in the highest business circles of his city. The C.P.R., he pointed out, drawing a contrast always popular in Montreal, paid dividends; the C.N.R. incurred deficits. ". . . the mad race of disastrous competition between the two companies" must be brought to an end. If the administration of the C.N.R. could be separated entirely from politics great benefits would result but he doubted that this was possible with a publicly owned system. ". . . the country cannot continue to pour out the sweat of its people and the gold they produce simply in order to have the false pride of having a national railway and exploiting it."[22] Just how he would solve this problem, which he mentioned as one of the two major ones facing the country along with trade policy, Patenaude did not say. However, it is not unreasonable to suppose that those in Montreal who were assisting him with money, publicity and moral support hoped to use him for their own purposes and through him to have a decisive influence in determining the substance of national policy. He was to be, in other words, the means by which they could at last gain that control over the Conservative party and its national leader which for so long had eluded them. But as well-laid plans have a habit of doing, theirs went very much awry and the opportunity they were trying to create failed to materialize.

The whole plan of the Patenaude campaign was thoroughly worked out, especially as far as maintaining the appearance of freedom from Meighen was concerned. The *Star* and the *Gazette* scarcely if ever mentioned Meighen in their editorial columns, confining themselves to condemnation of King and praise of Patenaude, whom both of them supported vigorously, the *Star* in its typically flamboyant fashion, the *Gazette* with more dignified restraint but equal devotion. Their news pages, too, gave the impression that the fight that counted was between Patenaude and King and their reports of Meighen's speeches in other parts of Canada became shorter, less frequent and more deeply buried on the inside pages as the battle wore on, as though he were a minor figure too insignificant to be of interest to the people of Quebec. Not only was Meighen himself ignored but those who had been associated with him in the past were ostracized by the Patenaude organization in an effort to get rid of the Meighen stigma. One of those who were adjudged guilty by reason of such association was Arthur Lalonde, a Montreal lawyer, who explained to Meighen that he had "not personally taken much part in the campaign as the organization that has carried on the work did not wish to place, in charge, or even, accept the help of myself as I have been '*to* [*sic*] *much near you.*' That I was told by the heads of the organization."[23] Monty, who ran and lost in Laurier-Outremont, got into a public altercation after the election with Cahan, who had been victorious in a Montreal riding. During the argument Monty declared: "I was isolated in my constituency. I was unable to get any publicity. There was a weekly paper to which I gave $8,500 in five years and when I wanted an article signed by my name in it I was unable to have it inserted. I was unable to go to headquarters. I was prevented from going because it was told me that nobody who had been in Meighen's Cabinet should go to headquarters."[24] Grattan O'Leary was evidently having the same kind of trouble in his fight against Rodolphe Lemieux in Gaspé. He suffered from the double handicap of being a very close friend of Meighen and having an opponent who was just the kind of good conservative Liberal the people in Montreal would be happy to see elected. "I am extremely sorry," Meighen wrote, "to hear from Grattan O'Leary that he is not being supported in Gaspé, as he had a right to expect. Have sent repeated wires in an endeavour to help him out but am of opinion that there is hostility at Montreal headquarters because of his well known friendship for myself."[25]

The one fatal flaw in all these elaborate efforts to expunge the name, memory and influence of Meighen from Quebec was that the Liberals very inconsiderately refused to play the game. To them Meighen and his alleged crimes were far too valuable as electioneering issues to be eliminated in this summary fashion. It was an ironical situation, as well as a bitter and humiliating one for Meighen. His supposed friends and allies in Quebec acted as though he was their most burdensome liability; his enemies found in him their greatest asset and sought to make him the central issue. For the Conservatives, labouring to demonstrate their independence of him, there was no Meighen, only Patenaude; for the Liberals, dependent on him as they were for campaign material, it was the other way around.

Early in the campaign Mackenzie King in the course of a speech at Alexandria, Ontario, accused Meighen of raising the race cry.

> Premier King cited Mr. Meighen as saying recently that the talk in Quebec in the last campaign was not of protection but of Mr. Meighen being responsible for the murder of their children.
> "In talk of that kind," the Prime Minister went on, "Mr. Meighen is starting to raise race prejudices right in the midst of this campaign. He is starting to revive, five or six years away from the war, all the storms, passions, prejudices and feelings aroused at the time, when all true citizens have tried to forget differences of the past. I say that kind of thing is diabolical in a campaign of this kind.[26]

To this, according to the Montreal *Star*'s report, King added "that any man trading upon racial or creedal prejudices, using pure and holy things for his own ends, was unworthy the countenance of his fellow citizens. The members of his Cabinet approached racial or creedal questions with the golden rule, and the spirit of brotherly love in mind."[27]

It was presumably this benign and Christian spirit which accounted for the character of the Liberal campaign in Quebec. One had to expect a certain amount of personal vilification in the midst of a rousing political contest, no less in Quebec than in other provinces, and King himself came in for his share, much of it insinuations about his "pro-Americanism" along the lines that Brigadier Meighen had been thinking of.[28] But this was as nothing compared with the cynical mendacity of the propaganda unleashed against Arthur Meighen in 1925. For King to accuse him of being the author rather than the victim of race prejudice was a piece of blatant nonsense and a nice illustration of his way of twisting the issue of national unity for his own purposes. Talk about "storms, passions, prejudices and feelings"! Unless King was entirely ignorant of the methods being used by his lieutenants in Quebec, and that is not easy to believe, he must have known that they were fanning anew the old flame, reviving again those "differences of the past" the very mention of which he professed to deplore.

This, of course, was nothing new and not unexpected. Meighen long since had predicted it and Patenaude when he spoke at Saint Laurent saw that his opponents, as he expressed it, proposed "to organize the elections by talking of Mr. Meighen and Conscription."[29] Their campaign was that of 1921 all over again but even more violent and extreme in exploiting the bitter memories of wartime as well as the credulity of the voters. And in addition to conscription they now had Chanak to talk about and Meighen's alleged willingness, nay, his eagerness at Britain's behest, to see Canadian blood spilled on the shores of the Straits, or anywhere else in the world for that matter. The fact that a new crisis loomed ominously in the Near East in the autumn of 1925 was grist for their mill and they extracted the last ounce of sustenance from it. "In Quebec," Meighen wrote a few days after the election, "our candidates faced a campaign of hatred and racial appeal even more bitter than that of 1921. Paid organizers went from house to house advising the voters, particularly the women, that if Meighen were elected Prime Minister a war with Turkey would be declared and that the entrails of their sons would be scattered on the streets of Constantinople."[30]

The tenor of the Liberal campaign in French Canada was well exemplified by the remark of one speaker at Three Rivers that "the duty of the hour is vengeance,"[31] and by a cartoon, widely circulated, it was alleged,[32] by using it as a wrapping paper in the country stores. Its title was "A Voice from the Beyond" and it consisted of two panels. In the left-hand panel a ruthless, not to say demoniacal, looking Meighen is depicted with whip in hand, driving Canadian soldiers to war. On the right the spirit of Laurier speaks to a voter on his way to the polls, followed by a women dressed in mourning: "My friend, do not repeat your error of 1911. Vote for Mr. King, who was fighting at my side in Tory Toronto in 1917."[33] Then there was the cartoon in *Le Soleil*. On the one side stand Meighen, Patenaude and L. J. Gauthier. Out of Meighen's mouth come the words: "The last *sou*, the last man for the Empire." On the other side King is standing in the foreground with three of his ministers, Ernest Lapointe, P. J. A. Cardin and Lucien Cannon, behind him. He is saying: "Not a *sou* will be expended, not a man will be mobilized for the Empire without consent of the people." In the foreground a woman about to vote is being clutched by one skeletal hand labelled "The victims of Borden-Meighen Imperialism," while the other hand points to Meighen to remind her that he is the author of death.[34] Still another cartoon was entitled "The Trafficker in Human Flesh." Meighen is pictured standing on a promontory overlooking the sea. From across the sea stretch hands, dripping in blood with long, talon-like nails, labelled "Imperialism." Into these hands Meighen is placing a human figure in uniform labelled "Canada." He is saying: "Aye! Aye!! Ready! Aye!! Ready we are!"[35]

Pictures could be effective but for the most part the ammunition consisted of words. And they really were extraordinary words, for example in *Le Soleil's* treatment of the pregnant topic, "Peace or War?":

> Conscription! Arthur Meighen!
> Blood spilt! The blood of our sons! Spilt in far away countries, on the other side of the ocean!
> If it is to fight in defence of the cause of justice, those who want to may go. Their action is noble and generous. But who will submit to compulsion?
> Who, on the shores of the St. Lawrence, homeland of the French Canadians, will agree to allow Arthur Meighen to take our boys and send them to Turkey, China and the Indies?
> To send them forward at the first word from England!
> Without consulting our members, the representatives of the people,—Parliament! Without consulting others than Meighen and England!
> When we have no interest in this affair!
> Who wants war under these conditions?
> War for every purpose, and no purpose at all!
> War because England has many interests to protect in the petroleum wells of Mesopotamia! . . .
> The blood of our sons shed, the public treasury emptied, the country disrupted, and national bankruptcy!
> He who wants all that will get it with Arthur Meighen.
> Peace!
> Labourer in your field, worker in your workshop, merchant behind your counter, prosperous manufacturer, father of a family, young man, mother, and sweetheart, do you not prefer peace?

Blessed peace!

Peace that makes all things flourish!

If your country, your own land, is not in danger, do you not prefer peace?

You are brave; you love your country, you own your land, and you would defend it with the vigor of a lion if it were in peril.

Mackenzie King, grandson of William Lyon Mackenzie, rebel of 1837, thinks as you do.

His country is Canada. His soil is Canadian. His land to protect is our homeland.

He will not seek out our sons in our homes and ship them to Turkey, China or the Indies.

He will not "park" them on ships to send them to Mesopotamia to defend the oil wells of big London financiers.

To the Lloyd Georges who ask for Canadian troops for that, he will reply politely but firmly "no."

And that "no" will signify for you peace in your field, in your workshop, by your counter, in your home, in your heart.

Do you wish for peace or war?

Choose between King and Meighen. . . .[36]

The charge that a Conservative victory would mean war was constantly repeated. "A vote for Davidson is a sure vote for Meighen, the father of conscription," announced a pamphlet distributed in Shefford County. "If you want your sons to go to war vote for Davidson." "If you wish to open your veins on the battlefields of Europe," echoed *Le Soleil*, "return Mr. Meighen to power."[37] Meighen's reputed responsibility for conscription and all its horrors was incessantly harped upon. He "is the author of the Conscription Act," declared Cannon, "he is the author of the orders in council authorizing the police to hunt the conscripts in our rural districts and even to make use of police dogs. Do you favour his election?" And J. E. Perreault, Quebec's Minister of Mines and Colonization, told an audience in Drummond-Arthabaska: "You are aware as well as I am that Mr. Meighen is the author of all the iniquities of the *bleu* regime. He is the author of the famous Conscription Act and he boasts about it. Young men of Victoriaville, you recall the sad days we lived through while Meighen was in power. You recall that even after the war, when all countries had pardoned the draftees who had not reported for military service, Mr. Meighen still kept on their trail and had his agents filling the Arthabaska jail." A four-page circular distributed to the electors of Matane County and bearing no imprimatur declared that Meighen

was the chief instigator of conscription, which was revolting to all the instincts of our nationality.

He hounded our young men in all public places, and even in their homes.

He provoked in the city of Quebec riots that had to be quelled in blood.

He allowed all his newspapers and a clown known as Harry Lauder to insult our race.

He did not have in his cabinet a single elected French Canadian minister.

He was one of the most energetic racial firebrands.

One of the most energetic campaigners in 1925 was Premier Taschereau, who appealed strongly to memories of 1917. "How many young men," he exclaimed to one audience, "came to us and asked us to have them exempted from military service? But the Meighen-Borden law was inexorable. They had to leave for Valcartier. Sixty thousand of our sons fell on European battlefields." It had evidently eluded the Premier's memory that the Military Service Act contained liberal provisions for exemption, that large numbers of exemptions were granted in Quebec, as elsewhere, and that of the total of sixty thousand Canadian dead not one was a conscript. Moving to another meeting a few days after this speech, Taschereau, elaborating on his theme, was reported in *Le Canada* as saying:

> In the present contest, you have to choose between two men—Mr. King and Mr. Meighen. I do not want to be without Christian charity but I believe that I am guilty of no fault when I say that Meighen is the man of conscription, that he has sent our boys to Flanders Fields. He it is who, with his conscription law, has filled the cemeteries of Flanders with 60,000 Canadians. Has he grown better since? Has he reformed? Has he had perfect contrition? No.[38]

Shortly after the campaign was over Meighen charged that "never in the history of elections in this Dominion has a great party stooped to methods at once so dishonest and so dangerous as did the Liberal party in the late campaign in the Province of Quebec." To illustrate he quoted these statements by Taschereau.[39] This called forth a lengthy explanation from Taschereau that he had been misquoted by *Le Canada*.[40] However, misquoted on that occasion or not, the Premier of Quebec had certainly joined with other Liberals in that province during the campaign as a whole in "trading upon racial or creedal prejudices, using pure and holy things" for their own political advantage. It is not exactly clear how means such as these served the sacred cause of national unity about which Mackenzie King was so fond of declaiming. The Ottawa *Citizen*, no friend of the Conservative party, spoke the obvious truth when it described them as "wholly destructive, tending only to stir up animosity and bitterness. They destroy confidence between French and English citizens of the Dominion. National unity is set back for another period of years, after every general election into which such base appeals to party passion are introduced."[41] But if these appeals did serve their real, intended purpose, King's extraordinary success becomes somewhat less mysterious and magical, somewhat less difficult to explain than has sometimes been believed.

When the campaign ended Meighen was in Ottawa and on election night he sat in his office awaiting the returns, as he had in 1921. This time there was much more to gladden his heart in the news that reached him, though it was several days before the final results were know. The Conservative party had made a spectacular comeback, in terms of seats gained the greatest recovery ever made by any party up until that time. Outside of Quebec it won sixty-two per cent of the seats, double its share in 1921 and an increase of unprecedented dimensions. Its gains were at the expense of both Liberals and Progressives and only one seat held by a Conservative at dissolution was lost. With 116 members in a House of 245 the party was the largest element, though short of an absolute majority. 101 Liberals had been returned and only twenty-four Progressives. Two Winnipeg ridings had elected Labour members and there were two Independents, A. W. Neill of British Columbia and Bourassa. Comparing the results with those of 1921, the Conservative share of the popular vote had risen from 31 to 46 per cent, that of the Liberals had declined very slightly from 41 to 40 and of the Progressives from 25 to 9 per cent. Whereas in 1921 the Conservatives had taken no seats in six of the nine provinces, now every one except Saskatchewan was represented in their ranks. Ontario led the way, giving them 68 of its 82 places. In British Columbia they took ten out of fourteen, in New Brunswick ten of eleven, in Nova Scotia eleven of fourteen and in Prince Edward Island half of the four. Conservatives were successful in seven of Manitoba's seventeen ridings but had to be content with three of Alberta's sixteen, all of them in the two large cities. They also captured the lone Yukon seat and four of Quebec's 65. The four Quebec Conservatives elected were all in the Montreal district, three in the city and the other in the suburbs. None of them was French-speaking.

Taking the country as a whole there was an unusually close correlation between the number of ballots and the number of seats given to each party. However, in individual provinces the usual wide discrepancies were to be found. In New Brunswick, for instance, the one Liberal victory was hardly commensurate with the 40 per cent of the popular vote received by that party. Equally glaring was the disproportion between the Conservatives' 34 per cent of the Quebec popular vote and their capture of only four seats, about six per cent. Again, in Saskatchewan the Conservatives elected no members but collected one-quarter of the vote, as compared with 16 per cent in 1921, while in Alberta they outpolled the Liberals but took one seat less.[42]

Le trafiquant de chair humaine

Cartoon in *Le Soleil*, Quebec City, October 23, 1925.

Cartoon in *Le Soleil*, Quebec City, October 24, 1925.

The results in those two prairie provinces were very disappointing from the Conservative standpoint but not wholly unexpected. The party had never found them to be good fighting ground since their creation in 1905. Leaving aside the 1917 election when party lines had been virtually obliterated, only two Alberta and two Saskatchewan constituencies had ever sent Conservatives to Ottawa. Added to this lack of long-established strength, indeed partly the cause of it, was a serious publicity problem. There was no Conservative press to speak of in Alberta outside of Calgary and Edmonton; in Saskatchewan there was none at all and various efforts to acquire or start a paper had fallen through. The area was blanketed with Liberal and Farmer publications with scarcely a Conservative voice raised editorially in opposition to them. The whole problem was compounded in 1925 by the important fact, which Meighen knew full well, that the fiscal policy with which he was appealing to the country was less popular on the prairies than he hoped it would be elsewhere.

But it was not the rather poor showing in Alberta nor the complete failure in Saskatchewan that most bothered Meighen. The really stunning disappointment was the outcome in Quebec, for he had been led to expect such big things from that province. It had done materially better this time, of course; four seats were an improvement over none at all and the increase of fourteen per cent in the Conservative popular vote in Quebec practically equalled the increase in the country at large. But where were the fifteen ridings that had been so confidently counted upon by the Patenaude organization? With the exception of the four and of Bourassa's they were all still safely in Liberal hands and this was a fact of far-reaching importance. Had there been fifteen Conservatives from Quebec, even "free" ones, along with the 112 from the rest of the nation, the party would have had a slim but absolute majority in the House of Commons. A change of government in all probability would have occurred at once and Lord Byng would have been spared the deplorable controversy that was to mar the closing phase of his years in Canada.

Who or what was to blame for the failure of Quebec to come through as anticipated? As the inevitable inquest got under way almost everyone seemed to agree that blame belonged somewhere, but just where was a matter of opinion. The Montreal Star, to no one's surprise, blamed Meighen, not for anything in particular he had done but simply for still being leader. Patenaude, it pointed out, "was pictured by the very large army of campaigners, mobilized by the Liberals, as no more than a stalking-horse for a leader who does not command the confidence of Quebec—and the burden proved too heavy for him to carry."[43] Others blamed it on the utterly base propaganda used by the Liberals, which had misled the thoughts of the people away from the issues of the present to the struggles and passions of the past. Still others attributed it to the lack of a virile French-language Conservative press and to the influence of Bourassa and *Le Devoir*. A different diagnosis was that the women's vote had been the downfall of the party. One defeated candidate informed Meighen that upon "examining the ballots given against me, I found that more than half bore the small crosses made by the women voters. I believe that it will be very hard to obtain control in this Province, as long as the women have the right to vote. They are not educated to it, and vote only in the fear of conscription." He went on to draw the obvious but most ungallant moral that the ladies of Quebec should be disfranchised![44]

The difficulty of combating the suspicion of French Canada so assiduously cultivated by the Liberals was the most formidable, baffling problem the Conservatives faced. As Meighen commented:

> The war and all the war's suffering and animosities form the groundwork upon which unscrupulous politicians can operate. It is not to my views on questions of Empire duty that the people of Quebec object, it is rather to a gross and false misrepresentation of my views persistently and resolutely indulged in by our political opponents. It has proven impossible so far to overtake this misrepresentation, first, because we have not a French press. We lost our French press as part of the price paid for doing right in the war. The second reason is that the use of the French language makes it very difficult for myself personally and the leaders of our party generally to overtake calumnies thus circulated.[45]

Patenaude had hoped to solve the problem by asserting his freedom from Meighen. He had failed, despite the gains that had been made, and much of the recrimination that inevitably ensued was directed against him, as well as against those in Montreal who were popularly believed to have inspired and directed his campaign. "They were out for your scalp," a friend in Toronto told Meighen, "and Mr. Patenaude was the knife they intended to use. . . . Look out for that Montreal crowd and keep a weather-eye peeled for our genial friend, Bob from the West, for I am not so sure he has not had a finger in the pie."[46] But Rogers, if active at all in Quebec (and Patenaude could not later remember having seen him once during the campaign),[47] was only a peripheral figure in that situation; he had been mainly concerned with winning his own personal contest in Winnipeg South, which he did. The culprits in Montreal singled out for abuse were chiefly Lord Atholstan, Smeaton White, their respective newspapers and the powerful business interests, especially the C.P.R., for which they spoke. Atholstan, perhaps the most widely disliked Canadian of his day, was the target of the bitterest criticism and this was not surprising. So loud had been the blare of the

Star's trumpets, so blood-tingling the insistent beat of its drums on Patenaude's behalf, that His Lordship, whose predilection for intrigue was no secret, was generally supposed to have been the guiding genius behind Patenaude. While this was probably an exaggeration of his actual influence, many people found grim satisfaction in the view that the failure in Quebec had at last given Atholstan his "come-uppance." "Curses both loud and deep," Frank Meighen reported to his cousin, "are being hurled at a certain gentleman for the way affairs were managed here. There is a feeling of pleasure that he failed so completely, and the hope is expressed that he is finished."[48] Senator Rufus Pope, a Conservative of the old school from the Eastern Townships, was one of those who were cursing:

> Some people said I was wrong in my speeches when I mentioned your name, but the smoke screen is gone I guess they all see that. The war is on in Turkey and will be on my friend so far as this Province is concerned for the next forty years. As Riel's hanging has lived so will conscription. The womans' [sic] vote will nourish the microbe of conscription as long as life lasts. Amen.
> Glad that His Lordship and gang had their way no one to disturb them. . . . I would rather be beaten without them than to win with them hanging on our necks. Of course I never saw or heard a word from any of them. No fear. They were out for murder, and got shot themselves on the trail when they were out for the other man's blood. Good riddance of an unscrupulous Bunch partly composed of crooks and the balance Fanatics. Arthur I know the Bastards from the ground up.[49]

A similar though less profane comment, passed on to Meighen by its recipient, was contributed by an unidentified New Brunswick Conservative: "The Gazette and Star instead of being loyal to Meighen and supporting him to the hilt, boomed Patenaude to Meighen's detriment. Meighen should have conducted his campaign in Quebec, the same as he did in every other Province. Results would not have been any worse and possibly they might have been better. The quicker that you people get after Lord Atholstan and Senator White, the better for the Conservative Party."[50] Of like mind were a number of French-speaking Conservatives, people who had not been or now claimed not to have been in sympathy with the notion of an independent movement, and some of whom had been shouldered aside by the Patenaude organization. For example Senator D. O. L'Espérance, proprietor of *L'Evénement,* the nearest thing there was to a French-language Conservative paper, assured Meighen that

> had the support given Patenaude and his group, been given to the men who stood by the Conservative Party and by yourself in the sombre days of the war, the result would not have been worse; on

the contrary, it would, in my humble but very firm opinion, have been very much better. I, in unison with thousands of my fellow compatriots, considered as a great personal injustice to yourself and also as a gratuitous insult on the French Canadians the fact that you were debarred from visiting the Province of Quebec during the . . . election. I am absolutely convinced that you would have been personally received and greeted as well, if not better, than Mr. King.

No permanent headway can be made in this Province until such time as you find and entrust with your confidence public men who are not afraid to espouse and defend the policies and ideals you profess yourself. A house divided amongst itself cannot reign. Our people are not what certain interested or ignorant people would have you believe. They love courage and sincerity and they would soon realise that you have these two virtues in abundance. But how can we make any headway against the liberal [sic] party, which is interested in blackmailing you, unless you surround yourself with men possessed of enough political sense to frankly and courageously stand by you?

. . . They may say what they like today; to save their face they will put forth all kind of excuses; but the fact remains that the same conspirators, who knifed you in 1921, were behind the Patenaude movement, at this election, and for the very same purpose they had then in view. Had Mr. Patenaude come with us openly and sincerely, it would no doubt have helped, but the moment he tied himself hands and feet to that group, he was heading towards certain defeat, while we, French Canadians, unjustly bear the stigma of having debarred you from visiting this Province, whose inhabitants count among the most generous, the most courteous and the most broadminded in this Dominion.[51]

Meighen agreed completely with the views expressed in these letters. It had been no choice of his that he stayed out of Quebec and he had no intention of repeating the error. "You may depend upon it," he declared, "every contest in the future will be fought in Quebec on exactly the same lines as in the rest of Canada, and I will go into that province and conduct the battle there just the same as in the other provinces of the Dominion."[52]

One of the grounds on which Patenaude was accused of having done a disservice to the cause, and Meighen himself felt this very strongly, was that by setting himself up as an independent leader he had implied his belief in the validity of the Liberal charges against Meighen. Also, he had created some uncertainty as to his own exact position. If, as the Liberals contended, he was not really free from Meighen, those who believed his claim that he was and supported him for that reason would be his dupes. On the other hand if he *was* really free, then he was neither a *Bleu* nor a *Rouge;* he and his followers would be in the hazardous and possibly powerless position of an isolated bloc in the House of Commons. It was not in the tradition of French Canada to elect representatives who were not in some way closely associated with one of the two national parties, not its habit, despite the recurring Nationalist movements, to entrust its interests at Ottawa to a purely Quebec party. Doubt about just where Patenaude really stood may have been an important factor in the discouraging results of his efforts. "The people prefer definite situations," remarked André Fauteux, "and never fail to appreciate acts of courage at their true value."[53] "Meighen is the leader," echoed Monty during the dispute with Cahan already referred to, "he is the right leader, he is the best man that we have got. . . . I am not for independent parties. We must be Liberal or Conservative. We must be for King or Meighen."[54] A Montreal manufacturer told Meighen that one of his "French-Canadian travellers from the Eastern Townships stated to me on Saturday last that had Patenaude come out as a straight 'Blue', and a supporter of yours, except with the reservation that in the event of conscription again becoming an issue he would oppose it, he would have carried fifteen seats. As it was the French-Canadian people in the Eastern Townships said 'What is he?' 'What confidence can we have in him?' "[55]

From the point of view of the election results the strictures passed on Patenaude were not entirely fair, even though the number of seats won had not come up to expectations. In almost every French-speaking riding the Liberal majority had been substantially reduced, in some cases drastically so, and this was perhaps as much as could have been reasonably hoped for at that time, whether Patenaude were free of Meighen or not. Another election, which the indecisive results of this one in the country as a whole appeared to make imminent, might well bring a further improvement and at long last send a number of French-Canadian Conservatives to Ottawa. Undeniably under Patenaude's direction real progress had been made. However, equal progress might have been achieved and the further advantage of party solidarity been secured had he come out courageously as a supporter of Meighen. No one could be sure what would have happened had things been managed differently but it was the opinion of many that, considering the trend towards the Conservatives across the country, little if anything had been gained by the whole elaborate independent strategy. As things stood Patenaude had failed to remove Meighen from his unenviable position as the favourite Liberal campaign issue in Quebec, which was to have been the most beneficial consequence of his "freedom." And, as the post-mortem letters received by Meighen made clear, the course taken had not healed the wounds within the Quebec section of the party and restored its unity and morale as Meighen had prayed that Patenaude would do. The bitter recriminations with which some of those letters were filled indicated that the party was still faced, as it had been since the war, with the urgent necessity of getting its dirty linen washed and put away at last.

However, for all his disappointment at the result in Quebec, Meighen could not bring himself to join in the condemnation of Patenaude which so many others expressed. He was, of course, hopeful that the man would remain in politics and play a more effective part in the future. But that expedient consideration aside, he believed Patenaude himself had acted in all sincerity, mistaken though he might have been. Some days after the voting he wrote a long and friendly letter to the French-Canadian leader, offering some reflections on what had happened in Quebec and expressing his appreciation of Patenaude's efforts.

> I have waited until the smoke cleared away before writing. My desire is merely to put in words an expression of admiration of the excellent campaign you conducted, and of sincere regret that greater results did not accrue.
>
> Without the least hesitation I say to you that I have no feelings toward you but feelings of gratitude and loyalty. Whether the course which you felt it best to pursue was wise or not is another question which I will refer to later only briefly. The fact is you adhered loyally to the statement of intention which you gave to me, and no doubt you adhered in the face of strong and persistent pressure. I can never cease to admire both the signal honesty which characterized your course and the notable energy with which it was pursued. The speeches you delivered were masterpieces of dignity and power.
>
> We both of course remember the rather long period which preceded your decision to enter the fray. Forgive me if I say again that I think the advice which I urged so persistently was right. I think you would have done better to have stayed definitely and unwaveringly with me, and that we had gone into battle and fought through to the end together. The dangers of the course which you conscientiously thought it best to take were pointed out by me at the time, and the experience of the contest has shown that these were the very dangers and difficulties which appeared.
>
> The above is stated not in any belief that I have anything in the way of personal strength in the province of Quebec; it is stated rather in the belief that the standing aside of the official Conservative party from direct association with myself as leader tended to convince the people that the disapproval in which many men held me was justified, and to leave my reputation after the campaign rather worse than better than it was when the campaign began. It is impossible for a party to win if the public feel that the man who will be at the head of the Government in the event of the party's success has not the confidence of the party itself. It is quite possible, of course, that there will be a reaction against the diabolical methods the Liberal leaders adopted repeatedly in recent elections, and put in practice in the most malevolent and dishonourable form in the late election. The statement you made to the press after the result was known was characterized both by justice and by truth. There can never be unity in Canada while a political party employs the base and poisonous weapons used by the Liberals in the late contest.

For the use of these weapons in this campaign there has not been the faintest shadow of excuse. In the rest of Canada we managed to get concentration of thought on the issues of to-day. There was nothing, even from the mouth of the most obscure speaker or the columns of the most irresponsible journal, in the way of racial appeal or appeal to the hostilities of years gone by.

May I ask you to count me, however, not as a critic but as an admirer. I can never forget your steadfast courage, your impressive eloquence and your undaunted Canadianism.[56]

CHAPTER THIRTEEN

HERESY AT HAMILTON

WHILE IT was all very well to talk about how different the results might have been in this or that part of the country had affairs been managed differently, no amount of argument or recrimination could alter the verdict of the voters. But what exactly was that verdict? The people had been heard but never since Confederation had their almighty voice spoken in such uncertain tones. Instead of that adequate majority which Mackenzie King had appealed for, they had elected a Parliament in which the opposing forces were far more evenly balanced than before. There were some certainties in the new situation, of course. The Government had received no fresh mandate, anything but a vote of confidence. Not only had it sixteen fewer members behind it than before (in a House of Commons now larger by ten seats), but the Prime Minister and eight of his ministerial colleagues had gone down to personal defeat. By no stretch of the imagination could this be described as a victory for the Liberal party, although King later counted it as one of the elections the party had "carried" under his leadership.[1] At the same time, however, the Conservatives had scored only a moral victory, impressive and unprecedented as the extent of their gains was. The one most ironical fact was that the Progressives, despite their heavy losses to both the old parties, would hold the balance of power much more decisively in the new Parliament than they had in the old; what happened when the House met would depend entirely on them.

It would depend on them, that is, if Parliament were allowed to meet. For several days after the election, while everyone waited for the final tabulation of results, speculation mounted concerning the course King would take. Would he resign, making way for Meighen, or would he meet the House, hoping that Independents, Labourites and enough of the Progressives would choose to sustain his regime? Meighen quickly became convinced that he planned to take the latter course and in an effort to prevent his doing so sent off a code telegram to leading Conservatives across the country:

Apparently Government intends hanging on obviously with intention getting new campaign fund. Strongly urge newspaper demand for resignation. Make plain that any second dissolution granted this government would be outrage. Resignation only course as Prime Minister declared only reason for election was to get clear party majority. Also all precedents show Government has only right count on its own supporters in estimating whether defeated or not. Pass this suggestion quietly to favourable papers your province.[2]

But were resignation or meeting Parliament the only alternatives in King's opinion, or was there still another possibility? Speaking at Erindale, Ontario, early in the campaign about the necessity of a government having an adequate parliamentary majority, he had declared: "If we should ever be faced again with conditions such as pertained in the last four years, I would not hesitate to again call upon the Governor-General to dissolve Parliament and would continue until some party secures a majority to enable it to carry on the affairs of the country."[3] This statement, which has been described by one authority as "quite the most extraordinary of Mr. King's career,"[4] indicated a belief on the latter's part that in the circumstances resulting from the election he could have another dissolution without the new Parliament ever assembling. That he did actually believe this was shown by a formal statement which he issued on November the fourth after consultations with his Cabinet and the Governor-General, ending the suspense about what he would do. There were, he said, three choices before him: he could resign, meet the new House, or advise "an immediate dissolution." He had chosen the second, not because the duly elected Parliament had a right to meet, but because he "felt it was not in the interests of the country to occasion the turmoil and expense of another general election until at least Parliament had been summoned and the people's representatives in Parliament had been afforded an opportunity of giving expression to their views."[5] In King's opinion, apparently, once those views had been expressed he could, if he wished, secure another dissolution.

That opinion was not shared by Lord Byng. Immediately after the election King had several interviews with the Governor-General which were described in a memorandum prepared by the latter's secretary, Arthur Sladen, and transmitted in January to L. S. Amery, Secretary of State for the Dominions.

> At these interviews the situation was thoroughly discussed in all its bearings. The result of the first interview was that the Prime Minister went away saying he would resign—though he had not come up to Government House to hand in his resignation—but had accepted the private and confidential view expressed by the Governor General that that was his proper course.
> The next day he came up again to see His Excellency, and announced that he had changed his mind and now thought it was his duty and his right to stay on as Prime Minister and meet the House of Commons.

His Excellency again tried to persuade him to take the dignified course of resigning . . . but told him that there was no constitutional reason against his continuing in office.

Several more interviews took place but the Prime Minister did not again change his mind. The only course then open to the Governor General was:—

(1) To insist on the Prime Minister calling the House of Commons to meet at the earliest possible moment.

(2) To make the Prime Minister understand that no political appointments (Senators, Judges, etc.) could be made in the interim—and that no contracts should be made for any public works.

His Excellency also gave the Prime Minister to understand that he would not grant him another dissolution.[6]

In acknowledging receipt of this report Amery wrote that "the political situation in Canada during the next few months is likely to be a matter of general Imperial interest. . . ." and added in a handwritten postscript: "A queer gentleman it is you are dealing with!"[7]

Neither King's Erindale statement, it has been well said, nor his claim after the election that he could advise "an immediate dissolution" could "be brought within any conceivable definition of parliamentary government. If Parliament has any rights at all, it must surely have the right to come into existence. Yet Mr. King asserted that the Prime Minister has the right to kill Parliament before it is born."[8] That this right of abortion existed was promptly denied by Meighen in a statement of his own. "The Premier," he said, "knows that his cabinet had no such alternative and could not get another dissolution no matter what they advised. They have made their appeal and they have been defeated." But Meighen went further than that, asserting that King had not the right to await the assembling of Parliament and should resign forthwith.

There never has been a case in Canada [he said] and none for a third of a century in Britain, where the leader of a minority group has waited for the calling of Parliament or has refused to resign immediately. Mr. Baldwin [in 1923] waited for Parliament but Mr. Baldwin emerged from the election the leader of by far the largest group.

Mr. King declared as the reason for his appeal to the people, that his Government could not satisfactorily conduct public business while dependent upon Progressive support. In defiance of this declaration he now decides to cling to office, though dependent infinitely more than before upon Progressive support. Of the twenty-seven Progressives, Independents and Labour candidates elected, eighteen of them denounced his record and defeated his candidates. The Premier himself and eight of his Ministers have been rejected. The popular majority against his Government is overwhelming. To cling to office under such circumstances is usurpation of power and contempt of the popular will.[9]

This last sentence was an irresistibly appropriate echo of King's sanctimonious accusations of usurpation against Meighen before the 1921 election. If there had been usurpation then King was guiltier of the same crime now, for Meighen had at least commanded a clear and certain majority in Parliament. But might not King also turn out to have a majority once Parliament was convened, sufficient to enable him to retain the confidence of the House, if not to solve national problems "in a reasonable and satisfactory manner"? It was true, as Meighen said, that there was no very recent British precedent, and no Canadian ones at all since 1867, for King's decision as leader of only the second largest group to await the verdict of Parliament. However, in 1892, the not very remote past, Lord Salisbury had met the British House of Commons as Prime Minister after an election which gave his party only the second largest number of seats, and King surely possessed the right to do the same now. If the House gave him its confidence all the requirements of the Constitution would be satisfied; if he were denied its confidence it would be time for him to resign in Meighen's favour. The danger to the Constitution would come if King, lacking a majority in Parliament, attempted to assert what he regarded as his right to another dissolution.[10]

Because of the highly unusual and uncertain situation arising from the election the opening of Parliament, set for the seventh of January, was awaited with much more than ordinary anticipation. For the same reason uncommon interest was aroused in a by-election in Bagot County, Quebec, necessitated by the death of J. E. Marcile, who had represented it for twenty-seven years. Marcile had defeated André Fauteux by fewer than eight hundred ballots out of more than six thousand cast and the Conservatives nominated Fauteux again, hopeful that the electors of the county would decide to climb on the party's bandwagon before it got rolling so fast that they were left behind. There was no thought of keeping up the elaborate masquerade of independent Conservatism in Quebec now; Fauteux was running as a straight Conservative and arrangements were made for Meighen to address several meetings in the riding. He welcomed the chance to do so, both because it had been alleged during the recent campaign that he was afraid to enter Quebec and because he had a pronouncement to make of a sort which he thought would appeal strongly to the French Canadians. This he had "had under review for months"[11] and, it may be, had intended to deliver it in Quebec before the general election until Patenaude's repudiation of him kept him out of the province.

As a matter of fact, though, the pronouncement was first made, not in Bagot County, but at a banquet in Hamilton, Ontario, on November the sixteenth where, after condemning the vile and slanderous campaign the Liberals had waged in Quebec, Meighen declared:

> In the late war, as in every war, the Government had to decide its course and submit that course to Parliament. . . . Never would any Government so much as dream of sending troops beyond our shores unless the authority of Parliament was first obtained. Indeed, I would go further. I do not anticipate that we of this generation will ever be called upon to take part in war again, and I earnestly hope that our children and our children's children may be free from the curse of war, but if ever the time should come when the spectre of 1914 should again appear I believe it would be best, not only that Parliament should be called, but that the decision of the Government, which, of course, would have to be given promptly, should be submitted to the judgement of the people at a general election before troops should leave our shores. This would contribute to the unity of our country in the months to come and would enable us best to do our duty. It would not mean delay. Under the stress of war delay might be fatal. Let me make clear what I mean. The Government would have to decide and decide quickly what was best in the interest of Canada. The Government would have to act on its judgement, but before there was anything in the way of participation involving the despatch of troops the will of the people of Canada should first be obtained. I have myself not the slightest fear but that if danger threatened the Empire, and therefore, threatened Canada again, this country would respond as it responded in 1914, but I believe in future it will be best for all that before a Government takes a step so momentous as the despatch of troops the will of the people should be known.[12]

Before enunciating this principle, that a general election should precede the sending of troops, Meighen had consulted a number of men whose judgment he trusted. Chief of these was Borden, with whom, in fact, he had discussed it more than once. Borden approved of it and so did others—Hugh Guthrie, Sir Edward Kemp, J. D. Reid, General Mewburn and Sir Henry Drayton. The one dissenter among those he conferred with was Howard Ferguson, whom Meighen stopped off to see on his way to Hamilton and who, "while not objecting to the procedure recommended in the speech," Meighen wrote shortly afterwards, "took the ground that it was unwise to disturb a good situation in Ontario. He was the only one to whom I ever mentioned the subject who did so advise. I am informed now of many who say they so urged me, but as a matter of fact no one else did. I had no conception there would be anything like the opposition that was raised."[13]

Opposition there was, and it was vociferous. Immediately after the Hamilton banquet Meighen left for a short holiday at Highland Pines, North Carolina (like Mackenzie King he sometimes holidayed in the United States!) and had been there only a few days when his friend, T.

A. Russell, telephoned from Toronto to warn him that a storm was brewing. Their conversation did not last long enough for Meighen to get many details—he regarded long-distance telephone calls as an unwarranted extravagance—but he gathered that he was being personally attacked by some Conservative newspapers and individuals who refused to be bound by his declaration at Hamilton.[14] Upon arriving back in Ottawa near the end of November he learned how true this was and when he repeated the gist of that declaration in French at meetings in Bagot during the first few days of December, further evidence of dissatisfaction accumulated, especially but not only in Ontario. Even in that province not all Conservatives were antagonistic, of course, probably not the great majority. R. J. Manion wrote from Fort William that he had just read the Hamilton speech. "Bully for you. You have 95% of Canada with you on that policy, at least as far as calling parliament before sending troops is concerned & probably all the way. A few *extreme* Imperialists may kick, but where can they go? You are on solid ground. I have heard this attitude upheld by ... many ... old line Tories. I am with you 100% (That ought to help! Don't laugh.)"[15] It did help and so did the approval of some newspapers like the Kingston *Standard,* the Hamilton *Herald,* the Sydney *Post,* and the Edmonton *Journal,* which rose to defend Meighen against his critics. But it was the bitterness of the criticism in some Tory circles that was most noticeable, as well as the failure of some of the leading Conservative papers to endorse his pronouncement. The *Mail and Empire,* with whose editor Meighen had briefly discussed on his way to Hamilton what he was going to say, gave it guarded approval but rather skirted the issue.[16] The Ottawa *Journal* remained ominously silent, indicating that Meighen had again incurred the august displeasure of of P. D. Ross, as indeed he had.

My conviction is strong [Ross wrote to him] that the principle of representative government which has carried the English-speaking peoples along safely so far is contravened by the idea of holding a plebiscite, for a general election upon a single issue would be practically that, in a moment of national crisis.

Without desiring to trouble you by argument, but to make my feeling clear, I think that to propose that a great national issue at an emergent time should be relegated to the judgment and delay of a great mass of individual voters, mostly ill informed, instead of having the decision made by representative and better informed men in Parliament, would ordinarily be to call for whatever opposition I might be able to give.

I feel obliged to keep silent at present, as far as public comment is concerned, the duty of the moment being I think to do nothing to hurt the possibility of this country getting back to an effective national policy industrially, but I want to be frank about the other matter at once, so that no misunderstanding can arise as to the Journal's motives if comment should seem necessary at a later date.[17]

Some other displeased editors and publishers were less forbearing than Ross. The Toronto *Telegram,* whose fiery editor, John R. Robinson, was no great respecter of party leaders or other persons, smote the Hamilton message hip and thigh, but warned that Conservatives should not be diverted by a feud among themselves from carrying on the battle against the real enemy. They must, it said, "postpone the duty of DELIVERING THE PARTY from a partnership of responsibility for the ultimate perils of Hon. Arthur Meighen's palaver at Hamilton until they have fulfilled their share in the duty of delivering the country from the immediate perils of Hon. W. L. M. King's PREMIERSHIP at Ottawa."[18] The Winnipeg *Tribune* was equally emphatic in its condemnation. The idea of holding an election before dispatching troops, it said, was one that might be expected to come from ultra-nationalists like Sir Clifford Sifton, Henri Bourassa or J. S. Ewart. "It comes strangely from the lips of Rt. Hon. Arthur Meighen." What would it mean in practice? "While other parts of the Empire were fighting Canadians would be voting. Bullets flying in the battle front and ballots flying in Canada. Battles with other parts of the Empire participating and stump speeches on the Canadian hustings. A war horror and an election horror as well. . . . If Mr. Meighen can contemplate such a spectacle with complacency he has been greatly misunderstood by his friends. His proposal is, of course, foolish and impractical. Its acceptance and its expression in fixed Canadian policy would be the beginning of the end if not the actual end of Canada's attachment to the British Empire."[19] The *Tribune* seemed to be particularly, and to Meighen surprisingly, apoplectic about this question. In a later editorial, prompted by his statement in Bagot that it was the policy of the Conservative party to go to the country before sending troops off to war, it stated:

> Mr. Meighen may properly be asked to explain when it became the policy of the Conservative party.
> So far as The Tribune is aware, when Mr. Meighen gave utterance to this policy in his recent speech at Hamilton, he voiced an idea absolutely new in Canadian political affairs. It came like a thunderclap from a clear sky.
> In the general elections the Conservative leader had addressed hundreds of meetings from Halifax to Vancouver. He had the opportunity of expounding every plank in Conservative policy, in fact it was his duty to do so. And not one word did he utter bearing on this vitally important policy which he now declares is endorsed by the Conservative party.
> The last public utterance Mr. Meighen made on this subject was on September 22, 1922, at Toronto. There, he said, referring to

the British government's cable asking Canada's support in the British-Turco crisis at Chanak:

> "When Britain's message came, then Canada should have said, 'Ready, aye ready; we stand by you!' I hope the time has not gone by when that declaration can yet be made. If that declaration is made then I will be at the back of the Government."

> That was Conservative policy in 1922, accepted as such because it was in line with every tradition of the Conservative party in Canada. It stood as Conservative policy until November, 1925, when Mr. Meighen spoke at Hamilton. Then he removed the keystone of the arch of Conservative policy, introduced this Bagot by-election monstrosity in place of it, and solemnly affirmed it to be the policy of the Conservative party.

> Why did he not proclaim this policy in the general election campaign, in order that the people might pass upon it?

> And having waited till the general elections were over why could he not have waited until Parliament convened? His followers had surely some right to consultation in advance of the disclosure of a policy that throws the Conservative party on its beam ends.

> Mr. Meighen could not or would not wait. A Quebec by-election was in the offing and a special Conservative platform had to be rigged for the occasion. But if to win one by-election the very foundation of Conservative policy must be rooted up and destroyed, and the Conservative party accepts that as a necessary expedient, then surely it has lost the spirit of its founders.[20]

This was the most outspoken attack ever made on Meighen by any Conservative paper outside of Montreal and no doubt it faithfully mirrored the views of many Conservatives across the land.[21]

Most of these people refrained from expressing their objections publicly but some of them let Meighen know privately what the feeling was. Senator Rufus Pope wrote in his typically blunt fashion: "I beg to report that your Hamilton speech, as far as its influence goes was very detrimental to you personally. Of course personally I do not feel bound by the personal views of yourself or any other individual, because I consider the Principles of the Conservative party transcendent to the utterances of any man."[22] "If the blessed day ever comes," Meighen retorted, "when even good friends don't take a swat at me once in a while I will consider I have arrived at political Paradise."[23] As he well knew, that paradise was not of this world. Fawcett Taylor, the Conservative leader in Manitoba, reported: "Our fellows here are not bothering much, they say we never had to apologize yet for anything you said; but at the same time don't like the idea of a general election before going to war."[24] But some "fellows" were bothering most decidedly and openly dissociating themselves from Meighen on the question. Thomas L. Church, a right-wing Tory imperialist M.P. from Toronto, stated that he did not "believe in Mr. Meighen's doctrine. We are part and parcel of the British

Empire and not a nation within ourselves. I will oppose Mr. Meighen's attitude on the floor of the House and in caucus. We do not need autonomy. . . . There are some people in this country who would like to do away with British ties."[25] C. H. Cahan took advantage of an invitation to address the Toronto Liberal-Conservative Business Men's Club, which, as it happened, had been extended to him at Meighen's suggestion,[26] to denounce the latter's utterance at Hamilton. After remarking that "efforts to adjust, without due consultation and consideration, serious questions of public policy, frequently serve to invite future dissensions." Cahan went on to say:

> It may be that the personal policy which Mr. Meighen recently announced . . . may turn the tide of local sentiment. But, speaking also personally, with a quite intimate knowledge of the views and sentiments which generally prevail in the province of Quebec, I do not believe that the Hamilton pronouncement will be regarded either in Quebec or the other provinces of Canada as binding upon the conscience and judgment of the Conservative party as a whole, or as controlling the discretion of Parliament whenever grave international complications may arise in the future. Nor do I believe that such a pronouncement, made by a political leader, however able and esteemed he may be, will serve to remove permanently the estrangement which at present exists between Quebec and the majority of the provinces outside of Quebec.[27]

The president of the club advised Meighen not to take this too seriously. "So far as Toronto is concerned," he wrote, "forget Cahan. I gave a dinner that night for Cahan . . . & we fought it out till midnight. Cahan got an earful. Your friends are loyal & true to you. Be of good cheer. . . ."[28] This was comforting and, after all, Cahan's reaction was not altogether to be wondered at in view of his effusion in the *Gazette* a year earlier. One could not help wondering whether he would have waxed so indignant had *he* been one of those consulted. As for Tommy Church, he could hardly be regarded as a power in the land and his contributions to the debates in the House during the past four sessions had frequently struck Meighen as both irrelevant and tedious.

But not all of his friends were as loyal and true as those in Toronto were said to be, or as discreet as Taylor and others in Manitoba. One vocal critic was Meighen's old journalist crony, Tom Blacklock, who in the past had always stood up for him through thick and thin and whose defection on this issue Meighen felt most keenly because of their close personal friendship. Blacklock was now Ottawa correspondent for the Detroit *Free Press,* to which he sent a dispatch enumerating the reasons why the Hamilton speech was unacceptable to many Conservatives and ending with some rather hard words: "There is no precedent in Canada for a leader with victory in his grasp, if he but remained silent, to deliberately jeopardize his success by an unnecessary and such an unprecedented speech. Mr. Meighen will probably survive the storm, but he has lost at least the enthusiastic support of scores of thousands of men and women who were loyal to him in his dark days."[29] To Meighen loyalty to one's friends was a virtue higher than almost any other and he was greatly shocked by these words of condemnation. "You will be astonished to learn," he told Manion, "that our mutual friend Tom Blacklock has become very much incensed over the subject. I have not seen him since and indeed he declines to have anything to do with me. . . . I am not sure that there is anything you can do but really Tom's conduct has hurt me far more than all the rest of them combined. He is one to whom I have felt under considerable obligation and I am most anxious not to allow his present action to interfere with, or impair the feeling toward him, which I have always held."[30]

The hubbub over the Hamilton speech was a windfall of good fortune for the Liberals, discomfited by the outcome of the recent election, and they made the most of it. Their editorialists gloated over the evidence of dissension in the Conservative camp and gleefully emphasized the apparent inconsistency between what Meighen had proposed at Hamilton and what he had said during the Chanak crisis three years before. However, the *Manitoba Free Press* welcomed the "inconsistency" which it thought amounted to "getting back on the right road." On this matter, said its editor, administering what he may have hoped was the kiss of death, Meighen had resumed "the attitude of statesmanship."[31] Apparently L. A. Taschereau and P. J. A. Cardin, campaigning in Bagot, thought the same, for they assured their audiences that what Meighen had enunciated at Hamilton and in Bagot itself was really the policy of the Liberal party. On the other hand the National Liberal Committee mailed out a leaflet under the Prime Minister's frank which, as Meighen observed, was clearly intended "to rouse the Conservatives of Ontario (and Liberals to [sic]) against my statement . . . on the ground that it is not sufficiently loyal to the British Empire."[32]

He was genuinely taken aback by all the fuss and furor over a proposal which several leading men, all of them from Ontario, had agreed with him beforehand was both a reasonable and a proper one to make. To Manion he wrote: "I do not know whether you have felt much of the repercussions up in Fort William or not but I have encountered much more difficulty than I expected as a consequence of the speech I made in Hamilton. First of all you may rest assured I am not going to swerve by a hairs [sic] breadth. The procedure there advised is the right procedure and if our friends will only do some thinking and act logically and fairly it will turn out of great advantage to the Conservative party as well as to the country."[33]

When Meighen returned to Ottawa from campaigning in Bagot he "was urged in the strongest terms to let the subject drop, or rather, let it lie quiet until immediate antipathies would cool down. To these importunities I, unfortunately, acceded. This, I frankly confess, was a mistake in tactics. I should have unhesitatingly defended my position and . . . arranged for immediate public speeches in Canada . . . and proclaimed the lines of the Hamilton speech as definitely my policy, and made it the policy of the Conservative Party. To my mind this was the only major, or at any rate the most important, mistake I made in public life. There would even so probably have been some who would have persevered in their antagonism, but they would have been very, very few, and there might have been none at all."[34] Because he refrained from taking his case to the country in a series of speeches the soundness of this opinion cannot be conclusively judged. He did, however, draft a lengthy letter, elaborating upon and defending his Hamilton proposal, which he sent to a large number of men in politics and journalism, at least some of whom he knew were not with him on the matter.

It was as though he were inviting an argument and was determined to bring them around, to make them see the logic and common sense of his position. If anyone was to give ground it would have to be they, not he, unless they were prepared to find a new leader for the party. What he had advocated, the letter emphasized,

> was not so much a policy, indeed not a policy at all, as regards Empire relations, but is merely a procedure in order to give, in the best way, effect to a policy. Never would I swerve from the great principle that a Government must always assume its responsibility and in the event of a crisis involving the likelihood of war being upon us, must declare its stand and upon that stand must live or die. . . .
> What the Hamilton speech involves is this, that without subtracting in the least from Governmental responsibility which responsibility of course would involve the immediate making of preparations, mobilization under the existing law, and all other steps necessary to carry out the declared intention of the Administration, there should as a condition previous to a despatch of troops from our shores, be a submission of the Government's policy to the people in the regular constitutional form of a general election. This should not, and would not involve delay. In 1914 we could have had two general elections before troops were actually despatched. Had we done so I believe much of the disunion which afterwards developed would probably have been avoided.
> . . . In this Dominion we absolutely must have regard to the composition of our people. I feel absolutely certain that the very assurance of their being consulted, as can without great inconvenience be done, will have a steady and quieting effect, and will tend rather to strengthen their faith in the fairness of their fellow citizens and

predispose them to join with us in any necessary steps to secure our ultimate security and peace.

The talk about a surrender to Bourassa is utter nonsense. Such a mistake arises through confusing policy with procedure. . . . Mr. Bourassa, just as I would have expected, has not accepted, but rather denounced the course to which I am committed.

Personally I believe very strongly that the peace of the world for many, many years, and probably for more than one generation, if not for many more, is now secure. In this belief the people of Canada I think generally share. Why then should we suffer that a large portion of our people should remain longer in a state of utterly unnecessary apprehension to the very great detriment of our strength as a Party, and consequently our usefulness to the Dominion.[35]

One of the numerous recipients of this was Sir John Willison, who replied that had he been consulted he would have advised against giving the undertaking Meighen had at Hamilton. Many Conservatives would refuse to accept the proposal, which was in any case "impracticable and impossible," and it would be "best that the letter of the Hamilton speech should be forgotten. . . ." What the party needed, he wrote, was not a new procedure to give effect to policy in war but a new war policy itself, namely, a declaration "that we would never apply conscription for a war outside Canada. That I think could be made the definite and positive policy of the Conservative party. Such a policy ought to satisfy Quebec which, when all is said, is in its own way reasonably loyal to British connection." At all event Meighen's suggestion involved more than procedure; it amounted to requiring the people to determine policy on the supreme issue of peace or war and there was a grave hazard in doing that. "If we had a general election in which Quebec declared against war and the rest of Canada for war we would have an even more serious situation than we had when we attempted to enforce conscription a few years ago. Bluntly, as I see it, we would split the country in two in the endeavour to unite it for war."[36]

A pledge of no conscription as recommended by Willison, was quite out of the question, of course, as long as Meighen remained Conservative leader. To give it would mean in effect a repudiation of the wartime administration and of a measure with the formulation and parliamentary discussion of which he had had a peculiarly close connection. It would necessitate a repentance, a tacit admission of error; like most men Meighen found it hard to admit that he might have been wrong about the big things that really mattered and far more than most he was ready to stand or fall by everything he had said and done. Not only that, it would be a mistake in Meighen's opinion to bind oneself to refrain from a certain *policy* which events might make desirable or necessary but it was safe to commit oneself to a *procedure* to be followed in event of war. As to the procedure he now advanced being, as Willison claimed, "impracticable and impossible," that was not so, Meighen answered. "We were, as a matter of fact, very close to taking that procedure in 1914. It was Liberal propaganda that deterred us. We would have been better if we had. . . ."[37] It was improbable, he thought, that an election at the start of war would tear the country apart instead of uniting its people, as Willison and others claimed. An election in 1914, he explained, would have made the opposition to "the Government which subsequently developed much less powerful. This also I feel free to say is the opinion of Sir Robert Borden. At all events if a government assumed office and subsequently faced a crisis having given such a pledge as I have given, then the reason for the election would be clear and the obligation of all Canadians to submit to the result of such election would be so emphasized that I don't believe the difficulties would be nearly so great as before."[38]

Another of those who received Meighen's widely distributed letter defending the Hamilton speech was Horatio C. Hocken, who represented one of the Toronto ridings in Parliament and, as editor of the *Orange Sentinel,* was a spokesman for the ultra-loyalist wing of the Conservative party. The Orange Order, with its strong Protestant flavour and its intense feeling of attachment to the mother country, was still a factor to be reckoned with in Canadian politics. Hocken's answer indicated, if he knew the minds of his audience as a good editor usually does, that the Orangemen were not apt to take kindly to what Meighen had proposed.

> The Sentinel [he wrote] has not made any comment on your Hamilton speech thus far. My intention is to avoid it altogether if possible, but I may not be able to carry out my intention, depending upon the amount of pressure coming from our leaders and lodges.
> I know you want me to speak frankly to you and I am bound to say that in my judgment the Hamilton speech was a mistake. I note in your letter you differentiate between policy and procedure. No doubt that is clear in your mind, but you cannot put that into the minds of the rank and file of the Conservative Party. The subject dealt with is one that touches their deepest sentiments, and no amount of argument or explanation can satisfy them that there is any difference between policy and procedure.
> I do not think that you can be aware of the extraordinary measure of support that you received in this Province at the recent election, because of the solid Quebec behind Mr. King. It was not merely among those whom I represent but from the loyal liberal element of this Province. Your candidates were supported because they are sick and tired of French Canadian domination in Federal affairs. Bearing that in mind I would ask you to consider how they would feel at you making such a pronouncement at the time you did. To such electors as I speak of, it had the appearance of a surrender to French-Canadian sentiment, and while there is no desire in this Province to deal unfairly with the French in Quebec,

there is deep-seated resentment at anything that has the appearance of making further concessions or promises to them.

If in your Hamilton speech you had pledged yourself to an appeal to the country before adopting conscription it would no doubt have been quite as influential among the French, and would no doubt have been quite satisfactory to the British sentiment of the Dominion. . . .

My own view of the course we should pursue at the present time is not to discuss your Hamilton speech, in the hope that feeling that has been aroused may gradually die away for lack of fuel to keep the fire burning. Certainly it cannot be widely discussed in this Province except to injure you personally, and act detrimentally upon the Party.[39]

Judging by this the tariff had not been the main election issue in Ontario any more than in Quebec. Meighen's reply to Hocken, and indeed the whole episode of the Hamilton speech and its aftermath, revealed the moderate man caught between two extreme points of view, a position familiar to all party leaders.

. . . Do not consider me guilty of the slightest egotism when you read the following words. They are certainly not animated by any such spirit. I have lived with this problem for many years, have naturally seen it at first hand and no doubt most impressively from the Western and Ontario angle. I have seen it also from the Quebec viewpoint and have mixed considerable [sic] with the Conservative party of that province for many years. I am necessarily in contact with them daily and have been throughout my entire term of leadership, and, indeed, for many years before. If I had made a statement such as you suggest it would have been utterly ruinous in Quebec. My meaning is this: It not only actually would have been valueless but would have been most injurious. It would have been accepted as an intimation utterly unnecessary at the present time, that we were quite prepared to launch conscription again, and would have tended much to revive the conscription issue. The Conservative party of Quebec leans very strongly to British connection, and, indeed, to co-operation within the Empire. It is my firm and immovable belief that given the safeguard contained in my Hamilton speech they will tend more and more to lean this way. I have nothing but friendship and the highest opinion of those of your friends whose sentiments are against the statement I made at Hamilton, but we simply must, in the interests of our country, get over the habit of thinking that anything is truckling to Quebec. We must consider every proposition strictly on its merits, and judge those merits by a calm consideration of the actual composition of our country. If the sentence just written does not embody common sense then I do not know what common sense is. It is the spirit of that sentence which animated me in what I have done. . . .

Meantime we have the advantage of quieting apprehensions on this side. We have the advantage of having contributed much to the unity of Canada. From a party standpoint we must never forget that we are jammed in between Quebec on the one hand and the Western low tariff sentiment on the other, and unable to gain the advantage of our strong position in point of policy. We must remember not only the composition of Quebec but the composition of other provinces. This we cannot change. We must deal with it as it is and we, who are by sentiment and by conviction the strong. est adherents of British connection, British tradition, and British destiny, must handle the situation wisely in our own land, having regard to the actual conditions which confront us.[40]

The one criticism of his Hamilton doctrine that bothered Meighen more than all others was that he had gone back on his famous "Ready, aye ready" speech of 1922. He set great store by consistency, far more than the average politician, and would as soon have sold his soul as resort to the kind of expedient shifting which he regarded as one of the besetting sins of Mackenzie King. Thus when even normally friendly papers like the Winnipeg *Tribune* and exalted Conservative personages like Cahan accused him of having deserted the ground he had stood on in 1922 he was at particular pains to refute the charge. Far from there being any discrepancy between the two speeches, he asserted in a letter to C.A.C. Jennings of the *Mail and Empire,* they were entirely on all fours.

What I dislike most in the criticism is the very casual and careless assumption that the procedure advocated at Hamilton is the slight-est contradiction from that declared in my speech . . . in September 1922. The fact is, there is not the faintest substance of contradic-tion.

In Toronto in 1922 I was dealing with the policy the Government should adopt, and indeed, with the policy it should adopt under very special circumstances, namely, the circumstance of an attack on a treaty signed and ratified by Canada. . . . Please observe that this speech was made before the King Administration had revealed the terms of the communication from the British Government. You will note that what I called for was . . . such a reply as would have shown to the world solidarity on the part of the Dominions who were parties to the Treaty. It was this declaration of solidarity which I called for. Observe also that I stated distinctly that there was no suggestion of the despatch of troops. . . .

On the other hand in the Hamilton speech I was dealing with procedure after the Government comes to its decision. I emphasized not only that the Government should come to its decision, and come to its decision rapidly, but act on its decision and go right ahead without, however, despatching troops abroad until the Government had, in the British way, submitted its policy to the people. No honest mind can see the slightest contradiction between this speech and the speech of 1922.

I find some, whose opinions I much respect, who fear that in the event of an adverse judgement by the people there would be a civil war in the country. Their sentiments are the same as mine, but their estimate of the possible situation is, to my mind, wholly unfounded and imaginary. . . . I know as certainly as I know anything that we never could participate [in war] in the future unless, not only a majority but an overwhelming majority, were in favour. A Government has to take account of the fact that as the struggle progresses, and great sacrifices are made, and poignant sorrow comes home to the masses of the people, there is always a falling away of the less virile and resolute members of the community. Indeed, the necessity of a very general, popular support will be far greater in the future than in the past owing to what will be the nature of future wars. In a word, there will be no danger in the world of any Government in Canada entering a conflict unless there is not only a majority but an undoubted and overwhelming majority demanding such participation.[41]

While answering his critics in these and other letters Meighen also busied himself in preparing another speech on the subject which he proposed to deliver at a meeting in Brandon he had promised to attend. He would bring together all the arguments that had been advanced against his suggestion, all the misconceptions and misinterpretations to which his Hamilton speech had given rise, and he would dispel each and every one of them in a way that would leave no opening to any logical mind for further dispute. Far from letting the Hamilton pledge be forgotten, as many thought it should be, he was bent on justifying it unanswerably. He got the Brandon speech ready, but on the urgent advice of some of his friends, who thought there should be no more rocking of the party boat, he decided not to deliver it. Regretfully it was put aside; there might be an opportunity later on to use it. In due course that opportunity arrived and Meighen seized it, causing even more commotion with his defence of the doctrine than he had with his original announcement of it.

That moment, however, was still some distance in the future. When it came Meighen's defence of the Hamilton speech proved to be a powerful one, logically almost impregnable. But logic does not govern politics or human affairs generally as much as one might wish, and as he thought, it did. The fact was, whatever were the merits of his idea and however much it may have been misunderstood and misinterpreted, that in presenting it he had caused a disruption in the party at the very moment when it seemed to stand on the threshold of power, a disruption which someone more sensitive to the intricately varied currents of public opinion might have anticipated and avoided. Had the looked-for advantage in Quebec been gained there would have been ample compensation; but it was not and it is not easy to understand the expectation that it would be. The day after the Hamilton meeting Fauteux wrote to Meighen: "This morning, in my office, I was visited by three friends from Bagot County who came to tell me of their satisfaction with the subject of the speech you have just delivered. . . . Here is what they said: If the voters of Bagot are not satisfied, we see nothing that can satisfy them."[42]   But the voters were far from satisfied and Fauteux was defeated again.   The margin against him this time was less than five hundred but the total vote was smaller than it had been in October.

One could attribute this disappointing result in part to untoward circumstances which happened to intrude just then, as well as to the normal Conservative handicap in Quebec.   The situation in the Near East took a turn for the worse, opening up the possibility that Great Britain might become militarily involved.   In addition Admiral Earl Jellicoe, for a time during the war commander of the British Home Fleet and later First Sea Lord of the Admiralty, chose this moment to publish a suggestion that Canada should contribute $36,000,000 annually for the next several years to the upkeep of the British navy.   Here was the old imperialism against which Laurier had contended raising its ugly head once again.   "Well the fight is over," Meighen wrote on the morrow of the by-election, "and while we did not win we put up a creditable contest.   When one considers the circumstances, two Governments against us, no newspaper, and, super-added to this, the senseless statement heralded through the press from Admiral Jellicoe, and, as well, the newspapers flaring again alleged rupture between Turkey and Great Britain, all these things were pretty hard to overcome."[43]   Indeed they were, but even had the Near Eastern situation been more stable and Jellicoe kept his opinions to himself it is doubtful that Meighen's Hamilton and Bagot speeches would have had the desired effect.   So thoroughly had the wells of public sentiment been poisoned by Liberal propaganda, so keen and bitter were memories of the war, that a people habituated to think in terms of its position as a minority would probably find little reassurance in the principle that the dispatch of troops must be sanctioned by the majority.   More important from the French-Canadian point of view would be the kind of manpower policy which a Conservative government, given that mandate, would adopt.   Thus while a case strong in logic and reason could be made for Meighen's proposal, and while he could not be blamed for seeking with the best will in the world some way of quieting the apprehensions of French Canada, this particular way was less well calculated than he imagined to do that and to counter the malicious slander spread by his opponents.

Aside from the merits or drawbacks of the procedure he advocated, the manner in which it was decided upon and announced was objected to by many.   John T. Haig, for example, wrote from Winnipeg that he approved of the proposal itself.   "The only question I raise is: Did you do it in the right way?   Does it not look a little as if you were bidding for

Bagot? Would it not have been better to have raised the question in caucus and had the Party endorse your stand? Or better still raised it in parliament by way of resolution as you did the question of tariff last year? There is a feeling abroad that the Party as a whole was not consulted and that you took too much authority into your own hands."[44] This was certainly the feeling of the *Telegram* and the *Tribune*, of Church and Pope, Cahan and Blacklock, of most of those Conservatives, in fact, who either publicly or privately took exception to the Hamilton speech. The authority of the party leader was nowhere clearly defined, of course; there was no party constitution which spelled out his rights or his duties. These were matters of custom and judgment and it is hard to avoid the conclusion that Meighen's judgment was faulty on this occasion. He was, as Haig put it, "bidding for Bagot" and beyond that for the confidence of French Canada, as he was both entitled and obligated to do. But it was understandable that many Conservatives were not only surprised but somehow disillusioned that Arthur Meighen, whose reluctance to make easy promises as election bait was one of his distinguishing features, should come out with an entirely new principle on the eve of an important by-election in Quebec. He would have been better advised to wait until the caucus was held and present his proposal then in the usual way. Some of the members undoubtedly would have resisted it strenuously but he would have been able to carry the great majority with him and have avoided the charge that he acted without due consultation. Then when another general election was called he could have argued the merits of his idea throughout Quebec and the rest of the country with greater authority in the knowledge that it had been duly considered and approved by his parliamentary followers.

In another respect, too, his method of introducing the idea was open to question from a strictly party point of view. How differently Mackenzie King would have proceeded had he been in Meighen's position! One may guess that he would have let Lapointe, Cardin, Cannon and others spread the word through Quebec that a Liberal government would go to the country before sending troops overseas. When word of this seeped through to Ontario King would have one of his ambiguous "explanations" all ready. The matter was not quite so simple, he would say; his policy was that there would be, not necessarily an election, but an election if necessary. It was typical of Meighen's straightforward approach to politics that he preferred to state his position unequivocally and to do so first, not in Bagot County, but in Hamilton, a stronghold of Ontario Conservatism. More than that, departing from his usual practice he had a prepared text of his speech, copies of which were distributed to the press just before the banquet. Since the matter he was going to discuss affected the whole country, he wanted the whole country to know exactly what he had said, so that there could be no mistake or confusion about it. Unlike King, who preferred to make real issues as blurred as possible so that they would not obscure unreal ones that might be politically more useful, Meighen's habit was to be as clear and explicit as he could so that no one would have any doubt about where he stood. This, he believed, was the only honest way of dealing with the people, the only honourable way in which the affairs of a democracy could be debated and conducted. Unfortunately it was also apt to embroil him in controversy with members of his own party, as it did in the autumn of 1925. One of the facts which Meighen, a man who believed in facing facts, failed to appreciate as yet was that not everyone thought or could be made to think as logically as he did himself, that people were often moved by their hearts, not guided by their heads. His proposal seemed to him completely sensible and right and he did not apprehend the deep-seated emotions that it would bring bubbling to the surface. Thus his astonishment when his forthright and well-publicized declaration at Hamilton at once embroiled him in a hornet's nest of angry, stinging argument. The result of it all, though less calamitous to the party than some then feared or than has sometimes been thought since, was that, with no great gain in Quebec by way of compensation, Conservatives fell to quarreling among themselves at the very moment when they needed to close their ranks for the crucial parliamentary struggle just ahead.

With a test of strength shaping up in the new Parliament between the two major powers, all depended on how the uncommitted members would act. Would the 24 Progressives, two Labourites and two Independents prefer to keep Mackenzie King in office or would enough of them desert him to cause his downfall? On the face of it the advantage here seemed to be all with the Liberals. The Progressives had generally supported the Government during the past four years and a goodly number of them were really crypto-Liberals, Liberals in a hurry to find their way back into the fold. Even to those who were not, King's views on policy, equivocal and evasive as they often were, might be more attractive than Meighen's. King, after all, had made some reductions in the tariff and had promised during the campaign to finish the Hudson Bay Railway. He was opposed to foreign entanglements and "militarism" and in general appeared to be more sympathetically disposed than his rival to the western agrarian point of view. As for the two Independents, Neill of Comox-Alberni was a Progressive in all but name while Bourassa was hardly likely when a showdown came to do anything that would help put Arthur Meighen in power. The two Labour members, Woodsworth and A. A. Heaps, despised both the old parties but, having run afoul of authority during the the Winnipeg general strike of 1919, could be expected to oppose Meighen, whom they regarded as the sinister power behind the measures by which the strike had been broken. When it came to a choice of evils they would in all probability decide that "Toryism" was the greater.

At the same time it was not impossible that enough of the uncommitted would join with the Conservatives to bring about a change of government. Being the largest group the Conservatives had a strong moral claim to power, even if the constitutional basis of their claim was not as strong as they thought. In addition the Progressives were sorely divided, with the members of the so-called "Ginger Group," which had broken away from the main body of the movement in the House in 1924, feeling considerable disillusionment with King's performance in office and with the crypto-Liberalism of many of their fellows. They represented the hard core of orthodox Progressivism as a revolt against both the old parties and against the party system itself; they regarded the Liberal party as being little if any better than the Conservative. Thus they were suspicious of anything that might lead to the absorption of the Progressive movement by the Liberals which King for years had been trying to accomplish. Therefore, while by no means enamoured of Meighen's policies, some of them at least might side with him when the crucial vote came in order to register their independence of Mackenzie King. The whole situation was surrounded by many uncertainties but about one thing there could be no doubt as the country awaited the opening of Parliament: never before had the Progressives been given so much flattering attention by the two parties. With their movement dying a slow death and their numbers in the House reduced by three-fifths, they nevertheless were going to play the decisive part in deciding who should govern. It was ironical that Meighen, who had often dismissed Progressivism with sardonic disdain as a temporary aberration from the norm of political good sense, should now when the movement was on its last legs be utterly dependent upon the Progressives in his bid for power. It was equally ironical that whatever support he might get from that direction would probably come from the most radical element in the Progressive camp.

Almost immediately after the general election letters began to come into his office containing news, rumours and speculations about the attitude of the Progressives and the two Labourites. One of the first to arrive was from J. T. Haig in Winnipeg, who reported a conversation he had had with some friends of his he met on the street. ". . . they told me Woodsworth and Heaps would probably vote to keep you in office, if they were sure of no opposition from our party in the next election. I told them I was not interested, but I thought I should pass the information on to you."[45] Meighen was not much interested either, even if Woodsworth and Heaps *were* of that mind, which was doubtful. "Would not feel," he replied, "like giving any undertaking whatever to the two representatives to whom you refer, at least none along the lines suggested."[46] Haig also had some news about one of the Manitoba Progressives, A. L. Beaubien, M.P. for Provencher. "Our friend here, Beaubien, although a Progressive, will vote for you any time he is sure the Government will be licked. He would prefer to keep you in power for years, but will not vote with you unless he is sure of defeating the Government."[47] Meighen had hoped for better than this from Beaubien, against whom the Conservatives had not run a candidate in the recent election. "Am very disappointed," he wrote, "at the very limited measure of support now suggested by the member. . . . My understanding was quite different. On the basis stated in your letter the support would be practically worthless because no one could know in advance what he insists on knowing. If this is the stand he takes we will know how to deal with the county in the future."[48] Meighen had misunderstood him, Haig answered. "You are a great man to hue [*sic*] to the line but when you are dealing with a Progressive Frenchman, the line sometimes moves. Beaubien has no love for Mackenzie King at all but what he says is this: 'If I vote for Meighen all the time, it will simply mean that I shall have no chance in an election for re-election; what I want to do is carry on for four years.' However, he has agreed to vote exactly as Aimé [Benard] and I ask him to when the time comes."[49]

Unusual importance seemed to be attached to Beaubien's vote because on the very day this latest letter from Haig was written Meighen learned that E. C. St. Père, Member of Parliament for Hochelaga, Quebec, was going all the way out to Winnipeg. The purpose of his visit, according to an unsigned memorandum which Meighen sent to M. E. Nichols of the *Tribune,* was "to make sure of the vote of Mr. Beaubien, M.P. in the first critical division in the House. My information is that in an unguarded moment [St. Père] stated he had authority to pay a large sum of money to make sure of Mr. Beaubien's vote."[50] St. Père, reported Haig a little later, "has been here for three or four days visiting with Beaubien. He went home this morning and I do not think he made any progress."[51] But either progress had been made or Haig and Senator Benard forgot to give Beaubien his instructions, for when the time came he voted with the Liberals in every division throughout the session.

So much for him but what of all the others? Meighen heard from Saskatoon "that those Progressive M.P.'s who like to think of themselves as the 'Ginger' group . . . would prefer to see you in control for the coming session rather than King. They realise that you cannot negotiate with them or they with you in any open or direct way." They might support Meighen if he would recommence the Hudson Bay Railway, provide financial assistance for the wheat pools, the farmers' new market-ing co-operatives, and leave the tariff as it was. "I know all this is rather vague and indefinite, and lacking in authority from the Prog ginger group. . . . The only tangible things in the suggestion are that they . . . have in mind a full session with its indemnity and that they are in the frame of mind to throw their support to you during that session on some encouragement."[52]   There were other intimations, as well, of the reputed willingness of some of the Progressives to side with the Conservatives in the House.   William Irvine, who was in close touch with sentiment in Alberta, advised Meighen from Calgary "that in my opinion, you have a very good chance of securing the support of the Alberta members after the opening of Parliament.   I also had a conference with Mr. Woodsworth and find that he is undecided but fully expect that he will consult you prior to arriving at a final decision. . . . If I can be of any service to you please let me know."[53]   Another report had it that four Saskatchewan Progressives "held a meeting at Regina quite recently and decided that they would not support King at Ottawa and at present are very favorably disposed towards yourself and may support you."[54]   From a Toronto source came word that Agnes MacPhail and seven other Progressives "will refrain from voting on any question coming up in the House, where it means a test of strength between the parties."[55]   And Hugh Clark, one of Meighen's cronies, passed on the word from his brother, who had just been in Alberta, that G. G. Coote, the Progressive member for Macleod and one of the Ginger Group, "will not support King as against Meighen —says Coote has nothing but contempt for King."[56]   Added to all these intimations of the support that might be forthcoming was the avowed opinion of an influential farm paper, *The Western Producer* of Saskatoon. The Progressives, it said, "should give Mr. Meighen a chance to form a government.   After it is formed, they should not take the responsibility of forcing another general election . . . unless the Conservative legislative program was definitely opposed to theirs."[57]

With so many such smoke signals coming up over the western horizon the possibility of overturning the King regime looked rather promising. But obviously one could not sit passively by and count on factors like Mr. Coote's contempt for Mackenzie King to do the trick.   The Pro-gressives felt a keen sense of responsibility to their constituents and they could hardly justify supporting Meighen unless they received satisfactory assurances regarding the policies a Conservative government would adopt.   There would have to be some kind of *quid pro quo* before their votes would be gained, some understanding with regard to subjects like the tariff, the Hudson Bay Railway, rural credits and the transfer of control over their natural resources to the three prairie provinces from the Dominion.   Meighen, however, was very loath to go too far in making promises and afraid that others, in their anxiety to gain supporters among the Progressives, might do so without proper authority. With the Liberals known to be courting the Progressive M.P.'s assiduously there was a danger that individual Conservatives playing the same game might try to outbid their opponents and give undertakings that could not be carried out. One of those engaged in this work with Meighen's knowledge was Manning Doherty, who had been Minister of Agriculture in the Farmers government in Ontario a few years before. Doherty had just resigned from his seat in the legislature of that province and announced that he intended to work in the interests of the Conservative party nationally, his reason being that Meighen was more favourably inclined to the encouragement of co-operative marketing of farm products than the other leaders. Late in November 1925 he visited the West to try to convince as many of the elected Progressives as possible that they should help to overthrow King and make Meighen Prime Minister. Early in December Senator Billy Sharpe wrote to the latter in some perturbation to say that he had found out in Winnipeg that Doherty "was up working with Rogers on the Progressives."[58] If Rogers was in the picture, and it was the kind of picture he would have found it torture to be kept out of, there was no telling what inducements were being held out to the Progressives. "I knew Mr. Doherty was West," Meighen told Sharpe, "but I did not know he was discussing the matter with the parties you refer to. This certainly was not in my mind. My information was he was discussing it solely with the members themselves."[59]

Throughout these anxious interim weeks between the election and the opening of Parliament Meighen was insistent, too much so to suit some of his own followers, that no deal should be made with the Progressives that would compromise the policies embraced by the Conservative party. "There are," he remarked, "various reports of the attitude of different Progressives in the West and I have reason to believe a great many of them would prefer supporting us. I have decided definitely that I will not start any log-rolling activities but will stand firmly on our principles. It is better to be in power effectively than to impatiently grasp for power and be there under impossible circumstances."[60] And again:

> I more and more lean to the view that we should not be too precipitate. We have a grip on the situation and can only lose it by being in too big a hurry, or by making some error in tactics. I do naturally, want to do everything possible for the West, and I have a high personal regard for most of the Progressive members elect. We should strive to get them in as favourable a mind toward us as possible, but be certain we can go on with any commitments which we undertake, and we can do so if these commitments are in line with our principles.[61]

In any event, as he observed in another letter, "There will be no such thing as getting these matters to a head until the members are down."[62] Once the House had assembled the disposition of the Progressives and the concessions they might insist upon could be more accurately learned.

Just before Parliament was opened on the seventh of January matters did begin to come to a head. Early in the month a straw vote among the Progressive members-elect showed twelve of them wanting to support the Conservatives with ten preferring to back the Government. Some of the minority were prepared to do more than that; they were ready virtually to merge themselves with the Liberal party and to have Robert Forke accept, as he wanted to, the invitation King extended to join the Government as Minister of Agriculture. However, the diehards among the Progressives refused to countenance its acceptance and Forke was compelled to decline. They saw that to join so fully and openly with the Liberals would mean the final collapse of the Progressive movement and necessitate the assumption of responsibility for everything the King administration did. They refused, therefore, to do more than co-operate independently with whichever of the old parties offered the more satisfactory legislative programme. The Alberta Progressives, among whom were included most of the members of the Ginger Group, had already decided, meeting by themselves, that they would sit to the Speaker's left so as to demonstrate that they were not in or of the Government. Then when the Progressive caucus was held they proposed that both Meighen and King should be asked by letter to state their positions on fourteen matters of policy. This would be a sign that they were willing to throw the weight of their support either way, that they were free from Mr. King even as they were free from Mr. Meighen. Instead of assuming, as crypto-Liberals like Forke were prone to do, that King's policies as a matter of course must be superior to Meighen's, they would receive and judiciously assess the evidence from both sides.

Accordingly Forke on January the sixth wrote to both the Prime Minister and the leader of the Opposition, soliciting their views on such subjects as the tariff, the Hudson Bay Railway, the statutory Crow's Nest freight rates on grain and flour, rural credits, the transfer of natural resources to the Prairie Provinces, co-operative marketing and the alternative vote.[63] The next day Woodsworth and Heaps similarly addressed the two leaders to find out whether either would "introduce at this session legislation with regard to (a) Provision for the unemployed; (b) Old Age Pensions."[64] The time had come for King and Meighen to put their chips down and play the hand.

Their responses to these inquiries illuminated the contrast between the two men. The former was in the desperate position of having to make generous commitments in order to remain in office; the latter, feeling that the tide of affairs was with him in any case, could afford to be more cautious. But even had their positions been reversed in this respect, it is improbable that their reactions to the situation would have been much different from what they were. King was by every habit and instinct given to bending with the wind in order to gain his objective, which was always power. He could thus, more easily than the relatively uncompromising Meighen, bring himself to offer the desired concessions to Progressives and Labourites. When it came to a matter of bargaining for support Meighen was almost certain to be outbid by King, and certainly he was on this occasion.

Replying to Forke, Meighen disposed of eight of the fourteen subjects, among them the tariff, the Hudson Bay Railway, statutory freight rates, public ownership of railways and transfer of natural resources, by remarking that "the stand of the Conservative Party has been fully and repeatedly outlined by myself in the House of Commons and along precisely the same lines elaborated in the country. So far as I know it has never been charged that my attitude as Leader on any of these subjects has been equivocal or obscure." With respect to the tariff he added the comment that he "could not in a few words better define our historic and present policy than to quote what the Right Honourable W. L. Mackenzie King on September 6th, in the County of Peel, in the Province of Ontario, declared to be the policy of the Liberal Party, namely —'a tariff which will help to give us what we need in the way of revenue, and, at the same time safeguard industrial development.'" From this the Progressives could draw a number of conclusions. A government headed by Meighen would maintain a consistently protective tariff. It would complete the railway to the Bay at once if this could be done for a sum in the neighbourhood of $3,000,000 and, if not, only when the finances of the country improved sufficiently to warrant a larger expenditure. It would probably repeal the Crow's Nest rates, since Meighen believed that the Government and Parliament should lay down only the general principles according to which all rates were to be set by the Board of Railway Commissioners, and not define specific rates by statute. The continued public ownership of the National Railways would, of course, be absolutely secure if Meighen were in power, whatever the desire of some Conservatives might be in that regard. As for the transfer of natural resources—unalienated land, timber and minerals—he would offer nothing more than a resumption of the earnest effort he had made while in office to work out a basis of transfer which would be financially acceptable to all the provinces as well as to the Dominion. That this was an extraordinarily difficult task both he and King knew very well. "As respects the Natural Resources," Meighen remarked a month before he received Forke's questionnaire, "it would not be honest to go farther than we have gone. As you know the restoration of these resources to the provinces is the right thing to do, but everything depends on the terms which they are demanding. As a matter of fact these resources should not have been withheld, but their being withheld all these years makes the omelette very hard to unscramble."[65]

With respect to the remaining items enumerated in Forke's letter Meighen was equally cautious. For example he favoured in principle the construction of a railway outlet for the Peace River district but thought it could not be built at the present time. He was "most anxious to see installed at the earliest possible date a sound and sane system of rural credits," of making mortgage money available to farmers at lower rates of interest than those charged by private leading agencies, but was opposed to any system of direct Government loans for this purpose. He promised that the "utmost possible assistance will be given to co-operative marketing of farm products of every kind" but on the other hand declared that the Conservative party was "definitely opposed" to the alternative vote, a method of balloting dear to many of the Progressives.

The general tone of his letter to Forke was not at all that of a party leader grasping desperately for power. Nor was his answer to Woodsworth and Heaps likely to win him their support in the House. The way to deal with the unemployment problem, he implied, was not to offer the palliative of unemployment insurance, which was advocated by the two Labour members, but to create employment by a consistently protective tariff. "The thing to do for the unemployed," he told Woodsworth, "is to get them work, and I have been often very disappointed that I have never been able to secure your co-operation in the least degree in an effort to extend the area of employment in this country." As for the other matter they had asked about, old-age pensions, he recognized the importance of this question but felt there were "other subjects demanding attention in more pressing form at the present time. . . ."

King's response to these inquiries from the Progressives and the Labourites went a great deal further in meeting their demands. While in due course he replied in writing to each, his real reply, to the Progressives at least, was contained in the speech from the throne. It was sprinkled with a number of enticing statements and promises. ". . . a general increase in the Customs Tariff would prove detrimental to the country's continued prosperity and prejudicial to national unity. . . . the incidence of this form of taxation should bear as lightly as possible upon the necessaries of life and on agriculture and other primary industries." ". . . a measure will be introduced offering wide facilities for rural credits." The Government would "submit provisions for the completion forthwith of the Hudson Bay Railway." ". . . a bill to provide for the transfer to the Province of Alberta of its natural resources" would be brought in.[66]

The throne speech, alluring as it must have sounded to the Progressives, contained nothing to satisfy the specific demands of Woodsworth and Heaps; there was no reference to either unemployment insurance or old-age pensions. However, after Woodsworth stated in the session's opening debate, which ended with the Government being sustained by only three votes, that he had no more confidence in the Liberals than in the Conservatives,[67] King took steps to help him see the light. Woodsworth was invited to join the Cabinet as Minister of Labour and when he declined was given a verbal assurance, later confirmed by King in writing, that a measure establishing a system of old-age pensions would be presented to Parliament. Furthermore King agreed to the demand for certain other legislation, which Woodsworth had attempted unsuccessfully to obtain since 1921 in a number of private member's Bills. Various enactments prompted by the Winnipeg strike were to be repealed, notably section 98 of the Criminal Code and a section in the Immigration Act which made British subjects not born in Canada liable to summary deportation.[68] It was surprising what King on the spur of the moment could undertake to do if the need were sufficiently urgent.

To all these concessions with respect to policy, and to his offer of Cabinet positions to Forke and Woodsworth, were added still further emblems of King's sudden and expedient identification of himself in a practical way with western interests and desires. It was announced that, having lost his own seat in North York, he would seek election to the House in Prince Albert, the riding being opened for him by the resignation of the elected member. In addition it was learned that he intended to bring Charles A. Dunning, Premier of Saskatchewan, into his government as Minister of Railways. The accession of Dunning, a powerful spokesman for the western farmer and a leading advocate of the Hudson Bay Railway, could be taken as an earnest of the Government's good intentions towards the prairies. ". . . the West having so long refused to come to King, King was at last going to the West."[69] In this kind of popularity contest Meighen was no match for his rival and that he had been outclassed was indicated by the results of another poll among the Progressives. This time all but five of them voted in favour of supporting the Government, which had promised them much of what they wanted.[70] If all but those stubborn five remained true to this decision, and were joined by Woodsworth and Heaps, Bourassa and Neill, the Government would, by the narrowest of margins, be safe.

CHAPTER FOURTEEN

MACKENZIE KING AT BAY

W HEN THE session opened Meighen felt confident that, whatever the Progressives might decide to do at the outset, a government so precariously situated as Mackenzie King's could not long survive. Opportunities to hasten its demise would appear as the session wore on, he thought, as debate exposed the administration's weakness and futility. The Conservatives, of course, were now in a much better position to keep the debating pressure applied relentlessly than they had been in the former Parliament with their corporal's guard of fifty. Not only were their numbers greater, their morale was high; they sensed that a triumph was at hand and they were eager to carry the war into the enemy's territory. Meighen felt also that, with few exceptions, they were united in support of his leadership and this enhanced the confidence with which he awaited the first debate. That there were exceptions was indisputable, as much so as it was predictable that they represented the old, familiar Montreal point of view. Of the four Conservatives elected in Quebec, Meighen counted on the fidelity to himself of only one—Sir George Perley. The other three, all Montrealers, could not be regarded as anything but hostile. R. S. White, who was returning to the Commons after an absence of thirty years, had been privy to the various efforts to oust Meighen which had consumed so many man hours of activity in Montreal since 1921. He was known to have strong feelings about the Hamilton speech, which he apparently regarded as just the latest of Meighen's many errors. So, of course, did the second of the three, Cahan, who was being touted by the Montreal *Star* to supplant Meighen. Everyone knew what Cahan thought of the latter, since he had taken the trouble to express himself publicly on the subject more than once, and early in the session he described himself as "a somewhat independent member."[1] The third Montreal member was Leslie Bell, who this time had secured the nomination in St. Antoine which had been denied him in the 1924 by-election and had won the seat. With memories of Meighen's intervention in the by-election still undoubtedly green, Bell could hardly be expected to regard the national leader with unqualified devotion.

Meighen was warned to beware of Cahan and Bell by Ballantyne, a not entirely unprejudiced counsellor, who wrote that both were "proving to be just what I advised you when they were chosen as candidates. Ca-han's speech in Toronto proves, if you need any further evidence, how opposed he is to you, and that he never has in the past nor ever will in the future, be a man that you can depend upon. I have no more con-fidence in Bell than I have in Cahan. Last night Bell met his committee of the St. Antoine Association and stated to those present that he did not want any of them to say that you were his leader. He wanted to remain perfectly neutral; indicating that there may be a change of leadership."[2] Meighen was so accustomed to news of this kind that by now it left him quite unfazed. "From what I have learned from Sir Robert Borden as to the first man you refer to," he replied, "his conduct has not at all surprised me. I suppose the second man feels he is playing safe. He will find out quite a lot after spending a few months in the House of Com-mons."[3]

It was true, as Bell's alleged remark to his workers in St. Antoine was said to indicate, that there was again—or perhaps one should say still—a movement afoot in Montreal to get rid of Meighen. Even after having led the party in its great comeback he was not to be spared the intrigues of the Montreal tycoons, whose indignation his Hamilton speech had rekindled. In the early part of 1926 there was much talk in Liberal newspapers about the desire of powerful interests in the Conservative party to replace Meighen with someone more to their liking and most of the gossip mentioned R. B. Bennett, who had now returned to the House after being absent since 1917. Bennett was known to hold more "business-like" opinions about railway matters than Meighen—people still remem-bered his famous description of the latter as "the gramophone of Mac-kenzie and Mann"[4]—and although he had joined the reconstructed Meighen government in September 1921, it was believed, rightly, that the two were not on particularly close or friendly terms. It was also believed that Bennett was ambitious for leadership and would not be inhibited by false modesty from grasping the mantle whenever it might fall from Meighen's shoulders. Consequently one could not help but wonder how vigorously he and the three Montrealers would engage in the present battle against Mackenzie King, victory in which would redound to Meigh-en's credit and strengthen his hold on the party. "The handling of affairs here has been anything but easy," Meighen told Ballantyne shortly after the session commenced. "As you know we have now 116 members and among them are many very able men. Some of them came down with a disposition not far removed from the critical, and all these things have to be taken account of in the handling of the party affairs in the House."[5] However, to all outward appearances morale was good. "Our Party is solid and united," Meighen wrote in high spirits a little later, "certainly there is not the slightest difficulty outside of one city . . . and the difficulty there while irritating will end in nothing. We have the most effective party on the floor of the House that I have even seen in the Commons."[6]

The manner in which the House commenced its proceedings was wholly unprecedented but this was only the first of several departures from precedent before the session and the fifteenth Parliament itself came to a tumultuous end less than six months later. The first step in the normal procedure of the Commons, after the members have returned from hearing the speech from the throne in the Senate chamber, is a motion for leave to introduce Bill No. 1, "An Act respecting the administration of oaths of office." This is a formality symbolizing the right of the Commons to take up such other business as it may wish before considering the speech from the throne and this Bill is never heard of again until the beginning of the following session. Next the Speaker announces that he has a copy of the Governor's speech, "which is as follows." Then there is a motion, ordinarily unopposed, that the throne speech be considered on such-and-such a day and that its consideration be given precedence over all other business until completed. When the debate on the speech is about to begin a supporter of the Government moves that an address be presented to the Governor-General expressing thanks for his speech. If the Opposition desires to move want of confidence in the Government at this stage it does so by offering an amendment to the motion for an address. In 1926, though, Meighen was not content to wait this long before attacking because it was his contention that the Liberals had no right to advise the Crown, no right to remain in office at all, and consequently no right to place a programme of legislation before Parliament through the mouth of His Excellency. Since there was no way in which he could formally raise this constitutional issue before Lord Byng had opened Parliament by reading the speech, the best he could do was to try to prevent consideration of the speech in the Commons and thus force the resignation of the Government.

Accordingly in consultation with a committee of his supporters he drew up a motion which he proposed to introduce as an amendment to the motion that the throne speech be considered on a certain day. While the House was awaiting the summons of the Gentleman Usher of the Black Rod to repair to the Senate chamber to hear the speech, Meighen sent a copy of his amendment to Lapointe, who was leading the House in King's absence, along with notice that it would be moved "at the first available opportunity." The amendment recited the reasons why "those who now assume to be His Excellency's advisers" had no right to retain office: the candidates supporting them had been "defeated in a large majority of the constituencies"; nine ministers including the Prime

Minister had been personally defeated and were without seats in Parliament; the Conservative party had secured the largest popular vote and elected the largest number of members. Without a Prime Minister holding a seat in either House, the amendment asserted, those who now claim to advise the Crown "are not competent to act as, or to become, the committee of parliament, commonly known as the government, or to address parliament through His Excellency, and their attempted continuance in office is a violation of the principles and practice of British constitutional government."[7]

When the Commoners returned to their places from the Senate chamber, Lapointe, instead of moving for leave to introduce Bill No. 1, presented a substantive motion:

> That in the opinion of this House, in view of the recent general election, the government was justified in retaining office and in summoning parliament, and the government is entitled to retain office, unless defeated by a vote of this House equivalent to a vote of want of confidence.[8]

It seems evident that this was improvised after Lapointe received the copy of Meighen's amendment. As the latter was a direct negative of this motion it would be ruled out of order as an amendment thereto, and if the motion carried it would be pointless for Meighen to bring in his amendment later on. Lapointe had clearly framed his motion to appeal to the Progressives, who were very much between the devil and the deep blue sea. They had often propounded the doctrine that the mere defeat of a Government measure in the House should not cause the Government's downfall, which ought only to follow the passage of a resolution expressly declaring want of confidence. Meighen's amendment obviously *was* a no-confidence motion whose terms those Progressives not already committed in their own minds to the Liberal cause might find it difficult to oppose with a clear conscience. But most of them were not in a mood to express lack of confidence in the Government just yet; they wanted to wait and see precisely what it would do in the way of legislation and that seemed to be all that Lapointe's motion asked for. It would get them off the hook by sidetracking an issue they would have been happy to avoid—the constitutionality of the Government. It would save them from having to express confidence or no confidence in one side or the other.

However, they were not to be rescued from their dilemma quite so easily. Meighen at once objected that the Lapointe motion was out of order, since the two days' notice required by the rules had not been given before it was moved. Not only that, there was not even any reference to the motion on the order of proceedings for the day which he had been handed earlier. After a complicated and heated procedural argument the Speaker announced that he would give his ruling on Meighen's point of order the following Monday. Thus Lapointe's motion was put aside for the time being and he was compelled, after the Speaker had made the customary announcement that he had a copy of the speech from the throne, to make the other, usual motion concerning consideration of the speech. As soon as he had done so Meighen moved his amendment, which therefore became the first question before the House as he had wanted it to be. This preliminary skirmish in which the opposing forces were manœuvring for position had been won by the Conservatives. How advantageous this would prove to be of course depended on the response of the twenty-eight members who were not in either of the major parties; the way in which many of them would respond was still anybody's guess.

The situation was not greatly clarified during the course of the debate on the amendment, which raged for five days with the public galleries almost always filled and long queues of people waiting vainly in the corridors for admission. The flood-tide of oratory was at the full and the chamber resounded to the cheers and desk-poundings of the back-benchers on either side as their spokesmen re-fought the election campaign, delved into constitutional precedents and set the welkin ringing with eloquent appeals to reason and justice, with loaded questions, sweeping charges, outright denials and defiant rejoinders. All the oratory on the floor and most of the attention of the galleries were directed towards the troubled twenty-eight, who would, however unwillingly, have to make the agonizing, fateful decision. Of those among them who took part in the debate a few made it known that they would oppose the amendment but several others were non-committal. Only two conclusions could be drawn from their remarks: they wished to be saved from having to vote confidence in either party but at the same time they wanted at least that session and if possible others to be completed before another election became necessary. It was the seeming incompatibility of these desires that put them in their quandary. If they voted against Meighen's amendment they might in effect be expressing a confidence in the King administration which they did not feel and could not justify to their constituents. On the other hand if they supported the amendment and it carried, Meighen would come into office, propose policies which they thought it improbable they would be able to support, for that reason suffer defeat in the House and then go to the country. If this should happen within the first fifty days of the session they would receive no indemnity, would suffer all the turmoil and expense of an election campaign so soon after the last one and, considering the downward tendency of Progressive fortunes in the country, might well lose their seats. It was a damnably uncomfortable position to be in.

Each of the two large parties made a considerate move to rescue these unhappy and reluctant arbiters from the horns of their dilemma. It fell to Hugh Guthrie to do so on behalf of the Conservatives. Trying to remove the fear of an early dissolution if there were a change of government, he said:

> . . . if we are tempted to consider ulterior results, then let me say this in the presence of my leader and with his authority, that if this motion carries, if this government resigns, and if he is called upon to form a government in this House, he will undertake the task. He will undertake to carry on that government from session to session without dissolution, and he will do so just so long as he receives parliamentary support.

To Meighen's embarrassment Guthrie did not stop there but continued:

> Hon. members who form the Progressive group in this House will realize this: Their position will be just as strong under a new administration as it is under the present one. They will occupy the same dominant position in the councils of this House as they do to-day, and if a new government were formed and legislation satisfactory to them introduced and proceeded with, there is no reason why such a government should not continue to the end of the parliamentary term. But the Progressives have this safety valve. Should legislation be introduced not acceptable to them, then on account of the peculiar position which they occupy, they would have the remedy in their own hands.[9]

Two days later George Boivin, the Minister of Customs, countered for the Liberals. They could vote against this want-of-confidence amendment moved by the leader of the Opposition, he assured the Progressives, without thereby expressing confidence in the Government, in the policies it had followed during the past four years or those it proposed to follow now. If they defeated the amendment they would simply be deciding that the Government had a right to bring its measures before Parliament, first in the speech from the throne and, if that were approved, in legislation.

This assurance proved to be enough for most of the all-powerful twenty-eight and more convincing than Guthrie's. The Progressives could not imagine themselves supporting what they thought would be the tariff policy of a Conservative government, to say nothing of Meighen's cautious attitude to other subjects like the Hudson Bay Railway and the transfer of natural resources. Knowing Meighen they thought it unlikely that he would modify his policies substantially in order to suit them. If he refused to do so and they opposed his government, it would fall and the election they wanted to postpone as long as possible would be brought on. It would be better to wait and see what Bills the present government came up with, especially as they could do so, on the authority of a minister of the Crown, without registering approval of its past performance or confidence in its present intentions. When the division bells rang shortly after midnight on the fifteenth of January only five Progressives, persuaded that Meighen was correct about the constitutional issue he had raised, voted for his amendment which was defeated by a count of 123 to 120.

That he was correct seems very doubtful, even though his moral claim to office was strong when one considers all the circumstances. One could also sympathize with his objections to the Government's crass bartering of promises to do this and that in return for support in the House and agree with his description of the situation.

> What [he wrote] strikes me as utterly insufferable about the present situation is this: A Government defeated at the polls comes to Parliament and through the mouth of a Minister declares that it does not ask for confidence and continuation in office on the basis of its past record, but that it offers a new series of promises of future conduct fulfillable at the expense of the Public Treasury to a small group of Progressives, and asks these Progressives on the face of such promises to maintain it in power. The Progressives even more frankly state that they are prepared to accept the offer and maintain the Government in office because of such offer. This is a shameless, brutal assault not only on the most sacred principles of British constitutional government but on common honesty. It is actually and indisputably what is going on to-day.[10]

Nevertheless, however much one might be justified in deprecating such behaviour, the fact remained that whoever commanded a majority in the House of Commons had a right to govern. There was apparently no exact precedent for a Prime Minister personally defeated, without a seat in either House and leading only the second largest group of elected members deciding to await Parliament's verdict instead of resigning. But because King lacked a seat for the time being did not mean, as Meighen in effect argued, that there was no government capable of advising the Crown and acting on behalf of the Crown in the Senate and Commons. A Prime Minister, he claimed, "is the sole via media between parliament, as parliament, and the crown or the representative of the crown."[11] But this amounted to a denial of the generally accepted constitutional principle that the Prime Minister, with all his admittedly enormous power, is merely *primus inter pares* and that, as all ministers are ministers of the Crown, the link between the Crown and the two Houses is the entire Cabinet, the Committee of the Privy Council. King could quite legitimately have taken the same action Meighen had in 1921 of making a nominal appointment of one of his supporters to the civil service in order to open a seat for himself but, having raised such a furious hue and cry on that occasion, he could not now follow suit without appearing completely ludicrous and dishonest. However, he obviously intended to reappear in Parliament as soon as possible after its opening and it is not easy to see why his temporary absence should have been deemed to render his retention of office and the continued functioning of his government unconstitutional.[12]

At any rate, the House had very narrowly decided that the King government should continue to function if it could and bring in its legislation. That it had little legislation ready and was too disorganized to operate effectively in its present condition became abundantly clear when Lapointe announced that he would ask to have the session adjourned for six weeks as soon as the throne-speech debate was over, "for the purpose of reorganizing the government in some way" as he put it.[13] Certainly as matters stood the Cabinet was a tattered remnant. Only a dozen ministers were left in Parliament and three of them were in the Senate. Five of the nine ministers in the Commons, and also the Solicitor-General, hailed from Quebec and—a fact without precedent—there was not a single minister in the House from Ontario. Neither New Brunswick, Prince Edward Island nor Manitoba had any members at all in the Cabinet, which was the most unbalanced and unrepresentative in history.

It was necessary to correct this imbalance as far as possible, to get the Prime Minister back into the House and to fill at least some of the portfolios left vacant by the electoral slaughter of the ministers. This would mean by-elections and by-elections would necessitate resignations from the Commons by some of the sitting Liberal members. But if such resignations occurred while the House was in session the Government might lose its precarious and very precious majority. Hence a proper reorganization could not be undertaken without an adjournment. Of course a recess would also make it easier to get some Bills ready for presentation. Not one Government measure was introduced until after the middle of March; never before had Parliament had to wait so long to be acquainted with the precise terms of the Government's policy. This lent credence to the belief of the Opposition that the promises contained in the speech from the throne, to say nothing of the undertaking given privately to Woodsworth and Heaps about old-age pensions, had been cooked up hurriedly without adequate consideration having been given to the means of actually implementing them. If this was the case one could readily understand the desire of the few harried ministers who remained to free themselves from attendance in the House so as to have more time to frame their Bills.

But there was still another reason for their wanting a six weeks' recess, or so it appeared to suspicious Conservative minds. One of the resolutions on the Order Paper at the start of the session in the name of H. H. Stevens called for the appointment of a special committee of the House to investigate evidence of irregular and corrupt conduct by officials of the Department of Customs and Excise. Stevens knew that the ministers were aware that all was not as it should be in that department and was afraid they might use an adjournment to head off the kind of investigation he wanted. His motion could not be reached until the throne-speech debate was over; if the House recessed for six weeks immediately after that debate, there was no telling when it would be reached and by the time it was, the Government might be in a position to say that steps had already been taken to put the affairs of the department in good order. Having in his possession some very damaging information, Stevens was naturally anxious, in the public as well as in the party interest, to have the matter thoroughly thrashed out, first in a parliamentary committee and then in Parliament itself.

Recognizing how advantageous a recess would be to the Government in these various ways, the Conservatives strenuously opposed Lapointe's motion on February the second that as soon as the debate on the address in reply to the speech from the throne was concluded the House should adjourn until the fifteenth of March. This motion came immediately after the House had voted down, 125 to 115, a want-of-confidence amendment Meighen had moved to the address and Lapointe perhaps hoped that, as that amendment had been discussed for two weeks, the members would now be ready to approve the address and give him his adjournment. When his motion was read out on the second of February the Conservatives waited for him to stand up and offer some explanation of why an adjournment was requested but he made no move to do so; he simply sat still and stared at the Opposition, whereupon Sir Henry Drayton rose to oppose the motion. It was indeed extraordinary that a minister of the Crown should ask Parliament to disband for a month and a half without offering any explanation whatsoever when it had not yet transacted any public business. ". . . the spectacle this House has witnessed," said Meighen, "is without parallel or approach in the history of this most extraordinary administration. Never has any member of the House in the last twenty years witnessed anything which in any way compares; and I fancy the records of this parliament, or of the parliament of any dominion of this empire, will be searched in vain for anything that could be called a precedent or could be called an excuse." The real significance of this request for an adjournment, he went on, "the ghastliest feature of the whole occasion is this: the government comes to parliament, convened at its own instance, brought here under its own auspices, declared to be brought here for the despatch of business; and before any business is despatched suggests that we go to our homes for six weeks because it is not in a position to carry on, and then refuses to give any single reason to parliament for not carrying on."[14]

If Lapointe had any thought that his motion would be accepted after a brief and perfunctory debate he was quickly disabused of the idea. One after another the Conservatives got up to speak against it. The afternoon passed without any of the one hundred Liberals rising to defend it and as the evening wore on the Opposition continued to hold the floor. Shortly after midnight a Conservative motion to adjourn the debate was defeated by ten votes, whereupon Stevens stood up to speak. By this time the galleries, which had been filled to capacity earlier in the day as during many of the sittings since the opening of the session, had begun to empty and the M.P.'s sat yawning in their chairs or hovered, smoking, in the corridors adjoining the chamber. However, what Stevens had to say brought them sharply to attention for he proceeded to divulge some of the facts in his possession concerning what had been going on in the Customs Department. It was a rather shocking and grisly story he had to tell. He told only part of it but his allegations were sufficiently documented to show that an investigation of the department was indeed desirable. He concluded with an amendment to Lapointe's motion to the effect that there should be no adjournment of the House until the public business referred to in the speech from the throne had been disposed of and until a special investigating committee of seven members had been appointed.

George Boivin, who had joined the Cabinet as Minister of Customs in September, inheriting the departmental mess left by his predecessor, Jacques Bureau, announced that the Government was quite willing to have an investigation. In fact he had intended, when Stevens' original resolution on the Order Paper was reached, to propose that the probe should be made broader and more thorough than the resolution would have permitted. As for the evidence that Stevens had now brought forward and the charges he had made, Boivin was ill prepared to reply and admitted as much. About all that he could say was that he had started to reform the department and most of his speech was devoted to an angry denunciation of the Opposition for trying to prevent an adjournment. When he finished speaking it was after three o'clock in the morning and the Conservatives again tried to adjourn the debate until that afternoon. Lapointe, who was evidently determined to get his six weeks' recess if he had to keep the House sitting all night, objected and the motion to adjourn the debate was defeated by one vote. Finally at four o'clock Lapointe agreed that Meighen should adjourn the debate on the understanding that the motion for a recess and Stevens' amendment thereto have precedence over all other business until disposed of.

When the weary but excited members returned to their places that afternoon Boivin announced that he was prepared to meet with Meighen to frame a motion appointing the committee Stevens had asked for.

Accordingly the two men got together and, not without some difficulty, worked out a mutually acceptable motion which the House approved on February the fifth, along with the names of the four Liberals, four Conservatives and one Progressive who were to form the committee. Later the same day Lapointe's motion for the recess was at last accepted by a margin of eight votes. However, it was one thing to have this passed and another to have the recess, which was to end on March the fifteenth and to begin upon completion of the debate on the address. Lapointe had hoped for six weeks but the Conservatives were uncooperative. They were not through debating the address yet by any means, and saw no reason why they should cease debating it until the Government introduced some legislation. On the eighth of February another Opposition amendment condemning the Government was moved and debate on this continued until the sixteenth when it was defeated. There was now less than a month to go before the House would have to come back from its recess—if the recess ever got started! It was known, in fact had been announced in the press, that Cahan was ready to move still another amendment, this one stating explicitly that the Government lacked the confidence of the House. If he got this in and it was supported at length by those around him, the fifteenth of March might arrive without the House ever having adjourned at all.

At this point one of the Progressives, the Reverend Thomas William Bird of Benito, Manitoba, came to the rescue of the Government. Here was a gentleman upon whom this session was to confer great notoriety, for this was the first of two occasions on which he came spectacularly to the fore. Showing what was in Conservative eyes a suspiciously sophisticated knowledge of the Rules of the House, Mr. Bird now moved "the previous question." If this motion, "that this question be now put," carried, there could be no further debate on the motion for an address, which would have to be put to a vote forthwith, and Cahan would not be able to move his amendment. The last time this seldom-invoked rule had been used was in 1913 when it had figured in the ingenious means devised by Meighen to have the new closure procedure embodied in the rules.[15] In 1913 the Liberals, engaged in the very same kind of obstruction the Conservatives were now practising, had thunderously denounced the moving of "the previous question" as a shameful, bare-faced stratagem to gag Parliament. Now they looked on with smiling complacency, delighted to see Meighen hoist with his own petard. This time, of course, it was not they but one of their Progressive friends who had done the dirty deed, done it, Cahan charged furiously, at their behest (which Bird hotly denied) because having made such a fuss in 1913 they were afraid to do it themselves.

In any event, whether there had been collusion or not, if Bird's motion carried, the debate on the address would be over and the recess would follow at once. But the motion that "this question be now put" could itself be debated, and for a long time with 116 Conservatives available for duty. For two weeks they kept at it while Lapointe, nervously watching the calendar, saw February slip by into the past. A most exceptional maiden speech, full of Latin phrases and allusions to mythology and literature as well as current events, replete with long words that some honourable members of the House may have been hearing for the first time, was delivered by a freshman Conservative from Ontario—"a milk white hind on the political lawn," as he described himself—while Meighen sat chuckling to himself in his front-row seat as the carefully rehearsed words rolled out. This speech was one of the few during that unusually acrimonious session that was entirely uninterrupted; it was as though the Liberals were transfixed with incredulity and thankful for some temporary comic relief from the hard round of argument. The speech resounded with such sentences as: "I am not one given to apotheosis and I made the statement with full premeditation, deliberation and sincerity. Wherefore, let us scrutinize the statement and examine into my rationalizations in this regard." And: ". . . most important of all is the Platonic element. We are forced to recognize the theory that the souls animating the frames of the various individuals in question had previously hobnobbed in some pre-natal sphere." A flowery tribute was paid to Mr. Speaker Lemieux, hearing which that urbane and dignified gentleman must have found it hard to maintain a suitably impassive countenance. For relief from the bitterness of partisan strife, said the "milk white hind," he sometimes turned "to the pages of Parkman, and in the transition, I have observed, Sir, with what facility, being within the shadow of the Speaker's chair, I enter into the esprit of an elder day— my point being, Sir, that you are not only a splendid specimen of our present-day compatriots of Norman extraction, but also to me, you are redolent of our grand and romantic Canadian past." At which, perhaps, the redolent Mr. Speaker gravely bowed.

There was also an eloquent eulogy of Meighen, whose "very aloofness and . . . penetrating analytical mind are phenocrysts of character and ability respectively. . . ." On the other hand Robert Forke did not fare quite so well: "I sat in this House and heard the Argus-eyed member for Brandon state in his usual Laodicean manner. . . ." As for the Progressives collectively, they heard a trenchant explanation of why they did not make common cause with the Conservatives. It "was due to what I should term their urban complex, meaning by this a more or less morbid pathological mental process resultant mostly from that diffidence, that timidity, that self-complacency, that parsimony, that narrowness, that simplicity incident to rusticity."[16] The next day Forke quoted this passage and protested with mock indignation, "This is terrible, Mr. Speaker! It is the worst that has ever been said about us."[17]

Perhaps this speech, coming on top of all the others, was just too much for Lapointe. At any rate as soon as it was over he gave notice that the next day he would move closure, for the first time by a member of a Liberal government, which meant that Bird's motion would have to be voted on not later than two o'clock the following morning and that no member could speak to it for longer than twenty minutes. When his turn to take twenty minutes came Meighen, to no one's surprise, used some of them to do a little reminiscing about what Lapointe had said about closure when it was incorporated into the rules in 1913.

> . . . of all hon. gentlemen opposite in numbers then almost what they are to-day who condemned this rule, its principle, its initiation, its application, who condemned it day and night with bell, book and candle, the most vociferous was himself, the then hon. member for Kamouraska. He declared that the application of this rule was the gag and disruption of a free parliament. As time is very precious I cannot quote much of what he said. If I could quote it all, I would piece together from the speeches of . . . the present Minister of Justice, a better speech than he delivered this afternoon but one wholly on the other side of the case. . . .
>
> I do not object to closure. I believe the closure rule is essential in all free parliaments. This doctrine I preached in 1913, and this doctrine we on this side of the House sought to drive home to hon. members opposite. This doctrine they repudiated and they declared that parliament debased itself by the adoption of such a rule. Has any explanation come from the Minister of Justice this afternoon of his change of front? Is there anything left for this government to swallow of all its professions throughout all its history? . . .
>
> The closure rule is all right; it is perfectly defensible, justifiable and necessary. But never in the history of any parliament was closure adopted for the purpose of giving its members a holiday. Those who stoutly resisted this rule when applied only for the purpose of learning the will of parliament on absolutely essential legislation, only for the purpose of getting the decision of this House in important legislation submitted by the government; those who fought day and night to prevent the application of closure for such purpose, come into parliament this afternoon and call upon all their own followers and their allies . . . to stand up and support closure in order that parliament may adjourn.[18]

This argument made no impression on the new-found friends of closure. Bird's motion was passed near midnight on March the second, as was the main motion for an address to the Governor-General, whereupon the House adjourned until the fifteenth. The Conservatives had succeeded in shortening the recess from six weeks to twelve days.

Because of this King was unable to carry out as thorough a reconstruction of his Cabinet as probably he had intended, since there was not enough time to have the necessary by-elections before the House re-assembled.   He himself was elected in Prince Albert on February the fifteenth, easily defeating an Independent who had unofficial Conservative support, and Dunning was returned by acclamation in Regina on the sixteenth of March.   The only other new face in the reorganized ministry was that of J. C. Elliott, a London lawyer.   For someone in his first session of Parliament Elliott suddenly became a very busy man.   He had been chosen to move the address to His Excellency in January; in Feb-ruary he was put on the committee to investigate the Customs Depart-ment; he was appointed Minister of Labour in March; in April he took on two additional portfolios, Soldiers' Civil Re-establishment and Health. Seldom had there been seen such a meteoric rise!

When the House reconvened on the fifteenth of March this still rather ramshackle Cabinet began to bring in its legislation at long last—legisla-tion the Progressives and Labourites were waiting for.   There were to be cash advances out of the Treasury to persons settling on Crown lands in order to stimulate rural settlement; there was to be (one of Forke's fourteen points) a revaluation on application by individual settlers of lands taken up under the Soldier Settlement Act of 1919, to take account of the drastic fall in land values since the war and thus permit a down-ward revision of the settler's payments; a system of old-age pensions would be set up under which the Dominion would pay half of a maximum pension of $240 per annum to needy persons living in provinces whose governments agreed to pay the other half.   When the resolutions preced-ing the introduction of these three Bills were read out Meighen invited the Government to give an estimate of what all this would cost.   "I do not expect a close estimate at all," he said sarcastically, "but say within a hundred million dollars."[19]   There was still more, of course.   The resolu-tion on which the promised transfer of Alberta's natural resources was to be based was presented, although this proved to be illusory when negotia-tions between Ottawa and Edmonton broke down with charges of bad faith on both sides.   A Bill providing for long-term loans to farmers, a form of rural credits, was brought in and in due course approved.   In the estimates of the Department of Railways there was an item of $3,000,000 to put the completed portion of the Hudson Bay Railway in operating condition.   The amendments to the Criminal Code and the Immigration Act demanded by Woodsworth were duly introduced.   And then there was the Budget, a most attractive affair this time.   Generous reductions in income tax were granted as well as lower tariffs on a num-ber of items, notably automobiles.   The sales tax was removed from such diverse items as articles for exhibitions, split peas and heirlooms and the old, popular penny postage on letters addressed to points in North America, which had vanished as part of the price of financing the war, was restored. It really looked as though the Government expected another election before very long.

After the twelve days' adjournment, as before, the Conservatives bent every effort to bring the Government down, lengthily opposing its measures and dividing the House whenever possible. The Government, however, creaked along with the help of Progressives, Labourites and Independents, being sustained by majorities as high as fifteen and as low as one. And then on June the eighteenth the special committee investigating the Customs Department presented its final report, a report which, if not heard around the world, at any rate shook the Government to its already feeble foundations and precipitated a series of sensational, climactic events which were to prove as unexpectedly disastrous to Arthur Meighen as they were surprisingly providential for Mackenzie King[20]

In the four and a half months of its existence the committee had met 115 times, examined dozens of witnesses and looked into such records of the department as it could get its hands on. Taken as a whole the evidence it gathered added up to a genuine scandal if ever there was one, a sordid story of debauchery and corruption among officials of the Customs Department. It showed beyond any doubt that they had not only connived at, but encouraged and profited from, smuggling on a large scale. It showed that prosecutions for smuggling had been discouraged —in some cases prevented—at the behest of the minister or certain of his subordinates in order to serve the interest of the Liberal party. It showed that fines imposed on convicted smugglers had often been remitted at the behest of politicians and on the order of the Minister. It proved that the Public Treasury had been defrauded of very large sums of money in unpaid customs duties, as well as sales and excise taxes. Under the best of conditions, of course, smuggling between Canada and the United States was bound always to be a serious problem for the authorities. Inevitably attempts would be made to bring lower-priced American goods into Canada without paying Canadian duties or taxes. The immense length of the border between the two countries and its openness made the task of policing most difficult, as did the extent of Canada's coastlines where small boats could land their illicit cargoes in secluded bays and coves without much fear of detection. The problem was enormously enlarged by the addition of the eighteenth Amendment, the prohibition amendment, to the Constitution of the United States. This made the smuggling of liquor into that country hugely profitable and increased the volume of American goods brought illegally into Canada, as the liquor carriers loaded up for their return trips.

The greater part of the committee's attention was devoted to the

Montreal Customs district, where the most flagrant violations of the law by organized smuggling rings seemed to occur. It turned out—indeed it was well known before the committee was appointed—that the man who until recently had been chief preventive officer there, with the duty of enforcing the law against smuggling, was one Bisaillon, a smuggler himself and a suspected perjurer and embezzler. In fact Bisaillon, who enjoyed the implicit confidence of Jacques Bureau, Minister of Customs until September 1924, was alleged to be, if not the guiding genius, at any rate one of the chief organizers and directors of smuggling in that district. Complaints were made to the Government about his activities as early as 1924 by the Commercial Protective Association, an organization of Canadian manufacturers and importers whose businesses were being adversely affected by the smuggling of American products, especially textiles. But the Government seemed strangely reluctant to proceed against him. Mackenzie King at length informed the association that, while he could not sanction the summary dismissal of Bisaillon, if specific charges were made a Royal Commission would be appointed to investigate. In due course charges were made but no commission resulted. When Bisaillon was finally dismissed, it was only near the end of 1925 when it became known that Stevens intended to press for a probe of the department's affairs.

While the Montreal district was the chief trouble spot and Bisaillon the most notoriously corrupt official, the degeneration of the department was to be found everywhere the committee looked. Some especially astonishing data concerning liquor-running from the ports of the Maritime Provinces came to light. Boats would load up with liquor bonded for export and on which, therefore, no excise tax had been paid. After receiving clearance from Customs officers who obviously must have known what was going on, they would set sail ostensibly for far distant places that would take weeks or months to reach and miraculously in a few days would reappear with their holds and decks empty at the port whence they had sailed and load up all over again. The schooner *Dorin,* for example, left Halifax on September the seventeenth, 1925, carrying a cargo of liquor to Lima, Peru. Four days later she was back in Halifax taking on a similar cargo for Havana. The schooner *Ena A. Moulton* made three round trips between Halifax and Nassau in eleven days, one of them in two days. Hardly less phenomenal was the *Ellice B.,* which completed two round trips between Halifax and Nassau and two between Halifax and Havana in less than two months, carrying in all these voyages a grand total of over forty thousand cases of liquor. While all this might be regarded as proof that Maritimers made the world's finest ships and that Canadian whisky enjoyed an enviable reputation in Latin America and the Caribbean, the fact was, of course, that with the connivance of the Customs officials at the ports concerned all these boats were sailed either down "Rum Row" to the United States or around to quiet places on the coasts of the Maritimes where their cargoes were unloaded and disposed of by bootleggers.

The Conservatives in Parliament were determined not to allow King and his ministers to absolve themselves of responsibility for the multitudinous instances of gross malfeasance revealed in the voluminous evidence gathered by the committee. The majority of the committee, however, the four Liberals and one Progressive, refused to include in its report any censure of the Government, contenting themselves with recommending certain reforms in the procedures of the department and the removal of various officials, in some cases by retirement, in others by dismissal. Consequently when the committee chairman moved that the House concur in the report, Stevens moved an amendment to the effect that the report should be referred back to the committee with instructions to add to it certain clauses censuring the Government in general and the Prime Minister and the new Minister of Customs, George Boivin, in particular. It was on this question of the responsibility of the Government, this motion of censure, that the climactic debate of 1926 took place.

The Government's defence, one that was thoroughly riddled by Stevens, Meighen and other Conservative speakers, was that effective measures had already been taken to reform the department, the need of whose reform even the Government had to admit. In 1925 the Customs Act had been amended to make the smuggling of goods valued at more than two hundred dollars an indictable offence punishable by imprisonment instead of merely by fine. However, it appeared that there had been very few prosecutions under the stiffened law. The Government had also requested and received from Parliament an increased appropriation for the preventive branch of the Customs service—but most of the money had not been expended. The infamous Bisaillon had been fired, without the prior investigation by a Royal Commission Mackenzie King had at one stage thought necessary, though not until it became clear that the administration of the department would be given a thorough parliamentary airing. Furthermore, and this went more to the heart of the matter, King had requested Bureau's resignation from the Government in September 1925 and Bureau had departed, taking with him to his home in Three Rivers, Stevens charged, nine filing cabinets full of departmental records and correspondence. The committee's report blamed the degeneration of the department very largely on Bureau, who, it said, had "failed to appreciate and properly discharge the responsibilities of his office," and King seemed content, once he had got rid of the man, to allow the blame to be laid at his door. Since Bureau had been the culprit and since he had been removed from the Government, the Government could not be implicated in his conduct or be held to share his guilt.

Bureau's departure from the Cabinet was followed by his appointment to the Senate—Senate reform at last!—and his replacement as Minister by the young, energetic and exceptionally able Boivin. But certain of Boivin's actions in office seemed to the Opposition to be not above reproach, especially in the case of Moses Aziz. This man, a Syrian resident of New Brunswick, had a predilection for the Liberal party and a tendency to run afoul of the laws against smuggling and bootlegging. In August 1925 he was convicted of being in possession of smuggled liquor, fined one hundred and fifty dollars and sentenced to three months in jail. The following month in the midst of the election campaign J. G. Robichaud, the Liberal candidate in Gloucester, New Brunswick, wrote Boivin to ask him to intercede with the Minister of Justice to have Aziz kept out of jail. "I attach the greatest importance to this affair," Robichaud wrote, "since in the actual circumstances I need the help of all my friends. . . . Mr. Aziz is the highest help for us during this campaign, and we cannot do without his services."[21] Lapointe, the Minister of Justice, was away from Ottawa at the time so Boivin, new in office but a first-rate lawyer who ought to have known better, took the advice of his deputy minister, who was not a lawyer at all, and had an order sent out that the warrant committing Aziz to jail should not be issued. After the election, which saw Robichaud return as the sole Liberal from New Brunswick, Boivin advised him that he could now see no reason why the sentence against Aziz should not be executed but Robichaud besought him to stay proceedings with the result that Aziz was not imprisoned until the spring of 1926 when the facts of the case were ascertained by the Customs probe committee. It was this interference with the course of justice that caused Stevens to include in his amendment, as a statement to be added to the committee's report, these words: "The conduct of the present minister of the department, the Hon. George H. Boivin, in the case of Moses Aziz is utterly unjustifiable."[22]

The debate on Stevens' amendment began on June the twenty-second before a nearly full House and crowded galleries. Often it became a shouting match rather than a debate and the Speaker, whose impartiality remained impeccable, was often hard put to it to maintain decorum in the uproar. The hoots and catcalls of the back-benchers, the frequent wrangling over points of order, the rousing cheers and derisive laughter, the loud applause and crude invective were all doubtless entertaining to the spectators, if less than edifying. Not for years had the House gone through such hectic sittings as the tension heightened and the tumult mounted in a windy crescendo. The prosecution's case, for it was a trial of sorts, was presented first of all by three of the four Conservative members of the committee, the fourth, R. B. Bennett, having decided, oddly enough that his presence was required more urgently in Alberta, where a provincial election campaign was going on in which the Conservatives had not the slightest chance of success, than in Ottawa where rather more stirring events were taking place. Each of the three, Stevens, C. W. Bell of Hamilton and A. J. Doucet of Kent, New Brunswick, dealt with different aspects of the evidence, Bell's speech being a particularly able presentation. Boivin led off for the defence and was seconded by Dugald Donaghy of Vancouver, one of the Liberal committee members, in a fighting five-hour address, by far the most effective effort of any on the Liberal side.

The first to be heard from of the twenty-eight "non-aligned" members on whom would depend the outcome was W. T. Lucas, an Alberta Progressive, who expressed his horror at the misconduct revealed in the Customs Department and his intention of voting for Stevens' amendment. Lucus was followed directly by Woodsworth, who saw the matter in a somewhat different light and sought to inject a note of sweet reasonableness into the discusion. He took the position that the whole business should be removed from the consideration of Parliament and made the subject of a judicial inquiry. To that end he moved an amendment to Stevens' amendment, not only calling for the appointment of a judicial commission but expunging all censure of the Government. Members of Parliament, he argued, could not possibly deal with a matter like this in an appropriately detached spirit; they would be governed by partisan prejudice and subjected to the outside influences of inflammatory editorials and of public opinion. "If the [Stevens] amendment carries," he said, "presumably the Liberals go out of office and the Conservatives come into office. Does anyone say that under these circumstances either Liberals or Conservatives can vote dispassionately on such a question as this?"[23] Of course they could not but what of Woodsworth himself, and Heaps, and the Progressives and Independents? After all it was they who held the balance of power and, being connected with neither of the old parties, they could presumably bring to bear that calm and impartial attitude without which there could be no just decision. Even if they had not read all the evidence from the committee hearings, and Woodsworth was probably only more honest than most in admitting he had not, even if they were unfamiliar with the exact terms of the Customs Act governing the administration of the department, which he confessed he was, they would surely be in a position to pronounce judgment on the basis of the facts before them as members of the high court of Parliament, which it was their right and duty to do.

As a matter of fact it became clear in the course of Woodsworth's speech that what really bothered him was not the impossibility of a dispassionate vote on the amendment but the possibility of a change of government if it carried, as it would if many of the Progressives were of the same mind as Lucas. One could not help wondering whether he would have been so deprecatory of people living in glass houses throwing stones and pots calling kettles black if the Conservatives had been in the dock instead of the Liberals. He thought it ought to be possible "to condemn certain actions of the government without necessarily replacing the government by another party or group in the House."[24] That some of its actions deserved condemnation he agreed, especially the appointment of Bureau to the Senate, which struck him "as the worst thing the present government has done in connection with the whole matter. . . ."[25] But to censure it for this or anything else, given the party system and the conventions of responsible parliamentary government as they actually were, would be to cause its downfall and the elevation of Meighen to power. It was this prospect, one suspects, which most profoundly troubled Woodsworth, not the unjudicial atmosphere of the House.

During his speech he began to dilate on the infamous means by which the Winnipeg general strike had been ended, a favourite topic of his and one that had been debated already that session, in order to remark that the very man, the leader of the Opposition, who now sought to have the King government censured and to install himself in power, had been the chief perpetrator of those means. At this point Meighen jumped to his feet to assert heatedly that this was irrelevant to the question before the House. The Speaker declared Woodsworth to be in order but admonished him not to wander too far afield, whereupon Woodsworth resumed his recital of the events of 1919. This led to another interruption by Meighen which resulted in his being required, for the first and only time in his career, to withdraw an unparliamentary remark. Rising to a point of order, he was greeted by a loud chorus of boos and shouts of "Sit down" from across the aisle and there ensued the following dialogue.

> Mr. MEIGHEN: I rise to a point of order.
> Some hon. MEMBERS: Sit down.
> Mr. MEIGHEN: I think the government and their followers have no proper respect for the rules of the House.
> Mr. MACDONALD (Antigonish): I rise to a point of order. The right hon. leader of the opposition has no right to make the statement he did and I ask that he be compelled to withdraw it.
> Mr. SPEAKER: I do not see why there should be so much heat in debate. This is one of the finest debates we have heard for some time, and I fail to see any reason for disorder. I hope the right hon. leader of the opposition on thinking the matter over will withdraw the expression he used with respect to hon. gentlemen to my right to the effect that they have scant respect for the rules of the House. All members have a great deal of respect for the rules of the House.

I am glad to acknowledge that at a time when I am celebrating the thirtieth anniversary of my first appearance in this House.

Mr. MEIGHEN: Whenever I rise to a point of order there invariably arises from the other side a chorus of boos. My retort is very mild indeed.

Mr. SPEAKER: I must ask the right hon. gentleman to withdraw the first expression used, that hon. gentlemen on the government side have scant respect for the rules of the House.

Meighen persisted in objecting to the Speaker's ruling but when Lemieux demanded that he withdraw his statement, he gave in.

Mr. MEIGHEN: Mr. Speaker, out of deference to your authority as Speaker of this House I obey your ruling, but I hope you will permit me to say that because I ask that hon. gentlemen shall not do what they have no right to do I do not necessarily offend them. My reason for rising to the point of order was this: It was to repeat what I had urged before, and I insist on doing it, that no hon. member has a right in any way to debate in this House a question which already has been decided in the same session. I do not know of any rule more firmly established or more clear. I was overruled by Your Honour then; I hope I shall not be overruled again.

Mr. SPEAKER: I fail to see where the hon. member (Mr. Woodsworth) is infringing the rules. I again ask that hon. members so conduct themselves as to obviate any necessity for a ruling by the Chair.

Mr. MEIGHEN: Mr. Speaker,—

Mr. SPEAKER: I must ask hon. gentlemen to remain within reasonable limits.

Mr. WOODSWORTH: I cannot hear you, Mr. Speaker.

Mr. SPEAKER: I am telling the right hon. gentleman [sic] not to dilate too much on branches of the main subject.

Mr. WOODSWORTH: I am glad to know that I am and have been in order. I shall try not to say anything that is out of order.

Mr. MEIGHEN: You cannot.[26]

As soon as Woodsworth had finished speaking Meighen claimed that the proposed subamendment was out of order on the grounds that it completely eliminated the substance of the Stevens amendment, on which the House would have no opportunity of voting if the subamendment carried. That argument was supported by several other Conservatives and opposed by three members of the Government and by Forke, all of whom understandably welcomed Woodsworth's effort to remove the possibility that the administration would be censured. After this point of order had been debated for about an hour the Speaker reserved his ruling until the next sitting when he declared the subamendment to be in order and it thus became the question before the House.

It was now the turn of the two leaders to speak, first King and then Meighen. With every allowance for the fact that the former was a drown-

ing man, clutching frantically at every straw, flailing wildly in every direction, while the latter was swimming coolly and confidently towards the
visible shore, to read these two speeches one after the other is to discover
much of the contrast of mind and manner between these totally dissimilar
men.[27] For over two hours on the afternoon of June the twenty-fourth
King held the floor in a desperate, do-or-die effort. He began by saying
that the Government endorsed the report of the committee and was prepared to implement its recommendations. It was also ready to accept
Woodsworth's "constructive" and "non-partisan" amendment as opposed
to the "political," "partisan" and "destructive" one offered by Stevens.
Then, after some general remarks about the problem of smuggling, he
began to review the dealings of his government with the Commercial
Protective Association and its president, R. P. Sparks, intending to show
that the association had received the fullest co-operation from the Government as they worked zealously together to suppress smuggling and punish
the guilty. To hear King tell it there had been practically a love feast
between the two bodies, so appreciative was the Government of the service rendered by the association in bringing the facts about smuggling
to light, so grateful was the association to the Government for taking
such energetic action. And then suddenly Sparks, a Liberal all his life,
had turned his coat, going to Stevens with his information about the
Customs Department just when a general election was called, and for a
financial consideration, King insinuated darkly. With Sparks sitting
listening in the gallery behind him the Prime Minister declared:

> Mr. Sparks' change of mind and heart is not difficult to see. In Sep-
> tember, after a general election was declared, Mr. Sparks was ten-
> dered a banquet in the Chateau Laurier here; he was given no end
> of praise for having secured the reforms which had been brought
> about, and I am told that as an additional recognition he was given
> an honorarium of $1,000.
>   Mr. STEVENS: That is too small for a prime minister—
>   Mr. MACKENZIE KING: It was too small; they should have
> given him $10,000. My point is—
>   Mr. STEVENS:—reflecting on a citizen who cannot defend him-
> self.
>   Mr. MACKENZIE KING: The point I am bringing out is that Mr.
> Sparks at that late date was allowing it to be believed that he
> had achieved a great purpose, that he had done a great service to the
> association and to the country. That was in September, just at the
> time a general election had been declared. And then what took
> place? Mr. Sparks began to associate with my right hon. friend
> opposite, just as he is doing from the gallery at the moment. They
> worked together back and forth during the campaign and when
> the election was over, just before parliament was summoned, in order
> to make things difficult and complicated for the government, he

supplied the hon. member for Vancouver Centre (Mr. Stevens) with the information. . . .

Mr. MEIGHEN: Will the Prime Minister be good enough to explain what he meant by saying that Mr. Sparks was in association with me from the gallery at the moment?

Mr. MACKENZIE KING: I have not been blind to my hon. friend's eyes.

Some hon. MEMBERS: Cheap!

Mr. MACKENZIE KING: Yes: if my hon. friend wishes to follow these methods I will admit that they are cheap. The whole business is pretty cheap when you get to the bottom of it.

So much for Sparks. Now what about Jacques Bureau, whose name had figured so prominently in the discussion? Unfortunately, said King, his health had broken down early in 1925 and he had not been able to give his usual close attention to departmental administration. In fact the Department of Customs had had to be put in charge of an acting minister, P. J. A. Cardin, and when Bureau's health had failed to improve by the autumn of 1925 King had regretfully asked him for his resignation. Until his illness Bureau had enjoyed an excellent reputation. Was there any member of the House, asked King, who would deny that, who would stand up now and say that between the beginning of 1922 and the end of 1924 he had not had "the highest respect for the integrity, the ability and the honesty of Hon. Jacques Bureau. If there is one such member I ask him to reply. . . . We will see how brave some men are." He had been criticized, the Prime Minister went on, for appointing Bureau to the Senate. ". . . . if there is anyone who will deny the esteem in which Mr. Bureau was held at the time he was appointed to the Senate, let him stand up in his seat [sic] and say so. Not one! That reveals better than words could do the regard in which Mr. Bureau was held at the time of his appointment to the Senate."

There was one thing about the committee's proceedings, said King, which troubled him more than anything else. "Why was Mr. Bureau not invited to testify before the committee? If hon. gentlemen opposite were going to attack him, why did they not invite him to appear before them?" He had not himself advised his former colleague to testify, King admitted in answer to a question. "I may say that I have not talked with Mr. Bureau from some time before the day the investigation began until this very morning; I deliberately refrained from so doing. . . ." However, Bureau had told him that morning of his surprise at not being summoned by the committee and of his willingness to appear before "a judicial body properly constituted. . . ." Then came some of King's patented rhetoric:

> . . . I am not going to be numbered among those who seek to destroy a man's life and the lives of those that are near and dear to him, and

his reputation as well, without affording him an opportunity to be heard in any and every particular before a properly constituted tribunal. If there is one thing more than another which men have to watch in politics it is to see that party persecution is not carried to the point where it ruins human lives and honour; and every hon. member in this chamber owes it to himself and to the position he occupies to see that men who enter public life are not slaughtered for the sake of party ends and party gain.

So the Government, having neglected to appoint a Royal Commission before and having agreed to an investigation by a special committee of the House, had now decided that a judicial inquiry as proposed by Woodsworth was preferable after all. Not only would it permit Bureau to be heard in his own defence but it would also enable the entire investigation to be completed, as the committee's report acknowledged it had not yet been. In this connection King was prompted to spring to the defence of national unity with a typical innuendo:

> Mr. MACKENZIE KING: The report states that the work has not been completed, that the committee have not reviewed all the matters that were referred to it [sic]—
> Mr. STEVENS: Hear, hear.
> Mr. MACKENZIE KING:—and mention was made of some particular matters that were not concluded. Now I do not say that the action of my hon. friends opposite was designated to prevent inquiry elsewhere, but there is a certain chivalrous attitude that needs consideration in this regard. It so happened that hon. gentlemen opposite sought to focus the whole inquiry on the province of Quebec.
> Some hon. MEMBERS: Oh, oh.
> Mr. MACKENZIE KING: They did not go much beyond that province.
> An hon. MEMBER: Shame!
> Mr. MACKENZIE KING: The facts speak for themselves.
> Some hon. MEMBERS: Shame! shame!
> An hon. MEMBER: Too small!

Having made his bow to Quebec, he now turned to the West and its Progressive representatives with a wildly irrelevant reference to the tariff issue. "What is the object of hon. gentlemen opposite?" he asked. "It is that they and their friends may again control the policies of this country; it is another device whereby those who favour higher and higher protection—." When the loud laughter from the Opposition benches had ceased he repeated the charge. "From the beginning to the close of this session hon. members opposite have sought in one way or another to get possession of the seals of office, in order that they might put their own policies into effect." That, as no one knew better than Mackenzie King, was what politics was all about but he hoped that the wavering Progressives would be brought to their senses by this reminder of what the Tories would do to the tariff.

After a brief defence of George Boivin, a tribute to his zeal and ability, King ended his remarks characteristically with a quotation from Scripture. "I say to hon. members, judge by the judgment wherewith you expect to be judged, 'for with what judgement ye judge, ye shall be judged; and with what measure ye mete, it shall be measured to you again.'" Again there was much mirth on the other side of the House and King retorted angrily: "My hon. friends may laugh. They laugh at Scripture. They laugh at anything and everything but they will find the truth of the words I have just uttered, because those words have stood through many centuries and will stand for many centuries to come."

With that he sat down, flushed and disheveled, to the mingled cheers and jeers of the members. Before the din had died away Meighen was standing austere and motionless behind his desk, ready to reply. The audience in the galleries leaned forward expectantly, the reporters in the crowded press gallery sat with pencils poised, the members subsided in their places. All of them waited, some with pleasurable anticipation, others with hate in their hearts, for the relentless, merciless dissection they knew they were about to witness. How Meighen had looked forward to this moment! There sat King, caught at last, so vulnerable, so ridiculous, so entirely contemptible. Little knowing that this was the last time he would ever address the House of Commons, Meighen set out to demolish the Government's defence, dissolving its elements with withering scorn and an orderly, precise analysis of the evidence. One by one the arguments advanced by Boivin and King were held up for examination and one by one they were refuted with calm, "un-get-aroundable" logic. As one of King's biographers has described it, "Meighen took the corruption of the Customs Department, the failure of Bureau, the whole sorry spectacle of the Government, and ushered them in faultless procession before the jury. Gestureless, his voice quiet, his face serene, he moved pitilessly from one perfect extemporaneous paragraph to another which still stand in the record like considered prose."[28]

Meighen turned first to King's address. "The Prime Minister," he said, "has just concluded a very laboured defence of the administration and his minister; and I will deal with his remarks with the respect which his office demands, with the respect which I owe to him and have always felt for him [sic!]. But I commence with this promise, that it will be my endeavour through every sentence which I utter, to keep just as far as I can from his method and his style." Now King had taken the committee, and especially its Conservative members, severely to task for not having invited Bureau to come before it; but was that criticism to be taken seriously? "I have practised law for some years," Meighen remarked,

". . . and I never learned of the doctrine that those who are said to be of the prosecution should see to it that the defence is called. Were there no doctrine to the contrary, which is so plain that a child would understand it, were there none at all, those of us who know the Hon. Jacques Bureau know this, that he does not need any instance from us, any summons or suggestion, to come and defend himself at a trial if he feels it is in his interest to come. Whatever may be said of him, no one will challenge his intelligence or his capacity to look after himself." In any event why had not the four Liberals on the committee or Boivin, "whose department was on trial, the friend and associate of Mr. Bureau," seen to it that the latter was called?

> The whole thing is humbug. It is such transparent, unspeakable nonsense that it is incapable of discussion. Senator Bureau would have come there if he had felt there was anything in his interests to be served by coming. Senator Bureau would stay away—if he felt it was in his interest to stay away. But to charge those who are not serving Senator Bureau, whose interests are not his but the interests of Canada, with being under an obligation to summon him, and especially to charge those of the opposite party—well it so shocks the intelligence that the sooner the subject is dismissed the better.

The Prime Minister had said that the report should be concurred in and at the same time had defended Bureau's record as a minister prior to his having fallen ill early in 1925. But what was the unanimous finding of the four Liberals, one Progressive and four Conservatives on the committee? Meighen read clause 6 of the report:

> The evidence submitted to the committee tends to the general conclusion that for a long time the Department of Customs and Excise has been slowly degenerating in efficiency and that the process was greatly accelerated in the last few years.
> Apparently the Hon. Jacques Bureau, then Minister of Customs, failed to appreciate and properly discharge the responsibilities of his office and as a result there was a lack of efficient, continuous and vigorous control of subordinates by the headquarters staff at Ottawa.

How did King square that with his defence of Bureau's honour and record as an administrator?

> I ask the Prime Minister: If he believes what he said of the Hon. Jacques Bureau this afternoon, of his record in that department, of his devotion to the public service, of his capacity, if he believes that all the Hon. Jacques Bureau was guilty of was being sick, is he honest to-day with Jacques Bureau; is he standing by Jacques Bureau, as a friend, as a citizen, in allowing this report to be adopted? I put it to hon. gentlemen behind him, those who agree with the words of the Prime Minister this afternoon, those who applauded his words that all that was the matter with Jacques Bureau was his illness. Do they consider that clause 6 fair to the Hon. Jacques Bureau?

Will anybody reply? If I believed as the Prime Minister says he believes, I would be a member of no government that would submit to the adoption of that report. If what the Prime Minister expects the House to believe this afternoon is true, the report is a calumny on the administration of the Hon. Jacques Bureau and on Jacques Bureau himself.

Meighen now turned his attention to the Commercial Protective Association and its relations with the Government, on which King had dwelt at great length. In this connection the Prime Minister had claimed during his speech that he had had various private conversations with R. P. Sparks at which things were said that contradicted some of Sparks' testimony before the committee. King himself had not gone to the committee with this contradictory information but now brought it out before the House; and Meighen took strong exception to his doing so.

> There is one comment of a general character which I desire to make. When a case has been tried and the evidence has been adduced; when every opportunity has been given, as is given in our courts and before our committees, for all parties concerned to come forward and state what they have to say either in support of prosecution or by way of defence; when all this has transpired then the case is decided upon the evidence so adduced. And if any party affected, having failed to take advantage of the opportunities afforded in the course of the trial, comes forward afterwards and seeks to address the court and establish facts or correct evidence . . . it is not very likely that he will be heard. If he came forward after the evidence was closed and said to the judge, "All this is wrong. I had a conversation with Mr. Sparks or Mr. So-and-So in my office, which conversation wholly contradicts what is clearly in the evidence, and I want you to find upon what I say now": what would happen? He would be told to sit down or the sheriff would take him by the shoulder and throw him out. It does not become an hon. member of this House to ask for a verdict on the faith of testimony which he seeks to give to parliament now but which he failed to adduce when he might have been subject to cross-examination and contradiction. I say, it does not become any member of this House to make that attempt, and when this intrusion is committed by the Prime Minister of our country, when this is the example he sets, how does he expect other members to act creditably and intelligently in respect of investigations and reports to parliament thereon? . . .
>
> Oh! how brave the Prime Minister is now. . . . He bravely thunders now the information that he had certain conversations, private conversations, with Mr. Sparks, and he relates these conversations at a time when the other party to them cannot by any possible means be heard.

The Government took great credit for having, at the instance of the Commercial Protective Association, put more teeth into the anti-smuggling provisions of the Customs Act with the amendment of 1925. That amendment had been approved by the Opposition, said Meighen, despite King's claim to the contrary, and in fact it had been two Liberal senators who had tried in vain to have the teeth removed by the upper House. "But after all, is the passing of this legislation, even with the approval of this side of the House, an approval with which I know the Prime Minister is not satisfied merely because there were certain inquiries as to its character in the course of its consideration in parliament—nothing but blind approval, three cheers and a tiger seems to suit the Prime Minister—is the passing of that legislation, I ask, an achievement worthy of an hour and a half of boasting? When all is said and done, is legislation any more than paper and parchment until it is enforced?" In fact it had not been enforced—that is, until it was known there would be a parliamentary investigation. And speaking of enforcement, what about the notorious Bisaillon, chief *preventive* officer, of all things? King had emphasized his determination to be fair to the man before taking action against him; hence his insistence that specific charges be laid so that a Royal Commission could be set up. "Who ever heard before," Meighen demanded indignantly, "the doctrine that a civil servant cannot be removed except after specific charges are laid before a royal commission? I ask how many members of the government sitting in front of me this afternoon ever appointed a royal commission before dismissing a civil servant. Not one." Take, for instance, the case of Dr. F. Torrance, a senior official of the Department of Agriculture, who had been summarily dismissed. "I put the question especially to the Minister of Agriculture (Mr. Motherwell). Will he name the party who laid the charges, will he name the royal commission whom he appointed to investigate specific charges before dismissing Dr. Torrance? I ask, why such solicitude for Mr. Bisaillon, and why such brutality for Dr. Torrance?"

The Prime Minister had charged Sparks with being a partisan, with having gone to Stevens with his information in order to injure the Government just when a general election had been announced. But this overlooked the fact that the Conservatives had not made corruption in the Customs Department an issue in the campaign and furthermore Sparks had written Meighen a letter, emphasizing the desire of his association to remain non-partisan and the fact that its membership was drawn from both political parties. "The Prime Minister says Mr. Sparks was against the government in the last election. So he was, and I venture to suggest that if any hon. member of this House, be he as strong a Liberal as Mr. Sparks has been all his life, had the same experience with this government as Mr. Sparks had, he would probably turn against the administration also."

It was always a pleasure for Meighen to castigate Mackenzie King, whom he thought so thoroughly despicable, but as he turned from the

Prime Minister to the Minister of Customs pleasure was replaced by a certain anguish and regret. He had great respect for George Boivin. He remembered, of course, how close Boivin had been to joining his own government in 1921 and how disappointed he had been when this most talented and promising young French Canadian had declined at the last moment. Perhaps he also remembered having written to Boivin: "I sincerely hope we will yet be found side by side in the public service."[29] Now that could never be. Instead here they were face to face, the hunted at bay, the hunter moving in for the kill but with some distaste for his duty. It was a moment not without poignancy.

Two days earlier, when Boivin had been defending his conduct in the Aziz case, Meighen had interjected the assurance that "all who vote against the minister will vote with regret." And Boivin, wrought up and troubled, had retorted: "I thank my right hon. friend for that statement, and I believe it. I believe the right hon. gentleman would crucify his own brother with regret but he would do it in order to serve the Conservative party."[30] Now, starting to review the evidence as it related to the Minister, Meighen repeated that assurance and spoke feelingly of Boivin's great capabilities.

> I am going to speak on this matter not without kindness, I hope, and certainly with no personal animosity; I am also going to speak with all the frankness in my power. When I sought to assure the minister of the good opinion personally which hon. gentlemen on this side of the House have always held of him he was pleased to hurl back what I thought a rather coarse gibe, but in what I have to say I shall not be influenced at all by any recollection of that incident. The minister is in the House, and one always feels more free to speak of hon. gentlemen who are in the House and able to defend themselves.

There followed a tribute to Boivin's attainments as a lawyer and a parliamentarian. "He is," said Meighen, "a man of extraordinary ability; on that score no stone can be cast against him, and no excuse can be made of his conduct on the ground of simplicity or inexperience. If he has done wrong he has done so knowing the right as perhaps very few hon. members of this House would know it; if he has sinned against the light it is not because he did not see the light. There is none more capable and none of a clearer mind."

Meighen then proceeded to deal with the two chief cases in which Boivin had been involved. The first had to do with the disposition of 16,000 gallons of contraband liquor seized from a barge, the barge *Tremblay,* in the St. Lawrence River. It had sat in a Government warehouse for some time until the Minister had arranged with W. J. Hushion, the same man who had won the famous by-election in St. Antoine, to sell it to Dominion Distillery Products, Limited, in which Hushion had an interest. It was bought ostensibly for denaturing purposes and when disposed of by the distillery as denatured alcohol would not be subject to excise tax. In fact, however, the distillery sold it for potable purposes, some in the United States in contravention of the laws of that country, the rest in Canada, and not a dollar of excise tax was paid, the Treasury being thus defrauded, Meighen estimated, of $100,000. The Minister ought to have known if he did not know, Meighen asserted, that no distillery would buy that much liquor all at once to turn into denatured alcohol, which could not legally be exported and for which the market in Canada was very small. But even if Dominion Distillery had intended to denature it instead of selling it for beverage use, it had still been the duty of the Minister to dispose of it to the Quebec Liquor Commission, which was willing to buy it, because such a sale would have brought the $100,000 in excise tax into the national exchequer. By the time he had got through reasoning this whole complicated matter out Meighen had made a shambles of Boivin's defence.

The other case was that of Moses Aziz. To the accompaniment of frequent interruptions and denials from Boivin and the Solicitor-General, Lucien Cannon, Meighen proved from the evidence and from Boivin's own speech in the House that the Minister of Customs, with full knowledge of what he was doing, had ordered that the jail sentence imposed on Aziz not be carried out. He also demonstrated that such executive interference with the judicial process was an indefensible violation of the fundamental principles of jurisprudence. There had been a good many strictures passed on J. G. Robichaud for writing his famous letter, even the doughty Donaghy of Vancouver denouncing him in stinging terms. But if the action of Robichaud in interceding for Aziz was as reprehensible as Donaghy said, "dishonourable and impossible of perpetration by any man with any sense of public decency, so gross that the hon. member would not dare to defend it out of self-respect," then, Meighen asked, "are we to condone the conduct of the minister who accedes to such a corrupt appeal?" Would Parliament allow itself to be put in the position of saying "that justice in this Dominion may be perverted after judgment has been pronounced by a judge, and that a minister of the crown, for political purposes and none other, may step in and save a prisoner from the execution of sentence?"

Now, he continued, it was not enough to attach blame to the Minister alone, or to two successive ministers of Customs. The whole government was collectively responsible for the sins of Bureau and the errors of Boivin. He asked the House to consider a case in Great Britain in which the Attorney-General, not for partisan reasons but for compassionate ones, not after sentence had been passed but before the trial was completed, had discontinued the prosecution of an accused man. The British Parliament had refused to sanction even that interference with the course of justice and, not the Attorney-General alone, but the entire government had fallen as a result. Should Canada not follow this example? Were they, the members of Canada's Parliament, to approve the dismissal of various subordinate officials of the Customs Department for corruption and at the same time "show by our vote that we have not the courage to bring home even censure to those who are responsible to this House for the administration of our affairs?" That would be the effect of their approving Woodsworth's subamendment, to which Meighen now turned his attention.

> The purpose of that amendment [he said] the merest tyro in parliamentary life can easily discern. In itself it is comparatively harmless. . . . But in order to get something to put in a subamendment, in order to get a bridge upon which timid members of parliament could pass over and get away from the main amendment—in order to do that, the amendment to the amendment says: you must appoint a royal commission to continue this investigation. And the Prime Minister stands up and says that unless we vote for this and oppose the other resolution, thus defeating the main amendment, there cannot be a continuation of the investigation. Imagine the Prime Minister suggesting such a thing to the members of this House! The investigation, if this report is adopted, must go on by order of this House.

Woodsworth's subamendment deplored "the common practice . . . of members of parliament and others appealing to the minister to relax the regulations of the department for personal advantage or political expediency." It seemed strange to Meighen that the condemnation had stopped there.

> May I ask the hon. member why he did not go on and say, "and of acceding to those appeals?" Why did he not say that? The member is very much absorbed. Do hon. gentlemen recall that the loudest assertion of his speech, that upon which he seemed to have the deepest conviction was a declaration that the most astounding fact of the whole thing was the appointment of Mr. Bureau to the Senate; that is what he denounced most. Will the hon. gentleman tell me where that is in his amendment? His amendment is a lot of eyewash, purposely eyewash, froth and foam, and he knows it. His only purpose was to—
> Mr. woodsworth: Mr. Speaker, as a matter of privilege—
> Mr. meighen: I have the floor.
> Mr. woodsworth: I rise to a question of privilege.
> Mr. meighen: I am accustomed to some of these privilege matters on the part of hon. gentlemen opposite.
> Mr. woodsworth: I assert that the purpose which I had in view was not that which the right hon. gentleman says it was. I tried last night—

An hon. MEMBER: That is not a question of privilege. . . .

Some hon. MEMBERS: Order.

An hon. MEMBER: You talked last night.

Mr. WOODSWORTH: I talked last night and set out my reasons, and while the hon. gentleman has always the right to say what the effect may be he has no right to say what my purpose was if that purpose is other than the one I stated.

Mr. MEIGHEN: If the hon. gentleman would prefer that instead of saying it was his purpose I should say it was its obvious, manifest and only effect, and that a child ten years of age could see it, I will put it in that form.

In conclusion Meighen summed up the choices which he believed confronted the House.

> . . . I leave the case so far as I am concerned in the hands of parliament. If parliament believes it is in the interests of Canada to condone this conduct, parliament should condone it. . . . But if, on the other hand, there is concern on the part of hon. members of this House, aside from all party proclivity, for the good name of our country; if we want to-night to show to our constituents, to the people, to the citizens of this Dominion, that we have some regard still for the honour of this nation, that we have some sense of our duty to hold ministers responsible for malfeasance, that we are not afraid—while visiting condign punishment upon officers of this government who are at our mercy, making them pay the full penalty of their delinquency—at the same time to bring home their guilt to men in high places even if they are members of this House and this government, then they will vote for the [Stevens] amendment. But if we are going to yield to this insidious appeal that every time an hon. member seeks to hold those in the seats of the mighty responsible, then he is playing politics, he is seeking to "get" his enemy, if we yield to such insidious appeal, then parliament is paralyzed and is no longer the guardian of the honour of the state. Between these two positions I place every hon. member of this House to-night, and I put my fellow members there with confidence that parliament at this momentous time will fufil [sic] its high purpose in our land and vindicate its name to the people of Canada.

One might have expected Meighen to be followed by Lapointe, next to King the leading member of the Government and one of the most effective debaters in the House, but that task was given instead to Cannon. Lapointe, in fact, remained strangely silent throughout the debate on the Customs scandal, except for one interjection to argue that the Woodsworth subamendment was in order. After Cannon came A. M. Boutillier of Alberta, a Progressive, to say that he would oppose the subamendment. The quarrelsome discussion continued the next day, June the twenty-fifth, the most striking occurrence being the announcement by still another Progressive, Milton Campbell, the only Saskatchewan member of the Ginger Group, that he would vote against Woodsworth's amendment and in favour of Stevens'. A rather heated altercation developed between Woodsworth and Campbell, who were personal friends, and the latter also denounced Robert Forke, who interrupted him at one stage, telling Forke bluntly that he had "never been able to speak for the Progressives and is not able to speak for them to-day."[31] Later in the day D. M. Kennedy, the lone Progressive on the Customs probe committee, joined his colleagues, Lucas, Boutillier and Campbell, in declared opposition to the Government. With a distinct possibility that two or three other Progressives would line up with these four, the fate of Woodsworth's subamendment was very much in doubt. The party whips were busy, making sure that every available member was on hand for the division expected to come that night and that all those who could not be present were paired; it was imperative that nothing that could be settled be left to chance.

Two members, both Progressives, were absent without pairs. A. M. Carmichael had been called home to Saskatchewan some weeks earlier because of serious illness in his family and Alfred Speakman was ill at his home in Alberta. Carmichael, a former Conservative, was one of the five Progressives who had voted against the Government in the first division of the session. Assuming that he still believed the Conservatives had a right to govern, he would probably now have lined up with them. Speakman, in contrast, had always stood with the Liberals so his vote and Carmichael's would have cancelled each other. Everyone else was present and nearly all were accounted for. With Speaker Lemieux neutralized except in the event of a tie, the Liberals could count on one hundred votes of their own, along with those of the two Labourites, two Independents and perhaps fifteen of the twenty-two Progressives present for a total of 119. It was not quite enough. On the other hand the Conservatives would receive the votes of five Progressives—the four already mentioned and W. R. Fansher of Saskatchewan—to add to their own 116. But two Progressives, G. G. Coote and Agnes MacPhail, could not be definitely identified with either side at the moment. If they both supported the subamendment when the division bells rang there would be an even split, the Speaker would cast the deciding vote and, if he chose to uphold the Government, Woodsworth's motion would just squeeze through. If, however, Coote and Miss MacPhail abstained or opposed the motion it would most certainly be defeated.

It was getting on for midnight when the bells rang. Singing patriotic ditties and drinking songs, each side trying to drown the other out, the members who were in the chamber waited for those who were not to come running. And then the Clerk of the House and the Clerk Assistant took the fateful poll, deciding whether Stevens' motion of censure would be erased or not. When their names were called Miss MacPhail and Coote abstained, having privately paired with each other. As a result the subamendment was rejected by a margin of two votes and there were resounding cheers from the Tory benches. As soon as the excitement died down Fansher moved another subamendment, which had the effect of adding to Stevens' amendment the one the House had just rejected, instead of substituting it therefor, as Woodsworth had intended. The Speaker declared this out of order and Meighen appealed from that ruling to the House, which overruled the Speaker, the margin again being two votes. On this occasion Miss MacPhail and Coote, giddily swinging from one position to another, joined with the Liberals, a really extraordinary feat for Coote who, having seconded Fansher's motion, now voted to uphold the Speaker's ruling that it was out of order! However, Woodsworth deserted the Liberals for the first and only time in the session and this momentary aberration was enough to sustain Meighen's appeal from the Chair.

With this new subamendment the question before the House the sitting went on and on. In the small hours of the morning A. L. Beaubien moved that the debate be adjourned but there were shouts of "No!" from the Conservatives and once more the division bells rang. Out of their offices or away from the parties which by this time were going on in some of the upstairs rooms come those tired M.P.'s who had left the chamber, to vote for the third time that night. Beaubien's motion was supported by the Liberals but, owing to the fact that one of their number was absent and could not be found, it was defeated by a single vote. On three divisions in a row the Government had found itself in a minority. It looked very much as though the Stevens amendment with Fansher's subamendment tacked on would carry. At length King announced that the Government would accept that subamendment, which was then approved unanimously, on the understanding that the Liberals reserved the right "to reject the amendment as amended, or to amend the amendment as amended, as the rules of the House may permit."[32] Their right to try to do either of these things was, of course, unquestionable; whether they any longer had the strength to do them was another matter. With the Fansher motion out of the way C. G. Power moved the adjournment of the debate and this was carried by one vote. When King thereupon moved that the House adjourn Meighen said: "Mr. Speaker, I desire to ask the government if the report which is current to-night that an order in council has been passed appointing certain civil service commissioners is true, and also if it is true that just recently another has been passed appointing a senator; and also if the Prime Minister intends to make any statement as to the attitude of the government following three defeats to-night." "Mr. Speaker," King retorted, "if my right hon. friend will retract the last statement he has just made, I will answer his former questions."[33] There was no retraction and the answer, which would have been in the affirmative, was not given.

It was now a quarter past five in the morning of Saturday, the twenty-sixth of June. Everyone stood while the Speaker wearily made his ceremonial exit with the Sergeant-at-Arms and the mace. Then the spectators in the still-crowded galleries began to head for the stairways, the yawning page boys filed out to go to bed at last, while the members on the floor cheered lustily and threw papers in the air as they left the chamber. It was terribly late but they would have the weekend to recuperate before the struggle was resumed. Little did they suspect, certainly Meighen did not suspect as he walked down Parliament Hill and across Wellington toward Cooper Street, what was in Mackenzie King's mind at that moment and how sensational the turn of events would be.

CHAPTER FIFTEEN

THE CONSTITUTIONAL CRISIS

ONE OF THE FACTS unknown to Meighen as he headed home in the dawn's early light, and to practically every other member of the House, was that during the hectic sitting just ended Mackenzie King had attempted to secure a dissolution of Parliament. According to a memorandum prepared at the time and endorsed as accurate by Arthur Sladen, the Governor-General's secretary, before the vote was taken on Woodsworth's subamendment "and while the House was in session, Mr. King rushed down to Government House and asked Lord Byng for a dissolution. Lord Byng . . . refused. . . . Mr. King thereupon got very angry, went back to the House and was beaten."[1] In some ways it would seem more probable that he made his visit to Rideau Hall after the Woodsworth motion was defeated rather than before. If the motion should carry, and it was not at all certain that it would not, he would be extricated from his difficulty and one would not expect him to want to go to the country, courting defeat at the polls, as long as there was a chance that the House would refrain from censuring his government.

However, the important thing is not the exact hour of the night or morning that the advice to dissolve was first given but the fact that it was given when Stevens' amendment had yet to be voted upon. It was odd indeed that the self-appointed defender of the rights of Parliament should take the wholly unprecedented step of trying to deprive Parliament of the right to pass judgment on his administration. ". . . no prisoner under trial in a lower Court is ever allowed, *while his trial is proceeding, and before the lower Court has had a chance to pronounce its verdict,* to bring the proceedings to an abrupt close by appealing to the higher Court. Why should a Cabinet, *while its trial in the House of Commons is proceeding,* and *before the House has had a chance to pronounce its verdict,* be allowed to bring the proceedings to an abrupt close by appealing to the electorate?"[2] In claiming immediately after the 1925 election that he could then advise an immediate dissolution King had denied the right of this Parliament even to come into existence. He now claimed the power to destroy it so that it might not destroy him and his attempt to do so made a mockery of responsible government. "The country has an absolute right to the judgment of Parliament on a motion censuring a Government for misconduct. No Prime Minister can ever justify denying the country that right. No Prime Minister except Mr. King ever ventured to try. Moreover, this is one right of Parliament and the people which the Crown alone can protect. If the Crown fails to do so, Parliament and the people are quite helpless to protect themselves."[3]

Following Lord Byng's first refusal King renewed his request, arguing the case with the Governor-General on Saturday afternoon and again on Sunday to no avail. At one o'clock on Monday afternoon he presented Byng with an Order-in-Council providing for the dissolution of Parliament which the Governor refused to sign. Thereupon King submitted his resignation which was immediately accepted. His letter of resignation read in part:

> Your Excellency will recall that in our recent conversations relative to dissolution I have on each occasion suggested to Your Excellency, as I have again urged this morning, that having regard to the possible very serious consequences of a refusal of the advice of your First Minister to dissolve Parliament you should, before definitely deciding on this step, cable the Secretary of State for the Dominions asking the British Government, from whom you have come to Canada under instructions, what, in the opinion of the Secretary of State for the Dominions, your course should be in the event of the Prime Minister presenting you with an Order in Council having reference to a dissolution.
>
> As a refusal by a Governor-General to accept the advice of a Prime Minister is a serious step at any time, and most serious under existing conditions in all parts of the British Empire to-day, there will be raised, I fear, by the refusal on Your Excellency's part to accept the advice tendered a grave constitutional question without precedent in the history of Great Britain for a century and in the history of Canada since Confederation.
>
> If there is anything which, having regard to my responsibilities as Prime Minister, I can even yet do to avert such a deplorable and, possibly, far-reaching crisis, I shall be glad so to do, and shall be pleased to have my resignation withheld at Your Excellency's request pending the time it may be necessary for Your Excellency to communicate with the Secretary of State for the Dominions.[4]

To this the Governor-General replied:

> In trying to condense all that has passed between us during the last week, it seems to my mind that there is really only one point at issue.
>
> You advise me "that as, in your opinion, Mr. Meighen is unable to govern the country, there should be another election with the present machinery to enable the people to decide." My contention is that Mr. Meighen has not been given a chance of trying to govern, or saying that he cannot do so, and that all reasonable expedients should be tried before resorting to another election.

> Permit me to say once more that, before deciding on my constitutional course on this matter, I gave the subject the most fair-minded and painstaking consideration which it was in my power to apply.[5]

Lord Byng promptly cabled copies of this correspondence to Leopold Amery, the Dominions Secretary in London, along with his own account of what had occurred. "A Governor General," he declared, "has the absolute right of granting dissolution or refusing it. The refusal is a very dangerous decision, it embodies the rejection of the advice of the accredited Minister, which is the bed-rock of Constitutional Government. Therefore nine times out of ten a Governor General should take the Prime Minister's advice on this as on other matters. But if the advice offered is considered by the Governor General to be wrong and unfair, and not for the welfare of the people, it behoves [sic] him to act in what he considers the best interests of the country." Regarding King's suggestion that he should consult Amery before finally declining to dissolve Parliament, Byng's dispatch said:

> While recognising to the full the help that this might afford me, I flatly refused, telling Mr. King that to ask advice from London, where the conditions of Canada were not as well known as they were to me, was to put the British Government in the unfortunate position of having to offer solution which might give people out here the feeling of a participation in their politics, which is to be strongly deprecated.
> There seemed to me to be one person, and one alone, who was responsible for the decision and that was myself. I should feel that the relationship of the Dominion to the Old Country would be liable to be seriously jeopardised by involving the Home Government; whereas the incompetent and unwise action of a Governor General can only involve himself.

His Excellency then added some further comments:

> I am glad to say that to the end I was able to maintain a friendly feeling with my late Prime Minister. Had it been otherwise, I should have offered my resignation at once. This point of view has been uppermost in my mind ever since he determined on retaining the reins of office (against my private advice) last November. It has not been always easy but it was imperative that a Governor General and a Prime Minister could not allow a divergent viewpoint to wreck their relationship without the greatest detriment to the country.
> Mr. King, whose bitterness was very marked Monday, will probably take a very vitriolic line against myself—that seems only natural. But I have to wait the verdict of history to prove my having adopted a wrong course and this I do with an easy conscience that, right or wrong, I have acted in the interests of Canada, and have implicated no one else in my decision.
> I would only add that at our last three interviews I appealed to

Mr. King not to put the Governor General in the position of having to make a controversial decision. He refused and it appeared that I could do no more.[6]

Amery, who stated in an official cable to the Governor-General that he would not have expressed any opinion had he been consulted as King suggested, acknowledged Byng's account of events in a personal letter.

I am truly sorry that at the close of your wonderfully successful term in Canada you should have had to face so difficult and unpleasant a situation as that which Mackenzie King's behaviour has created for you. It is not for me from here to attempt to judge the weight of all the factors which determined your decision that the possibilities of the Parliamentary situation were not exhausted and that you ought to give Meighen a chance of trying his hand. It was a courageous decision and a difficult one, and it is enough for me that you took it. I imagine that will be enough for the people of Canada too, who know quite well that no party or personal motive, nothing but your conviction of the public interest, could have influenced you. I can only add that it was no less wise than courageous of you to refuse flatly Mackenzie King's preposterous suggestion that you should cable to me for advice or instructions. He of all people, should have been the last to try and invoke, in his personal interest, that dependence of Canada upon an outside authority which he has always so strenuously denounced in public. He has cut a contemptible figure in the whole business. His letter to you, with its threat of an Empire wide agitation, was scandalous and nothing could have been better than your reply.[7]

Although a rumour had been circulating during the weekend that King was trying to obtain a dissolution, the first clear intimation Meighen had of these developments came in the early afternoon of Monday.[8] He was at home finishing lunch before going back for the regular two o'clock sitting of the House. Hugh Clark was with him and they had their heads together, assessing the situation. The telephone rang and at Meighen's request Clark answered it. Arthur Sladen was on the line and Clark said as he handed over the telephone, "Before the day is over you will be Prime Minister again." Sladen's message suggested as much: the Governor-General wished to see Meighen immediately following the afternoon sitting.[9] Consequently when the House met the latter had an inkling that matters had taken a sudden turn. However, he was not fully prepared for what proved to be his last parliamentary dialogue with Mackenzie King.

Once again the public galleries were filled to capacity as the Speaker made his entrance and the mace was placed on the table. At once King rose and began to read in a low voice from a slip of paper:

Mr. Speaker, I have a very important announcement, which,

I wish to make to the House before proceeding any further. The public interest demands a dissolution of this House of Commons. As Prime Minister I so advised His Excellency the Governor General shortly after noon to-day. His Excellency having declined to accept my advice to grant a dissolution, to which I believe under British practice I was entitled, I immediately tendered my resignation which His Excellency has been graciously pleased to accept. In the circumstances, as one of the members of the House of Commons, I would move that the House do now adjourn.

With that King sat down and Meighen stood up. "Mr. Speaker," he said, "if I caught the Prime Minister's words aright, they were that the House adjourn; that the government has resigned. I wish to add only this that I am—." He had gone no further when King interrupted him curtly: "I might say that this motion is not debatable." "I do not propose to debate it," Meighen answered, "but I presume the Prime Minister will agree that I have a right to make a statement. As the House knows we are close to the end of the session and the question of how the session should be finished is one of great importance to the country. I think there should be a conference between myself and the Prime Minister." Here Lucien Cannon echoed his leader's interruption: "I rise to a point of order. The motion is not debatable." This brought a rebuke from Speaker Lemieux, who intervened to protect Meighen's right to speak. "Everyone knows that a motion to adjourn is not debatable," he said, "but a grave and extraordinary situation has arisen. I do not see that there is any opposition to the motion to adjourn; but Bourinot at page 355 says plainly that under such circumstances the leaders in the House of Commons are allowed by courtesy of the House to make statements. I understand the right hon. gentleman is not debating the motion to adjourn. That would be out of order." Cannon persisted with the point of order, trying to prevent Meighen from speaking further, but King intervened to bring the attention of the House back to the real nub of the problem.

> May I make my position clear? At the present time there is no government. I am not Prime Minister; I cannot speak as Prime Minister. I can speak only as one member of this House, and it is as a humble member of this House that I submit that inasmuch as His Excellency is without an adviser, I do not think it would be proper for the House to proceed to discuss anything. If the House is to continue its proceedings, some one must assume, as His Excellency's adviser, the responsibility for His Excellency's refusal to grant a dissolution in the existing circumstances; and until His Excellency has an adviser who will assume this responsibility, I submit that this House should not proceed to discuss any matters whatever.

Again the Speaker declared that notwithstanding King's explanation Meighen had a right to make a statement. "The only statement I wish to make is this," Meighen said. "I think on the question of the completion of the session there should be a conference between the Prime Minister and myself, in which conference I am prepared to engage." It takes two to make a conference and King was decidedly not prepared to engage in one. "There is no Prime Minister—may I emphasize that?" he declared, the rising inflexion of his voice betraying his anger at what had befallen him. "When there is a Prime Minister he may come to this House and announce his policy and his wishes." With that Meighen gave up. "Until when is the House to adjourn?" he asked. "I assume," said Mackenzie King, "until to-morrow."[10]

All this had taken less than fifteen minutes. Before the astonished spectators had got themselves well settled to watch Friday's fray resume it was all over. The Speaker had left the Chair, the mace had left the table. There was, as King had said, no government; therefore there could be no debate, at least not in the House. The debate would continue in the rooms and corridors of the Parliament Buildings, on the street corners and in the lounges of the Chateau Laurier and now it would be less about the Customs scandal than about the constitutional questions raised by this new turn of events. As Meighen walked out of the chamber on his way to meet the Governor-General he was cheered to the echo by his followers, who then repaired to the Conservative caucus room on the fifth floor, singing, shouting, marching in celebration of their triumph. As for the Liberals they gathered disconsolately in small knots to hold their inquest and to speculate about an old rumour that suddenly gained new prominence, that King would also resign the leadership of their party and be succeeded by Charles Dunning. How little anyone at that stage could foresee what was to come!

Arriving at Rideau Hall, Meighen sat down to discuss affairs with the Governor-General. There was not then or ever in their later meetings any recrimination on Lord Byng's part against Mackenzie King. He simply explained what had happened and asked Meighen if he could form a government. Meighen replied that he would like to consider the situation before committing himself and Byng agreed to this. However, Meighen's apparent hesitancy seemed to trouble His Excellency, for as they were parting he said: "I feel justified in saying to you that I think my position should be considered." Concerning this remark Meighen wrote many years later:

> I had no doubt in my own mind as to what he meant. He meant to indicate that he had acted constitutionally in discharge of his duty, and that a refusal on my part would be, in some places anyway, regarded as a rebuke to him. In that I think he was right. I was quite certain at the time . . . that a refusal on my part would have been proclaimed at once as a rebuke to Lord Byng, and the more I

thought of the subject, the more I was convinced that it would be a rebuke he did not merit.   That was a consideration I did not think I had any right to ignore.[11]

Upon returning to Parliament Hill, Meighen closeted himself in his office with Borden.   Together they decided that, as Byng had acted correctly in refusing a dissolution while a vote of censure was pending, Meighen's inescapable duty was to try to form a government.   Shortly before midnight Meighen returned to Rideau Hall to tell the Governor-General that he would do so.

No decision he ever made was so often and unreservedly criticized as this one—later on when things turned out badly.   His greatest mistake, his fatal blunder, it has been said over and over again, was his acceptance of office in 1926.   He was too eager for power; he should have held his hand, since matters were moving favourably for him as things stood and he was almost certain to come strongly into power before very long. While it is true that Lord Byng's refusal to dissolve Parliament and Meighen's acceptance of office *proved* to be politically disastrous, assuming that the constitutional issue was a decisive factor in the election that was to come, no one could guess at the time that this would be so and, indeed, there was no good reason why it should turn out to be so.   There were, on the contrary, several compelling reasons why he had to take office, the very thing King was trying to prevent with his repeated requests for dissolution.   In the first place, leaving aside the constitutional aspects of the case for a moment, Meighen had declared right after the election that King had no right to a second dissolution and should resign forthwith.   Both then and repeatedly in the course of the session, especially during the climactic debate on the Customs scandal, he had announced his readiness to form an administration.   He would cut a sorry figure now if he refused when his chance had come and one can imagine the sport that newspapers like the Montreal *Star* and Toronto *Evening Telegram* would have had at his expense.   Furthermore, though it was not true as has sometimes been suggested that he allowed himself to be pushed into this "blunder" by his power-hungry followers, had he declined the Governor-General's invitation most of them would have been in the mood to hang, draw and quarter him.

However, these were not the ruling considerations.   He was in the position of having no honourable alternative to the acceptance of office and this was true for various reasons.   The paramount one was his conviction that the Governor had properly declined to follow most improper advice.   This being so Meighen could not hesitate to assume constitutional responsibility for that action as His Excellency's new First Minister.   Since Byng desired to give Meighen the chance he was entitled to as leader of the largest party in the House of Commons, the chance must be taken if there was a reasonable prospect of his forming a government that would command the confidence of the House. The political danger of accepting Byng's invitation was impressed upon him by two M.P.'s, R. B. Hanson and E. B. Ryckman, who waited upon him at his office while he was conferring with Borden. Earlier that day Arthur Beauchesne, the Clerk of the House of Commons, had asked Hanson to come to see him. ". . . he told me," Hanson wrote long afterwards to Grant Dexter of the *Winnipeg Free Press,* "that Meighen should not take office but let King have his dissolution. By no means was this advice based on the constitutional angle but that from the standpoint of pure political strategy he felt Meighen should refuse to form a government. It would follow that Byng would have to send for King and give him his dissolution and that he, King, would then have to go to the country, that he would be on the defensive all the way through and would probably be soundly beaten." Hanson did not want to take the sole responsibility of putting this point of view before Meighen. He looked in vain for Hugh Guthrie but found Ryckman, whom he took to see Beauchesne. Ryckman having been convinced by the Clerk, he and Hanson went to see Meighen and after waiting for some time were admitted to his office and expressed their opinion to Borden and him. "Both Sir Robert and Meighen were immediately seized of the point we were making and discussed it briefly. Both stated that for Meighen to refuse would mean that Byng would be left in a very bad position and would probably have to resign, and they both said that he should not and must not be sacrificed."[12]

One complicating factor to be considered was that King, upon the acceptance of his resignation, had precipitately left office; as he said in the Commons, there was "no Prime Minister" and "no government." The Crown was without advisers and no public business could legally be transacted. King's action in creating this situation, like his attempt to dissolve Parliament before the Stevens amendment could be voted on, was entirely unprecedented and violated the well-established conventions of constitutional practice. The Crown must have advisers; to assure that it had it was the custom, even in cases where dissolution was refused, for an outgoing Prime Minister and his colleagues to remain in office as a caretaker government until their successors were sworn in. Judging by Byng's reports to Amery he accepted the resignation at once without asking that King and the other ministers remain temporarily in charge of their departments until Meighen's attitude could be ascertained; perhaps he assumed that the traditional courtesies would be observed as a matter of course. Later in the Commons King declared that he "distinctly stated to His Excellency, and stated it in writing, that I was prepared, if His Excellency so desired and should ask me, to keep my resignation in abeyance until he had had the opportunity to take such further steps as he might wish to take."[13]   But what had King actually said in his letter of resignation?

> If there is anything which, having regard to my responsibilities as Prime Minister, I can even yet do to avert such a deplorable and, possibly, far-reaching crisis, I shall be glad so to do, and shall be pleased to have my resignation withheld at Your Excellency's request pending the time it may be necessary for Your Excellency to communicate with the Secretary of State for the Dominions.

The discrepancy between what he had said and what he claimed to have said is obvious.   He had offered to hold his resignation in abeyance, not so that Byng could "take such further steps as he might wish to take," but so that there might be a quite improper and unconstitutional reference to London, as King proposed.

King's justification for his having left the country without a government, which he gave to the House later, was based on the erroneous impression, one he seems to have had throughout his career, that an outgoing Prime Minister has a right to advise the Crown whom to send for as his successor and that that advice must be accepted.   When things were done that way, he said, a retiring ministry would indeed remain in office until its successor was ready to replace it.   But if a retiring Prime Minister could recommend no one to take his place there must be a dissolution.   And there was at that time no such person he could advise the Governor-General to send for, certainly not Meighen, who in King's opinion would not be able to command the confidence of the House.   In his own view King was irreplaceable as Prime Minister.   Responding to the Governor's acknowledgment of his letter of resignation, he wrote:

> In reply to Your Excellency's contention that Mr. Meighen had not been given a chance of trying to govern, or saying that he could not do so, I said that I could not advise Your Excellency to send for Mr. Meighen or for any other member of the present House of Commons to form an administration, as I did not believe any other administration could be formed which would command the confidence of the House. . . . The House of Commons having declined to express any confidence in Mr. Meighen throughout the entire session, I could not see wherein there was any probability of the House giving him the support which would enable him to carry on the Government, and . . . therefore I could not assume the responsibility of advising Your Excellency to send for him. . . . Dissolution . . . appeared to me to be the only course which I could advise, and I advised accordingly.[14]

When Byng rejected this extraordinary proposition that it was for King alone to judge whether Parliament would give its confidence to his rival and after deciding that it would not, to prevent it from expressing its lack of confidence in himself, King felt, as he explained to the Commons, that he could not remain His Excellency's adviser one minute longer and so left office without even waiting for a new government to be sworn in. In doing so, in leaving the Crown without ministers, the country without a government, he created a constitutional vacuum which Meighen felt in duty bound to fill. Had he not tried to fill it Byng's position would have become utterly untenable. He would have had to recall King to office and King undoubtedly would have made the dissolution of Parliament the condition of his acceptance. In other words, a refusal by Meighen to undertake the task of forming an administration would have necessitated consent by the Governor to advice which was clearly subversive of the Constitution. As Meighen put it in commenting on Hanson's letter to Dexter:

> . . . aside from the lesser question of political strategy, what was the situation on Monday afternoon, June 28th, when these men called? Mr. King had resigned because he was refused dissolution. There was no government. He had refused my request to consult with him. That it was the Governor-General's duty, when dissolution was applied for, to ascertain first whether I was ready to undertake the formation of a government is now, I think, beyond all cavil or question. If, when the Governor-General expressed this view to Mr. King on . . . June 28th, Mr. King had awaited such consultation by Lord Byng with myself, then I would have been quite free to have measured the matters of political strategy and decided accordingly, but on the contrary, Mr. King had thrown down the gauntlet to Lord Byng, and had definitely challenged his right to consult me at all on this single question. Either Mr. King was right or Lord Byng was right. If, in doing so, Mr. King was wrong and Lord Byng was right, then I had no option whatever. To have decided otherwise than I did decide would have been to do a cruel and unmerited wrong to Lord Byng.[15]

Of course in King's view it was not he but the Governor-General who had subverted the Constitution and threatened responsible government, an opinion which he and his followers lost no time in announcing to the country in tones of indignation and reproach. Inasmuch as Byng was precluded from defending himself before the public against these charges, Meighen felt called upon to issue a statement. "While it is highly undesirable," it began, "that a controversy should arise with respect to the conduct of the Governor General in respect to a matter upon which his duty compelled him to give a decision according to his best judgment, yet the attacks promulgated by, or under the direction of the late Prime Minister ought not to pass unnoticed, seeing that His Excellency in virtue of his office is not in a position to make reply." There were various situations in which the prerogative of dissolution must be exercised at the discretion of the Crown. One of these was when "a Prime Minister, having asked for and obtained dissolution, has failed to secure a majority. It is indisputable that in such a case a Prime Minister continuing in office and especially if confronted with a hostile majority upon a question involving lack of confidence in or censure upon his Administration is not entitled to a second appeal unless in the meantime some vital or highly important issue has arisen upon which the verdict of the people ought to be invited. This principle is of special force in the early stages of a new Parliament."

After reviewing events since the election down to the moment when King found himself faced with a vote of censure, Meighen wrote: "To avoid the impending censure Mr. King again advised dissolution in the midst of a session and before necessary provision had been made for the public service. His advice was properly and constitutionally declined by His Excellency. If it had been granted Mr. King, again appealing to the people and finding himself once more in a minority, could with equal reason apply at the next session for a third dissolution and so on indefinitely." Far from Lord Byng's having acted improperly in refusing to sanction this procedure, it was "manifest that His Excellency could not for a moment entertain a principle involving such extraordinary and unconstitutional results. His plain duty was to decline the advise which Mr. King had tendered on this subject and to accept that gentleman's resignation." The statement concluded by quoting the opinion of Herbert Asquith, the former Liberal Prime Minister of Great Britain, given as recently as 1923:

> The dissolution of Parliament is in this country one of the prerogatives of the Crown. It is a . . . part, and, I think, a useful part, of our constitutional system. It does not mean that the Crown should act voluntarily and without the advice of responsible ministers, but it does mean that the Crown is not bound to take the advice of a particular ministry to put its subjects to the tumult and turmoil of a series of general elections so long as it can find other ministers who are prepared to give it a trial. The notion that a minister who cannot command a majority in the House of Commons is invested with the right to demand a dissolution is as subversive of constitutional usage as it would, in my opinion, be pernicious to the general and paramount interests of the nation at large.[16]

It has sometimes been argued that King's only mistake in 1926 was asking for a dissolution while a motion of censure against his government was pending, that had he waited until that vote took place he would have been entitled to a dissolution, to appeal from the lower to the higher court. Meighen's statement just quoted denied even this, declaring it to be "indisputable" that in the circumstances no such entitlement existed. Meighen's view was, of course, disputed by King himself and by various writers on the Constitution. But Dr. Eugene Forsey points out:

> It seems obviously undesirable to allow a Cabinet to play a game of constitutional ping-pong in which, rejected by the electors, it appeals to the House, rejected by the House it appeals to the electorate again, and so on indefinitely; and this argument would seem to have a special force if the appeals took place at frequent intervals. A Cabinet which gets a dissolution, carries on for three or four years, is then defeated in the House and asks for a dissolution, seems, as a matter of public policy, to have a stronger case for getting it than one which has had a dissolution, carries on with the new House for less than a year, and then, on defeat in the House, asks for a second dissolution. Both precedent and authority provide strong ground for the view that the latter is not entitled to a second dissolution unless (a) meanwhile its opponents have either formed a Government and been defeated and resigned (declining to avail themselves of their right to dissolution), or have had a chance to form a Government and have declared themselves unable to carry on with the existing House, or (b) some great new issue of public policy has arisen, or (c) some major change has taken place in the position of parties, or (d) an effective alternative Government is clearly impossible.[17]

Meighen's acceptance of office reflected his belief that he could form "an effective alternative Government." Had there not been a reasonably good chance of his doing so Lord Byng would have been unable to decline Mackenzie King's advice and, indeed, that advice need not have been given. For it was the very evenness of the opposing forces in the House of Commons, where the shift of a few Progressives from one side to the other could decisively alter the balance of power, that both landed King in his trouble and made a change of government possible without another election. By the same token, however, Meighen's task of forming a ministry was surrounded with a number of unusual problems. It was in order to be able to decide how best to resolve these that he had asked Lord Byng for time to consider before agreeing to take office and his conference with Borden had been devoted largely to this matter.

As the law then was a member of Parliament upon accepting salaried office as minister of a department (minister with portfolio), automatically vacated his seat and had to seek re-election.[18] If the usual number of ministers with portfolio, fifteen or sixteen, were appointed in the ordinary way, they would all give up their places in the House until returned in by-elections. In their absence the new government's supporters would be outnumbered and defeat on the first vote in the Commons would be certain. It would, therefore, be impossible to finish the session if the customary practice were followed. One possible way of getting around this difficulty was to adjourn the House for a few weeks to permit by-elections for the new ministers, as Lapointe had unsuccessfully tried to do earlier. In this way the depletion of voting strength in the House would be avoided and Meighen was frequently criticized afterwards for not having done this. But he concluded, and had good reasons, that an adjournment was not only unnecessary but perhaps unobtainable. The Liberals would undoubtedly oppose an effort to recess the House, just as the Conservatives had resisted Lapointe's effort to do so. An adjournment would have been even more advantageous to the new government than to the old. Hence there was greater incentive for the Liberals to balk it now than for the Conservatives in February, and there was more chance of their doing so successfully. In February the Liberal government was in being, although decimated, and had the full muster of its supporters in the House. In June the Conservatives had to *form* a government in the midst of the session; if the usual number of ministers took office in the ordinary way, their seats would be vacated and Conservative voting strength on the motion to adjourn would be reduced by fifteen or sixteen. King's unwillingness to approve an adjournment was apparent from a couple of his remarks. When it was claimed that Meighen, after taking office, had the right to adjourn the House or the right of prorogation, King interjected, "He had not that right, I submit."[19] Later King said that he had known the Conservatives could only "form a Government by going back to the people for re-election" and "that if they attempted to do that they could not carry on successfully the business of this parliament."[20]

Nor were the Progressives, the all-powerful ones in that Parliament, likely to favour a lengthy recess, especially at that time of year. Most of them were farmers and if the House shut up shop for six weeks they would have to be back in Ottawa at the middle of August, just when the harvesting season began. They were anxious to finish the work of the session so they could get home to their farms and would be likely to vote against a recess at this stage.[21] Little parliamentary business remained to be disposed of. Supply for some departments had yet to be voted and some items of legislation had not passed through all their stages; but it was expected that once the debate on the report of the Customs probe committee was over the House could wind up the session in two or three days. That being so it seemed pointless, even assuming that a motion to adjourn would carry, to subject the members, especially those from distant parts, to the inconvenience of a recess with the necessity of returning later in the summer.

Thus both an adjournment and by-elections without an adjournment were discarded as impracticable. There remained two possible ways of forming a ministry, one of which Meighen overlooked, the other of which he adopted. The method he failed to use rested upon a statute passed in

1884 which stipulated that no member of Parliament accepting an office under the Crown vacated his seat "if, by his commission or other instrument, it is declared or provided" that he took office "without any salary, fees, wages, allowances, emolument or other profit of any kind attached thereto."[22] A government formed in accordance with this law would have been quite unprecedented but Meighen's failure to take advantage of it proved costly when the method he did follow, for which there was ample precedent, was erroneously but successfully attacked as unconstitutional in the Commons two days later.

What he decided to do as a temporary expedient was to construct a small Cabinet of ministers without portfolio who, as acting ministers of various departments, would be able to conduct the remaining business through Parliament and reach prorogation. He himself would be sworn in as Prime Minister, Secretary of State for External Affairs and President of the Privy Council and, accepting an office of emolument under the Crown, would automatically lose his seat in the House. He was told by authorities in the Department of Justice that there was no way in which he could become Prime Minister without surrendering his seat. His colleagues, however, would receive no remuneration as ministers without portfolio apart from their regular indemnity as members of Parliament. Their seats would therefore not be vacated and the voting strength of the Conservatives in the House would be maintained except for Meighen's own vote. His plan was to reconstruct the Cabinet as soon as possible after the end of the session, having the usual number of ministers of departments appointed in the usual way and returned in by-elections. Accordingly he was sworn in on the morning of June the twenty-ninth. Orders-in-Council were then passed appointing Sir Henry Drayton, R. J. Manion, Sir George Perley, H. H. Stevens, Hugh Guthrie and W. A. Black acting ministers of various departments.

With the method of Cabinet-making settled upon, the one great remaining question was whether the new regime could control the House of Commons and receive its confidence. As always during 1926 everything depended on the Progressives, and Meighen's acceptance of office was predicated on the belief that the government he formed would be supported by enough of them to enable it to carry on with a small majority. For one thing, he felt sure that the five Progressives who had joined the Conservatives in the series of divisions on the night of June the twenty-fifth to twenty-sixth would remain true; they would hardly vote to unseat one government and then turn upon its successor. In fact some of them had given him individually unsolicited assurances of support. Also, if the absent A. M. Carmichael returned from the West, as some reports had it he was going to do, he could be counted on to support the Conservatives, whose right to office he had affirmed early in the session. In addition there was a real possibility that some other Progressives might swing over. Agnes MacPhail and G. G. Coote had abstained from voting on the Woodsworth subamendment, which was a hopeful sign in view of their past voting habits and their friendship for Woodsworth, and it was rumoured that they and their *confrères* in the Ginger Group might swing their support behind the Conservatives. There was nothing very definite in all this that Meighen could include in his calculations but the general desire of many of the Progressives to postpone another election as long as possible was no secret and was a factor that he thought worked in his favour.

On the morning of June the twenty-ninth, after he had accepted office, the Progressive members met in caucus to decide what their attitude to the new government should be. Their meeting for such a purpose was not without its comic aspect because many of them were pronounced individualists, disinclined to be bound by a decision they did not like. While this conclave was in progress Forke was summoned by telephone to an audience with the Governor-General. Why Byng waited to ascertain the position of the Progressive group until after Meighen had agreed to form a Cabinet is something of a mystery. One would have expected Forke to be consulted by His Excellency, if at all, on the Monday, while Meighen was deliberating, so that the latter would have the advantage of learning the attitude of the Progressives before giving his answer to the Governor. At any rate it was Tuesday morning, apparently before Meighen was sworn in, when the call to Forke came and ere he set off on the well-worn path to Government House, the members of his group drew up a memorandum for him to carry to the interview. Two years later Meighen set down in writing what he recalled having heard about the circumstances surrounding this interview.

> Very close to the time of my being sworn in and to the best of my recollection some time during the same day, Mr. Forke came to see the Governor General. . . . This is information given me by His Excellency. He voluntarily presented to His Excellency a statement of the attitude of the Progressive Party. I have not a copy of the statement in my possession . . . but it was to the effect that the Progressive Party would support my Government for the balance of the Session. . . . My information from certain of these Members was that they would not trust Mr. Forke to present their attitude himself verbally, and consequently they had it put in writing and placed in his hands. I subsequently saw a copy of it; it was shown me by a Progressive Member. It is quite true that His Excellency did not ask Mr. Forke for any pledge, nor as I understand what took place, did he accept any pledge. He stated to Mr. Forke that he had nothing to do with securing support for me or for any political leader. The statement was simply presented by Mr. Forke to him.

So far as any relations between myself and Mr. Forke were concerned, I made no request of him for support and never even considered doing so. He gave me no pledge or undertaking of any kind.[23]

Whether Forke actually gave Lord Byng the copy of the memorandum or simply delivered the substance of it orally is not clear. In any event it read as follows:

Memo. for Mr. Forke from Progressive group before he visited the Governor-General.
Tuesday, 29th June, 1926.
Motion agreed to by Progressive group:
That we assist the new administration in completing the business of the session.
That we are in agreement of the necessity of continuing the investigation into the customs and excise department by a judicial commission.
We believe it advisable that no dissolution should take place until the judicial commission has finished its investigation into the Customs and Excise Department, and that Parliament be summoned to deal with the report.[24]

This document, the contents of which Meighen did not learn until later, seemed to vindicate his confidence that he would have the support of enough Progressives to finish that session at least.

It was also decided at the meeting of Progressives that while Forke was conferring with the Governor-General a deputation should visit Meighen to find out how he proposed to form a government and carry on. Half a dozen of them were selected to perform this mission, with E. J. Garland of Alberta their spokesman, and shortly they appeared at Meighen's office. He explained to them the expedient of the temporary government, his reasons for adopting it and his intention of reconstructing the Cabinet in the regular way after prorogation. He asked for no assurance of their support and they gave him none but they offered no objection to the procedure he outlined.

The House met at two o'clock that afternoon, again with the galleries packed. King now sat at the desk Meighen had occupied the day before. Meighen, of course, was not on hand, being no longer a member of Parliament, and he had selected Drayton to act as House leader in his stead, a choice he was to have cause to regret. Proceedings opened with Drayton reading a statement Meighen had prepared, explaining the formation of the new government of ministers without portfolio, acting ministers of departments. Then the debate on the investigation of the Customs Department was resumed. As matters stood the question before the House was Stevens' amendment as modified by Fansher's subamendment. This latter motion, which the House had approved, had the effect, it will be recalled, of adding to the Stevens amendment the same terms that Woodsworth had tried in vain to substitute for it. The first speaker in the renewed debate was Fernand Rinfret, who moved still another sub-amendment deleting censure of the former government and providing for the appointment of a commission of three judges to carry on the probe of the department. Drayton claimed this was out of order and a protracted argument over that point ensued. The Speaker finally ruled that the Rinfret subamendment was in order, whereupon the Conservatives appealed from his ruling, which, however, was sustained by one vote.[25] Discussion of the subamendment went on for the rest of the afternoon and into the night when it was defeated by twelve votes. The Stevens amendment was then carried by a majority of ten. The late government as a whole, and Mackenzie King and George Boivin in particular, had now been formally censured. On these two divisions eleven Progressives remained with the Liberals but ten joined the Conservatives.

The next day King, on a motion to go into Committee of Supply, moved an amendment expressing lack of confidence in what he assumed would be the new government's tariff policy, asserting that it "would prove detrimental to the country's continued prosperity and prejudicial to national unity."[26] Both the amendment itself and the speeches in support of it were obviously designed to win back the ten errant Progressives by raising the bogey of high protection but only one of them—Agnes MacPhail—came to her senses. The other nine remained obstinately with the Conservatives and King's amendment was defeated by seven votes. This division made one fact amply clear: the Progressive memorandum Forke had carried with him to Government House was meaningless, at least as far as Forke himself and eleven of his friends were concerned. For surely it was a strange way to "assist the new administration in completing the business of the session" to vote want of confidence in it at the first opportunity. Later on Forke denied that he had violated the terms of the memorandum, explaining that it had been based "on the distinct understanding that the new Government was able to function. If it had been sustained in the House, we would not have attempted to prevent the passage of the Supply Bill."[27] But in supporting King's amendment Forke voted against the House considering Supply, against allowing the Government to function. If this action was in accordance with the memorandum then words have no meaning.

The House had approved only a few items of Supply when King began to attack the constitutionality of the new administration, alleging that the acting ministers were not entitled to ask the House to vote public funds. "We are," he said, "now voting large sums of public money to different hon. gentlemen opposite who are supposed to be administering several departments of the government. Before we proceed any further

I would like to discover from those hon. gentlemen to what extent they have complied with constitutional practice in the matter of assuming office."[28] It was at this moment that Meighen's enforced absence from the House suddenly took on a crucial significance, for an astonishing scene was played out, one of King's most effective in the House of Commons, a scene which would have been played very differently had Meighen been in the cast. Assuming his beloved role of defender of the Constitution, King proceeded to cross-examine the ministers concerning their credentials and they, instead of protesting as they had every right to do that his questions required due notice and must be put on the Order Paper, one after the other and with perfect meekness answered him like a group of naughty boys faced by a wrathy mother who suspected them of raiding the cookie jar. The interrogation must have made a deep impression on the Progressives who were not learned in the law, and must have seemed very damaging to the Government. Without a great deal in the way of reply from the Conservative benches King succeeded in making out a plausible case, entirely founded though it was on misrepresentations and mis-statements of constitutional law and practice, for his claim that the country had no legally constituted administration.

What oaths of office, he asked the ministers in turn, had they taken before undertaking to govern the nation? They had all taken the oath as members of the Privy Council. When? One of them the day before, all the others some years earlier. Had they not sworn the oaths required of ministers who were heads of departments? No, because they were merely acting ministers of departments. What departments were each of them administering? They told him. How had they been appointed acting ministers of those departments? By Order-in-Council. Would they lay these Orders-in-Council on the table? They would. During this grilling Meighen, aware of what was happening, paced nervously up and down a nearby corridor where he was encountered by one of the friendly Progressives, Lucas. "Lord," Meighen said to Lucas, "how I wish *I* was in there!"[29] Had he been in there King would not have remained so confidently astride his snow-white steed of constitutionalism, wounding the dragon at every stroke, for Meighen could have easily demonstrated to the most bewildered Progressive that King's arguments were unadulterated nonsense from beginning to end. Drayton, whose good qualities Meighen genuinely admired, was a most inadequate substitute for his leader in this emergency. What was needed was a man with some hard steel in his makeup, who would talk back to King and put him in his place as Meighen could do so well. But Drayton responded to King's inquisition with rather genial and jocular good nature, not taking it very seriously and showing at times an embarrassing lack of familiarity with the law and custom of the Constitution. When he chose Drayton as

House leader Meighen had not expected that the constitutionality of his government would be disputed. Now that it was being challenged and Sir Henry was making a very poor fist of the defence, he regretted the choice and wished that he had selected Guthrie, who was more at home with constitutional matters, instead. But most of all he regretted the absence of Bennett. The latter had gone to Alberta with Meighen's approval to take part in the campaign there and was now on his way back to Ottawa. He could not arrive soon enough to suit Meighen, for, in addition to being an excellent lawyer, he was a tough, resourceful fighting man in the House of Commons where he was not noted for exhibiting the bluff good humour of a Drayton or the impeccable gentle-manliness of a Guthrie.[30] As it turned out, in the absence of Meighen and Bennett it was Cahan, and not any of the ministers, who put up the best defence against King in this debate which no one on the Conservative side expected or was prepared for. King was set right by Cahan on a number of constitutional points but was in no mood to accept corrections and even Cahan's efforts did not suffice to stem the righteous fury which the former Prime Minister directed against his successors.

The contentions advanced by King in challenging the constitutionality of the Meighen government, in an impassioned oration on the evening of June the thirtieth and again the following day, must be considered briefly in turn.[31] His main point was that the ministers had not sworn the necessary oaths of office, having taken only the oath of Privy Coun-cillors. "Those of us sitting on this side who composed the former government," he declared, "have taken the oath as privy councillors, but that does not entitle us to administer departments of the government at present. I want to make the position quite clear to hon. gentlemen opposite. I observe members in the government are former Privy Coun-cillors, men who have taken the oath as councillors . . . many years ago."[32] There was, of course, no such thing as a "former" Privy Councillor. Every minister of the Crown was required by law to be sworn of the King's Privy Council for Canada and remained a member of the Privy Council for life. But, said King,

> Privy councillors are not permitted to walk into the council cham-ber, sit around the table, and pass whatever orders they may like, to give each other official positions. If that were the case there is no reason why my erstwhile colleagues and myself should not have walked into the council chamber and sat down at the table with whoever was prepared to assume the position of Prime Minister of this country and assign positions to ourselves that would enable us to control the expenditure of public moneys to the extent necessary to carry on the administration of public affairs for a year.[33]

Here Cahan made the perfectly correct observation that only those

Privy Councillors who were invited to do so by the Prime Minister of the day entered the Council chamber. By custom this was how the composition of the Cabinet, the Committee of the Privy Council, was determined and without such an invitation no group of Privy Councillors could perform executive acts as advisers of the Crown. King, however, brushed this aside; it was too true to suit his argument. The important thing, he insisted, was that a minister of the Crown must not only be sworn of the Privy Council but must take an additional oath as head of a department.

> . . . what I want to make clear to the House and to the country this evening is that of this entire cabinet there is not a single member who has taken any oath to administer a single department of the government; and yet these gentlemen come before us with estimates and ask us to vote hundreds of millions of dollars. We have voted some thousands of dollars already just to see how calmly they would take the process, and how rapidly they are prepared to vote millions of dollars to themselves without having any authority whatever to ask this House for a single dollar. I say there is not a single minister of this administration sitting in his seat to-night who is entitled to ask the House to vote him a single dollar.[34]

It was not true that no member of the Cabinet had taken the oath required by custom of ministers with portfolio, ministers of departments; Meighen had done so. None of the others had but they were all ministers without portfolio, merely acting heads of the departments. Did that fact, as King asserted, debar them from asking for Supply and performing the other normal duties of the Crown's advisers? The answer is that it did not, that an "acting Minister of a department, while he is so acting, has, in fact, all the powers . . . of a Minister of that department . . . and can ask for Supply with the same authority."[35] On a great many occasions acting ministers had done so without their right being disputed. To mention only one, E. M. Macdonald had been Minister without Portfolio, Acting Minister of National Defence in King's own government for nearly four months in 1923 and had asked for and received Supply for that department from the House of Commons.

Connected with King's argument that in order to function the advisers of the Crown must have taken not only the Privy Councillor's oath but also the customary oath sworn by ministers of departments was his further claim that the failure of Meighen's ministers to have taken the latter oath invalidated the Orders-in-Council appointing them to their positions. Part of his lengthy discourse on the subject of oaths is worth quoting, both to give the content of his argument and to illustrate the style and manner which Meighen found so repugnant.

> . . . may I return again to the situation with which we are confronted? I asked hon. gentlemen opposite a moment ago whether

any of them had taken the oath of office. Not one has. I asked them how they were appointed? They said they were all appointed by order in council. Now look at the situation: We have a Prime Minister who has taken an oath. I ask hon. members to remember this—the Prime Minister has taken an oath. He has not given a mere promise or undertaking to do something, but has taken a solemn oath which relates to the crown itself, with all that pertains to the sacredness of parliamentary institutions. That oath obliges him to see that the crown's name in all particulars is protected; that the crown or its representative shall not by any act of his be brought into public discussion. May I say that [it] is only through the act of the present Prime Minister that any mention has come to be made of His Excellency the Governor General at the present time— only through his act. He has taken his oath to see that the government of this country is carried on in a manner which will not reflect upon the crown and all that the crown stands for in conserving the liberties and freedom of the people under responsible government. Now I shall give the Prime Minister the opportunity to-night of thinking over the position in which he has placed His Majesty's representative in this country, over the position in which he has placed the King himself,—because he is acting as one who is advising the crown through its representative—and I say to him that if he will read my words in the morning, if perchance he cannot hear them now, he should consider very carefully how much longer he is going to keep His Excellency in the position of great suspense which he must be in at the present time with respect to whether or not his act [in refusing dissolution] has been constitutional or justified, and for what he does in that regard the present Prime Minister will be judged by the people of this country and by posterity itself.

Now that right hon. gentleman, having taken the oath of office, proceeds to appoint his ministry. May I again recall to hon. gentlemen opposite what I said a moment ago about the manner in which orders in council are passed and what is essential in that regard. Four members of the cabinet are supposed to constitute a quorum. How was the first order in council passed, appointing hon. gentlemen opposite? I suppose the hon. gentleman who is leading the House at the moment was appointed by the first order in council. Therefore I ask my hon. friend who were present at the cabinet meeting when he was appointed? What was the quorum that enabled the Prime Minister to pass an order in council and present it to His Excellency? I say that if the Prime Minister of this country went to His Excellency the Governor General with an order in his hand appointing certain gentlemen opposite ministers of state or acting ministers of state, when there was only himself to sit in council and pass it, and asked His Excellency to sign that order, he committed the most autocratic and unconstitutional act that any individual in this country could commit.[36]

What King was saying here, to put it briefly, was that the four Privy Councillors required as the quorum he mistakenly claimed was necessary to pass any Order-in-Council must all have taken oaths as ministers of departments before passing any Order. But this is a logical impossibility when a new government is being formed, and therefore had never been the case in the past, since ministers or acting ministers of departments are normally appointed by Order-in-Council and cannot take an oath of office until the Order has been approved. The passage of the Order-in-Council, in other words, must precede the taking of the oath and the "quorum" consequently can consist only of four men who have sworn the Privy Councillor's oath and that oath alone. In any event there is no such thing as a quorum of the Privy Council. In 1896 Laurier was appointed President of the Privy Council by an Order-in-Council passed by a "committee" of the Privy Council consisting solely of himself. The Orders-in-Council appointing the members of the Meighen government of 1920, the Bennett government of 1930 and the King government of 1935 were, like those appointing the temporary government, passed by a "committee" consisting of the Prime Minister only in each case.

Another criticism of this government of ministers without portfolio, one raised by Cannon and reiterated by King with considerable emphasis, was that it could not be held accountable to Parliament. According to their reasoning the maintenance of a constitutionally responsible government demanded that some ministers of the Crown sitting in the Commons must have portfolios, have sworn the oath given to ministers of departments, have vacated their seats and been returned in by-elections. They did not venture to say how many ministers without portfolio might be permitted but they did confidently advance the theory, as Dr. Forsey has described it, "that Ministers without portfolio, acting Ministers of departments, are in some way constitutionally inferior to Ministers with portfolios; that Ministers without portfolio are not responsible and cannot answer for their acts; that Ministers with portfolio must assume a vicarious responsibility and answer for their inferior colleagues. It is a theory which at least has the virtue of novelty, but no one has attempted to suggest that there is any warrant for it in the procedure of either Cabinets or Parliaments."[37]

A Dominion government in which while Parliament was in session no minister sitting in the House of Commons held a portfolio was without precedent in Canada. However, there had been many cases in the Canadian provinces and in other parts of the Commonwealth in which, usually but not always for short periods, no one, not even the Prime Minister, had held a portfolio and many others in which most of the ministers had been without portfolio.[38] The notion that only ministers of the departments could be held responsible to Parliament had frequently been repudiated before 1926, among others by Edward Blake, a distinguished constitutional authority and one of King's predecessors in the leadership of the Liberal party. The responsibility of "a Minister of His Excellency," Blake said in 1871, "depended not upon his holding any Departmental office, but upon his being a member of His Excellency's Council."[39] In other words every Privy Councillor who was invited by the Prime Minister to deliberate at the Council table was responsible to Parliament whether he held a portfolio or not. The only requirement, by custom, was that all Privy Councillors so invited must be members of one of the Houses of Parliament or become members within a reasonable time after entering the Cabinet.

As for the idea, expressed in some of King's statements, that ministerial by-elections were necessary to the survival of responsible government, not only were there many parts of the Commonwealth where ministerial by-elections had never been required, there were also many others where the requirement had been abolished. At the very moment when this discussion was going on in the Canadian House of Commons, Great Britain herself was in process of abolishing them once and for all. Indeed they were done away with in Canada a few years later and this can hardly be blamed for any weakening of the responsibility of governments to Parliament which may have occurred since that time. The truth is, as Dr. Forsey makes abundantly clear, that the Meighen temporary government was no less responsible to Parliament than any other. All but one of its members were in the House of Commons. They could be and were asked questions which they did not refuse to answer. Supply could be refused by the House, motions of want of confidence or of censure could be moved and, if carried, as events were to show, result in the consequences usual under the Constitution. "Indeed the only means of enforcing responsibility which the House did not possess fully in this instance seems to be a motion to reduce a Minister's salary. It could do this with regard to the Prime Minister, but not the others [who received no salary]. Does the whole of responsible government hang on this one motion?"[40]

All of the long and continuously interrupted harangue to which King, in a loud voice and with an abundance of gesture, subjected the House on the evening of June the thirtieth had to do in one way or another with the "unconstitutional" results of Byng's having refused a dissolution. All the talk about ministers and acting ministers, about oaths and Orders-in-Council and the rest of it would have been unnecessary had the Governor-General only done the proper thing when asked to and put Parliament out of its misery. King did not claim that the Crown was powerless under any and all circumstances to decline to dissolve Parliament but he did assert that refusal was only justified when a properly constituted alternative government able to enjoy the support of the Commons was available. As, in his view, there was no such alternative in this case, the refusal had been unjustified. At one point he went so far as to state that if Meighen did not resign, the Governor-General should dismiss him and he, King, would take the responsibility for the dismissal. It is a maxim of the Constitution that the King can do no wrong, that his ministers must bear responsibility for all executive actions. It is therefore forbidden in Parliament to attack the Crown or its representative, and King, in denouncing the refusal of dissolution, sought to direct his attack against Meighen, who upon taking office had assumed responsibility for Byng's decision. But it was, after all, the alleged unconstitutionality of that decision, made at the Governor's discretion, that was the heart and centre of King's completely fallacious case and he came perilously close at times to transgressing the immunity of His Excellency from personal attack. At one stage of his discourse he was taunted by a Conservative for thinking of 1837.

> Mr. MACKENZIE KING: Yes, I am thinging of '37, and I tell my hon. friend that I was never prouder in my life than to have the privilege of standing in this parliament to-night and on behalf of British parliamentary institutions denouncing the irresponsible government of his party. Do hon. gentlemen opposite advocate that we shall go back to a condition of affairs in Canada worse than anything that existed in 1837?
>
> An hon. MEMBER: We have had it for the last eight months.
>
> Mr. MACKENZIE KING: 1837 was bad enough, but it was not a circumstance on the present condition of affairs. If at the instance of one individual a prime minister can be put into office and with a ministry which is not yet formed be permitted to vote all the supplies necessary to carry on the government of Canada for a year, we have reached a condition in this country that threatens constitutional liberty, freedom and right in all parts of the world.
>
> Mr. LADNER: Mr. Chairman—
>
> Some hon. MEMBERS: Sit down.
>
> Mr. LADNER: Will the right hon. gentleman state frankly and directly to the House who that individual is? Has he the courage to do so?
>
> Mr. MACKENZIE KING: The courage to do what?
>
> Mr. LADNER: To state the individual to whom he has referred in the last sentence of his remarks?
>
> Mr. CANNON: That is Arthur Meighen. Didn't you understand?

Of course it was not Arthur Meighen but Lord Byng that King was talking about and, realizing that he was skating on very thin ice, he did a quick pirouette and headed away.

> Mr. MACKENZIE KING: I said, and I repeat it, that a prime minister does not come into office by virtue of the will or the wish of any individual. A prime minister comes into office by virtue of

having the confidence of the people's representatives in the House of Commons.

Mr. LADNER: Will the right hon. gentleman for once answer a question directly?

Some hon. MEMBERS: Sit down.

Mr. MACKENZIE KING: I repeat what I have said.

Mr. LADNER: You are saying it differently now.

Mr. MACKENZIE KING: What did I say before?

An hon. MEMBER: Nothing.

Mr. LADNER: I am not afraid to repeat what he said. The right hon. gentleman stated that at the instance of one individual a government was able to be placed in power and to vote to themselves supplies for a year, and then he proceeded in a somewhat bumptious manner to describe the iniquities which might follow. His reflection was upon a person whom he must know he could not refer to, and whom he is ashamed to name.

Mr. MACKENZIE KING: I beg my hon. friend's pardon. I ask him, how does the present Prime Minister of Canada come to be in office?

Mr. LADNER: By a proper constitutional course.

Mr. MACKENZIE KING: What is the court?

Mr. LADNER: Course. Owing to the lack of confidence of the majority of the members of the House of Commons, due to the dereliction of duty of the former government.

Mr. MACKENZIE KING: My hon. friend is entirely mistaken. The government of which I had the honour to be the head never met with defeat from the day that it came into office to the day that it resigned.

Mr. BURY: Mr. Chairman—

Some hon. MEMBERS: Order. Sit down.

The CHAIRMAN: Order.

Mr. BURY: The right hon. leader of the opposition said a minute ago that the Prime Minister at the instance of one individual was allowed to get into power.

Some hon. MEMBERS: No, no.

Mr. BURY: He did.

An hon. MEMBER: Listen again. You are dreaming.

Mr. BURY: May I ask the right hon. leader of the opposition, who was the individual?

Mr. MACKENZIE KING: I repeat what I have said. The Prime Minister is in office to-day—

Mr. BURY: At the instance of one individual.

Mr. MACKENZIE KING: Yes, that is correct.

Some hon. MEMBERS: Who?

Mr. MACKENZIE KING: If hon. gentlemen opposite will not get so excited—

An hon. MEMBER: Name the individual.

Mr. MACKENZIE KING: May I say that the individual to whom I refer has, I believe, acted according to his conscience, honestly, sincerely, truly. I have nothing disrespectful to say of him in any particular. I have the greatest admiration for him.

Mr. BURY: Mr. Chairman, I rise to a point of order.

Some hon. MEMBERS: Sit down.

Mr. BURY: The right hon. leader of the opposition is referring to the action of His Excellency, and I do not think he has any right to discuss it.

Mr. MACKENZIE KING: My hon. friend was seeking to have me name an individual, and I am replying. The rules of this House do not say that individuals cannot be named; the rules say that individuals in certain positions cannot be spoken of disrespectfully. May I say that the individual of whom I am speaking is a gentleman for whom I have the greatest regard it is possible for one man to have for another. The individual of whom I am speaking is a gentleman for whom I have the greatest affection possible, and may I say further that the individual of whom I am speaking is, I believe, a gentleman who would never commit an act of any kind which he did not think right and proper in every particular. Let me make that clear.[41]

But this gentleman for whom King professed such deep affection and high regard had done something, if King's own reckoning of the matter were to be accepted, that created a situation which threatened "constitutional liberty, freedom and right in all parts of the world." How could Mackenzie King, of all men—friend of liberty, defender of Parliament, foe of autocracy and usurpation, indeed of evil in all its many forms— how could he respect and love a Governor-General who had refused to act on advice and had saddled the country with an unconstitutional government? How could Mackenzie King—valiant contender against colonialism, champion of autonomy, watch dog of national liberties and Nemesis of the imperialists—bring himself to express his devotion to a Governor whose refusal of dissolution, he alleged, relegated Canada to colonial status and placed in jeopardy the whole treasured tradition of self-government? At one stage of the debate he said:

My position, and I take it in the interest of this country, as a self-governing Dominion, is that the Prime Minister of Canada in advising His Excellency the Governor General is in precisely the same position as the Prime Minister of England advising His Majesty the King. . . . Any other theory of government reduces this Dominion of Canada from the status of a self-governing Dominion to the status of a crown colony. . . . For one hundred years in Great Britain there is not a single instance of a Prime Minister having asked for a dissolution and having been refused it. . . . The issue that we are face to face with at the present time is one which affects all parts of the British Empire, and it is amongst other reasons because of my belief in and my love for the British Empire that I take the stand I do in this matter. It is only by a recognition of the fact that the British Empire rests upon the corner stone of responsible self-government . . . that this great Empire can endure.[42]

Actually, of course, Lord Byng's decision had not the slightest bearing on the principle of self-government and could not have had unless that decision had been dictated from London.[43]   Coming from the man who had repeatedly urged Byng to consult Leopold Amery and to ask "the British Government, from whom you have come to Canada under instructions," whether a dissolution should be granted, all King's talk about the refusal of dissolution endangering Canada's freedom was the supreme effrontery.   Had Byng taken the advice and consulted Amery, and had Amery given an opinion or instructions, Canadians might then have had reason to be alarmed about their country's status.   The prerogative of dissolution resided then as it resides now in the Crown, in Canada as in Great Britain.   Save in most exceptional circumstances it was and is exercised on the advice of the Prime Minister but the circumstances of King's request for dissolution in 1926 were wholly exceptional and unprecedented.   For Byng to have accepted his request would have amounted to acquiescence in the proposition that the Prime Minister, a party leader, enjoys an absolute power of life and death over Parliament, the very negation of responsible government and parliamentary supremacy.

It had been decided shortly after the change of government that the House would meet on Dominion Day in an effort to finish up the business of the session as soon as possible.   That day, as it turned out, did finish the session but not in exactly the way the new government had hoped for.   First Ernest Lapointe, who thus far had taken little part in the discussion of the constitutional matters, raised a question of privilege which he said affected the independence of Parliament.   His contention was that, as the Orders-in-Council appointing the six gentlemen acting ministers of various departments did not expressly state that they were to receive no payment of any kind, it must be assumed that they were in receipt of the payment given ministers of departments and had therefore vacated their seats.   It followed that they were illegally sitting in the House of Commons.   Lapointe's argument supporting this proposition was a clever one but no one seems to have taken it very seriously, not even on the Liberal side of the House.   Certainly it was at variance with what Mackenzie King had been saying the night before and was to say again and again before that First of July was over.   Lapointe's view was that the new ministers could not function in the House because they had accepted offices of profit under the Crown; King's was, in effect, that they could not function as ministers because they had *not* accepted offices of profit under the Crown, and were only ordinary, private members of the House of Commons.   Clearly it was impossible for both of these charges to be true.   The fateful question Parliament was going to have to answer that day was whether either of them was true.

Lapointe was followed by Guthrie, who had done some homework in the company of Meighen since the adjournment of the House the night

before.   He was much better briefed than when King had been conducting his cross-examination and delivering his grandiloquent disquisition
on parliamentary government.   Guthrie had his precedents to cite and
his arguments well arranged; he not only disposed of Lapointe without
much trouble but gave a calm and well-reasoned reply to King's allegations about oaths and Orders-in-Council.   He had also secured the opinions of the Clerk of the Privy Council and the Deputy Minister of Justice
as to the procedure by which the temporary government had been formed.
Both testified in writing that the requirements of the law and the usages
of custom had been fully complied with.[44]

It was now that Cannon and then King turned to the question of
whether a government with no one but acting ministers in the House was
a responsible government and to the claim that responsibility entailed
ministerial by-elections.   And then before long King was reaffirming his
right to a dissolution, his belief that the acting ministers were not really
ministers at all and, of course, his devotion to the Crown and the Empire,
to justice, right, liberty and the supremacy of Parliament.   The discussion went on and on, from two o'clock in the afternoon until the supper
recess at six, from eight o'clock until shortly before ten.   During all that
time the only matter formally before the House was Lapointe's question
of privilege, the actual substance of which had, it seemed, been all but
forgotten.   But it was not quite forgotten, for now J. A. Robb came
forward with a motion which ingeniously combined Lapointe's contention
with the contradictory one advanced by King.   The Robb motion read:

> The actions in this House of the hon. members who have acted as
> ministers of the crown since the 29th of June, 1926 . . . are a viola-
> tion and an infringement of the privileges of this House for the
> following reasons:
>   1. That the said hon. gentlemen have no right to sit in this
> House, and should have vacated their seats therein, if they legally
> hold office as administrators of the various departments assigned to
> them by orders in council.
>   2. That if they do not hold such offices legally they have no
> right to control the business of government in the House and to ask
> for supply for the departments of which they state they are acting
> ministers.[45]

Implicit in this motion was the assertion that one of two things *must* be
true: *either* the ministers' seats had been vacated upon their appointment *or* they did not hold office legally.   If one accepted the view that
these were the only two possibilities then of course it followed inevitably
that Messrs. Drayton, Manion, Guthrie, Stevens, Perley and Black had no
right to exercise any of the powers or perform any of the duties of ministers in the House of Commons.   The fact, however, was that neither of
the propositions was true.   "Any Member of Parliament who supported

that Resolution," Meighen remarked later, "would have to plead in his defence either mad partisanship or idiocy."[46] Not having accepted offices of profit, the ministers without portfolio, acting ministers of departments, rightfully retained their seats; their appointments being valid in every respect, they had the fullest right to speak and act in Parliament as ministers of the Crown.

During this debate on the Constitution on June the thirtieth and July the first Meighen spent most of his time in the office near the Commons chamber provided for the use of the Prime Minister. There he talked over what was going on in the House with various supporters who came to consult him, and especially with his colleagues in the Government whom he tried to arm with facts and arguments with which to make answer to Mackenzie King. Sometimes he took a stance at the back of one of the galleries to watch proceedings, or at the door of the House lobby where he could listen to what was being said. He heard King's profuse expressions of respect for Lord Byng and was repelled, as often in the past, by what he regarded as the man's insufferable, blatant hypocrisy. As for King's remarks about the Constitution, the fact that almost everything he said was wrong could be explained in one of two ways: either he was sincere but woefully ignorant, incredibly so for a man of his experience; or he was deliberately attempting to mislead the members with his distinctive brand of constitutional demagoguery. Meighen, seldom if ever willing to give King whatever benefit of the doubt there might be, preferred the latter explanation; it seemed to accord better with what he had observed of the Liberal leader during the last seven years.

The question of immediate importance, though, was not whether King was sincere but whether those Progressives who had joined the Conservatives in censuring the late government because of the Customs matter would now join the Liberals in censuring its successor on the constitutional issue. Meighen found it hard to believe that they would do so, that they could have been swayed by King's emotional clap-trap about responsible government and national autonomy, rather than convinced by the reasonable, if insufficiently forceful, defence put up by the ministers. But the speech of the only member of the group who took part in the debate, E. J. Garland, was a straw in an adverse wind. Addressing the House just before Robb's motion was introduced, Garland dismissed the new regime as a "shadow government" and was strongly censorious of Meighen for having put the Governor-General in a false constitutional position by undertaking to form an administration with no assurance of the requisite support in the Commons. When someone asked him whether the fact that the new government had been sustained by vote of the House did not vindicate Meighen's belief that he would have the requisite support, Garland replied: "That is rather an absurd question."[47] Certainly it was an embarrassing question to put to a man who had cast his own vote to uphold a government which he now denounced as a phantom with no right to rule.

Only the night before Garland had spoken strongly against King's motion of non-confidence in Conservative tariff policy. He was not, he had said then, going "to be tricked into voting for any political motion . . . . Political questions such as this motion raises . . . have no reasonable bearing upon the vote of any hon. gentleman." It had been moved by King, he went on, because the "Liberal party is now so anxious to gain control of the election machinery in view of what they hope will be an appeal to the country that they are willing to go to any extreme to get that control. . . . The country does not want an election to-day. . . . That being the case, I say that we would be ill advised indeed to fall into any trap that may be set for us by hon. gentlemen to my right [the Liberals]. . . ."[48] Now here was Garland about to be tricked into voting for the Robb motion, which was just as "political" as it could be, and with gusto leading his friends into a trap which, if sprung successfully, would plunge the country needlessly into another election.

The debate on Robb's motion ended after half past one in the morning of July the second. The division bells rang again and the roll call began, while Meighen watched and listened from the lobby. There were fewer than two hundred M.P.'s in the chamber but the Liberal and Conservative whips had arranged pairs for twenty-three men on each side and all the members of these two parties were present or accounted for. The six members not accounted for in the record of the division[49] were all Progressives. The two who had been absent for weeks, Carmichael and Speakman, had still not returned. Two Liberal-minded Manitoba Progressives were away, W. J. Ward having been called home suddenly by the serious illness of his wife,[50] W. J. Lovie for unexplained reasons. Milton Campbell left for the West on business the very day the Robb motion was moved but in any case he and Ward had made a pair with one another.[51] The sixth man missing was D. M. Kennedy of Peace River, who was suffering from an indisposition and had retired about midnight to his lodgings to go to bed. Before leaving he had secured a pair for the vote on this one motion with his fellow Progressive, T. W. Bird.

The atmosphere in the great, high-ceilinged Gothic room had never been more highly charged with excitement than it was just then when the Clerk Assistant started to call out the names as the members stood up to be counted. Although the tumult and the shouting of the past three days now died down, the passions of the debate just over were not spent. They still seethed and flowed in the low, rippling hum of the politicians talking in undertones to their neighbours as they sat tensely in their places. The spectators thronging the galleries murmured to one another and leaned forward expectantly as each representative declared himself. One by one, row by row, the members of the Opposition, the "Yeas" in this case, rose, heard the Clerk Assistant call out their names and the Clerk repeat them as he marked his tally sheet. Then the "Nays," the Government's supporters, did the same. When the Clerk had completed his count he stood, faced the Speaker, bowed and said: "Yeas, *pour*: 96; Nays, *contre*: 95," whereupon the Speaker announced: "I declare the motion carried." Instantly there was an uproar among the Liberals. "Resign, resign!" they shouted, rising exultantly in a body as though they were ready to move across the aisle and throw the rascals out.[52]   When order was restored the Reverend Mr. Bird rose to make a confession and offer an apology: "I wish to explain to the House, and with extreme regret, that I was paired with the hon. member for Peace River (Mr. Kennedy) who had retired from the House on account of indisposition, and I cast my vote inadvertently." As the motion had carried by the margin of a single vote and as the Speaker, had he followed custom, would probably have cast his tie-breaking vote in favour of the Government, Bird's "inadvertence" was of some consequence. However, since the practice of pairing was purely unofficial and not recognized by the rules of the House, the Speaker decreed that Bird's vote must be counted.

Drayton then rose to move the adjournment of the House but before doing so became involved in an altercation with Cannon which went on against a background of turmoil and noise. When Drayton finally moved adjournment Mackenzie King said: "I shall assume in view of the decision that the House has given on a very important motion, that the Prime Minister who is advising His Excellency will immediately advise His Excellency that this House has declared that his government has no right to be in existence and that he has found it impossible to carry on." ". . . I would assume," answered Drayton, "that the Prime Minister, reporting to His Excellency according to the facts as they actually occurred, will have to tell His Excellency that in this House his administration stands at least nine votes better than my hon. friend's party."[53] This remark brought on a new pandemonium which reigned for some minutes. Several members stood, wildly gesticulating and yelling imprecations, trying to make themselves heard above the din of shouts and hoots and the pounding of desks. The Speaker stood on his podium calling "Order! Order!" to no avail and the deputy Sergeant-at-Arms moved up the aisle towards the mace. At last the Speaker was able to put Drayton's motion. "Carried!" shouted King and abruptly walked out of the chamber without waiting for the Speaker to make his exit first.[54] The other members stood as the mace was lifted from the table and with due dignity carried from the room, the Speaker and the Clerks behind. It was a quarter past two in the morning. Later in the day Meighen advised the Governor-General to dissolve Parliament and this was done, without royal assent having been given to a number of Bills awaiting His Excellency's signature.

The defeat was a stunning and unexpected blow for Meighen and his friends. Mackenzie King, of course, regarded it as a complete vindication of the assurance he had given Lord Byng that Meighen could not form a ministry which would have the confidence of the House. The passage of the Robb motion, King trumpeted over and over again during the next few weeks, proved how right he had been on that score and how wrong His Excellency had been to refuse dissolution in the absence of an acceptable alternative government. Most of all, he claimed, it showed that Meighen's opinion that he could form such a government had been totally unwarranted. Now this was all very well and may have convinced some people but surely there was no way of knowing on June the twenty-eighth what only became clear in the early morning of July the second. And, as the votes on Rinfret's subamendment, Stevens' amendment and King's want-of-confidence motion showed, there had been good reason to expect that the new administration would be sustained by a small majority. How could either Byng or Meighen have foreseen that most of the Progressives would be misled by an entirely spurious argument about the Constitution or that Mr. Bird would break a pair?

The usual explanation of the latter phenomenon is that Bird was nodding, that he was not a strong man and went to sleep in his seat, that when his turn came to vote his desk-mate nudged him to wake up and that he came to with a start and rose to hear the Assistant Clerk say his name before he could remember that he was paired.[55] If that is what happened it was one of the most decisive slumbers in history. With all due allowance for the lateness of the hour, however, and for Bird's lack of physical stamina, it is not easy to believe that anyone could have dozed off in that place at that moment with tension so high, with the noise of members trooping in for the vote and then the sound of the Clerks' voices as they began the poll. If Bird was wide awake, as everyone else present certainly was, but momentarily forgot his agreement with Kennedy, it must have been because he was fired up with Methodist indignation over the iniquities of the "illegal" government and the "unconstitutional" refusal of dissolution by the Governor. The Conservatives, however, were most sceptical of Bird's claim that he had voted unintentionally. They suspected collusion between him and the Liberals in this instance, just as they had when he moved "the previous question" in February. Perhaps the most sceptical of them all was J. A. Clark of Vancouver. He had met Kennedy in the lobby as the latter was about to go home and had tried to persuade him to stay. Kennedy refused but told Clark of the pair with Bird and asked him to inform the chief Conservative whip, W. A. Boys, of that arrangement. Entering the chamber Clark at once reported his conversation with Kennedy to Boys, adding that in his opinion Bird could not be trusted to honour his pair. Boys disagreed and said that at all events there was no way in which Bird's vote could be challenged if it were cast. Thereupon Clark went to his place and sat down, keeping his eyes on Bird as the roll call started. He was certain that the man was not dozing, that when his turn came he voted without hesitation and that there was no inadvertence on his part whatever.[56]

While Bird's dishonouring of his pair had tipped the scales, whatever the explanation of it, that lapse would have made no difference had certain other Progressives not shifted from one side to the other on this vote. During the crisis the Progressive party in Parliament was split into three distinct factions. On the one hand were the five who had swung their support to the Conservatives on the Customs scandal and who kept it there; they acted consistently throughout and the two who were not present to vote on the Robb motion, Campbell and Kennedy, had arranged pairs. On the other side were Forke and his group. They, too, were immune to the charge of inconsistency; they supported the Liberals after the change of government as before, ignoring the terms of their own memorandum of June the twenty-ninth from start to finish. The third faction was the decisive one. It consisted of four Albertans—E. J. Garland, G. G. Coote, Robert Gardiner and H. E. Spencer—and the not-so-gentle-representative of the gentler sex, Agnes MacPhail. For Meighen there was bitter irony in the fact that the fate of his government on the Robb motion, which had nothing to do with either policy or administration and concerned solely questions of law, was decided by a small group among whom there was not a single lawyer but who had more confidence in their own judgment than in that of the Clerk of the Privy Council and the Deputy Minister of Justice. None of them had actually voted against King before his resignation but the abstention of Miss MacPhail and Coote on the Woodsworth subamendment had caused its defeat, from King's point of view an ominous sign that may have determined him to seek a dissolution. After the change of government these five had voted to censure the former regime and, excepting Miss MacPhail, had opposed King's resolution regarding tariff policy. Now, however, they turned against the new regime and, upon its defeat and the dissolution of Parliament, were immediately and caustically attacked in the Conservative press for capricious and irresponsible behaviour.

To answer these attacks Garland issued a statement on July the third.[57] This, he said, was authorized by a conference of the Progressive group but clearly it was intended to justify the actions of himself and the other four changelings in censuring first one government and then another. The harshness of some of its language and its categorical tone suggest that they were sensitive on this score. The statement declared that the memorandum Forke had carried to Government House on the twenty-ninth of June was, first, "simply a guide for Mr. Forke; secondly, a general indication that we were prepared to act fairly with the new administration and facilitate the completion of the session's business, and, thirdly, was purely voluntary and in no sense could be regarded as a contract." But the memorandum set forth the terms of what it described as a "Motion agreed to by Progressive group," the first of which was "That we assist the new administration in completing the business of the session," and a motion agreed to is usually considered binding on the members of the group which passes it.

Of course, the statement continued, the contents of the memorandum had been "based on the assumption that the new ministry was legally constituted and capable of functioning." Had it been, "the Progressives would undoubtedly have given it assistance in completing the work of the session." As "proof" of this two "incidents" were mentioned:

(1) The Progressives requested an interview with Mr. Meighen and secured it at the very time when Mr. Forke was being consulted by His Excellency. In this interview no mention whatever was made of co-operation or assistance, and it was solely for the purpose of ascertaining the procedure Mr. Meighen intended to adopt.

(2) A majority of the Progressives rejected the purely partisan fiscal motion introduced by the Liberals.

The first of these items was an accurate account of the interview with Meighen but it "proved" absolutely nothing about Progressive intentions. The second was simply wrong: twelve of the twenty-one Progressives present voted for "the purely partisan fiscal motion." The statement then went on to list three reasons why the group had "assisted in dismissing the Conservative shadow Government":

(1) It was not legally capable of functioning either as to the introduction of money bills or estimates or in the letting of necessary contracts.

(2) The act of Mr. Meighen in attempting to usurp the functions of government in so illegal a manner is evident when it is known that the proper step for Mr. Meighen to have taken was to have sought adjournment for six weeks to have properly elected and sworn his Ministry.

(3) The action of the Governor-General in refusing to accept the advice of his adviser, the late Prime Minister, was unconstitutional, and calculated to restore Canada to a purely colonial status.

The first and third of these pronouncements rested on nothing more substantial than Mackenzie King's word and Garland and his friends had discovered these horrendous crimes rather late, after voting to up-hold a government which they now so confidently condemned as "illegal" and which had assumed responsibility for His Excellency's "unconstitu-tional" action. Not one of the Progressives who went to interview Meighen had questioned then the legality of the Government he had just formed. Not one had expressed a word of doubt as to whether Lord Byng had acted constitutionally. Nor had any of them suggested to Meighen that he should adjourn the session for by-elections instead of "attempting to usurp the functions of government" as they now accused him of having done. The claim, advanced in Garland's statement, when it was too late, that Meighen ought to have recessed the House fitted well into the laboured rationalization of the Progressives' actions, but it is very questionable whether they would have thought so well of a lengthy adjournment had Meighen proposed it upon accepting office.

Apparently believing that offence is the best form of defence, Gar-land ended his statement with some very severe strictures on Meighen for having sought a dissolution of Parliament and for having permitted it to occur before certain legislation passed by the two Houses and been given royal assent. Meighen was loudly denounced on the same grounds by the Liberals and the fact that he secured a dissolution when King had been denied one, along with the stranding of some legislation by the sudden demise of Parliament, created the last of the many constitutional "issues" arising from the events of those crowded, hectic few days.[58]

One of Mackenzie King's major grievances was that he had been grossly discriminated against by the Governor-General, that Byng had shown a partiality to Meighen. For after all the very dissolution which had been refused to one Prime Minister had been given to the other only four days later. In developing his case before the electors in the ensuing weeks King returned over and over again to what one of his biographers describes as an "undeniable and lethal" point: "Byng had accepted from Meighen the very advice which he had refused from King two [sic] days before. King, though undefeated in Parliament, had asked for a dissolu-tion in vain. Meighen, defeated in Parliament, had been granted it." And King's audiences "understood that inconsistency at once."[59] Now King may have peddled this intelligence, this so-called "inconsistency" with "lethal" effect on the Conservatives, he may have convinced his audiences that he had been most unjustly treated, but in fact there was no inconsistency on Lord Byng's part at all. In the first place he had not "accepted from Meighen the very advice which he had refused from King." King's advice was that a Parliament recently elected under his own auspices be dissolved *before* it could vote on the Stevens amendment and without Meighen's being given a chance to say whether he could form an administration. Meighen's advice was that Parliament be dissolved *after* it had shown a lack of confidence in both administrations. On June the twenty-eighth the possibility of an alternative government plainly existed; on July the second there was none. But surely an "undefeated" Prime Minister was more entitled to receive a dissolution, and whatever advantage control of the election machinery might give him, than was a defeated one? Of course in declining King's request the Governor had no way of knowing that Meighen's government would fall so soon but in any event was it not playing with words, as Meighen contended it was, to say that King was undefeated in the House?

> . . . It is my view that King's Ministry certainly was defeated both technically and in substance. The situation is different when there is a substantial third Party, as there was on this occasion. Without a question King got Woodsworth to move the amendment he did, and, no doubt at all framed the Woodsworth amendment. However, that cannot be asserted as a matter of history. A Motion, however, in the form of an amendment is made by Parliament [sic], which eliminates the element of censure on the Government itself from the main Motion. The Prime Minister announces his Government's support of this amendment. The amendment then goes to a vote and is defeated. There could be no more direct defeat than that. If the fact that someone else, and not a member of the Government, moved the amendment absolves the Government from the penalty, then no dangerous Motions would ever be made by a member of the Government.[60]

Even if one did not regard the rejection of Woodsworth's subamendment as tantamount to a defeat of the King ministry, the fact remained that King had sought to avoid unquestionable defeat by dissolving Parliament before it could pronounce judgment on the Stevens amendment. If the right of a Prime Minister to a dissolution in circumstances such as these were admitted, then no government would ever suffer defeat in the House of Commons and, indeed, the responsibility of the ministers to Parliament would be at an end. As Dr. Forsey puts it, if King "had simply resigned, without asking for dissolution, and if Mr. Meighen had taken office in these circumstances and after being sustained for a time, been defeated, his right to dissolution would then have been incontestable. To suggest that Mr. King could deprive him of that right by making a prior unconstitutional request for dissolution is once again to place the whole Constitution at the mercy of any Prime Minister's caprice, or lack of scruple, or ignorance of constitutional usage."[61]

Still, it has often been argued that Meighen ought to have resigned, advising His Excellency to recall King to office so that the latter might receive the dissolution which was allegedly his by some kind of prior right. But could the Governor-General recall a Prime Minister whose improper advice he had properly rejected and a ministry which had formally been censured by the House? Byng could not possibly have put himself in that position and remained true to the Constitution he was sworn to uphold.

The final count in the indictment against Meighen set forth in the statement issued by Garland, and one which figured prominently in Mackenzie King's election campaign, was the summary manner in which Parliament had been dissolved. Before requesting dissolution, it was asserted, Meighen should have advised the Governor-General to prorogue Parliament and to give royal assent to the Bills passed by Commons and Senate, by attending in the Senate chamber in the usual way. Instead the members had been left to learn of the dissolution casually and by chance in the corridors and Bourassa claimed to have heard it from "a wandering Asiatic consul."[62] Garland's statement declared roundly that the fact that Meighen

> advised the summary dismissal of Parliament, without either meeting Parliament or arranging for the assent to the legislation, constitutes not only a breach of faith to the people of Canada, but a disgusting insult to the people's representatives. But, worse still, by his advice to the Crown, Mr. Meighen made His Excellency the Governor-General of Canada a party to this deliberate theft of the people's legislation. But the Crown can do no wrong. Mr. Meighen alone stands responsible for the loss of the fruit of five years of effort by the Progressive group, and of the legislative work of the past five months of Parliament.[63]

These strong words were not fully justified by any means. It was simply untrue that the fruit "of the legislative work of the past five months of Parliament" had been lost. Seventeen public Bills, including four granting Supply to the Crown, and 131 private Bills had already been assented to. On July the second four public and twenty-three private Bills awaited assent.[64] It may be added that had Garland and his friends paid attention to the opinions of competent and impartial officers like the Deputy Minister of Justice and the Clerk of the Privy Council, instead of to the rantings of Mackenzie King, prorogation would have been reached and the legislation saved. Furthermore, if King had obtained the dissolution to which Garland now claimed he was entitled, some if not all of this legislation would have died, probably all of it. It is true that King afterwards claimed that he had intended to have prorogation and royal assent before dissolution. However, the circumstances of his several interviews with Byng during the fateful weekend, as well as the contents of his correspondence with the Governor and of the latter's reports to Amery, suggest very strongly that he wanted Parliament dissolved without any delay. Had Lord Byng signed the Order-in-Council

King presented to him just before the Monday sitting of the House, neither that sitting nor prorogation nor royal assent would have taken place. Meighen dealt with this whole matter a few weeks later in a speech at Sydney, Nova Scotia.

> Mr. King complained that we insulted Parliament by securing dissolution without completing the business of the session and having formal prorogation. If this is so, Sir Wilfrid Laurier insulted Parliament also in 1911, for the dissolution then was just as sudden; there was no formal prorogation, no finishing of business—the members learned of dissolution in the corridors and on the streets. No one then complained of Parliament being insulted because there was no one in politics at that time who had chronic constitutional phlebitis. Sir Wilfrid Laurier's course was perfectly proper, so was ours.
>
> Had Mr. King got his dissolution when he asked for it . . . the result to Parliament would have been exactly the same, and Mr. King and everyone who has the slightest knowledge of Parliament affairs knows it. Mr. King would like the country to believe now that all he asked the Governor-General for was assurance that some time later he could get dissolution; that is, after the session's work had been completed and formal prorogation had taken place. This, in face of the record, is just chatter and nonsense. . . .
>
> . . . When . . . dissolution was decided on, whether by Sir Wilfrid Laurier, by Mr. King, or by the Government of which I am the head, this superseded all else, and the assent of His Excellency thereto immediately dissolved Parliament.[65]

It appears, however, that Meighen could have advised the Governor to sign the Bills already approved before signing the dissolution Order but he had a defence of his failing to do so: that the Commons, in passing the Robb motion, had decreed that his government was unconstitutional and had not the legal right to meet Parliament at all or to advise the Crown to approve policy. ". . . the very nature of the Resolution passed by Parliament against us," he wrote, "put it out of the power of Parliament itself and of all those Members who supported the Resolution to complain about our declining to perform any subsequent act of Government. According to the terms of this Resolution, not only had we no right to transact any business in Parliament, but we had no right to transact any business anywhere as a Government. Of course, King's talk about what we should have done and what he intended to do in the event of his having obtained dissolution, is the most blatant and transparent hypocrisy."[66]

All of King's utterances about the constitutional crisis, indeed, both in its duration and later, Meighen regarded as "blatant and transparent hypocrisy." But, although King had led the narrowest possible majority of the House of Commons astray, Meighen went to the country with confidence, little fearing that the electorate would similarly permit itself to be misled.

CHAPTER SIXTEEN

THE 1926 ELECTION

A S THE TEMPORARY GOVERNMENT had been only a device to get through the remaining few days of the session, one of the first tasks awaiting Meighen after the dissolution of Parliament was to reconstruct his Cabinet. He was faced, of course, with the necessity of making it as representative a body as possible, instead of being free to choose the best man for each position, and was subjected to the usual barrage of claims for preferment and of conflicting advice about whom he should select. The makeup of the new ministry, announced on the thirteenth of July, reflected the normal compromises: some of its members had been chosen for their ability, others for no readily apparent reason except that they represented some provincial or regional interest, some ethnic or religious group. The names of all the ranking parliamentary men in the party were on the list: Bennett, Guthrie, Drayton, Stevens, Manion. Along with Meighen they formed the nucleus, the others being much more on the periphery. For the first time since Confederation there was an Ontario French-Canadian minister in the person of R. D. Morand, a young physician from Windsor. The only other French Canadian was Patenaude, who became Minister of Justice, although two more, Eugène Paquet and André Fauteux, were added a little later.

Patenaude's availability, which greatly simplified the job of Cabinet-making, was the result of several months of negotiations which were in progress during the recent sessions of Parliament. After the 1925 election he had dropped out of sight, becoming again the "master of silence." He took no part in the Bagot by-election and there were those in the party who were not displeased by this, who thought that after the fiasco of independence Patenaude could no longer be relied upon. But Meighen was not of that mind; though regretful that he had to start all over again to court the man, he was convinced that without him the party would get nowhere in Quebec. At the same time he wanted to avoid a repetition of 1925 when the Patenaude group had taken over control of the organization and the campaign, leaving members of the other groups—and Meighen himself—completely on the outside. The imperative requirement, of course, was a willingness to co-operate in overcoming the ruinous factionalism which the 1925 campaign had done nothing to assuage.

452

That another independent movement would not be tolerated, under Patenaude or anyone else, was shown by the appointment of Senator D. O. L'Espérance as chief Conservative organizer in Quebec. L'Espérance had little or no confidence in Patenaude and his friends, they little or none in him. His appointment signified that the party in Quebec was an integral component of the party nationally and not a separate segment going its own sweet way. It would, however, be fatal if Patenaude were driven irretrievably back into his shell, if he refused to participate because of L'Espérance's prominence in party affairs. Meighen dreaded that eventuality; it was obvious to him that unless the Conservatives of Quebec were prepared for once in their lives to work together there was absolutely no chance of adding to the four seats they had won there in the last election.

One of the projects which L'Espérance began to organize in the early spring of 1926, and by which he set great store, was a giant rally at the Montreal Forum, at which Meighen would be the chief speaker, to take place in June. Meighen was very anxious that Patenaude be persuaded to address the rally too. The appearance of the two men on the platform together would symbolize their union and demonstrate that Patenaude was no longer as free from Arthur Meighen as he was from Mackenzie King. Whether Patenaude would fall in with this plan Meighen had no idea when it was first mooted. Of one thing, though, he was positive: Lord Atholstan, whose newspaper was diligently attacking his conduct of the Opposition in Parliament that session, would do everything he could to prevent the achievement of a genuine Meighen-Patenaude alliance, unless he could be convinced at last of the futility of his long, remorseless vendetta against Meighen. In order to convey indirectly to His Lordship the fact that it was and always would be futile and to plant the idea that Patenaude should speak at the Forum meeting, Meighen wrote early in March to Murray Williams, a Montreal business man who had the ear of both Patenaude and Atholstan.

> . . . at the next meeting which I address in that city Mr. Patenaude as well as the Quebec members should speak. Whether this consummation so devoutly to be wished is going to be attained or not may be doubted. Certainly all that one of the newspapers can do to prevent it is being done. Nothing could exceed in dishonesty as well as treachery the two-column articles which have gone out from the Press Gallery here to that paper. In order to undermine whatever measure of confidence I may enjoy in the city of Montreal the writer of those articles has perverted facts, discoloured truth and suppressed every quality which the newspaper owes it to the public to employ. This, of course, he has done under instruction and with a definite end in view.
> . . . that there will ever be any change of attitude or even the

smallest modification on the part of the paper or its owner I have not the least hope. My purpose then is only to assure you of this, that while the members of Parliament remain in the mind they are in now the designs of no man living will ever bend my determination in the slightest.[1]

Meighen's first step in trying to clear up the situation in Quebec was to seek a meeting between himself, the Conservative members of Parliament from the province and Fauteux, Monty, Patenaude and Sauvé. If the Patenaude-Sauvé forces could be really aligned with those of Monty and Fauteux a great stride forward would be made. Accordingly he issued his invitations to Sauvé and Patenaude. Explaining that he had met with the four M.P.'s "to consider the position of the Conservative party in that province and especially to consider means of bringing about the union of our forces for the benefit both of the party federally and the party provincially," he urged them to come to Ottawa

> and see if we cannot together make an earnest effort to arrive at a basis of cooperation between us. I know you will agree with me at once when I say that nothing but keen appreciation of the absolute need of unity and a most earnest desire to help in every way in our power to bring such unity actuated the . . . Quebec members as well as myself in coming to this conclusion and extending this invitation. I am only fulfilling their desire when I go so far as to urge that you will endeavour to make it convenient to come and to assure you that your visit here will be exceedingly welcome and in our view undoubtedly helpful all around. . . . We do sincerely hope you can find it convenient to accede to this request.[2]

The phrasing of this letter, with its rather extravagant expressions of hope that the two men would make the supreme sacrifice of coming to Ottawa to talk to him, suggests that Meighen feared they would not. If so he was not surprised by their answers. Patenaude wired: "Your letter received impossible to attend meeting,"[3] and Sauvé similarly explained by telegram that owing to sickness he would not be present.[4]

Sauvé's trouble, however, was apparently not so much bodily illness as an aversion to being associated with the national party in any way, at least as long as it was led by Meighen. "His case," the latter was told, "is simply this—he thinks that politically it pays to 'avoid' Meighen."[5] Certainly Sauvé was convinced that Meighen was making no headway in gaining the confidence of the French Canadians and the outlook seemed to him hopeless. He had made "a small inquiry" in Quebec "concerning Mr. Meighen," he wrote to Sir George Perley,

> and I regret to be forced to say that it was not at all encouraging for the Conservative party. The situation is due, in a large part, to the educational campaign of the Liberal press in the Province, when our

party has no such power at its disposal to counterbalance this influence. It is also due to certain war measures of the former Government, to certain campaign [sic] against the Province of Quebec and French Canadians, to certain declarations of Mr. Meighen.

A leaflet was distributed in our colleges and to the parish-priests of the Province, containing Senator L'Espérance's speech, trying to justify the conscription and Mr. Meighen's attitude, and it is said that same has produced a very bad effect. Mr. L'Espérance's nomination has created a great division amongst our friends. The Patenaude group feels deeply offended by this nomination. I might also mention that the federal members of the Opposition do not all partake the same opinion as to the direction of the party, and that there is actually no organization whatsoever, and no proper organ in Montreal.

In the Province of Quebec, there is also amongst our federalist friends, many groups which are disputing as to the federal direction and organization, and so long as it will be so, it will be very difficult for me to consider definitely, the question of union.[6]

Sauvé elaborated on this last point in a letter to Meighen himself.

I regret sincerely and infinitely the fact that you have been wrongly advised as to your position in Quebec. This position was not created by the provincial conservative party.

The federal conservatives are divided in different groups in Quebec, without mentioning the other groups in Ottawa. However, I am not the one who has organized the Patenaude group, the Monty group, or the Fauteux group, nor the Lespérance [sic] group.

Federal conservatives have done everything they could to take away from me and the provincial legislature, the Hon. Mr. Patenaude and throw him into the federal arena.

As long as union does not exist between those groups, why ask from the provincial conservative party a cooperation which would be impossible or inefficacious amongst so divided elements.

Cooperate with which group?[7]

This seemed to mean that, while Meighen wanted Sauvé's assistance in achieving party unity, Sauvé was going to remain aloof because there was no unity. Obviously if this was Patenaude's attitude as well those two gentlemen might as well be written off. As matters stood there assuredly seemed little prospect of their being on the platform at the Forum in June and some of Meighen's friends thought that Patenaude's refusal even to attend the little meeting in Ottawa should bring an end to the wooing of the man. One of these was Lorne Webster, who wrote:

Murray Williams mentioned to me yesterday, a conversation he had with a friend of Mr. Patenaude who suggested you might call on Patenaude in Montreal rather than Patenaude calling on you in Ottawa. I expressed to Murray Williams that I thought such a suggestion was most unfair and undignified, further stating that you were the leader of the Party and that it was not becoming or wise that you should be asked to run after any individual. . . . Again, I thought that there had been too many requests made to our friend Mr. Patenaude, and if he cannot see the wisdom of being willing to act as a true soldier and offer his services rather than to be begged every week by somebody to come to our ranks, then the sooner we were either off or on with this gentleman the better it would be for our party. I have no doubt the situation is giving you a great deal of concern, as it has occupied my attention, but unless there is a genuine, open and sincere rally made by several of our well-known French-Canadian friends, I think we are better without them in the meantime, as they may only create or set up more difficulties later on.[8]

However, Meighen was not ready yet to give up, sorely disappointed though he was and severely tested as was his patience by the negative response of Patenaude and Sauvé to his overtures. It was not a time to stand on one's dignity or to be subdued by one's pride. Patenaude at least must be secured, really secured this time, and if with his help things began to look up in Quebec, Sauvé would come along too in due course. "The great thing," Meighen remarked, "is to make friends as carefully as possible with Mr. Patenaude's friends and indeed with Mr. Patenaude himself. . . . We will probably have to go ahead with our big meeting in Montreal without all of them joining it, but I want to get them as favourably disposed to it as possible. I very much fear that if I decline to go on with this meeting that [sic] our friends who have stood behind us all these years will get disgusted and quit. Therefore I think the thing to do is to go ahead and maintain a friendly attitude toward Mr. Patenaude, Mr. Sauvé, et al, and make the greatest possible success of our work. That, I think, will go a long way toward bringing them with us."[9]

His perseverance was rewarded. After further correspondence, mostly with Joseph Morin who acted as intermediary between Patenaude and Meighen, it was agreed that the latter should frame a declaration of principles regarding Imperial relations and French-Canadian rights. This would form part of his speech at the Forum and he would submit it in advance for their approval to Patenaude, Sauvé, Morin and J. L. St. Jacques, a member of the provincial legislature. These men would not take part in the proceedings at the Forum, but if they liked what Meighen said, and presumably if they thought the public response sufficiently favourable, Patenaude would then pronounce himself a supporter of Meighen with no reservation of freedom or independence. This rather tortuous procedure was not without an element of the absurd. Meighen had already given Patenaude a statement of his views on these subjects in their correspondence of 1920 and had reaffirmed and elaborated upon them in another long letter in 1925.[10] In addition he had at Hamilton and subsequently in Bagot County expressed himself on the subject of

Canada's participation in war. There was nothing really new that he could say. Still, he had to appear to say something new and different, to shift his position somewhat, so that Patenaude could justify his own sudden departure from the no-man's-land he had occupied in 1925.

On the twenty-fourth of May Meighen mailed a draft of his proposed declaration to Morin, who wrote two days later that Patenaude, St. Jacques and he had read it and approved of it decidedly. Morin also remarked that he had been summoned to an audience with Lord Athol-stan "and had a very interesting interview. Though I consider it of a rather confidential character, I can tell you that I made it clear to His Lordship that the interest of the party and of the country makes it impera-tive that we should be united, and that union had been too far delayed. I suppose he will draw deductions from this declaration."[11] The one deduction that could be drawn was that Patenaude was about to join forces with Meighen, who was encouraged to believe that this union would solve at long last the hitherto insoluble and supremely decisive problem in the Province of Quebec which for six years had perplexed and bedevilled him.

There were nearly eight thousand people from all parts of the prov-ince in the Forum when Meighen rose to speak on the evening of June the fourth and it was a reassuringly friendly audience. He had memo-rized the rather lengthy opening remarks he was going to deliver in French including the statement of principles already approved by Patenaude, St. Jacques and Morin, and though they were written out in front of him he had no need to consult the text. He began with a graceful apology for the imperfections of his spoken French.

> Since accepting the leadership of the Conservative party six years ago I have endeavoured whenever opportunity offered to discuss public affairs, and especially the record and policy of the party, with the people of the province of Quebec. To do this has always been a pleasant task because of the invariable kindness and courtesy extended by audiences of our French-Canadian people. It has, how-ever, not been easy, and this because of a too meagre knowledge of the French language. To improve that knowledge in the course of a very busy life is exceedingly difficult, and I never want any better argument than my own bitter experience for the teaching of our two great languages in the schools of Canada.

After a generous reference to the integrity, sincerity and ability Pate-naude had exhibited in the 1925 campaign, Meighen devoted a few mo-ments to denying, as he so frequently had when speaking in Quebec, that he was an inveterate enemy of French Canada.

> I have often said, and long to say again, to my French compatriots that in spite of the prejudices raised against me my opponents have never yet been able to prove that in the entire course of my public

career or in my private life, have I ever said or done anything which may be construed as other than friendly to the majority of the people of this Province.

Let those, whether friends or foes, who have occupied so much of their time in recent years in an endeavour to raise a storm of enmity against me, let them come forward and state when and where any language of mine has ever been uttered, or that I acted with more partiality against this province than in relation to the rest of Canada, and before this vast assembly I declare that if they can substantiate such an allegation I will consider myself unworthy of the successorship to the men of old who have led the Conservative party in paths of tolerance and honour, and I will immediately resign that trust.

Now it was time to announce the principles to which Patenaude attached so much importance. There was nothing exceptional here, nothing that differed one iota from what Meighen had said in Quebec on previous occasions. "We are a self-governing nation within the British Empire, and there we propose to remain because we believe that our future there is more secure and is larger and better than otherwise it could be. . . . It follows that if there were danger to the Empire and its existence there would be danger to us, but it is for us to judge what is our duty, what is our interest, and to be free to decide our course." With respect to active participation in war he made a brief reference to his Hamilton-Bagot proposal, "which I think, situate as Canada is, will tend to remove apprehensions wrongly but honestly held, to create a better feeling in this Dominion, and to make all our people better satisfied with their British citizenship."

He believed, Meighen went on, "in the fullest proportionate representation of our French-speaking people, not only in the Government itself, but in all branches of Government, in the Commons and in the Senate, and in those various organizations under the Government which do the executive work. Nothing in the world can be gained but everything can be lost by failure to accord generous treatment in this regard." Indeed, a spirit of generosity was the key to the whole problem, generosity and mutual respect and appreciation by each of the two peoples of the contribution the other had made and would yet make to the greatness of Canada.

> Experience has proven that the traditions of the two great races will survive, that there will be no merger of our French-speaking people with our English-speaking people on any extensive scale, and that the great problem of Canada is to respect the traditions of both races, jealously, scrupulously, and even generously accord and maintain the constitutional rights of all minorities, encourage so far as we can the mastery of both languages by our people, and thus not only extend among both the knowledge of our laws, but, what is still more important, a knowledge of each other.[12]

These remarks were received with much enthusiasm by the great crowd. "They treated him royally," the reporter for the *Gazette* wrote, "cheering him on as now and then he stumbled over a word in the course of his half-hour French address. . . ."[13] "General opinion," Morin assured him, "concedes that your french [*sic*] effort has been a 'véritable tour de force.' "[14] Everything considered, it seemed to Meighen that he had never had a more successful meeting anywhere. Even the failure of Cahan and Leslie Bell to make a single reference to him in the course of their own speeches, a very pointed snub, did not spoil things, especially as R. S. White rather unexpectedly came up with a splendid tribute to his prowess as a parliamentarian. All that remained now was for Patenaude to declare himself. He did so on June the tenth after having had a talk with the noble proprietor of the Montreal *Daily Star*. "As a sequence to my last interview with Lord Atholstan," Morin explained, "we thought good that Mr. Patenaude should meet him. Their interview took place yesterday afternoon; he was very cordial and approved the idea of a declaration by Mr. Patenaude."[15] As was to be expected Patenaude's statement interpreted Meighen's speech as having brought the Conservative party back to its ancient moorings, from which it had been wrenched away on a voyage across dangerous waters.

> The declarations which we have just heard coming from the mouth of our party chief on the question of autonomy, be it of Canada or of the rights of its provinces, of the rights of the minorities, of the French language and its influence throughout the country, bring the Conservative party back to its ancient traditions, and vindicate our campaign of last autumn. We preached then what we believed to be the true Conservative doctrine, and we are happy to find that doctrine again on the lips of the present chief of the Conservative party.
> Remembering the past, and inspired by the thoughts and aspirations of the Fathers of Confederation, Mr. Meighen is endeavouring to gain both unity within his own party and unity within the Dominion of Canada. Speaking in my own name, I desire to associate myself with those sentiments, and I have confidence that all true Conservatives will do the same.
> . . . I am happy today to hail with favor the declarations of Mr. Meighen and to align myself with him in his work for our country.[16]

Thus it was that Patenaude had become available by the time Meighen had to put a Cabinet together in the early days of July. No party leader had ever sought for so long to secure a colleague or encountered so many vicissitudes in the seeking. Expressing his gratitude for Patenaude's statement, Meighen wrote: "In its terms it was well designed and most handsomely expressed. The effect in the other provinces of Canada will be immediate and pronounced. It will strengthen confidence in our success. I need not speak of the reaction in Quebec. You will appreciate

that more accurately than I can."[17]   With the dissolution of Parliament
the time had come to discover just what the reaction of the people of
Quebec was.   Polling day, September the fourteenth, would tell the
story.

Meighen touched off his campaign at Ottawa on July the twentieth
and then started out on a series of tours across the country. Although
his ingrained habit was to worry and expect something less than the best,
he felt optimistic. Never, he thought, had any party leader had a stronger case against an opponent than he had against King. Whether one
considered the Customs scandal, trade policy, Imperial relations, the
constitutional crisis or the generally fumbling ineptitude of King's administration since 1921, his own position seemed favourable. The tide
had run powerfully for the Conservatives a year earlier and he could
think of no good reason why it should not run more powerfully now,
especially with Patenaude at his side and something resembling party
unity in Quebec. So it was with good cheer that he set off to meet the
voters again. With him on the campaign trail as his secretary went his
son, Ted, who had just graduated from Royal Military College and was
ready to enter Laval University in the autumn to study law. Never
before had this father and son been so close or for so long together. For
the younger man, twenty years of age, the experience was part of an education; for the older the burdens and the weariness that went with
campaigning were lightened by the companionship and assistance of the
son, one advantage, at least, that Mackenzie King could not enjoy. But
it was still a tiring business for one so unsparing of himself as Meighen.
A reporter for the *Manitoba Free Press* described his appearance at a
meeting in Winnipeg.

> Fighters who are master fighters can fight a good hard battle
> when they are unconscious, or out on their feet. Mr. Meighen is
> travel-tired; he is languid with fatigue; his throat is like a file; his
> voice is just a croak. He is pulled into a tight black coat and waist-
> coat; he has a stiff high collar around his neck. His face is red and
> moist with heat; he has been speaking for weeks; his eyes are pits
> beneath his forehead; his face is set in lines as firm as hardwood.
> And out he comes and into it he plunges. It is a beautiful congenial
> theme—the destruction of the Liberal party, the pulverization of Mr.
> King. And he has done it all so often. Here is a speech that Mr.
> Meighen could make even if he were chloroformed. He rolls his
> eyes around the enormous hall, over the banked-up masses of the
> audience, and throwing up his head begins to fight.[18]

Several issues vied with one another to dominate the campaign. The
tariff, although much to the fore in Meighen's own speeches, figured less
prominently in the appeal made by the Conservatives than it had the

year before. They stressed instead the Customs scandal, indeed over-stressed it. Scandals, unless of truly gargantuan proportions, are not particularly good fighting issues in a society not overly preoccupied with political and administrative morality and the electorate is apt to be re-pelled to some extent by a too censorious and self-righteous emphasis on virtue. Furthermore, instead of being content to publicize the evidence presented to the parliamentary committee, damaging enough in itself, certain Conservative candidates came up with some new charges which they were unable to substantiate and which seemed overdrawn and meanly spiteful. This tended to discredit their whole case, which was further weakened by the sudden, shocking death of George Boivin in the midst of the campaign. His friends promptly depicted him as a martyr whom the enemies of Quebec had hounded to his death. In addition to the scandal most of the usual subjects were discussed to some extent: trade policy, freight rates, the railway problem, and Maritime rights for exam-ple. However, as the campaign proceeded two factors appeared to loom ever larger. One was J. A. Robb's Budget, a sunshine Budget if ever there was one. Its promises of lower taxes, lower prices for automobiles and lower postage rates were bound to attract many voters and the Liberals pledged that, if they were returned to power, the next Budget would grant further sweeping reductions in taxation. No doubt that was enough to make some people forget the Aziz case, the barge *Tremblay,* those most remarkable Maritime schooners and all the rest of it.

The other leading factor, despite Meighen's scornful efforts at first to dismiss it as no issue at all, was the constitutional crisis—the various questions raised by the Governor-General's refusal to dissolve Parliament on King's request and by the events of the following few days. Meighen was right that there was no real constitutional issue here, at least none resulting from anything Lord Byng or he had done, but King went storm-ing about the country proclaiming emotionally that the refusal had been unconstitutional and destructive of Canada's liberty and self-government. "He loves to rave about usurpers," Meighen gibed in one speech, "and to be doubled up with constitutional pangs. Whenever Mr. King is out of power the Constitution is in danger."[19] Never was any subject more thoroughly misrepresented by any party leader than this one was by King; what he had to say about it may have been inspired nonsense but it was nonsense all the same.

At the invitation of *Maclean's Magazine* each of the two leaders pre-sented his case in its issue of September the first and each of them referred to the refusal of dissolution and its consequences.[20] King's presentation was written in characteristically orotund phraseology. The reason he had wanted a dissolution, to which "in accord with British practice" he

thought he was entitled, was that he had become convinced "that no leader could so control the business of the House as to enable government
to be carried on in a manner befitting British parliamentary institutions;
in other words, that the government of the country could not be conducted with the authority which should lie behind it. . . ." And again: ". . . as
to which political party had the right to govern, that was a matter which,
as I had pointed out after the last general elections, it was for Parliament
to decide, if Parliament were in a position so to do; that when Parliament
ceased to be in a position to make a satisfactory decision as to which
party should govern, it was then for the people to decide." Whether
government could "be carried on in a matter befitting British parliamentary institutions" and "with the authority that should lie behind it,"
whether Parliament was "in a position to make a satisfactory decision,"
was entirely for the Prime Minister of the moment to say. He had told
Lord Byng that it was not "a duty or a responsibility of the Governor-
General to make that decision. I stated that in my humble opinion it
was not for the Crown or its representative to be concerned with the
differences of political parties, and that the prerogative of dissolution, like
other prerogatives of the Crown, had come under British practice to be
exercised by the Sovereign on the advice of the Prime Minister."

It was apparently sheer coincidence that, after the session of this
incompetent Parliament had been going on for five long months, it had
suddenly come home to King on the night of June the twenty-fifth as a
vote on the Stevens amendment approached that government could no
longer be carried on in a fitting manner or with the necessary authority
behind it, that Parliament, that is, was no longer able to make a "satisfactory" decision as to which party should rule. At any rate it was not,
according to King, because he sensed that the defeat of his government
impended. On the contrary, when he had asked for dissolution "my
colleagues and I enjoyed the confidence of the House of Commons." In
the four and a half years since coming into power in 1921 "never once
as Prime Minister had I encountered defeat." What is "confidence,"
what constitutes "defeat"? In rejecting the Woodsworth subamendment,
of which, if Meighen's suspicions were well founded, King was the real
author and which deleted censure of the Government from Stevens'
amendment, the House had implicitly expressed the opinion, which it
made explicit after the change of government, that censure was deserved.
If that was not a defeat, if that indicated that King enjoyed the confidence
of the House up to the moment of his resignation, one could not balk at
being asked to believe that the cow *did* jump over the moon. And why,
if he had the confidence of the House, did King seek to prevent it from
voting on the motion before it? That awkward question he neglected
to answer for the benefit of the readers of *Maclean's*.

He did boldly assert, however, and this was utterly ludicrous in view of his own effort to escape the verdict of Parliament, that the "supremacy of Parliament, the rights, the dignities, the existence of Parliament have been challenged by the present Prime Minister in a manner that surpasses all belief." For what had Meighen done? He had constructed a Cabinet of ministers without portfolio, acting ministers of departments, "that in no sense of the word was a responsible ministry, and by his advice, knowingly, made the Crown, through its representative, a party to this unconstitutional course of procedure." He had advised the Crown with respect to public policy "without a single Minister sworn to office, save himself. He alone was the Government of Canada. . . . If that is not anarchy or absolutism in government I should like to know to what category political philosophy would assign" it. "Surely it will not be termed responsible self-government under the British parliamentary system." Of course it was neither anarchy nor absolutism (obviously it could not have been both) but a perfectly constitutional and responsible, if unusual, kind of government devised to fit a very temporary situation.

One item in his catalogue of grievances King only hinted at obliquely in his *Maclean's* article: that the refusal of dissolution had been an infringement of Canadian self-government reducing Canada to the status of a colony. Indeed he never explained clearly just why this was so but the allegation that it was so was prominent in the Liberal campaign, especially in Quebec where the tocsins urgently sounded the alarm. After all an English Governor had defied a Canadian Prime Minister and cries of "Downing Street interference" soon resounded on the hustings. This sort of thing was meat and drink to the Liberals of Quebec, a province in which the dangers of "imperialism" could always be exploited to good political advantage, and especially to Nationalists like Bourassa, who, while running in this election again as an Independent, gave King the strongest support on the constitutional "issue." Bourassa went so far as to express the opinion that Lord Byng had consulted London during the crisis; not having had the advantage of reading King's letter of resignation, he was unaware that that very course had been repeatedly urged upon Byng to no avail. He also claimed that "either Mr. Meighen had odiously fooled His Excellency or His Excellency had made himself the election agent of Mr. Meighen" and in a burst of grandiose eloquence, which even King could not have excelled, he said: "It is the slow but gradual conquest of our liberties which is in peril; it is the work of Macdonald and Cartier; it is the very spirit of Confederation in its relations with the metropolis of the Empire which is being sapped at the present moment by those who falsely claim for themselves the traditions of the Conservative party."[21] This sort of thing heavily discounted the intelligence of the voters but was well calculated to touch their heart strings and "Downing Street interference" superseded even conscription as the leading campaign issue in Quebec. Since Meighen could be made to appear an accomplice in the crime and its beneficiary, if not the mastermind behind it, the propaganda fitted perfectly into the tissue of falsehood surrounding his name which he had been trying in vain ever since 1920 to tear apart so that he might approach the French Canadians. In no way whatever had there been interference from Downing Street, in no way whatever had Canada's autonomous status been affected by the crisis and the claims to the contrary were of a piece with the other properties and paraphernalia of that constitutional wonderland through which Mr. Mackenzie King conducted his listeners and his readers in 1926.

In all King's heady rhetoric in his submission to *Maclean's,* as in his campaign oratory on the subject, there was scarcely a sentence that did not rest on a misapprehension of the Constitution or a misinterpretation of events. Meighen's comments in the same issue of the magazine were much more laconic.

> . . . I suppose some statement about the alleged constitutional issue, in which Mr. King is revelling with apparent great gusto, is expected. Well, to my mind, the Governor-General acted correctly, and well within his powers, and in conformity with established constitutional usage. I cannot, therefore, see that there is any real issue at all. The hysterical platform utterances of Mackenzie King and his new ally, Mr. Bourassa—who is always in his element when he is disturbing racial and religious peace—should serve only to amuse; they are not instructive, and they certainly do not create alarm. Our parliamentary and other liberties are still safe and unharmed, notwithstanding the somewhat violent fulminations of these self-styled guardians of the Constitution.

He then quoted from an editorial in the Toronto *Globe,* of whose fidelity to the Liberal party there could be no doubt, strongly deprecating the involvement of the Governor-General in political controversy and ridiculing the idea that his action in declining to dissolve Parliament was autocratic or a menace to self-government. After repeating a statement he had made in a speech at Ottawa—"never within a century, never in the history of parliamentary government, as we have it to-day, has any Prime Minister ever demeaned himself to ask for dissolution while a vote of censure of his Government was under debate"—Meighen finished his exposition of the Conservative case by writing: "Mr. King tried to run away from the just condemnation of himself and his Government by Parliament, but he was not permitted to do so; he thereupon hatched a constitutional issue to act as a smoke screen. That is the case in a nutshell." And so it was.

But would the electorate understand that that was the whole truth about the so-called constitutional issue? As the campaign neared its climax evidence mounted that King was making an impression on some voters with his patent misrepresentations. Ably but belatedly Meighen fought back, surveying the whole affair in a number of speeches. One of these was delivered at Cobourg, Ontario, on the very eve of the election.[22] It was a superbly clear and orderly recital of the facts and an unanswerably cogent argument based upon them. One by one the events relating to the matter passed in review before the audience: the result of the 1925 election; King's decision to meet Parliament, which Meighen now admitted he had had the right to do; the precarious survival of the King government for five months of the session; the Customs scandal and the report of the investigating committee; the Stevens amendment and Woodsworth's amendment thereto; Lord Byng's refusal of dissolution and King's precipitate withdrawal from office; Meighen's acceptance of office and the formation of his temporary government; the subsequent three divisions in the House which went against the Liberals; and finally the climactic division on the Robb motion, which he described as "a fantastic fabric of legal phraseology . . . a work of guile . . . a plant . . . a piece of verbal chicanery . . . a wily, sinister artifice to take advantage of men untrained in legal reasoning . . . in plain language, a fraud."

After quickly refuting King's charge that the temporary government had been unconstitutional Meighen turned to the main question: "Was the Governor-General right or wrong in refusing dissolution to Mr. King on June 28th?" He was right, Meighen answered, partly because the weight of precedent and the opinions of constitutional authorities were on his side but most of all because common sense and a true regard for the rights of Parliament decreed that a wrongful request for dissolution must be denied. If it were not, "a Prime Minister and Government can play fast and loose with the Constitution of our country. . . ." To illustrate this he quoted the description of King's argument offered by the *New Statesman,* certainly not in any sense a voice of Conservatism.

> When he finds he cannot control Parliament, he appeals to the electorate. The electorate rejects his appeal, and back he goes to Parliament and furbishes up a temporary majority. Parliament becomes tired of him and is ready to condemn him, and he asks the Governor General to allow him a second appeal to the voters. Presumably if Lord Byng had acceded to his demands and he had not improved his position at the election, he would again have claimed the right to meet Parliament and made another attempt to conjure up another majority, which would probably have been available until members earned another sessional indemnity. Then the majority would have crumbled away, and by his doctrine he could have demanded a third dissolution.

Against King's insistence that no request for dissolution could be refused (which was at variance with what he had said during the debate in the House and also in his first campaign speech) Meighen cited the authority of Burke, Peel, Gladstone, Disraeli, Lord John Russell, Sir John Simon, Asquith, Lloyd George and, from Canada, of Alexander Mackenzie, Edward Blake and Sir Richard Cartwright. He also, and with great relish, quoted the pre-1926 opinions of Arthur Berriedale Keith, a well-known British writer on constitutional questions, who when the crisis arose in Canada rushed into print in Mackenzie King's defence. "He is not a clear-thinking man," Meighen commented, "but one very much in need of what Macaulay described as 'purification of the intellectual eye.' Anyway he is the authority Mr. King depends on, so I am going to speak from his writings before he knew of this case." Whereupon, citing chapter and verse, he proceeded to demonstrate that everything Keith was now writing about the prerogative of dissolution contradicted what he had written in the past.

Summing up, Meighen asserted that since a "democracy has an absolute right to the judgment of Parliament on the behaviour or misbehaviour of its Administration," from "every angle of approach the Governor-General was right and Mr. King was wrong. For His Excellency to have yielded would have been to make himself an accomplice in an unheard of assault on the prerogatives of Parliament and people." And then this in conclusion:

> . . . Nobody claims, least of all the present Governor-General of Canada, any right on the part of the King's representative to choose as between parties the stamp or colour of Government. That is for Parliament alone. The King's representative, in the limited sphere as guardian of the Constitution still reserved for him, can only make sure that Parliament is not denied that right. It makes no difference to a free people, said Edward Blake, whether their rights, as reposed in their Parliament, are invaded by the Crown or by the Cabinet. What is important, he said, is to secure that their rights shall not be invaded at all. . . .
>
> In fidelity to this teaching, in simple performance of the duty it imposes, guided and directed as well by other great figures over a wide range in our present and our past, the Governor-General of Canada, in silence and in dignity, has done his part. His part being done, it has been my humble but proud privilege to stand at his side.
>
> The Lord Byng of Vimy is not on trial in this contest. His Court is the Court of Conscience and of History. The immediate fortunes of two political leaders and two political parties are before the tribunal of their masters. But more than they, and far more important than they, the people of Canada themselves are on trial. Not by showy strategy—to use a most flattering term—not by empty dexterities of politics can popular institutions either flourish or survive, but

only by all ranks seeking steadily the truth and toiling in its light, preserving from the past what has proven good, and thus building on foundations which are solid and abiding. Yes, the people of Canada are on trial. On the integrity of their thinking, as reflected in the verdict of tomorrow, will depend in no small measure the standard of our public life for years to come.

The verdict of the morrow was a shocking, disillusioning blow to Meighen. He was personally defeated in Portage la Prairie by Ewan A. McPherson, who had been his first law partner there twenty years before, and five of the other ministers, including all four French Canadians, likewise went down to defeat. The Liberals elected 118 members, his own party only ninety-one. As for the once mighty National Progressive party, it split into four more or less distinct entities during the campaign. Ten men calling themselves Liberal-Progressives and led by Robert Forke were returned, more than enough to assure King an absolute majority in the House. Nine unhyphenated Progressives were victorious, as were eleven candidates running under the banner of the United Farmers of Alberta. The fourth element consisted of Agnes MacPhail, who as in 1925 chose to describe herself as the nominee of the politically all-but-defunct United Farmers of Ontario.

No one can say with certainty why elections are won or lost. The mail received by Meighen contained the usual wide variety of explanations of why the Conservatives had not won this one. The party had been over-confident; its campaign had consisted too much of "destructive" criticism; the Liberals had had more money; faulty organization was to blame, or fortress Quebec, or the lack of a strong press in Quebec and the West. Meighen's stand on the tariff was blamed by some western Conservatives, his attitude to construction of the Hudson Bay Railway by others, his opposition to statutory freight rates for grain by others still. Another important factor from the western viewpoint was an incident at an election meeting near Toronto attended by Meighen. After his speech he had left to keep another engagement and so was not on hand to hear one of the speakers who followed him advance the astounding proposition that henceforth no immigrant who was not of British birth should be given the vote as long as he lived. This suggestion, J. T. Haig told Meighen, "played havoc with us in Manitoba; not only the Poles and Ukrainians, but the Swedes, Germans and Icelanders were affected by it and very seriously."[23] The Liberals seized upon it and publicized it in the West in such a way as to give the impression that Meighen had heard the proposal made and had not repudiated it. The defeated Conservative in the Saskatchewan riding of Qu'Appelle described what happened.

Up until ten days before the polling day the Customs scandal was the main issue of the campaign, but during the last ten days we were on the defensive, trying to convince the people that their freight rates would not be raised if the Conservative party was returned to power. A very energetic campaign was also carried on among the foreigners for the purpose of inducing them to believe that their franchise would be taken away from them if the party got elected, and in the foreign settlements pamphlets were issued in the languages of these people, reminding them of the war-time Elections Act, and that they might expect the same kind of legislation if a Conservative government was in power.[24]

Whatever the influence of these sundry factors the downfall of the Conservatives in 1926 has usually been attributed to three main causes: the popularity of the Robb Budget and the Liberals' promise of further tax reductions; the constitutional "issue"; and Meighen's alienation of many Conservatives by his Hamilton speech. Respecting the second of these it has been written:

On this issue King seized with the instinct of victory. It was such as to awaken all the atavistic colonial resentments of Grit democracy and French-Canadian nationalism. Lord Byng's offence was that he was an Englishman and a Lord, representing an outmoded imperial relationship. Canadians, sensitive on the score of their emerging nationalism, were easily persuaded that they had been treated as a colony might be treated, and the response was instant and decisive. The result of 1926 was the political expression of the new Canadian nationalism, sprung from the war, and since groping for expression. The constitutional crisis of 1926 first gave it a domestic issue of a traditional character on which the electorate could speak with point and emphasis.[25]

And one of Mackenzie King's biographers explains:

The campaign went against Meighen not by accident but by the sure logic of history. He had lost Quebec by his conscriptionist record to begin with. Now, in the rest of the country, he was caught between the deep cross-currents of Canadian life, between those who suspected him of surrendering Canada to an English Governor and those who feared that his actions struck at the British constitution and damaged the British connection.

Toward the end, Meighen realized what was happening to him. Desperately he tried to turn the tide. It could not be turned, because it welled out of Canada's whole past.[26]

It is impossible to measure the actual influence of the crisis, the Budget or the Hamilton speech, to say nothing of the innumerable local and personal factors that have a bearing on every election. Nor is it as easy as one might wish to be sure just what "the sure logic of history" is. A close look at the actual returns, however, leads one to think that such

conventional interpretations of the 1926 election are not altogether satisfactory, that "the new Canadian nationalism" expressed itself with less
"point and emphasis" and the response was less "instant and decisive"
than one might think at first glance.

Of one thing, at least, there was no doubt: unlike the 1925 election
when there had been a remarkably close correlation in the country at
large between the percentages of the popular vote and of the seats given
to each party, in this one the results were full of grotesque anomalies.
The Conservatives with forty-six per cent of the votes, the same as in
1925, won only thirty-seven per cent of the ridings, a drop of ten per cent.
Though by a smaller margin than last time, they again outpolled the
candidates of the Liberal party in Canada as a whole and in six of the
nine provinces, but won twenty-seven fewer seats than the Liberals. If
one lumps the Liberal-Progressives with the ordinary Liberals, where
for all practical purposes they belonged, one finds that the combined
popular vote of the two groups exceeded that of the Conservatives by
fewer than seven thousand but between them they captured thirty-seven
more seats. The total Conservative vote was larger than in 1925, though
it declined very slightly in four provinces, and all in all the figures do
not support the conclusion that any of the issues that had arisen since the
last contest had caused a loss of confidence in the party or its leader. The
figures for the popular vote also show, however, marked gains for the
Liberals. Was this because of the new nationalism, the heresy of Hamilton, the logic of history or what?

The Conservatives' net loss of twenty-five seats was accounted for
mainly by Ontario, where they dropped fifteen, and Manitoba, where
they received forty-two per cent of the popular vote but were beaten in
all the seven ridings they had won the year before. The Manitoba debacle was a genuine electoral absurdity, for the Liberals got four seats
with only eighteen per cent of the ballots, the Liberal-Progressives seven
seats with twenty per cent, straight Progressives four with eleven per
cent and Labourites two with nine per cent. Put differently, the Conservatives were defeated in all sixteen Manitoba constituencies (the
seventeenth went to the Liberal-Progressive A. L. Beaubien by acclamation) in spite of the fact that thirteen thousand more people voted for
them than in 1925. The explanation of this lay less in the impact on the
public of the various national issues that had arisen in the past year than
in the comparative absence of three-cornered battles. There had been
ten of these in the province the last time; now there were only three and
this meant that, except in those three ridings, the non-Conservative or
anti-Conservative vote was concentrated in each case behind a single
candidate. Save in Portage la Prairie the Liberals nominated no one

outside of greater Winnipeg, leaving the rural field to Liberal-Progressives like Forke or other Progressives such as T. W. Bird, who for some reason refused to take on the Liberal label, and organizing the Liberal vote behind them. A somewhat similar consolidation of the opposition vote occurred in the two Winnipeg ridings that had gone Conservative in 1925 in three-cornered contests. In both of them over three thousand ballots had been cast for Labour candidates, who were not in the field in 1926 and much of whose support probably shifted to the Liberals. The one Conservative riding in Manitoba where the outcome was not affected by the elimination of a third candidate was Meighen's own, which he had won back from Harry Leader in a straight two-way fight. To lose it again so soon after regaining it was a bitter pill but here, too, the result seems to have been due more to local factors than to national issues. In the last election Meighen had had the support of a good many Liberal townspeople who deserted him when one of their own in the person of the able and intelligent McPherson entered the lists. And the rural people who had backed Leader before now threw their strength behind McPherson in the absence of a Progressive nominee.

Disparities similar to, though less glaring than, those in Manitoba between the popular vote and seats won were evident in Ontario but there the situation was rather different. The Conservative vote declined by more than ten thousand, or about one and one-half per cent, while the Liberals polled nearly fifty thousand more than in 1925, a gain of over fifteen per cent. These shifts were enough to cost the Conservatives twenty-two per cent of their seats in the province and to more than double the Liberal representation but hardly enough to constitute an emphatic expression of "the atavistic colonial resentments of Grit democracy" or of "the new Canadian nationalism." In 1925 the Conservatives had won an abnormally large number of Ontario seats (68 out of 82), far more than their 56 per cent of the popular vote entitled them to, and a few losses were not to be wondered at. In eleven of the fifteen seats the party lost in 1926 its candidates actually received more votes than they had as winners the year before. In four of them they were defeated because they faced only one opposing nominee, instead of two as before. They were not on particularly good fighting ground in some of the others, such as Essex East, which was largely French Canadian and had been very narrowly won the last time, and Oxford North, which had never elected a Conservative until 1925. The charge of one over-zealous Conservative candidate that there was gross immorality in the civil service at Ottawa may have had something to do with the loss of the two seats in that city. In still another of the lost ridings, Elgin West, the Liberal victory was less a vindication of Mackenzie King than a personal triumph for a young man of whom much more was to be heard in the future, Mitchell Hepburn.

The improved showing of the Liberal party in Ontario seems to have been largely caused, though not entirely, by a transfer of support to its candidates from the Progressives, who fielded the same number as in 1925 but lost strength badly, and from Labourites and Independents, of whom there were fewer in the running. This transfer also explained in part the reduction of majorities in 36 of the 53 ridings that remained Conservative. So did the consolidation of the opposing forces by the absence of third candidates in a number of constituencies where they had been present in 1925 and, in a few cases, the replacement by less well-known nominees of prominent Conservatives who retired, for example General Mewburn in Hamilton East.

These assorted facts, so much more tedious to relate and so much less soul-satisfying to contemplate than the logic of history, are not without significance. They do not by any means indicate a large-scale repudiation by Ontario Conservatives of the party or its leader because of the constitutional crisis, the Hamilton speech or anything else. King's stand on the crisis may help to explain the increased vote received by his party for he had a plausible case and worked it for all it was worth. But outside of the Toronto area the Conservative vote also increased, by over thirty thousand. It was the city with its suburbs that was responsible for the net reduction of the party's Ontario poll. For some reason the citizens of Toronto were apathetic about this election and both Liberals and Conservatives stayed away from the polling booths in droves. The Conservative vote in the Toronto ridings (including York South and York West) was lower by almost forty-two thousand than in 1925 and in most of those ridings Liberal strength declined as well. How was this curious failure to get out the vote in the city to be explained? One reason, perhaps, was that most of those seats were so safely Conservative and had been won the last time by such handsome majorities that some Liberals thought it was useless to vote and many Conservatives thought it was needless. Insofar as Conservative absenteeism may have been caused by some national issue of the moment, one would imagine it to have been the Hamilton speech more than anything else. For Toronto was still a centre of ultra-British sentiment where the speech had caused considerable anger when it was delivered. However, despite the falling-off of the popular vote all the Toronto and York seats were retained and the results elsewhere in the province suggest that what Meighen had proposed at Hamilton did less damage to the Conservative cause than has often been supposed.

At the same time it did far less good in Quebec than it had been intended to. To Meighen the prospects in that province looked better than they had for many years. Patenaude's accession, he thought, would be a big factor and the purchase of *La Patrie* of Montreal by a group of financiers headed by Lorne Webster and J. W. McConnell gave the party a French-language voice in the city at last. Even Lord Atholstan seemed well-disposed for a change. Early in July Murray Williams reported that he had been talking to him.

> Every election adds five years to Lord A's life. A satisfied smile wreathes his face, he rubs his hands with glee. He loves elections and eats 'em alive. He told me to tell you it is his opinion that the date should be delayed as long as possible. Late in September, or better still in October, he thinks would be the ideal time for farmers and city men alike. He says people now stay out in the country very late and furthermore the travellers in Europe are not all back yet.
>
> He is going to back the party to the limit, and is much more friendly to you, but I do not anticipate an immediate editorial outburst on your personal behalf. If Ballantyne runs anywhere he intends to attack him, but all the other candidates will be fully supported. He thinks Cahan made a great showing this session, and hopes that you will fit him into the Cabinet somewhere. He rather thinks, too, it would be good politics not to overlook Bob Rogers.[27]

Even Meighen's failure to include either Cahan or Rogers in the Cabinet did not induce an Atholstanian tantrum. Acknowledging a note from Meighen, His Lordship wrote:

> I was very pleased to get your encouraging note, and sorry to hear that your pressing duties prevented your paying me a visit. I pay that penalty frequently for living away out in the country.
>
> I have followed your campaign in the Maritimes with close attention. Will you permit me to say that it seems to me that such speeches as yours deserve to win. I have given my editors instructions to report you fully, feeling that this is undoubtedly the best service we can do the cause.
>
> A "hot weather" election naturally finds the people lethargic, but you will doubtless waken them up before polling.[28]

But nothing, neither Meighen nor Patenaude nor the *Star* nor the new *La Patrie,* wakened the people of Quebec up in the way that Atholstan meant. The same four seats were won by the same four men as in 1925 but there were no gains, though the party's share of the vote in the province went up one point to thirty-five per cent. Patenaude, of course, faced very serious obstacles, quite apart from the habit of the public mind and the superior financial, journalistic and organizational strength of the Liberals. He had only three months in which to try to impose a peace on the factions, develop an organization and mount and conduct his campaign. Had he joined with Meighen before the 1925 election and remained at work thereafter things might have been in better shape when the crisis precipitated another campaign in the summer of 1926. As it was he had not enough time, nor was he able to produce a convincing reason for his having entered Meighen's government after pointedly proclaiming his independence of the national leader only ten months before. But it is doubtful whether under any circumstances he could have coped successfully with conscription, "Downing Street interference," and Meighen's alleged assault on responsible government. Sir Lomer Gouin was reported to have told Edmund Bristol: "I and a lot of other Protectionist Liberals in Quebec would like to back the Conservatives but we have abused Mr. Meighen so severely for ten years that we cannot with good countenance support him now."[29]

As for Conservative fortunes in the rest of the country, with a slightly reduced share of the popular vote in the Maritimes they suffered a net loss of three seats; Saskatchewan gave them a few more votes but still no seats; in Alberta they got the same proportion of ballots as before but lost two of their three ridings, Bennett being the only survivor; and in British Columbia their share of the vote was substantially increased and two seats were added to their previous total of ten.

One overriding fact, of course, no amount of analysis could obscure: whatever the causes, whatever anomalies one might discover in the returns, from the standpoint that really counted—the makeup of the new House of Commons—the Conservative party had been defeated. Accepting this harsh truth, Meighen at once submitted his resignation as Prime Minister but at Lord Byng's request remained in office ten days longer while King went about the work of constructing his Cabinet. Meighen never managed to reconcile himself to this defeat, which he thought as undeserved as it was unexpected, and it is not hard to understand his astonishment, his profound disappointment. Mackenzie King had been on the run, the prestige of his government and his own authority in the Liberal party slipping away. His sudden resignation from office on June the twenty-eighth had seemed to Meighen and other Conservatives likely to be the first step towards the extinction of his political career. And yet here he was, fresh from a victory at the polls, his indestructible Calvinistic faith strengthened in his own moral superiority as one of the elect. Defeat would have rankled for Meighen no matter who the adversary but to be beaten just when his own triumph looked assured by King of all men, in Meighen's eyes the living embodiment of deceit, unreason and hypocrisy, was an intolerable blow to his pride and one that weakened his hitherto genuine faith in the democratic process. That faith would have survived unimpaired defeat by Laurier or Blake or Mackenzie, the Liberal leaders his predecessors had faced, but King was of a different breed from these men. His victory, in Meighen's view of the case, meant that large masses of the voters could be swayed by demagogic appeals, impressed by soft, shapeless, confusing, meaningless verbiage, or seduced with proffers of public funds. It meant that the people either cared more for tax reductions than for the Constitution or had allowed themselves to be carried away by King's emotional and entirely ridiculous utterances about responsible government and national autonomy.

It was especially an affront to decency, honour and the fitness of things in a democracy that King had won the election over the constitutional "issue," as Meighen thought. For it was King, self-appointed champion of parliamentary supremacy, who in effect by word and deed had claimed the supremacy of Prime Minister over Parliament. It was King who had left the Crown without ministers, the country without a government, by his unprecedented withdrawal from office when dissolution was refused. It was King who had then rudely declined to confer with Meighen as to how the session might be finished. It was King who had dragged the name and office of the Governor-General through the mire of partisan controversy while sanctimoniously professing his devotion to Lord Byng. Finally, though Meighen did not yet know, he was shortly to discover that King, while insinuating that refusal of dissolution was a blow to Canadian status and allowing his cohorts to scream "Downing Street interference" from the rooftops, had urged Byng to invite the intervention of the British government in a purely Canadian affair. The constitutional crisis was probably less decisive in determining the outcome of the election than Meighen thought but it was natural for him to think it had been decisive in view of the central place it occupied in King's campaign. And, although he accepted the verdict with dignity, wasting no time in lamentations, he remained convinced to the end of his days that no party leader had ever been beaten on so contemptibly and transparently false an issue.

King interpreted the election results as a clear vindication of his stand on the dissolution controversy, not pausing to consider how cloudy the evidence of such vindication was. He remarked, however, that had the election gone the other way the question would have been "very far from settled."[30] Heads I win, tails you lose! A few days after taking office again he sailed for London to attend an Imperial Conference, determined, apparently, to obtain a formal declaration concerning the position of Governors-General which would conclusively uphold his own contention respecting exercise of the power of dissolution. "The conference heard him," one of his unofficial biographers writes, "as the first overseas statesman of the Commonwealth who had taught the Crown a lesson, destroyed the last vestigial remnants of the royal prerogative in the issue of parliamentary dissolution, and established the equality of the Dominions and their British mother beyond question."[31] Thus the folklore of the Liberal party. But it was not quite so simple, so gloriously an unfolding of "the sure logic of history" as that. A committee of the conference was appointed to consider and report on the constitutional aspect of Imperial relations. Its report contained the celebrated description of Great Britain and the Dominions as "autonomous Communities within the British Empire, equal in status, in no way subordinate one to another. . . ." It also defined the position of the Governor-General, who was declared to be "the representative of the Crown, holding in all essential respects the same position in relation to the administration of public affairs in the Dominion as is held by His Majesty the King in Great Britain, and . . . not the representative or agent of His Majesty's Government in Great Britain or of any Department of that Government."[32] Presumably this had Mackenzie King's approval, since he was a member of the committee, and it is therefore odd that he should so recently have pressed the representative of His Majesty, who was not an agent of the British government, to consult that government as to where his duty lay.

This definition introduced no principle that was not already generally accepted, and accepted certainly by Meighen, but it is often assumed that it settled the whole argument over the prerogative of dissolution in King's favour. Whether it did, whether he had in fact "destroyed the last vestigial remnants" of its free exercise by the Crown, depends on whether the King himself retained any discretionary power in this respect. In Meighen's opinion he did and would have acted precisely as Lord Byng had. That the King still held the right to refuse was shown by his response to Ramsay MacDonald's request for a dissolution in 1924, after his minority government had been defeated in Parliament. Far from accepting MacDonald's advice "immediately" and "without even considering whether the Government could be carried on without a dissolution," as Berriedale Keith described the King's response, George V granted a dissolution "with the utmost reluctance and only after he had ascertained from the leaders of the Conservative and Labour [sic] Parties that they themselves were unable or unwilling to form an Administration."[33] If the King could have refused in 1924 and if a Governor-General was on the same footing as His Majesty, then quite clearly Byng possessed the right to refuse in 1926.

That the prerogative of dissolution is no "vestigial remnant" has been affirmed in more recent years by both Winston Churchill and Clement Attlee. ". . . It does not rest with any Prime Minister to dissolve Parliament," the former said in 1944. "The utmost he can do is to tender advice to the Crown. . . . This is one of the exceptional occasions when the Prerogative of the Crown comes into play and where in doubtful circumstances the Crown would refer to other advisers. It has been done on several occasions. I must make it absolutely clear that it does not rest with the Government of the day."[34] Attlee was of the same opinion in 1952: "The monarch has the right to grant or refuse a prime minister's request for a dissolution of Parliament. . . . This is a very real power. It means that there is always someone other than a party leader who is available to take action in critical times."[35] Far from being subversive of liberty or a "vestigial remnant" from some dark and distant past, the possession of this power by the Crown, as Meighen affirmed and King denied in 1926, is an essential safeguard of parliamentary government. "The danger of royal absolutism," Dr. Forsey writes, "is past; but the danger of Cabinet absolutism, even of Prime Ministerial absolutism, is present and growing. Against that danger the reserve power of the Crown, and especially the power to force or refuse dissolution, is in some instances the only constitutional safeguard. The Crown is more than a quaint survival, a social ornament, a symbol. . . . It is an absolutely essential part of the parliamentary system. In certain circumstances, the Crown alone can preserve the Constitution, or ensure that if it is to be changed it shall be only by the deliberate will of the people."[36]

Shortly before Mackenzie King sailed for England Lord Byng preceded him. He had agreed to stay on in Canada past the normal end of his term until the general election was over. His last official act in Canada was to swear in the new ministers on September the twenty-fifth. The ceremony must have imposed on His Excellency a certain amount of strain after all the fuss and fury of the past weeks but no doubt he kept his feelings under a close rein. Meighen was much impressed by the wholly proper but in the circumstances remarkable fortitude and forbearance Byng displayed during the crisis and the ensuing campaign. Never once in Meighen's hearing did he let fall a word of reproach or complaint concerning the position in which King had put him, not a syllable to indicate that he had anything but the greatest respect for King, as for other Canadian public men. But something of Byng's true feelings about the victor of 1926 may be gathered from a letter he wrote after returning to London to his former aide-de-camp, Colonel H. Willis-O'Connor. He had been at the station when King arrived to attend the Imperial Conference and later a dinner had been given by the Canada Club in Byng's honour at the Savoy.

> I went to the station to meet Mackenzie King—a beau geste of perfection. He fell into my arms and produced a Niagara of gush—"How noble," "How thoughtful," "He would ever remember it." There was a considerable crowd. . . .
> Then, we had the Canada Club dinner. My speech may be said to have been an unqualified success owing to the enthusiastic applause

of W.L.M.K. who cheered every utterance.   It ran something like this:

SELF: Your Royal Highnesses—
KING: Hear! Hear!
SELF: Mr. Chairman—
KING: Très bien! Good. Good!
SELF: My Lords—
KING: Attaboy . . . Buono Oratorio (Italian)
SELF: And gentlemen—
KING: Banzai . . . fine . . . clap, clap, clap, and so on until the end.[37]

Lady Byng was much less reticent than her husband in discussing Canadian politics and politicians, even with the politicians themselves and their wives.   In temperament she was volatile, her opinions were emphatic and she expressed them with an amply forthright vocabulary that left no room for misunderstanding.   She made little or no effort while in Canada, especially after the crisis, to conceal her detestation of King and she did not forget or forgive.   Some years later the Meighens received an arresting and laugh-provoking communication from the Byngs' estate, Thorpe Hall, Thorpe-le-Soken, Essex. Across the top of the page was pasted a small clipping, a social notice, from the columns of *The Canadian Gazette:*

> Mr. Mackenzie King received 3,500 Christmas cards and messages.   The Prime Minister spent Christmas Day at Ottawa opening the messages.

Below this a few words were scrawled in Lady Byng's hand:

> I suppose you were both there helping our dear little roly poly friend.
>
> (sgd.) Evelyn Byng of Vimy
> Who did *not* send one of the 3,500 greetings.[38]

CHAPTER SEVENTEEN

POLITICS, FAREWELL

THE DEPARTURE of Lord and Lady Byng from Canada was soon followed by Meighen's exit from politics. For a few days after the election he was undecided as to what he ought to do. His inclination was to retire but he was deluged with hundreds of letters and telegrams urging him to stay on. These messages were full of glowing tributes to his personal qualities from people who had nothing to seek or to gain and they indicated the intensity of the loyalty to him as an individual which he aroused in so many hearts. But doubtless there were many others in the party who, whatever they thought of him personally, believed that he should now make way for someone else. This division of opinion was reflected in the Conservative press and an editorial debate developed between the *Mail and Empire* of Toronto and the *Gazette* of Montreal. The latter, which predictably enough wanted him to get out, based its opinion on the proven hostility to him of Quebec. "French-Canadian Quebec," said the *Gazette*, "has voted solidly against the Conservative party led by Mr. Meighen, and has done it thrice in succession, despite the admitted fact that the Conservative policy conforms absolutely to the social and economic requirements of the Province. There was no accident about these votes; they were given deliberately upon each occasion by an overwhelming majority—and upon one issue—Mr. Meighen." The question, it went on, was not whether this antipathy was fair. "The essential fact is that Quebec will not have Mr. Meighen, and it is a stubborn fact, one that is not affected in any way by debates as to whether the French-Canadian attitude is just or unjust."[1]

By the time his resignation as Prime Minister became effective on September the twenty-fifth Meighen had made up his mind. "We resign tomorrow morning," he wrote to his elder son. "I am retiring from the leadership. It is the best course now. And I will soon get down to work in another line and seek success again. My race is to quite an extent run. Yours has not opened. My two boys are my proudest possessions and may they always be the credit to me they are now. Good night my son. Be true every moment to yourself."[2] In announcing his retirement as leader Meighen summoned the Conservative senators, members of the

House and defeated candidates to a meeting in Ottawa on October the eleventh to choose a successor. While his departure caused pleasure, not to say rejoicing, in some quarters, in others it was cause for lament and many letters came in pleading with him to reconsider. The one that most impressed him was from the Reverend Canon Allan P. Shatford of Montreal, who remonstrated strongly against Meighen's decision to step down in this moment of adversity. The defeat, Canon Shatford assured him, was in no way a reflection on his leadership. "This is not the hour for any of us to nurse our wounds—it is the hour of crisis when we need experienced officers to command & loyal followers to fight on. Therefore I plead for your continuance in office."[3] But it was too late for reconsiderations. Meighen had made his choice and he answered:

> To put the case simply, I became convinced that to continue in the office of leader at the present time was to bring myself into a position not only insufferable from a personal standpoint, but one in which it was impossible for me to succeed. A man may lead a party while there is division in the ranks, and indeed while substantial numbers are opposed to him; but it is another matter to lead a party while prominent and influential newspaper organs of the same political faith are continually criticizing his conduct. This makes for dis-union. My conviction is that the evil can only be remedied by my stepping aside and giving the party a chance to unite upon another leader. It is not because of the defeat in itself, but because of the opinion above outlined that I have taken the step. . . . My duty now is to make the circumstances as favourable as they can be made for my successor and so far as in me lies, to give him every opportunity to succeed.[4]

Naturally there was a great deal of interest in who that successor would be. Sir Rodmond Roblin of Manitoba, who had had more success than Meighen in gaining and holding power, warned that intellectual ability was not the main quality to look for in a leader. The inference to be drawn was that the party should not repeat the mistake it had made on that score in 1920. Rather, said Roblin, it should choose a Roman Catholic who spoke French and he therefore recommended Robert Manion, who had the additional merit of being a good mixer who would attract support with his winning personality.[5] Instead, however, the meeting selected Hugh Guthrie as temporary leader for the approaching session of Parliament and appointed a committee to organize at last the national convention about which there had been so much talk and so little action ever since 1920. "I feel certain," Meighen answered Roblin, "that on the score of personal popularity alone [Manion] would have been elected, and between him and Mr. Guthrie, he is the more assiduous, diligent and aggressive. I fancy the other collateral fact though, [his religion] had practically everything to do with his being defeated."[6]

With these arrangements made regarding the succession Meighen's day in public life was over—or so it seemed. As he prepared to leave Ottawa and start a new life at the age of fifty-two he could not shake off a feeling of baffled incredulity at what had befallen him, mixed with a certain gnawing disillusionment. His departure, of course, brought forth numerous tributes in which his friends were joined by some of his foes. "He goes out without a stain upon his armour," the Ottawa *Journal* declared. "To his last fight he gave his all; it was not his fault if he did not reach the summit. He believed in himself, he believed in Canada, and he believed in his policies, and he was true to the last to all of them." The *Manitoba Free Press,* which Meighen regarded as a malign power whose influence largely accounted for the hostility of the the West to his party, was also generous in its comments now that he was safely out of the way: "To enter Parliament at thirty-four, one of a horde of undistinguished raw recruits, and to become almost immediately a parliamentary figure; to fight his way to the charmed government ranks in six years; to win premiership at forty-six, to attain and hold against all comers the position of the first swordsman of Parliament— these are achievements which will survive the disaster of to-day."[7]

But Meighen could not rest content on these laurels, impressive as they might be. The stark truth, with which he had to live henceforth and which no praise of his character or accomplishments could obscure, was that he had been bested by Mackenzie King when all the chips were down, when the struggle between them had come into its sharpest focus. The loss of an election was not in itself what really bothered him, because after all politics was a hazardous profession and elections had to be lost by someone. Rather, it was the nature, the mentality and the methods of his adversary, whom he regarded as the most despicable charlatan ever to darken the annals of Canadian politics and whose final victory seemed to undermine every precept instilled in Meighen as a child, every lesson life had taught him thus far. Above all it exposed to doubt the core of his moral code—the responsibility of the individual. It had been dinned into him, along with his brothers and sisters, "that our success or failure depended solely on ourselves; and the idea that we could attribute to others, or to the community or to the country, accountability for our own failure was never permitted to find lodgment in our minds."[8] Now after six years of unceasing effort and three general elections he had failed in his war with Mackenzie King, which until the very last he had been so confident of winning. Was this his fault? Or could it be attributed "to others, or to the community or to the country"? Meighen was torn between his innermost conviction that it was wrong to blame others for one's misfortunes and the belief that his political downfall had been brought about by causes over which he had no control and for which he was not responsible.

How much the fortunes of a party leader and the party he leads are determined by his own qualities and actions is one of the most fascinating yet unanswerable questions raised by the politics of democracy. Possibly in Meighen's day what the leader said and did, what image he projected, were less dominant factors than they have become since. In the 1920's the leader created his own image very largely, without resort to advertising agencies or the techniques of motivational research, without benefit of the mass media of radio and television. The impact of the leader's personality and character was perhaps less direct, their influence less pervasive, when most of the electorate never heard his voice or saw him either in the flesh or on the screen. The personality of one man did not override public issues, whether local or national, and reduce local candidates to insignificant anonymity as much as it has tended to do in more recent years when the image of the leader, the "cult of personality," has loomed increasingly large.

Nevertheless, in the 1920's as at all times the personality and conduct of the leader no doubt had great, if unmeasurable, importance and it has been fashionable to explain the outcome of the struggle between Meighen and Mackenzie King mainly in personal terms. There can be no doubt, of course, about the contrast between them or that the problems they faced at the outset were not dissimilar. Each inherited the leadership of a party in which the crisis of the war, culminating in 1917, had caused deep divisions. These divisions were hardly less grave in the Conservative party than in the Liberal for, if the latter under Laurier had surrendered much of its influence in English-speaking Canada by its opposition to conscription, the former under Borden had estranged its supporters in Quebec on the same issue and alienated many Conservatives elsewhere by the establishment of the Union Government. Therefore King and Meighen both were confronted with the task of healing wounds and making their respective parties truly national once again. In addition each of them had assumed leadership in the face of powerful opposition and both had to win the confidence of substantial elements within their parties who regarded them with suspicion. One would gather from the conventional wisdom that Meighen was hopelessly unsuited by temperament and King ideally suited to overcome these difficulties and that this accounts for the final triumph of the one over the other. One would gather that Meighen was like a spectacular rocket which explodes its flaring lights magnificently against the dark sky, arousing excited exclamations of admiration or of fear, and then subsides, forgotten, while King's light burned less arrestingly, with fewer pyrotechnics, but more steadily, reassuringly. In this view of things Meighen was a brilliant failure with small talent for party leadership, who fell inevitably because he lacked the superior perception that belonged to King, the deeper understanding of democracy, the aspirations of the Canadian people and the nature of the Canadian state. He was too rigid and uncompromising, too dogmatic and confident in the rightness of his own opinions, too obsessed with preserving his own consistency, too reluctant to accept any but the wrong advice from the wrong people. He took too much upon himself and failed to share either the work or the glory with others. His manner was overly austere, his language in controversy overly severe. He angered where he should have appeased, defied where he should have conceded, alienated where he should have conciliated, repelled where he should have attracted. This interpretation has all the beauty of simplicity but does not accord entirely with the facts.

To begin with, judged by the acid test of ability to attract votes Meighen was not a failure. Curiously, though his ultimate loss of the field to King has generally been ascribed to his own shortcomings, he has never received much credit for the revival of the Conservative party between 1922 and 1925. The credit was not all his, of course, nor would he have thought of claiming it, but if the personal factor of leadership was of any significance the impressive gains made by the Conservatives during that period must have been partly the result of his efforts. The 1921 election was a defeat, and a bad one, but in all probability had been lost before Sir Robert Borden ever retired as Prime Minister in the summer of 1920. The 1925 election, in contrast, was a victory, though not a decisive one, in which the Conservative popular vote exceeded the Liberal by over two hundred thousand. Even in 1926 the party outpolled the Liberals and came within a few thousand votes of equalling the poll of Liberals and Liberal-Progressives combined. Not for more than thirty years afterwards, with the single exception of 1930, were the Conservatives to win as many seats in the House or receive so large a share of the total vote as they did in two of the three general elections they fought with Meighen as their leader. These facts do not indicate that he was so inept politically, so much of a liability to the party, as has sometimes been thought.

But was the failure of the party to do even better under his direction and gain a secure hold on power due to his alleged defects as a public man? In part these sprang from the very qualities that made him most attractive as an individual. Meighen attempted to apply to public life the standards of private and personal conduct in which he believed, among which frankness, honesty and consistency ranked high. He tended to idealize politics as an intellectual competition, a continuous great debate which performed an educative function essential to the proper working of democracy. The duty of the leader and of all men in public life, indeed the purpose of the party system, was to define and clarify issues in such a way that the electorate, when the time came, could make an intelligent decision. One must take a clear stand, announce one's opinion or policy in such a way that there could be no mistaking what it was and try to convince the voters, either through Parliament or directly, that one was right. If Canada were to be more than a congeries of disparate sections, peoples and provinces, a national party must formulate a concept of the national interest, along with measures calculated to serve it, and be prepared when the opportunity arrived to put those measures into operation. It was incumbent on the politician, he thought, and especially on the leader of a party, to have the courage of consistency, to advance the same policies in all sections of the country, to say the same things no matter whom he was addressing, no matter whether what he said might prove popular or not. For the truth as one saw it was to be valued more highly than applause, even more highly than votes. That there was room for honest difference of opinion about almost any matter of public policy Meighen knew; that was why there were opposing parties—to crystallize these differences and bring them sharply into focus. Only in this way, through intelligent, vigorous controversy, could politics have that clarity, that rational order without which democracy made no sense. He was aware, of course, that one had to do more than win arguments in order to win elections. One needed organization and money and newspaper support, all of which the Conservative party was short of in the 1920's. Nor was he incapable of compromise; no one who was could have got as far as he did. He realized that one had to accommodate oneself in some degree to particular local pressures, to demands for jobs and favours and public works and services of various kinds. But most of all one needed to convince the judges of the debate, the jurors in the trial, with the weight of evidence, the logic of one's case and the effectiveness of its presentation.

This approach to politics, admirable in many ways, was perhaps not entirely suited to the realities of a far from perfect world. At any rate it was diametrically opposed—and this for Meighen was enough of a recommendation—to the theory and practice exemplified by King, which has been much celebrated as the only practicable one if not, indeed, the very acme of statesmanship. King's definition of the national interest seems to have consisted largely of the conviction that it could only be promoted by a Liberal government headed by himself, if, in fact, he did not believe that he was ordained to govern Canada by some divine right of King which rendered all his opponents either actual or would-be usurpers. To him the essence of the party leader's task was to listen to the many varied voices of the people. He was a "broker of ideas," to use a term much beloved of political scientists, taking from the infinitely complex and endlessly changing pattern of public opinion those thoughts, fears or desires which were politically important or exploitable. The leader, therefore, must respond to opinion, catering to it instead of trying to direct it along certain paths, and by being as many things as possible to as many people as possible seek to attract the support of the majority.

This intricate process was carried on by a compound of procrastination, inconsistency, compromise, equivocation, expediency and misrepresentation. It ruled out candour as a political virtue and supplanted it with the cult of ambiguity. It required the carefully contrived confusion of issues, the dulling of the sharp edge of disagreement so that men of diverse opinions could come together in the capacious political church built by Mackenzie King. There they could find common ground in the simple political theology, designedly acceptable to all, which he provided for them, a theology of gods and devils, saints and sinners, good and evil. It was seldom clear just where King stood on any actual issue of the moment but he never left any doubt that he was on the side of the angels, where he invited all liberally minded people to join him against the unregenerate and irredeemable Tories. Disliking to commit himself to a firm position on controversial public questions, he preferred to divert the attention of the people to the never-ending struggle between the wicked and the godly. Their support was invited in contending against usurpation, autocracy, militarism, the big interests and "Downing Street interference," in defending liberty, Parliament, peace and national unity. Meighen's attempt to gain support on the mundane issue of the tariff was pallid fare compared with the evangelical, moralistic fervour of his rival.

This was King's way of building a national party and, allegedly, of restoring national unity. Its logical end product was the unity of a one-party state, a state dominated by one massive, omnibus party which had something to offer to everybody and was bound to no fixed positions except an unremitting war against evil in which everyone could join with a good conscience. To Meighen it was all an outrageous debasement of politics. King's glossing-over of real questions in favour of fictitious ones, the contradictions between what he said here and what he said there, and between what he said almost anywhere and when he actually did, his tortuous twistings and turnings to avoid making decisions and giving direct answers, his willingness to shift ground for the sake of popularity and to barter promises in exchange for votes—all this was utterly repellent to Meighen, one of the least "promising" of party leaders; in his mind it added up to nothing but the philosophy of power at any price.

Because it was King who emerged triumphant in 1926, because his method of leadership and government resembled in some respects that of the illustrious Macdonald and Laurier and because he went on to govern for so long, it has generally been assumed that his was the only way in which so large and heterogeneous a country as Canada could be governed and a national party in a country like Canada be successfully led. According to this theory King's conquest of Meighen was pre-ordained, part of the inexorable "logic of history." This depressing conclusion not only exaggerates the similarity between King and his two most successful predecessors but places a heavy discount on the public intelligence. It also overlooks the fact that Meighen came within an ace of winning and King of being ousted, both from power and, it may be, from the leadership of the Liberal party. Assuming that Meighen was partly deserving of credit for the Conservative recovery revealed in the 1925 election, it may be said that his kind of leadership and his approach to politics had an appeal of their own, that forthrightness, consistency and reasoned argument proved more attractive to many voters than King's shapeless verbosity, incessant moralizing and calculated obscurities. Nor do the results of that election suggest that Meighen's manner on the hustings was a fatal handicap. That he faced the voters with anything but a sunny, outgoing disposition is true, but he paid them the compliment of taking it for granted that they had come to hear him discuss the public business as he saw it, not to soothe them with jokes or platitudes. There was, when he stood up on a platform and started to speak, something forbidding about him, even awesome: the unsmiling, drawn, tired-looking countenance; the brooding, deep-set eyes; the fierce, pitiless punishment of King meted out in carefully measured, faultless prose. But if some found him too austere in appearance, too remote in manner, too savagely bitter in his contempt for the enemy, others were impressed by his knowledge, captivated by his wit, searing though it might be, and enthralled by his matchless gift for constructing a case and presenting it with the utmost lucidity and succinctness. J. W. Dafoe of the *Winnipeg Free Press* recalled towards the close of his long life that as a young man he had been turned into a fighting Liberal by listening to the oratory of Edward Blake. There are people still living who attached themselves to the Conservative cause after listening to the oratory of Arthur Meighen, a man not unlike Blake in some ways.

It was in the House of Commons, if anywhere, rather than on the hustings, that Meighen's sharply controversial quality did him serious harm. In part it was his ability, in part his manner that aroused the intense dislike of many of his opponents, and in King's case an almost pathological fear and hatred. He was too clever, he knew too much, his memory was too dependable, he was too quick with the sharp riposte, the cutting sarcasm, too likely to be on hand with the final, devastating word, the clinching argument. By any standard of assessment he was "the first swordsman of Parliament." But those who felt the sharp point of the sword wanted nothing more than to retaliate, to get even, and their opportunities came in the ridings of the country where he did not confront them face to face. There, and particularly where he was weakest, the prairie West and Quebec, they attacked him with a kind of fury reserved especially for him, more vindictive, more venemous than might have been directed against some other leader who was less irritatingly and arrogantly supreme in the House. Long after he had left public life for good, in fact, his enemies continued to pursue him with a meanness and vindictiveness unparalleled in Canadian history.

These bitter personal attacks on the man were most decisive politically in Quebec. It was that province more than any other that enabled King to survive the 1925 election and prevented Meighen from coming into office then. The Conservatives were also sadly weak on the prairies, of course, especially in the two more westerly of the three provinces, but they had never been able to win more than one seat in Saskatchewan or more than three in Alberta since the establishment of those provinces, except in 1917 after the Union Government had been formed. With tariff protection the most conspicuous element in his programme Meighen had little expectation of doing better there until the western farmers were educated to see the indispensability of the tariff to the national interest. Quebec, however, was a different matter. It was true that it had been predominantly Liberal since the 1890's and that during Laurier's years in power the Conservatives had never captured more than twelve of the province's sixty-five seats until their alliance with the Nationalists in 1911. It was also true that in the wartime election the Union Government had won only three. But the Age of Laurier and the war were both over now and Meighen believed that with the help of the tariff issue the party could regain the ground it had lost in Quebec in recent years. Hence his efforts to exploit the prevalent suspicion there of western radicalism as represented by the Progressive movement and the fear that the Liberal party under King might tailor its policies to suit the West in order to absorb the Progressives or at least gain their support.

The failure of these efforts had various causes. One was that King was far too astute to alienate—over tariff policy or anything else—the province upon which he mostly depended and to which he largely owed his election as leader. Another was Meighen's association with policies especially unpopular in Quebec, chiefly two, public ownership of railways and conscription. Montreal was the centre of opposition to the first but antipathy prevailed throughout French Canada, of whose conservative social philosophy fear of "state socialism" and dislike of debts and deficits were natural expressions. Public ownership did not sit particularly well anywhere in the Province of Quebec and it both earned Meighen the inveterate animosity of the Conservative tycoons and provided the Liberals of the province with an issue which figured prominently in their appeal to the people. Conscription, though, was of more telling significance, arousing as it did the deep emotions associated with the ethnic dualism and tensions of Canadian history. The emphasis placed upon this subject by the Quebec Liberals in the elections of 1921 and 1925 more than offset the attempt by Meighen himself in the former campaign and Patenaude in the latter to concentrate public attention upon matters of the present rather than the past.

Of course, had no Liberal politician or orator uttered the word "conscription" on the hustings, had no Liberal or Nationalist editor filled his columns with scurrilous propaganda about it, the Conservatives would for a few years after the war at least have suffered to some extent in Quebec on that issue. Conscription itself was less easily forgotten than the fact that it had been demanded before it was introduced and supported afterwards by a great many English-speaking Liberals, some of whom like Fielding and Crerar later turned up as Cabinet colleagues of Mackenzie King. But the fact that the Conservatives remained as weak as they did in Quebec during the 1920's was presumably owing in some degree to the fantastic fabrications about Meighen's past deeds and future intentions with which the voters of the province were regaled in successive general election campaigns. The web of falsehood strung systematically across Quebec would have a strong emotional effect on many voters. Certainly it contributed to the continued disunity and demoralization of the Conservative party, causing Arthur Sauvé to conclude that "politically it pays to 'avoid' Meighen" and disposing Patenaude to go his separate way in 1925. It may be that Meighen suffered more in this respect than some other leader of the party would have, partly because he had drafted so much of the controversial, unpopular wartime legislation and had been so much to the fore in its defence, partly because he had so often and so triumphantly tangled in the House with representatives of Quebec who thirsted for revenge. In this sense his past was catching up with him but what that past actually had been and what his enemies in Quebec pictured it as having been were worlds apart.

At any rate conscription, with all it symbolized for French Canada, was an issue admirably suited to the immediate requirements of the Liberal party, however irrelevant it may have been in the post-war period. So were war with Turkey and "Downing Street interference" when in due course these alleged issues arose. They were not, however, well suited to the restoration and nourishment of national unity. King's devotion to that particular objective, so often affirmed, has usually been acknowledged as perhaps his most legitimate claim to the gratitude of his countrymen. However, it was the cultivation of discord and disunity by his followers in Quebec, especially in 1925, that spelled the difference for him between a defeat that might have meant oblivion and survival by a narrow margin that permitted the rest of his extraordinary career to assume the shape it did. For had the Conservatives in Quebec taken the fifteen ridings they expected to in 1925 King's day in power would have been over, for the time being anyway, and the crisis of 1926 with all its consequences would not have occurred. Thus there was no particular mystery or magic about King's success, no superhuman perception or political genius behind it. It rested simply on the hold which the Liberal party had over the Province of Quebec, a hold maintained in part by a flood of mendacity seldom if ever matched, at a time when the balance of public favour almost everywhere else was swinging towards Meighen and the Conservatives. This was an example of the practice described by the late John Farthing in a book deserving of a wider audience than it has received: "By no desire or intent of either [of the two peoples], differences have been used as a political lever with which to uproot or distort the essential traditions of the contrasting cultures, not in the interest of unity, but for the purpose of ensuring the perpetuity of power to one political group. Such a design may be the work of some kind of genius, but it is not a work that commends itself to honourable men of any race or tongue under heaven, or to any who have the slightest real desire for unity."[9]

Since Mackenzie King seems to have left affairs in Quebec pretty much to others, it cannot be said that he directly inspired the campaigning methods used by his friends there—the fostering of grievances, the exploitation and magnification of resentments, the sowing of suspicions that could only deepen and perpetuate disharmony, the assassination of Meighen's character by the telling of tall tales about what he had done and of taller prophecies of what he would do if in power. But elsewhere King himself advanced the cause of national unity in some rather peculiar ways. Unity is not served by crying that one's opponents are forever bent on its destruction or by falsely raising the spectre of disunity, as was King's invariable habit. The jagged edges of passion and animosity are not made smoother by constant reminders of the wounds they have inflicted in the past or by predictions that if one's opponent is elected the wounds will be reopened to fester and destroy. "The true unity of a nation," Farthing wrote, "can never be built on a basic assumption of disunity, and still less on the perpetuation of a situation marked by irreconcilable conflict. Yet that is precisely the basis on which the founder of the Kingsian school fabricated his false structure of Canadian unity; that is the basis of what still persists as the problem of Canadian unity. . . . But a problem is never to be resolved on the assumption of insolubility, and . . . unity will not be found by those who conceive of unity as but a means of attaining to power through a persisting threat of disunity."[10] It was ever King's custom to attribute to others what he was actually engaged in doing himself. The belief that he steadfastly promoted unity in Canada is a myth and a delusion.

Was Meighen responsible for his downfall or could it be ascribed "to others, or to the community or to the country"? Brooding over 1926 and all that had gone before, he could not bring himself to believe that, everything considered, he was really to blame. In this the weight of evidence is on his side.

No sooner had Meighen announced his retirement from public life than he began to receive offers of partnerships in law firms in different parts of the country, and also quite a lot of gratuitous but well-meant advice as to where he should settle and what he should do. One of the most attractive proposals came from Winnipeg but he declined it because, as he explained, "Winnipeg does not appeal to me as a place to live in now. . . ."[11] Another tempting one which he would have considered seriously had it not reached him too late was made by Leon J. Ladner, a Vancouver lawyer and Member of Parliament, who envisaged an amalgamation of his own firm and another with Meighen as senior member and counsel.[12] "While I am aware," Meighen told him, "that the possibilities of getting to a leading place in Law are rather more favourable in Toronto and Montreal than elsewhere, I have a great liking for Vancouver and quite agree with you that it probably presents the best prospects for the future, especially for the rising generation, of any city in Canada. Further, the suggestion you make is one that would have suited me perfectly." However, he had in the meantime "almost closed out an arrangement which takes me to Toronto. It has not as yet reached the stage of a final decision, but I have led my associates there to believe that [it] is almost, if not practically, certain. . . ."[13]

The Toronto proposition, which Meighen accepted, came from Watson Evans, President of Canadian General Securities Limited, an investment banking firm. Almost immediately after resigning as Prime Minister he went to Toronto where he had a long conversation with Evans about the affairs of the company and its future, and in November he accepted appointment as its vice-president and general counsel.

Accordingly the Meighens prepared to move. The house on Cooper Street which had been their home for eleven years, was sold and their personal belongings packed up. The two boys were not involved, Ted having gone to Quebec city and Max being enrolled at Royal Military College, but by the end of November Meighen, his wife and Lillian were installed in a rented house on Walmer Road in Toronto. Meighen had prudently decided not to invest in property there until he knew for sure that he was going to remain with Watson Evans. There was a good deal of speculation that he would not, that he would find the temptation to return to public life in some capacity irresistible. There were so many such rumours that he took occasion to deny that he had any intention of returning. "Sometimes," he said, "the hour strikes for a man when the best service he can render is to let someone else serve; that hour has struck for me."[14] But the belief persisted that the hour would strike for him to come back. This was the opinion, one would almost gather, the desire, of Dafoe of the *Free Press,* who wrote an editorial predicting that Meighen would return, as Winston Churchill, Herbert Asquith and Arthur Balfour had returned to British politics after suffering defeat.

> He has been Prime Minister, he is familiar with the most delicate parts of the political mechanism, he is profoundly learned in the intricacies of the national business; he has the inside positions and the most exclusive knowledge. He has got all this from nineteen years' work at Canadian politics; they represent, really, his professional stock-in-trade, and they are, after all, things for which, like surgery, like engineering, there is a national demand. Skill will not die easily in a man; it craves its outlet; and some day Mr. Meighen's skill will fret in him for usage, and then his attitude towards a political resumption will be less philosophic, less tinged with melancholy resignation.[15]

However, Meighen was genuinely interested in his new work. The challenge of making good at something entirely different from what he had ever done before appealed to him strongly, especially with the outlook as promising as it was in the developing boom of the late 1920's. Concerning an intimation that he might find a congenial place in the public life of England he wrote: ". . . I have sometimes regretted that my lot was not cast in England, because I would have enjoyed my Parliamentary career there more than in Canada. The population is British throughout and more responsive to British election methods and what one might describe as legitimate electioneering, than is the population of Canada. However, public life has its trials there as here, and by far the best course is neither to feel nor to utter a complaint. One can, by keeping busy and by concentration, become a master even of the art of forgetting."[16] But he could not really forget, no matter how busy he was. "I am entirely engrossed in this work," he assured R. B. Hanson, "and quite content with my lot." Just then, however, came a twinge of wistful nostalgia as he thought of Hanson and all the others battling it out in the House of Commons. "Suppose it would be different if I got among my old friends in the familiar haunts of Ottawa."[17]

Speculation about Meighen's possible return to politics increased as the time for the Conservative national convention approached in the autumn of 1927 and there were reports that he would not be averse to resuming the leadership if it should be thrust upon him. There was no foundation for these stories. He planned to stay with Canadian General Securities and in the late summer bought a fine house in Toronto, on Castle Frank Crescent overlooking the Rosedale ravine. "As acts speak more loudly than words," commented the Ottawa *Journal* à propos of this purchase, "Mr. Meighen has thus said more impressively than anybody else that he is not in the race for the leadership of the Conservative party."[18] "I don't intend to be a candidate for the Leadership at this Convention," he assured Ted. "It is impossible for me not to know that to secure it would be a very easy matter. I don't think I would be in a very strong position if I did secure it, and I don't think my accepting it would seem to the public very consistent with my retirement last fall. It is not impossible that at some time later I will feel like going back, but I don't think the time has come yet, and I may never feel like returning. One never knows."[19] He did not at first expect even to attend the convention, which was scheduled to open in Winnipeg on October the tenth. Although he knew that other dignitaries of the party from Sir Robert Borden down had been invited to be present on the platform, no invitation reached him until belatedly the committee in charge of arrangements decided in its wisdom that they would have to include him in the company. "As yet," he told Hugh Clark early in September, "I have had no communication from the Committee whatever—nothing but the usual circular letters from the secretary. It would look to me from this as if they thought the Convention would be better without me. Sir Robert Borden has been asked to be present, which I think was quite right. Under these circumstances you will realize that I don't feel very much like going, and . . . don't think it possible for me to go."[20]

Within a few days, however, he changed his mind. The committee duly invited him to be present in Winnipeg and to speak, and General A. D. McRae, M.P., chairman of the sub-committee on organization for the convention, called on him in his office to second the invitation. "The situation is now changed," Meighen reported to Clark. "The Committee has sent me the best possible form of letter, and I have had a call from the Chairman. I will be at Winnipeg all right."[21] His purpose in addressing the convention, as he informed McRae who raised no objection, would be to defend the Hamilton speech, which he knew had been widely blamed for the loss of the 1926 election. McRae evidently passed

the word along for when Meighen arrived at Winnipeg he was button-
holed by several delegates who urged him not to speak on that subject.
They feared that what was supposed to be a resurrection might turn into
an inquest instead, but he was determined to go on despite these entreaties and in spite of the fact that his name did not appear at all on the
official programme of the convention as one of those slated to address it.

The rickety old Amphitheatre Rink on Whitehall Avenue in Winnipeg was lavishly bedecked with flags and bunting, "transformed into a
great expanse of light and beauty" according to one description which,
if accurate, testified to the rare ingenuity and imaginativeness of the
decorating committee.[22]   There were about 2,500 delegates and alter-
nates on hand, along with a large complement of distinguished figures
in the party who were there as guests, and a very sizable contingent of
newspaper reporters from every corner of the country.   The platform at
the opening session on the morning of October the tenth was dominated
by the imposing, granitic presence of Borden, who was surrounded by
the three Conservative premiers—Ferguson of Ontario, Rhodes of Nova
Scotia, Baxter of New Brunswick—, the party leaders from the other
provinces, a sprinkling of former Lieutenant-Governors and a great
assortment of Privy Councillors.   Meighen had not yet made an appearance.   After the election of temporary officers, various addresses of welcome and replies thereto, Borden spoke briefly with all the weighty
authority of an elder statesman.   Among other topics he referred to the
obligation of the party to its leader, perhaps having in mind not only
some of his own experience but also what he knew to have been Meighen's.
"Once the Leader is selected you should stand by him.   Being human,
he may not always be right, but you are also human and sometimes when
you think he is wrong, he may be right.   Remember that he is primarily
responsible for policy.   There are great principles, of course, to which
the Liberal-Conservative Party has always been committed, but, as our
country develops, new considerations arise and a fresh outlook is necessary."[23]

At the outset of his remarks Borden observed that "in all his experience he had never seen anything so delightfully harmonious as the
opening of the present convention."[24]   The newspapermen watching the
proceedings, however, were struck less by the harmony prevailing than by
the listlessness, the lack of enthusiasm.   If this first morning session was
any indication, it looked as though they were in for a dull three days.
But shortly after lunch all the listlessness and a good deal of the harmony
abruptly vanished.   No sooner had the afternoon meeting started than
there was a commotion, a burst of cheering, at the far corner of the hall
from the platform.   Everybody craned his head in that direction and a

murmur passed rapidly through the crowd: "It's Meighen." Briskly down the aisle he came as the great crowd rose in a standing ovation, its cheers bursting wave on wave and swelling to a roaring crescendo as he climbed the steps to the platform and shook hands with Hugh Guthrie. "In that moment," one reporter wrote, "the convention was born, became alive, took a fire of enthusiasm which kindled it as nothing else had done."[25] As Meighen advanced to the microphone the demonstration went on and he stood there for more than two minutes, calmly, confidently, with a wistful half-smile on his face, acknowledging with nods of the head the tumultuous applause, the cheers and the shouts which reverberated up and down the hall. Someone struck up "For He's a Jolly Good Fellow" and the crowd joined in lustily. Then the Quebec delegation sang "Il a gagné ses épaulettes" while they waved hats and handkerchiefs in the air, Armand Lavergne acting as conductor and cheerleader. It was the high moment of the convention, a remarkable display of regard for a man who, in the popular imagination, was coldly intellectual and incapable of arousing "heart loyalty."

When the noise at last subsided Meighen began to speak. He both looked and sounded different from the haggard, weary fighter of the last election. He was a little heavier, having added to the meagre 128 pounds he had weighed when stumping the country in 1926. His cheeks were fuller, his face was no longer lined with fatigue, his voice had lost the rasping huskiness that beset him on a strenuous speaking tour. Retirement seemed to be agreeing with him physically, whatever nostalgia for the old scenes and the old faces he might feel. But his manner of speaking had not changed nor had his idea of what a speech should be. He started out quietly as was his custom, his voice rising, his manner becoming more forceful as the argument was developed, emphasizing the points he had to make less with gestures of the hands than with a bending of the knees. He was in his true element again, with something controversial to say in defence of his own record as a public man.

His defence of the proposal he had made at Hamilton—that a government having decided on participation in war should go to the people in a general election before troops left the country—rested on four facts. The first was that it had never been and was not likely to be Canadian policy to maintain a large standing army capable of fighting a war. Consequently "this country cannot send troops to participate abroad except after many long weeks of training and organization," long enough for a general election to take place. Secondly, an election would "not mean any delay or weakening of executive action, of preparation or of training. The experience of 1917 demonstrated clearly that not only preparations for the conflict, but, indeed, the conflict itself, may be carried on with relentless vigour while the judgment of the electors is being secured." His third fact was the big one.

> There exists in this country an apprehension, altogether unwarranted we all know, and most unjust, that if a Parliament is elected whose majority is Conservative, that Parliament is likely to plunge the country into war. This fiction has been dinned into the minds of vast numbers of our people, especially in the great Province of Quebec, by Liberal leaders and by the Liberal Press. A slander more malicious has never before stained the pages of our political history, but this very poisoning of the wells has been the chief occupation of Liberal leaders in that province for years, and their conduct has had its effect. It has had its effect especially on large sections of the women of our country. Such an apprehension in the minds of our people, whether French-Canadian or English-Canadian, is not only unjust to the Conservative party, but it is bad for Canada and it is bad for the Empire. Here, far away in Winnipeg, it may not be easy to realize how deeply seated this impression, this apprehension, has become, but there is not one man who knows this Dominion and has moved among all its people, who will not agree that I have understated rather than overstated the truth.

Finally, the Borden government in 1914 had been on the verge of adopting the very procedure Meighen had advocated at Hamilton in 1925. "It is not divulging any secret to say that the Conservative Government of that time never were closer to any step which was not taken than a decision to get the vote of the people approving of its course, and their mandate to carry on."

Reasoning on the basis of these facts, Meighen went on to defend his proposal and to answer one by one the various criticisms of it that had been made. The heart of his case was contained in two paragraphs.

> . . . Surely it is worth while of itself to demonstrate to the electors of a British country that their constitutional control of that country is real and not merely a sham. There may be nations where an autocracy is possible, but never a nation of British people. I know that no one suggests autocracy in Canada, but it is to my mind tremendously important that the voters of Canada do not harbour the idea that their control is nominal and farcical or applies only to matters of minor concern. There is nothing so certain to breed discontent as a belief down in the hearts of a people that they are not being trusted in the matter of great public policies, that they are victims of a pretense; that the very principle of democratic control is flouted at will by those in authority; and that while the masses are allowed to speak on matters of trivial consequence, they are really given no voice and are even warned in advance that they will have no voice when it comes to a question of great and momentous import. It is this very feeling which is the prolific breeder of suspicion and discontent and has been many times the mother of disturbance. So I say it is abundantly worth while in this country that

there go forth an assurance to the great masses of our people, men and women, that democratic control in Canada is not a farce and that their immediate responsibility is real and vital. I speak these words after many years of close contact with our affairs, and I believe the principle I am now trying to expound is not a mere lifeless platitude, not the empty heraldry of a demagogue, but a great and living truth.

Still further let me say that, in this Dominion, with its varied racial composition and in presence of the consequences of many years of propaganda designed to create in the minds especially of one of our two great parent races distrust of a Conservative majority in respect of this very issue, it surely is doubly important that the whole people be given renewed assurance that they will not be ignored. Speaking with a confidence born of some years of practical experience, a confidence which it is just possible a few years of trial will generate in others, I say it is worth while to quiet apprehensions honestly held by large and estimable sections of our country; that it tends to unity, harmony and goodwill to have all assured that these apprehensions are the product of nothing but mischievous party propaganda, and that in fact as well as in name the people are the real rulers of Canada.

Now, having made his defence, Meighen concluded with some words that were in the nature of a personal valedictory.

For almost two years I have been silent, but must now make plain to this Convention that if what I have said this afternoon is made the subject of attack, I claim the right to reply and intend from this platform to exercise that right.

To conclude, I will venture a word of some personal significance. It is spoken under the influence, perhaps under the handicap, of deep feeling. It has never been my custom, nor have I the needed gift, to kindle fires of sentiment or of passion. Whatever resources I may have were intended for another kind of appeal. But extraordinary occasions bring products meet for themselves, and this is a great and extraordinary occasion, moving in its retrospect, moving in the wonder of its outlook to none perhaps so much as to myself.

This great party is being born anew. Dark years of strife and cloud and pain lie behind it as they lie behind our country, behind the Empire, behind the scarred and suffering world. Among such years my lot of service and of leadership, and the task of my colleagues were cast. It was ours to cope with the subtle and sinister forces of the post-war interval, amid which all men, all parties, all nations were staggering to their feet. It is probable, far more than probable, that errors may have marked my course. But now that I stand apart, after nearly two decades, from public office and heavy responsibility, there is this conviction within me which means a great deal; I can look in the face of the Conservative party, of the whole Canadian people, and all the world who care to listen, and say there was no falsity or faltering, no act, no deed, no episode over which the pen of history need be shaded, no period or place into which the keenest enquirer may not go. There was no matter over which now I want to make petition. The book can be closed and I am content.

Looking again to the future, and bringing up the past only to shed its light, let me say: There will be more danger on the side of the party itself than on the side of the leader you will choose. Even here at this Convention the supreme consideration is not: who shall be the leader of this party? The supreme consideration is: what manner of party shall he have to lead? The chords of memory unite us with the past, and this is the time and this the place when all of us . . . should catch the spirit and hear the voice of the noble founders of our political faith. . . . If those men could speak . . . they would plead that we be loyal to each other and to those who serve for us. They would urge us to be conscious of our mighty heritage, proud of the Imperial Fountain of our freedom and of the flag that floats above us, worthy of those ideals of British liberty and justice which have sent their light forth and their truth among all races of men. To our history, our principles, our traditions let us be faithful to the end.

The speech, which occupied an hour and twenty minutes, had been frequently punctuated by applause, the Quebec contingent leading the way. As Meighen turned from the rostrum a fresh tide of enthusiasm swept over the audience, many of whom stood clapping frantically and cheering at the top of their lungs. At the height of this noise the short, pudgy figure of Howard Ferguson was seen to rise from its chair on the platform and make for the microphone. Ferguson, perhaps hoping to head off an incipient movement to draft Meighen for the leadership, looked like an angry cherub standing there, his rimless spectacles glinting in the light, as he struggled to gain the attention of the crowd. When he had done so he began to pour out his wrath. He had advised Meighen beforehand in 1925, he recalled, that what he proposed to say at Hamilton was "inappropriate" and "inadvisable." He had listened to the present defence of the Hamilton speech with profound regret. He objected to Meighen's "dragging in a corpse two years buried." "If Mr. Meighen can unnecessarily get on this platform and unnecessarily throw a firebrand into the peaceful spirit of this convention—" At this point there was a chorus of interruptions and a Saskatchewan delegate climbed on a chair and shouted, "Three cheers for Arthur Meighen!" A mixture of cheers and jeers echoed through the hall. "Sit down!" several voices called out. "Oh no," said Ferguson, "I won't sit down. I propose—" Again he was drowned out in an uproar of sound and fury, as demonstrations of support for Meighen were met by counter-demonstrations in Ferguson's favour.

In the midst of this bedlam J. B. M. Baxter got up from his place on the platform and had a word with the unfortunate chairman, N. K. Boyd, who was standing by helplessly. Thus prompted, Boyd pleaded with the convention to give Ferguson a fair hearing. "I propose to make my position clear," the latter resumed when the crowd had become comparatively silent. "If the Convention chooses to endorse Mr. Meighen, I would dissociate myself entirely from the activities of this Convention." With that Ferguson stumped, scowling, back to his seat while renewed disorder rocked the hall, partisans on either side vying with each other to show their spirit.[26]

After this unscheduled excitement it was not easy for the convention to settle down to the humdrum task of electing its committees and permanent officers; it was like following caviar with porridge. However, these things were done and the afternoon sitting adjourned. Immediately Meighen was surrounded by well-wishers, pumping his hand, congratulating him on his speech and urging him excitedly to stand for the leadership. And one French-Canadian woman was so agitated that she embraced him impulsively and said: "Je suis de Québec, mais je t'adore!" That evening and the next morning he was besieged by people wanting him to let his name stand and he believed that, had he given the word, he could have carried the convention and been reinstalled. He would have been more than human had he not been deeply affected by all the evidence of respect and confidence given him by the delegates as he strode down the aisle and stood before them and by the importunities of so many that he accept a nomination. To these, however, he turned a deaf ear; he had made his choice and had no alternative but to abide by it.

Meighen was probably not surprised, assuredly he had no right to be, to find himself taken severely to task for his performance by a number of Conservative newspaper editors. It was to be expected that the two English-language dailies in Montreal should view it with disfavour and alarm, and they did. The *Star* warmly complimented Ferguson for rescuing the convention from the emotionalism that Meighen's appearance on the scene and his address had aroused,[27] and the *Gazette*, when the convention was over, declared that it had been a great success despite "the most mischievous intervention. The unfortunate attempt made on Monday to divert the attention of the assembly to a personal grievance, and the unexpected reaction of the convention to that attempt, threatened to wreck the convention and might easily have done so."[28] The Toronto *Telegram*, whose editor, "Black Jack" Robinson—"the wild man who controls that paper," Meighen called him[29]—suffered paroxysms of rage whenever he thought of the Hamilton speech, chastised those at the convention who had cheered Meighen on. "Too many Conservative delegates . . . represented themselves and misrepresented their party in applause for the sentiments of the Hon. Arthur Meighen's Hamilton

speech and in hoots and hisses for the words of Howard Ferguson's protest against that speech. Such Canadian Conservative delegates were no
more delegates than they were Canadians or Conservatives."[30]   The
Winnipeg *Tribune,* which had been so upset over what Meighen had
said at Hamilton, now implied that he had deliberately waited to speak
on the subject again until the convention assembled so as to be able to
throw a monkey wrench into the proceedings, though it did not explain
why he should wish to do so.[31]

Not the least indignant of the many who were annoyed by Meighen's
action was the new leader chosen by the convention, R. B. Bennett. Upon
arriving at Winnipeg Meighen learned that Bennett was angrily opposed
to his speaking and the reception given Meighen must have been somewhat disconcerting to the man who confidently expected to be the new
chief of the party and the hero of the convention. After returning to
Toronto Meighen wrote to Bennett, congratulating him on his election
and remarking that he had all along looked forward to his being chosen.
He also expressed surprise that Bennett should have objected "to my
making a reasoned and certainly a non-provocative speech in my own
defence."[32]   This letter Bennett did not trouble to acknowledge but he
may well have reflected that if that had been a non-provocative speech
it was to be hoped that Meighen would never feel compelled to make
a provocative one.

Having had the satisfaction of unburdening himself in answer to his
critics and no longer having to bother much about what newspaper editors thought of him, Meighen wasted no time worrying over the hostile
editorial comments that burst from the pages of a section of the Conservative press. And there was, in any case, the additional satisfaction of
knowing, from the mail he received, that what he had said at Winnipeg,
as well as his having gone ahead and said it there, met with widespread
approval. One of the congratulatory letters he most appreciated came
from William Irvine, Labour member of Parliament from 1921 to 1925
and now back in the House again as a United Farmers of Alberta member
after having been defeated in 1925. Although he and Meighen were
usually far apart in their opinions about national policies he had more
than once over the years taken the trouble to drop Meighen a word of
congratulation or encouragement. Now someone had sent him a copy of
the convention speech and this provided him with a reason to write
again.

> As you may have noticed, I take great pleasure in the art of speaking,
> and have read the classics, and when all the circumstances of your
> address are considered, it stands as one of the best I have ever had
> the pleasure of reading. I have read it twice to-day, once aloud to

an audience of M.P.'s. It is a model in all the essential elements of the high art of oratory.

It has often been in my mind to write to you since last election, but some way or another I scarcely knew how to address you under the circumstances. But having just received a copy of your speech to-day, the opportunity to write to you has come in a very natural way. But before passing from the thought of your address, may I say that if I could achieve a triumph like that before I "shuffle off", I should think that life had been well worth while even if it yielded no other. Logical order, masterly argument, not cursed with superfluity or slush, built on a high plane, the right tone and the "inevitable word" in every sentence—this is a real oration.

Frankly and sincerely I regret the unfortunate combination of circumstances which has deprived Canada of your high gifts in that capacity in which you so recently served. Nor am I the only one with regrets. Even your bitterest foes—and you have some of them as all real men in public life have—have to concede that we have no one in Canadian public life so highly gifted. In spite of your splendid pleas for the democratic principle, to which I also adhere, it must be said that democracy at times is an unmitigated ass.

Well I must not allow this letter to become "slushy" with encomiums, coming too late to be of use. However, I have never regarded your resignation as the end of your public career. The issue and the hour will strike for you again, if you so desire. In spite of all, you hold the imagination of the Canadian people. . . . They will call on you again, and when they do I hope you will see your way to respond.[33]

But Meighen had no thought of being called back to public life. He had said farewell to politics, as he had earlier to teaching and then to the practice of law; he was now well launched on a fourth career, in business, which was proving to be both rewarding and interesting. He had given what he had to give in the public service without stint and what he had offered to the people had in the end been rejected. Sitting in his Bay Street office he felt remote and cut off from official Ottawa, and even from the Conservative party; he knew of no reason to doubt that a final period had been written to that chapter in the book of his life.

KEY TO ABBREVIATIONS USED IN THE NOTES

A.M.P.   Arthur Meighen Papers (Public Archives of Canada).

C.A.R.   *The Canadian Annual Review of Public Affairs,* J. Castell Hopkins, ed. Toronto: Annual Review Publishing Co. Ltd.

C.D.   *Canada, Debates of the House of Commons.*

N.M.   Notes and memoranda prepared for the author by the late Rt. Hon. Arthur Meighen.

P.A.C.   Public Archives of Canada.

NOTES

CHAPTER I: A TROUBLED LEGACY

[1] Meighen to Sir John Willison, Nov. 26, 1920 (Willison Papers, Public Archives of Canada, hereinafter cited as P.A.C.).

[2] See *Arthur Meighen, a Biography*, vol. I: *The Door of Opportunity, 1874-1920*, Roger Graham (Toronto: Clarke, Irwin & Co. Ltd., 1960), pp. 283 ff.

[3] R. L. Richardson to Meighen, Sept. 23, 1920, personal (Arthur Meighen Papers, hereinafter cited as *A.M.P.*, P.A.C.).

[4] J. A. Calder to Meighen, n.d. but received Oct. 9, 1920 (*ibid.*).

[5] C. A. C. Jennings to Meighen, Oct. 5, 1920 (*ibid.*).

[6] Meighen to Jennings, Oct. 7, 1920 (*ibid.*).

[7] Meighen to A. McAllister, May 28, 1921 (*ibid.*).

[8] W. A. Buchanan to Meighen, Nov. 4, 1920, personal and confidential; Meighen to Buchanan, Nov. 9, 1920 (*ibid.*).

[9] Meighen to J. L. Stansell, Sept. 24, 1920, personal (*ibid.*).

[10] *Daily Graphic* (Portage la Prairie), Aug. 3, 1920.

[11] *C.A.R.* (1920), p. 413.

[12] *Ibid.*, p. 412.

[13] *Ibid.*

[14] Copy of speech at Truro, N.S. (*A.M.P.*, P.A.C.).

[15] John Nelson to Meighen, Oct. 20, 1920 (*ibid.*).

[16] H. P. Whidden to Meighen, Nov. 6, 1920 (*ibid.*).

[17] Meighen to Whidden, Nov. 10, 1920 (*ibid.*).

[18] Meighen to Mrs. Robert Reford, Nov. 11, 1920 (*ibid.*).

[19] John MacNaughton to Meighen, Dec. 9, 1920 (*ibid.*).

[20] The writer of the letter apparently preferred not to give Graham his noble title of Baron Atholstan.

[21] Gaston Maillet to Meighen, Jan. 26, 1921, personal (*A.M.P.*, P.A.C.).

[22] J. F. Bissonnette to Meighen, Jan. 13, 1921, private and confidential (*ibid.*).

[23] Meighen to Mrs. Robert Reford, Nov. 11, 1920 (*ibid.*).

[24] E. L. Patenaude to Meighen, Sept. 16, 1920 (*ibid.*).

[25] Meighen to Patenaude, Oct. 22, 1920 (*ibid.*).

[26] Telegram, C. J. Doherty to Meighen, Oct. 27, 1920; telegram, Meighen to Doherty, Oct. 27, 1920; telegram, Doherty to Patenaude, Oct. 28, 1920 (*ibid.*).

[27] *Le Canada* (Montreal), Sept. 25, 1920. Quotations from a translation in the Meighen Papers. For a discussion of some of the matters referred to in this editorial see Roger Graham, *op. cit.*, pp. 163-70, 255-60

[28] See *ibid.*, pp. 250 ff.

[29] For example Aimé Dion *et al.* to Meighen, April 5, 1921 (*A.M.P.*, P.A.C.).

[30] *C.D.* (1921), vol. IV, pp. 3480-1.

[31] *Gazette* (Montreal), Oct. 9, 1925. Affidavit sworn to by L. P. Bernard. Meighen confirmed for the author Bernard's account of what took place.

[32] Meighen to G. H. Boivin, Sept. 19, 1921, personal (*A.M.P.*, P.A.C.).

[33] C. G. Power to the author, Sept. 8, 1952. I am indebted to Senator Power for permission to quote from this letter.

[34] H. B. Thomson to Meighen, Feb. 10, 1921, personal (*A.M.P.*, P.A.C.). On a copy of this letter submitted by the author to Meighen for his comments he wrote: "Good advice. . . . Fact is I did my utmost to press our men into combative service. A capacity to fight aggressively is possessed by few. Our ablest gladiators had dropped out (Liberal Unionists) or had been overworked. The situation was even worse after the election [of 1921]. I *had to* be over combative by reason of over modesty in the rank and file."

[35] F. D. L. Smith to Meighen, Feb. 7, 1921 (*ibid.*).

[36] C. G. Power to the author, Sept. 8, 1952.

[37] Quoted in *The Globe* (Toronto), July 9, 1920.

[38] S. C. Mewburn to Meighen, July 14, 1920 (*A.M.P.*, P.A.C.).

[39] Meighen to Mewburn, July 17, 1920 (*ibid.*).

[40] Meighen to Mewburn, July 26, 1920 (*ibid.*).

[41] F. B. McCurdy to Meighen, Aug. 13, 1920 (*ibid.*).

[42] Garrett Tyrrell to Meighen, Aug. 4, 1920 (*ibid.*).

[43] W. C. Mikel to Meighen, Feb. 8, 1921, personal (*ibid.*).

[44] F. A. Collins to Meighen, Jan. 21, 1921 (*ibid*)

[45] S. E. Richards to Meighen, Feb. 5, 1921 (*ibid.*).

[46] W. W. Richardson to Meighen, Feb. 9, 1921 (*ibid.*).

[47] Meighen to Richardson, Feb. 12, 1921 (*ibid.*).

[48] F. L. Schaffner to Meighen, June 3, 1921 (*ibid.*).

[49] Meighen to Schaffner, June 4, 1921 (*ibid.*).

[50] W. H. Dennis to Meighen, July 29, 1920 (*ibid.*).

[51] Meighen to J. J. Garland, Feb. 11, 1921, private (*ibid.*).

[52] J. H. Burnham to Meighen, July 8, 1920 (*ibid.*).

[53] Meighen to Burnham, July 19, 1920 (*ibid.*).

[54] Burnham to Meighen, July 22, 1920 (*ibid.*).

[55] Burnham to Meighen, Aug. 2, 1920; Meighen to Burnham, Aug. 9, 1920 (*ibid.*).

[56] Burnham to Meighen, Sept. 28, 1920, private (*ibid.*).

[57] Meighen to Burnham, Oct. 1, 1920 (*ibid.*).

[58] Meighen to S. D. Scott, Dec. 27, 1920 (*ibid.*).

[59] H. M. Mowat to Meighen, Feb. 8, 1921, private (*ibid.*).

[60] H. H. Stevens to Meighen, n.d. (*ibid.*).

[61] *C.A.R.* (1921), p. 368.

[62] B. F. Campbell to Meighen, May 31, 1921 (*A.M.P.*, P.A.C.).

[63] P. E. Blondin to Meighen, June 1, 1921, private (*ibid.*).

CHAPTER II: THE ANXIETY OF OFFICE

[1] Meighen to F. L. Schaffner, Sept. 25, 1920, personal (*A.M.P.*, P.A.C.).

[2] *C.D.* (1921), vol. I, p. 28.

[3] *Ibid.*, p. 32.

[4] *Ibid.*, pp. 27-8.

[5] *Ibid.*, p. 11.

[6] *Ibid.*, pp. 28-9.

[7] *Ibid.*, p. 33.

[8] *Ibid.*, vol. II, p. 1299.

[9] *Ibid.*, p. 1300.

[10] *Ibid.*, vol. IV, p. 3603.

[11] *Ibid.*, p. 3479.

[12] *Ibid.*, pp. 3155-6.

[13] *Ibid.*, pp. 3325 ff.

[14] Meighen to Sir John Willison, March 25, 1921 (*A.M.P.*, P.A.C.).

[15] *Canada, Sessional Papers* (1923), vol. 6, No. 32: "Annual Report of the Department of Railways and Canals, 1921-22," p. 20. This improvement was produced almost entirely by a decline in operating costs, although there was a slight increase in revenue. Lower costs were very largely accounted for by a drop in the payroll. This in turn resulted from two factors: a decrease of 7.66% in the number of employees, presumably made possible in the main by unification of the various lines; and a wage reduction of about 10.5% which became effective on North American railways generally in July 1921.

[16] *Ibid.*, p. 30. Cf. the statement by R. MacGregor Dawson in *William Lyon Mackenzie King, A Political Biography* (Toronto: University of Toronto Press, 1958), p. 389: "Legislation had been passed in 1919 authorizing the operation of these roads as one system; but two and a half years later, when the Meighen Government went out of office, nothing had been done." Although allowance must be made for Hanna's natural desire to put the best possible face on things, the Annual Reports of the Department of Railways and Canals indicate that his words are closer to the truth than Professor Dawson's and that the King Government had merely to carry to its fulfilment a process of railway unification which was well on the way to completion when it took office in December 1921. When King some years afterwards made the claim, later echoed by his biographer, that the whole task of unification had yet to be performed when he first came to power, Meighen made the following comments: "The Grand Trunk Acquisition Bill was before Parliament when Mr. King returned to the House after nearly nine years' absence. The first speech he made on his return was against the Bill. That speech ought to be read by anyone who really wishes to get his measure. . . . This Bill provided for the acquisition of the Grand Trunk, and contained a clause whereby the Governor-in-Council could declare the road part of the National System after the arbitration as to the value of the junior securities was completed. . . . Parliament was distinctly informed that . . . the Order-in-Council could not be put through until the arbitration was decided. This arbitration was on in 1921, and the decision was

appealed . . . to the Privy Council, and the Privy Council's judgement was returned only in May 1922, or five months after the King Government got into office. They waited until October and . . . passed the Order-in-Council which they were enabled to pass under our Bill, which Bill they had themselves resisted to the last ounce of their strength. Mr. King now says that he found the railways disjointed; that we had failed to bring in the Grand Trunk; and that he is the father of the unification. . . . It is fortunate that Hansard exists, because otherwise King would succeed in falsifying history. It would baffle the ingenuity of the most sinister of criminals to invent a course of conduct more alien in [*sic*] moral sense than that which has characterized Mr. King's whole relationship to the nationalization of our Railways." Meighen to G. R. Geary, May 27, 1929 (*A.M.P.*, P.A.C.).

[17] The foregoing quotations are from copies of the correspondence in *ibid*.

[18] *C.D.* (1921), vol. III, p. 2250.

[19] Shaughnessy to Meighen, April 6, 1921 (*A.M.P.*, P.A.C.).

[20] Shaughnessy to Meighen, April 15, 1921 and April 20, 1921; Meighen to Shaughnessy, April 21, 1921 (*ibid*.).

[21] Meighen to J. C. Hodgins, April 27, 1921 (*ibid*.).

[22] Flavelle to Meighen, April 7, 1921 (*ibid*.).

[23] Flavelle to Meighen, March 30, 1921 (*ibid*.).

[24] Meighen to Flavelle, April 4, 1921 (*ibid*.).

[25] Flavelle to Meighen, May 16, 1921 (*ibid*.).

[26] Meighen to Flavelle, May 18, 1921 (*ibid*.).

[27] Flavelle to Meighen, May 30, 1921 (*ibid*.).

[28] *Ibid*.

CHAPTER III: PROBLEMS OF EMPIRE

[1] See Roger Graham, *op. cit.*, pp. 197 ff.

[2] *C.D.* (1920), vol. III, p. 2178.

[3] Sir Charles Gordon to Meighen, Feb. 24, 1921 (*A.M.P.*, P.A.C.).

[4] *C.D.* (1921), vol. III, p. 2431.

[5] *Ibid.*, p. 2401.

[6] *Ibid.*, pp. 2931-2.

[7] *Ibid.*, p. 2404.

[8] Bennett to Meighen, n.d. but probably Nov. 1921.

[9] *C.D.* (1921), vol. III, p. 2400.

[10] *Ibid.*, p. 2430.

[11] Rowell to Meighen, March 3, 1921 (*A.M.P.*, P.A.C.).

[12] Meighen to Rowell, March 7, 1921 (*ibid*.).

[13] Telegram, Meighen to Borden, Nov. 7, 1921 (*ibid*.).

[14] Telegram, Borden to Meighen, Nov. 8, 1921 (*ibid*.).

[15] *The Development of Dominion Status, 1900-1936*, R. MacGregor Dawson (London, New York, Toronto: Oxford University Press, 1937), p. 175.

[16] See *Robert Laird Borden: His Memoirs*, Henry Borden, ed. (New York: Macmillan Co., 1938), vol. II, Chap. XXXVIII, and Roger Graham, *op. cit.*, Chap. XI.

[17] Governor-General to Colonial Secretary, Aug. 30, 1920, copy (*A.M.P.*, P.A.C.).

[18] *C.D.* (1921), vol. III, pp. 2504-05, 2637-8.

[19] *Ibid.*, pp. 2632-3.

[20] *Ibid.*, p. 2630.

[21] *Ibid.*, pp. 2633-4. There is no doubt that the British government intended naval policy to be one of the main subjects of the conference. It was placed second in a list of four on a proposed agenda sent out by Milner early in 1921. Colonial Secretary to Governor-General, Jan. 28, 1921, copy (*A.M.P.*, P.A.C.). The Canadian Minister of Marine, Ballantyne, told Meighen he agreed that defence should not be one the chief topics of discussion by the Prime Ministers. However, he pointed out, Australia regarded naval defence and the Anglo-Japanese Alliance as the two most important subjects. Ballantyne added that, along with ministers concerned from the other Dominions who would be present in London during the conference, he would probably have to engage in some consideration of naval defence with officials of the Admiralty. Ballantyne to Meighen, April 29, 1921 (*ibid.*).

[22] *C.D.* (1921), vol. III, pp. 2635-6.

[23] *Ibid.*, p. 2640.

[24] *Ibid.*, p. 2641.

[25] *Ibid.*, p. 2658.

[26] *Ibid.*, p. 2660.

[27] *Ibid.*, p. 2661.

[28] *Ibid.*, p. 2639.

[29] *Ibid.*, p. 2657.

[30] See *Canada and the Far East—1940*, A. R. M. Lower (New York: Institute of Pacific Relations, 1941), Chap. I.

[31] The view that it did not remove it was expressed by Bertram Lenox Simpson, a political adviser to the President of China, who argued that in the event of conflict between Japan and the United States, China would intervene against Japan and Great Britain would then be bound by the Alliance to enter the war against China, thus finding herself in effect at war with the United States. *C.A.R.* (1921), p. 99. See also Simpson's book, published under his pseudonym of Putnam Weale, *An Indiscreet Chronicle from the Pacific* (New York: Dodd, Mead & Co., 1922), pp. 59-60.

[32] See "Anglo-American-Canadian Relations, with Special Reference to Far Eastern and Naval Issues, 1918-1922," Michael G. Fry, Chap. VII. I am grateful to Mr. Fry for allowing me to make use of his forthcoming doctoral dissertation, and also for making available to me some of the important documentary material on which it is based.

[33] Governor-General to Colonial Secretary, Feb. 15, 1921, copy (Borden Papers, post-1921 series, reel 128, folder 253. Microfilm copy, University of Toronto Library).

[34] Colonial Secretary to Governor-General, Feb. 26, 1921, copy (*ibid.*).

[35] Memorandum, Christie to Meighen, March 3, 1921 (*ibid.*).

[36] Governor-General to Colonial Secretary, March 1921 (*ibid.*). The lack of a more precise date on this document may indicate that the message was not sent.

[37] Michael G. Fry, *loc. cit.*

[38] "Canada and the Conference," J. A. S[tevenson], *The New Statesman*, June 18, 1921, p. 296.

[39] In conversation with the author Meighen stated that he could not remember the suggestion that Borden accompany him having been made but that he would not have acceded to it for the reasons here given.

[40] Rowell to Meighen, Feb. 9, 1921 (*A.M.P.*, P.A.C.).

[41] See "Papers Respecting Conference of Prime Ministers, London, 1921" (*ibid.*). This is a bound volume of memoranda, etc., prepared by Christie for Meighen's use. Its contents indicate very considerable influence on Christie's part.

[42] Putnam Weale, *op. cit.*, pp. 52-3.

[43] Michael G. Fry, *loc. cit.*

[44] Dafoe to Brebner, April 25, 1935 (Dafoe Papers, P.A.C.).

[45] Brebner to Dafoe, April 30, 1935 (*ibid.*).

[46] Dispatch by Grattan O'Leary, Saskatoon *Phoenix*, June 15, 1921.

[47] *Manchester Guardian*, May 5, 1921. This statement was probably drafted by Christie. A version bearing emendations in Meighen's hand is in the bound volume of memoranda in the Meighen Papers referred to above. See note 41.

[48] *New Statesman*, June 18, 1921, p. 296.

CHAPTER IV: DEBUTANTE AND DOWAGERS

[1] Canadian Press dispatch, Saskatoon *Phoenix*, June 16, 1921.

[2] Clipping from unidentified English newspaper (Mrs. Meighen's scrapbooks).

[3] *Self-Portrait of an Artist: from her diaries and memoirs*, Kathleen Kennet (London: Musson, 1949). Transcript supplied by Mr. Meighen.

[4] Interview with John A. Stevenson, July 24, 1952.

[5] This and the opening statements of the other representatives are printed in the published summary, *Conference of the Prime Ministers etc.* (Cmd. 1474, H. M. Stationery Office, 1921), which contains material of very limited usefulness. The verbatim transcript of the proceedings has not yet been released from secrecy. Grattan O'Leary's dispatches to the Canadian Press show the good use a first-class journalist can make of reliable sources of information. An authoritative treatment of the discussions of the Anglo-Japanese Alliance, though in the opinion of the present writer it somewhat over-dramatizes the clash of ideas and personalities, exaggerating the measure of Meighen's triumph over W. M. Hughes, is "Canada the Anglo-Japanese Alliance and the Washington Conference," J. Bartlett Brebner, *Political Science Quarterly*, vol. L, No. 1 (March 1935). When this appeared Professor Brebner sent an offprint to Meighen, who wrote in acknowledgment: "It is a matter of amazement to me how you have succeeded in re-creating the scene of that period. My memory is fairly dependable and I cannot recall any feature of the series of proceedings covered by your article which is distorted or reproduced with the least infidelity. True, you do me honour much more than I deserve, but I may perhaps be permitted to observe that until your article appeared, I had received at the hands of the press and the historian rather less than I deserved. In truth I had quite given up all idea of any adequate account of those very important events ever being made known." Meighen to Brebner, March 20, 1935 (*A.M.P.*, P.A.C.). In addition the reader is referred to the following works: "The Imperial Conference of 1921 and the Washington Conference," John S. Galbraith, *Canadian Historical*

Review, vol. XXIX, No. 2 (June 1948); "More Light on the Abrogation of the Anglo-Japanese Alliance," Merze Tate and Fidele Foy, *Political Science Quarterly*, vol. LXXIV, No. 4 (Dec. 1959); "The Imperial Conference of 1921 and the Anglo-Japanese Alliance," J. Chal Vinson, *Pacific Historical Review*, vol. XXXI, No. 3 (August 1962). The most thorough treatment of the subject, as yet unpublished, will be found in Michael G. Fry, *op. cit.*, Chap. VII, which is based on a wider range of source material than are the other works mentioned here. See also *The Dominions and Diplomacy: the Canadian Contribution*, A. Gordon Dewey (London, New York, Toronto: Longmans, Green & Co., 1929), vol. II, pp. 62-80, and *The British Commonwealth and International Security: the Role of the Dominions 1919-1939*, Gwendolyn M. Carter (Toronto: Ryerson Press, 1947), pp. 37-47.

[6] *Development of Dominion Status*, R. M. Dawson, pp. 208-09; Cmd. 1474, pp. 9-10.

[7] *Canadian Constitutional Studies*, Sir Robert L. Borden (Toronto: University of Toronto Press, 1922), p. 113.

[8] *Ibid.*, pp. 115-16.

[9] On the very day that Meighen delivered this speech the House of Representatives approved the Resolution as an amendment to a Naval Appropriations Bill.

[10] Cmd. 1474, p. 19.

[11] Notes and memoranda prepared for the author by Arthur Meighen (hereinafter cited as *N.M.*), p. 100.

[12] Brebner, *op. cit.*, p. 57.

[13] C.B.C. broadcast, Aug. 11, 1960.

[14] W. L. Mackenzie King, had he been in Meighen's place, undoubtedly would have noted the coincidence and, with his predilection for seeing supernatural significance in such things, have regarded it as further proof that he was ever guided by an Invisible Hand.

[15] For this speech see *Unrevised and Unrepented: Debating Speeches and Others*, Arthur Meighen (Toronto: Clarke, Irwin & Co. Ltd., 1949), pp. 109 ff.

[16] It is remarkable that none of Curzon's biographers makes any reference whatever to the Anglo-Japanese Alliance, the Prime Ministers' Conference of 1921, or the genesis of the Washington Conference. See *Life of Lord Curzon*, Earl of Ronaldshay, 3 vols. (New York: Boni and Liveright; London: Ernest Benn Ltd., n.d.); *Curzon: the Last Phase, 1919-1925. A Study in Post-War Diplomacy*, Harold Nicolson (London: Constable & Co., 1934); *Glorious Fault: the Life of Lord Curzon*, Leonard Oswald Mosley (New York: Harcourt, Brace, 1960).

[17] *Charles Evans Hughes*, Merlo J. Pusey (New York: Macmillan Co., 1951), vol. II, p. 456.

[18] *A Diplomatic History of the American People*, Thomas A. Bailey (New York: Appleton-Century-Crofts, Inc., Fifth Edition, 1955), p. 688.

[19] *C.A.R.* (1921), pp. 108-09.

[20] Meighen to J. H. Woods *et al.*, July 19, 1921, personal (*A.M.P.*, P.A.C.).

[21] Cmd. 1474, p. 6.

[22] Quoted in dispatch by Grattan O'Leary, *Manitoba Free Press*, July 20, 1921.

[23] Fawcett Taylor to Meighen, Aug. 12, 1921, confidential (*A.M.P.*, P.A.C.).

[24] Meighen to Taylor, Aug. 15, 1921 (*ibid.*).

[25] Meighen to Lloyd George, Aug. 22, 1921. This cable and the subsequent correspondence are printed in *Development of Dominion Status*, R. M. Dawson, pp. 217-21. The quotations that follow are from this source unless otherwise acknowledged. For an excellent brief treatment of Dominion representation at the Washington Conference see G. M. Carter, *op. cit.*, pp. 47-50.

[26] Meighen to Lloyd George, Aug. 27, 1921.

[27] Lloyd George to Meighen, Oct. 3, 1921.

[28] Smuts to Meighen, Oct. 19, 1921.

[29] Memorandum from private secretary to Sir Jas. Lougheed to Prime Minister's office, Oct. 20, 1921 (*A.M.P.*, P.A.C.).

[30] Telegram, Meighen to Christie, Oct. 25, 1921 (*ibid.*).

[31] Meighen to Lloyd George, Oct. 27, 1921.

[32] Colonial Secretary to Governor-General, Oct. 26, 1921, copy (*A.M.P.*, P.A.C.).

[33] Transmitted in Sir George Perley to Meighen, July 6, 1921 (*ibid.*). Later Smuts wrote Borden that in London Meighen had been "depressed and hesitating" and "must have expected a set back. I liked him but he did not seem to have any real desire to ride the storm that was coming in Canada." Smuts to Borden, April 26, 1922 (Borden Papers, post-1921 series, reel 116, folder 69. Microfilm copy, University of Toronto Library).

[34] *Phoenix* (Saskatoon), Aug. 8, 1921.

[35] *C.A.R.* (1921), p. 220.

[36] *Ibid.*, p. 249.

[37] See "The Appointment of the Governor General: Responsible Government, Autonomy, and the Royal Prerogative," J. R. Mallory, *Canadian Journal of Economics and Political Science*, vol. 26, No. 1 (Feb. 1960), pp. 98-9.

[38] Meighen to Perley, March 28, 1921, confidential (*A.M.P.*, P.A.C.).

[39] Churchill to Meighen, March 25, 1921, private and confidential (*ibid.*).

[40] Mr. Meighen was unable to throw any light on this for the author. He was emphatic that he had selected Byng but the documents show that the selection was made only after other possibilities had fallen through.

[41] Devonshire to Meighen, May 5, 1921 (*A.M.P.*, P.A.C.).

[42] J. R. Mallory, *loc. cit.*

CHAPTER V: BACK TO EARTH IN OTTAWA

[1] Nelson Spencer to Meighen, Dec. 28, 1920 (*A.M.P.*, P.A.C.).

[2] Meighen to Spencer, June 3, 1921 (*ibid.*).

[3] George Buskard to Meighen, June 14, 1921 (*ibid.*).

[4] Meighen to C.A.C. Jennings, July 15, 1921, personal (*ibid.*). William Ivens was a former Methodist clergyman who was among those convicted of seditious conspiracy and imprisoned for their part in the Winnipeg general strike of 1919. In February 1921 he was paroled after being elected to the Manitoba legislature. Apparently he did not campaign in Medicine Hat but Meighen probably put him in this list as a sample of the kind of people the Progressives were associating with, and the kind of people who, in Meighen's opinion, would be influential if the Progressives came to power. Henry Wise Wood was President of the United Farmers of Alberta and the dominant agrarian leader in that province.

[5] H. H. Stevens to Meighen, July 11, 1921 (*ibid.*).

[6] Meighen to Stevens, Aug. 7, 1921 (*ibid.*).

[7] Memorandum, Aug. 22, 1921. Unsigned but bearing notation "Memorandum to be returned to Senator Sharpe" (*ibid.*).

[8] Drayton to Meighen, July 4, 1921, private and confidential (*ibid.*).

[9] *Phoenix* (Saskatoon), Sept. 15, 1921.

[10] J. J. Garland to Meighen, Sept. 3, 1921 (*A.M.P.*, P.A.C.).

[11] W. H. Dennis to Meighen, Sept. 16, 1921. Inscribed "For your personal consideration and strictly confidential" (*ibid.*).

[12] Meighen to Dennis, Sept. 19, 1921, personal (*ibid.*).

[13] C. A. B. Jennings to Meighen, Sept. 14, 1921 (*ibid.*).

[14] H. S. Clements to Meighen, July 13, 1920 (*ibid.*).

[15] Telegram, W. S. Montgomery to Meighen, Sept. 5, 1921 (*ibid.*).

[16] Meighen to Montgomery, Sept. 5, 1921 (*ibid.*).

[17] H. S. Clements to Meighen, Jan. 27, 1922 (*ibid.*).

[18] W. C. Mikel to Meighen, Oct. 6, 1921, personal (*ibid.*).

[19] George Buskard to Meighen, Oct. 4, 1921. Drayton lived in Toronto but represented Kingston in the Commons.

[20] W. A. Charlton to Meighen, Sept. 20, 1921 (*ibid.*).

[21] Meighen to Charlton, Sept. 21, 1921 (*ibid.*).

[22] J. W. Peart to Meighen, Sept. 14, 1921 (*ibid.*).

[23] Meighen to Peart, Sept. 19, 1921 (*ibid.*).

[24] *C.A.R.* (1921), p. 449.

[25] *Ibid.*, p. 458.

[26] *Ibid.*, p. 460.

[27] *William Lyon Mackenzie King*, R. M. Dawson, p. 353.

[28] King to Meighen, Oct. 21, 1921 (*A.M.P.*, P.A.C.).

[29] Telegram, Meighen to George Buskard, Oct. 22, 1921 (*ibid.*).

[30] Meighen to King, Oct. 22, 1921 (*ibid.*).

[31] *C.A.R.* (1921), pp. 496-7.

[32] *Ibid.*, p. 496.

[33] *Phoenix* (Saskatoon), Oct. 24, 1921.

[34] Hugh Guthrie to Meighen, Oct. 24, 1921 (*A.M.P.*, P.A.C.).

[35] Meighen to King, Oct. 25, 1921 (*ibid.*).

[36] Undated and unsigned memorandum (*ibid.*).

[37] *C.A.R.* (1921), p. 461.

[38] *Ibid.*

[39] *Ibid.*, p. 460.

[40] *Ibid.*, p. 457.

[41] *Ibid.*, pp. 459-60.

[42] *Ibid.*, p. 464.

[43] *Ibid.*, p. 462.

[44] E. H. Gurney to Meighen, Nov. 10, 1921, private and personal (*A.M.P.*, P.A.C.).

[45] *William Lyon Mackenzie King*, R. M. Dawson, p. 352.

[46] *Ibid.*

[47] *C.A.R.* (1921), p. 454.

[48] J. E. Walsh to George Buskard, Oct. 21, 1921; Buskard to Walsh, Oct. 25, 1921 (*A.M.P.*, P.A.C.).

[49] Meighen to W. H. Manning, Nov. 3, 1921 (*ibid.*).

[50] Meighen to Peter Cameron, Sept. 24, 1919 (*ibid.*).

[51] Meighen to Sir Thomas White, Sept. 5, 1919 (*ibid.*).

[52] Meighen to George Steele, Sept. 5, 1919 (*ibid.*).

[53] Meighen to W. H. Sharpe, Dec. 28, 1922 (*ibid.*).

[54] W. D. Staples to Meighen, Aug. 5, 1919, private (*ibid.*).

[55] Drayton to Meighen, Oct. 21, 1919 (*ibid.*).

[56] Meighen to Drayton, Oct. 22, 1919 (*ibid.*).

[57] Meighen to James Howie, Oct. 17, 1921 (*ibid.*).

[58] Meighen to Hugh McKellar, Jan. 20, 1921 (*ibid.*).

[59] *C.D.* (1919, second session), vol. I, p. 930.

[60] E. A. Partridge to Meighen, Oct. 20, 1921 (*A.M.P.*, P.A.C.).

[61] Meighen to Partridge, Oct. 29, 1921 (*ibid.*).

[62] Meighen to Partridge, Nov. 17, 1921 (*ibid.*).

[63] F. O. Fowler to Meighen, July 9, 1920, personal (*ibid.*).

CHAPTER VI: "ECRASONS MEIGHEN, C'EST LE TEMPS"

[1] L. C. Gravel to Meighen, Jan. 10, 1922 (*A.M.P.*, P.A.C.).

[2] *L'Union des Cantons de L'Est* (Arthabaska), Nov. 24, 1921. Author's translation.

[3] *Daily Star* (Montreal), Nov. 3, 1921.

[4] *Le Canada* (Montreal), Dec. 6, 1921.

[5] *Ibid.*, Nov. 30, 1921. Author's translation.

[6] *Ibid.*, Nov. 10, 1921. Author's translation.

[7] *Le Soleil* (Quebec), Oct. 4, 1921. Author's translation.

[8] *Ibid.*, Nov. 23, 1921. Author's translation.

[9] C. G. Power to the author, Sept. 8, 1952.

[10] *C.A.R.* (1921), p. 460.

[11] His memory was at fault on this detail. Borden introduced the Bill in Parliament but Meighen wrote it and in the main conducted it through the House.

[12] *Phoenix* (Saskatoon), Nov. 8, 1921.

[13] *Ibid.*, Sept. 20, 1921.

[14] *Ibid.*, Nov. 10, 1921.

[15] I.e. "Your cause is doomed anyway."

[16] This account of the meeting is based on the reports in *L'Evénement* and *L'Action Catholique* (Quebec), Nov. 9, 1921.

[17] *L'Evénement*, Nov. 9, 1921.

[18] *Morning Chronicle* (Quebec), Nov. 10, 1921.

[19] *L'Action Catholique*, Nov. 9, 1921.

[20] C. G. Power to the author, Sept. 8, 1952.

[21] *L'Action Catholique*, Nov. 9, 1921.

[22] G. G. Foster to Meighen, Nov. 10, 1921, private (*A.M.P.*, P.A.C.).

[23] Meighen to Smeaton White, Nov. 26, 1921 (*ibid.*).

[24] See Roger Graham, *op. cit.*, pp. 297-9.

[25] Diary of Sir Robert Borden, May 4, 1916.

[26] Meighen to H. P. Duchemin, Jan. 30, 1928 (*A.M.P.*, P.A.C.).

[27] Meighen to the author, Feb. 12, 1952.

[28] Meighen to the author, July 30, 1952.

[29] A remark attributed to Meighen by various persons in conversation with the author.

[30] Meighen to the author, Oct. 14, 1952.

[31] *Beatty of the C.P.R.*, D. H. Miller-Barstow (Toronto: McClelland & Stewart Ltd., 1951), p. 35.

[32] E. W. Beatty to Meighen, Oct. 4, 1920, private and confidential (*A.M.P.*, P.A.C.).

[33] Meighen to Mrs. Elsie Reford, Nov. 5, 1921 (*ibid.*).

[34] *Daily Star* (Montreal), Dec. 7, 1921.

[35] See Roger Graham, *op. cit.*, pp. 152-6.

[36] *Gazette* (Montreal), Sept. 22, 1926.

[37] *Daily Star* (Montreal), Dec. 7, 1921.

[38] *C.A.R.* (1921), p. 483.

[39] Drafts of letters in Lord Atholstan's handwriting (*A.M.P.*, P.A.C.). The one quoted is dated Sept. 17, 1921.

[40] Meighen to A. J. Brown, Oct. 3, 1921 (*ibid.*).

[41] J. A. Stewart to Meighen, Oct. 12, 1921, confidential (*ibid.*).

[42] *C.A.R.* (1921), p. 484.

[43] *Ibid.*, p. 482.

[44] *Ibid.*, p. 490.

[45] *Daily Star* (Montreal), Oct. 17, 1921.

[46] *Ibid.*, Nov. 24, 1921.

[47] *C.A.R.* (1921), p. 484.

[48] *Ibid.*, p. 489.

[49] Unsigned memorandum dated Aug. 2, 1921 and bearing notation, "Memorandum to be returned to Senator Sharpe." (*A.M.P.*, P.A.C.).

[50] T. A. Russell to Meighen, Nov. 5, 1921, personal (*ibid.*).

[51] Thomas Blacklock to Meighen, Nov. 2, 1921 (*ibid.*).

[52] Blacklock to Meighen, Nov. 21, 1921 (*ibid.*).

[53] Meighen to Blacklock, Nov. 22, 1921 (*ibid.*).

[54] Calder to Meighen, Nov. 20, 1921, confidential (*ibid.*).

[55] Telegram, C. G. MacNeil to Meighen, Nov. 25, 1921, personal (*ibid.*).

[56] Telegram, MacNeil to Meighen, Nov. 25, 1921 (*ibid.*).

[57] Telegram, Meighen to MacNeil, Nov. 26, 1921 (*ibid.*).

[58] *Daily Star*, (Montreal), Nov. 30, 1921.

[59] *Gazette* (Montreal), July 28, 1921.

[60] Flavelle to the editor, *Gazette*, Aug. 8, 1921, copy (*A.M.P.*, P.A.C.).

[61] *Daily Star* and *Gazette* (Montreal), Dec. 3, 1921.

[62] *Daily Star* (Montreal), Dec. 2, 1921

[63] *Ibid.*, Dec. 5, 1921.

[64] Telegram, J. A. Stewart to Meighen, Dec. 2, 1921 (*A.M.P.*, P.A.C.).

[65] Telegrams, J. F. Boyce to Meighen, Dec. 2 and 3, 1921 (*ibid.*).

[66] Telegram, Meighen to Boyce, Dec. 4, 1921 (*ibid.*).

[67] Meighen to Calder, Dec. 13, 1921 (*ibid.*).

[68] The entire correspondence and a laboured defence of the *Star*'s conduct in the affair were printed in its issue of Dec. 14, 1921.

[69] Meighen to A. R. Carman, Dec. 15, 1921 (*A.M.P.*, P.A.C.).

[70] *Gazette* (Montreal), Dec. 15, 1921.

CHAPTER VII: IN PURSUIT OF A PHANTOM GOVERNMENT

[1] Borden to Meighen, Dec. 2, 1921, personal (*A.M.P.*, P.A.C.).

[2] Meighen to Borden, Dec. 6, 1921 (*ibid.*).

[3] T. A. Hunt to Meighen, Dec. 17, 1921 (*ibid.*).

[4] Meighen to A. R. Hassard, Dec. 29, 1921 (*ibid.*).

[5] Meighen to W. H. Sharpe, Dec. 29, 1921 (*ibid.*).

[6] Meighen to A. R. Hassard, Dec. 29, 1921 (*ibid.*).

[7] Meighen to Hugh Ferguson, Dec. 21, 1921 (*ibid.*).

[8] Concerning the negotiations leading to the formation of the King government see *William Lyon Mackenzie King*, R. M. Dawson, pp. 357 ff., and *The Progressive Party in Canada*, W. L. Morton (Toronto: University of Toronto Press, 1950), pp. 130 ff.

[9] Meighen to Sharpe, Dec. 29, 1921 (*A.M.P.*, P.A.C.).

[10] Meighen to Hugh Ferguson, Dec. 21, 1921 (*ibid.*).

[11] Meighen to Howard Ferguson, Sept. 14, 1922 (*ibid.*).

[12] T. A. Russell to Meighen, Feb. 13, 1922, confidential; Meighen to Russell, Feb. 16, 1922, confidential (*ibid.*).

[13] Meighen to Russell, March 3, 1922 (*ibid.*).

[14] Meighen to Russell, March 13, 1922 (*ibid.*).

[15] Meighen to R. H. Roe, Jan. 20, 1922 (*ibid.*).

[16] *C.D.* (1919, second session), vol. I, p. 551.

[17] Borden to Meighen, Dec. 15, 1921, private (*A.M.P.*, P.A.C.).

[18] Meighen to Borden, Dec. 21, 1921 (*ibid.*).

[19] See *Revised Statutes of Canada* (1927), c. 145, sections 7, 9 and 13; c. 50, section 10.

[20] *Globe* (Toronto), Dec. 29, 1921.

[21] Meighen to H. A. Bruce, Dec. 29, 1921 (*A.M.P.*, P.A.C.).

[22] *Globe*, Jan. 20, 1922.

[23] *William Lyon Mackenzie King*, R. M. Dawson, p. 375. It is curious that in his treatment of the Casselman appointment Professor Dawson made no reference to the relevant circumstances which were well publicized at the time, namely, the

impossibility of submitting a resignation to the Speaker and the merely nominal nature of the appointment. Nor did he make clear just how it was an "attempt to circumvent the wishes of those whom the people of Canada had chosen."

[24] Quoted in *ibid.*, pp. 375-6.

[25] Meighen to the author, Jan. 22, 1959. It is fair to add that by this time Mr. Meighen's memory was not wholly reliable.

[26] *William Lyon Mackenzie King*, R. M. Dawson, p. 376.

[27] Calder to Meighen, Jan. 17, 1922, personal and confidential (*A.M.P.*, P.A.C.).

[28] Meighen to Ferguson, Sept. 4, 1922 (*ibid.*).

[29] Ferguson to Meighen, Sept. 12, 1922 (*ibid.*).

[30] Meighen to Sharpe, Jan. 7, 1922 (*ibid.*).

[31] J. C. Kyle to Meighen, Jan. 27, 1922 (*ibid.*).

[32] *Daily Star* (Montreal), Dec. 7, 1921.

[33] *Ibid.*, Jan. 4, 1922.

[34] *C.A.R.* (1922), p. 226.

[35] Meighen to R. Home Smith, Jan. 9, 1922 (*A.M.P.*, P.A.C.).

[36] *C.A.R.* (1922), p. 223.

[37] Calder to Meighen, Jan. 11, 1922, personal and confidential (*A.M.P.*, P.A.C.).

[38] Meighen to Calder, Jan. 27, 1922 (*ibid.*).

[39] Calder to Meighen, Feb. 6, 1922, personal and confidential; Meighen to Calder, Feb. 15, 1922 (*ibid.*).

[40] Calder to Meighen, Feb. 6, 1922, personal and confidential (*ibid.*).

[41] Meighen to John Ayers, March 6, 1922 (*ibid.*).

[42] *C.D.* (1924), vol. III, p. 2968.

[43] *N.M.*, p. 90.

[44] Meighen to Sir William Price, May 22, 1922 (*A.M.P.*, P.A.C.).

[45] Meighen to Tadoussac Hotel, June 8, 1922 (*ibid.*).

[46] Meighen to Mr. Maher, Jr., April 10, 1924 (*ibid.*).

[47] B. A. Macnab to Meighen, Sept. 19, 1923 (*ibid.*).

[48] English draft of speech (*A.M.P.*, P.A.C.).

[49] *N.M.*, p. 90.

[50] Interview with M. Grattan O'Leary, July 10, 1951.

[51] Quoted in the Ottawa *Citizen*, Sept. 20, 1923.

[52] Extract, supplied from memory, from speech at London, Aug. 19, 1925 (*A.M.P.*, P.A.C.).

[53] Germaine Bellemare to Meighen, July 17, 1924 (*ibid.*).

[54] Meighen to Loring Christie, July 1, 1924 (*ibid.*).

[55] Eight of the fifty, in addition to Meighen, had ministerial experience but four of these had held office only in the reconstructed Cabinet from September to December 1921. Of the remaining four, S. C. Mewburn and S. F. Tolmie were not particularly strong in the House of Commons. This left Sir Henry Drayton and Hugh Guthrie, on whom, along with H. H. Stevens, Meighen relied chiefly for assistance in the debates.

[56] Undated clipping in Mrs. Meighen's scrapbooks.

[57] *C.D.* (1922), vol. II, p. 1627.

[58] *Ibid.*, p. 1135.

[59] *Ibid.*, pp. 1578-9.

[60] *Ibid.*, pp. 1626-7.

[61] *Ibid.*, vol. IV, pp. 3426-32.

[62] *Ibid.*, vol. II, pp. 1103-04.

[63] *Ibid.*, pp. 1106-08.

[64] C.B.C. broadcast, Aug. 11, 1960.

[65] *Ibid.*

[66] *C.D.* (1922), vol. II, p. 1053.

CHAPTER VIII: "READY, AYE, READY!"

[1] *C.D.* (1922), vol. II, p. 1591.

[2] *Ibid.*, p. 1592.

[3] *Ibid.*, pp. 1620-23.

[4] Quoted in *Winston Churchill: Architect of Victory and of Peace*, Lewis Broad (London: Hutchinson, 1956), p. 193.

[5] Quoted in *William Lyon Mackenzie King*, R. M. Dawson, p. 408.

[6] G. M. Carter, *op. cit.*, p. 88.

[7] Quoted in *William Lyon Mackenzie King*, R. M. Dawson, p. 411.

[8] Quoted in *ibid.*, p. 409.

[9] Quoted in *ibid.*, p. 410.

[10] Quoted in *ibid.*, p. 413.

[11] *Ibid.*, pp. 412-13.

[12] Meighen to J. B. Laidlaw, Sept. 25, 1922 (*A.M.P.*, P.A.C.).

[13] *C.A.R.* (1922), pp. 184-5.

[14] *C.D.* (1914, special war session), p. 10.

[15] *Mail and Empire* (Toronto), Sept. 23, 1922.

[16] *C.D.* (1922), vol. III, p. 2935.

[17] G. M. Carter, *op. cit.*, p. 87.

[18] Meighen to J. B. Maclean, Oct. 23, 1922 (*A.M.P.*, P.A.C.).

[19] In law at that time ratification was an executive action performed by His Majesty on the advice of his British ministers, such action constituting ratification by the entire Empire. However, in practice it awaited approval of the treaty in question by the Dominions and in Canada the custom was to submit treaties to Parliament before consent to ratification was accorded by Order-in-Council. Such parliamentary approval was generally, if inaccurately, termed "ratification." The submission to Parliament took the form of a Bill "carrying into effect the Treaty of Peace between His Majesty" and a specified enemy state. Submission of the Bills respecting the treaties with Germany and Austria had been preceded in each case by the introduction of a resolution that "Parliament do approve of" the treaty. But there were no such resolutions in connection with the Bulgarian, Hungarian and Turkish treaties, the only action by Parliament in these cases being acceptance of the necessary Bills in the form and to the effect above mentioned. Passage of such a Bill, of course, amounted to approval of the terms of the treaty even in the absence

of a separate resolution. In 1922 Senator Raoul Dandurand, introducing in the upper House the Bill "carrying into effect" the treaties with Hungary and Turkey, explained that its purpose was to "ratify" those treaties. During the Chanak crisis, however, King denied that this had been its effect when he said: "By this Statute the Governor-in-Council was authorized to make such Orders-in-Council as appeared to him to be necessary, in certain contingencies, for carrying out what might become a Treaty with Turkey, and for giving effect to any of its provisions. No Order-in-Council has been passed under the Act referred to, so that it has never been ratified by Canada." *C.A.R.* (1922), p. 185. Thus according to this view, a rather curious one to come from King, it was for the Government and not for Parliament to decide whether Canada's consent to ratification should be given.

[20] *William Lyon Mackenzie King*, R. M. Dawson, p. 414.

[21] Meighen to B. E. Chaffey, Oct. 16, 1922 (*A.M.P.*, P.A.C.).

[22] *C.D.* (1924), vol. III, p. 2976.

[23] *C.A.R.* (1922), p. 187.

[24] *William Lyon Mackenzie King*, R. M. Dawson, pp. 422-3.

[25] *Ibid.*, p. 423.

[26] Colonial Secretary to Governor-General, Dec. 8, 1922; Governor-General to Colonial Secretary, Dec. 31, 1922. Quoted in *Development of Dominion Status*, R. M. Dawson, pp. 271, 266.

[27] At the Imperial Conference which King attended in the autumn of 1923 a resolution was approved to the effect that treaties imposing obligations on one part of the Empire were to be ratified at the instance of the Government of that part, while the ratification of treaties imposing obligations on more than one part was to be effected at the instance of the governments concerned. This principle was applied by King to the Lausanne Treaty.

[28] Governor-General to Colonial Secretary, March 24, 1924, *ibid.*, p. 272.

[29] Meighen to Christie, Jan. 13, 1926 (Christie Papers). I am indebted to Professor James Eayrs for calling my attention to this and other letters in these papers.

[30] See *The Art of the Possible: Government and Foreign Policy in Canada*, James Eayrs (Toronto: University of Toronto Press, 1961), p. 39.

[31] Meighen to Christie, April 14, 1924 (*A.M.P.*, P.A.C.).

[32] Meighen to Christie, May 12, 1924 (*ibid.*).

[33] *C.D.* (1924), vol. III, p. 2937.

[34] *Ibid.*, pp. 2937-52.

[35] Copy of speech at Vancouver, Aug. 27, 1922 (*A.M.P.*, P.A.C.).

CHAPTER IX: "THE WHISPER OF DEATH"

[1] Meighen to B. B. Smith, March 16, 1922 (*A.M.P.*, P.A.C.).

[2] Meighen to Sir C. H. Tupper, April 24, 1922 (*ibid.*).

[3] Ferguson to Meighen, Sept. 20, 1922, confidential (*ibid.*).

[4] Meighen to Ferguson, Sept. 27, 1922 (*ibid.*).

[5] I am indebted to Dr. A. R. Ford for allowing me to read this letter.

[6] Meighen to Sharpe, Feb. 21, 1923 (*A.M.P.*, P.A.C.).

[7] Stevens to Meighen, May 28, 1923 (*ibid.*).

[8] Meighen to F. B. McCurdy, July 2, 1923 (*ibid.*).

[9] D. B. Hanna to Meighen, March 21, 1923, personal (*ibid.*).

[10] *C.A.R.* (1922), p. 485.

[11] Flavelle to Meighen, June 19, 1923 (*A.M.P.*, P.A.C.).

[12] Meighen to Flavelle, July 2, 1923 (*ibid.*).

[13] Flavelle to Meighen, Oct. 11, 1922 (*ibid.*).

[14] For this speech see *C.D.* (1923), vol. II, pp. 1612 ff.

[15] See *ibid.*, vol. IV, pp. 3610 ff.

[16] *Ibid.* (1924), vol. V, p. 4724.

[17] *Ibid.* (1923), vol. III, pp. 3675-6.

[18] Meighen to P. D. Ross, June 9, 1923 (*A.M.P.*, P.A.C.).

[19] Ross to Meighen, June 12, 1923 (*ibid.*).

[20] Meighen to Ross, July 2, 1923 (*ibid.*).

[21] Flavelle to Meighen, June 12, 1923 (*ibid.*).

[22] Meighen to Flavelle, June 14, 1923 (*ibid.*).

[23] Flavelle to G. W. Allen, March 2, 1925, copy (Willison Papers, P.A.C.).

[24] *Herald* (Montreal), May 8, 1923.

[25] Meighen to Ballantyne, Dec. 4, 1922 (*A.M.P.*, P.A.C.).

[26] *Daily Star* (Montreal), July 12, 1923.

[27] *Ibid.*, July 25, 1923.

[28] *Ibid.*, Aug. 22, 1923.

[29] *Ibid.*, Aug. 30, 1923.

[30] *Ibid.*, Sept. 19, 1923.

[31] *C.A.R.* (1923), p. 166.

[32] Meighen to F. J. D. Barnjum, Aug. 15, 1923 (*A.M.P.*, P.A.C.).

[33] *Daily Star* (Montreal), Aug. 30, 1923.

[34] Meighen to J. D. Reid, Aug. 16, 1923 (*A.M.P.*, P.A.C.).

[35] *Le Matin* (Montreal), Aug. 4, 1923.

[36] B. A. Macnab to Meighen, Sept. 17, 1923, private (*A.M.P.*, P.A.C.).

[37] Webster to Meighen, Oct. 31, 1923 (*ibid.*).

[38] Ford to Meighen, Oct. 16, 1923 (*ibid.*).

[39] Meighen to Ford, Oct. 23, 1923 (*ibid.*).

[40] Ford to Meighen, Oct. 16, 1923 (*ibid.*).

[41] Meighen to Monty, Aug. 25, 1923, confidential (*ibid.*).

[42] Meighen to Kemp, Oct. 13, 1923, private and confidential (*ibid.*).

[43] Kemp to Meighen, Oct. 15, 1923, private and confidential (*ibid.*).

[44] Telegram, W. H. Dennis to Meighen, May 22, 1923 (*ibid.*).

[45] Meighen to Dennis, May 23, 1923 (*ibid.*).

[46] *Gazette* (Montreal), Sept. 3, 1923.

[47] *Tribune* (Winnipeg), Sept. 12, 1923.

[48] I am indebted to Mr. John A. Stevenson for calling this incident to my attention and to General J. A. Clark for his account of it.

[49] *Enterprise* (Yorkton), Sept. 25, 1923.

[50] *Herald* (Lethbridge), Oct. 1, 1923.

[51] Meighen to W. A. Boys, Nov. 25, 1923 (*A.M.P.*, P.A.C.).

[52] Meighen to F. B. Stacey, July 14, 1924 (*ibid.*).

[53] See *C.D.* (1923), vol. IV, p. 3640.

[54] Baxter to Meighen, Nov. 6, 1923 (*A.M.P.*, P.A.C.).

[55] *Daily Star* (Montreal), Nov. 9, 1923.

[56] Meighen to Baxter, Nov. 10, 1923 (*A.M.P.*, P.A.C.).

[57] Quoted in the *Chronicle* (Quebec), Nov. 26, 1923.

[58] *Ibid.*

[59] *Post* (Sydney), Nov. 29, 1923.

[60] *Standard* (Kingston), Nov. 30, 1923.

[61] *Herald* (Calgary), Dec. 1, 1923.

[62] S. A. Hamilton to Meighen, Nov. 29, 1923 (*A.M.P.*, P.A.C.).

[63] *C.A.R.* (1923), p. 717.

[64] *Ibid.*, p. 166.

[65] W. Ferguson to S. F. Tolmie, May 25, 1924 (*A.M.P.*, P.A.C.).

CHAPTER X: "O GOD! O MONTREAL!"

[1] J. G. Hossack to Meighen, March 17, 1924 (*A.M.P.*, P.A.C.).

[2] Meighen had certain correspondence on the subject with Mr. Vincent Massey, then President of Massey-Harris Company, but this I am not at liberty to use.

[3] For Meighen's speech on this subject in 1911 see *Unrevised and Unrepented*, pp. 3 ff.

[4] Ballantyne to Meighen, June 9, 1924 (*A.M.P.*, P.A.C.).

[5] Meighen to Ballantyne, June 13, 1924 (*ibid.*).

[6] Meighen to Ford, Sept. 12, 1924 (*ibid.*).

[7] Ballantyne to Meighen, May 27, 1924 (*ibid.*).

[8] Ballantyne to Meighen, June 10, 1924, private (*ibid.*).

[9] F. W. Stewart to Meighen, June 17, 1924 (*ibid.*).

[10] Monty to Meighen, June 17, 1924 (*ibid.*).

[11] Ballantyne to Meighen, June 27, 1924, personal (*ibid.*).

[12] Meighen to Ballantyne, May 30, 1924 (*ibid.*).

[13] According to his biographer Currie received an "offer" of the leadership in 1924 with a promise of financial assistance. Who took it upon himself to make the offer is not stated. See *Arthur Currie, The Biography of a Great Canadian*, Hugh M. Urquhart (Toronto, Vancouver: J. M. Dent & Sons Canada Ltd., 1950), p. 313.

[14] F. J. D. Barnjum to Meighen, July 7, 1924, private and confidential (*A.M.P.*, P.A.C.).

[15] *N.M.*, p. 49.

[16] Meighen to the author, April 2, 1952.

[17] Unsigned letter to Meighen, Aug. 4, 1924 (*A.M.P.*, P.A.C.). It is written on Senate letterhead and is obviously from Webster.

[18] Meighen to Monty, Aug. 6, 1924 (*ibid.*).

[19] *C.A.R.* (1924-25), p. 239.

[20] *Ibid.*, pp. 239-40.

[21] *Ibid.*, p. 239.

[22] *Gazette* (Montreal), Sept. 9, 1924.

[23] Quoted in *ibid.*, Sept. 19, 1924.

[24] Meighen to A. G. Penny, Nov. 27, 1924 (*A.M.P.*, P.A.C.).

[25] Penny to Meighen, Nov. 29, 1924, personal (*ibid.*).

[26] F. W. C. McCutcheon to Meighen, Sept. 13, 1924 (*ibid.*).

[27] Meighen to McCutcheon, Oct. 4, 1924 (*ibid.*).

[28] Wm. Irvine to Meighen, Sept. 25, 1924 (*ibid.*).

[29] E. G. Porter to Meighen, March 24, 1925 (*ibid.*).

[30] *C.A.R.* (1924-25), p. 241.

[31] *Ibid.*, p. 510.

[32] *C.D.* (1924), vol. IV, p. 3567.

[33] *Ibid.*, pp. 3744 ff.

[34] Meighen to F. W. C. McCutcheon, July 10, 1924 (*A.M.P.*, P.A.C.).

[35] *C.D.* (1924), vol. IV, pp. 3749 ff. Meighen's speech is also printed in *Unrevised and Unrepented*, pp. 114 ff.

[36] Meighen to F. B. Stacey, July 14, 1924 (*A.M.P.*, P.A.C.).

[37] R. A. Logie to Meighen, Sept. 12, 1924 (*ibid.*).

[38] B. M. Wylie to Meighen, June 27, 1924 (*ibid.*).

[39] Meighen to E. Leslie Pidgeon, Nov. 28, 1924 (*ibid.*).

[40] Pidgeon to Meighen, Dec. 8, 1924 (*ibid.*).

[41] Meighen to J. W. Woodside, June 16, 1925 (*ibid.*).

[42] Leslie Pidgeon to Meighen, Jan. 17, 1929 (*ibid.*).

[43] Baxter to Meighen, Dec. 3, 1924, confidential (*ibid.*).

[44] Baxter to Meighen, Dec. 4, 1924 (*ibid.*).

[45] Meighen to Baxter, Dec. 23, 1924 (*ibid.*).

[46] *Gazette* (Montreal), Dec. 10, 1924.

[47] Meighen to Cahan, Dec. 10, 1924 (*A.M.P.*, P.A.C.).

[48] Cahan to Meighen, Dec. 11, 1924 (*ibid.*).

[49] J. J. Carrick to Cahan, Dec. 11, 1924, copy (*ibid.*).

[50] Meighen to Carrick, Dec. 15, 1924 (*ibid.*).

[51] Carrick to Meighen, Dec. 18, 1924, confidential (*ibid.*).

[52] Meighen to Carrick, Dec. 19, 1924 (*ibid.*).

[53] Carrick to Meighen, Jan. 27, 1925 (*ibid.*).

[54] Carrick to Sir Herbert Holt, Jan. 9, 1925, private and confidential, copy (*ibid.*).

[55] Holt to Carrick, Jan. 13, 1925, private (*ibid.*).

[56] Meighen to L. J. Gauthier, Oct. 7, 1924 (*ibid.*).

[57] Meighen to Webster, Nov. 12, 1923 (*ibid.*).

[58] Webster to Meighen, n.d. (*ibid.*).

[59] W. R. Givens to Meighen, June 29, 1925, personal and confidential (*ibid.*).

[60] Meighen to Givens, June 30, 1925 (*ibid.*).

[61] Meighen to Price, Aug. 5, 1922, personal (*ibid.*).

[62] Price to Meighen, Aug. 12, 1922 (*ibid.*).

[63] Meighen to Chas. Smart, April 3, 1922 (*ibid.*).

[64] Smart to Meighen, April 11, 1922 (*ibid.*).

[65] Meighen to S. C. Robinson, March 24, 1924 (*ibid.*).

[66] Meighen to M. A. MacPherson, July 2, 1925 (*ibid.*).

[67] Tolmie to Meighen, Jan. 29, 1925 (*ibid.*).

[68] Memorandum accompanying letter, Borden to Meighen, Nov. 4, 1924, private (*ibid.*).

[69] Manion to Meighen, Jan. 10, 1925, personal (*ibid.*).

[70] Armand Lavergne to Meighen, April 2, 1925, confidential (*ibid.*).

[71] F. W. Stewart to Meighen, April 25, 1925 (*ibid.*).

[72] Meighen to Stewart, April 27, 1925, personal and confidential (*ibid.*).

[73] Webster to Meighen, Jan. 23, 1925, personal (*ibid.*).

[74] Quoted in Tolmie to Meighen, Dec. 19, 1924 (*ibid.*).

[75] See above, pp. 15-18.

[76] Meighen to Patenaude, April 27, 1925, confidential (*A.M.P.*, P.A.C.). The letter was sent in French, translated from this draft in English.

[77] Meighen to Robert Rogers, July 18, 1925 (*ibid.*).

CHAPTER XI: NATIONAL UNITY—A SPIRITUAL PROBLEM

[1] C. H. A. Armstrong to Meighen, May 15, 1925, private and personal (*A.M.P.*, P.A.C.).

[2] Meighen to Armstrong, May 19, 1925 (*ibid.*).

[3] G. E. Jackson to Meighen, May 22, 1925 (*ibid.*).

[4] Meighen to Jackson, May 25, 1925 (*ibid.*).

[5] F. L. Schaffner to Meighen, Dec. 3, 1924 (*ibid.*).

[6] Meighen to Schaffner, Dec. 23, 1924 (*ibid.*).

[7] Meighen to G. H. Hart, Sept. 25, 1924 (*ibid.*).

[8] T. A. Hunt to Meighen, Oct. 11, 1924 (*ibid.*).

[9] Meighen to Hunt, Oct. 15, 1924, personal (*ibid.*).

[10] Meighen to Chas. Peterson, May 11, 1925 (*ibid.*).

[11] Peterson to Meighen, April 14, 1924 (*ibid.*).

[12] Meighen to Peterson, April 12, 1924 (*ibid.*). Either this or Peterson's letter was misdated.

[13] Peterson to Meighen, June 3, 1924, private (*ibid.*).

[14] Meighen to J. M. Imrie, Dec. 9, 1924 (*ibid.*).

[15] Peterson to Meighen, April 13, 1925, personal (*ibid.*).

[16] Baxter to Meighen, Nov. 22, 1923 (*ibid.*).

[17] H. J. Congdon to Meighen, Jan. 4, 1924 (*ibid.*).

[18] Meighen to Congdon, Jan. 14, 1924 (*ibid.*).

[19] Meighen to Congdon, Sept. 10, 1924 (*ibid.*).

[20] Congdon to Meighen, Sept. 18, 1924 (*ibid.*).

[21] Meighen to W. A. Black, April 21, 1925 (*ibid.*).

[22] *Sun* (Vancouver), June 12, 1925.

[23] Meighen to R. J. Cromie, June 29, 1925, personal (*A.M.P.*, P.A.C.).

[24] *Globe* (Toronto), April 7, 1924.

[25] Meighen to Sir C. H. Tupper, Jan. 19, 1925 (*A.M.P.*, P.A.C.).

[26] Meighen to Michael Steele, Feb. 7, 1925 (*ibid.*).

[27] *C.D.* (1925), vol. IV, p. 3785.

[28] Meighen to A. B. Hogg, Feb. 13, 1925 (*A.M.P.*, P.A.C.).

[29] Peterson to Meighen, April 20, 1925, personal (*ibid.*).

[30] Meighen to Peterson, April 27, 1925 (*ibid.*).

[31] Peterson to Meighen, May 4, July 11, Aug. 21, 1925; Meighen to Peterson, May 11, July 18, 1925 (*ibid.*).

[32] Congdon to Meighen, May 25, 1925 (*ibid.*).

[33] *C.D.* (1925), vol. IV, pp. 3808-09.

[34] *Ibid.*, pp. 3811-12.

[35] Wm. Irvine to Meighen, undated but bearing notation: "filed 1.6.25." (*A.M.P.*, P.A.C.).

[36] See *C.D.* (1925), vol. II, pp. 1291 ff. A somewhat shortened version of the speech is in *Unrevised and Unrepented*, pp. 128 ff.

[37] *C.D.* (1925), vol. II, pp. 1301-02.

[38] *Ibid.*, vol. V, p. 4367.

[39] Meighen to Baxter, Aug. 17, 1925 (*A.M.P.*, P.A.C.).

[40] M. A. MacPherson to Meighen, July 19, 1925 (*ibid.*).

[41] Meighen to MacPherson, July 22, 1925 (*ibid.*).

[42] Rogers to Meighen, July 15, 1925, private (*ibid.*).

[43] Meighen to Rogers, July 18, 1925 (*ibid.*).

[44] J. S. Royer to Meighen, Aug. 28, 1925 (*ibid.*).

[45] L. J. Gauthier to Meighen, Aug. 26, 1925 (*ibid.*).

[46] Meighen to Gauthier, Aug. 31, 1925 (*ibid.*).

[47] Meighen to Lavergne, Aug. 31, 1925 (*ibid.*).

[48] Meighen to J. W. McConnell, Aug. 31, 1925, confidential (*ibid.*).

[49] P. C. Armstrong to Meighen, July 24, 1925 (*ibid.*).

[50] Telegram, A. W. Merriam to Meighen, Aug. 6, 1925 (*ibid.*). Meighen at the moment was in western Canada and the message was transmitted by his private secretary.

[51] Atholstan to Meighen, n.d. (*ibid.*).

[52] F. S. Meighen to Meighen, April 9, 1925, confidential (*ibid.*).

[53] Meighen to F. S. Meighen, April 10, 1925 (*ibid.*).

[54] F. S. Meighen to Meighen, June 11, 1925, confidential (*ibid.*).

[55] Meighen to F. S. Meighen, June 12, 1925 (*ibid.*).

[56] F. S. Meighen to Meighen, July 3, 1925, confidential (*ibid.*).

[57] Meighen to C. P. Beaubien, July 27, 1925 (*ibid.*).

[58] Beaubien to Meighen, Aug. 19, 1925; Meighen to Beaubien, Sept. 1, 1925 (*ibid.*).

[59] *Report of Speech Delivered at the Saint Laurent Meeting by Honorable E.-L. Patenaude on September 20, 1925* (n.p., n.d.), pp. 4-5. I am grateful to Mr. Patenaude for providing me with copies of this speech in French and in English.

CHAPTER XII: THE 1925 ELECTION

[1] Meighen to C. H. Smith, Nov. 9, 1925 (*A.M.P.*, P.A.C.).

[2] J. D. Reid to Meighen, July 20, 1925 (*ibid.*).

[3] A. H. Campbell to Meighen, Aug. 23, 1925 (*ibid.*).

[4] Meighen to Campbell, Aug. 28, 1925 (*ibid.*).

[5] N. K. Boyd to Meighen, Aug. 28, 1925 (*ibid.*).

[6] Meighen to Aimé Benard, Aug. 31, 1925, private (*ibid.*).

[7] Quoted in *The Royal Power of Dissolution of Parliament in the British Commonwealth*, Eugene A. Forsey (Toronto: Oxford University Press, 1943), pp. 174-5.

[8] This and the following quotations are from a copy of the speech in *A.M.P.*, P.A.C.

[9] Ballantyne to Meighen, Sept. 25, 1923 (*ibid.*).

[10] Meighen to Ballantyne, Oct. 15, 1923 (*ibid.*).

[11] G. H. Haney to Donald Sutherland, April 8, 1924 (*ibid.*).

[12] *Ibid.*

[13] Presumably a reference to the construction by the C.N.R. of a large office building in Toronto.

[14] *Daily Star* (Saskatoon), Sept. 29, 1925.

[15] *Ibid.*, Oct. 3, 1925.

[16] Lavergne to Meighen, Aug. 18, 1925, private and confidential (*A.M.P.*, P.A.C.).

[17] Meighen to Lavergne, Aug. 21, 1925, confidential (*ibid.*).

[18] *C.A.R.* (1925-26), p. 27.

[19] E. L. Patenaude to the author, March 24, 1953.

[20] Meighen to F. S. Meighen, Nov. 10, 1925 (*A.M.P.*, P.A.C.).

[21] *Daily Star* (Montreal), Sept. 23, 1925.

[22] *Report of Speech at Saint Laurent, p.* 10.

[23] Arthur Lalonde to Meighen, Oct. 31, 1925 (*A.M.P.*, P.A.C.).

[24] *Gazette* (Montreal), Nov. 23, 1925.

[25] Meighen to P. D. Ross, Oct. 23, 1925 (*A.M.P.*, P.A.C.).

[26] *Gazette* (Montreal), Sept. 14, 1925.

[27] *Daily Star* (Montreal), Sept. 14, 1925.

[28] The Toronto *Evening Telegram* carried on a particularly vicious campaign of defamation against King. See *C.D.* (1926), vol. I, pp. 353-5.

[29] *Report of Speech at Saint Laurent*, p. 14.

[30] Meighen to G. S. Henry, Nov. 24, 1925 (*A.M.P.*, P.A.C.).

[31] Quoted in a letter to *Daily Star* (Saskatoon), Nov. 28, 1925.

[32] By A. J. Doucet, M.P. in the session of 1926. He produced a collection of excerpts from Liberal editorials, circulars and speeches. See *C.D.* (1926), vol. I, pp. 301 ff. The following quotations are from this source unless otherwise acknowledged.

[33] There is a copy of this cartoon in *A.M.P.*, P.A.C.

[34] *Le Soleil* (Quebec), Oct. 24, 1925.

[35] *Ibid.*, Oct. 23, 1925.

36 *Ibid.*, Oct. 13, 1925.

37 Quoted in letter to *Daily Star* (Saskatoon), Nov. 28, 1925.

38 *Le Canada* (Montreal), Oct. 27, 1925. From a translation in *A.M.P.*, P.A.C.

39 *Journal* (Ottawa), Nov. 17, 1925.

40 *Free Press* (London), Nov. 18, 1925.

41 *Citizen* (Ottawa), Nov. 18, 1925.

42 For convenient tabular summaries of election results see *Party Politics in Canada*, Hugh G. Thorburn, ed. (Toronto: Prentice-Hall of Canada Ltd., 1963), pp. 156-67, and *The Conservative Party of Canada, 1920-1948*, John R. Williams (Durham, N.C.: Duke University Press, 1956), pp. 153, 154, 165. Only in the elections of 1874, 1878, 1882, 1911 and 1917 had the winning party taken a larger share of the non-Quebec seats than the Conservatives did in 1925.

43 *Daily Star* (Montreal), Oct. 30, 1925.

44 J. A. Sullivan to Meighen, Nov. 6, 1925 (*A.M.P.*, P.A.C.).

45 Meighen to J. R. Smith, Nov. 11, 1925 (*ibid.*).

46 Hugh Sutherland to Meighen, Nov. 11, 1925 (*ibid.*).

47 E. L. Patenaude to the author, March 24, 1953.

48 F. S. Meighen to Meighen, Nov. 2, 1925, confidential (*A.M.P.*, P.A.C.).

49 R. H. Pope to Meighen, Oct. 30, 1925 (*ibid.*).

50 Quoted in George Henderson to Meighen, Nov. 4, 1925, confidential (*ibid.*).

51 D. O. L'Espérance to Meighen, Oct. 31, 1925, private and confidential (*ibid.*).

52 Meighen to F. S. Meighen, Nov. 10, 1925 (*ibid.*).

53 Fauteux to Meighen, Oct. 31, 1925 (*ibid.*).

54 *Gazette* (Montreal), Nov. 23, 1925.

55 George Henderson to Meighen, Nov. 4, 1925, confidential (*A.M.P.*, P.A.C.).

56 Meighen to Patenaude, Nov. 4, 1925 (*ibid.*).

CHAPTER XIII: HERESY AT HAMILTON

1 *C.D.* (1947), vol. I, p. 69.

2 Telegram, Meighen to S. F. Tolmie, Nov. 1, 1925 (*A.M.P.*, P.A.C.).

3 *Daily Star*, (Montreal), Sept. 9, 1925.

4 "Mr. King and Parliamentary Government," Eugene Forsey, *Canadian Journal of Economics and Political Science*, vol. XVII, No. 1 (March 1951), p. 460.

5 Quoted in *ibid.*

6 Memorandum, Jan. 18, 1926, signed by Arthur Sladen (Byng Papers, P.A.C.). I am indebted to Dr. W. Kaye Lamb, Dominion Archivist, for his courtesy in giving me access to documents in this file.

7 L. S. Amery to Lord Byng, Feb. 12, 1926, secret and personal (*ibid.*).

8 "Mr. King and Parliamentary Government," Eugene Forsey, p. 460.

9 *Phoenix* (Saskatoon), Nov. 6, 1925.

10 I am indebted to Dr. Forsey for the opinion and the evidence to substantiate it, which is more extensive than that given here, that Meighen was mistaken from a constitutional point of view in his contention that King had no alternative but to

resign immediately.　Dr. Forsey remarks in his notes on the subject which he made available to me: "The constitution takes no cognizance of parties, but only of majorities or prospective majorities in the House of Commons, whether those majorities be composed of one party or of many."

[11] Meighen to P. D. Ross, Dec. 4, 1925 (*A.M.P.*, P.A.C.).

[12] Quoted in *Unrevised and Unrepented*, p. 193.

[13] Meighen to R. C. Matthews, Dec. 24, 1925 (*A.M.P.*, P.A.C.).

[14] *N.M.*, p. 40.

[15] Manion to Meighen, Nov. 19, 1925 (*A.M.P.*, P.A.C.).

[16] *Mail and Empire* (Toronto), Nov. 17, 1925.

[17] Ross to Meighen, Nov. 21, 1925 (*A.M.P.*, P.A.C.).

[18] *Evening Telegram* (Toronto), Nov. 19, 1925.

[19] *Tribune* (Winnipeg), Nov. 26, 1925.

[20] *Ibid.*, Dec. 3, 1925.

[21] M. E. Nichols, at that time editor of the *Tribune*, later repented.　On October 14, 1953 he wrote to Hugh Clark: "One of the great regrets of my life is the way I exploited [Meighen's] famous Hamilton speech.　I was honest about it, but stupidly honest in my failure to see that issue in its right proportions."　The late Col. Hugh Clark kindly brought this letter to my attention.

[22] R. H. Pope to Meighen, Jan. 16, 1926 (*A.M.P.*, P.A.C.).

[23] Meighen to Pope, Jan. 18, 1926 (*ibid.*).

[24] Fawcett Taylor to Meighen, Nov. 29, 1925 (*ibid.*).

[25] Quoted in the *Evening Telegram*, Nov. 19, 1925.

[26] *N.M.*, p. 40.

[27] *Gazette* (Montreal), Dec. 9, 1925.

[28] R. C. Matthews to Meighen, n.d. (*A.M.P.*, P.A.C.).

[29] *Free Press* (Detroit), Dec. 6, 1925.

[30] Meighen to Manion, Dec. 9, 1925 (*A.M.P.*, P.A.C.).

[31] Quoted in the Moose Jaw *Times-Herald*, Dec. 4, 1925.

[32] Meighen to Patenaude, Dec. 14, 1925 (*A.M.P.*, P.A.C.).

[33] Meighen to Manion, Dec. 9, 1925 (*ibid.*).

[34] *N.M.*, p. 42.

[35] Meighen to P. D. Ross, Dec. 4, 1925 (*A.M.P.*, P.A.C.).

[36] Willison to Meighen, Dec. 8, 1925 (*ibid.*).

[37] Meighen to Willison, Dec. 9, 1925 (*ibid.*).

[38] Meighen to Watson Griffin, Dec. 26, 1925 (*ibid.*).

[39] Hocken to Meighen, Dec. 9, 1925 (*ibid.*).

[40] Meighen to Hocken, Dec. 10, 1925 (*ibid.*).

[41] Meighen to C.A.C. Jennings, Dec. 13, 1925 (*ibid.*).

[42] Fauteux to Meighen, Nov. 17, 1925, strictly confidential (*ibid.*).

[43] Meighen to D. O. L'Espérance, Dec. 8, 1925 (*ibid.*).

[44] Haig to Meighen, Dec. 9, 1925, personal (*ibid.*).

[45] Haig to Meighen, Nov. 7, 1925, personal (*ibid.*).

[46] Meighen to Haig, Nov. 11, 1925 (*ibid.*).

[47] Haig to Meighen, Nov. 7, 1925, personal (*ibid.*).

[48] Meighen to Haig, Nov. 11, 1925 (*ibid.*).

[49] Haig to Meighen, Nov. 14, 1925 (*ibid.*).

[50] Unsigned memorandum accompanying letter, Meighen to Nichols, Nov. 14, 1925, private and personal (*ibid.*).

[51] Haig to Meighen, Nov. 23, 1925 (*ibid.*).

[52] Donald Maclean to Meighen, Nov. 23, 1925, personal (*ibid.*).

[53] Irvine to Meighen, Dec. 7, 1925 (*ibid.*).

[54] N. K. Boyd to Meighen, Dec. 8, 1925 (*ibid.*).

[55] D. Jamieson to Meighen, Jan. 6, 1926 (*ibid.*).

[56] Clark to Meighen, Jan. 4, 1926 (*ibid.*).

[57] *Western Producer* (Saskatoon), Nov. 26, 1925.

[58] Sharpe to Meighen, Dec. 5, 1925 (*A.M.P.*, P.A.C.).

[59] Meighen to Sharpe, Dec. 9, 1925 (*ibid.*).

[60] Meighen to F. Somerville, Nov. 30, 1925 (*ibid.*).

[61] Meighen to H. H. Stevens, Dec. 4, 1925, private (*ibid.*).

[62] Meighen to N. K. Boyd, Dec. 11, 1925 (*ibid.*).

[63] Forke to Meighen, Jan. 6, 1926. This letter and Meighen's reply are printed in *C.D.* (1926), vol. I, pp. 213-14. I have been unable to find a copy of King's reply.

[64] For this letter and the two replies see *ibid.*, pp. 560-1.

[65] Meighen to Stevens, Dec. 4, 1925, personal (*A.M.P.*, P.A.C.).

[66] *C.D.* (1926), vol. I, p. 11.

[67] *Ibid.*, p. 28.

[68] For the origins of these enactments see *The Winnipeg General Strike*, D. C. Masters (Toronto: University of Toronto Press, 1950), Chap. III; *A Prophet in Politics: a Biography of J. S. Woodsworth*, Kenneth McNaught (Toronto: University of Toronto Press, 1959), Chap. VIII; Roger Graham, *op. cit.*, Chap. IX. On the 1926 bargain between King and Woodsworth see McNaught, *op. cit.*, pp. 218-19; *J. S. Woodsworth, a Man to Remember*, Grace MacInnis (Toronto: Macmillan Co. of Canada, 1953), pp. 185 ff.

[69] W. L. Morton, *op. cit.*, p. 247. Dunning was appointed Minister of Railways in February and entered the Commons in March.

[70] *Ibid.*, p. 248.

CHAPTER XIV: MACKENZIE KING AT BAY

[1] *C.D.* (1926), vol. I, p. 789.

[2] Ballantyne to Meighen, Dec. 10, 1925, strictly confidential (*A.M.P.*, P.A.C.).

[3] Meighen to Ballantyne, Dec. 11, 1925 (*ibid.*).

[4] See Roger Graham, *op. cit.*, pp. 81-2.

[5] Meighen to Ballantyne, Jan. 28, 1926 (*A.M.P.*, P.A.C.).

[6] Meighen to Mrs. Elsie Reford, March 1, 1926 (*ibid.*).

[7] *C.D.* (1926), vol. I, p. 6.

[8] *Ibid.*, p. 4.

[9] *Ibid.*, p. 97.   Guthrie, according to Meighen, made these latter remarks without his sanction.   Meighen to A. G. Penny, Jan. 17, 1926 (*A.M.P.*, P.A.C.).

[10] Meighen to P. W. Pennefather, Feb. 19, 1926 (*ibid.*).

[11] *C.D.* (1926), vol. I, p. 15.

[12] I am grateful to Dr. Eugene Forsey for the benefit of his opinion on this point.

[13] *C.D.* (1926), vol. I, p. 496.

[14] *Ibid.*, pp. 673-4.

[15] See Roger Graham, *op. cit.*, pp. 70-2.

[16] *C.D.* (1926), vol. II, pp. 1422-4.

[17] *Ibid.*, p. 1441.

[18] *Ibid.*, pp. 1438-40.

[19] *Ibid.*, pp. 1664-5.

[20] For the report of the committee and the debate thereon see *ibid.*, vol. V, pp. 4694-7 and 4817 ff.

[21] *Ibid.*, p. 4865.

[22] *Ibid.*, p. 4832.

[23] *Ibid.*, p. 4926.

[24] *Ibid.*, p. 4927.

[25] *Ibid.*, p. 4922.

[26] *Ibid.*, pp. 4931-2.

[27] For King's speech see *ibid.*, pp. 4940 ff.   Meighen's follows immediately, pp. 4961 ff.

[28] *The Incredible Canadian.   A Candid Portrait of Mackenzie King: his works, his times and his nation*, Bruce Hutchison (Toronto, New York, London: Longmans, Green & Co., 1952), p. 116.

[29] Meighen to Boivin, Sept. 19, 1921, personal (*A.M.P.*, P.A.C.).

[30] *C.D.* (1926), vol. V, pp. 4838-9.

[31] *Ibid.*, p. 5017.

[32] *Ibid.*, p. 5095.

[33] *Ibid.*, p. 5096.

CHAPTER XV: THE CONSTITUTIONAL CRISIS

[1] Quoted in "Mr. King and Parliamentary Government," Eugene Forsey, p. 461, n. 60.

[2] *The Royal Power of Dissolution*, Eugene Forsey, p. 165.   Italics in the original.   For an intensive analysis of the various constitutional questions raised by King's request for a dissolution, Byng's refusal and consequent events the reader is referred to Chaps. V and VI of Dr. Forsey's book.   To those familiar with it my reliance upon his work will be obvious.

[3] *Ibid.*, p. 166.

[4] *Constitutional Issues in Canada, 1900-1931*, R. MacGregor Dawson (London: Oxford University Press, 1933), p. 73.

[5] *Ibid.*, pp. 73-4.

[6] Governor-General to Secretary of State for Dominion Affairs, June 30, 1926, secret (Byng Papers, P.A.C.).

[7] L. S. Amery to Byng, July 3, 1926 (*ibid.*).

[8] Byng had not consulted with Meighen at all up until then. There has been some speculation as to whom, if anyone, he did consult during the weekend. King later claimed to have told Byng that he would not object to Borden being asked "what was the right constitutional course. . . . I did not urge it, but I made the suggestion." *C.D.* (1926-27), vol. II, p. 1652. As far as the author knows Borden's opinion was not sought but certainly he would have advised against granting a dissolution. Meighen told Eugene Forsey afterwards that Byng had consulted Eugene Lafleur, one of the most eminent constitutional lawyers of that day. (Forsey to the author, March 5, 1963.) Forsey himself has recently been singled out as the man who must have advised Byng in 1926! Writing in "La Revue de l'Institut Canadienne-Francaise d'Ottawa," Sept. 1962, p. 27, Dr. Maurice Ollivier, Law Clerk of the House of Commons, states that he (Ollivier) was one of three persons requested by Lapointe to prepare opinions respecting the Governor's right to refuse dissolution. The others were O. D. Skelton, Under-Secretary of State for External Affairs, and Stuart Edwards, Deputy Minister of Justice. Their memoranda, according to Ollivier, were in Byng's hands during his interview with King. Ollivier implies that they argued that dissolution must be granted because he writes: "I have often asked myself where the contrary advice came from on which the Governor General based his action, probably from Dr. Eugene Forsey who, afterwards, published a remarkable work of erudition in which he attempted to justify Lord Byng's attitude." (Author's translation.) In 1926 Forsey was a twenty-two-year-old student.

[9] This was the late Col. Hugh Clark's recollection of what occurred, which he wrote out for my use. It differs slightly from the account given in a statement which Meighen prepared and which was read in the House the next day by Drayton. According to that statement Byng's summons came right after the sitting, which ended at 2.15 P.M. See *C.D.* (1926), vol. V, p. 5097.

[10] *Ibid.*, pp. 5096-7.

[11] Meighen to the author, Aug. 21, 1956.

[12] After Meighen's death in 1960 Dexter wrote a series of articles on the 1926 affair. This letter from Hanson is quoted in the third of these, "Consideration for Lord Byng," *Winnipeg Free Press*, Aug. 26, 1960. When the letter was called to Meighen's attention in 1950 he could not recall the visit of Hanson and Ryckman but fully accepted Hanson's word.

[13] *C.D.* (1926), vol. V, pp. 5231-2.

[14] *Constitutional Issues in Canada*, R. M. Dawson, p. 75.

[15] Meighen to Dexter, March 31, 1950. Quoted in the last of Dexter's articles, "The Decisive Factor," *Winnipeg Free Press*, Aug. 27, 1960.

[16] *Phoenix* (Saskatoon), July 2, 1926. Concerning Asquith's qualifications as a constitutional authority Meighen wrote later: "I would rather have his opinion on a subject like the Constitutional crisis of '26 after one hour's consideration, than I would have the opinion of any professional writers on the subject after a year's consideration. The reason lies not only in his probably unprecedented mastery of the principles of Parliamentary practice and Constitutional law, but in the fact that he lived with these problems throughout his life, in daily contact with them, and as a consequence the bigger meaning and significance of the conventions which had grown up, and all relating thereto, would be impressed upon him as upon no one else. . . ." Meighen to Eugene Forsey, April 28, 1941. I am indebted to Dr. Forsey for making this and other letters available to me.

[17] *The Royal Power of Dissolution*, Eugene Forsey, pp. 192-3. The Customs scandal, of course, was not a matter of policy but of administration.

[18] The single exception to this law was provided by a statute passed in 1884, which will be referred to presently.

[19] *C.D.* (1926), vol. V, p. 5179.

[20] *Ibid.*, p. 5253.

[21] This was later implicitly denied in a statement issued by the Progressives after the defeat of the Meighen government in the House. The denial is not wholly convincing for reasons which will be mentioned below.

[22] Quoted in *The Royal Power of Dissolution*, Eugene Forsey, pp. 224-5.

[23] Meighen to Harold Daly, March 3, 1928 (*A.M.P.*, P.A.C.).

[24] *Constitutional Issues in Canada*, R. M. Dawson, p. 85.

[25] Beauchesne, the Clerk of the House, felt so strongly that this ruling by the Speaker was wrong that he wrote to Sir T. Lonsdale Webster, Clerk of the British House, to get his opinion, which was the same as Beauchesne's. See the latter's *Rules and Forms of the House of Commons of Canada with Annotations, Comments and Precedents* (Toronto: Carswell Co. Ltd., Fourth Edition, 1958), p. 174.

[26] *C.D.* (1926), vol. V, p. 5176.

[27] *C.A.R.* (1926-27), p. 29.

[28] *C.D.* (1926), vol. V, p. 5211.

[29] Interview with W. T. Lucas.

[30] Some years later Meighen wrote: "If Mr. Bennett had been there . . . King would never have talked the diabolical and dishonest rot in which he indulged. He was a lot more careful when Bennett was across the floor, and he was equally careful when I was. Guthrie did well, but not as well as he could have done, by any means." Meighen to Forsey, Nov. 27, 1940. A recently published book about Bennett explains that he had agreed to address a Conservative rally in Calgary on June the twenty-sixth. He wired A. A. McGillivray, Conservative leader in Alberta, asking to be released from this engagement but McGillivray refused. See *R. B. Bennett. A Biography*, Ernest Watkins (Toronto: Kingswood House, 1963), p. 120.

[31] For the definitive discussion of them see *The Royal Power of Dissolution*, Eugene Forsey, pp. 206-32.

[32] *C.D.* (1926), vol. V, p. 5212.

[33] *Ibid.*, p. 5215.

[34] *Ibid.*

[35] *The Royal Power of Dissolution*, Eugene Forsey, p. 220.

[36] *C.D.* (1926), vol. V, p. 5225.

[37] *The Royal Power of Dissolution*, Eugene Forsey, p. 221.

[38] See Appendix B (*ibid.*).

[39] Quoted in *ibid.*, p. 223.

[40] *Ibid.*, pp. 227-8.

[41] *C.D.* (1926), vol. V, pp. 5220-2.

[42] *Ibid.*, p. 5224.

[43] On the question of whether the refusal of dissolution reduced Canada to colonial status see the statement by W.P.M. Kennedy quoted in *The Royal Power of*

Dissolution, Eugene Forsey, p. 244, and *The Statute of Westminster and Dominion Status,* K. C. Wheare (London: Oxford University Press, Fifth Edition, 1953), pp. 60-1.

[44] *C.D.* (1926), vol. V, pp. 5241, 5244.

[45] *Ibid.,* pp. 5285-6.

[46] Meighen to Harold Daly, March 6, 1928 (*A.M.P.,* P.A.C.).

[47] *C.D.* (1926), vol. V, p. 5280.

[48] *Ibid.,* pp. 5206-07.

[49] *Ibid.,* pp. 5310-11.

[50] W. J. Ward to the author, April 11, 1958.

[51] M. N. Campbell to the author, April 29, 1958.

[52] *Phoenix* (Saskatoon), July 2, 1926.

[53] *C.D.* (1926), vol. V, p. 5312.

[54] *Phoenix* (Saskatoon), July 2, 1926.

[55] W. J. Ward to the author, April 2, 1958.

[56] J. A. Clark to the author, Dec. 15, 1960 and Jan. 4, 1961.

[57] *Constitutional Issues in Canada,* R. M. Dawson, pp. 86-8.

[58] On these questions see *The Royal Power of Dissolution,* Eugene Forsey, pp. 232-43.

[63] *Ibid.,* pp. 87-8.

[64] *The Royal Power of Dissolution,* Eugene Forsey, p. 241.

[65] *Mail and Empire* (Toronto), July 27, 1926.

[66] Meighen to Forsey, March 30, 1943 (*A.M.P.,* P.A.C.).

CHAPTER XVI: THE 1926 ELECTION

[1] Meighen to Murray Williams, March 9, 1926 (*A.M.P.,* P.A.C.).

[2] Meighen to Patenaude, Meighen to Sauvé, April 7, 1926 (*ibid.*).

[3] Telegram, Patenaude to Meighen, April 9, 1926 (*ibid.*).

[4] Telegram, Sauvé to Meighen, April 10, 1926 (*ibid.*).

[5] Joseph Morin to Meighen, May 25, 1926 (*ibid.*).

[6] Sauvé to Perley, April 12, 1926, confidential, copy (*ibid.*).

[7] Sauvé to Meighen, April 14, 1926 (*ibid.*).

[8] Webster to Meighen, April 30, 1926 (*ibid.*).

[9] Meighen to J. W. McConnell, April 27, 1926 (*ibid.*).

[10] See above, pp. 15-18, 295-6.

[11] Morin to Meighen, May 26, 1926 (*A.M.P.,* P.A.C.).

[12] Speech at Montreal, June 4, 1926 (*A.M.P.,* P.A.C.).

[13] *Gazette* (Montreal), June 5, 1926.

[14] Morin to Meighen, June 10, 1926 (*A.M.P.,* P.A.C.).

[15] *Ibid.*

[59] *The Incredible Canadian,* Bruce Hutchison, p. 141.

[60] Meighen to Forsey, March 30, 1943 (*A.M.P.,* P.A.C.).

[61] *The Royal Power of Dissolution,* Eugene Forsey, p. 239.

[62] *Constitutional Issues in Canada,* R. M. Dawson, p. 85.

[16] *Daily Star* (Montreal), June 10, 1926.

[17] Meighen to Patenaude, June 12, 1926 (*A.M.P.*, P.A.C.).

[18] Quoted in *Conservative Party of Canada*, J. R. Williams, pp. 158-9.

[19] *Mail and Empire* (Toronto), July 27, 1926.

[20] See *Constitutional Issues in Canada*, R. M. Dawson, pp. 88-91.

[21] *C.A.R.* (1926-27), p. 33.

[22] This speech is printed in *Unrevised and Unrepented*, pp. 165 ff.

[23] Haig to Meighen, Sept. 20, 1926, personal (*A.M.P.*, P.A.C.).

[24] W. W. Lynd to Meighen, Oct. 8, 1926 (*Ibid.*).

[25] *Progressive Party in Canada*, W. L. Morton, p. 259.

[26] *The Incredible Canadian*, Bruce Hutchison, p. 145.

[27] Murray Williams to Meighen, July 4, 1926 (*A.M.P.*, P.A.C.).

[28] Atholstan to Meighen, Aug. 3, 1926, personal (*ibid.*).

[29] F. D. L. Smith to Meighen, Sept. 22, 1926 (*ibid.*).

[30] *C.D.* (1926-27), vol. II, p. 1652.

[31] *The Incredible Canadian*, Bruce Hutchison, p. 150.

[32] *Constitutional Issues in Canada*, R. M. Dawson, p. 91.

[33] *King George V: His Life and Reign*, Harold Nicolson (London: Constable & Co. Ltd., 1952), p. 400.

[34] *Parliamentary Debates* (Great Britain), Fifth Series, vol. 398, col. 1516.

[35] *Life*, Feb. 18, 1952, p. 31. In another article published in 1959 Lord Attlee wrote: "The two principal constitutional powers remaining to the Crown are the selection of the person to whom a commission to form a new administration should be entrusted and the granting or refusing a dissolution to a prime minister." The power of refusing a dissolution, he continued, might have come into play when his own government was in office. "It might well have arisen had the Labor Government been defeated in the House of Commons where there was only a majority of six. The King would have been within his rights in sending for the Leader of the Opposition if he thought that a working majority in the House could have been obtained by him." Lord Attlee, "Role of Constitutional Monarch in Britain," *Globe and Mail* (Toronto), Aug. 26, 1959.

[36] *The Royal Power of Dissolution*, Eugene Forsey, p. 259.

[37] *Inside Government House*, as told by Colonel H. Willis-O'Connor to Madge Macbeth (Toronto: Ryerson Press, 1954), pp. 31-2.

[38] Lady Byng to Mr. and Mrs. Meighen, n.d. (Mrs. Meighen's scrapbooks).

CHAPTER XVII: POLITICS, FAREWELL

[1] *C.A.R.* (1926-27), p. 98.

[2] Meighen to T. R. Meighen, Sept. 24, 1926. I am much indebted to Mr. T. R. Meighen for making available to me a large collection of letters from his father which are in his possession. This collection is hereinafter cited as T. R. Meighen Papers.

[3] A. P. Shatford to Meighen, Oct. 6, 1926 (*A.M.P.*, P.A.C.).

[4] Meighen to Shatford, Oct. 11, 1926 (*ibid.*).

[5] Sir R. Roblin to Meighen, Oct. 8, 1926, personal, private and confidential (*ibid.*).

[6] Meighen to Roblin, Oct. 12, 1926, personal (*ibid.*).

[7] *C.A.R.* (1926-27), p. 99.

[8] *N.M.*, p. 3.

[9] *Freedom Wears a Crown*, John Farthing, edited by Judith Robinson (Toronto: Kingswood House, 1957), pp. 114-15.

[10] *Ibid.*, p. 115.

[11] Meighen to L. J. Ladner, Oct. 25, 1926 (*A.M.P.*, P.A.C.).

[12] Ladner to Meighen, Oct. 8, 1926 (*ibid.*).

[13] Meighen to Ladner, Oct. 25, 1926 (*ibid.*).

[14] Quoted in the *Manitoba Free Press*, March 10, 1927.

[15] *Ibid.*

[16] Meighen to J. C. Hodgins, Sept. 17, 1929 (*A.M.P.*, P.A.C.).

[17] Meighen to Hanson, March 20, 1928 (*ibid.*).

[18] Quoted in the Winnipeg *Tribune*, Oct. 6, 1927.

[19] Meighen to T. R. Meighen, Sept. 26, 1927 (T. R. Meighen Papers).

[20] Meighen to Hugh Clark, Sept. 7, 1927. This and the letter cited in the following note were kindly put at my disposal by the late Col. Clark.

[21] Meighen to Hugh Clark, Sept. 10, 1927.

[22] *National Liberal-Conservative Convention Held at Winnipeg, Manitoba October 10th to 12th, 1927. A Review*, John R. MacNicol (Toronto: Southam Press Toronto Ltd., 1930), p. 17.

[23] *Ibid.*, p. 27.

[24] *Ibid.*, p. 26.

[25] *Tribune* (Winnipeg), Oct. 11, 1927.

[26] Based on accounts written by C. B. Pyper for the Winnipeg *Tribune*, D. B. MacRae for the *Manitoba Free Press* and J. B. McGeachy for the Saskatoon *Daily Star*, which appeared in those papers on Oct. 11, and also on *C.A.R.* (1926-27), pp. 45-8. Meighen's speech is in *Unrevised and Unrepented*, pp. 189 ff.

[27] *Daily Star* (Montreal), Oct. 11, 1927.

[28] *Gazette* (Montreal), Oct. 13, 1927.

[29] Meighen to Mrs. W. Garland Foster, Feb. 13, 1928 (*A.M.P.*, P.A.C.).

[30] Quoted in the Winnipeg *Tribune*, Oct. 12, 1927.

[31] *Ibid.*, Oct. 11, 1927.

[32] *N.M.*, p. 41.

[33] Irvine to Meighen, Jan. 25, 1928 (*A.M.P.*, P.A.C.).

INDEX